# American Socialism and Black Americans

# American Socialism and Black Americans

## FROM THE AGE OF JACKSON TO WORLD WAR II

# Philip S. Foner

CONTRIBUTIONS IN AFRO-AMERICAN AND AFRICAN
STUDIES, Number 33

GREENWOOD (G P) PRESS    Westport, Connecticut
London, England

Library of Congress Cataloging in Publication Data

Foner, Philip Sheldon, 1910-
    American socialism and Black Americans.

    (Contributions in Afro-American and African studies;
no. 33 ISSN 0069-9624)
    Bibliography: p.
  Includes index.
    1.  Socialism in the United States—History.
2.  United States—Race relations—History.  3.  Afro-
Americans—Politics and suffrage.  I.  Title.  II.  Series: Contributions in Afro-American and African
studies; no. 33.
HX83.F66        355'.00973        77-71858
ISBN 0-8371-9545-4

Library of Congress Catalog Card Number: 77-71858
ISBN: 0-8371-9545-4
ISSN: 0069-9624

First published in 1977

Greenwood Press, Inc.
51 Riverside Avenue, Westport, Connecticut 06880

Printed in the United States of America

The Negro Problem . . . is the great test of the American Socialist.

W.E.B. Du Bois,
"Socialism and the Negro Problem,"
*The New Review*, February 1, 1913, p. 140.

# Contents

# Preface

Few subjects in American radical history have generated as little published material as the relationship between American socialism and black Americans. While interest in the Communist Party's role in the black community during the 1930s has produced considerable literature, the relationship of Marxist organizations to blacks before the formation of the Communist party continues to be neglected. In his study *Negro Thought in America, 1880-1915*, August Meier found little interest in the attitude of black leaders toward radical movements of any kind, to say nothing of socialism, and even neglected to mention Peter H. Clark, the pioneer black socialist in the United States.[1] In the anthology *Black Protest Thought in the Twentieth Century*, which Meier, Elliott Rudwick, and Francis L. Broderick published in 1965, the first mention of blacks and socialism dates from 1907.[2] Herbert Aptheker's *A Documentary History of the Negro People in the United States from Colonial Times to 1910* does include a document or two on socialism, but it fails to publish more than a similar number by black socialists.[3] June Sachen's *The Unbridgeable Gap: Blacks and Their Quest for the American Dream, 1900-1930*[4] and Jervis Anderson's *A. Philip Randolph: A Biographical Portrait*[5] show no awareness of socialist influence in the black community prior to World War I. Charles V. Hamilton's *The Black Experience in American Politics*[6] does not contain a single mention of socialism. And

*Black Liberation and Socialism*, edited by Tony Thomas, confines its discussion of socialism entirely to the contemporary scene.[7]

Works devoted specifically to the history of American socialsim and the history of black Americans suffer from the same neglect. Morris Hillquit's *History of Socialism in the United States*[8] and John Hope Franklin's *From Slavery to Freedom: A History of Negro Americans* do not even indicate the existence of Negro socialists or that socialists paid any attention to the Negro question.[9] The same can be said of Daniel Bell's[10] and Howard H. Quint's[11] histories of American socialism. David Shannon's discussion is summed up in the observation that Negroes "were not important in the party, the party made no special effort to attract the Negro members, the party was generally disinterested in if not hostile to the efforts of Negroes to improve their conditions in American capitalist society."[12] Ira Kipnis' entire discussion criticizes the Socialist party for failing to champion the Negro's cause and to fight for his rights. Kipnis does not mention the existence of a single black socialist.[13] James Weinstein did advance the discussion of the Negro and the Socialist party somewhat by devoting a few pages of his book to the subject. In contrast to Kipnis, Weinstein saw the party as a real champion of the Negro. However, he merely listed one or two black socialists without discussing what they said or did.[14]

The truth is that only four published works — all of them articles — deal to any extent with the relationship between American socialism and black Americans.[15] Two are by the black scholar Earl Ofari: "Marxism, Nationalism, and Black Liberation," *Monthly Review*, March 1971,[16] and "Black Activists and 19th Century Radicalism," *Black Scholar*, February, 1974.[17] The other two are by white historians: R. Lawrence Moore's "Flawed Fraternity — American Socialist Response to the Negro, 1901-1912," *Historian*, November 1969,[18] and Sally M. Miller's "The Socialist Party and the Negro, 1901-1920," *Journal of Negro History*, July 1971.[19] All four are valuable in that they lay the groundwork for an understanding of the place of the Negro within the American socialist movement, although only Ofari's articles deal with this role during the nineteenth century. Moore's article suffers from a simplistic interpretation of the Socialist party's approach to the Negro question. In general, like most historians, he accepts the view that the Socialist party was almost completely racist, that its only analysis of the Negro's position was that the Negro was part of the general labor problem, and that the solution the party offered black Americans was the same as its solution for the whites — socialism — with the perspective that when socialism supplanted capitalism, the Negro problem would be solved. Finally, he gives the impression that the Negro question was rarely discussed in the Socialist party press.

That racism was well entrenched in the Socialist party and that the party's message to the Negro was often the one described by Moore will become abundantly clear below. But it will also become clear that few issues were more widely discussed in the party press than the Negro question, and that significant forces in the Socialist party fought racism in the party's ranks, took an advanced position on the Negro question, and did not confine themselves merely to parroting the usual line.

None of the three authors—Ofari, Moore, or Miller—discuss the writings or activities of a single black socialist apart from the *Messenger* editors. Nor do they make clear that socialist ideas and movements exercised an important influence upon several generations of black intellectuals and writers.

It was with the hope of filling the gap in the history of American socialism and the history of black Americans that I undertook to write a detailed study of the relationship between American socialism and black Americans from the Age of Jackson to World War II. Granted, nothing is easier than to throw rocks at other people's racial attitudes from the comfortable distance of one hundred, fifty, and even thirty years. It is, nevertheless, true that no book which seeks to present the views of a movement dedicated to the principles of solidarity of all workers can refrain from voicing criticism of ideas, concepts, and practices which flagrantly violated these principles. This I have done throughout. This work, the product of years of research, could not have been completed without the generous assistance of numerous libraries and historical societies. I wish to take this opportunity to express my sincere thanks to Dorothy Swanson and her staff at the Tamiment Institute, Elmer Holmes Bobst Library, New York University, for so kindly putting the vast collection on American socialism at my disposal over the years I was engaged in research on this project. I also wish to thank the staff of Duke University Library and the staff of the State Historical Society of Wisconsin for their assistance in the use of Socialist collections in those institutions. I owe a debt of gratitude also to the staffs of Boston Public Library, Butte (Montana) Public Library, Fisk University Library, Chicago Historical Society, Clinton (Iowa) Public Library, Columbia University Library, Cunningham Memorial Library, Indiana State University Library, John Crerar Library, Chicago, Galveston Public Library, Houghton Library, Harvard University Library, Howard-Tilton Memorial Library, Tulane University Library, Howard University Library, Institute of Marxism-Leninism, Moscow, Kansas State Historical Society, Louisiana State Library, Michigan State University Library, Montana Historical Society, University of Arkansas Library, Library of Congress, Missouri Historical Society, Nebraska State Historical Society, Bessemer (Alabama) Public Library, New York Public

Library, New York Public Library—Schomburg Collection, Omaha Public Library, Jackson (Mississippi) Public Library, University of Kentucky Library, University of Georgia Library, Oklahoma Department of Libraries, Archives and Records, Pratt Free Library, Baltimore, United Methodist Historical Society, Nebraska Wesleyan University Library, University of Florida Library, University of Tennessee Library, University of Nebraska Library, Bancroft Library, University of California, Los Angeles Library, San Diego Public Library, University of South Carolina Library, University of Pennsylvania Library, Department of Archives and History, State of Mississippi, Library Company of Philadelphia, University of Texas at Austin Library, University of Wisconsin Library, and Yale University Library. I also wish to thank the members of the library staff at Lincoln University, Pennsylvania, for their continuous assistance in obtaining materials through interlibrary loan from libraries, historical societies, and other institutions.

I wish to express my thanks to Dr. Brewster Chamberlin of the University of Maryland and Dr. Petter Hoffer of Lincoln University, Pennsylvania, for their valuable assistance in the translation of material in the German language. Neil Basen of the University of Iowa kindly directed me to a number of newspapers in the West that contained discussions of socialism and the Negro. Herbert Hill read portions of the manuscript and made several important suggestions. Finally, I wish to thank my brother, Henry Foner, who read the entire manuscript and made many valuable suggestions.

Although the bulk of the book relates to the Socialists and to the Socialist Party of America, the reader will find references in the latter sections to the emergence of the Communist party and some of its work among black Americans. I plan to follow the present volume with one on American communism and black Americans from 1919 to World War II, at the conclusion of which I will present my own analysis based on the experience of both the Socialist and the Communist movements.

Philip S. Foner
LINCOLN UNIVERSITY,
PENNSYLVANIA

# American
# Socialism and
# Black Americans

# Antebellum Socialism and Negro Slavery

Socialist tradition has usually been associated with Europe. As late as 1964 when Ronald Sanders and Albert Fried published *Socialist Thought*, they acknowledged that they had deliberately omitted American socialism because they regarded it as "a minor by-product of European Socialism." Later, on the basis of further study, Fried discovered that the socialist tradition was deeply embedded in American life. In fact, he found that enough socialist literature existed in this country to merit a separate volume, which was, in fact, published in 1970 under the title *Socialism in America*.

Most studies of antebellum socialism and communism in the United States have been concerned with the relative success or failure of these movements. Admittedly, neither movement has achieved its goal. As recent historical scholarship has emphasized, however, all forms of social movement, regardless of their manifest success or failure, must command the attention of historians.[1] Accordingly, let us briefly review the history of socialism and communism in pre-Civil War America.

## ANTEBELLUM COMMUNITARIAN MOVEMENTS

Socialism had its beginnings in the United States in the antebellum communitarian movements. A host of secular and religious utopian experiments were initiated in the four decades preceding the Civil War. These communitarian schemes included the Shaker villages, Owenite communities, and Fourieristic phalanxes, as well as a number of individualistic efforts such as Adin Ballou's Hopedale Community, Bronson Alcott's Fruitlands, and Etienne Cabet's Icaria. Although there were important differences in the experiments, especially on the question of complete or partial communal ownership of property, they shared some basic assumptions. First, all reflected a dissatisfaction with the social, cultural, and economic values institutionalized in nineteenth-century American society. Second, all assumed that heaven on earth was a viable goal; individual perfection and social harmony were not otherworldly realities. Third, the communitarians, for the most part, rejected individualism as the ultimate social unit of society. Collectivism and cooperation represented nobler ideals, even if as a means to achieving a higher individualism. Finally, the utopians emphasized voluntaristic compliance with the demands of the community. [2]

Religious communitarianism in America originally sought redemption for a small elect who adhered to the faith, but in the early nineteenth century, a number of plans for the universal regeneration of society emerged. These postulated the formation of cooperative communities that would, by example and radiation, eventually encompass all of society. These experiments, originated for the most part in Europe by such great utopian socialists [3] as Robert Owen and Charles Fourier, were either brought to America by their founders or propagated in this country by converts.

During 1820-1850, the American countryside was liberally dotted with communities established by searchers for the utopias promised by Owen and Fourier. Most of them failed within a few years after they were founded. Meanwhile, another group known as Agrarians or National Reformers were advancing their own utopian program. The land reformers, led by George Henry Evans, proclaimed that the workers were dominated and exploited because capitalists had engrossed the land. Land monopoly was the "king monopoly, the cause of the greatest evils," the only solution for which lay in restoring to the American workers their rights to ownership of the land and in creating Rural Republican Townships out of the public domain. [4]

The 1830s and 1840s brought an unprecedented influx of German immigrants into the United States. Among them were many who came as exiles from the Revolutions of 1830 and 1848. At first, the utopian socialist movements which populated America during the 1840s, especially Fourierism and land reform, were attractive to a number of German immigrants. In New York, Herman Kriege, a refugee from the Revolution of 1848, devoted himself to propagandizing the principles of George Henry Evans' land reform movement in his paper the *Volkstribun*. In *Die Republik der Arbeiter*, also published in New York, Wilhelm Weitling, another Forty-Eighter, spread his utopian schemes of cooperative handicraft enterprises and labor exchange banks to free workers from the prevailing system of wage slavery. Weitling was deeply influenced by Fourier, and in his later days he participated in a colonization project undertaken by disciples of the French utopian. Although Weitling styled himself a "communist," he was fundamentally a utopian.[5]

The history of Marxism in American began in November 1851, when Joseph Weydemeyer landed in New York. The son of a Prussian government official in Westphalia, educated in a Berlin military academy, and an artillery lieutenant at the age of twenty-four, Weydemeyer came under the influence of the Cologne *Rheinische Zeitung*, edited by the young Marx. Imbued by now with socialist ideas, Weydemeyer decided to quit the army after six years as a professional officer. From this time until the end of 1850, he worked as editor and collaborator on a series of socialist and radical-democratic journals. In 1846-1847, as a result of a visit to Marx in Brussels, he joined the Communist League, becoming both a warm personal friend and an organizational and literary colleague of Marx. During most of 1848 and for more than a year following, Weydemeyer was a full-time revolutionary journalist. With the decline of the revolutionary period in Germany, his position became increasingly precarious. He escaped from Germany in 1850 and, after a short stay in Switzerland, emigrated to America, well furnished with advice from his friends Marx and Engels about what he should do in this country to advance the cause of scientific socialism. He arrived in New York on November 7, 1851.[6]

As an active writer and militant in the German-American labor and socialist movement, Weydemeyer rapidly became the leading Marxist propagandist in the United States and remained so until his death in 1866. At that time, his place was taken by another Forty-Eighter, Friedrich Adolph Sorge. Sorge had fought in the Baden Revolution of 1848 and had fled to Switzerland shortly after its failure. In Geneva, he met Wilhelm Liebknecht and other members of the German Workers' Educational Society. He was expelled from Switzerland and, after a stay in Belgium and London, where he met Marx, he came to New York. Here he supported himself as a music teacher. He was active in circles of German freethinkers and socialists, but he did not become a confirmed Marxist until the 1860s.[7]

On October 25, 1857, some former members of the European Communist League in the New York metropolitan area formed the Communist Club, the first one in the Western Hemisphere. The club corresponded with Marx and with members of utopian settlements in America, including the Icarians at Nauvoo, Illinois. It also tried to stimulate the establishment here of a broad labor association to cooperate with similar movements in Europe. Weydemeyer, living at this time in Milwaukee, hailed the formation of the club and assisted in broadening its contacts among the communist refugees. By 1858, there were Communist Clubs in New York, Chicago, and Cincinnati.[8]

## UTOPIANS, MARXISTS, AND BLACK AMERICANS

The utopian and scientific socialists had fundamentally different approaches to the problems of black Americans. The first difference involved the acceptance of blacks in the movement. Robert Owen opposed slavery, attacked prejudice, and encouraged the education of Negroes. In his own colony at New Harmony, however, Negroes were excluded except as helpers "if necessary," or "if it be found useful, to prepare and enable them to become associated in Communities in Africa."[9] In the communities established by the Associationists, based on Fourier's principles, blacks were not even included as "helpers." One group which established a community in Wisconsin in 1854 invited all to join "regardless of age, sex, or color," but it disassociated itself from both the Owenites and Fourierites, emphasizing that there was to be "no combination of property or arbitrary control over the persons or property of others."[10]

Owenites, Associationists, and National Reformers justified their exclusion of blacks from their new society on the ground that they were still too "degenerate" to fit into white communities.[11] By contrast, the Communist Club of New York invited blacks to join as equal members. Its constitution required all members to "recognize the complete equality of all men—no matter of what color or sex."[12] At a meeting held in New York on April 22, 1858, sponsored by the Communist Club, the following declaration was unanimously adopted: "We recognize no distinction as to nationality or race, caste or status, color or sex; our goal is nothing less than the reconciliation of all human interests, freedom and happiness for mankind, and the realization and unification of a world republic."[13]

The second, and more important, major difference between utopian and scientific socialists on the issue of black Americans related to their approach to the one issue paramount in the black community before the Civil War—the abolition of slavery.

Slaveowners could join the communities organized by the Owenites, Associationists, and National Reformers as equal members, and once they joined, they were at no time required to dispose of their human property. On the other hand, the Communist Club of New York not only prohibited membership to slaveowners, but also expelled any member who manifested the slightest sympathy for the slaveowners' point of view.[14]

## OWENITES AND BLACK SLAVERY

The utopian socialists associated with Robert Owen believed that the solution to the problem of slavery required a combination of communitarianism and colonization. They believed, too, that just as the capitalists would accept their plan for the reconstruction of society, so the slaveholders could be persuaded to accept their plan to end slavery. The foremost proponent of this concept was Frances Wright, a Scottish-born reformer and freethinker who became a convert to Owenism. She was a militant champion of sexual equality, of the rights of labor, and of the abolition of family life as well as private property.[15]

After visiting the Rappite cooperative communities established by George Rapp at Harmony, Indiana, and later at Economy, Pennsylvania, and following a discussion with Robert Owen who was in the United States to establish New Harmony, Wright became convinced that a cooperative community was the best way to carry through her plan to end slavery. She published her plan in 1825, announcing that there would be a gradual emancipation of slaves based on cooperative labor. The slaves would be purchased by families to the greatest extent possible. It was calculated that a slave could pay for his cost, keep, and 6 percent interest on the capital invested in him by his labor within five years. The slaves would be trained in schools of industry, and their time would be divided equally between learning various trades and academic study. The children of the slaves would be taught trades and to read and write. When the slaves had completed their training, they would be colonized outside the United States in Haiti or Mexico, where they could build a life of their own. In this way, objections to the presence of free blacks in the South could be overcome. If the initial experiment succeeded—and of this Wright had no doubt—it would be extended throughout the whole South and would result in the complete disappearance of slavery in the United States. Then free white labor would come into the South to replace the Negroes who were freed, while the blacks, trained by Americans, would spread civilization to Africa, Mexico, and Central and South America. Wright's plan was thus a grandiose scheme that would benefit both white and black and the "backward" areas of the world as well as the United States.[16]

In September 1825, Wright purchased a few slaves and 300 acres in Shelby County, Tennessee, near Memphis and called her land "Nashoba," the Chickasaw Indian name for wolf. With the assistance of a group of idealistic whites (including her own sister), she began operating Nashoba in February 1826. During the spring, following a siege of malaria, Wright retired to New Harmony and became completely converted to Robert Owen's utopian socialist ideas. Together with Robert Dale Owen, eldest son of Robert Owen, she returned to Nashoba and began to operate the colony as an Owenite community modeled after New Harmony.

Both as a simple experiment in self-emancipation on the part of slaves and as a cooperative community, Nashoba was a miserable failure. Few slaves were involved, and those that were had to bear the burden of the enterprise. Even as members of a cooperative society, the Negroes were made responsible for obtaining enough money to pay their own way at Nashoba, to purchase their own freedom, and to pay the cost of eventual colonization. As a result, the slaves performed nearly all the work of operating the community, while the whites came to find in Nashoba "a place to spend time in lettered leisure." In short, the slaves did the hard work.[17]

When Wright at last decided to give up the experiment late in 1829, having herself lost some $16,000 on the venture, the only slaves who were liberated by the experiment were the remaining ones in Nashoba whom she personally brought to Haiti and placed under President Jean-Pierre Boyer—thirteen adults and eighteen children.[18]

In the first issue of the *New Harmony Gazette*, Robert Owen had published Frances Wright's "A Plan for the Gradual Abolition of Slavery in the United States, Without Danger of Loss to the Citizens of the South." In it, he had bestowed his blessings on Nashoba as presenting the best hope "for counteracting a national misfortune so pregnant with mischief as that of slavery; a misfortune which will, if not speedily averted, carry its dreadful consequences throughout our country, from the fire-side to the cabinet."[19] Gradually, Owen retreated from his insistence on the absolute necessity of the speedy elimination of Negro slavery. During his second visit to the United States in 1845, Owen addressed a convention of the New England Anti-Slavery Society and announced that while he remained opposed to Negro slavery, he no longer felt its speedy eradication was of prime importance. He said that he had seen worse slavery in England than chattel slavery in the South, and he was now dedicating himself to the battle to end the more evil form of slavery—"to contend for liberty for the white man, who was bound by the most arrant slavery of all."[20]

## FOURIERITES AND BLACK SLAVERY

The view that conditions of white wage slaves under capitalism were either as bad as or worse than those of black chattel slaves was already commonly shared by all utopians—Owenites, Associationists, and National Reformers. The Owenites and Associationists criticized the abolitionists for concentrating only on chattel slavery in the South and ignor-

ing "the slavery of capital, or the wage system at the North," and called
for an attack against all forms of slavery—"black slavery and white
slavery"—simultaneously.[21] Some Associationists, however, urged
that priority be given to ending wage slavery. One Associationist put it
this way in an appeal to New England workers:

> It is not slavery at the South which oppresses you, grinds you
> down with its iron heel, but slavery at the North. It is not chattel
> slavery, but wages slavery. It is the abolition of this which most
> immediately concerns you, which you are first to seek, and then
> you may battle to some purpose with slavery abroad.

Horace Greeley, the famous convert to Fourierism, refused to attend
an antislavery convention at Cincinnati in 1845 because he could see no
difference between slavery at the South and North. He asked the abolitionists:

> how can I devote myself to a crusade against servitude, when I
> discern its essence pervading my immediate community and
> neighborhood? Nay, when I have not yet succeeded in banishing
> it even from my humble household? Wherever may lie the sphere
> of duty of others, is not mine obviously here?

Associationist William West made the same point even more succinctly
when he insisted that American workers "do not hate chattel slavery
less, but they hate wage slavery more."[22]

The *Phalanx*, published in Paris by the followers of Fourier, declared
in 1843: "The French Fourierites are abolitionists, and women's rights
men, but they disdain to occupy themselves *specially* with these subjects, considering that slaves and women will be restored to their natural
rights, and their true social position, in the general operation of Fourier's
system, and that they can be by no other means." In like fashion, the
*Phalanx*, published by the followers of Fourier in the United States, went
into great detail explaining why chattel slavery could not be destroyed,
or the conditions of the Negroes improved, without the prior elimination
of wage slavery. "A thorough and complete extinction of slavery," it
argued, "can only be effected upon just and scientific principles." The institution of slavery could not be attacked impetuously as it was by the
Abolition party, which seemed to think that slavery was the "only social
evil to be exterminated." Such methods would lead only to violence and
revolution, and would produce "most meager and inadequate results."
For while the rights of the master would be "spoliated, and the slave
freed from personal bondage," the change "would only bring servitude

and oppression in another and more aggravated form." The emancipated Negroes would be transferred to the system operating under "Hired Labor or Labor for Wages," and that system was "but little better than slavery itself viewed in any light, and worse than slavery as a permanent institution." Since the wage system would therefore be a wretched substitution, the *Phalanx* concluded that "a new system of Industry had to be provided for" before attempting to abolish slavery in the South. 23

## NATIONAL REFORMERS AND BLACK SLAVERY

National Reformers, who followed the lead of George Henry Evans, vigorously took the position that the abolition of wage slavery was the only problem facing the working class. Since the controversy over chattel slavery distracted the workers from the main problem confronting them, they had better forget about the Negro. Then they could devote all their time and energy to the one program that would abolish wage slavery — land reform. Evans insisted, too, that land reform, once achieved, would then lead more quickly to the abolition of slavery than any number of abolitionist petitions and mass meetings. 24 He predicted, for example, that if Congress passed land reform in 1850, the following situation would exist twenty years later:

> In the Southern States chattel slavery is gradually dying out under the operation of the Free Public Land Law. . . . The emancipated Negroes have formed a settlement on the Public Lands almost large enough for a State and are debating whether they shall follow their brethren to Liberia or ask to be recognized as an independent State. 25

There would be no place for the emancipated blacks in the utopian society created in the United States under the operation of Evans' land reform program. They would have to be separated from the rest of society either through colonization or by being settled in their own communities somewhere in the West.

In his discussion of Evans' opinions, Herman Schlüter observes that "his hatred of the white slavery of the wage laborers came near turning into a defense of Negro slavery." 26 Schlüter was referring to the fact that Evans echoed Southern apologists for slavery when he argued that to free the Negro people for wage slavery would be a great disadvantage to the slaves as they would exchange their "surety of support in sickness and old age" for poverty and unemployment. At the same time, he maintained that the abolition of slavery would harm the Northern worker by throwing millions of blacks on the labor market and driving down the wages of the whole working class. Under these circumstances, the correct solution was to abolish wage slavery first. Thomas Devyr, one of Evans' disciples, expressed it this way: "Emancipate the white man first—free him from the thraldom of his unsupplied wants and the day this is done, we'll commence the manumission of the much wronged black man within our borders."[27]

## BLACK ABOLITIONISTS AND UTOPIAN SOCIALISTS

Black abolitionists bluntly accused the utopian reformers of allying themselves with Southern apologists for slavery. Nothing enraged the black abolitionists more than the cry that wage slavery was either as bad as or worse than chattel slavery. William P. Powell, a black militant in New York City who took his family to England in 1851 to remove them from the scourge of racism, encountered abroad the arguments advanced by utopian reformers when he addressed meetings to condemn Negro slavery in the United States. He angrily denounced the theory that the condition of white workers in English factories and mines was worse than that of the black slaves on Southern plantations, insisting that "they are, in effect, as far apart as the Poles." While the white workers had the protection of laws, where were the laws that protected the black slaves of the South? No white worker, he maintained, was subjected to the unlimited power the master class had over the Southern slave.[28]

Black abolitionists had no difficulty in deciding which form of slavery—wage or chattel—should be abolished first. They condemned the utopian socialists for raising the issue of priorities and thereby weakening the struggle against Negro slavery. In so doing, the utopians furnished the Southerners with ammunition to defend their "peculiar institution" and made it increasingly difficult to plead the cause of the slave without considering the issue of abolishing the wage system.

Early in his career in the antislavery movement, Frederick Douglass encountered the problem created by mixing utopian socialism with antislavery. Between 1841 and 1843, as a Garrisonian antislavery lecturer, he traveled frequently with John A. Collins, general agent of the Massachusetts Anti-Slavery Society. In his annual report to the society in 1842, Collins praised Douglass who had traveled with him to "upwards of sixty towns and villages," on a tour covering 3,500 miles, as a man "capable of performing a vast amount of good for his oppressed race." By 1843, however, Collins had become a convert to Fourierism, and he began advocating that the antislavery movement concern itself "not to free Negro slaves alone, but to remove the cause which makes us all slaves." At first

Douglass was sympathetic to Collins' socialist ideas. The *Herald of Freedom* of January 20, 1843, listed Douglass as one of the corresponding secretaries of the Society for Universal Inquiry and Reform, which was organized by Collins to seek the best method of reorganizing the existing social system and invited all to membership "without regard to sex, sect, condition, color, country, creed or character." Soon Douglass became alarmed that Collins' determination to build the Society would turn away people who had come to hear an antislavery lecture. "I held," he wrote later in his life, "that it was imposing an additional burden of unpopularity on our cause." In September 1843, at an antislavery convention at Syracuse, New York, the conflict came to a head. When Collins arrived in Syracuse, he set out to make converts for his new cause. At the antislavery meetings, he argued that the abolitionist movement was "a mere dabbling with effects," that if slavery were abolished and private property allowed to exist, it would simply be abolition in form and not in fact, and that the universal reform movement, spearheaded by the Associationists, would "do more for the Slave than the anti-slavery movement."

Douglass and Charles Lenox Remond, another great black antislavery orator, objected to Collins' tactic of organizing an antislavery meeting. After discoursing at length on the limitations of abolition, Collins would invite the audience to attend an Association meeting to be held immediately after in the same hall. The two blacks criticized Collins for preaching Fourierism to an audience that had come to hear about the evils of slavery, and they accused him of using the antislavery platform to convert the participants to Fourierism. Douglass made it clear that Collins had a perfect right to advocate the abolition of all property rights and the establishment of a new social system, and that he even had the right to advocate antislavery and universal reform at the same meeting. He maintained, however, that Collins decidedly had no right to attack abolitionism as useless and to insist that chattel slavery could only be abolished through the abolition of the existing social order. Douglass confided to Maria Weston Chapman of the Massachusetts Anti-Slavery Society that if the Board of Managers sanctioned Collins' conduct, he would be compelled to resign his connection with the society. But Collins resigned first to establish a cooperative community in New York State based on Fourieristic principles, and Douglass continued his work for the organization. [29]

While Douglass continued to uphold the utopian socialists' right—and even duty—to advocate their principles, he became increasingly hostile to their advocacy of the principle that the abolition of wage slavery should take priority and to their insistence that the struggle for the abolition of chattel slavery was meaningless unless the existing social order was first abolished. He attacked Greeley as a "queer and incomprehensible man" who could be full of remedies for "the poverty and misery of the poor white man in this country" through the formation of various associations, but "for the poor black man, he has neither sympathy, prophecy, nor plan. His advice to us may be stated in two words, and is such as is commonly addressed to dogs—'*Be gone.*'"

However, Douglass drew a distinction between those utopian reformers who condemned both chattel and wage slavery, and urged a simultaneous battle against both evils, and those who advocated relegating the struggle against chattel slavery to the background and who denigrated the contributions of the abolitionists. When the *National Reformer*, a land reform journal, ceased publication in 1849, Douglass mourned its demise because it had fought the evils of land monopoly and other evils in the existing social structure *without either sneering at the struggle against chattel slavery, or providing the slave owners with ammunition to use against those seeking to end Negro slavery.*[30]

At a meeting of the Pennsylvania Anti-Slavery Society in 1848, Remond announced that he "was out of patience" with land reformers who were indifferent to chattel slavery and argued that only wage slavery mattered. William Wells Brown, a fugitive slave who became a leading figure in the antislavery struggle, took a more conciliatory position, and even "wished success to the Land Reform movement." He went on:

> Their object is beneficent but it should not be mixed up with the Anti-Slavery cause. This reform is the first step towards ensuring their ultimate success. Labour is degraded by Slavery. Its abolition will elevate labour, and secure to *men* their manhood. Give me myself, and I will give myself a *home.* Robbed of myself, made a chattel, I can do neither—*manhood* is my first right and claim, we will talk of the *land* after this is gained. Give the slave his wife, his children, and the farm may come afterward.

Remond concluded the discussion with the observation that "the Anti-Slavery cause was the cause of labour, of man, of freedom, without regard to colour, and it was the duty of the workingmen to come to *our* platform, not for us to go to them."[31]

## GERMAN-AMERICAN MARXISTS AND BLACK SLAVERY

When the German Forty-Eighters arrived in the United States, they found the country in a ferment over the slavery question. The Mexican

War, the Wilmot Proviso with its demand for the abolition of slavery in the territories stolen from Mexico, the Compromise of 1850, and the Fugitive Slave Law which was part of the Compromise—all rubbed new salt into the wounds of the slavery controversy.

For several years, the German-American socialists played no role in the struggle against slavery. Herman Kriege argued that the slave system was essentially a question of property, and that if the abolitionist crusade succeeded, it would only increase competition among free workers and depress the white workers without elevating the blacks. "We feel constrained therefore to oppose abolition with all our might, despite all the importunities of sentimental Philistines, and despite all the political effusions of liberty-intoxicated ladies."

Wilhelm Weitling was no apologist for slavery. In his paper, *Die Republik der Arbeiter*, he denounced the Fugitive Slave Law, slave auctions, and the persecution of free blacks in the South, and he ridiculed the concept of racial superiority. His main emphasis, however, was on the abolition of wage slavery. Since he felt that concentrating on Negro slavery would divert attention from this more basic struggle, it became a "side issue" with him. In the first German Workers' Congress held in the United States in 1850, under Weitling's sponsorship, there was not a single reference to slavery. 32

Joseph Weydemeyer, the leading Marxist in America, came to grips with the slavery issue not too long after he arrived in the United States. Like Marx, Weydemeyer believed that the free labor movement could not develop as long as slavery existed and hampered the growth of industrial capitalism. In articles in the *Turn-Zeitung* and the Illinois *Staats-Zeitung*, Weydemeyer reiterated that the heart of the slavery controversy was the struggle between the industrial and slave economy, and that the success of the former through the abolition of chattel slavery would create new possibilities for the development of free labor. He brushed aside the contention of the utopian socialists, including Kriege and Weitling, that the abolition of wage slavery was the primary issue and the abolition of Negro slavery a "side issue." He insisted that wage workers could not advance further in American society until chattel slavery was eliminated, that they must play an important role in hastening its downfall, and that its demise would in turn strengthen their organization for the subsequent fight against capital.

Weydemeyer's articles were part of the literature distributed by the Communist Clubs in their effort to spread abolitionist propaganda. They reached an even wider audience when they were summarized in Friedrich Kapp's *Geschichte der Skalverei in den Vereinigten Staaten von America* (History of Slavery in the United States of America.) 33

When the Kansas-Nebraska bill to repeal the Missouri Compromise

and to open up territory reserved for freedom since 1820 was introduced
into Congress, Weydemeyer moved swiftly to enlist the German-American workers in the general movement of American workers against the
measure. At a mass meeting of the *Arbeiterbund* (Workers' League) on
March 1, 1854, a resolution introduced by Weydemeyer was adopted.
The resolution protested against the Nebraska bill because it favored the
capitalists and land speculators at the expense of the people, thereby furthering the extension of slavery. Denouncing "both white and black
slavery," the resolution branded every supporter of the bill a traitor to
the people. [34]


## ADOLPH DOUAI AND THE *SAN ANTONIO-ZEITUNG*

During the 1850s, the German-language papers were virtually the
only antislavery journals published in the South, and the *Turnerbunds*
were the only antislavery organizations in that region. Originally
devoted mainly to physical culture, the *Turnerbunds* became so influenced by socialist ideology that they were commonly referred to as the
*Sozialistiche Turnerbunds*. [35]

*Der Wecker* ("The Awakener") was established in Baltimore in 1851
by Carl Heinrich Schnauffer, the city's most famous Forty-Eighter, a
poet and revolutionist influenced by Marxism. The paper called for the
organization of trade unions, an eight-hour day, universal suffrage, and
the abolition of slavery. After Schnauffer's death in 1854, his wife edited
the paper for three years, when Wilhelm Rapp, another Forty-Eighter
and president of Baltimore's socialist *Turnerbund*, became editor. He
continued *Der Wecker* until April 1861, when a mob drove him and Mrs.
Schnauffer out of the city. [36]

Baltimore had two other German papers, both influenced by Marxism,
which called for the abolition of slavery: *Die Fackel* ("The Torch"), published by Dr. Samuel Ludvigh until 1859 when he was forced to move his
press to Cincinnati, and the *Turn-Zeitung*, published under the auspices
of the *Turnerbund*. [37] The *Deutsche Zeitung*, published in New Orleans,
also took a stand against slavery, and Marxist groups in that city supported it until it was forced to discontinue publication because of threats
of mob violence. [38]

In his *Journey Through Texas*, the second of his three great works on
the antebellum South, Frederick Law Olmsted told of antislavery radical
Germans in San Antonio, Texas, who, in 1853, raised, through small subscriptions, the capital for the purchase of a press, elected as editor "a
prominent exile, of literary experience," and thus made possible the issu-
ance of a weekly. "In his prospectus," Olmsted reported, "the editor

announced himself a radical democrat, and his determination to regard every political question from the point of view of social progress. Slavery could not, of course, be ignored."[39]

The paper was the *San Antonio-Zeitung*. The subhead printed boldly under the title of page 1, number 1, July 5, 1853, read: "Ein Sozial-Demokratisches Blatt für die Deutschen in West Texas" (A Social-Democratic Newspaper for the Germans in West Texas.) The editor was Adolf Douai, who was already a socialist, and as the subhead indicated, he was publishing a socialist paper in West Texas. In fact, the lead article in the first issue, "Die Sozialdemokratic," dealt with the major principles of socialism.

Dr. Carl Daniel Adolf Douai, a significant but neglected figure in the history of American antislavery struggle and socialism, was a descendant of a French Huguenot family and a native of Altenburg, Germany. From 1838 to 1841, he studied at the University of Leipzig, but his family was so poor that he was required to work at all sorts of jobs to continue his academic career. He graduated from Leipzig, but because of poverty he was unable to continue graduate studies at the University of Jena. Douai worked as a private tutor in Russia and at the same time successfully passed the examinations at the University of Dorpat, earning the title of doctor and the rank of professor. By the time he left Russia to return to Germany, Douai had come under the influence of socialist ideas and had become increasingly convinced that socialism was the proper form of society. He established a school at Altenburg but was sentenced to several prison terms because of his revolutionary writings and his activity in the Revolution of 1848. Unable to continue his school upon his release from prison, he emigrated to New Braunfels, Texas, in 1851 where he taught school.[40]

Douai's major work before he came to the United States was *Das ABC des Sozialismus*, published in 1851 at Altenburg. In the ninety-four-page booklet, Douai analyzed the evils of capitalist society and insisted that there was only one method of "quickly healing the sickness in the body of existing society—Socialism." Douai was not a utopian, but neither was he, at this stage, a Marxist, an ideological position he did not publicly espouse until after he had read the first volume of Marx's *Das Kapital*, published in German in 1867. In his 1851 pamphlet, Douai stressed currency reform and easy credit terms to workers and small entrepreneurs as a solution for many, though not all, of the evils of capitalism. (Even after the Civil War, when he became the most prolific popularizer of Marxism in the United States,[41] Douai still clung to his views on currency reform and credit extension, subjecting himself to sharp criticism from Marxists like Friedrich A. Sorge.)[42] In view of Douai's role in the slavery controversy in Texas, it is interesting that, in his first pamphlet on socialism, he emphasized that in a socialist society there would be equality of opportunity for all, regardless of race or color ("All will have the opportunity to become equal to others"), and that it would be a society in which slavery in any form would be banned. "That," he concluded, "is the much maligned Socialism in which there will exist freedom and equality for all, through the achievement of the Brotherhood of Man."[43]

At the time Douai arrived in Texas, only the eastern third of the state was populated to any large extent, and this area was, in many ways, an extension of the cotton culture of the Deep South. With the soil in this area excellent for cotton production and the rivers providing the necessary means of transportation, the slave-supported cotton crop boomed. Many Texans were convinced that, given enough slave labor, the state "could become the most important and richest state in the South, if not in the entire nation." Hence, any questioning of the necessity for slavery was viewed as tantamount to treason and "drew the harshest criticism from Texans." Moreover, while few Texans actually owned slaves (in 1860, only 25 percent of the families were slaveholders), many of the non-slaveholding whites had visions of becoming wealthy plantation owners in a state endowed with such vast agricultural resources. Exposed daily to the propaganda that the abolition of slavery would bring economic ruin and would place the lives of all whites — men, women, and children — in peril from "emancipated black savages," many nonslaveholding Texans were just as adamantly opposed to abolition as the slaveholders themselves. This was also true for the few settlers in western Texas who were linked to the cotton economy of the coastal areas.[44]

It is understandable then that in editing the *San Antonio-Zeitung*, Douai at first dealt with the slavery issue delicately. He feared that many of the 11,000 German colonists in western Texas, while theoretically opposed to slavery, would be quick to resent being identified with any publication that unequivocally opposed the institution. Instead, Douai concentrated on publishing material which would demonstrate that slavery was inimical to whites as well as blacks; he would let the reader draw his own conclusions from the evidence. A typical example is his account of the burning at the stake of a slave in Missouri accused of planning to rape a white woman. Douai published the report but went on to reveal that the slaveowner had acted loosely with white women in the presence of his slaves and had "talked derogatorily about the chastity and marital loyalty of white women," thus literally provoking his slaves to rape. He concluded that this incident was but "an example of how the white race is thrown into despairing immorality through the enslavement of the Negro." The Negro was demoralized by slavery, but the white slave-owner, by creating this demoralization, was himself reduced to a state of demoralization, as evidenced by this particular master's public display of contempt for the morals of white women. Douai hoped the Germans of western Texas would draw the logical conclusion from such a tragic story: that western Texas should be cleansed of such evils by being created as a state free of slavery. A free state in the West would operate as a magnet attracting runaway slaves from the eastern slaveholding state of Texas, and would, in time, make slavery so risky and unprofitable that its end all over Texas would be inevitable. [45]

The Joint Agreement of Annexation specified that when the increase of its population justified it, Texas could be divided into five states. Since there were only about 12,000 slaveowners (mainly Americans), 25,000 Mexicans who were unequivocally hostile to slavery, and a fairly large number of the 11,000 Germans who opposed slavery, there was a real possibility that western Texas might be created a free state by choice of its inhabitants, especially if antislavery Northerners could be persuaded to emigrate to western Texas. The proposed free state would include free blacks but not Indians who, Douai predicted, would soon be exterminated by the Texas Rangers. [46] Douai's contempt for the Indians is strange in view of his championship of the black cause. And, too, it is surprising that he did not even comment on the fact that among the Indians being exterminated in western Texas were the Seminoles, who had given refuge to fugitive slaves in Florida and had fled to west Texas after years of bitter warfare with American troops.

The openly antislavery Germans, most of them Forty-Eighters, had remained quiet on the subject of the free state for fear of stirring the slaveowners' wrath. In May 1854, they finally broke their silence. On May 17, a convention was held in San Antonio for the purpose of securing united action by Germans on political events. Some 120 delegates from various German settlements, societies, and clubs, the majority of whom were socialists, adopted a platform similar in many respects to that of the Richmond Social-Democratic Association. The most important section read:

> Slavery is an evil, the abolition of which is a requirement of democratic principles; but, as it affects only single states, we desire:

> That the federal government abstain from all interference in the question of slavery, but that, if a state resolves upon the abolition of the evil, such state may claim the assistance of the general government for the purpose of carrying out such resolve. [47]

Dr. Douai, who had played an important role in drawing up the platform, published its resolutions in the *San Antonio-Zeitung*. They were also published in English in the *Western Texan* of San Antonio. Those Germans who had been reluctant to tackle the slavery question head on became extremely alarmed and launched a bitter attack on the *San Antonio-Zeitung* for jeopardizing their status in the community. Until now, the slaveowners seemed to have ignored the platform, but the controversy among the Germans alerted them to the nature of the platform. They called upon the Germans to immediately prove that they were not guilty of "the charge of abolitionism and of any disposition to interfere with the laws and institutions of our country." The quickest way to prove it was to repudiate the *San Antonio-Zeitung*. The ever-hostile Austin *State Gazette* pointed out how the paper could be silenced: "The contiguity of the San Antonio River to the *Zeitung* office, we think suggests the suppression of that paper. Pitch in." To the editor of the paper, the *State Gazette* delivered the following warning: "If the editor of the *Zeitung* is a free soiler or an abolitionist, we would give him two alternatives, to desist from a doctrine which is to rob us of our property or take up his march." The *State Gazette* pointed out that in Louisiana Douai would have been indicted and found guilty under the state's statutes which provided for life imprisonment or the death penalty for any person publishing the type of editorials Douai was writing. The *State Gazette* then called for the Louisiana law to be enacted in Texas and promptly carried out. [48]

While threats of lynching did not intimidate Douai, the mounting attacks on the paper prompted the frightened stockholders to sell the weekly. Douai decided to buy it himself and to add an English-language section and perhaps even one in Spanish in order to bring his antislavery views to a wider audience and to build up sentiment for a free state in west Texas. Douai had met Frederick Law Olmsted and his brother, Dr. John Hull Olmsted, during their Texas trip the previous winter. Sharing a common interest in the creation of a "free" state in west Texas, the Olmsteds issued a circular to raise funds to sustain the *Zeitung*, "save it from the slaveholders," and enable its editor "to advocate the propriety and expedience of forming an ultimately free state in Western Texas." The fund-raising drive was successful. [49]

Douai began his career as owner of the *Zeitung* with considerable optimism. He assured the Olmsteds that west Texas could be made a free state. He was certain that all that was really needed was to induce Americans from the North, "supporters of Freedom, all of them citizens and voters," to join

a number of Americans, now enemies of Slavery, to pronounce their sentiments and form a liberty party. All over the South you find a number of free-thinking Americans—intimidated, it is true by slaveholder terrorism, but capable of uttering their feelings and forming a party as soon as they get hold of a firm phalanx of iron-souls. The Germans then will embrace—man by man—the new party. . . . With a nucleus of one or two thousand Northern Farmers, mechanics, etc., we will soon muster over thirty thousand votes for freedom in West Texas. And that will do.

Meanwhile, Douai did his part in the *Zeitung*, writing in both German and English. He conceded that his English was "full of blunders; but I had the option of not writing at all or writing as it was."[50] He soon discovered that the real problem was not how he wrote but what he wrote.

Rudolph L. Biesele, the leading authority on the German community of antebellum Texas, maintains that with the withdrawal of the stockholders from the *Zeitung*, the storm aroused by the San Antonio platform would probably have ended had not Douai "kept on agitation for abolition. Douai discussed all questions of public interest in the light of social progress and came out strongly in favor of abolition. The effect of his abolition agitation was to make the American press, generally speaking, believe that all Germans were abolitionists."[51] Actually, Douai did not come out strongly for the immediate abolition of slavery. He upheld the right of the slaveowner to his property so long as slavery existed, and he favored gradual, compensated emancipation. He also argued persistently that slavery was an evil institution that had to be abolished; that it injured the economy of the South, deprived it of a substantial middle class, held all Southerners up to the contempt of the world, and was, essentially, an uneconomical method of production as compared with free labor and should be replaced with a free labor system. Moreover, he exposed the humiliations to which free blacks were subjected in American society, both in the North and South; defended the rights of Mexican-Americans; spoke out in favor of equality for women; and denounced the special privileges granted to slaveowners under Texas law. He continually insisted on his right to discuss these issues, asserting boldly that his "rights to free speech" were as sacred as the property rights of slaveowners, "and to deny this is tending to the worst anarchy; for no state of society can exist when the equal rights of every one under the laws are not respected."[52] To one of the slaveowning organs which denounced him, he flung the following challenge:

Your idea that our articles are dangerous because they are printed in German, is from two causes unfounded: first because we have printed almost all of them which you please to call free soil articles, in English, and because the Germans do not need our aid to be convinced of the political evils that result from the institution [of slavery]. If you really wish to strike at the root of the matter, you must stop the immigration [of whites], which you can do more easily than by mobbing editors and presses. Just enact the following law:

"No person shall be allowed to write, print, publish, or circulate any sentiments or ideas opposed to the institution of slavery, and if any one shall so offend, he shall suffer an imprisonment of not less than" &c. &c.

Pass that law, Messrs. Editors, and you will drive and keep out of the state every man who has a spark of republicanism in his bosom. 53

It was all in vain. To the slaveowners it did not matter that the *Zeitung* upheld the rights of property in slavery while the institution existed. In their eyes, all this was but a subterfuge to hide Douai's real purposes. When Douai plainly and unmistakably declared, in the February 9, 1855, issue of the *Zeitung*, that western Texas must be free, he was immediately portrayed as devising "plans to improve our homely American institutions into the likeness of the bloody and drunken dreams of French and German liberty."54 Warned that they must prove beyond any shadow of doubt that they were not part of the conspiracy, the Germans of west Texas hastened to disassociate themselves from Douai and his paper. The Germans of New Braunfels met in a mass meeting on June 26, 1855, and unanimously resolved that they fully upheld the institutions of the state, that they were "not responsible for the sentiments expressed in the *San Antonio-Zeitung*," and that it was unjust to charge them with harboring designs against slavery. Several weeks later, a mass meeting of Germans in Lockhart recommended to all their kinsmen in Texas "to discountenance and suppress all attempts to disturb the institution of slavery."55

Douai had been so frequently threatened with lynching that he had provided for a friend to pay his debt to the Olmsteds if the threats were carried out. But his enemies hit upon a different approach. As Douai tells it, leading Germans responded "to the American and slaveholder opposition to my articles" by deciding "to drain the sources of my own existence and that of the 'Zeitung.'" The large San Antonio merchants withdrew their advertisements; subscriptions fell off rapidly; and old subscribers, convinced that the paper's days were numbered, refused to pay what they still owed. In addition, Douai's lithographing business failed, and his former partner in the operation spread the story that Douai had "sold [out] to the Northern Abolitionists," and was "serving for cash their purposes." "In short," Douai concluded, "I am in the most painful pecuniary embarrassment. It is time to try a *man's* soul."[56]

By August 1855, the paper's collapse was so complete that Douai was convinced that he could do nothing but sell out. "As soon as this will be done," he wrote, "I shall leave Texas, where for some years to come nothing can be done to advance our plans effectually."[57] Frederick Olmsted urged him to stay and did what he could to raise funds so that Douai could continue. "Our friend Douai is in a corner again," he wrote to Edward Everett Hale in Kansas, urging a campaign to enable the courageous editor to hold out against the lynch mobs. He felt that Douai "must be sustained" under all circumstances. Some funds were raised,[58] and Douai kept the *Zeitung* alive for nearly a year by setting type by himself and working and sleeping in the printing office. "It has been charged that we sold our paper to the abolitionists of the North," he wrote with a mixture of sadness and irony in the issue of February 16, 1856. "Half the city knows how poorly we live, never have fun, and work day and night, Sundays and holidays, that we never have money, and live worse than other people in the city." He did not mention that he also had a large family to support.[59]

The end came in the spring of 1856. The last issue of the *San Antonio-Zeitung* appeared on March 29. On April 27, *Der Pionier*, a paper published in New York City by Karl Heinzen, a Forty-Eighter and foe of slavery, carried the news that Douai had been threatened with either selling out or being strung up on the nearest lamp post and had finally decided to sell for enough to pay his debts and get his family to New York. The press had been bought by a group of San Antonio businessmen who changed the paper's name to *Staatszeitung* and announced that they would reestablish harmonious relations with the slaveowners.[60]

This outcome was a bitter one for Douai. He had held on, steadfastly hoping to obtain enough from the sale of the press to pay off his debts, including a note for $150 vouched for by the Olmsteds. Although he was originally determined not to sell to allies of the slaveowners, he was finally forced to sell the press for a pittance to the enemies of all he had sought to achieve.

The press did not remain forever in the hands of the enemies of the Negro people. In 1868, Douai received a newspaper from Texas which carried the following announcement in bold type at the head of the first column: "This paper, which is owned, edited, and whose types are set by Negroes, is printed upon the same press which Dr. Adolf Douai first battled for the emancipation of the black man. He has the gratitude of

the colored race who will ever remember his endeavors in behalf of freedom."[61]

## ADOLPH DOUAI AND *DER PIONIER*

When Douai left Texas, he first went to Philadelphia. The city's black
community, then the largest in the North, honored him at a public rally
and pledged to raise funds so that he might publish a newspaper in their
city. Douai settled instead in Boston where he helped establish a three-
class school with which a kindergarten was connected.[62] Douai did not
abandon the antislavery cause for the schoolroom. He campaigned for
the Republican party in the election of 1856 among the Germans of Massachusetts, Connecticut, and New York. In a speech in New York's
*Tabernacle*, he stated that, while he supported the Republican presidential candidate, John C. Fremont, he felt the party did not go far enough
on the slavery question by standing only for the limitation on the
extension of slavery in the territories. Answering the charge that a
radical abolitionist position would endanger the Union, he replied that he
preferred freeing the Negro to saving the Union.[63]

Nevertheless, Douai believed that it was essential that the German-
American workers support the Republican party. He expressed this idea
in "Ein Wort an die 'Arbeiter'" (A Word to the Worker), published during the presidential campaign of 1856 in *Der Pionier*.[64] A brilliant mixture of economic and moral arguments, the article explained why German-American workers should not only support the Republican candidates because of their opposition to the further extension of slavery in
the territories, but also take a firm stand against the entire system of
Negro slavery. Douai stressed that the existence of free or inexpensive
land in the West had up to that time offered an escape for workers of the
Northeast, preventing them from sinking to the status of proletarians, a
status that would have been even worse in the United States than in
Europe because of the higher cost of living in this country. But if the
slaveowners and their allies in the Democratic party were victorious,
slavery would spread everywhere, making the land in the West more
expensive and even pushing out free labor which could not compete with
slave labor. In such a situation, the proletarianization of the workers in
the East and their domination and exploitation by the capitalists would
become inevitable. Douai reasoned that with the possibility of western
emigration removed, the standard of living of the workers in the East
would decline rapidly. As a result, competition between native-born and
foreign-born workers would intensify, causing the native-born workers

to demand a halt to further immigration and also depriving those immigrants already in this country of their fundamental rights.

Apart from the economic arguments requiring the German-American
workers to take a stand against slavery and its further expansion, Douai
also insisted that there was the humanistic element. White workers, he
maintained, ought to have learned that if one class of workers was especially oppressed, as were the Negro slaves, no class of workers could
really be free. All oppressed peoples, and all workers who were oppressed,
had to sympathize with and assist those who were especially oppressed,
regardless of race or color. The oppressors knew the truth that a common
bond existed among them, and they acted to assist each other. Workers
must do the same. If the white workers failed to speak and vote against
slavery and its extension, they would have themselves to blame when
they found themselves enslaved. "Your own indifference to the enslavement of fellow workers will then go against you," he wrote. He closed his
article by expressing the hope that the German-American workers had
not "lost the hatred of every kind of slavery" and that they would
"acknowledge freedom for every one. But it is high time that you prove
this en masse, that you place humanity over narrow, selfish working
class interests, and that you put freedom over all." [65]

# 2

## The Election of 1860,
## the Civil War, and
## Reconstruction

THE ELECTION OF 1860

Douai left Boston early in 1860 to settle in New York
City. His departure was necessitated by a bitter campaign against him, led by Professor Louis Agassiz, who
held the chair of Natural History at Harvard. It was
spurred by a comment Douai made at a memorial meeting in honor of Alexander Von Humbolt. On this occasion, Douai declared that one of the services to humanity
of this great German naturalist was his assertion that
"he was not a believer in God."[1] Undismayed by
Agassiz's criticism that followed, Douai hit back at him
in a series of articles in *Der Pionier*. Douai proudly
acknowledged that he was a freethinker. He attacked
Agassiz not only as a reactionary but as a racist, noting
that his belief in Negro inferiority—as set forth in his
1850 essay "The Diversity of the Origin of the Human
Race"—helped to provide a rationale for slavery.[2] Douai
had already contended in a series of articles for *Der
Pionier*, entitled "Zur Geographie Den Menschen," that
slavery was responsible for whatever backwardness
might seem to exist among Negroes, but that fundamentally there were no superior and inferior races.[3] He
now found it necessary to expose Agassiz's own racism.

In New York, Douai joined forces with the Marxists.
While he did not become a member of the Communist
Club, he was so highly regarded by its membership that
he was invited to become coeditor of the club's journal,

the *New Yorker Demokrat*.[4] Together with Joseph Weydemeyer, Douai used the paper to mobilize support among German-American workers for the Republican party. Both conceded that the Republican party did not go far enough on social and economic issues, and that it did not even go far enough on the slavery question. They insisted, however, that it represented a movement that had mass support and stood a good chance of electing its presidential candidate in 1860, thus defeating the party of the slaveowners. Even its program of restricting the expansion of slavery, they maintained, was radical in the sense that a limitation on the expansion of slavery could deliver a death blow to that institution. It was the duty of socialists, they said, to form a radical, left corps inside the Republican party to prevent conservative forces from pushing it to the right, and then to continue the campaign to push the party in a more radical direction, especially in the direction of the total abolition of slavery.[5]

Weydemeyer and Douai had an opportunity to apply this principle. Weydemeyer, representing the Chicago Workingmen's Society, and Douai, as a representative of the German Republicans of Boston, were both delegates to the momentous national conference of German-Americans held in Deutsches Haus in Chicago on the eve of the presidential convention. The purpose of the conference was to exert the influence of the German-American community on the convention to guarantee that conservative forces in the Republican party would not dictate the platform and nominate the presidential candidate. They feared that moderate Republicans, influenced by the charge that they were "Black Republican" abolitionists, as well as by nativist "Know-Nothingism," would water down the party's stand against the further extension of slavery in the territories. They also feared that they would adopt a plank favoring the extension of the period required for foreigners to obtain the right to vote—just as the Massachusetts Republicans had done in pushing through the state legislature the notorious amendment which withheld suffrage for two years from those who had been naturalized.

Weydemeyer and Douai worked closely together at the Deutsches Haus conference. Their influence was seen in the resolutions adopted by the delegates. These resolutions based on those previously passed by the German-American Republican workingmen of New York City, insisted on a firm antislavery stand, opposition to the Massachusetts Amendment, support of a Homestead Act, admission of Kansas as a free state, and the nomination of candidates who would defend these planks. The resolutions were printed immediately after they had been accepted, and notice was served on the Republican convention that the German-Americans, a large number of whom were trade unionists, would give their votes to the Republican party only if its platform and candidates opposed Know-Nothingism and the further expansion of slavery. These votes could not be shrugged off lightly. It was widely acknowledged that the German-Americans could determine the outcome of the election in a number of crucial states. It is now generally conceded that the German-American influence was reflected not only in the Republican platform, but also in the defeat of candidates who were being groomed for the presidential nomination by the party's conservative forces and in the final nomination of Abraham Lincoln as the Republican standard bearer. [6]

Weydemeyer and Douai continued to work together after the Republican convention to help elect Lincoln, and they played an important role in the campaign in New York City. (Weydemeyer returned to New York after the conference and worked as an engineer and surveyor in the construction of Central Park.) The German-American workers, a significant voting element, were the target of a campaign to capture their votes for the ticket headed by Stephen A. Douglas. The campaign took the form of warnings that a Republican victory would be followed by the emancipation of four million slaves who would then come North and deprive white workers of their jobs. Another tactic used was sheer intimidation; in October, the large clothing houses began to curtail production, to fire workers, and to restrict supplies to the tailors, nearly all of them German-Americans, giving the excuse that the South was not placing any orders for fear of Lincoln's election. Since New York City depended so largely on the Southern trade, the German-American tailors were told that a Lincoln victory would force them out of business and that their workers would be reduced to starvation. [7]

The *New Yorker Demokrat* became the chief agent to counteract this campaign of terror. Douai's editorials, several of which were reprinted as leaflets and distributed among German-American workers, contrasted the Republican and Democratic platforms, exposed Douglas' "Popular Sovereignty" program as proslavery and racist, and warned workers that there was a more immediate danger that slavery would be extended to the workshops of the North than that emancipated slaves would take away their jobs in the event of a Republican triumph. The argument that slavery could only exist in a tropical climate and for the production of staple crops was characterized by Douai as a myth. Wherever slavery spread, he pointed out, free labor had to give way, and if the slaveowners had their way, it would have to give way in the North, too. [8]

At the request of the German Tailors' Union, Weydemeyer wrote an appeal, published in the *New Yorker Demokrat* and reprinted as a leaflet, calling upon German-American workers to "stand by Lincoln and freedom," and not to be intimidated into voting for the anti-Republican ticket. [9] When the employers called a meeting to counteract the leaflet, the Tailors' Union, the Turners (Singing Clubs), and the Communist Club took over the gathering. Weydemeyer delivered the main speech of the evening, pointing out that "the temporary layoffs in the large firms" were only a device to force the tailors to vote the anti-Republican ticket.

He emphasized that the election of Lincoln would "encourage social progress." 10

On election day, the pro-Southern New York *Herald* featured the following appeal:

### Irish and German Laborers

If Lincoln is elected to-day, you will have to compete with the labor of four million emancipated slaves. His election is but the forerunner of the ultimate dissolution of the Union. The North will be flooded with free negroes, and the labor of the white man will be depreciated and degraded. 11

The weeks of activity by the Communist Club, the *New Yorker Demokrat*, Weydemeyer, Douai, and the unions of German-American workers with whom they worked closely guaranteed that, so far as the German workers were concerned, the scare tactics would fail. The election results proved it. The German vote in New York City was overwhelmingly for Lincoln. After his victory, a Republican spokesman declared at a celebration gathering: "We owe a debt of gratitude to the laboring classes who gave us this victory, not to the mass of the merchants who were frightened by the cry of wolf." 12 It was a tribute to the majority of the workers of the city but especially to the German-American laborers.

In other cities like Chicago, Cincinnati, St. Louis, and even Baltimore, the Marxists and other socialists also played leading roles in rallying labor's support for the Republican ticket. While the view that German voters provided Lincoln's margin of victory in 1860 (especially in the Northwest) has been sharply criticized, it is clear that "after 1856 the Republicans did make inroads into Democratic German strength," and that in Illinois at least, the German vote was crucial in Lincoln's election. 13

The Marxist Joseph Weydemeyer and the near-Marxist Adolf Douai were under no illusion that they were working to elect a man who stood for the total abolition of slavery. They knew that Lincoln was no abolitionist and that he was opposed only to the further extension of slavery. But they believed that workers should play an active and independent role in the Republican party, pushing it in the direction of abolishing slavery, which they were convinced was essential for the next stage in the battle of labor — that against the capitalist system. By playing this role, they also believed, the workers would at the same time strengthen their organization for the subsequent fight against capital. Douai made this point of view quite clear in an editorial on November 10, 1860, three days after Lincoln's election, in the *New Yorker Demokrat*:

We have taken part in the campaign not as party-adherents, not for self-seeking reasons, but because the Republican Party is closest to our point of view and because we consider its victory a guarantee that still greater victories for the cause of humanity can be achieved in the future. It is therefore our special task to see to it that what has been achieved with our help is not again undone but is built up still more; and if reactionary elements in the Party of Reaction intend to do that, we must form a counter-weight to them and press forward to further gains.

Within the next few weeks Douai developed this theme. He elucidated three principles around which all friends of freedom should unite:

• Slavery must be abolished and there must be no more compromise which recognizes its right to exist or permits its spread of prolongation.

• The slave has in every condition the right and in certain conditions even the duty to free himself by every means possible from slavery.

• Every white man has the right to help him and under certain circumstances the duty to do so.

In the political arena, Douai called upon the friends of freedom and especially "our own countrymen," to begin organizing to "support only such parties which do not measure citizens by the place of their birth and human rights by the color of their skin." However, he believed that the best tactic was for such groups to function as "the left-wing of the Republican Party," for he was confident that it would be possible to achieve this dual program within that party. He reminded his readers that in a novel *Der Abolitionist*, which he had published serially in *Der Pionier*, he had predicted that if the slaveowners dissolved the Union, "the days of slavery are numbered."[14] He now added another prediction: "We predict that events in the near future will push the Republican Party more to the left, and that the whole North will become abolitionist."[15]

## SECESSION AND COMPROMISE

Late in February 1861, shortly before Lincoln's inauguration as president of the United States, a convention of slaveowners set up a provisional government at Montgomery, Alabama, with Jefferson Davis as the president of the Confederate States of America. Alexander H. Stephens, who was elected vice-president, said of the Confederacy: "Its foundations are laid, its cornerstone rests upon the great truth that the negro is not the equal of the white man; that slavery, subordination to the superior race, is his natural and normal condition." [16]

The weeks that followed witnessed frenzied efforts to persuade the Southern states that had seceded to return to the Union, and many Northern workingmen urged "Union and Compromise." [17] The workingmen of Massachusetts, meeting in Faneuil Hall in Boston in December 1860, summed up the prevalent attitude among many Northern workers: "We are weary of the question of slavery; it is a matter which does not concern us; and we wish only to attend to our business, and leave the South to attend to their own affairs without any interference from the North. The Workingmen of the United States have other duties." [18]

Not so, said the socialists and the German-American workers. En route to his inauguration, Lincoln was met at his hotel in Cincinnati by a delegation of 2,000 members of the German Workingmen's Society. Among the delegates were Marxists, one of whom—Fred Oberklein— delivered the address to Lincoln in which he said that the free workingmen of Cincinnati were opposed to "all compromises between the interests of free labor and slave labor." They regarded Lincoln as the champion of free labor and free homesteads, and they firmly adhered to the principles of liberty without compromise. They assured the president that if he needed men to maintain these principles, they and other workers would "rise as one man at your call ready to risk their lives in the effort to maintain the victory already won by freedom over slavery." [19]

In Baltimore, *Der Wecker* spoke out against secession; in St. Louis, the Germans, with the socialists in the vanguard, declared in their manifestos that "St. Louis stands for the Union," and pledged their "fortunes . . . sacred honors, and, if need be, our lives, to the maintenance of the Union, Federal Constitution, and the enforcement of the laws." While the development of railroad connections between Missouri and the Eastern market made the secession of this border state highly improbable in the long run, the Germans did not wait for the commercial and manufacturing middle classes to grasp the value of union with the East. The socialist *Turnvereins* formed themselves into military organizations and told the prosecessionists that "not mere words, but weapons will decide" this struggle. The result was put quite bluntly by John N. Edwards, a vehement pro-Southerner: "Twenty thousand Black Republicans, in and around St. Louis, composed largely of the German element, overawed, controlled, and finally possessed the State." [20]

## CIVIL WAR: BATTLE FRONT AND HOME FRONT

When the Civil War began with the attack on Fort Sumter, most of the organizations of the German radicals disappeared, since the majority of their members enlisted in the Union forces. The New York Communist Club did not meet for the duration of the war because most of its members had joined the Union Army. The *Turner* organizations, composed largely of German socialist workingmen, sent more than half of their members into the Union forces. Within days of Lincoln's first call for volunteers, the *Turners* organized a regiment in New York, and in many other communities, they sent one or more companies. There were three companies of *Turners* in the First Missouri Regiment, and the Seventeenth consisted almost entirely of *Turners*. In the assault on Camp Jackson, the German socialists of Missouri fought under their red regimental banner on which they had inscribed the symbol of a hammer smashing a shackle.

Many socialist leaders joined the Union Army, and some attained positions of high rank. Joseph Weydemeyer was commissioned as a colonel and assigned by Lincoln as commander of the military district of St. Louis. August Willich, a former Prussian officer and a friend of Karl Marx, who called him a "communist with a heart," took part in a number of engagements, was severely wounded, and left the army with the rank of brigadier-general. Robert Rosa, who had been a Prussian officer before he became a member of the New York Communist Club, was a major in the Forty-fifth Regiment of New York. Fritz Jacobi, vice-president of the Communist Club of New York, enlisted as a private, and was a lieutenant when he died on the field at Fredericksburg. [21]

The socialists also worked hard behind the lines for the Union cause. In 1863, when the *Cincinnati Volksfreund* endorsed the proslavery "Copperhead," anti-union policies of Representative Clement L. Vallindigham of Ohio and urged support for his sabotage of the war effort, the socialist *Arbeiterbund* of Cincinnati responded immediately by denouncing the paper and declaring that it was "deserving of the contempt of every loyal citizen." [22]

On July 11, 1863, the provost marshal's office in New York City opened for conscription. That same day wild mobs began to riot, and for five infamous days they stormed through the streets of the city, unleashing their hatred against the National Conscription Act and committing unspeakable atrocities against the black community. Any Negro they came upon was either murdered or maimed. The riots went unchecked until the secretary of war sent in eleven Union regiments to quell the rioters.

During the height of the draft riots, New York socialists posted a series of placards from the Battery to the Harlem River, calling upon the workers to *"stop and think"* before joining the riot. "Comrades!" they appealed. "Stand by the law! . . . Stand up as Democratic Workingmen should stand up before the world, and show the traitors of the South, and the friends of tyranny all over the world, that the *Workingmen of New York are able to govern themselves."* [23]

The socialists actively promoted the cause of abolitionism as well as that of the Union. They urged Lincoln to move toward a Proclamation of Emancipation, and when the provisions of the emancipation of slaves did not change the legal status of bondsmen in the border states, they began a battle to implement it in these states. In Missouri, a struggle for emancipation legislation had begun even before Lincoln's proclamation was issued on January 1, 1863. Joseph Weydemeyer joined the pro-emancipation forces upon the expiration of his term of service with the Second Missouri Artillery Regiment on September 21, 1863. He used the columns of *Neue Zeit*, where he served as a member of the editorial board, to urge the speedy emancipation of slaves in Missouri. His position was endorsed by a convention held in Cleveland on October 18-21, 1863, for the purpose of founding an organization of radical Germans. Among the delegates were Friedrich Sorge, representing the New York Communist Club, and several socialists from the Chicago *Arbeiter Verein* (Workingmen's Association.) Their resolutions voiced complete support for the "emancipationists who have been so furiously persecuted in Missouri," and declared that "more than any previous period, the present time compels us to recognize in the proclamation of equality of human rights in the Declaration of Independence . . . the fundamental law of Republican life." [24]

Weydemeyer and other German socialists persevered in the campaign for emancipation in Missouri. A state convention on January 6, 1865, at which German socialists were represented, passed an ordinance abolishing slavery immediately and without compensation. [25]


## MARX, THE BRITISH WORKERS, AND THE CIVIL WAR

"Events themselves drive to the promulgation of the decisive slogan—the emancipation of the slaves," Karl Marx wrote in the *Vienna Presse* of November 7, 1861. In the same issue, he emphasized that the Civil War was not a struggle between two countries or even territories, but a conflict between two different social systems. "The present struggle between the North and the South," he declared, "is . . . nothing but a struggle between the system of free and the system of slave labor." The self-interest of the working class in both America and Europe, he believed, required the freedom of the Negro people. 26

Marx was not content with merely enunciating this principle; he acted on it. He played a role in influencing the course of the British government during the Civil War. The British ruling class and Southern Confederate agents were busily engaged in pressuring the British government to declare war against the United States and align England with the Confederacy. The Union blockade of Southern ports had created a great scarcity of cotton in England, bringing widespread unemployment and misery to the British textile centers. The pro-Confederate forces were confident that the poverty-stricken workers would welcome a policy that would end the blockade and bring back both cotton and their jobs. 27

Some militant trade-union leaders did argue that, since there was "no great principle at stake in the Civil War," British intervention on behalf of the Confederates was the correct policy. 28 But Marx and his allies, along with others, helped organize the working people of England to oppose preparations to bring their country into the war on the side of the Confederacy. Even before the Emancipation Proclamation, meetings of workingmen resolved that "the distress prevailing in the manufacturing districts" was the result of the "rebellion of the Southern States against the American constitution." 29 As soon as the news reached England that Lincoln had issued the Emancipation Proclamation, Confederate hopes for England's intervention received a crushing blow. Large meetings of English workingmen were held in Manchester and London, and resolutions were adopted expressing support for the Union, urging Lincoln to pursue his policy until slavery was totally abolished, and warning Prime Minister Palmerston against intervention on the side of slavery. The most important and spectacular of these meetings was the gathering of the Trade Unions of London at St. James' Hall on March 26, 1863. Henry Adams, son of the American minister, attended the meeting and declared years later that he had "then understood and always since believed Marx's to have been the guiding hand in organizing the meeting." 30

Whatever may have been the extent of Marx's own personal activity in the matter, he was convinced that it was such workers' meetings that had "defeated repeated attempts of the ruling class to intervene on the side of the American slaveholders." Moreover, as Royden Harrison points out, these pro-Union activities "helped to widen the horizons of the British workers and prepared their leaders for participation in the International Working Men's Association." 31 On September 28, 1864, a mass meeting of European trade unionists was held in London which organized the International Workingmen's Association (IWA)—the

First International. Well known among European radicals as the author of the *Communist Manifesto* and for his activities in the campaign to prevent British intervention on the side of the Confederacy, Marx was elected to the General Council, even though he was not present at the meeting. Marx and his colleagues on the council announced from the outset that the fight against segregation and discrimination would be at the top of the IWA's agenda. The first of the Provision Rules of the Association announced that it stood for justice toward all men "without regard to colour, creed, or nationality."

Apparently, Marx almost immediately assumed leadership of the General Council, since he wrote the "Inaugural Address" which set forth the preliminary rules and program for the IWA. In one section, he wrote: "It was not the wisdom of the ruling classes, but the heroic resistance to their criminal folly by the working classes of England that saved the West of Europe from plunging headlong into an infamous crusade for the preparation and prolongation of slavery on the other side of the Atlantic." He added: "If the emancipation of the working classes requires their fraternal concurrence, how are they to fulfill that great mission with a foreign policy in pursuit of criminal design, playing upon national prejudices, and squandering in piratical wars the people's blood and treasure." 32

In November 1864, news of Lincoln's reelection reached London. This provided a new opportunity for the workers to organize protest meetings against the anti-American attitude of the Palmerston cabinet. The General Council of the IWA was involved in planning these meetings. When it was proposed in the council that the organization send an address to Lincoln congratulating him on his reelection, a committee was formed and Marx was asked to write the text of the address. His draft was approved, signed by all members of the council, and forwarded to President Lincoln through Charles Francis Adams, the United States minister. It was published on January 7, 1865, in the London *Bee-Hive*, the leading British labor paper.

In the address, Marx noted that the Civil War was of decisive consequence for the destiny of the working class throughout Europe, and he pointed out that the emancipation of the Negro slaves would remove the major obstacle to the further advance of the American working class. "The workingmen of Europe," he wrote, "feel sure that, as the American War of Independence initiated a new era of ascendancy for the middle-class, so the new American Anti-Slavery War will do for the working classes." 33

Three years later, in the first volume of *Das Kapital*, Marx enunciated the famous principle that the self-interest of the American working class as a whole had necessitated the abolition of slavery and would require the complete liberation of the black workers: "In the United States of America, every independent movement of the workers was paralysed as long as slavery disfigured a part of the republic. Labour cannot emancipate itself in the white skin where in the black it is branded." [34]

## JOHNSON'S RECONSTRUCTION POLICIES

In two addresses on behalf of the IWA General Council—one to President Andrew Johnson (who had succeeded the assassinated Lincoln to the presidency) and the other to the "People of the United States"—Marx urged a policy of reconstruction that would include full equality for the ex-slaves. He warned, too, that unless this equality was achieved, the victory over slavery would not be complete, and that this failure would sow the seeds of future civil strife. "Remove every shackle from freedom's limbs," his message urged. "Let your citizens . . . be free and equal, without reserve." [35]

In May 1865, Marx had great hopes for Andrew Johnson, a "former poor white," who he believed would pursue a radical policy of reconstruction. The disillusionment came quickly, however, and in June 1865, he criticized Johnson's policy as "extremely vacillating and weak in substance." A month later, Marx labeled Johnson's reconstruction policy completely reactionary and predicted that under its operation, the former slaveowners would be restored to power and the freedmen returned to a status of quasislavery. [36]

The reconstruction policy that alarmed Marx had evolved from the bare outlines of a policy that Johnson inherited from Lincoln. After an initial outburst of indignation against the slaveowners, whom he blamed for the Civil War, Johnson decided on a program of amnesty for all Southerners who would swear future loyalty to the Union. Under his plan, delegates elected to state constitutional conventions in the states that had seceded would amend their constitutions to abolish slavery, ratify the Thirteenth Amendment to the U.S. Constitution, repudiate all debts contracted by the Confederate governments, and nullify the secession ordinances. Having done that, Southerners could organize elections to establish regular civil governments. Since Johnson freely granted pardons to former leaders of the South, the dominant forces in Reconstruction were the former slaveowners and leaders of the Confederacy. The ex-slaves, deprived of the right to vote and without land, were thus left to the mercies of their former masters. Instead of receiving land and their political and civil rights, they were given the "Black Codes," [37] which, as the Freedmen's Bureau reported to Congress, "actually served to secure to the former slaveholding class the unpaid labor they had been accustomed to enjoy before the war." 38

German-American socialists shared Marx's alarm over these developments. In July 1865, the German *Unionbund* of New York, led by and composed mainly of socialists, issued a manifesto condemning Johnsonian Reconstruction. It pointed out that since Congress was not in session, there was no power to limit the president's plan to restore the former slaveowners to power, and it urged the immediate convening of Congress. "If the Southern States are reconstructed on the President's plan," it warned, "the colored population, to whose protection and liberation the Nation is in honor bound, will fall back under the exclusive rule of its enemies." In language similar to that used by Marx, the manifesto observed: "The President's policy of Reconstruction is the beginning of reaction; its consequences will be fatal." Furthermore, it emphasized that even the granting of equal political rights to blacks was not enough to place Reconstruction on a solid foundation. "The landless inhabitants of the South—the whites as well as the blacks—must obtain possession, by purchase or donation, of the confiscated estates of the aristocracy, in order that they become really independent citizens of the regenerated republic." The manifesto closed with an appeal to all liberal-minded German-Americans "to join in ranks, in order to labor together with the American-born citizens of the same conviction for the realization of the principles of our great revolution." 39

In Chicago, the socialist-dominated *Arbeiter Verein* sponsored a mass meeting "for the advocacy of a radical policy on the part of the government in the reconstruction of the Southern States." The meeting was attended by hundreds of German-American workers. After speakers had denounced Johnson's Reconstruction policy, resolutions were adopted declaring that the success of the policy meant "the victory of the old-Southern aristocracy," and that therefore Congress should not accept it. Rather, they advocated that Congress adopt one that would decree universal suffrage for black and white alike and provide an economic foundation, through land distribution for the ex-slaves, without which even political and civil rights would become meaningless. 40

## AMERICAN SECTIONS OF THE INTERNATIONAL ON THE NEGRO QUESTION

In 1867, the revived Communist Club of New York voted to become a section of the IWA. Soon afterward, Sorge received detailed directions from the headquarters of the organization in Geneva in the form of a communication from Johann Philip Becker on how the cause should be advanced in the United States. "Once you have a secure basis in New York," Becker wrote, "you should attempt to found the same organization in other cities in North America." Each section should have its own statutes in accordance with local conditions, except that they could not contradict the General Statutes in any way. Becker then emphasized: "Our sections must maintain everywhere in every affair concerning labor problems the initiative, they must be the inspiring, organizing and indoctrinating element." [41]

Some actions by the American sections of the International did indicate "initiative" and "inspiration" on the Negro question. For example, when the Communist Club of New York joined with German trade unionists in 1868 to form the short-lived Social party of New York and Vicinity, one of its planks demanded the repeal of all discriminatory laws, and another "favored the eligibility of all citizens . . . for office." [42] In December 1869, Section 1 of the International in America appointed a committee to promote the organization of Negro workers. [43] However, it sent no delegate to the convention of the Colored National Labor Union held that same month in Washington, even though it was widely publicized that whites would be welcomed as fraternal delegates. [44]

Black members of a waiters' union and Negro plasterers took part in the great mass demonstration for the eight-hour day in New York City on September 13, 1871, marching with the International section behind the red flag and a large banner on which were inscribed the words "Liberty, Equality, and Fraternity." This was certainly a great advance in the metropolis which eight years earlier had been the scene of draft riots. [45]

On December 17, 1871, 10,000 men and women marched in New York under the International's sponsorship to honor the martyrs of the Paris Commune. A catafalque, wreathed with flowers and draped in red, moved slowly along Fifth Avenue to the muffled drumbeats of a Negro guard. In the line of march were Cuban, French, German, and Irish societies and, to the surprise of the reporter for the *New York World*, the "Skidmore Light Guard, a negro military organization numbering about forty men." The black contingent, he noted, was "loudly cheered." He also pointed out that the delegation of the Cuban League included

quite a number not of the Caucasian race . . . , but nevertheless placed in the ranks without the least distinction as to race or color, the Cuban mulatto and black being found in many files side by side with his fellow-countrymen of the fairer race, all in perfect concordance no doubt with the International's demand for "liberty, equality, and fraternity," particularly the two last. [46]

It is quite understandable that in the Southern press the words "social equality" were equated with "communist." [47] When Robert Nelson, the Texas agent of the Colored National Labor Union, issued a call for a convention of "the Laborers' Union Association of the state of Texas," which led to the formation of a branch of the Colored Labor Union in Houston, the Galveston Daily News warned editorially: "The beginning is here—the little rippling stream, so weak as to be insignificant—the end is like that of Paris. It is the Commune with its sea of blood and its ocean of fire." [48]

The fears expressed by the editor must have come back to haunt him the next year when Section 44 of the IWA was organized in Galveston. A meeting for the "formation of a Workingmen's Association," held on the evening of February 19, 1872, was attended by about twenty-five men, many of whom were members of the various craft unions. John McMakin, a leader of the Painters' Union, explained that a branch of the IWA was needed because "the rights of the working men are ignored, and [because] the slavery they endured was worse than that which was endured by the negroes." He explained the objectives of the International to the meeting, and while conceding that it had been responsible for the shedding of such blood, he observed that "it was but a lake beside the ocean of blood spilled by the aristocracy."

By April 1872, the Galveston section of the International had some 200 members. At its third meeting, the race issue came to the fore when a motion was made to appoint a committee to "wait upon the colored working men to ascertain if they would cooperate with the society." A white worker, Bert Lochrey, took the floor in opposition to the proposal:

> Gentlemen, I came here to-night to join, if agreeable, your society. I have co-operated with every society, wherever I have lived that had for its object the amelioration of the condition of the working man. But if I understand by the resolution that the colored man is to be taken into full fellowship in this society, socially and politically, I must decline to become a member.

Lochrey was followed by McMakin who spoke at length in favor of the resolution, pointing out that the failure in the past to unite black and white in Galveston in a common struggle against common oppressors had enabled the capitalists to triumph. His logic prevailed, and the resolution was adopted. Moreover, the meeting also adopted a "platform of principles of the Association" that included the following provision: "As the Declaration of American Independence affirms that all just governments derive their power from the consent of the governed, therefore, the right of suffrage should be secured to every citizen of mature age, regardless of nationality, sex or condition."

The *Galveston Daily News* had predicted that "the negro question will prove a subject of discord in the society." It proved to be an accurate prophet. When the charter for Section 44 arrived from International headquarters, it contained a section providing for "complete political and social equality to all, without regard to nationality, sex, or condition." Although the words "race" or "color" did not appear, all at the meeting knew that Section 44 would have to practice racial equality if it was to continue as a branch of the IWA. (Why this should have come as a surprise to anyone at the meeting is difficult to understand since the International was already known for its stand in favor of racial equality.) The fact that McMakin was out of town during the meeting seriously weakened the forces in favor of accepting the charter with the controversial provision. In the end, the meeting voted to accept the charter, but immediately thereafter members began to hand in their resignations. In an effort to halt the departures, J. E. Gallagher, Section secretary, assured all members that the provision did not mean that the Section had to endorse "social equality." His assurance did not stem the tide, and soon most of the 200 members had left. By June 1872, Section 44 was dead. [49]

Strangely enough, the reports of the American sections of the International did not even mention the few occasions on which they took what was, *for the time*, an advanced position on the Negro question. The only exception to this pattern was Sorge's description of the demonstration of September 13, 1871, in which blacks participated. The report of the Central Committee of the International Workingmen's Association for North America to the General Council in London described the participation of its local section in the mass demonstrations and the "deafening cheers" which greeted their red flag. It added: "Equally significant was the participation of colored (negro) organizations for the first time in a demonstration got up by the English speaking unions. (The German unions having treated them as equals already years ago.)" [50]

## IWA GENERAL COUNCIL AND THE NEGRO QUESTION

At its founding convention in 1869, the Colored National Labor Union decided to send Reverend J. Sella Martin as a delegate to the Congress of the First International scheduled to meet in Paris in 1870. The Franco-German War forced its postponement. The General Council, however, was apparently not interested in pursuing the relationship. While it sent invitations to its European congresses to almost every convention of the National Labor Union, it never extended one to the black organization. [51]

Unfortunately, this neglect was typical of the General Council as regards the Negro question. The minutes of the council reveal that while from 1866 on, American affairs loomed large in its thinking, the Negro question never entered into its deliberations. Six pages of the published minutes for August 27, 1867, were devoted to the annual report of the American secretary of the General Council—Peter Fox. [52] Three years later, on August 30, 1870, the minutes of the General Council noted that an American, Osborn C. Ward, who was about to return to the United States, delivered a lengthy speech on the situation and problems in that country and the tasks confronting the American sections. [53] On November 1, 1870, Marx informed the General Council that he had received, through Sorge, an address presented by the German and French sections in New York to the workers of Europe on the problems facing American labor. Marx then read the lengthy document. [54] In none of these cases was there a mention of Reconstruction or any other aspect of the Negro question. Moreover, neither Marx nor any other member of the General Council bothered to ask why these issues were not discussed.

On April 9, 1870, Marx wrote to Siegfried Meyer and August Vogt, two organizers for the IWA in New York, comparing the treatment of Negroes in the South with that of the Irish in England. The "ordinary English worker," Marx observed, cherished "religious, social, and national prejudices against the Irish worker. His attitude toward him is much the same as that of the 'poor whites' to the Negroes in the former slave states of the U. S. A." Marx went on to urge the IWA in New York to make Irish independence a major demand as the General Council had already done in Europe. In conclusion, he advised the IWA organizers: *"A coalition of the German Workers with the Irish* (as well as with those English and American workers who are ready to do so) is the most important job you could start at the present time." [55]

Marx's letter to his American friends has been cited as evidence of his interest in the Negro question during the Reconstruction era. [56] The letter actually provides evidence to the contrary. He did not advise the IWA organizers to seek a coalition with the oppressed Negro in the South or to seek to educate the "poor whites" to the realization that their antagonism toward the Negro was being kept alive and intensified, like the hostility of the British worker to the Irish, "by the press, the pulpit, the comic papers, in short by all the means at the disposal of the ruling classes." [57]

It may be argued that black workers were so insignificant a part of the industrial working class during this period that Marx was justified in not being concerned over their problems. It may also be contended that the vast majority of blacks in the South were sharecroppers and tenant farmers; they lived in communities where even the attempt to bring them into a coalition with white workers would have brought wholesale arrests, imprisonments, and lynchings, and would have been doomed to failure.

In his letter, Marx observed that the antagonism between the English and Irish workers, created by the ruling class, was "the *secret of the impotence of the English working class*, despite their organization." [58] Marx knew that the antagonism between whites and blacks in America was the secret of the weakness of the working class in America. After all, as mentioned earlier, he had noted in 1867 that labor in the United States could not "emancipate itself in the white skin where in the black it is branded." [59] His failure to make the analogy clear to his American correspondents is proof that the issue of black-white relations was a minor one in his mind at this time. [60]

Robert Hume of Long Island, the General Council's propagandist among native Americans, informed the IWA's Executive Committee that he was distributing widely the address of the "International Workingmen's Association on the Irish Amnesty Affair." He added the shrewd comment: "The enemy has triumphed by sowing division between the two grand sections of producers, viz., the agricultural and manufacturing laborers. With us between the Whites and Blacks, with you between English and Irish laborers." [61] There is no record, however, that Hume ever distributed any International literature on how to combat the efforts of "the enemy" to sow division "between the Whites and Blacks."

In his article "Marxist Theory in Search of America," Harvey Klehr points out that "Marx and Engels devoted most of their prodigious energy to understanding and influencing events in Europe," and that when Marx wrote about America, "he generally ignored the South." [62] This is only partially true. Klehr himself is aware that the correspondence Marx and Engels had with Americans regarding the problems in the United States fills a volume. Yet little of this correspondence, particularly after the Civil War, deals with the South. Along with Marx, American Marxists viewed the struggle to end slavery as crucial, not only in order to liberate blacks from the most brutal system of exploitation, but also to remove the major obstacle in the development of free labor. The Marxists had attacked Weitling's view that the struggle to end Negro slavery was a "side issue" and that the paramount battle was to end wage slavery. They had insisted instead that a free labor movement could not develop as long as slavery existed and hampered the growth of industrial capitalism. The abolition of chattel slavery, they insisted, was a necessary precursor for the emergence of an independent working-class movement in the United States.

The Marxists apparently believed that a vigorous independent working-class movement, prepared to do battle with capital, was emerging in the United States, and that it was not the time to divert that movement with other issues. The problem of black liberation would have to wait until after the successful organization of the independent working class.

The fundamental error in this thinking, an error that the history of the American working class since the Civil War has demonstrated, is that a vigorous, effective independent working-class movement could not develop in the United States unless black liberation was an integral part of its struggle at all stages. Indeed, such an important aspect of the struggle should have demanded continuous and special attention. But such attention would have required that the American Marxists conduct as consistent a struggle against racism in white working-class circles as they had waged in convincing the antebellum Northern workers to give priority to the abolition of Negro slavery. For many reasons, one being that they themselves were not entirely free of racism, they failed to do so.

## WORKINGMEN'S PARTY OF THE UNITED STATES

In 1872, the International moved its headquarters from London to New York in order to try to prevent the anarchists from taking it over. Sorge was entrusted with the task of preserving the organization until such time as it could be returned to Europe. It was never to return. On July 15, 1876, ten delegates met in Philadelphia and dissolved the International Workingmen's Association—the First International.

The following day the same delegates gathered together to hear Sorge's advice on how to spread the ideas of the International among native Americans. In his presentation, Sorge emphasized the need to avoid foreign models, especially the German, and to achieve closer relations with the trade unions. A major concentration, he advised, should be in New England, a vital center of American industry, where the textile workers were showing every indication of being ready for organization. 63

But Sorge said nothing about another need—that of championing the cause of black Americans. That same year, 1876, Sorge published his only piece of writing in English, *Socialism and the Worker*. In the entire booklet there is not a single mention of the Negro.

As Sorge was speaking and writing, the counterrevolution to wipe out Radical Reconstruction was making rapid headway in the South. Amnesty was being granted to Confederate leaders, and Union troops were being withdrawn from state after state. Violence was being used on an ever-increasing scale to suppress the Negro vote and to keep the freedmen economically oppressed, and the blacks were left with no protection to face the armed might of the Ku Klux Klan. In the Northern industries, blacks were more and more being eliminated from the skilled trades, and the unions were still largely lily-white.

The most influential Marxist in the United States, and the one closest to Marx, had nothing to say about these issues.

Shortly after the dissolution of the First International, at a Unity Congress of Marxists and Lassalleans, [64] the Workingmen's party of the United States was formed. Its platform was a compromise between the principles of the two groups. It adopted the economic policies of the Marxists, asserting that the economic organization of the workers should precede the political movement of labor, and that the new party would "in the first place direct its efforts to the economical struggle." It also incorporated the Lassalleans' request that a national instead of an international organization be established.

Since neither the Marxists nor the Lassalleans had paid any attention to the Negro question during the decade preceding the formation of the Workingmen's party, [65] it is not surprising that neither the new party's declaration or principles nor any of the eleven specific measures proposed "as a means to improve the condition of the working classes" dealt with this issue. The resolution that was adopted dealing with woman's rights is worth mentioning since it foreshadowed what was to become standard socialist policy on the Negro question for many years to come. It read in part: "The emancipation of women will be accomplished with the emancipation of men, and the so-called woman's rights question will be solved with the labor question. All evils and wrongs of the present society can be abolished only when economical freedom is conquered for men as well as women." [66] If one substitutes the words "Negro workers" for "women" and "white workers" for "men," one has an accurate prediction of what the socialist policy toward the Negro would become.

Although the party began to function at the time of the final overthrow of Reconstruction, none of the twenty-four party papers—eight in English, including a daily, two in French, and fourteen in German, half of which were dailies [67]—concerned themselves with the issues of the final phases of Reconstruction, the organization of black workers, or even the recruiting of Negroes. Even when the disputed election of 1876 was followed by the removal of federal troops from South Carolina by Rutherford B. Hayes as part of his bargain with the Southern Democrats, an action that assured the complete triumph of the counterrevolution in the South, [68] there was only one comment in the party press on the campaign and the "great betrayal" of the blacks. This comment appeared in the *Labor Standard* (formerly *The Socialist*), the leading English-language party organ. The paper was edited by J. P. McDonnell, an Irish-American Fenian and labor leader, and a colleague and correspondent of Marx. In its issue of September 23, 1876, the *Labor Standard* noted that when the black laborers on the rice plantations of South Carolina went on strike for an increase of fifty cents in wages, D. H. Chamberlin, Republican governor of the state, ordered the sheriff to call out the militia to protect strikebreakers. This was followed by the comment: "The interests of black and white laborers are the same and when they strike they find their friend: the Republicans, the Democrats, and the Greenbackers all agreed upon shooting them down."

The implication was that only the Workingmen's party of the United States was the true friend of blacks. The blacks, however, aware that the socialists, including the Marxists, stood aloof from the battle for full civil and economic rights for Negroes, were apathetic to this argument. The failure of American socialism to exert any influence in the black community during Reconstruction is manifest in the fact that the histories of the First International in America list not a single Negro member and only a handful of activities associated with blacks. [69] Given the isolationist tendencies of the German-American Marxists, the absence of guidance from their theoretical leaders, and the chasm between the European-born urban radicals and the recently emancipated Southern-born blacks, it is probably hardly surprising that the issues crucial for blacks in post-Civil War America were never of major concern for American Marxists. Nevertheless, the fact remains that American socialism emerged from the crucial years of Reconstruction without the semblance of a meaningful policy for black Americans and without providing any guidance on the Negro question for American socialism in the future.

# The Post-Reconstruction
# Era, 1877-1890

PETER H. CLARK, PIONEER BLACK SOCIALIST

In March 1877, at a socialist meeting at Robinson's
Opera House in Cincinnati, Ohio, the first black American to identify himself publicly with socialism announced his support of the Workingmen's party of the
United States. The pioneer black socialist was Peter H.
Clark, principal of the Colored High School in Cincinnati.

Peter Humphries Clark (popularly known as Peter H.
Clark) was born in Cincinnati in March 1829. His grandfather, William Clark, was the Clark of the Lewis-Clark
expedition which President Thomas Jefferson commissioned in 1804 to explore the continent and find a route to
the Pacific. Clark was a Southern white who had fathered
several children by a black women. Fearing that he
might not return from the expedition and that his family
living in the South might be enslaved, he moved them
from the South to Cincinnati with enough money for
their support during his absence. One of his children,
Michael Clark, was the father of Peter H. Clark.[1]

In choosing Cincinnati, William Clark selected the
gateway to the South, and a city which was anything but
receptive to Negroes. The Black Laws passed in 1804 required Negroes to secure a $1,500 bond signed by two
"approved" white men who would guarantee their behavior and support. Twenty-five years later, the city's
attempt to enforce the law rigidly produced an anti-

Negro riot in which black lives and property were lost, and as a result, 1,200 Negroes left Cincinnati for Canada. There were other riots in 1836 and 1841. [2]

Cincinnati had no public schools for blacks until the nineteenth century was well advanced. Peter H. Clark began attending high school in 1844 at the Cincinnati High School, the first high school established for the education of the free black youths of the city and surrounding area. Many of its graduates went on to Oberlin College or other colleges that drew no line on color. Clark left the school in 1848, refusing a job with his father, a barber, "because it would make him move around at the dictates of every class of white men," and apprenticed himself to a liberal artisan, Thomas Varney, to learning stereotyping. [3]

In 1849, Clark became a teacher in the colored public schools established in Cincinnati. But since the law establishing free schools for colored children authorized blacks to elect their school directors, the racist school authorities, backed by the city officials of Cincinnati, challenged its constitutionality and refused meanwhile to turn over the money necessary to maintain the schools. Clark taught for two years without a salary until the courts upheld the law's constitutionality and ordered the city to pay the salaries of colored teachers from the time the schools were established. The suit against the city had been very costly for Cincinnati's blacks, and Clark, upon receiving his back pay, turned over the entire sum of $105 to the fund to defray the cost. This gesture, all who knew him declared, was typical of the man. In his work, "The Colored Schools of Cincinnati," L. D. Easton writes:

> For a number of years, Mr. Peter H. Clark labored, after school hours, instructing advanced classes of young people, and preparing teachers to maintain the supply demanded by the colored schools within a large radius of Cincinnati. In fact, it is safe to say that from 1859 to 1895 not a teacher in the colored schools, but had been trained by him. No one realized as he did, the pressing need of a high school for colored youth, and in 1865 he began to advocate its establishment. Always timid and apprehensive of its cost, a majority of the Board opposed the scheme, but in July, 1866, the measure received a majority of one vote, and in September the school was opened under the title of Gaines' High School with . . . Peter H. Clark, principal. [4]

Even though he was a principal and teacher, Clark found time to participate in the developing struggle against slavery and for equality for free blacks. He served as a conductor on the Underground Railroad and was associated with Frederick Douglass in the editorial management of

*The North Star.* [5] He was a Republican from the mid-1850s on, but not an uncritical one. In 1858, when the Republicans of Ohio refused to take a firm stand against the state's "black codes" and other aspects of the persuasive racial prejudice in the state, Clark told a convention of colored men in Cincinnati that "the rights of the Negro were no safer with the Republicans than with the Democrats" and that blacks should let it be known that their support was not to be taken for granted. [6]

After the Civil War, Clark remained a Republican but he began moving steadily to the left. He was instrumental in organizing the black teachers into the Colored Teachers Co-operative Association, which, from all available evidence, appears to have been the first trade union of teachers in American history. Clark represented the Colored Teachers Co-operative Association as a delegate to the 1870 convention of the National Labor Union. [7] Here he met another delegate from Cincinnati, William Haller, representing the "Workingmen's Organization." Haller, a former militant abolitionist, had become Cincinnati's "foremost voice of socialist protest in the post-Civil War years," and was the editor of the leading English-language socialist paper of the Midwest, *The Emancipator.* [8] Haller and Clark became life-long friends, and eventually, the black teacher became convinced that the socialist ideology Haller propounded offered the best answer to the problems facing the Negro people in the United States. [9]

In 1872, enraged by the failure of the Republicans to protect the citizen rights of his people in the South, and concerned over the growing influence of industrial capitalists in the party, Clark joined the Liberal Republicans. He soon became disillusioned with that movement, after it nominated Horace Greeley for president. At a meeting in Cincinnati, August 15, 1872, Clark rejected Charles Sumner's plea for Greeley and criticized the longtime editor of the *New York Tribune* for having advised President Lincoln to offer the slaveholders $400 million for their slaves:

> This earnest Abolitionist, whom Mr. Sumner so much admired, and for whom he advises us to vote, was willing to burden the laboring man of the North with a debt of four hundred millions of dollars to pay the masters of the South that sum for releasing their unfounded claims to the bodies and souls of their slaves. Had the proposed donation been to the slaves, there would have been some justice to the demand.

Although he returned to the Republican fold, Clark made it clear again that he considered it unwise for the Negro vote to be "concentrated in one party." [10]

In August 1875, Clark addressed the convention of Colored Newspaper Men in Cincinnati. He called for a militant black press both to "express our wants" and to educate blacks on the vital social and economic issues of the day, issues "which are for the most part unheeded by the press of the country." 11 In November 1875, he addressed the local Sovereigns of Industry in Cincinnati, 12 an organization concerned mainly with establishing cooperatives for the distribution of the necessities of life among wage earners. Clark vigorously supported its program of producer and consumer cooperatives, condemned extreme wealth and poverty alike as "curses," and urged the regulation of capital. The Republican *Cincinnati Commercial*, describing Clark's speech as "an intelligent review of the relations of capital and labor," summarized his remarks:

> The question most pertinent to the poor man is whether it is better to give him a benevolent loaf of bread, or put him in the way of earning it. He was decidedly in favor of the latter. Any other way of helping the poor man was a delusion and a snare. All methods at mere benevolence crushed the manhood out of him, and degraded and debased him. 13

However, Clark still remained a Republican; he attended the 1876 Republican National Convention and publicly supported the candidacy of Rutherford B. Hayes. 14 Toward the end of that year, his radicalism began to emerge clearly. On December 10, he addressed the Cincinnati Workingmen's Society on "Wages' Slavery and the Remedy." In the course of his speech, he condemned the "inordinate concentration of capital" and "large fortunes" as being "contrary to the welfare of society and to the interests of capital itself." He urged "the gradual reformation of the laws of society and of Government" as well as "thorough, intelligent, honest, and faithful labor organizations." Capital, he maintained, had to "give up some of its assumed selfish rights and give labor its share." 15

When Clark announced his renunciation of the Republican party and his support of the Workingmen's party on March 26, 1877, the socialists who were gathered at Robinson's Opera House "heartily applauded," and they interrupted his speech with cheers. Clark bitterly denounced the notion that the interests of capital and labor were the same and argued that the conflict between them "drenched the streets of Paris with blood, accounted for . . . strikes in England, the eviction of small tenants in Ireland, and the denial to the freedmen of the South of the right to purchase the land they till." He went on:

> Go to the South and see the capitalists banded together over the poor whites. They carefully calculate how much, and no more, it

will require to feed the black laborer and keep him alive from one year to another. That much they will give him for his hard labor, on which the aristocracy live, and not a cent more will they give him. Not a foot of land will they sell to the oppressed race who are trying to crowd out the degradation into which capital has plunged them. And here in Ohio nothing but the bayonet of the militia alone has kept the miners of the Southwestern part of the State groveling in the dust. Here in Cincinnati we have the working woman working hour after hour with her needle to eke out a bare existence. The great middle class of society is being crushed out.

The black educator pointed out that, while the middle class was being pushed into the ranks of the working class, the "millionaires" were growing in number. Only a few years before, he said, there had been just a few "millionaires" in American society, "but now they jostle each other in the streets while the men — the great mass of men — who toiled . . . to make the city what it is, have passed away in poverty and obscurity." He described his own bitter experience: unemployed for months on end, his wife and baby starving, and so desperate that he felt "like throwing himself in the river, and thus ending all his misery." It was then that he first understood what it meant to be unable to find work in the existing society through no fault of his own. Clark insisted that he did not hope for violence and that reforms would come "one by one." But he continued: "Capital must not rule, but be ruled and regulated. Capital must be taught that man, and not money, is supreme, and that legislation must be had for man." Dismissing the argument of the *laissez-faire* school that the less government the better, he insisted that government "is good; it is not an evil" if it were used in the interests of the working people. It was the government's duty "to so organize society that honest labor should not feel such oppression to drive it to desperation" as he had been driven during his months of unemployment. [16]

It was a remarkably moving speech, and William Haller, who had recruited Clark as a member of the party, rejoiced in his paper *The Emancipator*. It was one of the best speeches he had heard and "decidedly the best of the evening." [17]

Having joined the Workingmen's party of Cincinnati, Clark began to speak for the cause at street-corner meetings and trade-union gatherings. [18] It was not until the great railroad strike of 1877, however, that his name became widely known in the working-class circles of Cincinnati.

In the hot mid-July of 1877, exactly one year after the celebration of America's one hundredth birthday, with the nation prostrate after three and one-half years of severe depression, a general railroad strike developed into a national conflagration that brought the country closer to a social revolution than at any other time in its century of existence.

The strike came after the third 10-percent wage cut since the beginning of the depression. On Tuesday, July 16, 1877, railroad workers at Martinsburg, West Virginia, went on strike against the wage cut imposed by the Baltimore & Ohio Railroad. As the militia was called out and violence broke out, the strike extended up the B & O line and spread rapidly to other lines. Other workers came to the support of the railroad strikers, and by the weekend, angry crowds of workers were attacking the railroads and fighting with militia in the cities of West Virginia, Pennsylvania, and Ohio. The local militia generally sided with the strikers, and for the first time since Andrew Jackson's administration, federal troops were called in to suppress a strike. [19]

The headline in the *Cincinnati Enquirer* of July 23, 1877, read: "THE RED FLAG. IT CASTS ITS UGLY SHADOW OVER OUR QUEENLY CITY."

On the day before, the *Enquirer* had carried the following notice inserted by the Workingmen's party of Cincinnati:

### GREAT MASS-MEETING THIS AFTERNOON

At 2 o'clock at the Court Street Market Place.
All Good Citizens Are Invited to Appear.
Subject.

### THE GREAT STRIKE OF THE RAILROAD MEN.

At two in the afternoon, many workers fell in behind members of the German, Bohemian, and English-speaking sections of the Workingmen's party, led by the Eureka Brass Band, headed by a man carrying "the blood-red flag of the Commune." [20] An "immense crowd," estimated in the thousands, filled the marketplace and was divided into four sections—two for the German-speaking contingent and two for the English. Resolutions were presented and adopted. They charged the Baltimore & Ohio Railroad Company "and similar monopolies" with having reduced the wages of their "employees to a starvation point, and thereby forced them to desperate measures in order to better their condition"; condemned the governors of West Virginia, Pennsylvania, and Maryland and President Rutherford B. Hayes for using the military powers "in favor of said monopolies, regardless of the will of the people, and against the people, slaughtering innocent men, women, and children," and concluded by pledging to "use all *lawful* means to support the downtrodden, outraged railroad employees now on strike." [21]

Then came the key speech of the afternoon, which was delivered by

Peter H. Clark, black member of the English-speaking section. He condemned the railroad companies and their political allies, denounced the slaughter of workers by federal troops and state militia, and analyzed at length the causes of the economic crisis and its impact on the working class. "I sympathize in this struggle with the strikers," he declared, "and I feel sure that in this I have the cooperation of nine-tenths of my fellow citizens." But sympathy, he said, was not enough. It was necessary to create a society in which the widespread suffering that provoked the strike would be eliminated. "Every railroad in the land should be owned or controlled by the government. The title of private owners should be extinguished, and the ownership vested in the people." And this was only the beginning. Machinery—indeed all the means of production—had to be appropriated and used for the benefit of the people and not for private gain. There was only one "remedy for the evils of society"—socialism. "Choose ye this day which course ye shall pursue," Clark concluded to thunderous applause. The *Cincinnati Commercial*, which published Clark's speech in full under the heading "Socialism: The Remedy for the Evils of Society," reported that he was "well received." *The Emancipator* found his speech "characterized by that deep pathos of feeling that is to be expected of one who can look back at the time when the wrong and injustice of capital abused his race, which by its labors and sorrows helped to build the greatness of this nation." [22] Clark's speech to the railroad strikers was probably the first widely publicized proposal for socialism by a black American, and *The Emancipator*'s comment on it was probably the first recognition by an American socialist organ of the contributions of blacks to the building of American society.

Although the *Cincinnati Commercial* had published Clark's speech, it emphasized that it did not agree with him. "Mr. Peter H. Clark," it noted editorially, "can not understand why it is that the military are always against the strikers. It ought not to be a great mystery to a man of his analytic powers." According to the newspaper, a worker had the right to leave his employment if he was not satisfied with his wages, but he had no right to take possession of his employer's property and dictate to him what he should or should not do. The employer had a perfect right to appeal for protection, and if the sheriff could not provide it, the governor of the state was perfectly justified in calling out the militia. The worker, having "done an unlawful thing," had "put himself outside the law, defied the civil authority," and "made himself penally liable." That was all there was to it. "It seems to us if Mr. Clark would give his mind to the subject for a few hours he would be able to discover why it is that the military are in such crisis as the present on the side of law and order." [23]

Clark, however, was not persuaded. In "A Plea for the Strikers," he reminded the newspaper that he had experienced enough of what it meant to be poor to understand the meaning of the words in "Ecclesiastics": "I

beheld the tears of such as were oppressed and they had no comforter."
"With this fact imprinted on my memory by many years' sympathy with
and service in unpopular causes, I do not marvel when I see the oppression of the poor, and violent perverting of judgment and justice." As for
himself, he was "in every fiber and nerve a law-abiding citizen," one, indeed, who deprecated "violent words and violent deeds as much as any
one can. I am, sir, emphatically a law-and-order man." But not all the violent deeds and words were "on the part of the strikers and their friends."
The advocates of "law and order" boasted openly that they were prepared to "wipe out the strikers and their sympathizers. Thumbs have
been drawn significantly across the throats, and law-and-order men have
pulled at imaginary ropes to give me an inkling of the throat-cuttings
and hangings in reserve." The press, Clark pointed out, had no words of
condemnation for such conduct. The workers could hardly be blamed if
they took such threats seriously and also took steps to defend themselves. Nor should the reaction of the workers to what they saw about
them on the railroads be considered surprising. They were told that
wages must be reduced because the railroads were losing money:

> But when they see high railroad officials receiving the salaries of
> princes, when they hear of dividends on stock and interest on
> bonds, they cannot understand why there is no money for the
> man whose labors earn these vast sums. . . . When they complain,
> they are told that they are at liberty to quit and take their ser-
> vices elsewhere. This is equivalent to telling them that they are
> at liberty to go and starve. . . . Hence they make the effort to ob-
> tain an increase of wages and to retain their places at the same
> time. Understanding their motive, and the dire necessity by
> which they are driven, I pity, but I can not condemn them. . . .

> Then too, the door of justice seemed shut in their faces. They
> have no representation on the Board of Directors. Every State
> has laws punishing conspiracy, punishing riot and unlawful as-
> semblages, but no State has laws providing for the examination
> and redress of the grievances of which these men complain. The
> whole force of the State and National Governments may be in-
> voked by the railroad managers, but the laborer has nothing.

Clark declared that the right to resist wrong resided in every man and
that no laws could take this right away from him. "Hedged in and despairing, the railroad men have exercised this right," yet as the newspapers could attest, "the strikers themselves, are neither destructive nor
men of blood."

Clark concluded by defending the Workingmen's party against the charge that it had stirred up the strikers to acts of violence. Actually, he maintained, there was probably "not a section of that party in any one of the centers of disturbance." Had there been there would have been less tendency to disturbance: "When workingmen understand that there are peaceful influences at work to relieve them of the thraldom of wages slavery, they will be more patient." Clark even proposed that the railroad managers "plant a section of the Workingmen's party at every station. They would guard their property more effectually than the whole United States army can do it."[24]

*The Emancipator* applauded Clark's advice to the railway management and called it "correct every word of it." Clark, it observed, had put his finger on the real reason for "mob violence"—the refusal of the capitalists to permit the workers to organize and defend themselves against exploitation. "In endeavoring to weaken the power of the working people to protect their rights, by preventing organization, employers have increased the danger to their possessions an hundredfold. Gentlemen, the way to prevent another reign of terror is to help organize the laborers of the country."[25]

Both Clark and *The Emancipator* demonstrated genuine sympathy for understanding the problems of the strikers. However, they also advanced a naive proposal as to how the Workingmen's party of the United States could contribute to the elimination of the class struggle.

In a letter to Engels on July 25, 1877, Marx asked: "What do you think of the workers in the United States?" He was referring to the great railroad strike, which he called "the first uprising against the oligarchy of capital, which has arisen since the Civil War." Even though it was crushed, this explosion, coming after President Hayes' betrayal of the Negro people in the South, appeared to Marx to open up the real possibility for the establishment "of a serious workers' party in the United States," in which the blacks would become "allies of the workers."[26]

It is significant that Marx emphasized the special role the Negroes of the South (along with the white farmers) could play allied to the workers in this new party. It would appear that he believed that, up to that point, the Negro people had been too closely linked to and not sufficiently disillusioned with the Republican party to be potential allies in an independent labor party. Perhaps this was the reason for his indifference to the Negro question throughout the Reconstruction era, after his initial rebuke of Johnson's policy. Whatever interpretation Marx's comments in July 1877 are susceptible to, it is a fact that apart from his reference to the hostility of the poor whites in the South against Negroes in his 1870 letter to Meyer and Vogt, they represent his only reference to the Negro question in his correspondence during the twelve years following the Civil War. Research on Marx's still unpublished correspondence in the archives of the Institute of Marxism-Leninism in the Soviet Union and the Institut Für Marxismus-Leninismus in the German Democratic Republic has failed to turn up any evidence to contradict this conclusion.

Since Marx, in his correspondence with American Marxists, never raised the possibility that the Southern Negro might now become an ally of the white workers, it cannot be said that this view guided them in their activities in the newly formed Workingmen's party. Nevertheless, it appears that the railroad strike of 1877 did produce increased efforts in the party's ranks to build a Negro-labor alliance. Even though the Workingmen's party did not initiate the strike, once it began its members became involved in the struggle in every important city. And, as was the case with Clark in Cincinnati, they were addressing large audiences of strikers. In Chicago, the party's leadership was given a share in the command, and in St. Louis, where there was actually a general strike, a party-sponsored Executive Committee organized and led the strike and was even in power temporarily.

Although sporadic flareups continued throughout the country well into August, the great uprising of 1877 was over by the end of July—crushed by local police, state militia, and especially by 3,000 federal troops who had been moved into the strike areas by President Rutherford B. Hayes. "The strikers have been put down by force," President Hayes wrote in his diary. More than 100 of them had been killed in the process. [27]

After the strike had been crushed through government intervention and "social peace" was restored, the *Labor Standard* called attention to several highlights of the struggle waged on such an unprecedented national scale. One of the themes it stressed was the high level of black-white unity that had emerged. Addressing a meeting of the Amalgamated Trade Unions in New York City, J. P. McDonnell, a leading American Marxist and editor of the *Labor Standard*, declared:

> It was a grand sight to see in West Virginia, white and colored men standing together, men of all nationalities in one supreme contest for the common rights of workingmen. (*Loud cheers*). The barriers of ignorance and prejudice were fast falling before the growing intelligence of the masses. Hereafter there shall be no north, no south, no east, no west, only one land of labor and the workingmen must own and possess it. (*Tremendous applause*). [28]

There was some truth to this proud declaration, but there were also limitations caused by the continued presence of racism within the ranks of the Workingmen's party of the United States. A case in point is St.

Louis. At a mass meeting sponsored by the sections of the party in that city on July 24, it was suggested "that the colored men should have a chance." At that, a Negro steamboat man mounted the stand and described the plight of the blacks who worked on the levees and steamboats. "We work in the summer for $20 a month," he said, "and in winter time we can't find the man we work for." He asked the crowd if they would stand behind strikers, "regardless of color," and the shout came back immediately, "We will." 29

The black steamboat man had had reason to raise the question. Since the end of slavery, neither the trade unions nor the socialist organizations of St. Louis had displayed any willingness to cooperate with black workers, and the Workingmen's party of St. Louis had not made the slightest effort to recruit blacks during its year of existence. The answer of the crowd, "We will," had encouraged the black workers. They began to join with white workers in the general strike that developed in St. Louis, and they also joined with them in mass meetings sponsored by the Workingmen's party. One reporter wrote:

> Great crowds of strikers and some 300 Negro laborers on the levee visited a large number of manufacturing establishments in the southern part of the city, compelling all employees to stop work, putting out all fires in the engine rooms and closing the building. . . . The colored part of the crowd marched up the levee and forced all steamboat companies and officers of independent steamers to sign pledges to increase the wages of all classes of steamboat and levee laborers sixty to one hundred per cent.

After they had obtained written promises of higher pay, the workers "of all colors" headed triumphantly to join a great procession of strikers under the sponsorship of the Workingmen's party. 30

A reporter for the *New York Sun* noted that the Negro participation with white workers in the general strike was "a novel feature of the times." This "novel feature" soon disturbed both the establishment of St. Louis and the white supremacists in the Workingmen's party. The establishment was quite naturally shocked to see blacks abandoning their assigned role of "contented banjo-strummers" and asserting their rights just as if they were white. In its description of the Negro strikers who paraded on the levee before joining the great procession, the *Missouri Republican* labeled them "a dangerous-looking set of men." It observed, almost in terror, that "there was something blood-curdling in the manner in which they shouldered their clubs and started up the levee whooping." As blacks began to appear in processions and at the mass meetings sponsored by the Workingmen's party, the press, particularly the *Missouri Republican*, painted a picture of a movement that was being taken over by "notorious Negroes." It was all the result, they charged, of the "insidious influence of the International," and the Workingmen's party was accused of being responsible for these "outrages" against the social values of the community. [31]

This was enough for the white supremacists in the Workingmen's party. After the strike, Albert Currlin, a leader of the German section and a prominent member of the Executive Committee of the Workingmen's party of the United States, which had organized and was leading the general strike, was interviewed by the *St. Louis Times*. In the course of the interview, Currlin stressed that the Executive Committee had been shocked by the role the "niggers" had assumed in the parades and mass meetings, and that it had tried to dissuade white workers "from going with the niggers." (The derogatory term is Currlin's.) One sure way of keeping blacks out of mass meetings and white workers from going with black workers was not to hold mass meetings. There is little doubt that racism played an important part in the Executive Committee's decision to hold no further mass meetings — a decision that guaranteed the disintegration of the great upheaval. [32]

Throughout the nation, the bitterness evoked by the alliance of employers and the government during the strikes caused a political upheaval as labor turned to independent political action to redress its grievances. The Workingmen's party of the United States campaigned actively for the socialist candidates in the fall elections of 1877. In Maryland, the Workingmen's party appealed to workers and all citizens, "without regard to race, nationality or political creed," to support its candidates. In Cincinnati, the party nominated Peter H. Clark for state superintendent of schools. The other candidates on the socialist ticket were a white native American, a Bohemian, a German cigar maker, and an Irish stonecutter. In the party's official organ, *The Emancipator*, William Haller called for special efforts to pile up a big vote for the black candidate:

> Peter H. Clark of all the candidates on the ticket most thoroughly represents the contest between laborers and capitalists, of the proscribed race, whose sorrows made the name of the United States the synonym of robbery and murder throughout the world; his nomination is therefore above all others the finest vindication of the claim that the Workingmen's Party is a purely cosmopolitan organization.

> But a long time since this man of learning and culture, now the principal of our colored schools, was a youth, on the streets of

Cincinnati battling for a living as a newspaper carrier, hated and proscribed because he belonged to a class whose labors had opened every field in the South, and whose woes and miseries had ladened every breeze with appeals to the hearts of the just for the wrong and injustice of slavery to be lifted off of Africa's outraged sons and daughters. [33]

Clark campaigned enthusiastically for the Workingmen's party. That summer and fall he spoke for the Socialists in Louisville and in Jeffersonville, Indiana. A Louisville socialist wrote: "Clark for reasoning can't be beat." Clark's "reasoning" consisted of pointing out to working-class audiences that the Great Strike had proved the socialist contention that the local, state, and national governments of the United States were controlled by, of, and for the capitalists. He counseled that, just as the capitalists were preparing for future labor conflicts by building up the armed forces, so the workers should prepare by electing socialists to office to guarantee that these forces would not be used to break strikes.

The socialist ticket fared badly in the fall election, but Clark ran ahead of the entire ticket. In 1878, he was chosen a member of the National Executive Committee of the newly formed Socialist Labor party. [34]

Although the role of the Workingmen's party in the railroad strike contributed to an increase in both its membership and the circulation of its press, soon after the strike the rift between the Lassalleans and the Marxists widened into a split. When the party sanctioned participation in the electoral campaign with an independent party ticket, thus reversing the policy that the former Internationalists had made a condition of unity, they seceded, leaving the Workingmen's party in the hands of the Lassalleans. In December 1877, the Lassallean "politicals" formed the Socialist Labor party.

## THE SOCIALIST LABOR PARTY AND BLACKS

Originally called the *Sozialistiche Arbeiter-Partei*, or in its English version, the Socialistic Labor party (SLP), a title that was changed fifteen years later to Socialist Labor party, the SLP was the only socialist party in post-Civil War United States to survive and maintain its existence over any extended period of time. [35] The records of the SLP's founding convention in December 1877 reveal that it took no stand on the Negro question in the platform, constitution, or discussions of the delegates, and no resolutions on the subject were introduced or adopted. This neglect persisted until 1879 when the SLP platform for that year declared itself in favor of "universal and equal rights of suffrage without regard to color, creed, or sex." At this convention, Philip Van Patten, SLP general secretary, told the delegates that in Ohio, "Peter H. Clark, a colored man," had been a party candidate for Congress the preceding fall, together with Solomon Ruthenberg. He pointed with pride to the fact that the first socialist congressional nominees in American history were one black and one white. [36]

This pride was justified, and the *Conservator*, a Chicago black weekly, reported early in 1879 that "a colored man named George Mack has joined the Socialist party in New York." It also noted that he was "the first colored man to wear the red badge." *The Socialist*, the leading English-language SLP organ, also published in Chicago, was quick to point out that not only had Peter H. Clark "for some time past been a member of the organization . . . [and] has been for the past year a member of the National Executive committee," but that many other "colored men" in Chicago and other cities had "lately joined the party." How many and just who they were was never made clear in the reports of the various sections of the SLP.

The *Conservator* had urged the socialists to move into the South, predicting an enthusiastic response from Southern blacks but at the same time warning that if a black socialist like George Mack went organizing for the party in South Carolina, he would be "wise to insure his life before he attempts to work it." *The Socialist* assured the *Conservator* that, risk or no risk, the SLP would bring its message to blacks in the South and would seek to convince them that through socialism they would secure real emancipation. [37]

But deeds rarely followed words when it came to socialism and black Americans, and this pledge was no exception. [38] Only twice after this pledge did *The Socialist* even mention blacks in the South, and on both occasions the reference was to the Negro exodus of 1879, when blacks moved from the South in large numbers to escape mob law and violence, poverty, inadequate educational opportunities, and the loss of their political rights. Many of them headed for the "Promised Land" of Kansas, though quite a few remained stranded, penniless and destitute, in St. Louis. [39] *The Socialist* did little to enlighten the SLP membership on the causes and scope of the exodus. [40] All it offered to Southern blacks was the advice to remain in the South, where they might come to realize that they were entitled to the full fruits of their labor on the soil, at which time they "would soon have the pleasure of seeing their present taskmaster work alongside them." [41] It is difficult to understand how a socialist organ could believe that such advice would convince the poverty-stricken blacks that the party it spoke for offered them a way out of their misery. Had *The Socialist* reported the destitute state of the "exodusters" (the name given to blacks involved in the exodus), stranded in St. Louis, and had it appealed for relief from the party members, or had its section in St. Louis organized its members to demand that the city officials become involved in the relief of the migrants, the socialists could have enhanced their reputation in the black community. But the SLP appears not even to have been aware of the plight of the exodusters. While Section New Orleans boasted that it had raised funds for the relief of yellow fever sufferers in that city, Section St. Louis never once mentioned the black migrants in its reports to national headquarters. Finally, in Kansas itself, the socialists not only did nothing to aid the indigent black migrants, but G. C. Clemens, the leading socialist in that state, condemned the blacks for overrunning the West and characterized the exodusters as "petty-thieving colored paupers." [42]

It is small wonder, then, that, despite *The Socialist*'s optimistic prediction, the SLP recruited few blacks in the following years and that those already in the party abandoned the movement. In the summer of 1879, Peter H. Clark announced his departure. He stated that his decision was made not because of any lessening in his belief in socialism, for, as he pointed out, he had remained with the party despite threats that he would lose his job as principal of Gaines High School in Cincinnati if he did not resign and repudiate socialism. The campaign failed, Clark proudly noted, "when the colored people of Cincinnati, who had stood by me all my life-time, came to my rescue just as if I had been a son and brother. They laid aside political prejudices and religious prejudices, and came out as one man and protested my removal." [43]

Still, Clark found the Cincinnati SLP more and more disappointing as a force through which blacks might redress their grievances. For one thing, William Haller's influence in the party declined after 1877, as a result of which the Negro question was played down in the party press and activities. [44] For another, intense factionalism plagued the party, and more time was spent in personal recriminations than in discussing concrete issues. Clark found the factional strife and the party's failure to concern itself with the problems of blacks too much to ignore. [45] In his farewell address as a member of the SLP on July 21, 1879, Clark announced that he was still a "socialist" but would wait for a movement of socialism to arise which would speak in the interests of his people. "The welfare of the Negro is my controlling political motive," he told his white comrades as he urged them to abandon their factional disputes and begin paying some attention to issues that might make the party attractive to blacks. [46]

That Clark remained a socialist for some time after he left the SLP is indicated in the moving eulogy he delivered at the funeral services for

William Haller, his old friend in the socialist cause, who died on March 1, 1881. He began by thanking Haller for having introduced him to social-ism, and he went on to praise him as an agitator for social justice:

> He had dreams of the millennium. Those visions which have in-spired the prophets and sages of the past. To him Utopia was not Utopian; he believed that the day might come when the "lion and the lamb" should lie down together, and a little child should lead them. The New Jerusalem of his hope was not in a different life and beyond the sky, but here—here upon earth, and dwelt in by living men.

In his quest for social justice and racial equality, Haller had demon-strated that "such lives . . . beating themselves out in strife with hoary wrongs, shall not be lived in vain." [47]

"The welfare of the Negro is my controlling political motive," Clark re-peatedly insisted, [48] but the SLP rarely concerned itself with the "wel-fare of the Negro." To be sure, the party's demand for "equal rights of suffrage without regard to color" was a feature of every SLP platform during the 1880s, but the Party did nothing to implement this general statement. Discussions at party conventions, editorials, and letters in the party press, together with the records and correspondence of the national office and the various sections, all reveal that the SLP leaders and members were oblivious to the increasing attacks on the political rights of blacks in the South. They were also oblivious to the deteriora-ting economic position of the black sharecroppers and craftsmen, and the exclusion of blacks from Northern industry in a decade of increasing in-dustrial growth and of mounting importation of workers from Europe to meet the labor needs of industry. [49]

While the first secretary of the SLP was a native American, it is esti-mated that not more than 10 percent of the membership in the early years was native born. Of the 90 percent who were of foreign origin, Germans were the most numerous, many of them refugees from Bismarck's repres-sive regime in Germany. [50] Few of them settled in the South.

The role of the German-American socialists was the subject of lengthy discussion by Frederick Engels. After Marx's death in March 1883, Engels was the man to whom leading socialists in various countries turned for advice and help. [51] While Engels devoted most of his attention in the 1880s to the movements in France and Germany, he had much to say about the role of the socialists in the United States. Throughout the decade, Engels castigated the German-American socialists for their sec-tarian approach to the American working class. He complained that they did not appreciate the fact that "our theory" was not "a credo," but "a guide for action," something that was living, not dead. Their refusal, on principle, to learn English was to him an example not only of their narrowmindedness, but also of their political ineptitude. It is no wonder that in a letter to Sorge, Engels declared in exasperation that "if the whole *German* Socialist Party went to pieces . . . it would be a gain, but we can hardly expect anything so good as that."[52]

Engels' criticism of the German-American socialists for refusing to learn English and for confining their activities to German-speaking workers was echoed by John Swinton, labor champion and admirer of Karl Marx. In 1885, Swinton resigned his editorship of the *New York Sun* and started his own paper, a weekly labor organ called *John Swinton's Paper*. In the February 21, 1886, issue, Swinton chided the German-American socialists for isolating themselves from the "general life" of the nation by refusing to "speak, read and write the American language . . . which is spoken by over fifty millions of our progressive population white and black." That Swinton mentioned blacks as part of the American "progressive population" which the SLP was failing to reach reflected his awareness, as a former abolitionist, that the SLP was making no special effort to address itself to the needs of black Americans. He commented, too, that, although the party continued to come out in its platform for universal suffrage regardless of race or color, it included no other specific demands for the Negro people and appeared to believe that this one issue which it did raise would be self-fulfilling.[53]

Unfortunately, in his extensive correspondence with American socialists during the 1880s, Engels never once mentioned this serious shortcoming in the SLP's platform and activities, or used his influence to correct it. His failure to do so did not stem from charges by enemies of Marxism that he had no right to issue commands to individual national parties. Indeed, when this charge was leveled against Marx in 1881, Engels wrote:

> Through theoretical and practical work achievements Marx has gained for himself such a position that the best people in all the working-class movements throughout the world have full confidence in him. At critical junctures they turn to him for advice and then usually find that his counsel is the best. . . . It is therefore not a case of Marx forcing his opinion, and still less his will, on the people, but of the people coming to him of themselves. . . . It would only harm us to try to influence people against their will, it would destroy the old confidence dating back to the time of the International.[54]

Engels believed that what he had written about Marx was valid for himself. His failure to advise American socialists on the Negro question at a time when he was pointing out the weaknesses of their work can only be

ascribed to the small importance he attributed to this issue in his evaluation of the American scene.

Nor was Engels the only leading European socialist who did not advise
American socialists about their failure to deal with the problems of black
Americans. In the fall of 1886, the Socialist Labor party played host to
three important European visitors. At its invitation, Wilhelm Liebknecht, German socialist leader and long time co-worker of Marx and
Engels, Dr. Edward Aveling, an English physiologist and socialist, and
his wife, Eleanor Marx, the daughter of Karl Marx, undertook an extended lecture tour through the United States. In New York, Boston,
Washington, Pittsburgh, Milwaukee, St. Louis, Minneapolis, Chicago,
and other cities, they addressed enthusiastic rallies of American socialists and their sympathizers. Although their primary purpose was to raise
money for socialist party struggles in Europe, the three guests took the
opportunity to lecture on socialist doctrine and sought to influence the
socialists to play a more active role in the struggles of the American
workers. Despite their position as recognized leaders of the European
Marxist movement, not once did they lecture the socialists on their neglect of the basic problems facing blacks. Indeed, they never even mentioned the Negro question. Nor did they deal with it in the published
accounts of their visit to the United States. One searches in vain in
Liebknecht's *Ein Blick in die Neue Welt* (A View of the New World), a
volume consisting of letters and daily sketches written aboard boats and
trains and first published in Stuttgart in 1887; in Edward and Eleanor
Marx Aveling's *The Working-Class Movement in America*, published in
book form in 1888 (although much of the account had appeared earlier in
various journals); or in Edward Aveling's *An American Journey*, a collection of articles written en route, for any significant reference to blacks.
*The Working-Class Movement in America* contains a chapter on "The
Cowboys," but the only mention of blacks is the sentence "It is worth
noting that the immense coloured population of Kansas is beginning to
understand the wage-slavery question." [55] The fact that German-American socialists were doing so little to increase this "understanding" did
not merit comment.

The failure of socialist leadership to express even a passing concern for
the problems of black Americans in 1886 contributed to the SLP's continued neglect of this issue throughout the decade.


## KNIGHTS OF LABOR, SOCIALISTS, AND RACISM

In his letters to American correspondents, Engels urged the socialists
to work within the Knights of Labor to arouse the masses. Despite the

fact that he characterized the Order as having "confused principles and . . . ridiculous organizations," he urged American Marxists to "form within this quite plastic mass a core of people who understand the movement and its aims." From all he had heard, "the K. of L. are a real power, especially in New England and the West, and are becoming more so every day owing to the brutal opposition of the capitalists." Therefore, he maintained, it was urgent that the American Marxists "work inside them" and influence their policies. 56

Engels evidently did not know that some American Marxists, members of the Socialist Labor party, were already working inside the Knights of Labor and helping to build an alliance of black and white workers.

In 1869, nine Philadelphia garment cutters, whose union had been shattered and its members blacklisted, formed a secret society and named it the Noble Order of the Knights of Labor. The Knights opened its membership to anyone eighteen years of age or older who worked for a living, except for lawyers, doctors, bankers, and those engaged in the sale of liquor. Women were not eligible for membership until 1881, but from the outset, the Knights of Labor did not exclude any male workers because of color or race, political or religious belief, or place of birth — unless he was Chinese. It was founded and grew on the rock of labor solidarity as expressed in its slogan: "An injury to one is the concern of all."

Estimates of the membership of the Knights of Labor at its peak in 1886 vary from 700,000 to more than a million. Whatever the actual figure, the fact is that the Knights achieved what no labor group before it had accomplished — the organization and unification of the American working class. The Order did not wage a constant, determined campaign to eliminate racism from its ranks, but it did, for the first time, bring large numbers of skilled and unskilled black workers into the predominantly white labor movement. At the height of its strength, in 1886, there were no less than 60,000 Negroes in its ranks, and it was estimated that there were over 400 all-Negro locals in the organization, most of them in the South. 57

For a short time, the Knights were instrumental in establishing and maintaining many producers' and consumers' cooperatives. This effort attracted many blacks in the South who saw in the cooperatives, not so much a means of escaping wage slavery, but rather a method of escaping price-gouging landlord-storekeepers. Most of the all-Negro assemblies in the Southern and border states had cooperative stores associated with them; a black assembly in Little Rock, Arkansas, established a steam cotton gin cooperative, and in Richmond, Virginia, black and white Knights jointly operated a cooperative soap factory. 58

The Knights were not able to counter the racial injustices of the South on any lasting basis, or to develop a pattern of genuine equal participation of blacks in the Order. Local assemblies were always established on a segregated basis in the South; black candidates in both the North and South were sometimes barred from local offices solely on the basis of color, and the Knights never really made a dent in the exclusionary practices that kept blacks out of the major industries and restricted them mainly to farming and domestic service. But black-white unity was created in the Order on a scale unprecedented up to that time in the history of American labor, and in New York, where the socialists were a prominent element in the Order, such unity was achieved to a very high degree.

A Brooklyn Knight wrote to John Swinton: "I am connected with an assembly of the Knights of Labor which contains 450 members, 25 of whom are colored, and there has not been a single outburst of feeling on account of color. I am a colored man myself, and am Worthy Treasurer, an office which was forced upon me for the third time." [59] The Brooklyn local assembly was part of the powerful District Assembly 49 of New York in which socialists exerted a dominant influence, and its policy of electing blacks to leadership positions reflected the influence of these socialists. [60]

Among District Assembly 49's leaders were white socialists like Timothy Quinn, district master workman, Victor Drury, formerly a leading figure in the French sections of the First International in the United States, and Thomas B. Maguire, an Irish-American labor spokesman. Its secretary-treasurer was the second important black socialist in the United States and the most famous Negro in the Knights of Labor — Frank J. Ferrell. Ferrell, a New York City machinist and stationary engineer, had been recruited into the Socialist Labor party soon after he joined the Order. An effective speaker, he soon rose to prominence in District 49 and addressed meetings of the local assemblies that made up the district on trade unionism and socialism. Although none of his speeches is available, the black press reported that they were influential in building black-white solidarity in District 49. [61]

The white socialists and the black socialist of District 49 were leaders in the effort to organize Chinese workers. Ferrell made this a special issue, noting that blacks, exploited and discriminated against because of race or color, were opposed to the anti-Chinese position of the Knights' leadership as set forth by the erratic grand master workman, Terence V. Powderly. Powderly issued an edict soon after he assumed his position that Asians could not be members of the Order and, furthermore, that they were unfit even to reside in the United States. Together, Ferrell and Timothy Quinn organized two groups of Chinese in New York City. When an effort was made to secure charters for them as regular local assemblies, opposition arose, particularly among Knights on the West

Coast, where anti-Chinese propaganda, playing on workers' fears of job competition, had long been standard. A majority of the General Executive Board was opposed to granting the charters, but a minority, composed mainly of the representatives of District 49—Drury, Maguire, and Ferrell—spoke out in favor of the request. In the minority report, signed by these three and by Captain Mazzi, an Italian exile and master workman of an Italian local, emphasis was placed on the fact that "the first and basic principle of the organization was the obliteration of lines of distinction in creed, color or nationality." It further argued that the only remedy for the problem created by the employers' use of the Chinese to cut the wages of other workers was, as in the case of blacks, to organize the Chinese. Pointing to the fact that the Chinese had conducted a militant strike for higher wages in California in 1884, the report concluded that this group could make a valuable contribution to the labor movement when they were organized. [62]

Nevertheless, the opposition was too strong and the charters were denied. Even after the Chinese assemblies were dissolved and transferred to "mixed" assemblies, however, they were welcomed into District 49. It was largely because of the black and white socialists in the Order that Powderly grudgingly informed the public that "we have some Chinese Knights of Labor." [63]

## FERRELL AND THE 1886 KNIGHTS OF LABOR CONVENTION

District 49's most famous stand in favor of racial equality occurred at the Richmond convention of the Knights of Labor in 1886. A few months before the convention, master workman Quinn sent a delegation to Richmond to see which hotels would be available for the sixty delegates, including Ferrell, the only black delegate from the district. On the basis of this report, the district officers made arrangements for all the delegates to stay at the hotel of Colonel Murphy, a Confederate war veteran. When the colonel discovered that one of his guests would be a Negro, he canceled the contract, arguing that Negroes would not be allowed in many Northern hotels and that "customs here must be respected." He offered to provide Ferrell with quarters at a Negro hotel. [64]

When District 49 learned that they could have accommodations at the hotel only if Ferrell were excluded, it unanimously adopted the following resolution, introduced by master workman Quinn: "That no arrangements be made for hotel accommodations for the delegates from this district that excludes any delegates without regard to color, creed or nationality." District 49's delegates, most of them socialists, came to Richmond carrying tents, as an indication that they would under no cir-

cumstances abandon their Negro brother. The *New York Times* correspondent from Richmond, noting that these delegates were not only
Knights but also members of the SLP, remarked:

> These delegates are determined to fight the color line right in the
> midst of that part of the country where race prejudice is the
> strongest, and they will insist on carrying on what they claim is a
> fundamental principle of their Order—that the black man is the
> equal of the white socially as well as politically, and that all races
> stand upon an equal footing in all respects.[65]

The delegates from District 49 immediately proceeded to demonstrate
that the *Times'* correspondent had quoted them accurately. They succeeded in getting board with several Negro families, and a dozen delegates worshipped at the only Negro Catholic Church in Richmond. They
also attended, in a body, a performance of *Hamlet* at the Mozart
Academy of Music in Richmond. Ferrell, seated between two of his white
socialist brothers in the orchestra, became the first Negro in Richmond's
history to occupy an orchestra seat in a theater.[66]

Before the convention opened, Quinn approached Powderly, explained
to him what had happened at Colonel Murphy's hotel, and requested that
Ferrell be allowed to introduce the governor of Virginia, Fitzhugh Lee, to
the assembly. Powderly objected on the ground that "it would not be
pleasant for either the Governor or the convention to attempt to set at
defiance a long established usage." He suggested instead that Ferrell introduce him (Powderly) after the governor had spoken. This compromise
was accepted.

With over 800 delegates assembled in the Armory Hall of the First
Virginia Regiment, the largest hall in the city, delegate Ferrell, a black
socialist member of the Order's General Executive Board, pointed out to
the delegates and to the governor of Virginia, who was seated on the platform, that one objective of the Knights of Labor was "the abolition of
those distinctions which are maintained by creed or color."[67]

The dispute over Ferrell's introductory speech was not the only occasion on which Powderly stepped in to tone down District 49's bold attempt to assert the Order's equalitarianism. On behalf of the district,
Quinn introduced a resolution to the convention declaring that the
Knights of Labor recognized "the civil and political equality of all men
and women in the broad field of labor, and recognizes no distinction on
account of color." Powderly, fearful of antagonizing Southern white
opinion, including that of the white delegates from Southern assemblies,
insisted that the resolution be amended by adding the words "but it has

no purpose to interfere with or disrupt the social relations which may exist between different races in any portion of the country." Over District 49's objection, this concession to white supremacy was adopted. [68]

Ferrell's prominent role at the convention, the refusal of white socialist delegates to accept hotel accommodations and seats in the theaters because Negroes were excluded, and the high degree, for that time, of Negro-white solidarity expressed at Richmond caused the Southern press to accuse the Knights of being an agency of "the Socialist conspiracy to overthrow existing social relations in our communities." The Negro press, while criticizing Powderly for his capitulations to racism, had only words of the highest praise for the Order. Negro newspapers which had earlier expressed distrust of unions were now specifically recommending that blacks join the Knights of Labor. "Taking all things into consideration, time, place, surroundings," the *Cleveland Gazette* editorialized, "it is the most remarkable thing since emancipation. The race's cause has secured a needed ally in the Knights of Labor organization." It urged all Negro newspapers, especially in the South, to spur their readers into joining the Knights since it was "generally seen and admitted that it is a grand organization and will do more for them than any other agency in existence." [69]

The *New York Freeman*, the leading black newspaper, edited by the foremost black journalist T. Thomas Fortune, not only praised the Order for the display of labor solidarity at Richmond, but singled out District 49 for special commendation: "District Assembly 49 of New York should be placed at the head of the class for a square-toed manifestation of true manhood and most unusual courage." [70]

The black community of Richmond expressed its attitude in a banquet honoring District Assembly 49. Inside Harris Hall, 100 delegates and their friends were "seated without reference to color" around two tables "stretched the length of the hall." In a speech to the diners, Victor Drury pointed out that District 49 was applying the fundamental principles of socialism. A reporter, observing that Drury "seemed to be inspired by the occasion to a flight of oratory unusual even in him," paraphrased him as follows:

> that what Forty-Eight was to the oppressed millions of Europe, it was hoped Forty-Nine might be to the struggling masses of Americans in this day, and this play upon words and reference to a red-letter period of revolutionary spirit nearly forty years ago abroad were received with cheers. He declared that if it were their fate to die, as three great champions of the brotherhood of man had died—Socrates by the poison hemlock, Christ upon the

cross, and John Brown upon the scaffold—they would go to their fate saying with Christ, "forgive them, Father, for they know not what they do." [71]

## THE SLP AND THE NEGRO, 1887-1890

Anyone who relied on the SLP press for information would have been unaware that party members were making the question of race discrimination and black-white labor unity national issues. Actually, none of the events involving District 49 and black workers received any attention in SLP publications—not even the testimonial dinner in honor of District 49 tendered by Richmond's black community. The *Workmen's Advocate*, the English-language SLP organ published in New York City and New Haven, carried no news at all about the contributions of socialist Knights in the battle against racism. But then, in its entire career between 1885 and 1889, the socialist weekly published only two articles relating to blacks. [72]

The 1887 SLP convention did adopt the report of its committee on the "attitude of socialists towards trades unions and the Order of the Knights of Labor," which urged members to "foster our democratic principles in any . . . K. of L. Assembly in which they may hold membership," and to likewise foster the recognition of "the solidarity of all wage workers." [73] But the committee accorded no special praise to SLP members in the Knights of Labor for their work in this very connection so far as the Negro question was concerned, nor did it acknowledge that other members might learn from their experiences. It is no wonder that in the section of his *History of Socialism in the United States* dealing with the SLP and the Knights of Labor, based only on the party press and convention proceedings, Morris Hillquit does not even mention District 49 and its role in upholding the principles of racial equality in the Order. In fact, he writes that "only when the Order was already on the decline, toward the beginning of the nineties, did the socialists gain actual influence in the organization." [74] This was the period when, as we shall see, the party press and publications first dealt with the role of socialists in the Knights of Labor.

The truth is that the SLP leadership maintained that black workers were workers just like white workers, and that since only socialism could solve the problems of workers, only activity for socialism could be judged socialist activity. The contributions of socialist Knights in pointing out the special problems facing black workers, and their role in combatting the special forms of racism burdening black workers, particularly in the South, were not considered socialist contributions. Hence, they received no attention in the party press, convention proceedings, or in the correspondence between American and European socialist leaders.

The special character of the problems facing black Americans was becoming clearer as the decade advanced. The resurgence of white supremacy in the South, the disfranchisement of the Negro by terrorism and undemocratic political maneuvers, the Supreme Court decision invalidating the Civil Rights Act of 1875, the neglect of the Negro's welfare by Republican and Democratic administrations alike, and the continuing inability of the black worker to find a place in Northern industry—all these were manifestations of the special character of the Negro question. [75] The SLP ignored them all, just as it ignored the battle for black-white unity in the Knights of Labor and contented itself with repeating, convention after convention, that it stood for "universal and equal rights of suffrage without regard to color, creed or sex."

# 4

## The Decade of the Nineties: From De Leon and De Leonism to Debs and Social Democracy

In the 1890s, the Socialist Labor party came under the guidance and leadership of the brilliant, though erratic, Daniel De Leon. De Leon lost his position as a Columbia University lecturer when he became involved in labor's campaign to elect Henry George mayor of New York City in 1886. He joined the SLP following a brief sojourn in Edward Bellamy's utopian Nationalist movement and after some intense reading of the works of Marx and Engels. He first achieved a position of importance in the SLP in the spring of 1891 when he was appointed national lecturer and was sent on an agitational tour across the country. The tour was part of an effort to reach English-speaking audiences with the party's message and marked the launching of a serious attempt to break with the past concentration on foreign-language groups. The new English-language organ, *The People*, at first a weekly and later a daily in New York City, was also begun in the spring of 1891, succeeding the defunct *Workmen's Advocate*.

On his return to New York, De Leon was appointed assistant editor of *The People* under Lucien Sanial, a veteran socialist and former French naval officer. When Sanial was named SLP delegate to the Brussels Congress of the Socialist International in August 1891, the ex-professor was given the post of editor, a position he held until his death in May 1914.

De Leon espoused a dizzying combination of half-baked Marxism and anarchosyndicalism. He translated and popularized some of Marx's works that had been unavailable in English up to that time, but he usually omitted sections with which he did not agree. In general, he brought the ideas of the SLP to a much broader audience than before. His service both in this respect and in exposing the class-collaboration policies of the trade-union leadership of the period was seriously weakened by his dogmatism, his sectarian policies, and by his view that all immediate demands for improvements under capitalism were "banana peels under the feet of the workers," retarding the struggle to achieve socialism. [1]

Under Sanial's and De Leon's editorship, *The People* continued the neglect of black Americans that had characterized its predecessor, the *Workmen's Advocate*. [2] This neglect was also reflected in De Leon's reports to the paper during his national tour as party lecturer. [3] However, by 1896, articles dealing with blacks began to appear in *The People*, and by the turn of the century they were a regular feature. Therefore, whatever his other shortcomings, De Leon deserves credit for being the first American socialist leader since the Civil War to address himself to the Negro question.

## THE SLP ON THE "NEGRO QUESTION"

The August 29, 1897, issue of *The People* marks a great landmark in the history of American socialism and black Americans. For the first time since the abolition of slavery, an American socialist paper carried an article entitled "The Negro Question in America." It was written by J. Howard Sharp, an SLP member who lived in the Deep South and resided then in Tennessee. It opened with a discussion of the efforts of African Methodist Episcopal Bishop Henry McNeil Turner to organize a mass migration of blacks to Africa. Sharp rejected this scheme as impractical, but he observed that since "the American negro's future is indelibly linked with that of the United States, it will be well that we as Socialists examine his condition, surroundings and prospects for as a wage worker the destiny of the negro is part of our own." Never before had an American socialist called upon his party to perform such a task. Sharp's analysis of what the socialists could do to win black support was weak, since he believed that, in view of the difficulty of making headway against racism in the South, where the majority of blacks lived, any efforts would be fruitless. Nevertheless, he also believed that capitalism would soon bring about real changes in the South and with them "enlarged opportunities for the spread of Socialism." Meanwhile, the best that could be expected was to make converts among the "more intelligent and honest negroes; furnish them with means and literature, and leave it to them to carry on the work among their race." The article closed with what was becoming a typical theme in socialist literature—that only through socialism could the race problem be solved. The very last sentence reiterated the main point of the article: "The negro is a wage-slave, and as such he deserves our thought and efforts."

Not long after this article appeared, news about blacks became a fairly regular feature of *The People*. Beginning in 1898, it was not unusual for material on blacks and their problems to appear every few weeks in *The People*. By 1900, there were even news reports and articles on a daily basis, including reports of the mounting anti-Negro riots in the North as well as the South. [4] At a time when the Negro was being caricatured and derided in the regular commerical press, *The People* reported the plight of black Americans, Whatever his other weaknesses, De Leon deserves credit for bringing the Negro question to the attention of *The People*'s readers. While James Benjamin Stolvey is correct when he writes in his unpublished biography of De Leon that "*The People* did not at any time make the Negro question a 'special feature,'"[5] it was nevertheless the first American socialist paper to feature it at all.

The coverage of the Negro in *The People* was marred by De Leon's approach to the Negro question. For one thing, as did all other socialists, he repeatedly argued that Negroes were just workers like white workers and had no special problems apart from those facing all workers under capitalism; therefore, their grievances merited no special attention. Moreover, just as a socialist republic would solve the problems of white workers, it would do the same for blacks. Hence, any attention paid to such issues as segregation, lynching, and race riots was a waste of time and distracted from the struggle to achieve the only real solution for the problems of blacks in American society—a socialist republic. The only exception De Leon made related to disfranchisement, partly because he saw the move in the Southern states to deprive the Negro of the right to vote as an attack on him as a worker which, if successful, would pave the way for the disfranchisement of the white worker, in the North as well as the South. Again, if the Negro's solution lay in the establishment of a socialist republic when the SLP came into power, it was necessary that he be able to vote for the party that would liberate him from the evils he suffered under capitalism. Apart from the suffrage, all the evils under which blacks were forced to live were inherent in capitalism and could never be eliminated so long as the capitalist system prevailed. Hence, any black leader, no matter how militant he may have been in the struggle against lynching or the denial of civil rights and job discrimination, was a "fakir" (an expression De Leon loved dearly) if he did not endorse socialism as the *only* remedy for his people's problems. Indeed, De Leon took a perverse pleasure in publishing lengthy interviews with black spokesmen mainly to demonstrate that they were hopelessly naive or opportunistically corrupt because they either did not understand or refused to acknowledge that the Negro's salvation could only be achieved through socialism. The interviews made clear De Leon's belief that the only thing both white and black Americans could or should do en route to the socialist paradise was to vote for candidates of the Socialist Labor party. 6

Given this approach, it is hardly surprising that De Leon neither used *The People* to mobilize the socialists for a militant stand against the political, economic, and social oppression suffered by blacks, nor sought to build alliances with nonsocialist forces in order to resist the rising tide of racism in American life during the 1890s.

## THE SLP IN THE SOUTH

In 1892, when De Leon became leader of the Socialist Labor party, most blacks lived in Southern rural areas, with the vast majority on farms. There were a few black landowners and an even smaller group of cash tenants—men who owned their animals and work tools and paid a fixed sum for the use of land. Most black farmers, however, were at the bottom of the economic ladder—either *sharecroppers*, that is, farm tenants, who, in return for tilling the soil and harvesting the crops, received one-half (and usually less after debts owed the landlord-storekeeper were deducted) of the crops produced, or *wage hands*, who earned a daily or weekly wage, usually paid in scrip that was good only at the employer's store, and who had even less income and security than the sharecroppers. 7

Although often nullified by employer pressure, violence, and the fraudulent manipulation of ballots, the Negro vote in the early 1890s was still a political factor in the South. Late in 1895, Charles G. Baylor, a black member of the Socialist Labor party (and indeed the only black to publicly acknowledge his membership at this time), expressed his desire in a personal letter to De Leon to go South and organize blacks into the party. Pointing out that Southern Negroes could still vote in many communities, he urged making "the Southern Negro a special feature of the *People*. . . . This attitude of the SLP and the *People* will give us and the paper not only a stronghold on the southern Negro population but in the colored population of the north. I believe it alone [will] add 10,000 names to your subscription list. . . . I should like to hear from you." De Leon did not even bother to reply. 8

That same year, *The People* carried an extensive report on the beginnings of the process of disfranchisement of the blacks—the Constitutional Convention of 1895 in South Carolina. Under the heading "Populism Drops the Mask," the article pointed out that the Southern Populists were in the forefront of the movement to eliminate the Negro from political life in the South through such devices as the poll tax and literacy tests, and warned that once blacks were disfranchised, white workers would be the next to be deprived of the vote. But it did not call upon the Socialist Labor party to move into the South and attempt to forge unity with the blacks. The only solution was for all workers, white and black, to vote the Socialist Labor party ticket. Socialism was the real answer to disfranchisement. 9

*The People* reported that SLP organizers in the South encountered bitter opposition when they sought to bring blacks into white sections. But it reported with pride that in April 1898 the first all-black section of an American socialist party had come into existence. It was set up by a Southern SLP organizer in Pocahontas, a mining town in southwest Virginia. 10

The Roanoke, Virginia, Section of the SLP was the first group of Southern socialists to mobilize a mass campaign around an issue of importance to blacks. It related to the efforts in 1901 to defeat the move to disfranchise Negroes in Virginia. The manifesto issued by the Roanoke SLP was a brilliant analysis, demonstrating how the oppression of blacks opened the door to similar oppression of white workers. The campaign initiated by the Roanoke Section, and joined in by sections in Richmond and Newport News, did not succeed in defeating the white supremacists, but the Virginia socialists at least did not confine themselves to simply proclaiming that socialism was the answer to the threat of disfranchisement. 11

## DEBATE AT THE 1900 SLP CONVENTION

The tenth national convention of the Socialist Labor party, held in New York City in June 1900, adopted a platform that included the customary reference to the party's advocacy of "universal and equal suffrage without regard to color, creed or sex." For the first time since the SLP was founded in 1876, however, a party national convention devoted time to a discussion involving blacks. The discussion grew out of a resolution relating to a bitter strike in Coeur d'Alene, Idaho, in the spring of 1899. The strike was aimed at raising wages at the Bunker Hill and Sullivan Mining Company, the property of the Standard Oil trust, and at bringing the rates in these mines up to the levels in the rest of the district, which had been unionized by the Western Federation of Miners. Federal troops, including black soldiers, were called into Idaho; martial law was declared as soon as the troops arrived, and at least some 600 men were arrested without warrant, of whom hundreds were held for months in a hastily constructed and filthy "bull pen." [12] The SLP resolution charged the Standard Oil Company with attempting to smash the union by erecting the bull pen and surrounding it "with colored soldiers." A controversy broke out over the use of the word "colored," and several delegates insisted that the word be retained in order to demonstrate that blacks were ready to be used by the capitalist class to destroy the efforts of white workers to unionize. De Leon insisted that the resolution should read "and in pursuance of its policy of dividing the working class on the lines of color, race and religion, they [the capitalists] sent colored troops to shoot white workingmen in the North, the same as before that they sent white workingmen to shoot colored men in the South." Capitalists, he reminded the delegates, invariably used racial and national prejudices "to divide the workers," and it would be wrong to single out the blacks for special condemnation.

A Southern delegate endorsed De Leon's amendment, pointing out the capitalists "spare no man, race or color, in the pursuit of their vile interests." The amendment was then carried. [13]

In this instance, De Leon was at least consistent. Just as he opposed singling out the Negro problem for special attention, he opposed singling him out as a special tool of the capitalist class. In any case, the stand he took at the 1900 convention was a vast improvement over that which involved the introduction of black workers into a Southern textile mill. The August 6, 1899, issue of the *Daily People* featured a manifesto written by the socialist members of the executive committee of striking mill workers at the Fulton Cotton Mills in Atlanta, Georgia. The strike was in response to the company's introduction of a number of black women into the plant when the whites threatened to organize. The white workers refused to work with the blacks. The manifesto explained that they were not striking against blacks, but against cheap labor which would undercut the existing miserable standards.

So impressed was De Leon with the manifesto, which he called "a strong indictment against capitalism," that he reproduced it in its entirety without even commenting on the fact that the socialists who had drawn it up had made no effort to convince the white workers of the necessity of bringing the blacks into their union in order to present a common front against the employers. Nor did he comment on the fact that the white workers had called off the strike when the company offered to discharge the blacks if the white workers would extend their working hours without extra pay, which they agreed to do. [14]

Not surprisingly, the report of the committee on organization at the 1900 national convention, written by De Leon, emphasized that the outlook for the SLP in the one area of the country where blacks were concentrated was anything but promising. It noted gloomily: "The South, even with regard to such states as have some industrial development does not as yet offer conditions favorable to the maintenance of SLP organizations."[15] It recommended that the issue of organizing blacks be postponed for a more opportune time. Clearly, despite the greater attention paid to the Negro question since 1894, the SLP at the beginning of this century had written off any real prospect of recruiting blacks.

This, unfortunately, continued to be true after 1900. To be sure, as in the 1890s, De Leon made a number of positive contributions after the turn of the century to the struggle against racism. He was uncompromising in his criticism of the exclusionist Jim Crow policies of the AFL,[16] opposed the formation of segregated locals in the South,[17] and played an important part at conventions of the Second International in combatting the racist attitudes of some of the delegates who favored restrictions on the entrance into their countries of the so-called inferior races.[18] He asked:

> Where is the line that separates "inferior" from "superior" races? What serious man, if he is a Socialist, what Socialist if he is a serious man, would indulge in "etc." in such important matters? To the native American proletariat, the Irish was made to appear an "inferior" race; to the Irish, the German; to the German, the Italian; to the Italian — and so down the line through the Swedes, the Poles, the Jews, the Armenians, the Japanese, to the end of the gamut. Socialism knows not such insulting iniquitous distinctions as "inferior" and "superior" races among the proletariat. It is for capitalism to fan the fires of such sentiments in its scheme to keep the proletariat divided.[19]

Yet, under De Leon's leadership, the Socialist Labor party (or whatever remained of it following the split in its ranks and the formation of the Socialist party in 1901) never once launched a drive to organize the Southern Negro. Even when De Leon went South on a lecture tour in 1907, he made no effort to contact blacks.[20]

During the early years of the twentieth century, R. T. Sims was the only black member of the SLP. Sims attended the 1906 Industrial Workers of the World (IWW) convention as a delegate from the Socialist Trade and Labor Alliance, De Leon's brainchild. He was appointed to the "Good and Welfare Committee" and introduced a resolution protesting lynchings of Negroes and antiblack riots as "a blot on the garment of civilization," and calling for the elimination of "such wanton and atrocious acts." The resolution was adopted. Sims became the first black organizer for the IWW. [21] However, he seems to have done little to recruit blacks into the SLP. De Leon's attitude certainly did not encourage him to do so.

De Leon seems to have believed that the Negro's heritage of slavery presented an insuperable obstacle to his conversion to socialism. "In no economic respect is he different from his fellow wage slaves of other races," he argued, "yet by reason of his race, which long was identified with serfdom, the rays of the social question reached his mind through such broken prisms that they are refracted into all the colors of the rainbow, preventing him from appreciating the white light of the question." Since slavery, he went on, the Negro had "been wandering in the wilderness," and there was little hope that socialists might lead him into the promised land. It was thus the Negro's own duty to join the socialist camp. [22]

In short, De Leon's attitude toward the Negro was a web of contradictions. There were no "inferior" races, but slavery had practically set the Negro into an "inferior" category. Then again, the Negro was part of the working class, just like the white worker, yet he was of a nonworking-class, quasifeudal background which blinded him to his true proletarian identity and would render useless any efforts to convert him to socialism. At the time of his death on May 11, 1914, De Leon had still not succeeded in extricating himself from this dilemma. Nor had he altered in the slightest his view "that there is no such thing as a race or 'Negro question'. . . . There is only a *social*, or *labor* question, and no racial or religious question so far as the Socialist and labor movements were concerned." [23]

Apart from De Leon's own writings on the subject, *The People* was barren of any discussions of the Negro question until the fall of 1911, when a debate on the issue appeared in the form of letters from members of the SLP. [24] Actually, there was not much of a debate; all the SLP members who participated agreed that the Negro had serious defects of character and was on the lowest possible level of civilization. The disagreement came over (1) whether this was because of innate, inherent factors or because of special exploitation under capitalism, "all purely proletarian vices must of necessity in him appear multiplied," and (2) the issue of whether under socialism these defects inherent in the Negro would be eradicated. While all of the participants finally agreed that the evils in the Negro's character were a product of his exploitation under capitalism, they could not concur on whether these defects would be eradicated under socialism. Indeed, the majority position was that the Negro had become so backward and so childlike, had such a primitive conception of morality, and was so shiftless and erratic in his work habits—all products to be sure of capitalist exploitation—that not even socialism could help the race. As one party member summed it up:

> even should the Socialist Republic be established the Negro
> would not know how to profit by the new conditions and oppor-
> tunities; he would keep on disseminating disease; his civic in-
> efficiency would remain a clog in the wheel of good government
> and administration; and by interbreeding would tend to lower
> the status of our own race. 25

*The People* published this racist, scurrilous attack without even an editorial rebuke.

For four and a half years after the 1911 debate, *The People* did not
carry a single discussion of the Negro. Then, suddenly on May 27, 1916,
the socialist weekly reported that the Socialist Labor party had held a
meeting near Thomasville, Georgia, "which was attended by a good
sized audience of colored people." At the close of the meeting, two subscriptions to the *Weekly People* were obtained, and five pamphlets sold.
Nothing was said about any blacks joining the SLP, and since this was
the last notice of an appeal to the Negro, it is unlikely that any did.

And such was the total result of whatever work the Socialist Labor
party did to win Negro support. It was indeed a sorry story.


## THE ANARCHISTS

Throughout the early decades of its existence, the Socialist Labor
party was torn by internal disputes and controversies. Party members
came more and more to believe that the emphasis on the peaceful acquisi-
tion of power through the ballot box was an illusion, and they actually
played into the hands of the capitalists. In 1880, those who advocated
direct action, including arming party members and training them in techniques of self-defense, seceded from the SLP and formed Social Revolutionary Clubs. The Chicago Club, led by Albert R. Parsons, a native
American, and August Spies, a German immigrant, was the most important. The club advocated the anarchist doctrine that "propaganda by
deed" educated the masses better than scores of political campaigns.
They also believed in the trade unions as "a great lever" by which the
working class could be economically emancipated. This brand of anarchosyndicalism became very influential in Chicago. 26

In October 1883, a congress of American anarchists at Pittsburgh
formed the International Working People's Association, the black International. During the debates and discussions at Pittsburgh, not a single
reference was made to the Negro question. Indeed, the only mention of
blacks in the entire proceedings was the oblique one in the fifth declara-

tion of what the new anarchist movement would achieve. It read: "Equal rights for all without reference to sex or race." [27]

The neglect of the Negro question is not surprising. None of the anarchist papers published before the Pittsburgh congress had ever mentioned the issue, although some did publish articles about the Irish and Jewish questions. Nor did any carry news about blacks, except the *Alarm*, [28] the English-language anarchist paper published fortnightly, edited in Chicago by Albert R. Parsons and frequently contributed to by his wife, Lucy Parsons. [29]

The *Alarm* featured two articles on the Negro. One, signed by "A.A.," advised the Negro to stop expecting to end his miserable status in American society through the use of the franchise. It even counseled the blacks against any efforts to gain the right to vote where they were disfranchised. Instead, it urged them to get for themselves what the ruling class used for its own purpose against the masses — "the gun, the rifle, the dagger, and the ready explosives." It expressed confidence that any Negro who studied the problem carefully would give up the quest for "the elective franchise" and instead would "swear on a keg of dynamite that he will never rest until even the best government is destroyed." [30]

The other article was somewhat less incendiary. It was by Lucy Parsons and was entitled "The Negro," with the subtitle "Let Him Leave Politics to the Politicians and Prayers to the Preacher." In it she asked:

> Who, surrounded even as we are in the midst of organizations whose mission it is to depict the wrongs to which the propertyless class is subjected, could help but stand aghast and heave a sigh and perchance drop a tear as they read the graphic account flashed to us of the awful massacre of the poor and defenceless wage slaves in Carrolton, in the state of Mississippi? Defenceless, poverty-stricken, hemmed about by their deadly enemies; victims not only to their misfortunes, but to deep-seated, blind, relentless, prejudice, those our fellow-beings are being murdered without quarter.

Could anyone be so stupid, she asked, as to believe that these outrages "have been, are being and will be heaped upon the Negro because he is black? Not at all. It is because he is *poor*. It is because he is dependent. Because he is poorer as a class than his white wage slave brother of the North."

How long, she went on, would the Negro continue to seek to solve his problems by votes and prayers? And to the Negro people she put the question: "Has it done you any good?" The only course to pursue in the future, she urged, "if you value real freedom, is to leave politics to the politician, and prayer to those who can show wherein it has done them more good than it was ever done for you, and join hands with those who are striving for economic freedom." As for what to do in the meantime, she answered that if she were in the same position, her advice would be: "You are not absolutely defenceless. For the torch of the incendiary, which has been known to show murderers and tyrants the danger line, beyond which they may not venture with impunity, cannot be wrested from you." [31]

The January 1896 issue of *The Rebel*, a Boston-based "Anarchist Communist journal devoted to the solution of the Labor Question," carried a piece entitled "The American Negro." Written by "A White Southerner," it urged the black man to shun political action and the white man's religion and to concentrate instead on efforts to "unify his fiscal and industrial strength in united co-operative effort," thereby emulating what the Jews had been doing successfully for centuries. In this way, the Negro would be ready when the "final conflict" came, at which time the white wage slaves would also be "sufficiently educated" to join forces with the blacks for "mutual deliverance." The confused article ended somewhat immodestly: "We have pointed out the road of emancipation for the Negro. Let him enter upon it at once." [32]

Although it was not uncommon for black workers who went on strike in the South to be denounced in the white press as "anarchists and fanatical denouncers of authority," [33] the first real charge that blacks were turning to anarchist methods, if not to the philosophy of anarchism itself, came in the early 1890s. On May 21, 1892, the *Boston Republican*, a black weekly, featured an article under the caption "Black Dynamiters in Boston," which was widely reprinted in the nation's press. It began: "The facts have just come to light that there are colored men in Boston and Cambridge who have banded themselves together with an oath to make dynamite and bombs to be used in the South to protect themselves against tyranny and despotism." The paper noted that the existence of "Black Dynamiters" should come as no surprise:

> We do not encourage dynamiters and bomb-throwers where no cause exists for indulging in such a warfare, as in the case of the Chicago anarchists of a few years ago. . . . But who will aver that there is respect for law and order in sections of the South where colored men are being lynched daily by the twos and threes and often-times more? . . . The only thing left for a people thus crushed and trodden down, is to have recourse to the mode of warfare which other people, similarly situated in other lands, employ. These are either dynamite, the dagger, or the bomb. [34]

Frederick Douglass, too, expressed no surprise at the existence of "Black Dynamiters." He declared:

> If the Southern outrages on the Colored race continue the Negro will become a chemist. Other men besides Anarchists can be goaded into making and throwing bombs. This terrible thirst for the blood of men must cease in the South or as sure as night follows day there will be an insurrection. Anarchists have not a monopoly of bomb-making, and the Negro will learn to handle the terrible engine of destruction unless the wrongs against him cease. [35]

Following the assassination of President William McKinley by an anarchist in September 1901, the virtues, or lack of them, of anarchism as a solution for the problems of black Americans were debated in the black press. In *The Colored American*, a black weekly, the debate was highlighted by a piece by John E. Bruce ("Bruce Grit") in which the militant black journalist condemned the nationwide hysterical call for the imprisonment of all native-born anarchists and the deportion of all who were foreign-born. Bruce argued that efforts to eliminate the anarchists were doomed to failure since the contradictions in American society represented by the few who were wealthy and the poverty-stricken masses were increasing and were laying the foundation for the continued emergence of radical movements, including the anarchists. He concluded:

> There is a deeper meaning and significance in this movement to rid the country of anarchists than appears on the surface. The rich and powerful are more concerned about it than the common people. They are alarmed, and well they may be, for they cannot be indifferent to the fact that their wealth has been used to the prejudice of the helpless and dependent who after all are the creators in one way and another of the great wealth which is used to keep them in subjection and to make them dependent upon the favor and smiles of these autocrats whose will and word is law, a fact which cannot be disguised by any argument however plausible and ingenious. [36]

Never again, however, were the anarchist journals to issue an appeal to Negroes. Indeed, in the entire period from 1903 to 1914, the Negro question was raised only twice in the anarchist press. The first occasion was in 1903 when several anarchist journals, in refuting President Theodore Roosevelt's charge that lynching was just another form of "anarchism," stated that anarchism was unalterably opposed to antiblack violence. [37] Apart from a brief notice attacking "the attitude of the Socialists toward the negro problem," [38] the only other time that blacks were mentioned was in a vivid description of the Southern chain gang in the August 1907 issue of *Mother Earth*, the anarchist monthly edited by Emma Goldman. [39] Even though she was a prolific speaker and writer, and the foremost twentieth-century American advocate of anarchism, Emma Goldman never addressed herself to the Negro question in a major way. [40]

## EDWARD BELLAMY, NATIONALISTS, AND BLACKS

While the SLP lost members to anarchism, it recruited others from the Nationalist movement which was inspired by Edward Bellamy's *Looking Backward*. Published in 1887, *Looking Backward* quickly sold a million copies and at one point was selling at the rate of 1,000 per day. Picturing a utopian socialist society in the year 2000 A.D., Bellamy explained how socialism had grown out of monopolies that stifled competition. The citizens of the new society found it difficult to understand why the people of the late nineteenth century tolerated "the imbecility of the system of private enterprise as a method of enriching a nation . . . in an age of such general poverty and want of everything," an age in which "workmen rioted and burned because they could find no work to do."

Bellamy's principal plan, the nationalization of industry, stimulated the growth of a short-lived socialistic movement, consisting of Nationalist Clubs which began in Boston in 1888 and spread overnight across the country. Linked loosely together through correspondence and exchange of lectures, and recruiting their membership mainly from the urban middle class, the Nationalist groups sought to remedy the fundamental evils of capitalism by nationalizing the functions of production and distribution. When nationalization was accomplished, they predicted that a "true democratic and popular society will become possible as never before; for the first time in history, the world will behold a true republic, full-minded, full-ordered, complete—a republic, social, industrial, political." [41]

For many Americans, *Looking Backward* constituted their first introduction to socialism. It taught them nothing about the Negro question for the simple reason that blacks figured neither in Bellamy's portrait of the evils existing under the system of private industry nor in his picture of how the new society would abolish these evils. [42] The platforms of the Nationalist party did include the demand for the abolition of the contract-labor system but said nothing about Negro suffrage and civil rights. [43]

In fact, the only time the Negro question emerged in the discussions of the new society envisaged by the Nationalists was in an anonymous article in *The Nationalist* of 1890. Entitled "The Negro's Part in Nationalism," it argued that the Negro had "done almost nothing" with the freedom he had enjoyed for twenty-five years. This, it insisted, was not surprising in view of the vast prejudice blacks had had to face since emancipation. So terrible were the social conditions under which most blacks lived that the race was actually deteriorating. The Negro was losing the virtues which were the by-products of slavery and gaining none to replace them in freedom.

What could be done to solve the problem? To let the situation remain as it was would be to risk a war of races in which the Negroes, being numerically weaker, would be exterminated. To admit the Negro to "perfect political and social equality" would bring about the same result in the end, for it would invite intermarriage which, in turn, would create a race of octoroons. This race, being physically inferior to both the white and the Negro, would be doomed to speedy extinction.

What, then, did the Negro have to look forward to in this new society? *The Nationalist*'s answer was that, once land and industry had been nationalized and the new nation created, a territory would be set aside for the Negro where he would have full opportunity "for the development of every faculty." While some force might be needed to get the Negro to settle apart from the rest of the population, once established, the separate black section would be kept going by "its own cohesive force." In time, perhaps, individual blacks would be allowed to reside elsewhere, but a mass migration from the area set aside would not be countenanced.

The article conceded that there was something wrong in forcing blacks to live apart in the new socialist society. It insisted, however, that it was necessary to be realistic and to understand that the solution to the Negro question was a difficult one, even under the best of circumstances, and that by giving the Negro a sphere of his own, the question, in time, would settle itself. [44]

## CHRISTIAN SOCIALISTS, FABIANS, AND BLACKS

If *Looking Backward* was the bible of the Nationalist Clubs, the New Testament itself stimulated a small group of ministers, led by William D.P. Bliss and George D. Herron, several of them active members of the Boston Nationalist Club, to form the Society of Christian Socialists. The

Declaration of Principles of the Christian Socialist Movement, adopted on April 15, 1889, asserted that its object was "to show that the aim of Socialism is embraced in the aim of Christianity." It called for the establishment of a system of "social, political and industrial relations . . . based on the Fatherhood of God and the Brotherhood of man, in the spirit and according to the teachings of Jesus Christ." All who agreed with this outlook were invited to join and form chapters of the society of Christian Socialists. Such chapters did spring up in various parts of the country, with their members dedicated to the peaceful establishment of a socialist society. They subscribed to *Dawn*, the movement's official publication edited by Bliss, and distributed copies of Bliss's pamphlet, *What Is Christian Socialism?*, which called for municipal ownership of light, heating, and transit companies; the nationalization of the telegraph and railroads; and the establishment of postal savings banks—all as preparatory steps to the complete socialization of all industries. It also advocated levying taxes as an interim measure to reduce the glaring inequalities of wealth. But as a solution for the evils of American capitalism, Christian Socialism gained few adherents. By the late 1890s, it was all but dead; *Dawn* had ceased publication in 1896, and soon afterwards, the chapters closed their doors. [45]

This, too, was the experience of the American Fabian Society, modeled after the British Fabians who had founded their first society in 1884. It was organized in 1895 by many of the same men who had been associated with the Society of Christian Socialists, and it emphasized the achievement of socialism without the necessity of a class struggle. It established branches in New York, Boston, Philadelphia, San Francisco, and a few other cities, and published the *American Fabian*, its official monthly publication. The journal ceased publication in 1900, and the society disbanded soon afterward. [46]

The Christian Socialist and Fabian movements were short-lived and fleeting, but they left a deeper mark on black Americans than did any of the other organized groups seeking to achieve socialism. This was not because they made greater appeals to blacks or discussed the Negro question more frequently. On the contrary, neither in the Declaration of Principles nor in any of its official journals, such as *Dawn* or *The Social Gospel*, or any of its widely distributed pamphlets, was the Negro question ever discussed by the Christian Socialist movement. As for the American Fabian Society, the only reference it made to blacks was in its "Political Demands" adopted in February 1896, which included the familiar call for "universal and equal right of suffrage without regard to color, creed or sex." [47] Rather, it was by harkening back to the principles of the early Christians, by viewing the cooperative commonwealth as the material expression of the teachings of Christ, and by emphasizing the gradualist, peaceable approach to socialism that these movements appealed to a number of black ministers. Since the church was a dominant influence in the black community, more black Americans learned of socialism through the debates in the columns of *The Christian Recorder* and the *AME Church Review*—both organs of the African Methodist Episcopal Church—than through all the publications of the various socialist groups combined. Those who wrote on the subject in *The Christian Recorder* upheld the view that blacks should shun socialism as a "pernicious doctrine" akin to anarchism, and rejected the notion, dear to Christian Socialists, that Christ was the "original Socialist." On the other hand, those who wrote in the *AME Church Review* argued forcefully that socialism was the proper form of society for all workers, including blacks, and cited the Bible and contemporary social scientists to reinforce their arguments. Yet, even those black leaders who condemned socialism conceded that, theoretically, blacks had the best reason to demand a fundamental change in American society along the lines proposed by the socialists. As one of them, Alexander Clark, stated: "They might be excused for listening to the siren voices of the Socialists." [48]

"Socialism is the subject now uppermost in all minds, almost to the exclusion of every other thought in this closing decade of the nineteenth century," Reverend James T. Holly wrote at the beginning of his article "Socialism from the Biblical Point of View." The former shoemaker, an ardent advocate of the emigration of black Americans to Haiti, had sent the article to the *AME Church Review* from Port-au-Prince where he lived. In a far-ranging discussion, Reverend Holly called for the application of "biblical socialism" to cure the evils of modern capitalist society. [49] Several years later, the talented Reverend Reverdy C. Ransom, later elected bishop of the AME Zion Church, published "The Negro and Socialism" in the *AME Church Review*. After painting a picture of the "spirit of unrest" which pervaded every avenue of American life, he declared: "The present social order with its poverty and vast reserve army of unemployed, cannot be accepted as final, as the ultimate goal for which ages have been in travail." According to Ransom, socialism was both the logical and inevitable answer. It was a form of society especially suited for the American Negro who, although belonging "almost wholly to the proletarian or industrial class," was finding it increasingly difficult to obtain work because of opposition from both employers and labor unions. Reverend Ransom predicted that when the Negro "comes to realize that socialism offers him freedom of opportunity to cooperate with all men upon terms of equality in every avenue of life, he will not be slow to accept his social emancipation." [50]

Editorially, the *AME Church Review* urged its readers to give Reverend Ransom's defense of socialism the "careful reading" it deserved. [51]

When Reverend W. H. Coston of Ohio, in a critical review of Reverend Ransom's article in *The Christian Recorder*, confused socialism and anarchism, the *AME Church Review* criticized Coston for having distorted what Reverend Ransom had actually said. It pointed out that Ransom had made it very clear that the two movements were quite different in theory, methods, and objectives. [52]

While many Christian Socialists, including Bliss himself, later became less involved in socialist affairs, and some even turned conservative, several of the black ministers continued to adhere to socialist principles after the Christian Socialist movement faded away, and eventually joined the Socialist party. In the 1890s, they had had no relationship with the Socialist Labor party, but in the next decade they and other black ministers became an integral part of the Socialist party, endorsing its principles and program and carrying its message to their congregations.

## EUGENE V. DEBS, THE SOCIAL DEMOCRATS, AND BLACKS

On January 1, 1897, Eugene V. Debs officially resigned from the People's (Populist) party and joined the socialist movement. In a letter to members of the American Railway Union, the industrial union of railroad workers he had founded in 1893 and led to enormous successes, only to see it shattered in the Pullman strike of 1894, Debs urged workers to follow him into the socialist movement. He was convinced that the issue was "Socialism vs. Capitalism," and he was for socialism, he said, because he was for humanity.

In June 1897, Debs wound up the affairs of the American Railway Union and merged it with the Social Democracy, then being formed at a convention in Chicago. Several months later, the Social Democracy gained the support of two important groups in the Socialist Labor party — the Jewish socialists of the East and the Milwaukee socialists led by Victor L. Berger. Both groups were opposed to De Leon's trade-union tactics and his tendency to resort to insult and derision in combatting his opponents. The *Jewish Daily Forward*, the organ of the Jewish socialists who had split with De Leon, became the spokesman for the Social Democracy among Yiddish-speaking workers, while the Milwaukee *Vorwaerts*, edited by Berger, performed the same role for the German-speaking workers. [53]

The Social Democracy reached English-speaking workers and farmers through several publications. One of them, *The Coming Nation*, [54] became the organ of the Brotherhood of the Cooperative Commonwealth, whose program, temporarily adopted by the Social Democracy, called for establishing socialism by combining the techniques of colonization and voting. Socialist colonies would be established in some sparsely populted western state. After socialists had migrated in large numbers into that state, they would gain control of the political offices in free elections and would usher in socialism. As the movement spread throughout the nation, a socialist United States would be created.

Debs eagerly endorsed the idea of developing a model cooperative colony, seeing it as a means of escape for unemployed workers during the economic crisis. If the idea succeeded with the pilot group, he envisaged the possibility of organizing thousands of workers into a cooperative that would set up factories in basic industries, control them, and return the profits to laborers. Step by step, a socialist society would evolve. In the meantime, the movement would recruit new members of the party. [55]

The colonization scheme encountered opposition from Berger and others who felt it detracted from concentration on political action and smacked too much of utopianism. In time, Debs, too, became convinced that concentration on colonization diverted attention from recruiting members among the trade unions, especially in times of strikes. On June 10, 1898, at the Social Democratic party convention in Chicago, Debs joined Berger in opposing colonization in favor of political action. When the majority of the delegates endorsed colonization, Debs and Berger led a group out of the convention hall and founded a new Social Democratic party with emphasis on political action. [56]

A firm believer in black-white labor unity. Debs had fought a losing battle in the American Railway Union (ARU) to gain admission for blacks. (The first annual ARU convention voted down his proposal to admit Negroes by 113 to 102.) Convinced that the union's defeat in the Pullman strike was partly the result of its racism which had encouraged blacks to act as strikebreakers, [57] Debs entered the socialist movement, determined to bring this lesson home sharply to the membership. Supporters of the Cooperative Commonwealth colony favored settling Negroes apart in colonies of their own as a solution for the race problem, and *The Coming Nation* carried a long article outlining how such a black cooperative colony would operate. [58] In developing his pilot colony, Debs rejected segregation for blacks and insisted that in the cooperative commonwealth, blacks, like women, must be equal politically and have the right to vote as well as hold office. In his cooperative commonwealth, too, blacks would have equality of opportunity in obtaining employment in the factories to be operated by the commonwealth. [59]

Debs abandoned the colonization plan, but he continued to insist on black-white unity. He brought this message to workers even in the South while lecturing to large audiences under the auspices of the Social Democratic party. While speaking in Louisville, Montgomery, Macon, Savannah, and other Southern cities, as well as in the North and West, he insisted that meetings be open to all regardless of race or color. [60] Following his tour of the South early in 1900, the *Social Democratic Herald* reported that "interest in Comrade Debs' work is not confined to any class; neither has it been to one color or one sex. All sorts and conditions of men and women—black and white—are moved to action by his earnest appeals." [61]

At the time this comment appeared, the Social Democratic party boasted a dues-paying membership of 4,636 in 226 branches, organized in thirty-two states. The only black to publicly announce himself as a Social Democrat in the period 1897 to 1900 was J. M. Moore, pastor of the AME Church of West Pratt, Alabama. On March 5, 1898, the *Birmingham Labor Advocate* reported that Reverend Moore had uttered "sensible remarks" in an address to the meeting of the United Mine Workers in which he defended the Social Democracy.

The Social Democracy espoused the most advanced view on the need for black-white unity up to that point in the history of American socialism. Yet, the fact that the party press rarely carried such clearcut appeals would seem to indicate that, apart from Debs, the issue of black-white unity did not loom particularly large in the thinking of the leadership. Neither the *Jewish Daily Forward* nor the Milwaukee *Vorwaerts* carried articles on the Negro question or news about blacks. [62] Apart from the publication of the article in *The Coming Nation*, mentioned above, discussion of the Negro question appeared only in the pages of the *Appeal to Reason*, the *International Socialist Review*, and the *Worker's Call*, the organ of Local Chicago—and then only occasionally. [63]

Still, this was no small contribution at a time when the Supreme Court endorsed the "separate-but-equal" doctrine, when Jim Crow laws were being passed all over the South, and when much of the labor movement had become solidly racist and exclusionist, consenting to organize a few blacks only in second-class and segregated locals. It was a period, too, in which white Americans, North and South—united under the banner of white supremacy—were forcing blacks to face the edict that they must abandon politics and the battle for civil rights and accept the clear and unmistakable domination of the white man. The progressive concern with the Negro by Republican politicians had, of course, long disappeared. Instead, in this period, with the rise of American imperialism, the view was firmly established in Republican circles that the destiny of Southern blacks should be left in the hands of those who understood them best—the white supremacists. This meant abandoning the blacks to a life of sharecropping and imprisonment under the vicious convict lease system, and subject to repeated acts of violence. It was a period, in short, that, as Floyd J. Miller puts it, "was not the time for a black protest organization to succeed—even exist—in the South." [64]

Against this background, the position of the socialists was at least unique in the sense that it proclaimed the principle of black-white equality. They proclaimed it, moreover, in the face of a well-organized campaign to turn blacks against radicalism in any form.

## EMERGENCE OF THE IDEOLOGY OF BOOKER T. WASHINGTON

Blacks had formed an important element in the Greenback-Labor party of the late 1870s, [65] the Knights of Labor, the Colored Farmers' National Alliance and Cooperative Union (which claimed more than a million members in twelve state organizations in 1891), [66] and, for a time in the Populist party. While their objective was primarily to redress immediate grievances, especially the vicious system of peonage, they also raised the necessity of changing the existing economic structure through cooperatives and the redistribution of land. The 1890 convention of the Colored Farmers' National Alliance asserted that "land is not property; can never be made property . . . the land belongs to the sovereign people." [67]

To no small extent, this view was influenced by the distribution among blacks of T. Thomas Fortune's great work *Black and White: Land, Labor, and Politics in the South*, published in 1884. Fortune did not shrink from association with socialists, and in his weekly, *The Freeman*, he called for an understanding of socialistic ideas, terming them of "vital, exigent importance, seeing the whole world is being shaken by dynamite and revolutionary agitation." [68] Nevertheless, in *Black and White*, he advanced the single-tax idea of Henry George rather than the principles of socialism, [69] arguing that at the root of economic and social miseries lay "land monopoly"—control by the few of the land that belonged to the people as a whole. Land monopoly had given birth before the war to chattel slavery, and after the conflict, because of the failure to break up large plantations and give the freedmen forty acres and a mule, had also given birth to *"industrial slavery*: a slavery more excruciating in its exactions, more irresponsible in its machinations than any other slavery."

Fortune felt that, as in the case of the Northern worker, the Southern white and black workers had a common cause and a common destiny. He praised the Knights of Labor for including workers of all races and saw this move as a portent of the rising conflict of labor against the "odious and unjust tyranny" of capital. "The revolution is upon us," he declared, "and since we are largely of the laboring population, it is very natural that we should take sides with the labor forces in their fight for a juster distribution of the results of labor." [70]

Fortune was convinced that the future struggle in the South would take place not between the whites and blacks, but between capital and labor and landlord and tenant. The conclusion to *Black and White* expresses this view dramatically:

> The hour is approaching when the laboring classes of our country . . . will recognize that they have a *common cause*, a *common humanity* and a *common enemy*; and that, therefore, if they would triumph over wrong and place the laurel wreath upon triumphant justice . . . *they must unite*!

> When the issue is properly joined, the rich, be they black or be they white, will be found on the same side; and the poor, be they black or be they white, will be found on the same side.

> *Necessity knows no law and discriminates in favor of no man or race.* [71]

The publication of *Black and White* marked the first time that a black spokesman had stated with such clarity and vigor the thesis of class conflict and the identity of interests of black and white workers. Not even Peter H. Clark had analyzed the class forces in American society and the inevitability of the struggle as cogently as T. Thomas Fortune. But while Peter H. Clark had drawn the conclusion that the nature of American capitalist society made it necessary for blacks to involve themselves in the struggle for socialism, Fortune shrank from the direction in which his own analysis was leading him. In fact, coupled with his clarion calls for black and white labor solidarity in the face of predatory wealth was a plea for accommodation to the very society he condemned. Society, he argued, was governed by iron-clad, immutable laws, and the Negro could only survive if he adjusted to them, instead of seeking to change them. The key to the Negro's future was his understanding of the need not to change the existing social structure, but to find a way to partake of its material benefits. [72]

By the 1890s, whatever radicalism had existed in Fortune's *Black and White* had been overwhelmed by a concentration upon the need for the Negro to make his peace with the existing society and shun any alliance with radical forces. The man who had predicted and favored the alliance of black and white laborers in the South against their common enemy now condemned every example of such unity in the Alliance and Populist movements. The Colored Farmers' National Alliance, the greatest mass organization of black sharecroppers and tenant farmers up to that time in American history, was to Fortune "offensively Socialistic in most of its demands." That one of its demands—the end of land monopoly through a progressive tax system—was taken from *Black and White* made no difference to Fortune. "We warn Afro-Americans everywhere," he wrote in the *New York Age*, "to be cautious of committing themselves to the support of the Farmers' Alliance and its revolutionary purposes and aims." [73]

During the agrarian revolt of the 1890s, it was *Black and White* rather than Fortune's conservative editorials which influenced many blacks in the South, especially the million and a half who joined the Colored Farmers' National Alliance and Cooperative Union. With the collapse of the revolt in 1896, and the rising tide of the movement for the complete disfranchisement of the Negro in which white Populists and Conservatives joined forces, radical influences among blacks receded. While the more radical elements among the Populists joined the socialists or were swallowed up by the Democrats, those blacks who had organized in the Alliance and Populist movements, even though separately, either returned to the Republican party or began to look for new means of continuing the struggle for a place in Southern society. With politics closed off as an avenue of expression, many followed the lead of Booker T. Washington, principal of the Tuskegee Institute in Alabama—for whom T. Thomas Fortune was to become a ghost writer and apologist [74]—and turned to self-help through such institutions as churches, business leagues, schools, fraternal societies, women's clubs, and farmers' societies. Many of these organizations had been in existence for a long time, but blacks turned to them with increasing vigor after 1900 in the hope that self-improvement might lead to entry into the mainstream of American life.

Essential to the philosophy of Booker T. Washington, now becoming dominant in the Southern black community and even making an impact among Northern blacks, was a rejection of any activity that might not meet the approval of the whites. Washington urged his people not to join unions, to remain aloof from conflict, and to accept any wage rather than be idle. The Negro Farmers Improvement Society of Texas, claiming 3,000 members in over 100 branches in October 1901, voiced this conservative outlook in its prospectus which stated that the organization was not involved in any religious or political controversies and was "not in any way in sympathy with Union Labor Organizations." [75]

Washington's emphasis was on the "cash nexus." The Negro might not be able to vote or to exercise his civil rights, but by satisfying the wants of the white man, he would achieve his full manhood rights. "Friction between the races," he wrote in 1896, "will pass away in proportion as the black man, by reason of his skill, intelligence and character, can produce something that the white man wants or respects in the commercial world." [76] "The struggle toward economic success" held "compensations for the losses [blacks] had suffered in other directions." Channeling politics into capital accumulation would adequately compensate for the abandonment of political struggle and lay the basis for future political viability. Independence, the realization of manhood, as Washington saw it, was founded upon ownership of business enterprise—upon achievement of a place within the framework of the capitalist order. [77]

Washington insisted that the main threat to the black masses came not from the capitalist class, but from the white workers. The Tuskegee leader claimed that the Negro had an "open sesame" to jobs in the South because of his buffer role against unionism. He followed this up with appeals to businessmen, urging them to

> remember that you are in debt to the black man for furnishing you with labor that is almost a stranger to strikes, lock-outs and labor wars; labor that is law-abiding, peaceful, teachable; labor that is one with you in language, sympathy, religion, and patriotism; labor that has never been tempted to follow the red flag of anarchy but always the safe flag of his country and the spotless banner of the cross. [78]

Conceding that socialism, with its condemnation of the evils of capitalist society, had a built-in appeal for Negroes, Washington's disciples argued that Tuskegee itself personified a socialist community. While socialists "dream of a land where, and in a time in the remote future, when and where men and women shall live in perfect peace," Washington, through his genius, had actually built such a community at Tuskegee:

> There are about fourteen hundred active, industrious intelligent young men and women at Tuskegee, and the splendid order, sympathetic and respectful attention these young people show for each other, speaks eloquently for the purely Negro community. In this community the system of government is simple, and yet the laws almost preclude the possibility of wrong-doing being overlooked. . . . The way to dignify a man is to place upon his shoulders the responsibility of the community. This is done at Tuskegee.

Tuskegee, in short, provided the model of socialism for the Negro, a socialism that rejected class conflict and sought to build for blacks within their own communities a self-contained economic independence which, in time, would influence the white society as well:

> This socialism of the Negro warrants the belief that the health, prosperity, comfort and happiness of the people of the United States, under the new social system toward which they seem to be rapidly floating, will depend largely upon the industrious examples of the Southern Negro in his own community, who seems to be pioneering the way to a higher Christian social order. [79]

The socialists scornfully charged that this vision was nothing more than a capitalist segregated society with a socialist label. Just as scornfully, they pointed out the contradiction in Washington's advice to blacks that they both achieve a middle-class status in a segregated society and regard the capitalist as the black man's best friend and the white worker as his main enemy. The Negro was proletarian, but his enemy was the white worker; he was cruelly denied the rights and opportunities of the capitalist order, but his friend was the capitalist. The socialists urged blacks to repudiate such subservience to capitalism, and, out of self-interest, to ally themselves with the one movement that served white and black labor, and that would, if successful, liberate both.

\*        \*        \*

On the eve of the formation of the Socialist party, founded in 1901 as the final product of a process of division, regrouping, and amalgamation of the various socialist forces of the 1890s, the battle between the ideologists of capitalism and socialism to win the support of black labor entered a new stage. "May the negro wage slave become awakened to his own interests, the interests of the class of which he is a member," wrote Charles H. Vail in concluding his article "The Negro Problem" in the *International Socialist Review* of February 1901, "and cast his ballot for the only party that stands for human emancipation—the Socialist Party. When socialism supplants capitalism the negro problem will be forever solved." [80]

In the chapters that follow, we will see to what extent this type of appeal produced results in the twentieth century.

# The Socialist Party and
# Black Americans, 1901-1904

## THE NEGRO QUESTION AT THE FOUNDING
## CONVENTION OF THE SOCIALIST PARTY

On January 29, 1900, at a convention held in Rochester, New York, fifty-nine members of the Socialist Labor
party, led by Morris Hillquit, Job Harriman, and Max
Hayes, repudiated the sectarianism of the SLP and its
Socialist Trade and Labor Alliance, under Daniel De
Leon's leadership, and with only a single dissenting
vote, voted for unification with the Social Democratic
party, headed by Eugene V. Debs. A committee was appointed to work out the details of unification and the
Social Democrats were invited to appoint a similar committee. [1] After many conferences, delegates representing
all socialist groups in the country, except the followers of
De Leon, met in Indianapolis in July 1901 to found a
united socialist movement—the Socialist party of
America.

Reports of the Indianapolis convention in the socialist
press emphasized "the great preponderance of native
Americans" among the delegates," indicating that at
long last interest in socialism was no longer confined
mainly to the foreign born, especially the German-
Americans. *The Workers' Call* of Chicago stated: "Another feature worthy of mention and conveying a special
significance of its own was the presence of three colored
men as delegates, holding credentials for branches. [Wil-
liam] Costley representing San Francisco, Cal. [John H.]

Adams and [Edward D.] McKay, delegates from Brazil and Richmond, Ind. respectively." *The Worker*, a socialist weekly published in New York City, noted that "among the natives we were all glad to see the three Afro-Americans, Costley, Adams and McKay," and pointed with pride to the fact that Adams and McKay were "coal miners."[2] No mention was made of the fact that Costley was also a worker.

The socialist press also emphasized that the three black delegates made a special contribution to the deliberations, which they emphatically did. Max Hayes, himself a delegate, wrote in the *Cleveland Citizen* that the blacks "surpassed some of their white brethren with their logic and understanding of the socialist movement."[3] *The Worker*'s correspondent observed that they were "fine orators," and added emotionally:

> I, for one, should have liked to see Wendell Phillips in the hall as they rose one after the other to voice the sentiments of their race and of their class; they used the language of the great abolitionist to give utterance to the teachings of Karl Marx. Old Phillips would have felt fully compensated for the Boston mob of which his friend, William Lloyd Garrison was the victim, and he a heartbroken witness in 1832, could he have heard our colored friends talk."[4]

According to *The Worker*, their oratorical skill "showed a firm grasp of Socialism and of the Socialist conception of the race question."[5] While no socialist paper published the discussion on this question at the convention, the unpublished proceedings reveal that the black delegates were involved with the issue throughout the sessions. Furthermore, the discussion on the Negro question and the final resolution adopted by the delegates revealed both the advanced position of American socialists at the turn of the century, compared to that of any other political party, and the weakness of the approach of many of them to this question.

The original resolution submitted by the Resolutions Committee noted that the socialist movement demanded "equal rights for all human beings without distinction of color, race or sex." It pointed out that Negro workers were "suffering under direct exploitation and oppression by the ruling class," and it urged their organization into trade unions and affiliation with the socialist movement "in order to bring about the final emancipation of the entire wage working class, without distinction of color or race."

Several white delegates immediately opposed the resolution on the ground that there was no need to single out the Negroes. The Negroes, they said, were only a division of the working class, and, consequently,

the general demands of labor would also cover black needs. Morris Hillquit, the New York Jewish lawyer who was soon to occupy a position in
the party second only to that of Debs, declared that there was no more
reason "for singling out the negro race especially . . . than for singling out
the Jews or Germans or any other nationality, race or creed here
present." It was inconsistent, or so the argument went, for a party that
proudly professed itself to be color blind to focus attention on color in a
special Negro resolution.

Two of the three black delegates (Adams and McKay of Indiana) initially supported this view, insisting, as Adams put it, that the Negro
"must stand up with every other man, without special favor." But Costley argued that special attention must be paid to the Negro people, that it
was not correct to view the black worker simply as a part of the general
working class, and, indeed, that "the Negro as a part of the great working class occupies a distinct and peculiar position in contradiction to
other laboring elements in the United States." He thereupon introduced
a substitute resolution which noted that the Negro people, because of
their history under slavery and their color, "occupy a peculiar position
among the laboring class." Costley pointed out that since black workers
were compelled under capitalism to accept lower wages and to work
longer hours than white workers, they were the victims of hatred and
prejudice on the part of both the white laborer and the white capitalist.
Included in the resolution was a denunciation of "lynching, burning and
disfranchisement" of black Americans in the South. It closed with an expression of sympathy with blacks in their plight, and an invitation to
Negroes "to join hands with the Socialist Party and work for the emancipation of all workers from the present condition of wage slavery, degradation and injustice."

Adams indicated that, even though he still believed there was no need
for a special Negro resolution, he would go along with Costley's substitute if it made clear that no "special favor" for Negroes was intended.
However, when Costley's resolution, slightly reworded, was submitted
by the Resolutions Committee to the delegates, a great deal of controversy arose. Algie M. Simons, socialist editor and historian, moved to
strike out the clause referring to lynching and disfranchisement and admitted frankly that this suggestion was out of deference to the Southern
delegates. He predicted that if the resolution was adopted, it would
"make a great deal of trouble in the South." He was promptly attacked
by Adams, who, for all his unwillingness to see a special resolution on the
Negro question adopted, still recognized capitulation to racism when he
saw it. He insisted that the resolution be passed without alteration;
otherwise, he said, the convention would be properly held up "to ridicule
and scorn." Costley, too, fought vigorously for the resolution. The blacks

were supported in their demand by Max Hayes of the Printers' Union, Reverend George D. Herron, John Collins of the Machinists' Union, William Hamilton of the United Mine Workers, and William Mailley, soon to become party secretary. The substance of their position was that it was high time that American socialists stopped vacillating on the race question and, regardless of the consequences as far as the South was concerned, came out unequivocally for a meaningful resolution on this issue. In this way a clear distinction could be marked between the new Socialist party and any other existing institution in the United States. "I would prefer that we lost every white vote in the South than to evade the question which is presented today in that resolution," Reverend Herron declared dramatically. Hamilton insisted that the socialists must do even more than pass the resolution unchanged; they had to become the vanguard force operating within the trade unions, especially in the South, educating the white workers as to the absolute necessity for black-white unity if the struggle against capitalist exploitation was to be successful. He predicted, too, that the socialists would meet with a more positive response from both black and white workers in the South than was generally believed. As proof that this confidence was not just wishful thinking, he cited his own experience in organizing black and white miners into the United Mine Workers of Alabama.

The delegates who supported Simons' proposal to eliminate the clause in question warned that failure to do so would doom the new party in the South. The convention thereupon voted to submit the resolution to a committee of one—Reverend Herron—who would report it back to the floor, presumably with its language refined but with its basic content unaltered. Just what happened next is not clear, but when Herron resubmitted the resolution to the convention, the clause that specifically condemned "lynching, burning and disfranchisement" was missing. The resolution was then adopted as read without further discussion. Evidently, those who had insisted that the party "must not fail to meet the moral issue" had yielded to pressure from the Southern delegates and from those who envisaged a powerful socialist movement in the South which would, they felt, vanish if the original resolution was adopted.

The omission of the clause cast a shadow over the Socialist party's future relations with black Americans. All the same, it is remarkable that any resolution on the Negro question was actually adopted. The discussions at the convention revealed that quite a few of the delegates would have preferred not to mention the issue at all and that they yielded only reluctantly to pressure from the black delegates and their supporters in accepting a resolution on the Negro question. The whole subject was, as one delegate phrased it, so "very delicate" that he felt the convention would do best to appoint a committee to study the issue in detail and come up with some recommendations—which is another way of saying that the entire matter should be dropped. Those who supported this approach indicated that the massive legal disfranchisement of black voters in the South and the fact that the small number of blacks still able to vote supported the Republican party meant that the new Socialist party would literally be risking destruction if it took a forthright position in favor of black equality. In short, they asked, was winning a few thousand black votes worth jeopardizing the future of the movement?

The supporters of this position considered it "realistic" and "pragmatic," but the black delegates and their white allies called it opportunistic and in basic contradiction to the avowed principles of socialism. They considered it unthinkable that a party that fought for the political and economic liberation of the "exploited masses" should ignore the most exploited of those masses simply because they happened to be black. With powerful eloquence, John H. Adams denounced the efforts to "bury" the Negro question and warned that if they were successful, his people would write off the socialists as just another group of betrayers, like the Republicans and Democrats. Leon Greenbaum, soon to become the party's national secretary, also insisted that the Negro question could no longer be tabled and forgotten, or even dealt with in meaningless generalities. "This is one of the questions that have been ignored too much, I think, by the Socialists," he declared. While these warnings were not sufficient to prevent the elimination of the disputed clause from the Negro resolution, they nevertheless kept the convention from burying the issue.

The resolution on the Negro question that was finally adopted by the founding convention of the Socialist party of America went far beyond the old cliché urging equality "without distinction of color, race, sex or creed," so typical of socialist resolutions from 1879 to the turn of the century. This one acknowledged that Negroes, "because of their long training in slavery and but recent emancipation therefrom, occupy a peculiar position in the working class." In this situation, it went on, the capitalist class sought "to foster and increase color prejudice and race hatred between the white worker and the black." It pictured the Negro as betrayed by the old parties and even by religious and educational institutions "in his present helpless struggle against disfranchisement and violence," and totally identified black labor with white workers. Finally, it projected socialism as the solution and cordially invited Negroes to "membership and fellowship with us in the world movement for economic emancipation." What it lacked was any forthright reference to either lynching or segregation. [6]

Even with this failing, the resolution was hailed in the socialist press as the most advanced stand on the Negro of any political party. The fact that it had been introduced by a black socialist and drawn up "with the assistance of the colored delegates" was a source of special pride. [7] The *Appeal to Reason*, the most widely circulated socialist weekly, noted that it lacked sufficient space to publish all of the resolutions adopted by the Indianapolis convention. Nevertheless, it felt that the text of the Negro resolution should be made known, and it published it in full. The journal emphasized, too, the uniqueness in contemporary political life of the theme stressed at Indianapolis of "the identity of interest between all workers in unions or out, in shop, field or mine and *without regard to color, race, sex or present kind of servitude.*" [8]

This 1901 resolution, which aroused such enthusiasm in the socialist press immediately after the convention and was even reprinted as a leaflet and distributed by the Socialist party shortly after the convention had adjourned, had a very strange history. It was never reaffirmed at any other party convention, and it was so rarely published in the socialist press or official party literature that most members did not even know of its existence. On April 18, 1910, the *Chicago Daily Socialist* reported that the national office had received "many communications . . . inquiring about the negro resolution adopted by the Socialist party," and it was therefore publishing the text at the request of the national secretary. In its issue of April 13, 1911, the *Prolucutor*, a socialist paper published in Garden City, Kansas, reprinted the resolution to answer "Nigger Haters" who objected to the paper's championing of Negro rights. When William English Walling issued *The Socialism of Today* in 1916, he announced that he was reprinting the 1901 resolution "in answer to numerous inquiries" from socialists who knew nothing of its text. "The party since then," he explained, "has taken no position on this question." [9]

Despite its weakness when adopted, and its almost total neglect thereafter, the 1901 resolution justifies C. Vann Woodward's characterization of it as outstanding for its time in "inviting the Negro to join the party on a status equal with white men." The resolution, he notes, indicates that the Socialist party of America, for all the contradictory elements within the organization, did "get off to a strong start" so far as black Americans were concerned. [10] To this statement, one should add that the discussion on the resolution not only marks the first time in the history of American socialism that the Negro question received more than a cursory examination at a party convention, but it also was the most detailed and analytical of any in the entire history of Socialist party conventions. Moreover, it was a discussion in which blacks played more than token roles. The discussion, reported in full here for the first time, touched on every aspect related to the Negro question that was to confront American socialism in the years ahead: the conflict between socialism and "Southernism"; the vanguard role that socialists should play in combatting racism in the trade unions and among unorganized workers; and the question of whether the Negroes were a specially exploited section of the working class or just a general division of that class who had no need for special attention and whose problems would be solved, as would those of all workers, with the ushering in of socialism.


## DEBATE ON SOCIALISM IN THE BLACK PRESS, 1901

Throughout the discussion of the Negro resolution at the Indianapolis convention, its proponents emphasized that a special resolution dealing with the problems of black Americans was necessary in order to begin to make "an inroad" in the black community. "I would like to see it adopted," Leon Greenbaum argued, "because it will give us the means of putting in something there for propaganda and agitation purposes, which we cannot provide in any other way." Indeed, some delegates announced that they were willing to support the resolution because it was directed primarily to gain converts among blacks and could be "soft-pedaled" among whites. [11]

The convention had barely adjourned when some socialists proceeded to make use of the Negro resolution to gain support among blacks. Francis B. Livesey, a Maryland socialist, addressed *The Colored American*, a black weekly published in the nation's capital, criticizing it for an editorial on the steel strike of 1901, [12] in which the paper had stated its conviction "that the Negro must side with the capitalists." [13] Livesey used this criticism as a means of introducing the Negro resolution adopted by the Socialist party. "It should therefore be interesting to you and your readers to hear what the Socialists propose for the Negro," he wrote, including the text of the Negro resolution. *The Colored American* published the resolution under the heading "The Socialists invite Afro-Americans to their ranks and hold out Flattering Inducements." [14]

While the resolution did not arouse much discussion, the position of *The Colored American* in urging blacks to act as strikebreakers in the steel strike did. Although *The Worker* bitterly condemned the black weekly, [15] much of the black press defended it. [16] A debate developed in the weekly itself over the role blacks should play in strikes. In the course of the dialogue, the socialist approach was made clear. It began with a letter from E. D. Gibson, a sergeant in the United States Army, who wrote scornfully of a speech by T. J. Shaffer, president of the Amalgamated Association of Iron, Steel and Tin Workers—the union conducting the steel strike—in which Shaffer urged that blacks be admitted to membership. Gibson advised blacks to reject the invitation. Echoing Booker T. Washington, whom he praised, Gibson denounced trade unions as the main enemy of black workers and called upon his people to join forces with the capitalists, their true friends, and to fill the vacancies created by white strikers. [17]

Socialist Charles L. Wood of Washington, Iowa, criticized Gibson and called upon blacks to reject his advice. He conceded that, as a white man, he was far from proud of the record of the trade unions with respect to blacks; in fact, he admitted, it had been "shameful in the extreme, and without cause." However, he insisted that to follow the course Gibson advocated would be disastrous for black workers. Inadequate as they were as far as blacks were concerned, the trade unions had raised the general standard of wages throughout the entire nation, and black workers benefited even though they were not members. If the unions were destroyed, no power would exist to restrain the capitalist class from subjugating both white and black labor. The capitalists were not the friends of the black workers; they only appeared to play this role in order to use blacks "as tools" to "subjugate white labor." Once this objective was achieved, they would use their unbridled power to reduce blacks to total subjection. They were the enemies of all workers, black and white, and all workers had to unite to defeat their common enemy. Wherever unions admitted blacks, they should join, and where they were excluded, they should form their own organizations and cooperate with the white unions. In no case should they permit themselves to be used as strike-breakers.

Turning to political parties, Wood called attention to the betrayal of blacks by the Republicans, while the Democrats had already demonstrated their hostility to everything blacks valued. Only the socialists stood for a policy that was meaningful and beneficial to blacks. Regarding "the colored man [as] a fellow being and a brother," the socialists urged him to join their ranks and unite "for industrial and political liberty." Wood urged blacks to read the Negro resolution just adopted by the Socialist party, as well as other party literature, "and whenever you have a vote unite with ours at the polls." [18]

Sergeant Gibson was not convinced. He was evidently aware of what had happened to the Negro resolution as originally introduced by Costley, for he asked if socialists like Wood had "ever raised a voice against lynching." The major part of Gibson's reply took the form of a bitter attack on socialism as dangerous to American institutions and indistinguishable from anarchism. [19] Following in the path of their great leaders, he declared, blacks had to ally themselves with the respectable elements in society and follow "the law and order route." [20]

Wood, for his part, closed the debate with a defense of his activity in behalf of the rights of blacks. He assured Gibson that socialists believed "in rights for the Negro that we demand for ourselves." The socialists also believed in law and order, but above all, they believed in the establishment of a society in which blacks as well as whites would be relieved of hunger and want, and would have the opportunity to benefit from all that God had given to mankind. [21]

Wood's letters to *The Colored American* made a valuable contribution to the debate raging at the time in the labor, socialist, and black press over black strikebreaking. [22] Unfortunately, apart from making statements about the need for working-class solidarity and for including blacks in working-class organizations, the newly organized Socialist party did little to break down the barriers against blacks in the trade unions. The truth is that the socialists were mainly concerned with trying to integrate themselves into the American Federation of Labor (AFL) in the hope that they could somehow influence the direction of that body and thereby win it over to the support of a socialist program. With rare exceptions, the socialist delegates to AFL conventions and those of its affiliates played a passive role on the question of the unions' hostility toward black workers. They failed to raise the demand to end constitutional or ritual clauses barring black members or to challenge the general policy of Jim-Crow unionism in the AFL. Nor did they call for any special program to organize black workers. [23]

To be sure, some socialists met the issue squarely—members of the United Mine Workers of America who called for a consistent policy of black-white unity; for example, men like John Collins of the Machinists' Union, who sought in vain to eliminate the barriers against black membership, and Taral T. Frickstad of the Carpenters' and Joiners' Union, who wrote in its official journal about the necessity of having "all the colored people organized in unions" as the prerequisite for establishing a government that would serve the interests of all workers. In general, however, the record of socialists in the trade unions was not one that could impress blacks, and it seriously reduced the effectiveness of appeals about the evils of strikebreaking. The socialists appear to have ignored the fact that blacks often found in strikebreaking the only way they could obtain industrial employment, and that this was the only reason they resorted to it. It is significant that when *The Worker* reprinted the editorial of *The Colored American* favoring black strikebreaking during the steel strike of 1901, and proceeded to condemn this action as currying favor with the capitalists, it omitted the following section of the same editorial:

> The Negro responds to the call [to act as strikebreaker], because he needs the bread that labor will bring to himself and loved ones at home. It is not that he wishes to defeat any just demand by white workmen. It is not that he is the servant of those who

would grind the poor to powder. He is not the tool of soulless operators. It's because the white labor organizations refuse to make common cause with him and decline to give him the opportunity that is rightfully his to provide for his family. It is because his sympathy is alienated by treatment that drives him to the capitalist in self-defense. The corporation offers bread. The labor unions turn him away with a stone. Who can blame the Negro for thanking the Almighty for the situation that grants him what the unions deny, and establishes his power as a labor factor among those who think more of quality of servance than of the color of the servant. 25

*The Colored American* was indeed naive in believing that the capitalist used black labor during strikes because they appreciated the "quality" of their work. Nevertheless, the socialists could not reasonably expect blacks to listen to their advice on strikebreaking when they failed to understand the forces that compelled black workers to turn to strikebreaking, and when they did nothing significant to convince the unions that it was their exclusionist and discriminatory policies that spurred black workers to such actions.

## THE NEGRO QUESTION IN THE SOCIALIST PRESS, 1901-1903

The debate in *The Colored American* was the last discussion of socialism in the black press until the presidential campaign of 1904. 26 Discussion of the Negro question continued in the socialist press. Between the end of the Indianapolis convention and the 1904 national convention of the Socialist party, the *International Socialist Review, The Worker*, the *Appeal to Reason*, the *Chicago Socialist*, the *Seattle Socialist*, and the *Social Democratic Herald* all presented articles on one aspect or another of the Negro question, and the *International Socialist Review* usually had one article in each issue. Indeed, apart from the question of the farmers' role in the Socialist party, the Negro question was the most widely debated issue in American socialist circles during the opening years of the twentieth century. The participants in the discussion were almost exclusively white party officials and members. 27 The lone exception was J. Johnston of Chicago, who contributed a short piece to *The Socialist* of that city that was critical of Booker T. Washington and asserted that blacks should concern themselves with the evils of capitalism rather than with social equality.

The first pamphlet published by the Socialist party on the Negro was *Socialism and the Negro Problem* by Reverend Charles H. Vail, issued in

1902 by the Comrade Publishing Company of New York. Reverend Vail, the first permanent national organizer of the Socialist party, presented much that was in other socialist publications, but he did place more than usual emphasis on the elimination of race prejudice under socialism:

> But it may be said that although Socialism would emancipate the negro from economic servitude, it would not completely solve the negro problem unless its advent would destroy race prejudices. This is precisely what Socialism would do. Of course, it would not accomplish it all at once, but race prejudices cannot exist with true enlightenment. Socialism would educate and enlighten the race. It would secure to the laborers, whether black or white, the full opportunities for education of their children. . . . Socialism recognizes no class nor race distinction. It draws no line of exclusion. Under Socialism the negro will enjoy, equally with the whites, the advantages and opportunities for culture and refinement. In this higher education we may be sure race prejudices will be obliterated.
>
> Not only will universal enlightenment destroy this low prejudice but abolition of competition will aid in working the same result. The struggle between the black and white to sell themselves in the auction of the new slave market has, in many quarters, engendered bitter race feeling, and that they might bid the fiercer against each other the masters have fanned this prejudice into hate. . . . Socialism emphasizes the fact that the interests of all laborers are identical regardless of race or sex. In this common class interest race distinctions are forgotten. If this is true of Socialists to-day, how much more will it be true when humanity is lifted to the higher plane where the economic interests of all are identical?

Reverend Vail concluded on a distinctly positive note: "When Socialism supplants capitalism the negro problem will be forever solved." [28]

The discussion in the socialist press revealed that, on the Negro question, the Socialist party was anything but a monolithic organization. Opinions ranged from the outright racist advocacy of white supremacy, through the idea that the Negro question was a class problem and nothing more, to the position that the Socialist party should conduct a consistent and persistent struggle against racism. This range of views refers only to those socialist publications that actually discussed the Negro question. The truth is that many publications never even dealt with the issue during their existence—often brief—while still others referred to it only once or twice. But the fact that a socialist publication discussed the issue frequently was no guarantee that its approach was constructive, or vice versa. Thus, the *Colorado Chronicle*, published in Denver, carried only one editorial on the Negro during its three years of existence (1901-1903), but that one, in its issue of July 15, 1903, was an effective attack on "representatives of the modern church in America" for opposing "the unqualified freedom of the negro." The socialist weekly accused leading clerical figures of "great antipathy . . . for the negro as a free man. As a slave the negro is all right, but as a free man he is all wrong, according to many of these ecclesiastical dignitaries," who believed that, being inferior to whites, the Negro

> must be content with any condition in life that the superior is willing to allow. If this whim takes the form of a mob and results in brutal murder and terrible torture at the stake, the church still apologizes and excuses, and in some cases actually indorses, the cruelties by the statement that the "crime" of the victim of the mobs' fury was very atrocious, etc.

Ironically the *Colorado Chronicle* seemed to be totally unaware that the same criticism it leveled at elements of the American church could have been applied almost to the letter to groups within the very party for which it spoke.

Take, for example, the position of Victor Berger, the first socialist elected to Congress, the architect of the party's impressive electoral victories in Milwaukee, the strongest socialist city, and the dominant influence in that city's trade-union movement. He also represented the most blatant racists in the party. It was this group that publicly proclaimed, in the North as well as in the South, that the Negro belonged to an inferior race. Racial animosity, they argued, was deeply rooted in human nature and was not simply a product of a capitalist conspiracy to divide the working class. In fact, it would even survive in the Cooperative Commonwealth. In 1902, Berger wrote in his widely circulated weekly, the *Social Democratic Herald*:

> There can be no doubt that the negroes and mulattoes constitute a lower race—that the Caucasian and indeed the Mongolian have the start of them in civilization by many thousand years—so that negroes will find it difficult ever to overtake them. The many cases of rape which occur whenever negroes are settled in large numbers prove, moreover, that the free contact with the whites has led to the further degeneration of the negroes, as of all other inferior races. The "negro question" will one day give the

Socialists a good deal of headache, and will never be settled by mere well-phrased resolutions. [29]

There is no difference between this comment and the white-supremacist utterances of the racist propagandists Madison Grant and Lothrop Stoddard. Berger, however, was a leading spokesman for a party that preached the universal brotherhood of man.

Berger was also a delegate to all the AFL conventions and was one of the party trade unionists who regularly courted the AFL's leadership. He shared Samuel Gompers' belief that the Negro was unorganizable and a "natural scab." His general view was that the Negro was a burden of which the Socialist party would do well to rid itself. He had only contempt for the "Negro Resolution" adopted in 1901, viewing it as a sentimental expression in direct conflict with biological realities. [30]

William Noyes was even more vitriolic in his statements against the blacks than Berger. He wrote in the *International Socialist Review*:

Physically, the negroes are as a race repulsive to us. Their features are the opposite of what we call beautiful. This includes, not their facial features alone, but the shape of their heads and hands and feet, and general slovenliness of carriage. The odor, even of the cleanest of them, differs perceptively from ours. In a word, they seem like a caricature and mockery of our ideas of the "human form divine." An intimate knowledge of negroes still further enables one to sympathize with the common dislike of them."

Like Berger, Noyes wished that the Negro would just go away and leave the Socialist party alone, although he conceded that this was unlikely. [31] Max Hayes, the prominent socialist trade-union leader, criticized any efforts to raise the Negro question within the party. Not only did he consider the issue divisive, but he also felt that it tended "to obscure the economic problems that press for solution" and to undermine the party's influence within the trade unions. [32]

Other prominent socialists who shared Berger's and Noyes' white supremacist views included H. Gaylord Wilshire, Reverend J. Stitt Wilson of California, and Alexander Jonas of New York. None, however, went as far as Berger and Noyes in their racism. Wilshire usually ignored the Negro in his West Coast publications, *The Challenge* and *Wilshire's Magazine*. In over 400 pages of articles and editorials from Wilshire's, published in 1906, there is not a single reference to the Negro. [33]

One socialist who later joined his white supremacist comrades was

Ernest Untermann. During this period, however, as associate editor of the *Appeal to Reason*, Untermann contributed a number of powerful attacks on anti-Negro racism. Most significant of these was his article "The American Kishineff," published on July 25, 1903, in which he dealt with an issue of major concern to blacks. Blacks were becoming increasingly bitter because the federal government refused to protect their rights guaranteed in the Fourteenth and Fifteenth Amendments, and instead remained silent in the face of the increasing number of lynchings and race riots. They were especially angry when this same government sent diplomatic protests to Romania and Russia over the treatment of Jews in those countries. Black newspapers stated that, while they condemned the pogroms against Jews, they found it hard to understand why the government could act so swiftly in behalf of citizens of foreign countries while it dragged its feet over the persecution of its own black citizens. [34] The issue reached a climax in 1903 as a result of the pogroms incited by Tsarist Minister Plehve at Kishinev, during which scores of Jews were killed, several hundred wounded, and hundreds of Jewish homes wrecked and plundered. When President Theodore Roosevelt transmitted to the tsar the petition presented to him in June by the B'nai B'rith denouncing the Kishineff massacre, his action received almost universal acclaim in the American press, both North and South. One exception was the black press. A number of black newspapers pointed out that the same people who had signed the petition to the tsar, and the same newspapers that supported it, were "dumb, when they do not approve, the savage outrages against Negroes at home." [35] For example, they pointed out, the signatures to the petition included the names of the mayor and City Council members of Evansville, Indiana, where, just one month later, a riot against Negroes drove over 1,000 blacks from their homes and forced them to seek shelter in the woods. "Negroes are fleeing from the American Kishineff, Evansville, Indiana," *The Freeman*, a black weekly published in Indianapolis wrote bitterly. "Shall the Negroes look to the Tsar of Russia for protection, since neither the President of the United States nor the Mayor of Evansville seems interested in protecting them?" [36]

Untermann addressed himself to this question in his moving article. He drew a parallel between the Jews who fled from Kishinev and the Negroes who had been forced to abandon their homes in Evansville, and he insisted that it was the same group of men—the capitalists—who were responsible for the persecution of the Jews in Russia and the lynching of Negroes in the United States. Pogroms in Russia and race riots in the United States, he said, were both fruits of the capitalist system: "Capitalism is only furnishing new proofs that humanity is living a lie

under the profit system." Neither the Jews nor the Negroes could expect
any aid from governments controlled by the capitalists. But there was a
hope for both:

> the Socialist party of the world is raising its warning voice and
> rallying the workers of all countries for their emancipation.
> Workers unite! Whether Jews or Gentiles, whether black or
> white or red, or yellow, your battles are the same all over the
> world! Your curse is capitalism, your only hope is Socialism. [37]

Unlike many other socialist publications, the *Appeal to Reason*, which
featured Untermann's article on its first page, could hardly be called indifferent to the Negro question. In the pages of this most widely circulated of all socialist newspapers, editor Julius A. Wayland condemned
"the continuation of lynching outlawry," the disfranchisement of the
Negro, and the convict lease system in the South. He also attacked the
trade-union restrictions which prevented black workers from making
common cause with the white, pointing out that workers of all colors
would have to join hands before the chains of wage slavery could be
broken. [38]

And yet, despite these positions, Wayland was a strict segregationist.
He insisted that wage earners preferred to work among others of their
own kind, and that only the present slave conditions of capitalism forced
races into unwanted mutual association. Given a truly free selection
under socialism, the races would drift into completely separate communities. The Negroes, he wrote, preferred "to live in communities of their
own just as Caucasians do. They will naturally have cities of their own
where none other will desire to interfere. They will live in nice homes if
they want them" and "have just as fine machinery and excellent conditions of labor as other people." Under socialism, workers would decide
who would labor beside them in the factories. In each factory, a majority
of the workers would have the right to consent to the employment of any
man. Logically, therefore, whites would decide to work only with members of their race, while blacks would seek employment in factories run
by members of their race. In short, the socialist society would be segregated from top to bottom. [39]

But in the same state of Kansas where the *Appeal to Reason* was published, a leading socialist was a pioneer in the struggle against segregation. In 1879, the Kansas legislature had passed a law that sanctioned
separate elementary schools for black children in the "first class" cities.
In 1903, William Reynolds, a black resident of Topeka, attempted to
enroll his child in a white school. The child was refused admittance, and
Reynolds initiated *mandamus* proceedings against the city's board of

education. One of his two attorneys was G. C. Clemens, the veteran Kansas socialist, who had formerly exhibited an anti-Negro attitude.

In the brief submitted to the court, Clemens argued that the statute violated the state constitution requiring that Kansas establish a uniform system of common schools. He contended "'common' means to *the people—all* the people—regardless of color, race, social standing or religious belief, or it has *no* particular meaning—is meaningless. *Every* school was to be a 'common' school. No school was to be a *select* or *class* school." The brief also emphasized that the school law violated the Fourteenth Amendment to the Constitution, and it cited Justice Harlan's dissenting opinion in Plessy *v.* Ferguson (1896) for support. The brief further declared that the Kansas statute did not even measure up to the "separate but equal" doctrine of the majority opinion in the Plessy case because the Kansas law did not require equal facilities for the segregated schools. The school board "may build an educational palace for the whites and give the colored children a hovel." It stated that "the mingling of the races at school is itself educative," and it minced no words in its conclusion:

> The discrimination goes far beyond simple segregation. The insult is made more galling by added circumstances of contumely. Not even health is regarded. The excuse must be that having expended so much in providing an elegant school for the whites, little was left the defendant to expend on the children of African descent. But does the Fourteenth Amendment recognize such an excuse?
>
> If the defendant is vested with discretion to provide separate schools, the testimony shows that it has so abused that discretion that its action is void.

The court ruled unanimously against the black plaintiff and upheld the constitutionality of segregation. Shortly thereafter, Clemens persuaded the court to decide against segregation in Coffeyville, a Kansas city of the second class. [40] This remarkable Kansas socialist should have been alive in 1954, when the United States Supreme Court, in the famous case contesting segregation in Topeka, completely vindicated the position set forth in the brief he had drawn up in 1903, and declared separate schools everywhere to be unconstitutional.

While few socialists preached a theory of separate societies on so elaborate a scale as did Julius A. Wayland, the idea of separate communities for blacks under socialism continued to find a place in the Socialist party's literature. Even the official party publication *Songs of Socialism*, published in 1902 and frequently reprinted, contained a distinct reference to a segregated society under socialism. One of the songs written by Harvey P. Moyer, the editor of the collection, was "The Darkies' Kingdom," a title reflecting the lack of sensitivity to blacks. In the song, blacks describe, in dialect, their plight under capitalism and the hope held out for them by the socialist party. Under socialism, they rejoiced, there would be

> in sun-ny Dix-ie, A
> state for all de dark-ies,
> Uncle Sam will gib to us alone. [41]

Many socialists made it clear that the party did not require social equality between the races. The party press took pains to highlight evidence that blacks themselves were only interested in economic and political, not social, equality, and it insisted that this approach was basically the correct one. Writing in the *International Socialist Review*, A. T. Cruzner strongly defended civil rights for Negroes and criticized socialists who hesitated to challenge the prejudices of Southern members. He hastened to add, however, that the Negro only wanted political and economic rights, and had no desire to mix with the white race—which he considered an intelligent conception of their real problems. [42] *The Worker* carried several editorials emphasizing that socialism did not mean social equality of the races. In one, it used a frequently repeated phrase that the Socialist party "does not trouble itself about the bugbear of 'social equality.'" Explaining this statement further, it declared: "Whether white men and black men shall sit at the same dinner-table is a matter, we say, for individual white men and black men to decide." No white Southerner, *The Worker* insisted, need hesitate to join the Socialist party for fear that it would upset the system of public segregation in the South. Eventually under socialism, when the Negro would have the "opportunity for education and culture" to develop to a point where he would no longer be 'inferior,' and consequently no longer repellant or uncongenial," social equality would be possible. Until then, the Socialist party would insist only that black and white achieve equality in the political and economic arena. [43]

## EUGENE V. DEBS ON THE NEGRO QUESTION

In common with many socialists of the period, *The Worker* believed that Negroes occupied a lower position on the evolutionary scale than whites. Unlike Berger, however, the paper believed that blacks could in

time advance themselves sufficiently to be entitled to enjoy social equality. In the meantime, it felt that there was a place even for the "inferior"
Negroes in the ranks of the Socialist party. Even Eugene V. Debs, a man
who opposed discrimination and toured the South speaking in defense of
Negro rights and calling on blacks to reject the false doctrines of "meekness and humility," [44] accepted the view that the Negro was not yet the
equal of the white. It was therefore pointless, he said, to talk about social
equality. Debs was never entirely consistent when he dealt with the
Negro question. On the one hand, he angrily denied the charge that the
socialists of Evansville, Illinois, were responsible for the tragic anti-
Negro riots in that city, declaring: "The Socialists are the only ones who
recognize not merely the political and economic equality of the negro, but
his social equality as well." On another occasion, he said: "Of course the
negro will 'not be satisfied with equality with reservation.' Why should
he be" Would you?" On the other hand, he would add, with no apparent
awareness of his inconsistency: "Social equality, forsooth! . . . is pure
fraud and serves to mask the real issue, which is not *social equality*, BUT
ECONOMIC FREEDOM." Debs did not rule out the possibility that
under the right circumstances, meaning socialism, the Negro could become fully the equal of the white. He wrote:

> The negro, like the white man, is subject to the laws of physical,
> mental and moral development. But in his case these laws have
> been suspended. Socialism simply proposes that the negro shall
> have full opportunity to develop his mind and soul, and this will
> in time emancipate the race from animalism, so repulsive to
> those especially whose fortunes are built on it. [45]

It must be added that Debs did not equate the elimination of the demand for social equality as a socialist principle with the acceptance of the
pattern of public segregation that prevailed in the South. In fact, he invariably refused to speak to segregated audiences. While he insisted that
socialism would not force a white man to invite a Negro into his home or
associate with him in private, he nevertheless maintained that no socialist worthy of the name could countenance segregation of public facilities.

Clarence Meily was another socialist who made it absolutely clear that
equal access to public facilities was included in the socialist concept of
economic equality. He wrote in the *International Socialist Review*:

> Absolute equality for white and black, covering perfect uniform-
> ity not only in opportunities for labor, but also in those public
> services such as education, transportation (including, let it be
> added, hotel accommodations), entertainment, etc., which may

be collectively rendered together with complete recognition of political rights, must be insisted on more strenuously by the socialist than ever they could have been by any abolitionist agitator. [46]

In an interview in Fort Worth, Texas, in October 1903, Debs was asked "about the attitude of Socialism towards the negro." He replied that socialism "preaches economic equality for all men, each according to his ability," and continued: "Socialism has not yet made progress enough to make a decision in the race question. That is a question that will be settled fairly and squarely when reached." [47] To help settle the question, he published a series of articles in late 1903 and early 1904 on the Negro question. While he went beyond the simple statement he made in Fort Worth, it can hardly be said that he contributed to settling the question "fairly and squarely."

The first article took the form of a letter to the editor of the *Indianapolis World* in response to an inquiry concerning the socialist leader's attitude toward Booker T. Washington and his plan for industrial education. Debs discussed the praise heaped upon Washington by David M. Parry, president of the National Association of Manufacturers and the guiding spirit of the antiunion "open-shop" drive. Condemning organized labor for its opposition to the entrance of black workers into the trades and industry, Parry praised Washington for training blacks in industrial education as a means of furnishing employment, and he hailed his advice to black workers that they take jobs vacated by strikers. Debs' reply was, of course, a bitter denunciation of strikebreaking. In words that sounded strange coming from a man not known for courting the AFL and the Railroad Brotherhoods and one who was certainly aware of the increasingly exclusionist trend in organized labor toward black workers, Debs wrote that "the labor movement in general, in America . . . stands unequivocally committed to receive and treat the negro upon terms of absolute equality." Therefore, he went on, Booker T. Washington was serving as a tool of the capitalists when he advocated a policy that would weaken black labor's staunchest ally. [48]

This was too much for George Washington Cable, the Southern author whose forthright denunciation of repression of the Negro and the convict system had caused him to take up residence in the North. [49] Cable wrote to the *Indianapolis World*: "We fear that Mr. Debs does not know the extent to which the colored worker is opposed by organized labor, which accounts for the general distrust which the colored man has for trade-unionism." Cable believed that, ultimately, the trade unions, out of sheer economic necessity, would "accept and treat the colored man as a fellow worker." He was also convinced "that the vast majority of American working men have a long way to travel before they reach the lofty plane on which Mr. Debs stands." [50]

Cable could also, if he had known of it, have called attention to Debs' own condemnation of the miners' union of Evansville, Illinois, for attacking black workers. [51] He could have pointed out that, since the United Mine Workers was supposed to be in advance of most unions on the Negro question, Debs' uncritical evaluation of organized labor was excessive, to say the least.

Debs' letter to the *Indianapolis World* was widely reprinted in the socialist press, but none of the papers even mentioned Cable's criticism of Debs' unqualified endorsement of organized labor's racial policies. This was not because these papers were unaware of the validity of Cable's arguments. In fact, *The Worker* published an editorial on the "Duty and Interest of Organized Labor" in overcoming the influence of Booker T. Washington's antiunionist, procapitalist ideology on blacks. The editorial urged "the trade unions of all crafts in all parts of the country" to make their contribution "by putting aside the race prejudice which some of them still entertain," and to regard blacks "simply as fellow workingmen."

*The Worker* hardly contributed to this worthwhile goal when it published, without comment, a lengthy article entitled, "The Race Question A Class Question" by C. L. (undoubtedly Courtney Lemon, later a leading editorial writer for the *New York Call.*) In order to prove that color had nothing to do with the black worker's status, the writer made the point that white workers, too, faced discrimination by being excluded from social contact with rich capitalists and their "fine ladies." Equating the exclusion of white workingmen from rich society with the daily humiliation blacks faced in a segregated society was a typical argument of those socialists who insisted that the Negro question was only one of class.

Nor did *The Worker* contribute to overcoming "race prejudice" in the trade unions when it constantly harped on the theme that blacks, having "a tradition of servility," were not yet ready for trade unionism. White workers, it wrote, had "a tradition of revolt to inspire them, rather than a tradition of servility to weigh them down," while black workers had inherited from slavery "a willingness to consider themselves inferior beings and to be humble and grateful to their 'betters.'" *The Worker* even attributed the high incidence of peonage among blacks in the South to the fact that "their general ignorance and habit of timidity and obedience, inherited from the past, makes it easier to bring them under the lash." Nonetheless, *The Worker* struck a fundamentally correct note— unfortunately not sufficiently emphasized in the socialist press—when it declared: "The organized working class alone has the interest as well as the power to settle the race question by the exercise of patient and class-conscious intelligence and the teaching and practicing of proletarian solidarity."[52]

In his letter Debs mentioned in passing that there was no Negro problem "apart from the general labor problem" and that blacks were "not one whit worse off" than white workers under capitalism, and therefore required no special attention. He developed this theme, a central aspect of his approach to the Negro question, in articles in the *International Socialist Review*. He advanced the concept that the Negro question was a class problem, and nothing more, and that formulating special programs for the Negro would constitute a kind of racism in reverse, antithetical to the egalitarian principles of the Socialist party. Indeed, the Negro question was a creation of, and problem for, the capitalist class only:

> We [the Socialists] have nothing to do with it, for it is their [the capitalists'] fight. We have simply to open the eyes of as many negroes as we can and do battle for emancipation from wage slavery, and when the working class have triumphed in the class struggle and stand forth economic as well as political free men, the race problem will disappear.

Until it disappeared, he observed, there was no need for special attention to the Negro question: "We have nothing special to offer the Negro, and we cannot make separate appeals to all the races. The Socialist Party is the Party of the whole working class regardless of color." And even though, in reply to a Southern socialist who criticized him for advocating equality for the Negro, Debs proudly published the "Negro Resolution" adopted at the 1901 convention, it is not surprising that he called upon the next convention to repeal the resolution as both unnecessary and contrary to the correct approach to the Negro question.[53] Victor Berger applauded Debs for his wisdom, declaring that it showed "Comrade Debs at his best."[54]

Of course, there was a world of difference between Berger's and Debs' positions on the Negro question. Compared with the racist Berger, Debs was a forthright supporter of Negro rights. Despite all the ideological weaknesses of his 1903 writings on the Negro question, these writings also demonstrate that as early as 1903 he clearly understood that "the history of the Negro in the United States is a history of crime without a parallel." His test for a socialist when it came to the Negro was simple: "Socialists should with pride proclaim their sympathy with and fealty to the black race, and if any there be who hesitate to avow themselves in the face of ignorant and unreasoning prejudice, they lack the true spirit of the slavery-destroying revolutionary movement."[55]

## CAROLINE HOLLINGSWORTH PEMBERTON, SOCIALIST CHAMPION OF BLACK EQUALITY

Of all the discussions on the Negro question in the socialist press between the 1901 and 1904 national conventions, the least compromising and most advanced came from the pen of the assistant secretary of the Pennsylvania State Committee of the Socialist party, Miss Caroline Hollingsworth Pemberton. [56] Pemberton was descended from an old Quaker family; her father was Henry Pemberton, scholar, scientist, and author of *The Path of Evolution* among other works, and her uncle was General John C. Pemberton of the Confederate Army. As a young girl, she spent months with her uncle's household in the South and came to know at first hand the conditions of the Southern blacks. [57]

The fact that the niece of a Confederate general—the defender of Vicksburg—should write so sympathetically about the Negro question did not escape attention in the contemporary press. Currently, however, her name does not appear in any work on American socialism and is not even listed among the hunderds of entries in *Index to Women of the World*, published in 1970.

The story of Caroline Pemberton's first writings on the Negro question before she became a socialist merits some attention in explaining the advanced position she took on the question once she joined the party. In 1897, Pemberton was in the Deep South, probably Alabama, and she drew upon her experiences there in writing her novel *Stephen the Black*. The novel reveals both the author's knowledge of the conditions under which Southern blacks lived and her indignation over what she had seen during her visit. It also reflects her disdain of white Philadelphia's indifference to these conditions and of the hypocrisy of many of those in her social set who were prepared to contribute to black educational institutions in the South but were unwilling to offer blacks opportunities to use the talents they acquired in these institutions. She felt they were primarily interested in seeing that the Negro remained in his place doing menial work.

*Stephen the Black* opens with a lucid picture of the failure of legal emancipation to change fundamentally the poverty-stricken status of Southern blacks: "Ignorance enveloped them still, as in the days of slavery. They worked steadily and uncomplainingly, but only a very few of them had land, houses, money, or education. They lived in the same miserable cabins; they toiled for the benefit of others; they reaped not what they sowed." She describes the vicious sharecropping system which replaced plantation slavery, and she relates how the master received the bulk of what the blacks produced. "They had all they could do to keep alive that year: and the master remarked grimly, 'Fill up your stomach with freedom boys,' when he saw their disappointed looks and heard the apprehensive murmur that the supply of food received in exchange for cotton would not last them until the next crop was grown and picked." [58] Later, she describes the division after the cotton had been sold, and how little was received by the sharecropper. The cotton the sharecropper had raised "had been sold by his landlord, who after deducting the expenses of living, the price of the ox, and the interest of his mortgage, returned to him a statement in which it appeared that Wesley [Anderson, a former slave] was still in arrears for the interest that had been accumulating on the ox." Pemberton tells of how the illiterate Anderson was cheated by the landlord-storekeeper who kept the accounts, charged the sharecroppers whatever he wished for supplies, and falsified the amounts he purchased so that the black was literally being swindled out of his "just earnings." [59]

Stephen Wells (*Stephen the Black*), with whom the sharecropper discusses his sad plight, is a graduate of Tuskegee Institute and starts a school in this typical Southern community. Stephen leaves for Philadelphia to raise money for his school, having been told while at Tuskegee that there are "wealthy philanthropists" in the City of Brotherly Love interested in helping the Southern Negro. He quickly discovers that these white philanthropists are ready to help certain Southern black colleges miles away from where they might possibly come into contact with those who were being helped. They have no interest in meeting blacks personally; they are embarrassed and not a little frightened when approached by Stephen. Stephen dimly discerns "what may be described as the national attitude of the average white American toward the black. For thirty years it has been his habit of mind to look over, by or beyond the black man, but never at him. Though northern cities may teem with representatives of the liberated race, the white American of the North knows the black only by the dreadful things he reads about him in southern dispatches." [60]

Unable to make any headway among rich whites, Stephen is compelled to look for work. But he is wise in the ways of Northern society and knows that his training at Tuskegee will not help him in his pursuit of work for which he has been trained:

> Although Stephen was a good penman, an accurate accountant and a clever carpenter, he was too well acquainted with the pecu-

liar form of race prejudice in the North to waste time seeking employment in any of these lines. Through the efforts of a friend, he secured a position as a waiter in a large summer hotel situated at a fashionable seaside resort, and as it was now open and guests were pouring in plentifully, his services began without delay.

Among his fellow-waiters were graduates of training schools established for the industrial development of the race. They had become skilled craftsmen and were striking examples of the satirical benevolence of the North which bestows the handsome accomplishment of a trade on a black, and then commands him to starve or steal rather than live by it.

The head-waiter was a graduate of Harvard and had been selected with great care, not because of his Greek and Hebrew accomplishments (of which the proprietor indeed knew nothing) but because his honesty was unquestioned, his habits beyond reproach, and his command of men, napkins and china equal to that of a great general over an army. His name was Henry Howard; he was a coal-black negro of good height and heavy build; his expression was thoughtful and his smile pleasing. [61]

As the waiters are excellent singers, the headwaiter suggests, after he learns of Stephen's mission, that they give a concert for the benefit of his school. The waiters respond enthusiastically and sell tickets to the wealthy white guests. Before the concert is to begin, Stephen delivers a short speech in which he describes his school and his hopes for his people. When he concludes, a wealthy guest observes that she had once been a great friend of the Negro but finally concluded that "a great deal of money had been thrown away on educating him above his position. The race had become shiftless and good-for-nothing. The colored people needed to be made to work. Freedom had done them no good." Furious, Stephen, forgetting that he is supposed to act the role of a menial, cries out angrily: "My people have never eaten bread that they've not earned—they've paid double the price of every mouthful that the white man has paid." [62]

The "great lady" rises from her chair in indignation, sweeps majestically out of the room, and promptly tells the other guests about the insulting conduct of the Negro waiter. The result is that, except for the nurses and children, no one comes to the concert. The receipts amount to next to nothing. Stephen's hopes are crushed: "To add to his depression, the evening papers told a terrible tale of massacre in one of the southern states—the victims being as usual, accused, untried, defenceless blacks." [63]

Out of despair, Stephen all but gives up hope for his school and his people. White America was too powerful and black Americans too degraded by centuries of exploitation ever to make possible any hope for a change. Howard, the headwaiter, reminds him that he knows nothing of the history of his people, that black Americans are descended from the Ethiopians and other great civilized people of ancient times. In time, black Americans would regain their heritage. It would require patience and the kind of work Stephen had been doing in his Southern community. But their rise was inevitable.

Encouraged, Stephen continues at his work. When a Quaker family, learning of his plans for his school, add to his earnings with a check for two hundred dollars, he has enough to pay his schools' expenses for several months.

When Stephen returns to the Southern community, he and several other blacks organize a society for the study of improved agricultural methods. The plan is to purchase land, sell it in small lots to members on credit, and gradually enable the blacks to escape from sharecropping and become independent farmers and homeowners. When the officers of the association try to purchase land, however, they discover that whites will not sell at any price. The blacks are forced to remain tenants: "This kept them poor and at the mercy of their landlords." [64]

Meanwhile, the school is progressing—so much so that the whites become alarmed and threaten to burn down the building. The blacks arm themselves and guard the school every night, drilling during part of the day with their arms. Fearing that this action will bring on a race riot with an orgy of lynchings, Stephen threatens to leave the community unless the armed patrol is disbanded. After an exciting debate, the blacks agree to cease the patrol on condition that a dozen be permitted to sleep in the building: "They came late, slept on the floor with a blanket apiece to cover them, and departed early in the morning." Learning of these safety precautions, the whites abandon their plans to destroy the school. [65]

*Stephen the Black* ends with the murder by white vigilantes of Theresa, a black woman who has secretly married Ralph Aikens, a wealthy white man who had fallen in love with her. Stephen buries her and dedicates his life to continuing his work for his people in the small Southern community.

*Stephen the Black* is not great American fiction. Nor is it free of ideological weaknesses; for example, there is a good deal of labored discussion of the conflict between the white and black blood in both Stephen and Theresa. Despite this particular weakness and its stilted language the book was, for its time, a remarkable novel. It was fully as important as *Doctor Huguet*, Ignatius Donnelly's novel published in 1891 about a white man turned black, who learns the daily humiliation of being a

Negro in American society. [66] Moreover, it provides a better picture than does Donnelly's novel of the terrible system of peonage under which millions of Southern blacks lived; the hypocrisy of Northern white philanthropy; the failure of industrial education to solve the economic problems of young blacks; and the inability of Southern blacks to purchase land, even when they had mastered scientific agriculture, in order to escape peonage. Furthermore, the novel portrays sympathetically the efforts of blacks to resist their exploitation and to achieve a better way of life. It bluntly points out that it was not through any lack of initiative or self-effort, but rather because of Southern violence and Northern indifference that they had not been successful. Indeed, the novel was a good antidote to the feeling so common in the United States at the time that white America had done enough for the Negro, that blacks had not known how to use their freedom, and that the solution of the "race problem" should be left to white Southerners who best understood the Negro.

Pemberton also sent several letters to the *Springfield Republican*, *City and State*, and *The Christian Recorder* dealing with the Negro question at the turn of the century. [67] In her letters, she criticized the apparent indifference of Northern whites to the reign of terror against blacks in the South; denounced Northern newspapers for assuming the guilt of Negroes lynched by Southern mobs, pointing out that the victims of lynch mobs were "put to death without evidence, identification or trial"; and accused Northern capitalists of hypocrisy because they believed that they had done their duty to the Negro by mailing a check "to the principal of a colored industrial training school" while denying the graduates jobs in their shops and factories:

> What the negro needs more than anything else is a diversified opportunity for industry. This the average white man seems determined he shall not have, and even the philanthropist shuts his door on the negro who appeals to him for work, after having benefitted by his liberality to the extent of a "free scholarship." What a satire this is on the white man's logic. [68]

Pemberton's letters were widely reprinted, especially her vigorous response to an address on "The Negro Problem in the South" by Charles Dudley Warner, president of the American Social Science Association, before the association's meeting in Washington, D.C., in 1900. In his address, published in the *Springfield Republican* of May 10, 1900, Warner contrasted the beneficial effects of slavery on the Negro with the injurious effects wrought by the attempts since his freedom to give him a higher education. Warner contended that under slavery "the negro was taught to work, to be an agriculturist, a mechanic, a material producer of something useful," while "our higher education applied to him in his present development operates in exactly the opposite direction." Warner concluded that the condition of blacks in the South was "lower than it was several years ago, and that the influence of the higher education had been in the wrong direction."

Warner's address was widely applauded. It fit neatly into the general view that the Southern Negro was destined to be only "the hewer of wood and drawer of water" and should be contented with this status. In her response, Pemberton graphically described the sad condition of blacks under slavery and noted the small likelihood of their obtaining the industrial education Warner believed was one of the benefits of slavery. There was not the slightest danger, she noted, of the Southern Negro becoming overeducated. The Negro masses, except in the towns and cities, had little opportunity "to obtain even the rudiments of an education."

> A public-school system of three-months' schooling, without text-books or school-houses, and which opens its schools in deserted log cabins or colored meeting-houses five, ten, or fifteen miles apart, is not likely to prepare many pupils for the "negro colleges" that Mr. Warner so much dreads. The public schools in the Philippine Islands would probably compare favorably with those provided for negro children in many of our Southern States — that is, for negro children on the plantations, where illiteracy often claims 70 per cent of the population. [69]

In reprinting sections of her letter, the *Literary Digest* called attention to the fact that she was the niece of a Confederate general, "an able defender of the colored race, and is the author of the recent novel, 'Stephen the Black.'" The *Boston Transcript* reprinted her letter in full and commented: "In this woman's quick intelligence, sound intuition, deep sympathy, and undoubted knowledge of the facts of the situation there seem to be gathered up more truth and justice than in any of the labored and pretentious attempts to state the problem and furnish a solution." [70]

Caroline H. Pemberton brought these qualities, especially "deep sympathy and undoubted knowledge of the situation," with her when she became a member and official of the Socialist party. [71]

On November 7, 1901, *The Worker* carried the first of a series of four articles by Pemberton, entitled "The American Negro's Problem: Another View of the Race Question Considered in the Light of Economic Conditions." The editor introduced the series with the notice that since Pemberton was a member of a family that "distinguished itself on the Confederate side in the Civil War," and had "closely observed conditions in the South in recent years," she was "especially qualified to discuss the

negro question without being open to the charge of Northern prejudice." [72] No further explanation was offered on just what constituted
"Northern prejudice" on the Negro question. Perhaps the editor had in
mind the complaints by Southern delegates at the Indianapolis convention that their comrades in the North simply did not understand the
Negro question in the South.

Pemberton's articles furnished no comfort to Southern socialists who
hoped the party would understand the white point of view in that section.
The first article attacked the concept that the Southern Negro was fundamentally "an idle, lazy brute, who knows not how to earn a living
either with his hands or his brain," or that he was a "heavy burden on the
white population," and was likely to remain so "until Northern philanthropists start enough industrial schools to teach him 'how to work.'"
She emphasized instead that the Negro had been and still was "the basis
of every form of industrial enterprise south of Mason and Dixon's line,"
and that whatever he had received since brought to this country, he had
"paid for many times over with his toil."

Pemberton then challenged the mythology, prevalent even in some
socialist literature, that slavery had been the best of all possible institutions for "helpless negroes" and that bondage had offered the Negro the
guiding intellect and "moral support" of the superior race, enabling him
to be trained "to habits of industry, and disciplined to good order" and
thereby lifting blacks up from savagery. According to the mythology,
blacks were worse off as a result of the demise of slavery. No longer provided for by a benevolent and paternalistic master, they were suddenly
"turned loose on their hands — and not knowing how to 'earn a living.'" [73]
Pemberton noted that slavery had existed for the "sole purpose" of furnishing "cheap and efficient labor for Southern cotton fields, and other
branches of industry." Negro slaves were not kept for "pets," but for
what they could produce by their labor for a capitalistic system of exploitation to achieve the greatest profits. Since the treatment of slaves
was geared to the extraction of the greatest profits, it was not surprising
that they had inadequate food, clothing, and housing. Even if the house
slaves were "better housed and fed" than the field hands, they rarely constituted more than 5 percent of the slave population. Then, to complete
the picture of the so-called benevolent institution, there were the horrors
of the domestic slave trade and the breeding of slaves in the Upper South
to be sold to the Cotton Kingdom where they would be put to work "in
gangs under the lash of overseers whose only interest in them was the
amount of work they could be made to perform at the smallest possible
cost to their owners."

Finally, Pemberton attacked the myth that American slavery was
characterized by a considerable degree of contentedness and docility

among the slaves, and that, during the Civil War, the slaves were remarkably loyal to their masters. She noted the thorough systems of
control developed by the Southern ruling class, especially the elaborate
and complex system of military control, to maintain its domination over
the slaves. She also mentioned the existence, in the face of these methods
of suppression and oppression, of resistance to slavery, and observed
that "every fugitive slave was a whole insurrection in itself." As for the
"loyalty" of the slaves during the Civil War, the records in the War Department gave the answer: "One hundred and eighty thousand ex-slaves
fought for freedom in the ranks of the union army against their former
masters. No one denies that they fought bravely. In many cases whole
regiments of blacks perished under fire rather than fall alive into the
hands of their late masters."

Pemberton concluded her first article with the observation that while
martial courage ranked low "as a civic virtue in the estimation of Socialists," for whatever it was worth, "the American black soldier is entitled
to the credit of having at least a fair share of it." [74]

A comparison of Pemberton's article with the writings of Algie M.
Simons, then the foremost socialist authority on American history,
shows how advanced she was on the Negro question. When Simons'
*Class Struggle in America* was first published in 1901, it did not even include a discussion of Negro slavery. Later, he conceded his oversight and
published three articles in the *International Socialist Review* of 1903 on
"Economic Aspects of Chattel Slavery in America." [75] Nowhere in these
articles, however, did Simons include a single sentence on the Negro
slaves themselves or challenge the myth of the "docile slave." Instead,
he argued that it was immaterial whether the Negro slaves helped free
themselves or were freed without their own participation, since the war
"freed nobody and least of all the negro." In what was probably an
attack on Pemberton's first article, Simons declared that the attempts of
"some Socialists" to prove that the Negro slaves had participated in
their emancipation "are essentially meaningless." [76]

Later studies in the history of American slavery would authoritatively
demolish the mythology of the benevolent, paternalistic institution, the
rarity of manifestations of slave unrest, and the "loyalty" of Southern
slaves during the Civil War. [77] Pemberton, of course, predated these
studies; even so, her conclusions were basically correct and were truly
advanced for her time. Her first article was a unique contribution to the
socialist approach to the Negro question.

Her second article dealt with the post-Civil War South. While she mentioned the robbing of blacks of their hard-won civil and political rights
after Reconstruction, she did not deal with another myth that influenced
a good deal of socialist thinking on the Negro question, particularly in
the South—namely, that during Radical Reconstruction, black voters

had been ignorant and easily exploited. They were portrayed as the passive pawns of scheming Northern white "Carpetbaggers" and Radical politicians, their leaders corrupt and incompetent; the Republican administrations in Southern states were characterized as a tragedy for black and white alike and without the slightest redeeming features. [78] (Since it was not until W.E.B. Du Bois read a paper, "Reconstruction and Its Benefits," before the American Historical Association in 1910 that the standard accounts of Reconstruction were challenged, it is understandable that Pemberton decided it best to avoid discussion of the question.) Her article concentrated on the process by which most blacks after slavery became sharecroppers or tenant farmers, rather than independent, landowning farmers, living and working on the land owned by white men and constantly in debt to their landlords. She showed, too, how the superexploitation of Southern blacks adversely affected the conditions of white labor nationwide, and how "all other forms of labor" were exploited "in exact proportion" to the exploitation of blacks:

> As long as the tiny black child is robbed of school and home to gather cotton from the growing plant, so long must the tiny white child be robbed of school and home to stand by a loom and weave that same cotton into cloth to undersell the cotton mills of the North. As long as the mills of the South can employ labor at 40 cents a day (and children all night), the mills of the North will have to adjust their wage scale to suit, or shut down half the year. . . . Unquestionably the white man pays somewhere for everything the negro is robbed of.

Yet, Pemberton emphasized at the beginning of her third article that black and white labor were not exploited equally under American capitalism. One had to conclude from her analysis that it was not correct to argue that the Negro question was simply a "labor question" no different for black than for white workers, and that therefore socialists need not pay any special attention to this question. Pemberton put it succinctly:

> The dark skin of the negro is the livery of the laboring class in the South. He needs no leather apron or cotton blouse to mark his calling. The Northern white laborer can doff his apron and hide his blouse when it suits his capitalist masters to lift him out of his class and make him one of themselves. With all the old ear-marks carefully obliterated even his old comrades can now hardly recognize him, and his place in their ranks closes up as if it had never been.

But the negro can not shed his skin. The white South not only adheres firmly to its traditional scorn of the laborer, but enjoys the immense advantage of dealing with its laborer as a race rather than as a class. If he dare rise above his fellows, he can be pushed back in the ranks and denied the benefits that capitalism is generally willing to bestow on those who can beat it at its own game. [79]

In short, the Negro question was both a class and a race question. The blacks faced special forms of exploitation under American capitalism that were not experienced by white workers and that required special attention and understanding on the part of American socialists.

Pemberton then proceeded to illustrate how the white South applied different principles to different Negroes. As long as the Negro occupied the servile status white Southerners had established for him, he could be accepted, even in the white community. But "uppity" blacks who, by dint of enormous hard work and self-sacrifice, overcame the insuperable obstacles confronting the Southern Negro to achieve a higher economic status had to be put in their place and were the main targets of the rigid exclusionist policy. The Negro, in other words, was acceptable so long as he was docile and knew his subordinate place in the Southern scheme of things. Those blacks who were not were guilty of insolence and had to be segregated, deported, or even, as a last resort, exterminated. [80]

While this analysis was an oversimplification, one has but to read the writings and speeches of William Gannaway Brownlow, Henry Watterson, Thomas Nelson Page, Thomas E. Watson, James K. Vardaman, and other ideologists of white supremacy [81] to realize that her discussion was based on solid evidence.

In her final article, Pemberton boldly tackled an issue socialists were reluctant to deal with—lynching. The 1901 convention had bowed to the Southern socialists and had eliminated the antilynching clause in the "Negro Resolution." Yet, the increasing number of black victims of lynch mobs and the mounting evidence of torture, dismemberment, and burning at the stake during the lynchings kept forcing the issue to the forefront. Many socialists, however, contented themselves with accepting the usual justification for lynching, namely, that it was necessary in order to protect white women from the primitive sexual lust of the black man. Victor Berger did more than accept this thesis. He embroidered it with descriptions of Negroes as depraved degenerates who went around "raping women [and] children," and referred to the "many cases of rape which occurred wherever negroes are settled in large numbers." [82] Debs never stooped to such shocking racism, but he also spoke of the "animalism" of blacks, [83] a term that was part of the vocabulary of justifications for lynchings.

Black spokesmen like Frederick Douglass and especially Ida B. Wells-Barnett had already exploded the myth that lynchings resulted from the attempt of Negro men to rape white women. [84] Their efforts seem to have had no influence in socialist circles. Pemberton's final article was the first effort to deal realistically with this "sensitive" subject in the socialist press. She demolished the "rape" argument with evidence from American history, from her own personal experience in the Black Belt of the South, and by reference to statistics on lynching. These statistics showed that not more than 25 percent of all the Negroes lynched since 1885 were even accused of such an offense as rape, and that many of those accused and brutally murdered were indeed, clearly innocent. She concluded that this justification of lynching persisted despite all evidence proving it to be baseless because it was part of the apparatus of Southern white supremacy to keep the Negro in total subjugation and part also of "the Southern capitalists' inherited antipathy to the existence of a growing class of comparatively independent negroes." [85]

Summing up her view of "The American Negro Problem," Pemberton described it as both a Southern and a national problem. In the South, the Negro's problem was "how to steer his way . . . through a community that wants his work and denies all the rights of his manhood; how to escape his class conditions without letting his exploiter know that he has escaped." Nationwide, the Negro's problem was "the labor problem plus the inherited prejudices of employer and fellow workmen in the North, plus the bitter jealousy in the South of a proud people who were conquered by the sword while defending their beloved dogma that 'the negro is not a man.'" [86]

Unlike nearly all socialist writings of the period on the Negro question, Pemberton's did not close with the assurance that socialism would solve the Negro problem and that, therefore, victory for the Socialist party was the only real answer. She merely said that the solution was the most difficult task ever placed before any race or nation, and she left it to her comrades in the Socialist party to do something to help in the solution besides passing resolutions.

Although Pemberton's four articles in *The Worker* contained a number of oversimplifications, they made everything else written by socialists of this period on the Negro question seem superficial by comparison. Nevertheless, they were neither reprinted in any other socialist publication nor commented on in editorials or in letters to editors.

During the Kishineff massacre of 1093 in Russia, the International Socialist Bureau issued an appeal "To the Laborers of All Countries," urging them to protest the anti-Jewish pogroms. Perhaps because it was aware of the anger in the U.S. black community over the absence of protests against lynchings, the International Socialist Bureau sent an inquiry to the National Quorum, the executive board of the Socialist party of America, asking for the policy of its American affiliate on lynching in the United States, "especially the lynching of Negroes." The answer came in the form of a resolution adopted by the National Quorum on the motion of Victor Berger. It condemned "the frequent lynchings which have been occurring in the United States" and blamed them on the economic conditions under capitalism which stimulated "race hatred" and fostered brutal instincts leading to crimes. These "crimes" then produced lynchings. As to what to do about it, the National Quorum had only one answer:

> The Socialist Party points out the fact that nothing less than the abolition of the capitalist system and the substitution of the Socialist system can provide conditions under which the hunger maniacs, kleptomaniacs, sexual maniacs and all other offensive and lynchable human degenerates will cease to be begotten or produced.

Even if one could penetrate this murky language, the conclusions one would have to draw from the stand of the Socialist party on lynching were (1) that the victims of lynch mobs were guilty of the crimes, including rape, which had caused their deaths; (2) that the crimes which infuriated lynch mobs were produced by the capitalist system; and (3) that until a new type of human being was created under socialism who would not be so fiendish as to commit such crimes, nothing could be done to halt the rising tide of brutal lynchings. It is easy to understand why Victor Berger moved the adoption of this resolution. It is not so easy to understand why every other member of the National Quorum allowed it to be adopted without even the slightest discussion, or why the International Socialist Bureau did not criticize its American affiliate for its shameful action. It did, however, issue a flaming appeal to the workers of all countries to take a stand against the persecution of blacks in the United States, and it minced no words in describing the nature of this persecution. "The Negro," declared the bureau's manifesto,

> works under the regime of the lash and club. He sometimes dies without regaining consciousness from the blows. To make certain that this every-day martyr does not flee, he is forced to work nude. The women, children and men of the black race are imprisoned, shot, massacred; their homes are burned; they them-

selves are burned alive thanks to the complaisance even the encouragement of the authorities, in cooperation with the land-lords.

Pointing out that in 1902 there were 103 lynchings of blacks in a single state, the manifesto asked to what degree had their conditions improved since slavery. While legal emancipation had been made a fact in the United States, lynchings, peonage, and persecution of all kinds had re-duced the Negro to a state of semislavery. At the same time, capitalists in the United States were stirring up racial antagonisms among the workers, hoping to seek a way out of the contradictions of their system "through a race war." Appealing directly to the socialists in the United States to defeat this capitalist conspiracy, the manifesto concluded:

> This shall not be! Capitalism makes no distinction when it is a question of living on the work of others. In its own interests the working class must unite whatever the differences of race and religion, in order to assure complete emancipation. Slavery is neither white, yellow or black. It is proletarian. The revolt against capitalist exploitation must be a united one.
>
> The interests of the working class demands the unity of all workers without distinction of race, and it demands the energetic protest of Socialist Democracy against the abominable acts com-mitted daily in the United States against the Negro. [87]

The manifesto was signed by members of the International Socialist Bureau representing nineteen countries, including the United States, However, the representative of the Socialist party of America, George Herron, signed only reluctantly. As he explained later, he believed the manifesto "extreme" in its declaration of worker solidarity embracing all colors. He signed knowing it would be ignored by comrades in the United States. [88] This is exactly what did happen.

One thing is clear. None of the members of the National Quorum appears to have read Caroline H. Pemberton's article in *The Worker* which pointed out the falsity of the charge that rape "explained" lynch-ing and which exposed it as a major device for maintaining the subjuga-tion of blacks under semifeudal conditions. It was probably fortunate, insofar as the prestige of the Socialist party in the black community is concerned, that the disgraceful resolution of the National Quorum received little publicity and saw the light of day only in the *Chicago Socialist*.

# The Louisiana and Other Southern Issues and the Elections of 1904 and 1908

## THE LOUISIANA SOCIALISTS AND THE NEGRO

The most widely publicized issue relating to the Negro in the early history of the Socialist party involved the Louisiana Socialist party, which was organized during the Southern drive that got under way shortly after the Indianapolis convention. The drive was directed primarily at recruiting former and existing Populists into the socialist fold. It made so much headway at first that in December 1902, Jno. A. Parker, chairman of the Allied People's party, wrote from Dallas: "Everything seems to be turning to Socialism. Everybody is talking about Socialism, and I much fear that we will be engulfed by the tide." [1]

Encouraged by this development, Eugene V. Debs and William Mailly, party secretary, agreed that the socialists should focus their efforts on the South. Mailly informed Debs early in 1903 that he had taken steps to send an organizer through the Southern states and was convinced that "a good many locals can be formed in that section and the way made ready for lecture tours by our best speakers." [2] The national office sponsored John C. Chase, the former socialist mayor of Haverhill, Massachusetts, "to carry out systematic propaganda into the 'Solid South,'" and appointed George H. Goebel as regional organizer. Debs himself traveled to the South and Southwest along with Mother Jones, the veteran mine workers' organizer. [3]

When the national office proved too impoverished to provide much assistance and the state offices were still too hard pressed for funds to carry the burden, the *Appeal to Reason* stepped in and filled much of the gap. It introduced many former Populists to socialism for the first time, and editor Wayland's agents helped to build socialist locals in many areas that regular organizers were unable to reach. [4] Together, the party and *Appeal* organizers established the foundation of the Socialist party in the South and Southwest. While the early rush of Populists to the party tapered off as die-hard Southern Populists refused to abandon their old party for socialism, the Socialist party still drew many of its Southern recruits from the Populist strongholds. Others were young tenant farmers who had not been affected by populism, and workers in the cities and industrial towns, especially where the United Mine Workers was making inroads. The party also drew support from immigrant trade unionists in the larger Southern cities. It had its greatest success in Houston, where the Socialist Labor party had an active Italian local in the 1890s; in San Antonio, where John Chase organized a few locals among the city's militant craft unions; in Dallas, where the *Laborer*, edited by two socialists, became the official organ of the city's Central Labor Union; in Bessemer, Alabama, where *The Southern Socialist* made its appearance as a monthly in July 1903, featuring on its cover the picture of Clarence K. Spencer, candidate for mayor of Bessemer on the socialist ticket; in Oklahoma City, where the party won the endorsement of *Labor Signal*, an AFL paper, and gained a foothold among the unions of construction and transportation workers; and in New Orleans, the largest and most cosmopolitan city in the Southwest, where German socialists, Italian and Spanish anarchists, and exiled Mexican revolutionaries who worked on the docks furnished a fertile recruiting ground for the new party of socialism. [5]

As might have been expected, the organizers in the South and Southwest had barely begun their recruiting drives when they encountered the Negro question. Reporting on "Socialism in the South" in the spring of 1903, John Chase listed the "race question" as "above all others, the question of the South." Many Southerners, he explained, were thoroughly disgusted with the Democratic party, and an "almost unlimited" number "would vote for Socialism if they could understand the difference between social and industrial equality. This particular phase is the one above all others that makes it hard to win people from the Democracy to the Socialist Party." [6] George H. Goebel confirmed this estimate and reported that everywhere he went, he was accused of being a "Northern nigger-lover" representing a party that was trying to impose social equality on the South. [7] Still another organizer, Charles G. Towner, wrote: "The negro is the bogey man that the old party politician is constantly holding up before the working class." Whenever he organized a meeting, he reported, Southern white workers were told that he would introduce "social equality" into the community. [8]

Most Southern organizers met the issue by simply ignoring the Negro, but A. W. Ricker, the leading *Appeal to Reason* organizer in the South, refused to cater to the prejudices of Southern socialists. When he was told that he would be wasting his time trying to recruit blacks since the Negro had no vote in the South, he answered: "You have forgotten something friend, for while the Negro has no vote, he has all the qualifications for a soldier of capitalism." He put the issue bluntly: "Shall we leave the Negro ignorant of Socialism, ignorant of the class struggle, ostracize him from our ranks, and thus turn him over to the capitalist, as a soldier to shoot submission into us? What folly this would be!" He asked if it was not high time "to be reasonable on the race question," and appealed: "Socialists of the South, be wise. LEAVE NO BLACK RECRUITING GROUND FOR CAPITALIST SOLDIERS." [9]

Ricker received no support from the socialist press for his educational efforts among white Southerners. Although the *Appeal to Reason* published numerous manifestos to assist its organizers in the South, not one referred to the Negro. [10] Similarly, in all the appeals in *The Southern Socialist*, the Negro was never mentioned as a potential socialist in the South. Indeed, the only references to the Negro in the publication were in the September 1903 issue. One was in connection with a street-corner speech by national party organizer John M. Ray in Bessemer. In summarizing his speech, the newspaper reported: "He pictured the present system in words so plain that even the most ignorant negro could understand the way he was 'injoying' the luxuries of a pick and shovel and ten hours a day for a dollar." The other reference grew out of a protest against the police of Bessemer for having arrested Comrade McGuire during a street-corner speech in Bessemer and thrown him into jail with "a lot of drunken men of all colors." It was not clear whether *The Southern Socialist*'s objection was to the arrest or to the company the comrade was forced to keep while in jail. The same issue of the paper published the constitution of the Socialist party of Alabama. There was no mention of the Negro, disfranchisement, segregation, or lynching. Nor were any of these mentioned in the report of the state convention of the Socialist party of Alabama published in the *Birmingham Labor Advocate*. [11]

Still, some blacks were organized during the Southern drive. John Chase emphasized in his speeches that the Socialist party did not stand for "social equality." He made the point even stronger by addressing whites and blacks on separate occasions—the whites in the afternoon and blacks in the evening. He reported that he could usually bring enough people to these meetings to organize locals—separate ones for whites and blacks. [12] W. R. Healey, the party secretary in Florida, reported to *The Worker* early in 1903 that he had organized a colored branch in Orlando with twenty-two members and had urged all locals in the state to take up the "work of organizing the negroes" into similar branches. [13]

These reports in the socialist press that separate branches were being set up for blacks in the South brought no objection from the national office. However, in 1903, when the leadership of the Louisiana Socialist party attempted to deny a charter to a local of black sawmill workers in Lutcher, the national office overruled it. [14] Later that same year, the first major battle over the Negro question erupted in the Socialist party over another action of the Louisiana socialists.

Louisiana had had a section of the IWA (First International) — French Section 15, but apart from providing a background for the formation of the Socialist party of Louisiana, it never accomplished very much.

On September 18 and 19, 1903, delegates from socialist locals in Louisiana met in convention in New Orleans to form a state organization and adopted a platform. In many respects, it was a far-reaching document for its time, especially in the Deep South. It called for the collective ownership and control of all sources and machinery of production and distribution "to the end that wage slavery shall be abolished and the worker receive the full product of his toil"; the adoption of the initiative and referendum and recall by the government of Louisiana; the abolition of child labor; absolute home rule for all towns and cities of the state; equal civil and political rights for men and women; and compulsory universal education, with the state to be required to furnish the necessary books and other implements. The platform also demanded the enfranchisement of all races, declaring that "the State has no right to disbar any citizen from the franchise." At the same time, it advocated the "separation of the black and white races into separate communities, each race to have charge of its own affairs." [15] The Louisiana State party then applied for a charter from the national committee. The "Negro Clause" soon produced a controversy between the committee and the Louisiana party.

The clause would probably not have aroused much action by the national committee if it had not provoked discussion in the outside press. The *New Orleans Daily Picayune* declared editorially that, while the stand of the Louisiana socialists was "a concession to overwhelming sentiment in the South," it certainly did not "comport with the fundamental idea of equality" that was supposed to be "a fundamental principle" of socialism. [16] The *Dallas Morning News* went further and remarked sternly that, while the doctrine upheld by the Socialist party was "sound" and its vision of a new society "workable," there was "no reason why all the children of men should not share the benefits." It continued:

"If the Negro is unworthy, and if he should be shut out because of his want of merit, why should not others be shut out for similar cause. If others are shut out what becomes of a 'Socialism' that reaches only part of the way around?" [17]

The action of the Louisiana socialists even provoked comment abroad. The *Edinburgh Review* viewed the news from Louisiana as proof that even socialists had to be practical if they wanted to make progress in the Southern states. They simply could not "afford to run counter to the overwhelming sentiment of the South on this question." It noted that, in theory, socialism demanded "absolute equality," and it was quite obvious that what the Louisiana socialists had done was "incompatible with the fundamental idea of equality." But then, it commented wryly, "even a theorist cannot stand outside of his environment." [18]

With this kind of publicity, the national leadership of the Socialist party could hardly ignore the action of the Louisiana socialists. To do nothing would only invite further ridicule from the press, and while some of the Southern commentators would probably have condemned the Louisiana socialists bitterly had they included black and white equality in their platform, the fact was that they now had the national leadership in a situation where it had to stand up and be counted. Did the Socialist party stand for universal equality, or was it simply a political movement that said one thing in its platform and did the opposite in practice, just like all the other parties on the American scene?

## DEBATE ON THE LOUISIANA ISSUE

On October 16, 1903, national secretary William Mailly asked P. Aloysius Molyneaux, the acting secretary of the Louisiana party, to explain the resolution in the platform requiring separation of the races. Mailly informed him that no action would be taken on the charter until such an explanation was made. In a lengthy reply, Molyneaux explained that the plank reflected the view of Louisiana socialists that "race instincts" would never allow whites and blacks "to intermingle in a co-operative society," and that they could see "no compromise of Socialistic principles" in this stand, since it included "no denial of economic equality." Any other position, he said, would only provide ammunition for the Democratic party to prove that socialism favored "social equality"; if Southern whites were convinced of the truth of this charge, the cause of socialism in the South would become "hopeless." Molyneaux reminded the national secretary that blacks in Louisiana had been eliminated from the electoral process, and that it was on the whites alone that the socialists had to rely in the political arena. (He was referring to the fact that

Louisiana had written the "Grandfather Clause" into its constitution which gave the vote to those whose fathers and grandfathers had voted on January 1, 1867, when no Negroes were qualified to vote in Louisiana. All others had to meet education and property qualifications. Following the adoption of this clause, the number of qualified Negro voters had dropped from 130,344 in 1896 to only 5,320 in 1900.) To antagonize whites while courting the voteless Negro, Molyneaux argued, made no political sense. The proper procedure, he maintained, was to organize the party in Louisiana "on the same lines followed by the American Federation of Labor—that is, to take in both races, but to organize them into separate locals. To follow any other course will be to commit political suicide." He concluded by assuring Mailly that the Louisiana socialists would abide by whatever decision was reached by the national committee, but he warned that an unfavorable decision would doom the party in Louisiana. [19]

When Molyneaux maintained that the Louisiana socialists were pursuing "the same lines followed by the American Federation of Labor," he was giving the AFL too much credit. The AFL sanctioned not only "Jim Crow" unionism, but also the total barring of blacks by a number of its leading affiliates, some of which explicitly excluded them in their constitutions. [20]

John Kerrigan of Texas, replying for the National Committee, explained that it was he who had been responsible for delaying the granting of the Louisiana charter. He emphasized the unfavorable publicity caused by the stand of the Louisiana socialists and called Molyneaux's attention to the editorial in the *Dallas Morning News*, which he enclosed, observing that it indicated "what use can be made of this declaration of the Louisiana Socialists." He also enclosed what he called "a slip that sets forth the position of the party on the Negro question," the main thrust of which was that the Socialist party aimed at economic, and not racial, equality. According to Kerrigan, the literature of socialism revealed that racial tensions were the result of capitalism's forcing white and black to work together, whereas under socialism, it would be the absolute "PREROGATIVE OF EVERY HUMAN BEING TO ASSOCIATE WITH THOSE ONLY WHO ARE AGREEABLE TO HIM." Kerrigan deplored the fact that the Louisiana socialists had bungled the handling of the race question. In Texas, he pointed out, the socialists had never declared their stand publicly, leaving it to each member to settle the question for himself: "We did not feel like placing in the hands of the enemy any weapon that we could keep out of them." Since the Louisiana socialists had so foolishly already stated their position publicly, the National Committee had no choice but to withhold the charter. To permit Louisiana to be admitted with its declaration intact would constitute an admission that socialism meant a "different thing" in that state than anywhere else, and Molyneaux knew "that the boast of Socialism is that whether it be in Dallas, Texas or St. Petersburg, Russia, Socialism is Socialism." If the Louisiana socialists would correct their "misunderstanding" of the party's position and vote to strike the "objectionable resolution" from the records, the charter would be quickly forthcoming.

Molyneaux replied that the Louisiana socialists would not hide their position from the public. While criticism in the Southern press could not be ignored, it could be easily answered. In any case, it would fool no one, or "at worst will fool only a few ignorant negroes who can do the party no possible harm." Molyneaux's chief argument now was that the Louisiana socialists were not guilty of any "misunderstanding" of socialism but had based their decision on common sense. If they had omitted the enfranchisement clause, the capitalist press would have said that the party was not honest in demanding economic and political equality. On the other hand, if they had omitted the reservation about the mingling of the races, the same papers would have raised the cry of "Negro supremacy" and "social equality," a cry that would have crushed the Louisiana party in its "infancy." Since the Louisiana socialists favored economic equality, and Kerrigan had indicated that this was all socialism stood for, what reason could the National Committee have for refusing them a charter? [21]

National Committeeman John Talbott of Minnesota supported the Louisiana socialists. Having himself lived in the South, he said, he found nothing in their platform that was contrary to socialist principles. Moreover, he felt they should be complimented for being "Southern Socialist diplomats" who knew "how to hedge in the Democratic Party" by depriving it of its chief weapon against the socialists—the cry of "race equality." Like Molyneaux, he emphasized that since blacks were either totally disfranchised in the South, or about to be, the socialists had absolutely nothing to gain and everything to lose by championing the equality of black and white. [22]

Between them, *The Worker* and the *Social Democratic Herald* published all of the correspondence between Molyneaux and the National Committee, but neither paper commented editorially. Thus arose the curious situation in which the capitalist press commented on the segregationist stand of the Louisiana socialists, while the socialist press remained silent. Caroline F. Pemberton pointedly asked *The Worker* why it could find "ample space" to discuss the appointments made by Mayor "Golden Rule" Jones of Toledo, yet remained silent on "the vastly more important question involved in the Constitution of the Louisiana 'Socialists,' so-called, who have embodied in their manifesto a declaration denouncing any semblance of equality or union between the white and colored races." She then proceeded to read the Louisiana socialists a stern lecture. It had been demonstrated again and again, she said, that the capitalist class had established the myth that the Negro was "inferior" in order to profit from his "illegal and enforced 'inferiority.'" Therefore, clearly one of socialism's "most vital principles" was that "such schemes be exposed and traced to their selfish, commercialized sources." It was as important that this be done in Louisiana as in Pennsylvania: "If the Louisiana people cannot bear the truth of the Socialist point of view, is it not a proof that they are not yet ready to uphold the cause of Socialism?" "No compromise with capitalism," she insisted, must be the socialist motto, in the South as well as elsewhere. If socialists refused to unite with capitalist parties in the North "to secure a temporary advantage," how could they unite with the "political, social, and economic powers of the South to crush the dark-skinned proletariat for the sake of the profit that lies in his degradation?"

Pemberton applauded the National Committee for withholding a charter from the Louisiana socialists because of their stand "in favor of 'racial distinctions'—a smug phrase for negro degradation." As she explained: "Such a sentiment has no place in any Socialist constitution in any country that the sun shines upon. To admit it for the sake of expediency is to lower our standard and convict ourselves of shameful hypocrisy." 23

Several weeks later, *The Worker* carried its first editorial on the Louisiana controversy. The editorial was what might have been expected from a paper that had contributed the phrase "the bugbear of 'social equality'" to the armory of white supremacists in the Socialist party and that had already asserted that the Negro was "repellant" to whites as an "inferior" species of the human race. There could be no real objection, *The Worker* declared, to separate branches in the Socialist party for blacks, just as there was none to separate nationality branches for Germans, Jews, Poles, Italians, and Scandinavians. (This point, of course, overlooked the fact that these nationalities insisted on separate branches to better serve their needs, while the blacks were being forced to organize into separate branches.) But to proclaim the principle of permanent separation of whites and blacks and to incorporate this principle in a party platform was quite a different matter and could not be countenanced. The blacks, through no fault of their own, were "inferior" to whites, but it was the duty of socialists to lift them up to a higher level of civilization. Their ability to perform this noble work would be frustrated if the two races were permanently separated: "While capitalism lasts, it is the duty of the Socialist Party so far as it deals with the Negro question as such, to use its influence in favor of the educational and especially the economic uplifting of the black." Under socialism, however, a segregated place for the Negro would become a viable solution of the race question. "Social equality" at any time was not part of the objective of socialism, and the Southern socialists could rest content that the national office would make no effort to force this upon them. Finally, *The Worker* took a swipe at National Committeeman Talbott's characterization of the Louisiana socialists as "Southern Socialist diplomats" for their action: "For us — and we believe we speak for the party — we do not wish to be led by 'diplomats.' Diplomacy is the wise policy for parties that are morally and economically wrong. We are right and have . . . no need and no place in our policy for what is commonly called diplomacy."[24]

*The Worker*'s editorial won applause from a Texas socialist who agreed with its contention that to compromise in order to win votes in the South was a violation of socialist principles. He insisted that "the work of the Socialist in the South in the immediate future lies not so much in making Socialist voters as in breaking down race prejudice."[25] Pemberton was skeptical that the editorial would help break down race prejudice. She complimented the socialist weekly for supporting the withholding of the Louisiana charter; however, she disagreed that the Negro was clearly an "inferior race" and that it was the duty of the "superior" white socialists to adopt a benevolent policy toward the "inferior" race and "charitably uplift it": "Since when, may I ask, have you, a Socialist, become converted to the doctrine of 'benevolence' as a working force to bring about the reign of truth and practice?" Speaking not only as a socialist but also as simply "a fellow human being to the negro," Pemberton insisted that no race that "rises to the measure of its opportunities" could be classified as "inferior." The so-called Negro race of America, of whom the majorities were "mixtures of various nationalities," could justly be said to have risen to the measure of its opportunities:

> Where the environment has been favorable, it has produced (from its working population, too) in a few decades, an astonishingly large number of educated, refined, self-controlled and gifted men and women, who, in obscurity, and often poverty, are leading blameless lives as teachers, professors, clergymen, writers and artists — not to speak of the still larger class who are producing wealth for the masters as peasants and laborers, and whose so-called "degradation" is certainly not greater than that of the despised peasants and laborers of Russia, Italy and other European countries.

Pemberton warned that, once the socialists held out to the Southerner the "attractive bait" of future "negro segregation" as an inducement for his acceptance of socialism, the way would be open to offer inducements to the Christian who objected to the Jew, the American who objected to the Chinese—and so on endlessly. She concluded:

> If we believe in international Socialism, we cannot judge any race by its progress in what is called "civilization." Our civilization must first be cured and purified before we can reproach any race because it has not yet learned to wallow in the foul depths of our own hypocrisy and corruption. [26]

## RESOLUTION OF THE LOUISIANA ISSUE

On December 11, 1903, the National Committee voted 14 to 5, with eight abstentions, to withhold Louisiana's charter until the "Negro Clause" was deleted from the platform. George Dobbs of Kentucky, one of those who voted in favor of granting the charter, argued simply that the objectionable clause did not "contravene any established Socialist principle." Kerrigan of Texas, speaking for those who voted to withhold the charter, began by asserting that socialists must conduct themselves in accordance with the principle laid down by Wilhelm Liebknecht, the famous leader of the German socialists who had said "No Compromise, No Political Trading." Kerrigan then launched into an analysis of the Southern way of life in which he emphasized that the real enemies of the Negro were the ignorant poor white masses, while the "educated Southern white man" accepted and even respected the black man "in his place." Of course, this "place" never included "social equality," but it did offer a place for the blacks. So long, then, as socialism in the South based itself on the intelligent, educated classes, the "race question" would be as easy to solve "from the Socialist standpoint" below the Mason-Dixon line as elsewhere. [27] With the Louisiana socialists insisting throughout the controversy that they were willing to accept the Negro "in his place" and Kerrigan seeming to approve this approach as a principled socialist answer to the Negro question in the South, it is clear that an enormous confusion permeated the thinking of the Socialist party's national leadership on the Negro question.

Louisiana capitulated. It removed the offending clause from its platform, received its charter, and then established separate locals for blacks without any objection from the national Socialist party office. In an article in the *International Socialist Review* of January 1905, Eraste Virden, a member of the Louisiana party, urged separate locals for Negroes on the ground that comrades of the "gentler sex" would not be comfortable in a mixed local. He then reported the existence of a separate

Negro local in Letcher, Louisiana. [28] The National Committee of the Socialist party ignored the report.

Strangely, during the National Committee's entire discussion of the Louisiana platform, it was never mentioned that the document affirmed the adherence of the Louisiana socialists to the principles enunciated in the platform adopted at Indianapolis in July 1901. Was not the "Negro Clause" in the Louisiana platform a contradiction of this statement? How did the Louisiana socialists reconcile their clause with the "Negro Resolution" adopted at Indianapolis? Evidently, the National Committee did not want to be reminded of the "Negro Resolution."

## 1904 NATIONAL SP CONVENTION

On the eve of the national convention of the Socialist party scheduled for Chicago in May 1904, the *International Socialist Review* devoted its entire issue to a "Symposium of Problems" facing the convention and to "Some General Suggestions" for the delegates. Editorially, the *Review* praised the discussion as

> one of which we feel the Socialist Party of America may well be proud. It constitutes the most thorough attempt ever made by any political party to work out the details of its organization and policy in a democratic manner. The large number of contributors represent every phase of thought that will appear at the convention, and the wide circulation which this number will receive makes it certain that these opinions will have great influence in determining the work of the convention and the future policy of Socialism in America. [29]

Insofar as black Americans were concerned, the highly praised discussion indicated that the Socialist party leaders, far from advancing, had retreated since 1901, and that if it reflected the "future policy of Socialism in America," then the promise held out in the "Negro Resolution" adopted at Indianapolis was still just a promise.

Not a single Negro participated in the discussion, and of the twenty-six whites who did, only six referred to the Negro at all. A. W. Ricker observed: "As we enter the southern field we meet the race question, and are thus compelled to define our attitude toward the negro." [30] What that "attitude" should be was left unanswered. Four of the contributors — Ernest Untermann, H. B. Weaver, Gaylord Wilshire, and Charles Dobbs — called for repeal of the "Negro Resolution" adopted in 1901. Untermann insisted that it be replaced by a declaration of principles stating that the Socialist party "seeks to develop the political class struggle in the interest of all proletarians regardless of race, color, creed and occupation." [31] Weaver recommended its replacement by a manifesto in which it would be made clear "to the negro that the race question will be settled only when the class war is ended." [32] Wilshire wanted no statement at all in place of the "Negro Resolution," suggesting "the less slush and slop we Socialists indulge in about our red, white, black and yellow brothers the better." [33] Dobbs called the 1901 resolution "a mistake," characterized by "a sentimental—not to say hysterical—spirit." While he would not "shut the door in the face of the black man," he was convinced that "as a race the negro worker of the South lacks the brain and the backbone to make a Socialist." [34]

Two contributors, Joseph Wanhope of New York and Herman F. Titus, editor of the *Seattle Socialist*, favored a special Negro resolution. Wanhope merely stated that the 1901 resolution "should stand" and left it at that. [35] Titus, on the other hand, introduced a new special "Negro Resolution" which should read:

> *Resolved*, That the Negro wage slave is robbed of the greater part of his product, the same as the white wage-slave, and the Socialist Party is his only hope of emancipation. We therefore welcome the negro vote as we do the vote of all wage slaves, without respect to color, sex, or nationality, and we advocate propaganda and organization among the negro population of the United States. [36]

Although this position was the most advanced of any taken during the entire discussion, it eliminated from the 1901 resolution the reference to the Negro's "peculiar position in the working class and in society at large," the condemnation of "disfranchisement and violence," and the expression of "sympathy" with the Negro workers "in their subjection to lawlessness and oppression." It added nothing on the subject of lynching which had already been condemned, even if in peculiar terminology, by the party's National Quorum.

One contributor, John H. Baxter of Tullahoma, Tennessee, whose piece was described as an "Ex-Slave Holder on the Negro Question," favored Ernest Utermann's proposal for a general declaration of principles, and he went on record as sharing "verbatim" Eugene V. Debs' "sentiments on the Negro question." The rest of his contribution was the most sympathetic discussion of the Negro question, even though it used some of the objectionable epithets. Baxter attacked Southern "nigger-haters" for their lack of appreciation of the Negro's contribution to the South, derided the myth of the "negro rapist" by pointing to the safety and security of Southern white women left alone on plantations with scores of blacks during the Civil War, and described how he was fed by one of the family slaves during the war when he was starving, even though he was fighting in the Confederate Army to keep blacks "in this miserable state of bondage." The ex-slaveholder socialist concluded:

> I am determined to defend the colored race's political and eco-
> nomic rights in spite of all the "critics" in and out of Hades. As to
> their social right, I will say that I would rather be associated with
> a nigger that would feed me than with a white man that would
> starve me. [37]

Although the preconvention discussion included only six references to the Negro, some of them derogatory, compared to the convention itself it was an advanced social document. While one of the delegates, Reverend George W. Woodbey, a cleric from California and a party member for years, was black, during the entire six days of proceedings there was not a single mention of the Negro. No Negro resolution was introduced or adopted, and the 1901 resolution was neither mentioned nor reaffirmed. No reference to the Negro appeared in the national platform adopted by the convention or in the state or municipal programs that were likewise adopted. In the entire 300 pages of proceedings, the Negro is conspicuous by his absence, and the word "Negro" does not even appear in the index. [38]

## ELECTION OF 1904

Eugene V. Debs, nominated for president of the United States by the Chicago convention, added nothing to the socialist platform during his campaign as far as the Negro was concerned. Yet, disillusionment with the Republican party was becoming so strong in Negro circles that the socialist ticket commanded more attention there than it had in any previous presidential campaign. In its August 1904 issue, *The Comrade*, an official party publication founded in 1901, reprinted editorials from two newspapers "published by and for negroes" — *The Broadax* of Chicago and *The Bee* of Washington, D.C. These papers hailed Debs as a champion of the rights of black Americans and urged blacks by the thousands to cast their votes for the socialist ticket. [39] A similar editorial stand was taken by a third black paper, *The Voice of the Negro*, published in Atlanta, Georgia, by the militant Jesse Max Barber. [40] When one realizes that 1904 saw the first Negro to be nominated for the presidency of the United States — George Edwin Taylor, candidate of the National Liberty party [41] — these endorsements indicate that for all its vacillations and retreats on the Negro question, by the summer and fall of 1904, the Socialist party was beginning to command the attention of influential elements in the black community.

While it welcomed these editorial endorsements, *The Worker* made it plain that the Socialist party had no special message for the Negro, nor was it looking for "the Negro vote." It sought the votes of all workers, blacks as well as others, for the Socialist party was the party of all alike. Under capitalism, black and white workers were similarly exploited, it declared, and the wisest thing for the blacks to do was to realize that there was no fundamental difference in the status of the two:

> You are denied civil and political rights and are kept in economic subjection under Republican and Democratic administrations alike. Well, so are we. Your troubles in Alabama and Virginia are matched by our troubles in Colorado. We are all oppressed alike because the capitalist class can make profit out of our oppression.

Reminding blacks that the Socialist party viewed the question of "social equality" as a matter for individuals to decide, *The Worker* once again emphasized that socialists made no "bid" for the Negro vote. It concluded:

> Here are our Socialist principles; here is our Socialist policy; we believe that it promises real freedom for the whole working class, real peace and progress for all mankind; we ask you all to think of it, and if you agree with us, to vote as you think. [42]

In equating the exploitation of black and white workers, *The Worker* chose an effective analogy. Precisely at that time, the Mine Owners' Association in Colorado, in an effort to smash the militant Western Federation of Miners, and with the aid of a mob organized by the Citizens' Alliance and the troops of the state militia, rounded up union miners and threw them into makeshift stockades or "bull pens" where they remained for months. Nearly 200 men were forced into box cars, transported to the Kansas or New Mexico line, and left on the prairies with orders never to return to Colorado. [43] What *The Worker* overlooked, however, was that blacks in the South faced a special oppression daily in the form of the deprivation of their constitutional rights and violence, including death by lynching. Brutal as were the conditions that the Colorado miners encountered, they were not as terrible as the exploitation imposed on the majority of the Negro people in the South under the semifeudal plantation, sharecropping economy, an environment that combined the most abject poverty with legalized terror.


## POSTELECTION TRENDS

Two events occurred in 1905 that reflected the contradictions within the Socialist party with respect to the Negro question. On May 5, *Line-Up*, a socialist weekly in Kansas City, Kansas, headlined the following sensational news on its front page: "The Only Negro Socialist Ever Elected." The reference was to the fact that M. R. Smith had just been elected social park commissioner in Kansas City on the socialist ticket. "Comrade Smith," *Line-Up* continued, "is a negro—the first of his race to be elected by the class-conscious proletarians anywhere outside the negro island in the Indian ocean [Madagascar]—and better than anything else Comrade Smith is a revolutionary Socialist, thoroughly class-conscious and fully realizing the absolute need of education along the lines of scientific principles rather than the hub-hub and glimmer of a POLITICAL movement. . . . As an official Comrade Smith will do honor to Socialism, and by his record attract investigation to its principles." Most important of all: "Nothing could speak such volumes for race equality of opportunity as stood for by socialists as the election of Com[rade] M. R. Smith to the first office in a first-class city to be held by a Socialist in this state." The *Kansas City Gazette* of April 8 provided some details omitted from the *Line-Up* account:

> M. R. Smith, who was elected park commissioner, is the only negro who was elected on any of the four tickets in the field. Mr. Smith is a socialist, and was the only man on the Socialist ticket elected. He had no opposition. Mr. Smith was issued a certificate of election and duly sworn in by the city clerk.

At exactly the same time, the *Appeal to Reason*, the socialist weekly published in Girard, Kansas, began serializing a novel by the socialist Upton Sinclair, *The Jungle*, dealing with conditions in the Chicago meat-packing industry. Readers were drawn to the work mainly by its accounts of rotten meat, but Sinclair's principal interest was in describing the exploitation of immigrant workers and their march from ignorance to socialism. Negroes, however, were not considered worthy of joining this parade. Blacks appear in the socialist muckraker's novel "only as scabs quite devoid of humanity." [44] Sinclair filled paragraph after paragraph with vicious racist descriptions of "stupid black Negroes," and he drew horrifying racist pictures of sexual contact between Negro males and white females. He wrote of

> young white girls from the country rubbing elbows with big buck Negroes with daggers in their boots, while rows of wooly heads peered out. . . . The ancestors of these black people had been savages. . . . Now for the first time they were free—free to gratify every passion, free to wreck themselves. [45]

Not a single socialist objected to this racist portrayal of Negroes in a leading socialist weekly. Moreover, when Sinclair, who had found it impossible to secure a publisher, decided to publish the book himself and appealed for support in the *Appeal to Reason*, [46] not a single socialist suggested that the racist passages be eliminated or modified before the novel appear in book form. When the book was published, it became an instant best seller and contributed effectively toward the enactment of the Pure Food and Drug Act. It also contributed to racist fears of the Negro, but none of this concerned the Socialist party, which was proud that one of its members was a nationwide celebrity. It was only one measure of how the Negro question was diminishing in importance in the deliberations of the Socialist party. Thus, the National Committee said nothing about the anti-Negro Atlanta riot of September 24, 1906, during which at least ten blacks (including two women) and two whites were killed, sixty Negroes and ten whites seriously injured, and scores of Negro homes looted and burned. [47] Moreover, it refused even to take a stand on an issue of tremendous significance to the black community—the Brownsville Affair. In August 1906, three companies of the Twenty-Fifth Regiment, composed of blacks, were involved in a riot in Brownsville, Texas. On the basis of an unsubstantiated report of an inspector who had said that the Negroes had murdered and maimed the citizens of Brownsville, President Theodore Roosevelt dismissed the entire battalion without honor and disqualified its members for service in either the military or the civil service of the United States. [48] The socialist press simply ignored the harsh, unjust treatment of the Negro soldiers and the bitter reaction of the black community. Only one socialist paper, *Itta Bena Progress*, published in Jackson, Mississippi, even noted the event. Its March 30, 1907, issue contained the item: "Member of discharged Negro regiment arrested in connection with confession on Brownsville affair. Will be put through rigid examination."[49]

In January 1907, at a meeting of the National Committee, George Ufert of New Jersey proposed that the Socialist party protest Roosevelt's order dismissing the Negro soldiers. La Rue of Alabama objected, pointing out that the president's action had the "entire approval of Southern Socialists," and accused Ufert of trying to "inject the negro question into the Socialist Party" where it did not belong. He argued further that the dismissal of the soldiers was not a concern of the working class. Even if it were, only the Southerner fully understood the character of the Negro, and the National Committee should be guided in this matter by the views of the Southern socialists. After some more give and take, the National Committee rejected Ufert's motion. [50]

The same fate befell a proposal by Algernon Lee, National Committee member from New York, to place the committee on record in favor of a campaign for equality of minority groups in American society. This outcome was hastened by Lee's retreat in the face of opposition. At the March 1907 meeting of the National Committee, Lee introduced a resolution that called upon the committee to assert that it was the "duty of all party members and sympathizers, in their activity as Socialists, as members of labor organizations, and as citizens"

1. To seek to procure and protect for all residents of the United States, regardless of race or nativity, full and equal civil and political rights, including the right of naturalization for all and admission on equal terms to the benefits of the schools and other public institutions;

2. To promote the enrollment of workers of alien race or nativity in the political and industrial organizations of the working class and the cultivation of a mutual good understanding and fraternal relations between them and the mass of native white workers;

3. By all means to further the assimilation of all such alien elements on a basis of common interest as wage-workers and to rebuke all appeals to racial, national or religious prejudices against or among them. [51]

At the next meeting of the National Committee, G. F. Bentley, a committeeman from Oklahoma, amended Lee's resolution by adding the following: "And that whenever states provide separate schools, equal and ample facilities shall be provided for all races regardless of numbers living in school districts." Defending the Jim Crow amendment, Bentley declared flatly:

We, in the South, find it absolutely out of the question to consider mixed schools. . . . It is absolutely essential for the negro's good that they be separated as much as possible in a social way. . . . Most of the negro states provide fairly equitable systems of separate schools, and they have done wonders for the negro race and they would close every public school in the South, rather than have them mixed."

Lee promptly retreated. His resolution, he emphasized, only laid down general principles: "It does not pretend to cover all details, nor would it be practicable to do so." The establishment of separate schools for blacks did not, in any sense, imply an inferior status for them: "We have separate schools for the blind, the deaf mutes, and for other special categories of pupils, without any suspicion of inequality." Hence, the amendment was not relevant since it was quite logical to affirm the principle that all residents of the United States, regardless of race or nativity, should have access "on equal terms to the benefits of the schools and other public institutions" without disturbing the existing segregation pattern of schools in the South and Southwest.

The Southern members of the National Committee were not as confident as Lee. Fearing even the assertion of the general principle of equality, they were able to have Lee's original resolution rejected. [52] That Lee should equate the second-class education received by blacks in the segregated schools of the South with separate schools for the blind and deaf is an indication of how little even socialists who called themselves champions of equality understood about the life of black Americans.


## 1908 NATIONAL SOCIALIST PARTY CONVENTION: THE IMMIGRATION ISSUE

The 1908 convention was dominated by the issue of immigration, the problem of how to deal with the influx of "new" immigrants in the United States — Southern and Eastern European by birth — and especially the question of Asian exclusion. While some socialists simultaneously urged the party to adopt a policy of actively seeking Negro members, and yet favored immigration barriers, the white supremacists in the party tied the two issues together. The racism of the white supremacist socialists that had been directed against Negroes was now turned especially against Asians. Again and again, they spoke of "alien elements" in the United Staes such as "the Negroes and the Chinese, and other Asiatic workers." [53]

At the 1907 International Socialist Congress held in Stuttgart, Germany, Morris Hillquit was vice-president of the Commission on Emigration and Immigration. In that capacity, he opposed a resolution introduced by the Argentine delegate condemning restrictions based on race or nationality and called for the organizing of immigrants for political and economic rights. Hillquit, insisting that the resolution was misguided, proposed that the Congress take a stand against the importation of those foreign workers whose presence would destroy worker organizations, lower standards of living, and retard the realization of socialism. In his remarks, Hillquit singled out Orientals as unorganizable and artificially imposed on American workers. Denying prejudice, he maintained that the American position advanced the class struggle while the Argentine resolution handicapped it. 54

Condemned for his racist views, Hillquit reversed himself and supported the successful resolution condemning exclusion of any nationality. His stand infuriated the racists in the Socialist party of America. At a meeting of the Socialist party's National Executive Committee in December 1907, Victor Berger introduced a motion censuring Hillquit for pledging support for the Stuttgart resolution. It was a matter of racial purity, he insisted: "We have one race question here now, the negro question. . . . If we admit Asiatic labor without restriction, this country is absolutely sure to become a black-and-yellow country within a few generations." 55

The National Executive Committee, and later the National Committee, rejected the Stuttgart resolution and came out for the exclusion of workers from Oriental and other "backward countries." 56 The question was then put before the national convention in 1908 in the form of a resolution sponsored by John Spargo. It said in part: "To deny the right of workers to protect themselves against injury to their interests, caused by the competition of imported foreign laborers whose standards of living are materially lower than their own, is to set a bourgeois Utopian ideal above the class struggle." The resolution also specified socialist opposition to "all immigration which is subsidized or stimulated by the capitalist class, and all contract labor immigration." It proposed that the question of exclusion based on race—primarily Asian—be left to the next convention, with a committee elected to study it in the meantime. 57

In the debate that followed, Ernest Untermann, a fervent supporter of the resolution, linked the issues of black and yellow:

> This is not only an economic question, but also a race question, and I am not afraid to say so. . . . Everyone familiar with conditions in the southern states knows very well what would be the fate of the Socialist Party if we attempted to organize mixed locals of colored and white people there. Everyone familiar with conditions on the Pacific and in the Rocky Mountain states knows that the same result would follow if we attempted to orga-

nize mixed locals of orientals and whites. . . . I am determined
that my race shall not go the way of the Aztec and the Indian. . . .
I am determined that my race shall be supreme in this country
and in the world. 58

As might be expected, Berger fully endorsed the opposition to the mixing of races in socialist locals and reaffirmed his stand that white Anglo-
Saxons must remain supreme. Guy E. Miller of Colorado declared:

I want to say to you again, on the question of immigration, that
there are biological reasons as well as sociological and economic
ones to be considered upon this matter. There has never been a
mixture and amalgamation of races that did not end disastrously
for the amalgamated. 59

It was useless for the opponents of the resolution to point out the inconsistency between it and the signs that encircled the convention hall
proclaiming Marx's great slogan "Workingmen of the World, Unite."
Max Hayes replied that if Marx had investigated conditions on the Pacific Coast, he would have realized that the slogan did not apply everywhere. 60

The Spargo resolution was adopted by a voice vote. The convention
elected four racists—Ernest Untermann, Victor Berger, Joseph Wanhope, and Guy Miller—and the equivocal John Spargo to the permanent
committee on immigration. 61

Apart from linking the Negro and immigration questions, the 1908
Socialist party national convention was a replay of the 1904 gathering
with regard to blacks. Once again there was a single Negro delegate
present—Reverend George W. Woodbey of California, who had also been
the sole black delegate in 1904. Once again no resolution was adopted on
the Negro question, and once again the party platform and the Declaration of Principles contained not a single reference to the Negro. On both
occasions, the word did not even appear in the index to the published proceedings.

ELECTION OF 1908

Eugene V. Debs, who typically did not attend the 1908 convention,
was, as in 1904, the party candidate for president of the United States.
Unlike 1904, however, this time both the party and its candidate paid
considerable attention to the Negro vote. When a correspondent asked
the *New York Call* whether the socialists were "trying to secure" the

Negro vote, and voiced the opinion that it was the Socialist party into which many militant blacks wished to go, "but . . . are not sufficiently sure of their reception," the socialist daily did little to encourage these blacks. Once again blacks were told that the Socialist party would do nothing "to secure the Negro vote," and could offer them only what it offered "any other member of society," which boiled down to "equality of opportunity." [62] Nevertheless, the 1908 campaign was distinguished by the fact that there were special appeals to blacks to vote for Debs. The Wilshire Book Company published, and the party distributed, a pamphlet entitled *Eugene V. Debs on "The Color Question"* by W. W. Passage, a black socialist. [63] The cover depicted, through cartoons, the theme that blacks had exchanged one form of slavery under capitalism — chattel slavery — for another — wage slavery — and suggested that they had been better off under the first than they were under the second. The cartoons were followed by a quotation from John C. Calhoun, the antebellum senator from South Carolina and leading proslavery apologist, which read:

> The Southern Capitalist owns the laborer, and his interest is that the laborer be well provided for. In the North the Capitalist owns the *instruments of labor* and he seeks to draw out of the laborer all the profits, leaving him to shift for himself in old age and disease.

The pamphlet made no mention of the fact that Calhoun had envisioned a union between slaveholders of the South and mill owners and other capitalists of the North to keep both black and white labor in total subjugation.

The rest of the pamphlet was devoted to Passage's appeal to blacks to vote for Debs and to extracts from Debs' speeches and writings which, Passage observed, "will explain why the colored people are coming to appreciate and love him, even as they love and revere the memory of John Brown, William Lloyd Garrison, Wendell Phillips, Charles Sumner and Abraham Lincoln, and for the same reasons." These extracts were from Debs' article on John Brown in *Appeal to Reason*, and his two articles in the *International Socialist Review* — "The Negro in the Class Struggle" and "The Negro and His Nemesis." [64] Also included was the text of a letter Debs wrote in response to an invitation from Reverend J. Milton Waldron, president of the National Negro American Political League, urging the socialists to join in a campaign to defeat William Howard Taft, the presidential candidate of the Republican party. [65] In his reply, Debs agreed that Negroes were wise to have at last shed the illusion that the Republican party was interested in their welfare. He proceeded to prove the Republicans' lack of concern by illustrating their repeated failure to stand up for the rights of blacks. He also indicated that he had no sympathy for the idea, initiated by the Negro League, that a Republican defeat in 1908 required the support of the Democratic party candidate. Debs noted: "as for the Democratic Party, which is even now depriving negro wage slaves of their political franchise in the South, it is not necessary to even raise the question as to where it stands." There was nothing to choose between the two major parties, he maintained, since both were instruments of the capitalist class, and only the Socialist party offered the Negro voter a meaningful choice. At the same time, he said that the socialists would not try to win the Negro vote by "trickery." The party wanted only the vote of those Negroes who came to this decision intelligently and honestly, understanding clearly what the socialists had to offer black Americans.

Finally, the pamphlet included an appeal by the *Cleveland Gazette*, the black weekly, urging all Negroes who did not wish to vote for Taft to support Debs, a man who was "right on the so-called race question, and has the courage of his convictions." Passage made a similar appeal in which he hailed Debs as "the John Brown and William Lloyd Garrison and Frederick Douglass and Wendell Phillips and Abraham Lincoln of the new emancipation rolled into one." The pamphlet concluded with an analysis of the Socialist party platform to demonstrate that the party was continuing the "heroic work" of the abolitionists by seeking to abolish the new and even worse form of slavery — wage slavery. "Therefore, my colored fellow workers," Passage ended, "let us arise, and by the power of our united ballots march into the promised land of ownership."

*Eugene V. Debs on "The Color Question"* reflected a number of trends in the socialist approach to the Negro question. One, of course, was the failure to deal with any specific or special problems of blacks, and the complete reliance on the party's advocacy of political and economic equality for Negroes in the future cooperative commonwealth, along with Debs' firm belief in universal brotherhood. Another was the emphasis on the theme that blacks had actually been better off under chattel slavery than they were under wage slavery, an idea that went back to the concepts advanced before the Civil War by the Southern proslavery apologists and the utopian socialists reformers. [66] (At least the *Chicago Daily Socialist* did carry one article during the presidential campaign in which the writer, probably a black, pointed out that, while Negroes may have been better cared for under chattel slavery than they were under wage slavery, they now had the right, in the North at any rate, to do something to change their condition by voting for the Socialist party — a right that no chattel slave could ever have exercised. [67] ) Still another theme was that the socialists, with Eugene V. Debs in the vanguard,

were continuing the tradition of the abolitionists and were the inheritors
of the contributions of Garrison, Phillips, and John Brown. (Socialists
repeatedly let the world know that, just as the abolitionists were honored
"because they led in the eternal march of man," the socialists would be
honored because they led "the cause of the greater freedom, the economic
emancipation of all men." [68] ) In one respect, however, the 1908 pamphlet
went beyond the usual references to abolitionists in socialist literature: it
included Frederick Douglass, greatest of the black abolitionists, as part
of the tradition inherited by the socialists. This was the first time a Socialist party publication ever mentioned that blacks had been part of the
antislavery movement before the Civil War and had contributed to the
abolition of slavery. It was also to be the last reference to this theme for
many years to come, except for the article in the *New York Call* of February 1911 on Sojourner Truth, the great black woman (described by the
*Call* as a "wonderful old negress") who, born a slave in New York,
became a noted abolitionist organizer and speaker and a champion of
woman's rights. [69] There was no mention in socialist publications of the
even more heroic black woman abolitionist, Harriet Tubman, who won
glory as a conductor on the Underground Railroad, returning to the
South after her own escape from slavery to liberate hundreds still in
bondage, and who was a guerrilla fighter during the Civil War.

*Eugene V. Debs on "The Color Question"* was only one of several special efforts made by the Socialist party, mainly by black socialists, to win
support for Debs from Negroes during the 1908 presidential campaign.
In his letter to Reverend Waldron, Debs noted that the Socialist party
"already has several [black] organizers in the field and expects to have
more in the near future." It is impossible to determine just how many
black votes these black organizers won for Debs in 1908. In his study *The
Brownsville Affair*, John D. Weaver claims that Debs "seemed to have
little appeal" for black voters in the 1908 election, but he offers no evidence for this assertion. [70] If it is true, as it appears to be, that the
Brownsville Affair greatly influenced the black vote, the fact that the
socialist press never carried any editorial comment on it, that the National Committee refused to condemn President Roosevelt, and that the
literature directed toward blacks urging them to vote for Debs did not
deal with it at all, makes it likely that many blacks who bolted the Republican party because of this issue did not consider the Socialist party the
logical champion of their cause.

Yet, the fact that there were black organizers who worked actively for
the Socialist party in the 1908 campaign is a significant aspect of the relationship between American socialism and black Americans, and one that
requires special attention and discussion.

# Black Socialist Preachers

REVEREND GEORGE WASHINGTON WOODBEY

In the *Ohio Socialist Bulletin* of February 1909, Reverend Richard Euell, a black minister of Milford, Ohio, published "A Plan to Reach the Negro." The Negro, he wrote, "belongs to the working class and must be taught class consciousness." Blacks could be recruited more rapidly into the Socialist party if the Socialists would go to them in their churches and point out "the way to freedom and plenty." Most of them had no experience with any organization other than the church and could not think of committing themselves to action except in religious terms. The Bible and even motion pictures about the "Passion Play" could be used effectively to imbue religion with radicalism and convince the black working class of the evils of the capitalist system and the virtues of socialism. [1]

The first black socialist to conduct the type of work Reverend Euell recommended was Reverend George Washington Woodbey (sometimes spelled Woodby). He had already been performing this function for the socialist cause for several years, even before "A Plan to Reach the Negro" was published.

Woodbey, the leading Negro socialist in the first decade of the twentieth century, was born a slave in Johnson County, Tennessee, on October 5, 1854, the son of Charles and Rachel (Wagner) Woodbey. Nothing is known about his early life except that he learned to read after he was freed and was self-educated, except for two terms in a common school, and that his life was one of "hard work and hard study carried on together." A fellow socialist who knew him wrote: "He has worked in mines, factories, on the streets, and at everything which would supply food, clothing and shelter."

Woodbey was ordained a Baptist minister in Emporia, Kansas, in 1874. He was active in the Republican party in Missouri and Kansas. He was also a leader of the Prohibition party, and when he moved to Nebraska, he became a prominent force in the prohibition movement in that state. In 1896, Woodbey ran for lieutenant governor and Congress on the Prohibition ticket in Nebraska.

That same year, he made his first acquaintance with the principles of socialism when he read Edward Bellamy's *Looking Backward*. His interest was further aroused by copies of the *Appeal to Reason* which he came across. Although he subscribed to the *Appeal*, he did not join the socialists. Instead, he moved into the Populist party, and in 1900, he supported William Jennings Bryan, the Democratic and Populist candidate for president. He also heard Eugene V. Debs speak during the presidential campaign and was so impressed that when the Democratic party asked Woodbey to speak for Bryan, he agreed to do so; the speeches he delivered, however, were geared more to the ideas advanced by Debs than to those of the Democratic candidate. After several such speeches, the Democrats stopped scheduling him and the black minister came to the conclusion that his place was in the socialist camp. He resigned his pulpit and announced to his friends that from then on his life "would be consecrated to the Socialist movement." A Nebraska socialist recalled: "We remember him in the stirring days of the inception of the Socialist movement in Omaha. Night after night he spoke on the streets and in the parks of that city. Omaha had never had the crowds that attended Woodbey's meetings."[2]

When Woodbey visited San Diego to see his mother in the spring of 1902, he immediately made an impression on the comrades in southern California. A dispatch to the *Los Angeles Socialist* on May 31, 1902, read:

> Socialism is on the boom here in this county and city. We have had Rev. G. W. Woodbey, the Colored Socialist orator of Nebraska with us for nearly a month during which time he has delivered 23 addresses and will speak again tonight, and then he will do some work in the country districts where he has been invited to speak. . . .
>
> Comrade Woodbey is great and is a favorite with all classes. He came here unannounced ostensibly to see his mother who re-

sides here but as he says that he is "so anxious to be free," that he feels impressed to work for the cause constantly. He has had very respectable audiences both on the streets and in the halls. He likes to speak on the street and it is the general verdict that he has done more good for the cause than any of our most eloquent speakers who have preceded him. He is full of resources and never repeats his speeches, but gives them something new every time. He requested me to state in my notes to the "Socialist" that he desires to visit Los Angeles later on if you folks can find a place for him. He makes no charges but depends entirely on pasing the hat for his support. 3

Los Angeles did find a place for Woodbey, and he delivered a series of soap-box speeches and lectures in its leading hall. When, after one of his speeches, Woodbey was denied admittance to the Southern Hotel and Northern Restaurant because of his color, the Los Angeles Socialist party organized a boycott of the establishments and distributed leaflets reading:

> We demand as trade unionists and socialists, that every wage-worker in Los Angeles bear well in mind these two places that depend on public patronage—the Northern Restaurant and the Southern Hotel—keep away from them. They draw the color line. 4

The boycott had the desired effect.

Woodbey accepted an offer to become minister of the Mount Zion Baptist Church in San Diego, and for the next two decades, he made his home in California. He was elected a member of the state executive board of the Socialist party and soon became widely known in the state as "The Great Negro Socialist Orator." In a Los Angeles debate with Archibald Huntley, Ph.D., in which Woodbey took the affirmative of the topic "Resolved That Socialism Is the True Interpretation of Economic Conditions and That It Is the Solution of the Labor Problem," he was listed as a "well-known Socialist Lecturer. Quaint, Direct, Forceful. Has spoken to great audiences in all parts of the United States." 5

An announcement that Woodbey would deliver a reply to Booker T. Washington's "Capitalist Argument for the Negro" packed Los Angeles' leading hall on May 1, 1903. He paid tribute to Washington "as a gentleman" and educator, but added: "He has all the ability necessary to make a good servant of capitalism by educating other servants for capitalism." Woodbey charged that, whether consciously or not, Tuskegee Institute fulfilled the role of providing black workers to be pitted against white workers so as to bring about a general lowering of wage scales.

What Washington failed to understand, he said, was that there was basically no unity between capitalists, white or black, and workers, white or black: "There is no race division industrially, but an ever-growing antagonism between the exploiting capitalists black or white, and the exploited workers, black or white." In this "industrial struggle," the working class was bound to "ultimately triumph": "And then the men of all races will share in the results of production according to their services in the process of production. This is Socialism and the only solution to the race problem."[6]

As a socialist soap-box speaker, Woodbey was a frequent target of the police of San Diego, Los Angeles, San Francisco, and other California communities. He was in and out of jail several times between 1902 and 1908, and was hospitalized more than once as a result of police brutality. Nonetheless, he refused to retreat. When he was attacked and driven off a street corner in San Diego in July 1905 by Police Officer George H. Cooley, Woodbey led a group of protesters to the police station to lodge a complaint. There Cooley again attacked the black socialist, "using at the same time oaths and language too mean and vile to print." Woodbey was literally thrown bodily out of the station house. He immediately brought charges against the police officer for assault and battery, and informed his California comrades: "In the days of chattel slavery the masters had a patrol force to keep the negroes in their place and protect the interests of the masters. Today the capitalists use the police for the same purpose." He added that the slaves had rebelled despite the patrols and that he was following that tradition in telling the police they could not get away with their brutalities against the enemies of the capitalist system.

Woodbey's case against the police was prosecuted by the county attorney, assisted by California's leading socialist attorney, Job Harriman. All witnesses testified that the Negro socialist's conduct had been "perfectly gentlemanly" and that he had a perfectly lawful right to be at the station house. Nevertheless, the jury, composed of conservative property owners, took only fifteen minutes to find the defendant not guilty. Woodbey was furious and published the names of the members of the jury, urging all decent citizens to have nothing to do with them. He then returned immediately to the soap box in San Diego and held one of the biggest street-corner meetings held in the city up to that time. As he wrote:

> The case has made more Socialists than I could possibly have made in many speeches. Had I not gone to the court with the matter the public would forever have contended that I was doubtless doing or saying something that I had no right to do or

say. And when I complained I would have been told that if I had gone to the courts I would have got justice. Now, as it is, nothing of the kind can be said, and the responsibility is placed where it rightly belongs.

Many nonsocialists in San Diego, Woodbey noted, were learning the truth of the socialist contention that "the police force are the watch dogs of capitalism."[7]

In more than one California city, Woodbey was arrested and hauled off to jail for trying to sell copies of his socialist booklets.[8] The writings made his name known throughout the entire party in the United States, and even internationally. A white socialist described him as "the greatest living negro in America" and noted that "his style is simple and his logic invincible. He knows the race question, and one of his most popular lectures relates to the settlement of this vexed question under Socialism." Because of Woodbey's ability to explain socialism in simple terms, he was asked to "embody some of the things he has said to the thousands who have listened to his talks, in a written form." The response was the pamphlet *What to Do and How to Do It or Socialism vs. Capitalism*. A copy of a small edition, privately printed, fell into the hands of A. W. Ricker, the socialist organizer in the West and South. While at the home of socialist publisher Julius A. Wayland in Girard, Kansas, Ricker read it aloud to the Wayland family. "At the conclusion," he wrote, "we decided that the book ought to be in the hands of millions of American wage slaves, and we forthwith wrote to Rev. Mr. Woodbey for the right to bring it out."[9]

It was published as No. 40 of the widely distributed *Wayland's Monthly* in August 1903. Ricker gave it a sendoff in the *Appeal to Reason*, writing:

> The book in many respects is the equal of "Merrie England," and in the matter of its clear teaching of the class struggle, it is superior. It has been read by every negro in Girard, and has made Socialists of those who were susceptible of understanding after every other effort had failed to shake their unreasoning adherence to the republican party. A good supply should be ordered by every local in the land, and gotten in the hands of negroes especially. In our humble judgment, there is no book in the language that will excel it in propaganda value, and we expect to see it pass through one edition after another, so soon as it is read by the comrades.[10]

Since Robert Blatchford's *Merrie England*, published in England in

1894 and in the United States in 1900, was considered one of the best of the socialist educational publications, the tribute to Reverend Woodbey's pamphlet was well understood by the readers of the *Appeal to Reason.*

Woodbey's forty-four-page booklet carried this moving dedication:

> This little book is dedicated to that class of citizens who desire to know what the Socialists want to do and how they propose to do it. By one who was once a chattel slave freed by the proclamation and wishes to be free from the slavery of capitalism. [11]

In his preface, Woodbey acknowledged that there was "nothing original" in his little book, his aim being simply to make the subjects treated "as plain as possible to the reader." It was not directed to those who were already convinced of the superiority of socialism over capitalism, but rather to "meet the demands of that large and increasing class of persons who have not yet accepted Socialism, but would do so if they could see any possible way of putting it into practice." Within this framework, Reverend Woodbey's booklet is an effective piece of socialist propaganda. It was so highly thought of in socialist circles that by 1908 it had been translated into three languages and had gained an international reputation of its author. [12]

Basically, the booklet consists of a dialogue between the author and his mother, whom he has rejoined after nearly seventeen years of separation. She expresses her astonishment upon learning that her son has become a socialist. "Have you given up the Bible and the ministry and gone into politics?" she asks. Her son tries to convince her that it is precisely because of his devotion to the principles enunciated in the Bible that he became a socialist and that, as the years passed, he became more and more convinced of the correctness of his decision. When his mother points out that among his comrades are many who believe in neither God nor the Bible, he readily agrees but reminds her that he found "a still larger number of unbelievers in the Republican Party before I left it some twenty years ago" and that other parties had their "equal portion" of nonbelievers. More important, while he believed in the Biblical account of God and the origin of the earth and of man, and members of his party did not, he and they were able to agree that "man is here, and the earth is here, and that it is the present home of the race, at least." To be sure, they did not see eye to eye about the "hereafter," but he was ready and willing to join hands with all who were "willing to make things better here, which the Bible teaches is essential to the hereafter." Since socialism was "a scheme for bettering things here first," he could be a "good Socialist" without surrendering his belief in God or the Bible. There was room in the

Socialist party for those who were interested only in what it could do for mankind in the present world and for those, like himself, who were "Socialists because they think that mankind is entitled to the best of everything in both this world and the next." Finally, his mother could rest assured that under socialism persons would be free to have "their own religion or none, just as they please, so long as they do not interfere with others." [13]

Having laid to rest his mother's anxiety and made her willing to listen to the fundamental principles of a movement that had obviously not destroyed her son's religious convictions, Woodbey proceeds to explain to her the evils of capitalist society and the way by which socialism, gaining power through the ballot box, would set out to eliminate these evils. After he takes his mother through such subjects as rent, interest, and profits, which are all gained from labor's production, and value, which is created only by labor but whose fruits are appropriated entirely by the capitalists, she expresses bewilderment at the meaning of these words. Her son then illustrates what they mean in simple language and in terms of daily experience. Here, for example, is his explanation of surplus value:

> Why didn't the slave have wealth at the close of the war? He worked hard.
>
> "Because his master got it," mother replied.
>
> The wage worker's master got what he produced, too.
>
> "But wasn't he paid for his work?" asked mother.
>
> Yes, about seventeen cents on every dollar's worth of wealth he created.

Under socialism, he continues, the capitalist would have to turn over to the state a "large amount of capital created by labor" which he had taken from the worker. The worker, meanwhile, having been deprived of all he produced under capitalism, would have nothing to turn over. The very rich man would have no reason to complain

> since he and his children, who have done nothing but live off the labor of those who have nothing to turn over, are to be given an equal share of interest with those who have produced it all, so you see we Socialists are not such bad fellows as you thought. We propose to do good unto those who spitefully use us, and to those

who curse us, by giving them an equal show with ourselves, provided that they will hereafter do their share of the useful work. [14]

His mother expresses concern that the capitalists will not yield peacefully to having the "land, factories, and means of production" turned
over to the cooperative commonwealth by a socialist Congress elected by
the people, and that they would start a war to retain their holdings. Her
son concedes that this would quite likely occur, just as the slaveholders
had refused to abide by Lincoln's electoral victory and had precipitated a
civil war. But the capitalists would never succeed in the war they would
seek to stimulate, since the majority of the people had clearly become
convinced that socialism was the only solution to their problems, or else
the socialists could not have won their electoral victories. Hence, the
capitalists would have no one to do the fighting for them:

> The slaveholder did not dare to arm the negro, on his side, with-
> out proclaiming emancipation, and to do that was to lose his
> cause; so with the capitalist, if he dares to offer all to the poor
> man who must fight his battles, he has lost his cause; and with
> this condition confronting the capitalist, there is no danger in
> taking over the entire industrial plant as soon as the Socialists
> can be elected and pass the necessary laws. And the Socialist
> party will go into power just as soon as the majority finds that
> the only way to secure to itself its entire product is to vote that
> ticket. [15]

His mother has only one question left about the transition from capitalism to socialism: "Have the people a right to do this?" Her son reminds her of the Declaration of Independence which clearly affirms the
right of the people, when any form of government becomes destructive of
the rights of life, liberty and the pursuit of happiness, "to alter and
abolish it and institute a new government" which would be most likely to
effect "their safety and happiness." On this "the Socialists stand," the
son declares firmly. Moreover, it was none other than Abraham Lincoln
who, in his speech of January 12, 1840, in the House of Representatives
had said "just what the Socialists now say." He had then declared: "Any
people anywhere being inclined and having the power have the right to
rise up and shake off the existing government and form a new one that
suits them better." [16]

His mother by now fully satisfied, the son proceeds to describe how different departments of government—agriculture, manufacturing, transportation, distribution, intelligence, education, and health—will operate
under socialism, providing for the needs of the people, and not for the

profits of the capitalist as under capitalism. The mother occasionally interrupts the narrative with questions that bring answers that satisfy her. Thus, when she asks whether the workers who would own and operate the factories under socialism "would know how to do the work," the answer reassures her:

> Why, the workers are the only ones who do know how to run a factory. The stockholders who own the concern know nothing about doing the work. If the girl who weaves in the factory should be told that Socialism is now established and that henceforth she is to have shorter hours of labor, a beautiful sanitary place to work in, and an equal share of all the wealth of the nation, to be taken in any kind of thing she wants, do you think she would forget how to work? And if on the other hand, all she produces is to go to the girl who does nothing but own the stocks, then she can work right along? Seems to me, you might see the absurdity of that, mother. "I believe I do see, now," she said, after a moment's hesitation. Then apply that illustration about the girls, to all the workers, and you will get my meaning. [17]

As might be expected, the mother asks, "Like all other women, I want to know where we are to come in." Her son assures her that it was in the interest of "the women, more than the men, if possible, to be Socialists because they suffer more from capitalism than anyone else." For one thing, the socialist platform demands "the absolute equality of the sexes before the law, and the repeal of all law that in any way discriminates against women." Then again, under socialism, each woman would, like each man, have her own independent income and would become "an equal shareholder in the industries of the nation." Under such liberating conditions, a woman would have no need "to sell herself through a so-called marriage to someone she did not love in order to get a living," and, for the first time in history, she could marry only for love. Under capitalism, the working man was a slave, "and his wife . . . the slave of a slave." Socialism would liberate both, but since it would give women political equality and economic freedom it would actually do more for women than for men. [18]

By now, his mother has been converted totally. The booklet ends with the comment: " 'Well, you have convinced me that I am about as much of a slave now as I was in the South, and I am ready to accept any way out of this drudgery,' mother remarked as the conversation turned on other subjects." [19]

Here and there, *What to Do and How to Do It* reflects Bellamy's influence on Woodbey. In fact, sections of the 1903 pamphlet are somewhat similar to parts of the 1887 *Looking Backward*. [20] In the main, however, the pamphlet revealed that the black minister had broken with Bellamy's utopianism. While Bellamy emphasized "equitable" distribution of wealth under Nationalism, Woodbey was convinced that the solution lay closer to Marx's maxim, "From each according to his ability, to each according to his needs." Bellamy rejected the label socialism as dangerous and un-American. [21] In contrast, Woodbey welcomed it and believed its principles were in keeping with the best in the American tradition. Like many in the Socialist party, Woodbey believed that, with the capture of sufficient political offices through the ballot box, socialism could be rapidly achieved. He was one of the very few in the party in 1903, however, who recognized the danger that the capitalists would not calmly allow their control of society to be eliminated by legislative enactments, but instead would, like the slaveowners in 1860, resort to violence to prevent the people's will from being carried out. Woodbey differed from Jack London, who, in his great 1908 novel, *The Iron Heel*, predicted that the oligarchy of American capitalists would seize power from the socialists and destroy the democratic process by violence. Woodbey, on the other hand, was confident that the capitalists would fail. [22] Nevertheless, by even raising this issue in his pamphlet, Woodbey was in advance of nearly all Christian Socialists.

Early in *What to Do and How to Do It*, Woodbey assures his mother that at a future date he would tell her "more about what the Bible teaches on the subject" of socialism. [23] A year later, he fulfilled his promise with *The Bible and Socialism: A Conversation Between Two Preachers*, published in San Diego by the author. The ninety-six-page pamphlet was dedicated to "the Preachers and Members of the Churches, and all others who are interested in knowing what the Bible teaches on the question at issue between the Socialists and the Capitalists, by one who began preaching twenty-nine years ago, and still continues." [24]

As the subtitle indicates, *The Bible and Socialism* consists of a dialogue between Woodbey and another clergyman. The latter is a local pastor to whom Woodbey's mother has given a copy of the 1903 pamphlet and has invited to her home to hear her son convince him that he was wrong in contending that "there is no Socialism in the Bible." The skeptical pastor questions Woodbey about the socialist claim that Karl Marx discovered the principles of scientific socialism and points out that this was centuries after the Bible was written. In response, Woodbey notes, first, that no new idea is ever entirely new and is in some way based on what went before, and, second, that

> Marx, the greatest philosopher of modern times, belonged to the same wonderful Hebrew race that gave to the world Moses, the

Lawgiver, the kings and prophets, and Christ the Son of the Highest, with his apostles, who, together, gave us the Bible that, we claim, teaches Socialism. Doubtless Marx, like the young Hebrews, was made acquainted with the economic teachings of Moses, and all the rest of the Old Testament sages and prophets, whatever we find him believing in after life.

If we are able to show that the Bible opposes both rent, interest, and profits, and the exploiting of the poor, then it stands just where the Socialists do. [25]

Woodbey agrees that Marx was not a Christian but notes that this was of no significance since socialism had nothing to do with a man's religion or lack of it. He devotes the rest of his pamphlet to detailed references, quotations, and citations to convince the pastor that since the Bible—both the Old and New Testaments—did actually oppose "rent, interest, and profits, and the exploiting of the poor," it was a socialist document with close affinity to such classics as *The Communist Manifesto, Das Kapital*, and other writings of Marx. As a Jew, Woodbey emphasizes, Marx was able to do "the greatly needed work of reasoning out from the standpoint of the philosopher what his ancestors, the writers of the Old and New Testaments, had already done from a moral and religious standpoint." [26] This is not to say, he continues, that there is no difference between a socialism based merely on a "moral and religious standpoint" and scientific socialism, just as there was a fundamental difference between the socialism advanced by utopian reformers prior to Marx and that set forth by the father of scientific socialism. For scientific socialism was based on the class struggle which had dominated all history and all existing relationships in capitalist society. When the pastor asks Woodbey if the class struggle also exists in the church, there is the following discussion in which the mother joins:

Master and slave, before the war, all belonged to the same church. They met on Sunday and prayed together, and one church member sold the other the next day. So now, in many cases, master and wage slave belong to the same church, meet on Sunday and pray together, and the one turns the other off from even the pittance he allowed him to take out of his earnings as wages or sets him out of house and home for non-payment of rent, or under mortgage, the next day. All that, notwithstanding the Bible says love brother and the stranger as oneself.

It took the abolitionist, in and out of the church, to show the inconsistency of slavery and force a division, as the Socialists are now doing.

> "Yes," said mother, "I belonged to one of that kind of churches, myself, before the war." [27]

Just as his mother was converted at the end of the 1903 pamphlet, so, too, is the pastor by the close of *The Bible and Socialism*. He confesses that he learned little of economics while in college, and since he joined the ministry, he has been too busy to give more than a casual thought to the Bible's "economic teachings" and to whether the churches adhered to them. As a result of the "interesting evening conversations," he was a changed man, "being convinced that Socialism is but the carrying out of the economic teachings of the Bible, I shall endeavor to study it and lay it before my people to the best of my ability." [28]

Woodbey's pamphlet offered little new for white, religiously inclined socialists since the Christian Socialists had already published a considerable body of literature demonstrating to their satisfaction that the Bible and socialism were compatible. To black churchgoers, however, much of what was in the pamphlet was new and certainly must have had an impressive impact. Moreover, while many Christian Socialists preached an emotional propaganda replete with Christian ethics, they tended to ignore the class struggle or to relate their Biblical references to the contemporary scene. Not so Woodbey; he was a firm believer in the class struggle, had read Marx, and was not in the least reluctant to couple discussions of the Old and New Testaments with those about the specific evils in twentieth-century American society.

Woodbey's third and last socialist pamphlet was *The Distribution of Wealth*, published in 1910 in San Diego by the author. The sixty-eight-page booklet consists of a series of letters to a J. Jones, a California rancher friend of the author. The pamphlet describes how the distribution of wealth created by productive labor would operate "after Socialism has overthrown the capitalist method of production." Pointing out in his preface that there was little in socialist literature about how the future cooperative commonwealth would function, Woodbey, without the slightest hesitation, declared he would attempt to fill the gap. Affirming his right to do so, he noted:

> If the socialist movement is based upon truth, it cannot be destroyed by the utmost freedom of discussion, nor is the movement or the party necessarily in danger, because your views or mine are not at once adopted even should they be correct. All I ask of the reader is a fair, honest consideration of what I have written. [29]

What he wrote is an interesting elaboration of how the different institutions under capitalism would operate in the new socialist society. Some of this had already been explained in his 1903 *What to Do and How to Do It*, but here he develops it further. In 1903, it will be recalled, Woodbey had conceded that the capitalists would resort to armed resistance to prevent the socialist society from coming into being. Now, however, he appears to believe that, while the capitalists would resist the transition to socialism with "tremendous opposition," it would not necessarily lead to war. Once socialism had proved its superiority over capitalism, even the capitalists and their children would acquiesce and decide to live under it—a clear throwback to *Looking Backward*. He writes:

> Let us go back, for instance, to the slaveholder, by way of illustration. He declared that he would go to war before he would permit himself and family to labor like the negro slave and live in poverty, rags and ignorance. He had been taught to believe that that was the necessary outgrowth of labor. And I submit that the condition of labor under chattel slavery was a poor school in which to teach the child of the master a desire to labor. So the capitalist of today and his children look upon the workers as he has them in the sweatshops, mines and factories of the country, putting in long hours for a bare existence, under the most unsanitary conditions, living in the worst of places, and eating of the worst of food; and, like his brother, the slaveholder, he is determined that he and his shall not be reduced to such straits. It has not yet dawned upon him that when the people who work own the industries in place of him, all of these disagreeable conditions will at once disappear.... It is my opinion that, notwithstanding the false education of the children of the wealthy, even they in the first generation will have so much of their distaste for labor taken away that we will have little or no trouble with them when the majority have changed conditions.[30]

Woodbey's rancher friend keeps asking whether people would work under socialism, once the fear of poverty and unemployment was removed. Woodbey's answer is interesting:

> when chattel slavery prevailed, as we said, men thought that labor must continue to be always what it was then, and that because the slave sought to escape he wouldn't work for wages. So now the capitalist, and those who believe in capitalism, think that labor must continue always to be just what it is now; and that some people won't work under the new and better conditions.

It is a wonder to me that men are so willing to work as they are now under the present conditions. The fact is, the mind of the child is such that it accepts what it is taught now, and will do the same then.

The boy that was born a slave thought that it was natural for him to be one, and the young master took it for granted that he was intended to be master. But the boy that is born free, never thinks that anyone ought to own him; nor does the youngster born at the same time with him think that he ought to own him. But instead, they both go to school often in the same class. They at once accept the conditions under which they were born. No, my friend, there is no danger of the children not at once accept- ing the new conditions under Socialism, and we have proved there will be so little loss through idlers, even in the first genera- tion of old folks, that it will not be found worth bothering about. And as the old and infirm should of necessity be looked after with the best of everything from the very beginning, it will be found when the time comes that the thing to do will be to let everyone work and be sure that we have abundance of everything for all, and then let everybody help themselves, wherever they may be, to what we have on hand, as we do with what the public now owns. Indeed, they can be better trusted then than now, with all fear of the future banished forever. [31]

It is perhaps significant that this is the only one of Woodbey's three pamphlets that ends with the second party still unconverted to social- ism. Woodbey himself may have realized that he had tackled a difficult subject and that his presentation was too tentative to achieve total con- version. At any rate, he ends his last letter:

Hoping that I have been able to make it clear to you that under Socialism it will be possible to equitably distribute the products of industry and that you and your family will at once join the movement, I will close this somewhat lengthy correspondence by saying that I would be pleased to hear from you soon.
Yours for the cause of the revolution,
G. W. Woodbey [32]

Reverend Woodbey was a delegate to the Socialist party conventions of 1904 and 1908; indeed, as noted earlier, he was the only Negro at these two gatherings. At the 1904 convention, Woodbey took the floor twice. On the first occasion, he expressed his opinion on the seating of A. T.

Gridley of Indiana, who was being challenged because he had accepted a position in the state government after passing a civil service examination. The question at issue was whether Gridley had violated the socialist principle of not accepting a position under a capitalist government. Woodbey spoke in favor of seating Gridley, arguing that in Germany the socialists boasted of the number of comrades in the army, and noting that certainly such socialists were doing work for a capitalist government. "We all know," he continued, "that we work for capitalists when we work at all, and we would be pretty poor if we did not work for capitalists at all." [33] On the second occasion, he supported the party national secretary receiving a salary of $1,500 a year, which he called "not a dollar too much." [34] He had nothing to say about the convention's failure to deal with the Negro question in the party platform or about the delegates' complete silence on the issue during the entire convention.

At the 1908 convention, Woodbey took the floor four times. On one occasion, in a discussion of franchises held by private corporations, he advanced what, for the Socialist party, was the bold proposition that the socialists declare themselves

> in favor as fast as they can get in possession in any locality, of taking everything without a cent, and forcing the issue as to whether there is to be compensation or not. (*Applause*). I take the ground that you have already paid for these franchises — already paid more than they are worth, and we are simply proposing to take possession of what we have already paid for. [35]

On another occasion, Woodbey recommended that the National Committee elect its own executive committee from among its own members. On a third, he opposed the imposition of a time limit before a party member could be nominated for office on the socialist ticket in order to insure that he would not betray the movement. Woodbey argued that the danger of such persons "selling out" was just as great if they were members for years instead of months: "In my judgment, a man who understand its [the party's] principles is no more liable to do it after he has been in the Party six months than five years." [36]

The fourth occasion on which Woodbey spoke at the 1908 convention marked the only time during the two national gatherings that he commented on an issue related to the race question. That was when he took a firm stand, during the discussion of the immigration resolution, against Oriental exclusion and, indeed, against exclusion of any immigrants. His speech, coming as it did from a California delegate, was a remarkable statement and was certainly not calculated to win friends among socialists in his state. But it was in keeping with the tradition of black Americans since the Reconstruction era: in 1869, the Colored National Labor Union had gone on record against the exclusion of Chinese immigrants. Woodbey conceded that it was generally believed that all who lived on the Pacific Coast were as "a unit" in opposing Oriental immigration. Although he was a delegate from California, he did not share this view:

> I am in favor of throwing the entire world open to the inhabitants of the world. (*Applause*). There are no foreigners, and cannot be unless some person comes down from Mars, or Jupiter, or some place.
>
> I stand on the declaration of Thomas Paine when he said "The world is my country." (*Applause*). It would be a curious state of affairs for immigrants or descendants of immigrants from Europe themselves to get control of affairs in this country, and then say to the Oriental immigrants that they should not come here. So far as making this a mere matter of race, I disagree decidedly with the committee, that we need any kind of a committee to decide this matter from a scientific standpoint. We know what we think upon the question of race now as well as we would know two years from now or any other time. [37]

Woodbey scoffed at the idea that the entrance of Oriental immigrants would reduce the existing standard of living. He argued that, immigration or no immigration, it was the "natural tendency of capitalism" to reduce the standard of living of the working class, and that if they could not get Oriental labor to do work more cheaply in the United States, they would export their production to the Oriental countries where goods could be produced more cheaply than in this country. [38] Woodbey's prediction that American capitalists would export production to cheap-labor countries of the Orient was, as American workers today can testify, quite accurate.

Continuing, Woodbey spoke eloquently of the contradiction between immigration restrictions and the principles of international socialism. As he saw it, socialism was based "upon the Brotherhood of Man," and any stand in opposition to immigration would be "opposed to the very spirit of the Brotherhood of Man." Reminding the delegates that socialists were organized in China and Japan as well as in other countries, he asked:

> Are the Socialists of this country to say to the Socialists of Germany, or the Socialists of Sweden, Norway, Japan, China, or any other country, that they are not to go anywhere on the face of the

earth? It seems to me absurd to take that position. Therefore, I
hope and move that any sort of restriction of immigration will be
stricken out of the committee's resolution. (*Applause*). 39

It is unfortunate that, while he had the floor, Woodbey did not attack
delegates like Ernest Untermann and Victor Berger for the anti-Negro
character of their arguments in favor of Oriental exclusion. Nevertheless,
Woodbey's speech on the immigration resolution should rank high in
socialist literature, even though it has heretofore been ignored by all students of the subject. 40

Only once at either the 1904 or 1908 conventions did the delegates take
public notice that Woodbey was black. That was when his name was
placed in nomination as Debs' running mate in the presidential election
of 1908. Delegate Ellis Jones of Ohio presented his name to the convention in a brief but moving speech: "Comrades . . . the nomination that I
want to make for our Vice-President . . . is a man who is well known in the
movement for many years. The Socialist Party is a party that does not
recognize race prejudice and in order that we may attest this to the world,
I offer the name of Comrade Woodbey of California." Woodbey received
only one vote—that of Jones. 41 The nomination went to Ben Hanford,
who had been Debs' running mate in 1904. 42 Possibly if Debs, who did
not attend the convention, had wired the delegates that Woodbey's
nomination would constitute a major contribution by American socialism to the struggle against racism, the vote might have been different.
Debs, however, did not believe that the party should do anything special
on the Negro question; this view was shared by everyone at the convention except for the one delegate who nominated and voted for Woodbey.
Since the fact that Woodbey was even placed in nomination has escaped
the attention of every historian of the Socialist party, 43 it is clear that
the significance of the one vote he received has been generally overlooked.

Following the 1908 convention, Woodbey began a tour of Northern
cities with fairly large black populations and delivered a series of soap-
box speeches in favor of the socialist ticket. 44 In addition, the national
office of the Socialist party circulated his four-page leaflet, "Why the
Negro Should Vote the Socialist Ticket." The author was described as a
member of the State Executive Committee of the California Socialist
party, and formerly pastor of the African Church of Omaha, Nebraska.
As was typical of Woodbey's propaganda technique, the leaflet consisted
mainly of a speech, supposedly delivered by a Reverend Mr. Johnson,
pastor of the African Baptist Church, who had called his congregation
together to explain why he had decided "to vote the Socialist ticket at the
coming election."

The socialist movement, he pointed out, sought to bring together all working people into a party of their own, so that through such a party "they may look after the interest of all who work regardless of race or color." Since Negroes were nearly all wage workers, surely only such a party could really represent them: "All other parties have abandoned the negro, and if he wants an equal chance with everyone else, he can get it in no other way than by voting the Socialist ticket." No other party, including the Republicans, stood for eliminating poverty, and just as at one time, the elimination of slavery was crucial for the Negro, so today was the elimination of poverty. Socialism would create a society without poverty, a society in which the land, mines, factories, shops, railroads, and the like would be owned collectively, and in which the Negro, "being a part of the public, will have an equal ownership in all that the public owns, and this will entitle him to an equal part in all the good things produced by the nation." In this future society, moreover, he would not have to abandon his belief in religion. On the contrary, by providing all with sufficient to eat and decent places in which to live, socialism would be fulfilling the fundamental ideas set down in the Bible.

Finally, Woodbey called for the unity of white and black workers, urging them to "lay aside their prejudices and get together for their common good. We poor whites and blacks have fought each other long enough, and while we have fought, the capitalists have been taking everything from both of us." The socialist movement was the embodiment of this unifying principle, for it was "part of a great world movement which includes all races and both sexes and has for its motto: 'Workers of the world, unite. You have nothing to lose but your chains; you have a world to win.'" [45]

Woodbey's first published appeal directly to his people in behalf of the Socialist party is an excellent illustration of the black minister's ability to take a complex subject and simplify it so that even a political illiterate could understand it.

Woodbey expanded on several points in his leaflet in articles written early in 1909 in the *Chicago Daily Socialist*. In "The New Emancipation," he emphasized the common interests of black and white workers under capitalism, and he condemned black strikebreaking and the doctrine that Negroes should seek to solve their problems by the accumulation of wealth. Even if a few Negroes could become wealthy, the fact still remained that "their brothers are getting poorer every day." What then was the answer?

> Give the negro along with others the full product of his labor by wrenching the industries out of the hands of the capitalist and putting them into the hands of the workers and what is known as the race problem will be settled forever. Socialism is only another

one of those great world movements which is coming to bless mankind. The Socialist Party is simply the instrument for bringing it about, and the negro and all other races regardless of former conditions, are invited into its folds. [46]

In another article, "Socialist Agitation," Woodbey called for the use of all forms of educational techniques to reach the black masses—"the press, the pulpit, the rostrum and private conversation." Socialist agitators had to be made to understand that they would face imprisonment and other forms of maltreatment, but such persecution was to be expected when one sought to overthrow an evil system: "For attempting to overthrow the slave system, Lincoln and Lovejoy were shot, John Brown was hung, while Garrison, Phillips and Fred Douglass were mobbed." Naturally, socialist agitators were "equally hated and despised," and they faced constant distortion of what they stood for:

> Because the Socialists recognize the existence of a class struggle they are sometimes accused of stirring up class hatred. But, instead, they simply recognize the fact that capitalism, by its unequal distribution of wealth, has forced on us a class struggle, which the Socialists are organizing to put down and bring on the long talked of period of universal brotherhood. [47]

When Woodbey advised socialist agitators to expect to be persecuted, he spoke from personal experience. At the time he was a delegate to the 1908 socialist convention, he was out on bail, having been arrested in San Francisco early in the year with thirty other socialist speakers for defying a ban against street-corner meetings. The arrest occurred in the midst of the economic crisis following the Panic of 1907 when the socialists were holding meetings to demand relief for the unemployed.

Even before the IWW made free speech fights famous, socialists had engaged in such battles and had used specific aspects of the strategy followed by the Wobblies in their spectacular free speech struggles. [48] In the case of the 1908 San Francisco free speech fight, the socialists deliberately violated a city ordinance forbidding street meetings without police permits for all organizations except religious groups. When a speaker was arrested for speaking without a permit, his place was speedily filled upon the soap box. Speaker after speaker—men and women, black and white—mounted the soap box, were arrested, and dragged off to jail. Woodbey was one of the first to be arrested and jailed. Along with his comrades, he was released on bail. [49]

"The police can't stop us," Woodbey told a reporter during the 1908 convention. "They can and do arrest us when we speak, but they can't stem the tide that has been started no more than they can the ocean. The more they ill treat us, the more Socialists there are." Despite police opposition, the socialists were determined to obtain relief for "the hordes of honest working men [in San Francisco] who are starving because they can't get the work they so earnestly desire." [50]

With the aid of liberals and labor groups, the socialists were able to force the City Council of San francisco to repeal the objectionable ordinance, and the charges against Woodbey were dropped. [51] He continued to participate in free speech fights, and in 1912, he was a key figure in what was probably the most famous free speech fight in American history—the one in San Diego. This of course, was Woodbey's home town. Here he had been the pastor of the Mount Zion Church for several years until he was removed because, as one who knew him wrote, he "loosened up his flock with the Bible, then finished his sermon with an oration on Socialism." [52]

On January 8, 1912, the San Diego City Council passed an ordinance creating a "restricted" district of forty-nine blocks in the center of town, on which no street-corner meetings could be held. Unlike ordinances in other cities banning street speaking, the one in San Diego made no exception for religious speeches. All street speaking was banned in the so-called congested district. The reason given was that the meetings blocked traffic, but it was clear that the real purpose was to suppress the IWW's effort "to educate the floating and out-of-work population to a true understanding of the interests of labor as a whole," as well as the organization's determination to organize the workers in San Diego who had been neglected by the AFL. Among these neglected workers were the mill, lumber, and laundry workers and streetcar conductors and motormen. The IWW's actions had infuriated John D. Spreckels, the millionaire sugar capitalist and owner of the streetcar franchise; he and other employers had applied pressure on the council to pass the ordinance. Certainly, San Diego had plenty of room for her traffic, and no one believed that this little town in southern California would suffer a transportation crisis if street-corner meetings continued. [53]

Two days before the ordinance was to go into effect, the IWW and the socialists held a meeting in the center of the restricted area at which Woodbey was a leading speaker. The police broke up the meeting but did not intimidate the free speech fighters. On January 8, 1912, the *San Diego Union* carried the following on its front page:

SOCIALISTS PROPOSE FIGHT TO FINISH FOR FREE SPEECH

> Following a near-riot Saturday night during a clash between the police department, on the one hand, and Socialists and Industrial Workers of the World on the other, the Socialists and IWW members held a running street meeting last night at Fifth and H

streets, but the meeting was orderly, and there was not any semblance of trouble.

During the meeting members of the organizations policed the
sidewalks and kept them clear, so that the city police would have
no objection to make. Among the speakers were Mrs. Laura
Emerson, Messrs. Hubbard and Gordon for the Industrial Workers of the World, and George Washington Woodbey, Kaspar
Bauer and Attorney E. F. Kirk for the Socialists.

The part played by the police in the affair of Saturday evening
was denounced, but none of the speakers grew radical. It was announced that the fight for free speech will be waged with vigor,
but in a dignified manner.

Aided by vigilantes, the police responded with more than vigor and in
anything but a dignified manner. The brutality used against the free
speech fighters in San Diego was so terrible that after an investigation
ordered by Governor Hiram Johnson, Colonel Harris Weinstock reported:

> Your commissioner has visited Russia and while there has heard
> many horrible tales of high-handed proceedings and outrageous
> treatment of innocent people at the hands of despotic and tyran-
> nic Russian authorities. Your commissioner is frank to confess
> that when he became satisfied of the truth of the stories, as re-
> lated by those unfortunate men [victims of police and vigilante
> brutality in San Diego], it was hard for him to believe that he was
> not still sojourning in Russia, conducting his investigation there,
> instead of in this alleged "land of the free and home of the
> brave." 54

On several occasions, Woodbey was beaten up as he insisted on exercising his right of free speech. He filed charges of "malicious and unoffi-
cial" conduct against the chief of police, the captain of the detectives,
and several policemen whom he accused of brutality. 55 As a leading figure in the Free Speech League, the organization coordinating the free
speech fight, Woodbey was frequently threatened by vigilantes, and on
one occasion, he barely escaped death. *The Citizen*, the official organ of
the labor unions of southern California, reported in mid-April 1912:

> Rev. Woodbey, a negro preacher, has been threatened for his
> activity. A few nights ago he was taken to his home by a commit-
> tee from the Free Speech League. As the party left the car at a

corner near Woodbey's home an automobile was noticed in front of the house. Upon examination it was found to contain two armed men. Across the street another vigilante was stationed, and in the alley two more armed men were found. The strength of the committee with Woodbey probably saved his life, as members of the League challenged the vigilantes to do their dirty work. The preacher's house was patrolled by armed men from the League all night. [56]

The free speech fight in "barbarous San Diego" was still in full swing in late April 1912 when Woodbey left to attend the Socialist party national convention as a delegate from California. By the time he returned, the struggle was still continuing. He did what he could to help the cause, which was faced with certain defeat because of the power of the police, vigilantes, and state government. Wobblies continued to be clubbed and arrested, and there was little that could be done to prevent the wholesale violation of their civil rights. "They have the courts, the jails and funds," Laura Payne Emerson lamented. It was not until 1914 that the right of the IWW to hold street meetings was established. Although the ordinance still remained on the statute books, the police no longer interfered when Wobblies spoke at street corners in the forbidden district. On the invitation of the IWW, Reverend Woodbey was one of the regular speakers at such meetings. [57]

Woodbey's associations with the IWW may not have pleased some California socialists, and his role in the free speech fights probably disturbed members of his congregation. All the same, he was candidate for state treasurer on the socialist ticket in 1914, and he was still listed as pastor of Mount Zion Church in San Diego and a member of the state executive board of the Socialist party in *The Christian Socialist* of February 1915, which published two of his articles. These Woodbey's last known writings on socialism, were "What the Socialists Want" and "Why the Socialists Must Reach the Churches with Their Message." The first was in the form of a dialogue—a familiar Woodbey technique—between the minister (here called Parker) and George Stephenson, a black mail carrier. Stephenson asks to be told "in short, and the simplest way possible, just what it is you Socialists are trying to get anyway." Woodbey proceeds to enlighten him, pointing out the features of the socialist society which he had presented in greater detail in his earlier pamphlets. When the mail carrier leaves, convinced that there was no way to answer the arguments in favor of socialism, his teacher shouts after him: "Hold on a minute, we would solve the race problem of this and all other countries, by establishing the brotherhood of man which Christ taught."

In the second piece, Woodbey insists that the socialists would never succeed unless they won over "the millions of working people who belong to the various churches of the country," and he proceeds to indicate how he did his part in this endeavor. His chief weapon was to play up the point that "the economic teaching of the Bible and of Socialism are the same, and that for that reason he [the church member] must accept Socialism in order to stand consistently by the teaching of his own religion." After having shown the church member that the Bible, "in every line of it," was "with the poor and against their oppressors," it was necessary to convince him that the solution for the ills of society was not charity, which was at best "only a temporary relief," but the collective ownership and operation of the industries. The last point had to be reached slowly and step by step, but if the socialist agitator kept using the Bible as his authority, he would carry the church member along to that conclusion. The danger was, Woodbey maintained, that too many socialists antagonized church members by linking antireligion with socialism. Therefore, he advised against using agitators "who do not understand the Christian people, to carry this message, for the reason that they are sure to say something that will spoil the whole thing."

We know nothing of Reverend Woodbey after 1915, but at this point in his career, he was still as confirmed a socialist as ever. "I would not vote for my own wife on a platform which did not have the Socialist message in it," he told an audience in December 1914. [58]

Just how many blacks Woodbey converted by the method he outlined in his last socialist writing is impossible to determine. Hubert H. Harrison, a militant black socialist in New York, said of Woodbey's work as a national party organizer: "He has been very effective." [59] At least one prominent black socialist attributed his conversion to socialism to Reverend Woodbey. In the *Chicago Daily Socialist* of September 29, 1908, Reverend George W. Slater, Jr., pastor of the Zion Tabernacle in that city, wrote:

> For years I have felt that there was something wrong with our government. A few weeks ago I heard Comrade Woodbey, a colored national organizer of the Socialist Party, speaking on the streets of Chicago. He showed me plainly the trouble and the remedy. From that time on I have been an ardent supporter of the Socialist cause.

## REVEREND GEORGE W. SLATER, JR.

We know little about Reverend Slater before he became a socialist. The *Chicago Daily Socialist* engaged him to write a series of articles for the paper under the general heading "Negroes Becoming Socialists," but it did not bother to introduce him to its readers with any biographical sketch. However, in the first article of this series, "How and Why I Became a Socialist," Reverend Slater reveals that during the winter of 1907-1908, a period of rising unemployment and economic distress resulting from the Panic of 1907 and the ensuing business recession, he had tried to alleviate the sufferings of his black parishioners by organizing a cooperative enterprise through which they might purchase goods at savings of between 25 and 30 percent. The giant manufacturers frowned upon the venture, however, and he was unable to purchase supplies. The salesmen for the companies told him frankly that any dealer furnishing him with supplies would be driven out of business by the manufacturers. [60]

This experience opened his eyes to the futility of trying to alleviate the sufferings of poor blacks under the existing economic system. When he heard Woodbey's analysis of how only socialism could help abolish poverty, he was immediately converted and joined the Socialist party. Once converted, Slater eagerly assumed the task of recruiting blacks for the party. This he did by means of weekly sermons in his church, by the distribution of his pamphlet *Blackmen, Strike for Liberty*, and especially through the articles he published in the *Chicago Daily Socialist*, beginning with the issue of September 8, 1908, and ending with that of March 27, 1909. Although they appeared for only a limited time, Slater's articles marked the first time in American history that a socialist organ carried writings by a black American on a regular basis.

In several ways, Slater's articles reflected the Socialist party position on the Negro question. When asked by black correspondents what the socialists would do for the Negro, he fell back on quoting answers to these questions already published in the *Appeal to Reason* and the *Chicago Daily Socialist*, the main tenor of which was that they would do nothing except give the Negro the same opportunities as those enjoyed by whites. [61] Again, in his article "Booker T. Washington's Error," Slater leaned on arguments familiar to readers of the socialist press. He insisted that industrial training would actually hurt the black worker, since it would enable him to compete more effectively with whites. The trained black worker, being less inclined to unionization and strikes than the white worker, would be preferred by the capitalists and thus displace the whites. This, in turn, would exacerbate antiblack prejudice in white working-class circles. What, then, was the solution? It was not to deprive blacks of education and training, but

> to remove from the realm of competition the exertions of men in the full life, liberty and the pursuit of happiness, and the right to earn an honest and adequate livelihood for themselves and loved ones, and to place such endeavors in the realm of collective

cooperation wherein the government guarantees every man equal justice and opportunity.

In short, under capitalism, the education and training of black workers would only make their plight worse since it would intensify hostility toward them, while under socialism, with competition to earn a living no longer a problem, it would be a useful tool. 62

In socialist literature, blacks trained in the industrial schools and "brainwashed" by Booker T. Washington to avoid unions and strikes were said to be preferred by capitalists and to be displacing white workers. In real life, however, the blacks with such industrial training found that, owing to the racist policies and practices of employers and unions alike, they could not obtain employment at the trades for which they had been trained. 63 Ida B. Wells-Barnett, the militant black Chicago woman, was closer to the truth than Slater when she wrote at about the same time as his article on Booker T. Washington appeared:

> The black man who has a trade at his fingers' ends finds all forces combined to prevent him from making a living thereby. First, the employer tells him that he has no prejudice against color, but that his employes will object and make his business suffer. If perchance the Negro gets by, is given a chance to make good, the employes in the office, factory and workshop combine to injure his work and to make life miserable for him. 64

Even in the South, the skilled black craftsman found it increasingly difficult to obtain employment. By 1899, the Virginia commissioner of labor reported that there were "fewer skilled Negro laborers in the state than there were before the Civil War." 65 Substantially the same picture emerged from reports from other Southern states. In the next few years, this trend intensified and was documented by W.E.B. Du Bois in *The Negro Artisan*. 66

The trouble was that blacks as good as or better than white workers had little chance to earn a living as skilled artisans. Reverend C. S. Smith of Nashville, a critic of Booker T. Washington, asked: "How can the multiplication of Negro mechanics help to solve the so-called race problem, when those who are already skilled cannot obtain employment?" 67 Even Slater himself had a glimpse of this problem, for in his article "Pullman Porter Pity," he seemed to understand that a job as a Pullman porter was often the only work an educated, trained black could obtain. 68

Slater's article on the Pullman porter is typical of his concern with immediate political and economic issues rather than with the religious aspects of socialism. He was more interested in trying to prove that Lincoln was a socialist than that Christ had espoused ideals similar to those ad-vocated by scientific socialism. Of course, in the process, he exaggerated and distorted Lincoln's position. He correctly quoted Lincoln's state-ments on labor and capital, such as his declaration that "Labor is prior to, and independent of capital . . . in fact, capital is the fruit of labor" and that "to secure to each laborer the whole product of his labor, as nearly as possible, is a worthy object of any government." But he overlooked Lin-coln's emphasis on the identity of the interests of labor and capital, and his belief that because equality of opportunity existed in American soci-ety, the laborer could easily become a capitalist. He certainly did not quote (if he knew it) Lincoln's advice to workingmen: "Let not him who is houseless, pull down the house of another; but let him labor diligently and build one for himself, thus by example assuring that his own shall be safe from violence when built." While Lincoln was an advocate of the rights of labor, he was certainly no believer in socialism. 69

Despite such exaggerations and the limitations inherent in his ap-proach because of the influence of socialist ideology on the Negro ques-tion, Slater dealt with political and economic issues boldly and effec-tively. His article on the Pullman porter is not only one of the earliest discussions in print of the problems facing these workers, but it is also a masterful destruction of the myths surrounding their work. His criticism of the Republican and Democratic candidates in the 1908 election and his arguments as to why blacks should vote for Debs went beyond rhetoric. He filled his articles with statistics on the terrible conditions facing the working class, discussed the indifference of both Republican and Demo-cratic candidates to this problem, and then contrasted this position with that of the socialist candidate. He emphasized that blacks would have the most to gain from a socialist victory:

> The colored man is the worst off of all the working class of people. This is because he gets less wages, less protection, less educa-tion, pays more for food, clothing, house rent, etc.
>
> Why is this so? It is because this government is so run that the necessities of life, such as food, clothing, houses, etc., are pro-duced more for the purpose of permitting a few men to make profit out of them rather than to use them for the benefit of all the people. That is, that in order for the rich men to make money you must work for him for much less than you produce for him. There-fore, the colored man, being the weakest and least-protected, is at the greatest disadvantage, hence he is the most ill-treated. . . .
>
> Let me urge you to get a Socialist Party platform and read it very carefully, and then vote for your own interests as poor peo-

ple for your wife and children—by voting the Socialist ticket straight. 70

Slater proudly announced that he had set himself the "task of reaching 1,000,000 colored people with the great message of Socialism," and he urged comrades to help him distribute his literature in black communities. 71 In the *Chicago Daily Socialist* of January 4, 1909, John H. Cummings, himself a black socialist, reported that Slater was "reaching thousands of our people with the great message of Socialism," and he urged every "colored man or woman" to "write to him."

There is no way of knowing just how many blacks Slater actually reached or how many he converted. Since the number of black delegates to Socialist party national conventions remained the same after the campaign to reach one million as it had been before—that is, one delegate— the likelihood is that he did not get very far. However, Slater certainly impressed leading white socialists. His descriptions of the welcome he received from white comrades, especially among Jewish socialists, 72 his emphasis that socialists were the "New Abolitionists," 73 his advice to black workers not to allow themselves under any circumstances to be used as strikebreakers, 74 and his repeated insistence that only through socialism could the problems of all workers, regardless of race or color, be solved—all appealed to white socialists. Since he never criticized the Socialist party for failing to mount a campaign against disfranchisement, segregation, lynching, and peonage in the South—subjects he himself never discussed—white comrades had little reason to feel embarrassed by his writings. At any rate, Eugene V. Debs hailed Slater as an "educated, wide-awake teacher of his race" who was "doing excellent work in educating the black men and women of the country and showing them that their proper place is in the Socialist movement." Fred D. Warren, editor of the *Appeal to Reason*, congratulated Slater on his "splendid work" and urged the party to assist him in his endeavor to reach blacks. Other white socialists wrote of how deeply they were moved by his articles and how happy they were that the socialist press was enabling such writings to appear in print. A typical letter went:

> I have been reading some of your valuable articles in the Chicago Daily Socialist.
>
> A few days ago, when I read your account of the meeting at which the Jew clasped your hand and exclaimed: "Isn't this great?" I said, "yes, that is great, that a Jew could clasp hands in so righteous a cause with the black man."

I extend to you, dear comrade, my hand across the long miles and thank you for your good work for the greatest of all causes — Socialism. Your work is a grand one. Few of us realize what an influence for our cause you are putting into being. . . .

I am rated with the Caucasian race, but I don't think my heart or hopes are whiter than yours. I know my work can never be as grand as yours promises to be. [75]

Slater's last article in the *Chicago Daily Socialist* was a summary of his lecture on "The Race Problem" before the Labor Lyceum of Rochester, New York. In this lecture, he criticized the ideas of Booker T. Washington, dismissed emigration as a solution for the problem, assured his listeners that blacks were not "trying to secure social equality with the whites," and stressed that the "solution" of the race problem lay only in socialism. He concluded: "The Socialist party, which teaches these things in its program, is the party which will solve the problems of the black man, as well as those of his white brother." [76]

Although he stopped contributing to the *Chicago Daily Socialist* after March 1909, Slater did not cease his work for the party. When Local New York of the Socialist party attempted to win Negro votes in the municipal campaign of the fall of 1911, it called upon Slater for aid. He furnished it with a pamphlet, "The Colored Man's Case As Socialism Sees It," which was widely distributed in Negro circles. [77] (All copies of the pamphlet, along with other pamphlets by Slater, have disappeared.) From 1912 to 1919, Reverend Slater is listed in the city directory of Clinton, Iowa, as pastor of the Bethel African Church. [78] From that city, he distributed a prosocialist monthly, *Western Evangel*, no copies of which are in existence. In addition, in the fall of 1912, the *Cleveland Citizen* reported that Slater had formed a "Negro Socialist Literature and Lecture Bureau," and was sponsoring a national conference of colored men in Chicago "to create a nationwide interest in socialism." [79] It is doubtful that the conference ever took place, since there is no report of it in the Chicago press, including the *Chicago Daily Socialist*.

In 1913, Slater was appointed secretary to the Colored Race for the Christian Socialist Fellowship. In that capacity, he published several articles in *The Christian Socialist*. One was "The Negro and Socialism," in which he assured his readers that a great opportunity existed for spreading socialist ideology among blacks. Not only were they "almost to a man . . . of the working class" and thus naturally receptive to such ideas, but even black professionals, including clergymen, were beginning to evince interest in socialism. Apart from the fact that the work of reaching them had been "woefully neglected," it could only be effectively conducted by supplying blacks with "simple literature on the subject written by some colored man. The fact that some colored person wrote it will get their attention and they will read it through carefully."[80] Fortunately, Slater indicated he had just the literature needed — his own *Blackmen, Strike for Liberty* and Dr. J. T. Whitson's *The Advantages Socialism Offers to the Negro*. He informed the comrades that they could obtain copies in quantity by writing to him in Clinton.

In the other articles, Slater again argued that Lincoln had been basically a socialist, buttressing this argument with quotations from his statements favoring labor over capital.[81] He took issue with R. R. Wright, the editor of *The Christian Recorder*, who contended that while socialism had much about it that was praiseworthy, it could not replace the social service of the church in meeting the needs of the poorer classes. Here, for the first time, Slater dealt with socialism from a religious viewpoint. In the manner made familiar by Reverend Woodbey, he pointed out that "Scientific Socialism is the only systematic expression of the social message of Jesus." Social service dealt merely with symptoms, while socialism addressed itself to the abolition of wage slavery, "the main root of our social misery." Since socialism took no account of religions, and since its doctrines were the logical fulfillment of what the prophets, Jesus, and the Apostles had sought, "should not Christians, the Church, and its social service element say Amen?" he asked. [82]

After 1919, Slater's name disappeared from the Clinton directory, but he probably remained in that area. In a letter of March 27, 1921, from that city to John Fitzpatrick, president of the Chicago Federation of Labor, he listed himself as "evangelist, Biblical, Economic, Spiritual" operating in the Iowa town, and that his special subjects were "Jesus," "The Modern Dance, "Assimilation vs. Isolation," "Courtship and Marriage," "Racial Problems," and "The Rustic City." The last-named appears to have been a cooperative interracial venture that Slater sponsored. Evidently, Fitzpatrick was sufficiently interested in "The Rustic City" to ask Slater for more information. In his reply, the Iowa evangelist enclosed a rough plan which, unfortunately, is no longer in the Fitzpatrick Papers. In his letter accompanying the plan, Slater wrote:

> With great appreciation, I note what you say of our efficient activity in bringing about a better understanding between the labor unions and the leaders of the colored people. For many years I have had the opinion that a more thorough understanding and cooperation on the part of both the colored people and labor unions would do very appreciably much to eradicate the cause of the most vexatious feature of their common problems. For after all the cause of the racial element of the industrial prob-

lem is basically economic. All workers are in the same maelstrom, and it will take the combined effort of all of them to get out. [83]

## OTHER BLACK CHRISTIAN SOCIALISTS

The February 1915 issue of *The Christian Socialist*, dedicated to the memory of Abraham Lincoln, was the first in that socialist monthly to devote significant attention to the Negro. In addition to articles by Reverends Woodbey and Slater, it included one by Reverend S. C. Garrison, pastor of the Negro Church of Montpelier, Indiana. Garrison's article linked Jesus, Lincoln, and John Brown to the activities of the Socialist party, and noted particularly that "while the great Lincoln freed our bodies Socialism will free our minds, then there will be a greater spiritual development. Until we have a more sane system of production and distribution it is insane to expect further spiritual development." [84] The same issue also included the piece "A Potato Patch Philosopher: Socialism As Seen by a Negro Sage Who Works All Day in His Garden and Philosophizes All Night." The author, C. V. Auguste, was described as "a negro philosopher of St. Petersburg, Fla."

In presenting this special issue, *The Christian Socialist* announced that "the sons of the black slaves are showing white serfs how they may both be freed." It acknowledged that there might be white workers who would "scorn to read a negro's word," but it advised them to bear in mind that with black strikebreaking on the increase, white workers would only be fooling themselves if they believed they could solve their problems by ignoring those of the Negro: "If the white workers should organize, even to the last man, and leave the negro unorganized, their efforts are utterly in vain. Six million negro workmen will stand ready to leap into the places of their white brethren—unless they understand SOLIDARITY." Hence, every worker, regardless of color, should be reached with this special issue. [85]

It is open to question whether *The Christian Socialist* converted any blacks to socialism. The truth is that all black Christian Socialists overlooked the fact that their people were primarily concerned with how to earn a living, how to halt the daily threats to their lives, how to educate their children, how to escape peonage and the convict labor system, and how to end their status of disfranchised, segregated second-class citizenship. Promising them a future life in a cooperative commonwealth without these burdens was hardly conducive to winning many to the cause of socialism.

With all their shortcomings, the black Christian Socialists were outstanding propagandists for the cause. They did not hide either their hatred of capitalism or their belief in socialism. Most of them suffered for their convictions and one, Reverend Woodbey, went to jail for upholding the right of socialists and workers in general to bring their message to the people. Even though they are hardly ever mentioned in studies of American socialism, [86] and not at all in those of Christian Socialism, they deserve a high place in the history of black protest.

*        *        *

Not all black socialist ministers were concerned primarily with convincing their people that their problems could only be solved in the new socialist society. At least one devoted himself to the battle to eliminate their grievances in the present society. He was Reverend George Frazier Miller.

Born in South Carolina in 1864, Miller was educated at Howard, the General Theological Seminary, and New York University. He served in churches in the Carolinas, but from 1896 until his death in 1943, he was the rector of St. Augustine's Church in Brooklyn, New York. Early in the twentieth century, he was elected president of the National Equal Rights League, an organization dedicated to combatting disfranchisement, segregation, and every other aspect of second-class citizenship for black Americans. [87] Thus, by the time Reverend Miller became a socialist, he already had a career as a militant black spokesman, a friend of W.E.B. Du Bois, and one who was concerned with the day-to-day problems of his people. To this he now added the conviction that socialism was a vastly superior form of society to capitalism. At the same time, he never adopted the attitude that one had to await the creation of this superior society in order to solve many of the problems facing blacks.

Miller's entrance into the Socialist party occurred in the fall of 1906 and was noted in the following report in *The Worker* of October 27, 1906, over the heading "Conversion of a Negro Preacher":

> Comrades and friends of the Socialist cause, crowding Silver Hall [in New York City] to its utmost capacity, cheered and applauded a new colored comrade who, in the course of a remarkable address, announced his adhesion to the tenets of Socialism.
>
> Rev. George Frazier Miller wore for the first time on a public platform the red button with the arm and torch. He was fittingly introduced by Comrade Passage, our nominee for state treasurer.

*The Worker* did not publish any part of Miller's "remarkable address," but, as we shall see in the next section, the "new colored comrade" was now to become part of a group of New York socialists who were to bring a new dimension to the party's approach to the Negro question.

# 8

# The Socialists and the Founding of the National Association for the Advancement of Colored People

## THE NIAGARA MOVEMENT

In his classic *The Souls of Black Folk*, published in April 1903, W.E.B. Du Bois rejected Booker T. Washington's policies, basically on the ground that they had failed to fulfill their promises. He pointed out that in his "Atlanta Compromise" speech of 1895 and in subsequent addresses, Washington had urged blacks to "cast your buckets where you are," to forgo political and civil rights, and to concentrate on proving their worthiness for these rights by acquiring skills through industrial education and the ownership of land. Moreover, Washington had held out the promise that, by accumulating material resources, blacks would ultimately gain equality and respect among whites. To all of this, Du Bois asked, what had happened since 1895? And he answered: "1. The disfranchisement of the Negro. 2. The legal creation of a distinct status of civil inferiority. 3. The steady withdrawal of aid from institutions for the higher training of the Negro." [1]

In June 1905, Du Bois sent the following letter to selected Negro leaders — mostly professionals and intellectuals, but including a few businessmen: "The time seems more than ripe for organized, determined and aggressive action on the part of men who believe in Negro freedom and growth. Movements are on foot threatening individual freedom and our self respect. I write you to propose a Conference during the coming summer." [2]

The conference was planned to be held near Buffalo, New York, in July. Du Bois requested accommodations on the New York side of Niagara Falls, but the hotels refused him. The hotels on the Canadian side opened their facilities to the black Americans. Since the meeting was held near the Falls, they called it the Niagara Movement. A set of principles was adopted denouncing the deprivation of suffrage and the denial of civil liberties, economic and educational opportunities, and equality before the law," and condemning those American institutions, including the trade unions, which cooperated in drawing the color line in the nation's life. 3

These significant developments in the black liberation struggle were for the most part ignored by the socialists. As we have seen Booker T. Washington had long been a target of socialist criticism, mainly because of his advice that blacks should offer themselves as a pool of cheap, reliable labor; shun alliances with white workers, especially in labor unions; and seek an alliance instead with their "natural friends," the capitalists. On the question of Washington's willingness to surrender political and civil rights, the socialists, themselves no great champions of these rights for blacks, were usually silent. Moreover, Washington's advice to blacks that they should assure whites "that their privileges of social equality will not be challenged by us" was certainly not a position that socialists would be inclined to criticize, since they, too, denied favoring "social equality." Therefore, it is not surprising that Du Bois' *The Souls of Black Folk*, although it was widely reviewed at the time of its publication, 4 went almost unnoticed in the socialist press. In fact, the only socialist who commented on the work was Horace L. Traubel, and this was in his own Philadelphia-based paper, the *Conservator*. Traubel praised the book for its "eloquence" and for its demands for justice for black Americans. However, he criticized Du Bois for failing to understand, as the socialists did, that the problem of the black worker was essentially the same as that of the white worker: "Du Bois falls down when he shows that he fails to see how the true labor problems north and south are one problem. The negro suffers more than the usual handicap. That I admit. But his trouble on the whole is the trouble of the factory operative or miner." 5

The socialist press completely ignored the formation of the Niagara Movement in the summer of 1905. Indeed, the first notice of the movement's existence came in *The Worker* of October 20, 1906, fully fifteen months after its historic founding meeting. 6 Despite its tardiness, the notice is significant in the history of American socialism and black Americans, since it also announced the existence of a group of socialists in New York City who were seeking to assist the struggle for full equality launched by the Niagara Movement. Soon, indeed, the two were to unite forces in a common struggle to achieve this goal.

## THE COSMOPOLITAN CLUB

André Tridon, a French psychiatrist who had become an important figure in the New York Socialist party and was an editor of *Wilshire's Magazine*, commented on the Niagara Movement in his article "Socialism and the Race Question" in *The Worker*. He began his article with the observation that the manifesto drawn up by the movement indicated that the Negro was "becoming tired of aping the white man and of submitting without protest to the white man's social and political whims." Booker T. Washington's advice to blacks to "keep quiet and try to be popular" was evidently losing its influence. One indication of this, Tridon noted (after a discussion of the Negro's "criminal tendency," which was not without racist overtones) was the existence in New York of a society composed of blacks and whites who met regularly in each other's homes to discuss how to struggle against the "rising tide" of oppression. Its aim, according to its constitution and bylaws, was "to study the grievances of the various downtrodden races (with a special reference to the colored races), and as far as possible to devise ways and means to improve their condition." According to Tridon, the members of the society were reaching the conclusion that socialism was "the remedy long looked for and hoped for in the fight against race prejudice." Indeed, the society had already converted two Brooklyn clergymen "to the idea that Socialism is a good thing." (Although he did not name names, it is clear that one of the converts was Reverend George Frazier Miller, the black clergyman.) The article closed: "Any one desiring further information regarding the Cosmopolitan Society can secure the same by addressing André Tridon, 229 East Twenty-First Street, New York City." [7]

Tridon's article in *The Worker* was the first public notice of the existence of the Cosmopolitan Club. Three weeks earlier, Mary White Ovington, a young settlement house worker who was descended from Massachusetts abolitionists and who had immersed herself in the study of the Negro question, had written to Oswald Garrison Villard, grandson of the great abolitionist and editor of the *New York Evening Post*, informing him of the existence of the Cosmopolitan Club. She stated that it was composed of "white and colored people," as well as "a charming Hindoo gentleman." The club met at the houses of its different members where discussions were held "on race questions, usually." It had been in existence for four months, but had not done anything in the way of "practical work." As far as Ovington knew, it was "the only club in which the two races appear in almost equal numbers in the city." [8] She did not indicate how many members the club had, but from other evidence, it is clear that there were about fifty. Again, although Ovington was a socialist, she said nothing in her letter about discussions of socialism at club meetings.

While socialists were active in forming and promoting the club, it is likely that Tridon exaggerated the extent to which the members were becoming convinced that socialism offered "the remedy long looked and hoped for in the fight against race prejudice."

The Cosmopolitan Club probably grew out of the Cosmopolitan Club movement which began on March 12, 1903, at the University of Wisconsin, where sixteen foreign and two native-American students, representing eleven nationalities, met in the apartment of a young Japanese. They formed the Cosmopolitan Club in which "the representatives of every nation in the university were to meet on a basis of equality and brotherhood." As the name indicated, it was to be a *cosmopolitan* organization, "with universal brotherhood as its cornerstone." It was to be based on the principle that all races and people were equal and that such inequality as existed was the product of erroneous ideas as to the natural inferiority of certain races and peoples. The idea spread rapidly in American universities, and in 1907, a National Association of Cosmopolitan Clubs was formed. [9]

It was likely from this movement that Ovington obtained the idea of an interracial association in New York City for discussions of the racial problems in the United States. After interesting others, she called the first meeting in her home in Brooklyn Heights.

All of the black members were convinced that Booker T. Washington's approach to the problems of the Negro people—narrow economic advancement at the price of social equality, together with limited vocational education and subordinate political status—was to a large extent responsible for the steady deterioration of the Negro's position in American life. Most of them applauded Du Bois' attack on Washington in 1903 and had joined with him in the Niagara Movement. The white members were composed of men like John E. Milholland, a wealthy Republican who had founded the Constitutional League of the United States in 1903 because he was convinced that establishing the constitutional rights of Negroes could best be accomplished through court actions. These men had at first supported Washington and his work, but they were becoming increasingly alarmed by his program's failure to prevent the Negro from slipping further and further into the ranks of second-class citizenship and peonage. They were especially troubled by the absence of any white voices in the North in defense of the Negro and his rights, while there was a proliferation of voices expressing approval of white supremacy in the South as the correct solution of the Negro question. Where, they asked, did the descendants of the abolitionists stand? Most were either silent or were concurring in the view that the entire post-Civil War effort to elevate the Negro to full citizenship had been a mistake. [10]

Some of the white members of the Cosmopolitan Club, like Milholland, had been active in the anti-imperialist movement at the turn of the century; they had seen how imperialism intensified racism by propounding the doctrine of "the white man's burden." They saw, too, how the imperialists sought to justify their depriving the nonwhite populations of the Philippines, Puerto Rico, Hawaii, and Cuba of the right to determine their own destiny. They did this by employing the argument that the white South had been correct in insisting on the dominance of the Anglo-Saxon in Southern society, with the Negro firmly fixed "in his place" — at the bottom. These club members had also observed that even anti-imperialists utilized racism in their arguments by maintaining that the United States should not obtain colonial possessions overseas since it already had enough inferior nonwhite people within its own borders. 11

It was by now the dominant view in the North that the South knew the Negro best and that it should be left to solve the Negro question as it saw fit — which meant total white supremacy and the lynching of any Negro who challenged this state of affairs. It was against this trend that the members of the Cosmopolitan Club sought, cautiously and privately, to develop a counterforce.

Among the members of the Cosmopolitan Club were some socialists, men and women who had reached the conclusion that the main problem facing the Negro was economic; that capitalism, North and South, was intensifying the use of racism as a weapon to keep the working class divided and weakened; and that the Northern capitalists lavishly supported Washington's program in order to assure themselves of a docile labor force to utilize against a militant labor organization. The socialists in the Cosmopolitan Club were not content to echo the party contention that the Negro question was *only economic*. They refused to accept the belief that "social equality" was of no consequence and should be shunted aside, and that disfranchisement, segregation, and even lynching were only secondary issues that should not divert attention from the need for creating a socialist society in which the problems of the Negro workers, as well as those of the white working class, would automatically be solved. They saw the necessity of waging a struggle for the full civil and political rights of Negroes under the existing socioeconomic system. They believed that this struggle should take priority over the battle to achieve liberation for the Negro through the establishment of a socialist society. Indeed, they feared that, unless such a battle was waged, the Negroes would be pushed so deeply into an inferior status that there would be little hope of rescuing them by any change in the system.

Mary White Ovington was typical of this group of socialists. Daughter of a well-to-do New York merchant, educated in exclusive private schools and at Radcliffe College, she was expected by her family to take her proper place in society. But, like Caroline H. Pemberton of Philadelphia, she came into contact with "how the other half lived." "I found out about conditions in my own city of which I was utterly ignorant," she wrote later. In 1896, Ovington opened a settlement house "among the white working-class people" in Greenpoint, Brooklyn. Her five-room house grew into a forty-room settlement in the seven years she remained there. "That I should later work for the Negro never entered my mind," she wrote. 12

This statement may seem strange coming from a descendant of abolitionists who as a child had listened to tales of the Underground Railroad and of the riots against abolitionists who dared to speak up for freedom for the slaves. Garrison, she recalled, "was my childhood's greatest hero." But after 1870, the Ovingtons, like most abolitionists, believed they had accomplished their goal. Slavery was ended, and under the Fourteenth and Fifteenth Amendments, Negroes had been made at least legally equal American citizens. It was time to turn their attention to other issues, such as civil service reform and tariff reductions. To be sure, James M. McPherson rejects this view in his recent study, *The Abolitionist Legacy: From Reconstruction to the NAACP*, and argues that abolitionists, especially the former followers of William Lloyd Garrison, remained active in racial reform efforts down to the twentieth century. However, the evidence he marshalls is not very convincing. 13

In any case, Mary White Ovington gradually came to realize that, even though slavery had ended, much more remained to be done. Part of this realization came from hearing Booker T. Washington speak before the Social Reform Club of New York City, of which she was a member. Although, as she later recalled, Washington "did not shine particularly that night," he made her aware of the fact that "there was a Negro problem in my city. I had honestly never thought of it before." 14

Booker T. Washington may have reawakened Ovington's interest in the Negro people, but it was W.E.B. Du Bois who gave it concrete direction. She had read Du Bois' articles on "The Black North" in the *New York Times Magazine* in 1901. Two of them dealt with New York City, and these inspired her to begin an intensive study of the New York Negro. 15 In the summer of 1904, she received a fellowship from the Committee on Social Investigations, connected with Greenwich House, for a one-year study of conditions among New York blacks. Her work culminated in the publication in 1911 of *Half A Man: The Status of the Negro in New York*, with a foreword by the distinguished anthropologist Franz Boas. Only a year after she began her studies, she revealed her deepening understanding of the problem in an article "The Negro Family in New York," published in *Charities* of October 1905. Here she broke with the idea, so popular in settlement house circles, that "philanthropy" was the answer for the black poor. Already a socialist, she also dissented from the common conception in the party that Negroes were just like any other workers under capitalism. "I accepted the Negro as any other element in the population," she wrote later of her view soon after she became a socialist. "That he suffered more from poverty, from segregation, from prejudice, than any other race in the city was a new idea to me." [16] In her article, Ovington pointed out that Negroes were among many poor in New York City, but she noted that a higher percentage of them were poverty-stricken than any other group. While many of the other working-class groups were poor, "the greatest majority of Negroes of New York live in poverty" and were mired in unskilled, menial occupations. Sixty-two percent of the men were in domestic and personal services, and in large stores and factories, "they do the work of porter or general utility man, not the better tasks." Only a very few practiced a trade. Black women were not able "in any numbers" to obtain work in a factory or shop. "The result," she concluded, "is a group of people receiving a low wage, and the character of their homes must be largely determined by their economic position."

She found, too, that the Negro faced a double exploitation. Not only did blacks, like the poor in general, live in slum tenements, but "the Negroes pay more and get less for their money than any other tenants." Restricted by racism to a narrow area in which to live, they were forced to pay whatever the landlord charged. For the same reason, Negroes in New York paid higher prices for inferior food than did white workers. Thus, while all of New York's immigrant working-class population faced poverty, abuse, and ridicule, the Negro faced all this and more. His case was "an exaggerated one," since he was treated as a member of a population basically of an "inherent and eternal inferiority," excluded from most of the trade unions and deprived of the opportunity to move out of his place on the lowest rung of the economic ladder. [17]

Ovington therefore rejected the view so common in the Socialist party that there was no special Negro question and that under capitalism all workers were exploited equally. She also rejected the view that "social equality" was not an important issue, for she became convinced, on the basis of her studies, that it was precisely because whites had so little close contacts with blacks that the view that Negroes were inherently inferior had gained currency.

Ovington practiced what she preached. Together with John E. Milholland, she went to see Henry Phipps, steel magnate and philanthropist, who had constructed model tenement houses for immigrants in New York City, to persuade him to construct a model tenement for the Negroes of San Juan Hill. When the Tuskegee Apartments were completed on West 63rd Street in 1907—a fireproof, steam-heated, roof-gardened, six-story house—Ovington moved into them, the only white person in the entire house. [18]

Mary White Ovington represented a different, though minor, strain in the American socialism of the early twentieth century. As a socialist, she was convinced that the collective ownership of the means of production and distribution was the only real answer to the Negro question. But she did not believe that the struggle for the Negro's civil and political rights should be neglected while the struggle for socialism was being waged. (In fact, so important did she regard the campaign for civil and political rights that, for all her understanding of the economic hardships black New Yorkers faced, she tended at times to overlook the need for a struggle on the economic front.) She believed, moreover, that the Negro could not be forced into seeing the virtues of socialism. He had to make his own decisions. The chances of winning him to socialism were much greater if he could identify the Socialist party with the struggle to solve his day-to-day problems in the existing society. This view was shared by the other socialist members of the Cosmopolitan Club. [19]

The club, whose membership had grown to eighty by early 1908, might have continued as a little-known medium for interracial cooperation between black and white New Yorkers had it not been for the first event sponsored by the club outside of the private meetings at members' homes. At Ovington's suggestion, it was decided to hold a public dinner to which guests would be invited. The gathering took place in Peck's Restaurant on lower Fulton Street, where Ovington had recently attended a socialist dinner. About a hundred persons were present, including Ovington, Oswald Garrison Villard, Hamilton Holt, editor of *The Independent*, John Spargo, the socialist editor and lecturer, Max Barber of *The Voice of the Negro*, Reverend George F. Miller, and A. B. Humphrey of the Constitutional League. One Hindu, a club member, was also present at the interracial dinner.

Dr. O. M. Waller, black secretary of the Cosmopolitan Club, chaired the meeting and introduced the after-dinner speakers. The principal object of the occasion, he declared, was to bring together "white, black and yellow races in order that they may exchange thoughts and become better acquainted." [20] The speakers included Villard, Barber, André Tridon, Reverend Miller, Holt, Ovington, Spargo, and Miss M. R. Lyons, a Brooklyn school teacher. While there was some discussion of intermarriage, it was deliberately played down. The following day, Villard wrote his uncle, Francis Jackson Garrison, that he thought the dinner was "a really remarkable gathering. . . . The speaking was of a high order." Unfortunately, he added, the newspapers had "made a great sensation" out of the dinner, and as a result, he doubted if the work of the club could "go on for the present at least." [21]

What had happened was that halfway through the dinner, reporters entered the dining room and a photographer stood on a chair to take flash pictures of black men, white men, black women, and white women dining together. After messages of protest were sent to the head table, they were prohibited from taking pictures. But the next day, New York newspapers filled in with words what the photographs would have shown, and added interpretations that the pictures would not have revealed. The New York *World* headlined its report soberly: "The Cosmopolitans to Aid the Negro. Race Speakers Discuss the Problem at Society's Dinner, Crisis in North Also, Says One." [22] The headlines in other papers screamed: "Social Equality! Intermarriage Advocated! White Women and Negro Men Dine Together!" [23] The *New York American*, a Hearst paper, reported: "Social equality and intermarriage between the races were advocated last night at a banquet where twenty white girls and women dined side by side at table with negro men and women." [24] The *New York Times* not only outdid the *American* in the luridness of its report, but also carried an editorial that Villard described as "villainous" and one that "outsoutherns the Southerns." The editorial, headed "As an Admonition," denounced the dinner as a socialist plot to destroy American society by secretly establishing intermarriage of whites and blacks while publicly parading behind the slogan of "brotherhood." [25]

As the news of the dinner spread southward, it became more and more titillating; the sober diners were depicted as "making love at a Bacchanal feast." The *New York Herald* filled columns with reports of how the South was "Roused by Mixed Race Feast." Headlines in the *Washington Evening Post*, *Richmond Times-Dispatch*, *Charleston News & Courier*, and *Savannah News* blared: "Racial Equality Feast. White Girls Seated Next to Colored Men at Dinner. Cheers for Intermarriage. Socialism and Free Love the Solution of the Race Problem." [26] Editorially, the Southern press condemned the "disgraceful performances" in New York City. "This miscegenation dinner," raged the *St. Louis Dispatch*, "was loathsome enough to consign the whole fraternity of persons who participated in it to undying infamy." Southern blacks were warned not to expect that a new era was opening in which they could marry white women. "Racial purity" would always remain the way of life in the South, they averred, no matter what Northern Socialists and their liberal dupes sought to accomplish. [27]

Southern judges, governors, and congressmen joined the chorus of denunciation. Judge Norwood of Savannah observed that it was bad enough that Ovington had invited Negro men to her home, but "the horror of it is she could take white girls into that den." [28] Congressman Tom Heflin of Alabama was brief and to the point: "The sensible negro had better take stock and study the sign of caution. There is danger ahead if the New York 'preachment' is followed by the negro." The implication was clear that whatever lynchings resulted could be placed directly at the door of the New York socialists and their miscegenationists allies. [29]

Ovington, Hamilton Holt, and André Tridon tried to halt the flood of denunciations by noting in letters to the press and in interviews that amalgamation of the races had not been advocated at the dinner. The only object of the gathering, they said, had been to enable blacks and whites to get to know each other better and together to explore the various aspects of the racial question. [30] The accounts in the press, Ovington commented, were not only vulgar distortions of what had actually happened, but they also served the purpose of teaching whites "a little of what the colored race has long encountered." [31] But the attacks continued, and Ovington received such obscene mail that she was forced to have her letters opened by her male relatives. [32]

Still, the Cosmopolitan Club dinner was not without its defenders. Writing in *The Public*, the progressive single-tax weekly published in Chicago, James F. Morton, Jr., denounced the press for "its work of falsification," observed that it revealed how racially bigoted editors, both North and South, were, and particularly condemned the Southern press for demanding that the North treat blacks as in the South. [33] While some blacks wrote to the press condemning the "extremists and faddists" at the dinner for having injured the cause of the Negro, [34] the black press, in general, attacked the white newspapers and defended the Cosmopolitan Club. The *New York Age* called the reports of the dinner "yellow journalism" at its worst, and praised the men and women who were present for seeking to create "a more friendly and God-like feeling among the various races of the country." [35] Writing in *Horizon*, the official organ of the Niagara Movement, Lafayette M. Hersaw, one of the regular contributors, commented under the heading "Forbidding to Do Good":

> The treatment of the Cosmopolitan Club of New York, by the daily press serves to call to attention several things about the attitude of mind of the American people towards the Negro. Foremost is the fact that there is a general sentiment which not only tolerates unfair treatment of the Negro, but actually demands it. This sentiment exhibits itself in the redicule, abuse and misrepresentation of those who try to bring to its normal condition the public mind when thinking of the Negro. Another thing is the fact that certain organs of public opinion wilfully, deliberately and maliciously lie about Negroes and the friends of Negroes. The dinner of the Cosmopolitan Club is a case in point. With but a few exceptions the daily papers have misrepresented and misstated not only the aims and purposes of the Cosmopolitan Club, but also what actually was said at the dinner. [36]

It is shameful that not a single socialist paper praised the Cosmopolitan Club and the diners, and that only one—the *Chicago Daily Social-*

*ist*—even commented on the affair. Its comment was a condemnation of the daily press, not so much for its distortion of what had taken place, but for promoting the idea that the dinner was sponsored and approved of by socialists. Its headline read: "Negro Banquet Used As Excuse to Take Rap at Socialists"; what followed was devoted largely to reporting the *New York Times'* editorial and then refuting it with the observation: "The Socialists had nothing to do with this affair." [37] The *Chicago Daily Socialist* conveniently overlooked such evidence as the fact that the dinner had been suggested by socialist Mary White Ovington and that socialists like Spargo, Tridon, and Reverend Miller, along with Ovington, had been among the speakers.

Since *The Worker* had expired on March 28, 1908, and the *New York Call* did not appear until May 30, 1908, New York City was without a socialist paper when the dinner took place. However, a month after the event, the *Call* did carry an interview with John E. Milholland in which it quoted the liberal Republican capitalist as calling the press criticism of the Cosmopolitan dinner "outrageous un-American" and as illustrating "how tenaciously our civilization clings to the past, when men and women were ostracized on account of race, color and other conditions for which they were not responsible." [38] The interview gave the *Call* the opportunity to comment editorially that socialists who had sponsored and participated in the dinner were of a different breed. Instead, the paper remained silent, clearly not anxious to associate the Socialist party with the social mingling of whites and blacks on an equal footing.

This position was actually that of the Socialist party's National Executive Committee. Among the Socialist party papers at Duke university Library is a document indicating that Spargo was called on the carpet following reports in the press that he had been one of the speakers at the Cosmopolitan Club dinner and that he had advocated "racial equality." The undated document is entitled "Race Question—John Spargo" and consists of Spargo's answer to the question: "Did John Spargo advocate racial equality at a socialist dinner in New York, April, 1908?" [39] (It is interesting that the National Executive Committee viewed the event as a "socialist dinner," while the *Chicago Daily Socialist* had sought to disassociate the movement from the affair.) Spargo's answer revealed his usual tendency to retreat in the face of criticism. According to press reports, he had told the diners that marriage was a personal matter to be decided by the parties involved. [40] In his report to the party, however, Spargo insisted that he spoke "with all the emphasis I could command against miscegenation and intermarriage as a peril to both black and white. I urged the negro leaders present not to give any support to the mistaken plea for intermarriage in the name of racial equality." Spargo assured the party leadership that he could have made his speech "in any great southern city without arousing the hostility of intelligent white citizens." It is difficult to understand just what he meant, in view of the paranoid reaction to the dinner by Southern editors, judges, and legislators.

Oswald Garrison Villard was convinced that the press campaign had sealed the doom of the Cosmopolitan Club. [41] Booker T. Washington shared this conviction. In fact, there is more than a suspicion that Washington may have inspired the adverse publicity in order to destroy an organization which, however small, threatened his leadership and policies. Charles Flint Kellogg asserts: "It is clear that Washington had arranged for derogatory publicity and that he had helped to promote the lurid headlines." [42] Louis R. Harlan, Washington's biographer and editor of his papers, does not go so far, but he does state that "Washington's secret cooperation with the racially biased white press in reporting another Cosmopolitan Club dinner in 1911 strongly suggests that he may have inspired the 1908 publicity also." [43] We shall discuss the 1911 dinner below, but here it should be noted that the fact that the Cosmopolitan Club was alive and well in 1911 shows that Villard's fear that the fury over the interracial dinner would destroy the organization was unwarranted. Ovington put it more accurately when she wrote in response to the vicious press campaign:

> We shall not be discouraged in our purpose to bring men and women together who need to learn of one another's problems, and we believe that the meal we shared was a pleasant bond that will make us a little kinder to one another, a little less ready to look for faults, as we work upon the great problem of helping two dissimilar races to dwell together in the United States. [44]

Later, she wrote with justifiable pride: "We at the Cosmopolitan Club were pioneers. We suffered the notoriety of pioneers, but we did a good piece of work." [45]

One last word is in order about the "infamous dinner." Essentially, the men and women who attended were intellectuals and professionals whose contacts with the black masses were limited. The blacks were part of what Du Bois called the "talented tenth" of the Negro people who would use their knowledge to improve the status of the black masses, but apart from Reverend George Frazier Miller, whose parish was in a black working-class district, their contact with these masses was almost nonexistent. As for the whites, only Mary White Ovington could be said to have had any association with lower class blacks, and she acknowledged having learned much from them. More typical was André Tridon, who told a reporter: "I would not associate with a negro menial any quicker than I would with a white menial—not from any aristocratic notion but because there is nothing in the conversation of the menial of either race to interest me." (It says something about a socialist who felt he had nothing to learn from a member of the working class which his party was seeking to emancipate.) In the same interview, Tridon took an unequivocal position in favor of the right of blacks and whites to marry, asserting that the issue was purely a "personal one, just as personal as whether a man should shave or wear a beard." [46]

As the Cosmopolitan Club continued and grew in membership, the influence of socialist ideas in the organization also increased. [47] At the same time, many of the black militants in the Niagara Movement, especially Du Bois himself, were also moving closer to the Socialist party. At Harvard, Du Bois learned very little, if anything, about Marxism and socialism in general. In his postgraduate German years at the University of Berlin, however, he learned more about socialism, and after attending meetings of the Socialist Club at the University, he joined the organization. [48] Nevertheless, in his 1903 *Souls of Black Folk*, Du Bois rejected "a cheap and dangerous socialism," and, in the chapter on the Black Belt, he came close to equating the advocacy of socialism with criminality. But he was changing rapidly, and a year later, his lectures were emphasizing the economics of racism and were indicating sympathy with the socialist objective. In November 1904, Isaac Max Rubinow, an outstanding socialist economist and statistician whose approach to the Negro question, as we shall see, was far in advance of that of most party members, wrote to Du Bois, urging him to consider allying himself with the socialist party. Despite the weaknesses and limitations of the party's approach to the Negro question, of which Rubinow was well aware, he was convinced that Du Bois would agree it was "the only organization in the country that moves in the right direction." In his reply, Du Bois wrote: "While I would scarcely describe myself as a socialist still I have much sympathy with the movement & I have many socialistic beliefs." [49] In the February 1907 issue of *Horizon*, Du Bois defined himself as a "Socialist-of-the-Path," meaning, he said, one who saw the need for the public ownership of railroads, coal mines, and many factories. In the same issue, his "Negro and Socialism" appeared, in which he declared that "in the socialistic trend . . . lies the one group hope of Negro America." He added that he did not agree with the socialists in everything, "but in trend and ideal they are the salt of this present earth." In 1907 and 1908, *Horizon* carried articles on "Why the Socialistic Flag Is Red" and recommended books on socialism by Spargo, Jack London, and William J. Ghent. [50] The February 1908 issue had this advice: "To Black Voters: In all cases remember that the only party today which treats Negroes as men, North and South, are the Socialists."

This statement was not quite true, and Du Bois himself did not endorse Debs in the 1908 presidential election, allying himself, instead,
with Reverend J. M. Waldron in supporting Bryan through the National
Negro Political League. Nevertheless, the fact is that Du Bois was moving closer to the Socialist party while he was general secretary of the Niagara Movement. This process was undoubtedly hastened by his respect
for Mary White Ovington and other socialists in the New York Cosmopolitan Club. In 1907, Du Bois invited Ovington to be the first white person to join the all-Negro Niagara Movement, and she indicated her
willingness to do so "if the members really want me."[51]

In August 1909, Du Bois invited Henry L. Slobodin, a prominent New
York socialist to address the Niagara Conference. (He was one of two
white men who addressed the gathering, and both were socialists.) Slobodin wrote later: "I lost no time in informing my auditors of my Socialist
point of view. The clearer my Socialism appeared, the warmer my
remarks were received."[52]

It was these few socialists in New York City who, more than any
others, provided the impetus for the formation of the National Association for the Advancement of Colored People (NAACP). Undoubtedly,
too, Du Bois' respect for their stand on the Negro question influenced his
decision to ally the Niagara Movement with these and other white people
to create the NAACP.


## THE SPRINGFIELD RIOT AND ITS REPERCUSSIONS

During August 14 and 15, 1908, a wave of anti-Negro violence swept
Springfield, Illinois—the home of Abraham Lincoln—and resulted in
lynching and other less deadly but equally forceful pressures upon blacks
to flee the city. Before over 4,000 militiamen could bring the riots under
control, two persons had been lynched, six killed, fifty wounded, and
more than 2,000 Negroes had fled the city, with hundreds taking shelter
in the militia camps.[53]

The riots brought reporters to Springfield to probe into the causes of
the lawlessness. Among them were the socialists William English Walling and his wife, Anna Strunsky Walling. Walling was a Southerner and
the descendant of a slaveowning family, but he traveled extensively both
in the North and abroad, and had manifested a deep interest in a variety
of social and humanitarian causes before joining the Socialist party. He
had moved from such causes as factory inspection, settlement house
social service, and the National Women's Trade Union League, to socialism. He joined the party in 1908 and immediately associated himself with
the left wing and became a bitter opponent of Victor Berger's reformism

and white chauvinism. Walling had married Anna Strunsky, a socialist who had come to the United States after having been imprisoned in her native Russia for revolutionary activities. (She had come to know Jack London in San Francisco and had tried in vain to clear up some of the contradictions in his socialist thinking, including his racist belief in Nordic supremacy.) [54] The Wallings had just returned from a visit to Czarist Russia when they went to Springfield to investigate the riot. They were thus in a position to compare the anti-Jewish pogroms in Russia with the anti-Negro pogrom in the city in which Lincoln had lived and was buried. [55]

Walling sent dispatches from Springfield to the *Chicago Daily Socialist* emphasizing that the riot was being used "by whites of all classes, except the organized workingmen, to rob, plunder and exploit the negro," and, in general, to eliminate blacks from all jobs and business enterprises so that whites could take over their places. Since Springfield had practically no trade-union movement and "no Socialism," these racist elements in the city were able to operate unhampered. Walling also noted that at least half of the mob leaders had originally come from the South and were introducing the Southern way of life into the North along with "the Russian idea" of pogroms. [56]

The *Chicago Daily Socialist* proudly featured Walling's point that no socialists or trade unionists had been involved in the riot. It praised the United Mine Workers in Illinois for disassociating itself from the rioters and defending its black members against attempts to drive them out of the mines. Here was proof, it said, that organized labor and the socialists were the Negro's best friends and that "labor is once more proving itself to be the most powerful force in present society that works for human brotherhood and social solidarity." [57] The New York *Call* reprinted several of the reports on the riot originally published in the *Chicago Daily Socialist*. However, editorially it confined itself to the comment that the citizens of Springfield "have done their best to maintain the reputation of the United States as the most lawless country in the civilized world. And they haven't the excuse which the Jew-baiting Russians have of being totally uneducated and living under a despotic government." [58] Clearly, nothing in the two leading socialist papers was designed to produce any definite action to combat the rising tide of racism.

The stimulus was provided by Walling's article "The Race War in the North," published in *The Independent* of September 3, 1908. Walling revealed that he and his wife were amazed to discover that "Springfield had no shame. She stood for the action of the mob." Indeed, prominent citizens, including "a leading white minister," recommended that the riot be followed by disfranchising all Negroes, as had already been done in the South, while others insisted that "lynching" was "the only way" to teach the Negro his place. It may be argued that there was a strong

Southern element in the town, and a good number of its citizens were originally from the South. But the fact was that almost the entire community accepted the Southern point of view—no doubt because the white workers and small businessmen wanted to eliminate Negro competition. Walling warned that if the Springfield rioters could eliminate Negroes from jobs and small businesses, then they would "offer every temptation to similar white elements in other towns to imitate Springfield's example," and "every community indulging in an outburst of race hatred will be assured of great and certain financial reward, and all the lies, ignorance and brutality on which race-hatred is based will spread over the land."

All this was but a prologue to Walling's main warning. As he saw it, the Springfield riot marked the turning point in the North's approach to the Negro. Therefore, he concluded with a moving plea:

> Either the spirit of the abolitionists, of Lincoln and of Lovejoy must be revived and we must come to treat the negro on a plane of absolute political and social equality, or Vardaman and Tillman will soon have transferred the race war to the North. . . .

> The day these methods become general in the North every hope of political democracy will be dead, other weaker races and classes will be persecuted in the North as in the South. . . .

> Yet who realizes the seriousness of the situation, and what large and powerful body of citizens is ready to come to their aid? [59]

The New York *Evening Call* reprinted parts of Walling's article, but it omitted both his warning that Southern methods would become prevalent in the North, and his plea that the seriousness of the situation be recognized and that action be initiated to aid the Negro. [60] Mary White Ovington read the article by her fellow socialist in *The Independent* and immediately wrote to Walling. She informed him that she supported his call for an organization of black and white Americans that would both secure the rights still remaining to the Negro and reclaim those that had been lost. Later, she attended a lecture by Walling on Russia at Cooper Union, in the course of which he stated that the race situation in America was worse, in some respects, than anything in Russia under Czarism. After the lecture, Ovington informed Walling that she had heard of his plan for a national biracial organization of "fair-minded whites and intelligent blacks" to help right the wrongs of the Negro. She proposed that they undertake at once to form such an organization. [61]

During the first week of January 1909, Ovington went to a meeting at

Walling's New York apartment to plan the initial steps for founding the new organization. Charles Edward Russell, Walling's friend and fellow socialist, was also scheduled to be present. Russell had joined the Socialist party in 1908. As a result of his regular appearance in the pages of the *Appeal to Reason*, *The Coming Nation*, and the muckraking magazine *Everybody's*, he had risen rapidly through the party ranks. The son of Edward Russell, an abolitionist editor of a small newspaper in Davenport, Iowa, Charles had established a scholarship for "young colored men" at Fisk University in memory of his father. In his writings in both the socialist and general press, he repeatedly insisted that the rising tide of anti-Negro sentiment and action must be halted and reversed if the nation was to survive. [62]

Together with Walling and Ovington, Russell was to become one of the most important figures in the early history of the NAACP, but he was unable to attend the initial meeting at Walling's New York apartment. The third person present was Dr. Henry Moskowitz, a social worker active among New York immigrants and, like Walling and Ovington, a member of the Socialist party. These three socialists — "one . . . a descendant of an old-time abolitionist, the second a Jew, and the third a Southerner" — took an important step at their meeting. They decided that Lincoln's birthday, February 12, 1909, should mark the launching of a campaign to secure the support of a large and powerful body of citizens in the struggle for Negro rights. [63]

The original trio was soon joined by Russell and Oswald Garrison Villard. The group then became biracial by including two prominent Negro clergymen, Bishop Alexander Walters and Reverend William Henry Brooks. Florence Kelley, the noted social worker, socialist, and close friend and correspondent of Frederick Engels, also joined the group. [64]

On February 12, 1909, a "Call" for a "Lincoln Emancipation Conference to Discuss Means for Securing Political and Civil Equality for the Negro," written by Oswald Garrison Villard, was issued by a group of sixty prominent Negroes and whites. Among them were W.E.B. Du Bois, Ida Wells-Barnett, Mrs. Mary Church Terrell, Reverend Francis H. Grimké, Bishop Alexander Walters, Dr. J. Milton Waldron, John E. Milholland, William Dean Howells, Jane Addams, Lincoln Steffens, Rabbi Stephen S. Wise, Oswald Garrison Villard, and such socialists as Charles Edward Russell, William English Walling, Mary White Ovington, Florence Kelley, and Dr. Henry Moskowitz. [65]

Russell and Walling not only signed the "Call" but also issued their own. On February 13, 1909, the *Chicago Daily Socialist*'s headline read: "Would Free Negro Again. Strong Appeal Is Made in Document by C. E. Russell and W. E. Walling." Three days later, the *New York Evening Call* announced: "A National Conference for the Emancipation of the

Negro. An Appeal to All the Forces of Genuine Democracy in the United
States, by Charles Edward Russell and William English Walling." Both
papers carried the full text of the Russell-Walling "Call."

There was a great deal of difference between the "Calls" of Villard and
Russell-Walling. Villard's emphasized the civil and political rights of
Negroes, and said nothing at all about economic problems. The Russell-
Walling "Call" also referred to "wholesale disfranchisement" and deprivation of civil rights, but spoke of them as part of a process of reen-
slavement of the Negro. They insisted that this "new form of slavery"
must lead to "a new abolition movement" which, unlike the previous one,
would lead to a compelte emancipation—which was their way of referring
to the establishment of socialism. The two socialists also pointed out
that the same reactionary ruling class in the South that had reenslaved
the Negro subjugated the poor whites as well, and that the struggle for
Negro emancipation was intimately linked to the liberation of the exploited poor whites. They noted, too, that the Southern ruling class,
whether reactionary or conservative, was determined to keep the Negro
confined to the most inferior occupations, and that his only future was to
become "a better servant-workingman." This situation, they insisted,
had to be changed.

Both "Calls" maintained that it was necessary for all believers in
democracy to abandon their silence, to dispel Northern indifference, and
to join in a national conference for the discussion of the present evils and
for the renewal of the struggle for Negro rights. Here, too, the difference
lay in the fact that Villard referred only to "civil and political rights,"
while Russell and Walling added a call for an end to "social and economic
persecution." [66]

Only the socialist press published the Russell-Walling "Call," [67] and
all accounts of the founding of the NAACP mention only the Villard
"Call." [68] But it is important to note that two of the socialists who
founded the NAACP were thinking in terms of the economic problems of
the Negro as well as his civil and political rights, and saw in the movement they were helping to launch an instrument that would serve the
class interests of poor whites as well as blacks against their common
exploiters.


## NATIONAL NEGRO CONFERENCE AND THE NAACP

The National Negro Conference took place in New York City on May
31 and June 1, 1909, and led to the formation of the National Negro Committee. The opening session was attended by about 300 men and women
of both races. Leading scientists presented detailed scientific evidence

exploding theories that the Negro was inherently inferior because of differences in brain structure—evidence that, as Dr. Du Bois observed,
"left no doubt in the minds of listeners that the whole argument by which
Negroes were pronounced absolutely and inevitably inferior to whites
was utterly without scientific basis." [69] Papers and addresses were presented by Du Bois, William L. Bulkley, leading Negro educator in New
York City, Ida B. Wells-Barnett, and others, dealing with various aspects of the Negro problem. Different proposals were advanced for solving the problem. [70] Only one speaker, however, raised the question of socialism. He was Reverend George Frazier Miller. After listening to Du
Bois' paper, "Politics and Industry," in which he argued that there
would be no solution of the Negro problem until the Negro in the South
could cast a free and intelligent vote, and after hearing J. Max Barber's
comment that at bottom, the Negro problem "lies not in economics but in
politics," Miller took the floor to insist that "economics is at the foundation of the whole thing." He pointed out that "the great Socialist party ...
stands for economic independence." He concluded: "Under Socialism we
have economic independence. Everyone has the right to work and every
man to the full reward of his labors." [71]

The reporter for the New York *Call* was convinced that the conference
was "the most important gathering of scientists and radicals" ever
brought together to deal with the "wrongs and needs of the black, and for
the uniting of the two races upon remedial schemes." [72] The editorial
pages of the socialist press did not share this enthusiasm. Robert
Hunter, a regular columnist for the *Chicago Daily Socialist* and *New
York Call*, greeted the conference skeptically: "That men meet for this
purpose is an encouraging sign. We fear, however, it will not avail
much." Resolutions, papers, and addresses, however well-intended,
could not solve the Negro problem. Only the Negro himself could do this,
and then only after he abandoned bourgeois ideology and developed class
consciousness in the same manner as white workers. And only when
black workers ceased serving the interests of the capitalists and showed
they were ready to take advantage of the opportunities white workers
were offering them to join their unions and political campaigns, would
there be "much hope for the negro in the South." Until that time, Hunter
concluded, conferences could do little except for "a few of the more
educated, intelligent property-owning blacks." [73]

The New York *Call* was not as cynical as Hunter about the conference,
but it saw only one virtue in the gathering: the possibility that the discussion had made "clearer both to colored people and to their white sympathizers, the truth, too little recognized by either, that the so-called
negro question is not simply a race question, but is much more a class
question." [74] Although the *Call* published the resolutions adopted by the

conference demanding "for negroes, as for every other race," equal civil, political and educational rights, the right to work, protection against violence, murder, and intimidation, and the strict enforcement of the Fourteenth and Fifteenth Amendments, [75] neither it nor any other socialist paper called upon the party to contribute to the campaign to achieve these goals.

Despite the lack of enthusiasm in party circles for the biracial movement, the socialists involved in organizing it pursued their activities energetically. On May 17, 1910, Oswald Garrison Villard wrote to his uncle concerning the newly named National Association for the Advancement of Colored People: "The most ardent workers who are really accomplishing something, Miss Ovington, Miss Blascoer, Walling, Mrs. Maclean, etc., are all Socialists." To this group was now added the "Socialist-of-the-Path" Dr. W.E.B. Du Bois. Having led most of the Negro leadership involved in the Niagara Movement into the new biracial organization, Dr. Du Bois accepted the offer to become the NAACP's director of publicity and research and editor of its publication, *The Crisis*, whose first number appeared in November 1910.

Few believed that the new organization would survive long in the face of opposition from the pro-Washington forces. In the spring of 1912, when the NAACP held its fourth annual conference in Chicago, there were only 329 members and three branches in the organization. [76] Nevertheless, the *Chicago Daily Socialist* pointed to the association as evidence of socialist influence in the solution of the Negro question. It reported that Charles Edward Russell, a socialist, and Professor W.E.B. Du Bois, "a well-known Socialist leader of his people," would deliver key addresses at the conference, [77] and that Mary White Ovington, NAACP secretary, also "a well-known Socialist," would leave the conference after it was over to attend the Socialist party's national convention. In general, socialists were "prominent in the councils of the association," and, led by Russell, they were crusading for national action to solve the race question. The *Chicago Daily Socialist* urged all Americans, especially all socialists, to commit to memory these words of Russell: "The nation cannot endure half with rights and half with none any more than it could endure half slave and half free. Every time justice has been perverted to wreak popular prejudice on a colored man the whole system has been weakened for everybody." [78]

# Local New York, the Colored Socialist Club, Hubert H. Harrison, and W.E.B. Du Bois

## ISAAC MAX RUBINOW'S PLEA

It will be recalled that in November 1904, Rubinow wrote to W.E.B. Du Bois asking him to give serious thought to joining the Socialist party. In the same letter, however, Rubinow conceded that "even among certain groups of socialists the Negro problem is not fully understood, and the new Southern members of the movement have not altogether succeeded in freeing themselves from the prejudices that arose in chattel slavery, and persist in wage slavery."[1] The failure of the Socialist party to come to grips with this problem induced Rubinow to prepare and publish a study which, he hoped, would help overcome this serious weakness in his party. He submitted his study in a series of articles to the *International Socialist Review*. By the time the series was concluded, it included fifteen separate articles under the general title "The Economic Aspects of the Negro Problem." Published under the pseudonym I. M. Robbins, the series appeared between February 1908 and June 1910.[2]

Rubinow (Robbins) began his series with one of W.E.B. Du Bois' most frequently quoted passages: "The problem of the twentieth century is the problem of the color line, the relation of the darker to the lighter races."[3] He noted that, despite the significance of the problem and the fact that "the vast majority of the negroes in this country belong to the proletarian class," the party that claimed to represent that class had troubled itself "very little about the negro problem." Apart from a few articles in the *International Socialist Review* and other socialist publications, some of dubious value, the socialists had been content to believe that the theory that "the negro problem was only one aspect of the labor problem" precluded any need for further study of the question. The result of this vacuum was "a universal lack of understanding of the complicated aspects of this problem among working socialists" and the existence in party ranks of either "antiquated prejudices" or "a purely platonic sympathy to the poor negroes." Rubinow then asked bluntly:

> Do the Socialists of this country really expect to attract the ten million negro proletarians into their ranks with such a policy of indifference? Or do they really think they can succeed in this country with these ten millions of proletarians left on the outside? Or do they simply sit and wait, until the International Socialist Congress will take up this momentous question, just as they were willing to leave the entire question of immigration alone to be discussed by the comrades from the countries of Europe?[4]

After discussing the history of slavery, the Civil War and Reconstruction, the post-Reconstruction disfranchisement of the Negro and the establishment of a Jim Crow society in the South which reduced blacks to second-class status, the crime of lynching, the conflict between Booker T. Washington and W.E.B. Du Bois, and the issue of social equality, Rubinow returned to the theme he had stressed in the first of his fifteen articles—Socialist party indifference to the Negro. Not even Debs escaped his criticism as Rubinow attacked his repeated assertions that the Socialist party had "nothing special to offer the negro." It was not correct to say, as Debs did, that the party had nothing to do with the "Negro question" because it was a problem of capitalist society. Could the Socialist party continue to ignore an issue of such great concern to the working class? "No, comrades, it will not do to avoid the issue." It was essential to convince the Negro that the socialist movement was "his movement." This meant not merely repeating endlessly that the party sought "to secure to every man, white and black alike, economic justice and equality in the full enjoyment of the product of his labor." Nor was it enough to assume that the "Socialist philosophy" was "incompatible with negro oppression." For one thing, how was the Negro to know it? For another, were party members "so very sure that the cooperative commonwealth is unthinkable with Jim Crow cars, and other characteristic virtues of modern Southern life?" (Since socialists like Julius A. Wayland actually envisioned a segregated society in the cooperative commonwealth, the answer would seem to be that not only was it thinkable, but it also was actually being planned.) All this meant that the Socialist party had indeed to take a "definite attitude" on the Negro problem and should not be afraid to proclaim it. This "attitude" must include "something a good deal more tangible than the promise of full products of one's labor in the cooperative commonwealth." It had to include "a clear, unmistakable demand for the entire abolition of all *legal* restrictions of the rights of the negro," and "social equality" in the sense of equality in all aspects of public life. And unless every party member, in the South as well as the North, stood unequivocally "against any discrimination against the negro, the Socialist will not have done his entire duty by the negro, nor by the rest of the American working class."[5]

Rubinow's fifteen installments closed with the following question directed to the Socialist party: "Will it be wise enough to do it?"[6] The only positive response came from Local New York of the Socialist party.

## LOCAL NEW YORK TURNS ATTENTION TO THE NEGRO QUESTION

Local New York, the Manhattan local of the Socialist party, was deeply involved in work with the trade unions, especially in the needle trades, and between 1908 and 1910, it conducted a series of recruiting drives among foreign-born and women workers. Prior to 1911, however, Local New York never once discussed the recruiting of Negroes, nor did it raise any specific demands of interest to blacks in the platforms it adopted for municipal campaigns. Only two branches—5 and 7 of Harlem—had more than one or two black members.[7]

In the opening years of the twentieth century, Harlem was populated largely by East European Jews, the Irish, and Italians, but there was already a substantial Negro population in the neighborhood. Branches 5 and 7 had originally been composed of Jewish, Italian, and Irish socialists, but as the expanding Negro population of New York City, seeking housing accommodations, spilled into Harlem in increasing numbers,[8] the branches began to recruit a number of blacks. As early as June 1906, the branches' Harlem Socialist Agitation Committee included black comrades among their speakers at open-air meetings. At their "grand outing and entertainment" at Fort Lee, New Jersey, in August of that year, a black comrade recited Wendell Phillips' "great speech on Toussaint L'Ouverture—the black Napoleon of San Domingo."[9]

By 1910, discussions of the Negro question had become a regular feature of Branch 5. Early in 1911, Thomas Sweeney, a member of the branch, notified the *New York Call* that several of his comrades were asking why Negroes were not joining the party. "Why don't they take to Socialism?" was a question raised at each meeting. In his letter, Sweeney presented the answer arrived at in the branch. What it boiled down to was that the Negroes' lack of interest in socialism was "the fault of the Socialist Party. With it and with it alone lies the blame." The party, the branch members felt, was simply indifferent to the Negro, neglected repeated opportunities to bring its message to blacks, and offered the Negro nothing to justify his support. Praising the stand taken by the Oklahoma socialists on the Negro question (which will be discussed in the next section), Sweeney urged Local New York to show similar concern for the problems and needs of blacks. He was confident that if the Socialist party took "a determined stand on the question of racial equality," showed the Negro "that it really stands for him and his interests," and supported the Negro "in his fight for betterment and advancement of the race," the blacks would "flock to the Socialist party by the thousand." The party was confronted with "a grand opportunity." Sweeney closed with the question: "Will it recognize and utilize the opportunity for the advancement of the grand and noble cause of Socialism or will it blindly let it slip? This is the important, the vital question. I, as a member and worker in the Socialist party, call upon it to answer." [10]

Sweeney's letter was endorsed by Thomas Potter, a black socialist from Paterson, New Jersey. "Let me say in most emphatic terms, he wrote to the *Call*, "that if there is one blot on the record of the Socialist party, it is that of its utter apathy and indifference toward the negro." He accused the party of being "as silent as a clam on every question that affects the negro," and urged the sending of "colored comrades as speakers" where blacks gathered "because they are always more ready to listen to one of their own race." [11]

Both Local New York and the *Call* ignored the criticism and suggestion. The *Call*, in fact, paid little attention to the criticism by another member of Branch 5 who called the party to account for its policy of speling Negro with a small "n." The *Call* defended itself with the weak argument that it was not in its style (or that of 99 percent of the papers in the United States) to capitalize a common noun, and since the word "negro" came under that heading, there was no more need to capitalize it than to capitalize the word "white." [12] Not so, responded W.E.B. Du Bois, defending the Branch 5 critic. Du Bois pointed out that all British papers and many "reputable" papers in the United States capitalized "Negro." He concluded with the hope "that the Call may early see its way clear to discontinue this policy of insult." 13 The *Call* paid no more attention to this distinguished scholar than it had to the original criticism. The correspondence does show, however, that the leadership of the New York Socialist party was coming under increasing criticism for its indifference to the Negro.

Branch 7, however, refused to wait until the leadership awoke to its responsibilities. On January 20, 1911, the branch sponsored a lecture at Lenox Casino at 116th Street and Lenox Avenue, at which W.E.B. Du Bois spoke on "The Race Problem." Every effort was made to fill the casino with blacks; advertisements were inserted in the Negro press, thousands of circulars were distributed throughout Negro Harlem, and admission was set at 10 cents per person in order to allow as many as possible to attend. "Nothing is left undone in the way of bringing this to the attention of the colored race," the branch noted proudly. Prodded by this unusual action, the *New York Call* ran an editorial urging, "Hear W.E.B. Du Bois Speak!" But after the lecture, matters returned to normal, and the question of organizing Negroes into the party was forgotten. 14

On October 12, 1911, Samuel M. Romansky, recording secretary of Branch 5, sent a letter to Julius Gerber, executive secretary of Local New York, informing him that Hubert H. Harrison, one of the black members of Branch 5, had already exhibited "a profound and practical familiarity with the history, the traits, the habits and inclinations of his race," and had demonstrated great capacity as a speaker: "He is a close friend of Professor Du Bois who recommends him highly as a man of intelligence and ability." Branch 5 now proposed that Comrade Harrison be made "a paid speaker and organizer for Local New York for special work in negro districts." Since Branch 5 was situated in the area with the largest Negro population in the city, it was "especially anxious" to be able to use "Com. Harrison's services as early as possible." Finally, since Branch 5 was fully aware of the "lack of true facts, data and general information that prevails among socialists regarding the negro problem confronting the Socialist Party," it requested that Local New York arrange a meeting for party members "at which Comrade Harrison will speak on 'How to reach the Negro vote.'" 15

Romansky's letter marked the first time since the formation of the Socialist party in 1901 that a party branch had called for *special attention* to the Negro question and for a *special campaign* among blacks.

Gerber referred the request to Local New York's Executive Committee, and on October 18, 1911, that body engaged Harrison as a speaker for the remainder of the election campaign at $18 per week "to do special propaganda work among the colored people." A committee of three was elected to meet with Harrison "to devise ways and means of doing effective agitation work among the colored race." 16

## HUBERT H. HARRISON AND THE COLORED SOCIALIST CLUB

Hubert H. Harrison was born in St. Croix, Virgin Islands, on April 27, 1883. At an early age, he left the islands to tour the world as a cabin boy. In 1906, he came to New York where he obtained work as a hallboy in a hotel and as an elevator operator, and in other menial jobs. He attended high school and made a very favorable impression on his instructor. A prolific reader, he immersed himself in books on the history of the Negro. Through continuous self-study, Harrison became an expert on African and Afro-American history.

Harrison was not interested merely in history; he also wanted to help change the existing status of the Negro. He became more and more convinced that, unless a militant struggle was waged against economic oppression, disfranchisement, segregation, and lynching, blacks in the United States would fall deeper and deeper under the "iron heel" of white supremacy. He was also convinced that the philosophy of Booker T. Washington was dangerous for the Negro, and in 1911, he published two letters in the *New York Sun* condemning Washington's leadership. 17

Harrison never knew it, but his letters caused an abrupt change in his life. In 1907, he had become a clerk in the New York City post office, a position he held for four years until he was suddenly dismissed. The reason for his discharge can be found in two letters in the Booker T. Washington Papers which provide some insight into the operations of the "Tuskegee Machine." 18 Charles W. Anderson, Negro Republican leader of New York City and a faithful follower of Washington, wrote the principal of Tuskegee Institute: "Do you remember Hubert H. Harrison? He is the man who wrote two nasty letters against you in the New York 'Sun.' He is a clerk in the Post Office. The Postmaster is my personal friend. . . . Can you see the hand? I think you can. Please destroy this, that it may not fall under another eye. . . . If he escapes me he is a dandy." Six weeks later, Anderson wrote: "I am sure you will regret to learn that Mr. Hubert H. Harrison has been dismissed from his position as clerk in the New York Post Office." 19

The sudden discharge hastened Branch 5's decision that Harrison, now without any means of livelihood, should be employed as a paid party organizer. Harrison had joined the Socialist party in 1909 and had quickly impressed his comrades of Branch 5 with his knowledge of African and Afro-American history. In fact, he had been asked to deliver lectures on these subjects to the members. He also became known as a street speaker, addressing audiences first in Wall Street and Madison Square, and then in Harlem. By the fall of 1911, he was already a familiar figure at party rallies.

Once he was hired by Local New York for the remainder of the municipal campaign of 1911, Harrison threw himself energetically into the work of winning Negro votes for the party. He spoke daily on street corners in Harlem and distributed copies of the pamphlet "The Colored Man's Case as Socialism Sees It," written for Local New York by Reverend George W. Slater, Jr., of Chicago. After the campaign, Harrison described how he and a few other comrades had operated:

> We would take one of these pamphlets and hold it so that the title showed plainly and walk up to a colored man with it. As soon as his eyes fell on the words "Colored Man's Case," his attention was arrested. Hide bound Republican heelers and Democratic politicians would take it, where they would put aside any less special literature with a wave of impatience. And having taken it, they would read it, and stop to listen to our street speaker. . . . Then there was the special form of address. Our arguments were the ABC arguments. But we crammed them full of facts—facts for the most part drawn from the Negro's own history and experience and hitting the bull's eye of his own affairs every time. That did not deprive our speeches of any general effectivenesses, for very often from a third to a half of our audiences would be made up of white people, whose attention and interest were held just the same. On the Tuesday before election, when we stampeded the crowd from the opposite corner, where they had women speakers as well as men, a large wagon and music, and held all of them for two hours in a driving rain—about two-fifths of the crowd were white people. So we demonstrated again the tremendous power of special addresses. And in that district they are talking about it yet—all of them—doctors, lawyers, longshoremen, clerks and waiters. 20

The socialist vote in the 1911 election increased by 6,000, and this included a rise in the black vote. Harrison's work was praised for "the increased interest in Socialism taken . . . by the colored voters." 21 Immediately following the election, the committee of three designated on October 18 by Local New York to work out a plan "for the agitation and organization of Negroes" reported to the Executive Committee. It recommended, first, the immediate organization of a new branch to be made up of black members and the transfer of Negro members in existing branches to the new branch; second, the establishment of permanent headquarters "in the negro district," or the rental, temporarily, of a place for weekly meetings; third, the printing of special literature "suitable for negroes"; and fourth, the appointment of a permanent organizer for work among the Negroes. The cost of this program was estimated to be $31 per week. It was proposed that a special fund be raised through the party press and that all branches and language groups be asked to contribute $1 per week to make this amount available.

After a good deal of discussion, Local New York's Executive Committee voted to engage Harrison to begin agitation work "for the purpose of establishing a nucleus of an organization among the colored," and that a call be issued immediately to raise the "special fund" for this purpose. [22] On November 28, 1911, the *New York Call* made public Local New York's decision under the headline "To Push Agitation Among the Negroes." Now at last, New York socialists knew that a plan had been adopted to take definite steps to bring socialism to the Negro, that a new branch consisting of black members would be established in Harlem, that special literature suitable for distribution among blacks would be published, and that Hubert H. Harrison would be in charge of this entire effort.

Harrison began his work with great enthusiasm. To build support among his comrades for the undertaking, he published a series of articles in the *New York Call* under the general heading "The Negro and Socialism." In these, the first of many articles on the subject to appear in the socialist press under his byline, he sought to explain to party members the basis of the oppression of Negroes and the best means of securing its elimination. He reminded the socialists that, historically, the roots of the race problem were to be found in slavery:

> Since the Negroes were brought here as chattels, their social status was fixed by that fact. To the credit of our common human nature, it was found necessary to reconcile the public mind to the system of slavery. This was effected by building up the belief that the slaves were not really human, that they belonged to a different order of beings. . . . And wherever the system was most profitable, the belief that the slave was not human was strongest. This belief dies hard, and, before it finally vanished, assumed many curious forms. In the early part of the nineteenth century, defenders of American slavery argued that the Negro was a beast. Later they conceded that he was a man of an inferior sort, consigned to slavery by God as the only human condition that was good for him. Then, when the freed black began to produce men of mark and lift themselves far above the slave level, it was argued that certain craniological peculiarities would prevent

them from assimilating the learning and culture of Europe. Finally, when they gave such evidence of that assimilation as even their friends could not deny, it was suddenly discovered that this is a white man's country.

Since the United States was considered a "white man's country," it followed that "all other occupants of it must be pariahs subsisting on sufference." Harrison then turned to a theme he was to stress in speeches and writings. The Negro problem, he emphasized, was essentially an economic problem. Race prejudice was the fruit of economic subjection and a fixed economic status. The Negro obtained less work, worked longer hours under worse conditions, and suffered from all forms of discrimination. His inferior status had been created in the first place and was perpetuated because it suited the purpose of the capitalist class to "use it as a club for the other workers." Since the capitalists were interested in keeping the average wage of all workers as low as possible, they pegged that of the blacks at the lowest level, thus making it difficult for other workers to raise theirs much higher. In this capitalist conspiracy, race prejudice proved to be "a very useful tool" since it served to divide the workers. Hence the campaign of deprecation and vilification of the Negro in the capitalist press; hence the association of blacks with criminal conduct and sexual assault of white women: "Thus public opinion is built up in favor of race prejudice."

Having acquainted his comrades with the roots of the oppression of the Negro people, Harrison turned next to the role they should play in eliminating this oppression. Basic to this role was the requirement that party members develop an understanding of how to spread socialism among Negroes. That blacks were ready to listen was evident from the increasing tendency of the Negro vote in the North to express itself independently. But to reach the Negro with the message of socialism required both literature of "a special nature" and "special work." For such work, "a special equipment was necessary":

> One must know the people, their history, their manner of life, and modes of thinking and feeling. You have to know the psychology of the Negro, for if you don't you will fail to attract or impress him. You will fail to make him think—and feel. For many of your arguments must be addressed to his heart as well as to his head. This is more true of him than of most other American groups.

> It stands to reason that this work can be better done by men who are themselves Negroes to whom these considerations come by second nature. If they are intelligent and well versed in the

principles of Socialism they can drive home an argument with such effectiveness that white Socialists must despair of achieving.

Once this approach was understood by white comrades, it was their duty at once to support Local New York's campaign for contributions for the "special work" of agitation among Negroes: "When negroes shall have joined the party in sufficiently large numbers, there will be no further need for a special fund. The work will be self-sustaining." Until that time, each socialist had the opportunity to prove that the party was sincere in claiming to represent the entire working class regardless of race or color—by supporting Local New York's campaign. [23]

The headline in the *New York Call* of December 12, 1911, read: "Help the Negroes to See the Light. Funds Needed for Socialist Propaganda Work Among Colored People." Then followed the full text of "An Appeal" from Local New York's Executive Committee. In it, for the first time, a leading official socialist body conceded that the party had been negligent in its work among Negroes and, too, that it was not enough to expect the Negro to come to the party: "We have gone to all others, native and foreign." Why not, then, to the Negro? Besides, the Negro was justifiably suspicious of every political movement in the United States, knowing from bitter experience that all such movements "broke down when they crossed the color line." Logically, he assumed that the same was true of the Socialist party: "Do you blame him? It is for us to enlighten his ignorance, remove his suspicion and enlist his self-interest upon our side in this great struggle of the working class." For this purpose, Local New York had launched a plan for work among Negroes. Since the local's regular income did not permit the appropriation of funds for this special work, the organization appealed to "the Branches, Party members, sympathizers and all those who recognize the necessity of Socialist agitation among the Negroes to contribute to the fund and make their work a success." [24]

This historical "Appeal" was unsigned. Not unlikely, it was written by Isaac Max Rubinow, a member of the committee of three set up by Local New York for the special agitation among Negroes. [25]

Shortly after the "Appeal" was issued, the *Call* announced that a "Colored Socialist Club" had been organized and had rented a hall on West 134th Street in Harlem for its meetings. Additional reports in the *Call* announced that both black and white socialists would lecture at the club's hall, and that Hubert H. Harrison would offer a course of five or more lectures on Negro history in the near future "for the benefit of the colored Comrades and others who may be interested." [26]

The drive to recruit blacks into the party had barely started when it ran into controversy. Both Reverend George Frazier Miller and W.E.B. Du Bois voiced concern that the plan to establish a separate branch for Negroes to which all blacks in existing branches would be transferred smacked of "segregation." Miller was willing to concede that a separate branch would be useful if its purpose was to advance the education of Negro comrades, but it seemed possible to him that the real aim was to spare white socialists the need to have contact with blacks. If it turned out to be so, he declared, then not only would it justifiably pour shame on a party that boasted of its "claim to equality and brotherhood," but it also would doom Local New York's campaign to recruit blacks. [27] Du Bois, on the other hand, refused to concede that the plan for a separate branch for blacks had even the slightest virtue. He did endorse the plan to interest blacks in socialism and praised Local New York for appointing a Negro organizer. But he insisted that

> his function should be to recruit members for the existing locals, and they should be distributed through these locals. In that way they would not only learn the principles of Socialism, but what is much more important, they and their white fellows would come to know each other as human beings.

Under no circumstances, Du Bois insisted, must there be a separation of black and white comrades. [28]

Local New York was probably too stunned by the criticism of its plan to respond. Harrison finally did answer, but it was not a response that could satisfy the critics of the "Colored Socialist Club." He maintained that Du Bois' fear that separate locals would be established for Negroes was based on a "misapprehension" since no such plan was envisaged. Separate locals were "an impossibility," he said, and therefore Du Bois had evidently meant "separate branches." (Just what this distinction proved was not quite clear.) Even then, Harrison continued, there was "no intention to establish separate branches or separate Socialist organizations for colored people." Yet, as Du Bois himself acknowledged, he went on, blacks had been historically conditioned to be suspicious of whites, so that they could not "effectively be approached by the average Socialist branch." They had to be proselytized by men of their own race, and the work had to be done where most blacks lived; hence the location of the Colored Socialist Club in Harlem. However, the party policy was clear: "When colored men or women become members of the Socialist party, they join the branch in whose territory they live." Thus, no segregation was intended; had it been, he would have been the most unlikely person selected for such work. "Those who know me well will realize this," Harrison insisted. [29]

At first, the controversy did not seem to affect the campaign to recruit blacks. The Colored Socialist Club continued to meet, and the *Call* announced proudly that "the last four meetings have been well attended." 30 White comrades were urged to help the black club members distribute literature in Harlem inviting the residents to attend the club meetings. A special inducement would be the opportunity to hear Hubert H. Harrison speak on "Socialism and the Negro" and also cover highlights of Afro-American history. 31

Chairman Gerber of Local New York also exuded confidence. On January 20, 1912, he announced that the fund drive initiated by the local "for carrying on special agitation among the Negroes has already awakened interest." Further, he stated that the plan envisaged "the establishment of a permanent clubroom in the heart of the greatest Negro population, an organizer who shall devote his entire time to the work of propaganda and the holding of meetings and circulation of suitable literature and addresses." "The field here is considered to be of great promise," Gerber declared, and the future prospects were indeed bright, especially since in Harrison, Local New York had "an eager exponent of the plans to agitate among his own race." Gerber concluded with the prediction that, as soon as "sufficient funds" were received, "the full plan will be inaugurated." 32

Then, a month later, without warning, Local New York abandoned the entire project. On February 23, 1912, the local's Executive Committee heard a report from the Committee on Agitation Among Negroes which recommended that, in view of the "depleted condition of the Party Treasury and the poor attendance of the meetings of the Colored Socialist Club," the "present method of agitation among Negroes" should be terminated. Instead, it was recommended that, rather than urge blacks to come to meetings of the Socialist party, speakers should be sent to Negro organizations to proselytize their members. Since there were numerous Negro literary and debating societies that would welcome a socialist speaker if one were furnished without charge, the opportunity to reach blacks would exist, and it would be better to obtain speakers, both black and white, to undertake such work without any cost to the party. One other reason given may have been more important than any of the others. The Executive Committee concluded that "the idea of segregation of the Negroes into a separate club is likely to have a false impression to the intension [*sic*] of the Socialist Party." 33 Evidently, Reverend Miller's warning had had some substance.

Harrison was very much upset by the Executive Committee's recommendation that "the present method of agitation among the Negroes be discontinued." He urged the body to reconsider what he felt was a hasty decision based on inadequate evidence. He conceded that attendance at the Colored Socialist Club had been poor, but he emphasized that, as a result of the agitation spearheaded by the club, there had been a "tremendous increase of Socialist sentiment among the Negroes of Harlem." He was convinced that attendance at the club could be increased, and he urged consideration of a proposal to accomplish this goal. Finally, he delivered a justifiable thrust at his white comrades:

> Let me remind you, comrades, that the local has established the Club but has not done anything else. Certainly it has not done its full duties yet, and I think that Local New York should support this work in a manner worthy of itself. That it may know how easily this can be done I shall attend the meeting of the Central Committee for Feb. 24th to endeavor to explain to you. [34]

It was all in vain. Local New York's leadership had decided to forget the whole business. The Colored Socialist Club was allowed to pass out of existence, and the campaign for special agitation among Negroes, begun with such enthusiasm, expired. In its report for the year 1912, Local New York's Central Committee did not even mention the campaign and reverted to type as far as the Negro was concerned—that is, neglect and indifference. It reported that it had admitted 2,309 new members, and it spoke of the activities of the foreign-language and women's branches. There was also a new English-speaking branch organized "in the Upper Harlem District"—Branch 12, consisting of members from Branch 7, which was "doing good work and progressing." Nothing was said, however, to indicate that the new Harlem Branch had any Negro members. [35] Thus, Local New York had retreated not only from separate organization of Negroes, but also from any special attention to the organization of blacks.

Harrison continued to function as a lecturer for the Socialist party, earning a modest living from lecture fees. [36] In one period, he delivered a series of lectures at Branch 5's headquarters, six open lectures at 39th Street and Broadway under the auspices of Branch 4, and a course of six lectures at the Outdoor Forum on the southeast corner of 116th Street and Lenox Avenue, under the auspices of Branch 5. In these lectures, he covered such subjects as "The Negro in American History," "Socialism: What It Is and Why It Is," "The Socialist Indictment," "The Nation's Wealth: Who Makes It, Who Gets It," "The Class Struggle and the Road to Power," "Socialism and the City," "The Socialist Party," [37] and "What Socialism Means to the Negro." [38] His conclusion in the last lecture was as follows:

> Socialism stands for the emancipation of the wage slaves. Are

you a wage slave? Do you want to be emancipated? Then join hands with the Socialists. Hear what they have to say. Read some of their literature. Get a Socialist leaflet, a pamphlet, or, better still, a book. You will be convinced of two things: that Socialism is right, and that it is inevitable. It is right because any order of things in which those who work have least while those who work them have most, is wrong. It is inevitable because a system under which the wealth produced by the labor of human hands amounts to more than two hundred and twenty billions a year while many millions live on the verge of starvation, is bound to break down. Therefore, if you wish to join with the other class-conscious, intelligent wage earners—in putting an end to such a system; if you want to better living conditions for black men as well as for white men; to make this woeful world of ours a little better for your children and your children's children, study Socialism—and think and work your way out. 39

As he had in his speeches, Harrison emphasized in his writings that "the Negro problem was essentially an economic problem." Race prejudice was "the fruit of economic subjection and fixed economic status" and the product of a conspiracy of the capitalist class to use one section of the working class against another so as to more effectively exploit all workers. As long as capitalism existed, this strategy would be employed, thereby making the need for socialism especially crucial for the working class and for black workers in particular. This was not to say that the party that claimed to be leading the working class toward the goal of socialism was capable of fulfilling its mission. Harrison was extremely sharp in his criticism of the Socialist party for its failure to eliminate racist elements within its ranks and for its tendency to retreat when white Southern socialists opposed any firm stand in favor of full racial equality.

As Joel August Rogers, the black historian, points out, through his oratory and his pen Hubert H. Harrison "labored for the emancipation of the working man." 40 In this labor, he was handicapped by a deteriorating relationship with the white leadership of Local New York. This bad relationship stemmed in part from Harrison's bitterness over the abrupt way in which the Colored Socialist Club had been scuttled and the agitation to recruit blacks abandoned. As long as he lived, Harrison could not forget the refusal of Local New York's Central Committee to grant him one more chance to prove the effectiveness of his campaign. He grew suspicious that perhaps Reverend Miller had been correct when he hinted that the real purpose of the campaign was to insulate white socialists from the black members. For their part, the white leaders of Local New

York resented Harrison's sharp tongue and pen and his proud defense of the Negro member's right to criticize his white comrades. 41

More serious, however, was the fact that Harrison was publicly allying himself with the pro-IWW forces in the Socialist party, while the leadership of Local New York was hostile to the IWW. Harrison firmly believed that much of the special exploitation of the black worker grew out of the racist policies of the craft unions in the AFL and Railroad Brotherhoods:

> The Negro worker gets less for his work—thanks to exclusion from the craft unions—than any other worker; he works longer hours as a rule and under worse conditions than any other worker; and his rent in any large city is much higher than that which the white worker pays for the same tenement. In short, the exploitation of the Negro worker is keener than that of any group of white workers in America. 42

So basic did Harrison consider the question of craft union discrimination that, in December 1911, he insisted that the Socialist party bring to the forefront "the suicidal policy of certain trades unions in excluding negroes from membership and to condemn them." 43 When the party proved to be too closely linked to the AFL officialdom to take such a stand, Harrison turned to the IWW. He was quickly impressed by the IWW argument that political action, emphasized by the Socialist party as the chief means of redressing grievances, meant little to the Negroes who were denied the right to vote by "Grandfather" and literacy clauses and by white primaries. He was also impressed by their argument that the real solution for blacks lay in industrial unionism and "direct action" on the job. Harrison attended the debate held early in 1912 in New York's Cooper Union between William D. ("Big Bill") Haywood, a leader of the IWW and the most outspoken defender of the Wobblies in the Socialist party, and Morris Hillquit, a defender of the AFL and a leading Socialist opponent of the IWW. The topic was "What Shall the Attitude of the Socialist Party Be Toward the Economic Organization of the Workers?" Harrison was very much impressed by Haywood's condemnation of the AFL for its craft unionism and racism, and not at all by Hillquit's defense of the AFL and his prediction that "within five years and no longer, the American Federation and its rank and file will be socialistic." After the debate was over, Harrison approached Haywood and reminded him that "while Douglas had won the debate, Lincoln had carried the country." Haywood took this comment to mean that although "Hillquit had won the debate, the workers of the nation were with me." 44

Whether or not the workers were, Harrison certainly was. Early in

1913, he signed the "Resolution of Protest" attacking the removal of Haywood from the Socialist party's National Executive Committee as "unwise and unwarranted." [45] Later that same year, he took an active part in the silk workers' strike in Paterson, New Jersey, sharing the soap box with Haywood and Elizabeth Gurley Flynn. [46] Moreover, in his speeches to socialist gatherings, Harrison continually praised the IWW position, and in his writings, he argued that industrial unionism and direct action would give the voteless black workers in the South a powerful weapon against capitalism. [47]

All this, of course, infuriated the leadership of Local New York. To them, it was not permissible for a black man, speaking as an official socialist lecturer, to publicly condemn the AFL for its racism and praise the IWW for its egalitarianism. By the summer of 1913, Local New York's Executive Committee noted that it was receiving "a number of complaints . . . against Harrison concerning phases of his talks," but it decided to take no action against him. [48] Later that year, however, the Executive Committee insisted that Harrison not speak as a party representative in a debate in which he would favor "Industrial Action" over "Political Action." Harrison ignored the order. When in March 1914, the Executive Committee ordered him not to debate Frank Urban, an opponent of socialism, under the auspices of the 3rd and 10th Assembly District of the party, Harrison shot back angrily: "Please tell the Executive Committee to go please chase itself." He added the significant postscript: "By the way if my color has anything to do with it this time I should thank you to let me know." [49]

Enraged, Local New York's Executive Committee voted to bring charges against Harrison for "contempt" and for disobeying the order. Harrison was ordered to appear before the Grievance Committee to answer the charges. "I shall be down," Harrison notified the committee. "If the Socialist Party and its principles can not stand the attacks of an Urban, then I give up hope." At his trial, Harrison defended himself with the argument that the Central Committee was "picking at him all the time." He pointed out that since he earned his living as a lecturer, cancellation of the debate would have meant a loss of $5. He insisted that "the executive committee can not prescribe a member of the S. P. how he shall earn his bread & butter." [50]

By a vote of three to one, Harrison was found guilty of the charges and suspended for a period of three months. He was notified of the suspension on May 18, 1914, [51] but by that time Harrison had had his fill of the Socialist party and had left the fold. For a number of years, he had become more and more convinced that the party was not basically concerned with promoting the interests of the Negro. He had tried to prod it to adopt a different policy, even if it meant losing support in the South.

By 1914, he had decided that all his efforts were futile, and would always be so. [52]

## W.E.B. DUBOIS AND THE SOCIALIST PARTY

Even before Harrison left the Socialist party, W.E.B. Du Bois had preceded him. Du Bois (whom one biographer calls "the off-again-on-again Socialist") [53] did not remain a member for long. Just how long it is difficult to determine, since it is not known precisely when he joined the party. The closest we can come to determining this date is the statement by Herbert Aptheker, editor of Du Bois' papers, that "by the year Mrs. Sotheran's article appeared in the organ of the Socialist Party, Du Bois had joined that Party." [54] Alice Hyneman Sotheran was an active socialist lecturer; the article referred to was a criticism of *The Souls of Black Folk* because of the author's failure, as she saw it, to understand that economic oppression lay at the root of Negro exploitation. Since it was published in the *New York Call* on January 12 and 20, 1911, [55] we may conclude that Du Bois joined the Socialist party some time later that year. He left the party to support Woodrow Wilson in the 1912 presidential election, dating his "resignation as member of the Socialist Party" on November 6, 1912. [56]

Du Bois' departure, like Harrison's, was hastened by his disillusionment with the party's stand on the race question. In fact, he had warned a group of socialists in New York City that the party would never succeed in attracting the Negro "so long as the international socialist movement puts up the bars against any race whether it be yellow or black. . . . So long as the Socialist movement can put a ban upon any race because of its color, whether that color be yellow or black, the negro will not feel at home in it." [57] Clearly, even though Du Bois' general sympathies were with the socialists for another generation, [58] he did not "feel at home" in the Socialist party. Early in 1913, he explained why in two articles in the radical journal, the *New Review*. In the first sentence of the first article, "A Field for Socialists," he set the theme of his discussion: "There is a group of ten million persons in the United States toward whom the Socialists would better turn serious attention." He treated party members to a lesson in the history of the relations between the white labor movement and black labor from the pre-Civil War era to the formation of the American Federation of Labor, and he demonstrated that racism had influenced the policies of the vast majority of the labor organizations. Consequently, with rare exceptions, the black worker had either been totally excluded from the unions or, if allowed to join, was forced into separate Jim Crow locals with the result that his condition was worse than that of other union members, even if he did belong to organized labor. "The net result of all this," Du Bois noted, "has been to convince the American Negro that his greatest enemy is not the employer who robs him, but his white fellow workman." He asked the Socialist party whether it had learned anything from this history and what it had to say to the black worker: "Is it going to ignore them, or segregate them, or complain because they do not forthwith adopt a program of revolution of which they know nothing or a movement which they are not invited to join?"

In less than a month, Du Bois returned to this question in "Socialism and the Negro Problem." Again he pointed out that one out of every five workers in the United States was black, and yet the Socialist party had nothing concrete to offer them. Instead, of coming to grips with this problem, the party was showing signs of yielding to "race hatred" in the hope of winning support among white Southerners. With extraordinary prophetic sense, Du Bois emphasized: "The Negro Problem is the great test of the American socialist." 59

If Du Bois was an "off-again-on-again Socialist," Local New York followed a similar path in its approach to the Negro question. From indifference, it had moved dramatically to launch the first campaign to recruit Negroes and had employed an outstanding black organizer and orator to carry through this campaign. At the first sign that the drive was faltering, Local New York quickly abandoned not only the campaign but also all other efforts to reach the increasing Negro population of New York City. By its neglect of the Negro question and its antagonistic attitude toward militant black socialist spokesmen, Local New York also succeeded in alienating precisely those Negroes whom it needed most if blacks were to be recruited.

# Oklahoma Socialists
# and the Negro

## THE SOUTHERN SOCIALIST
## PRESS AND THE NEGRO

On January 9, 1915, *The Rebel*, a socialist weekly published in Texas, observed: "The Socialist Party of the South is now being generally recognized as the only party that has anything definite to propose for the present situation of the South." *The Rebel* did not bother to discuss whether what the party had "to propose" contained anything of value to the Negro population of the South. It assumed that, since Negroes shared common problems and enemies with exploited whites, any program that dealt with the needs of whites would serve theirs as well. Of course, the problem was not that simple, and *The Rebel* itself proved it. Its December 3, 1911, issue featured a letter from its editor, Tom Hickey, which fairly reeked of racism. Having been informed that a Negro was running for office in Los Angeles on the socialist ticket and that this would give the Democrats "some ground to harp on negro equality," Hickey launched into a vicious tirade. He accused the Democrats of fathering mulattos and of establishing Negro locals in their organizations in Northern cities, and he insisted that wherever the Democrats gained control there were bound to be "mixed marriages," which, of course, went with "social equality." So bad had the situation become, he complained, that in cities in Texas, black and white workers were employed in the same factories, and in the public works of Temple, Houston, Galveston, and elsewhere, one could see "negro and white men alternating with the scrapers and drinking out of the same cups." This situation, Hickey insisted, clearly demonstrated a fundamental truth: "Capitalism has driven the workers into a social equality that would not be possible in Socialism. Socialism says to the negro 'we guarantee you economic equality' and that is all." [1]

Even as this letter was being published, Hickey was organizing the Renters' Union in Texas — and ignoring the black tenants. From its outset, union membership was restricted to "all white persons over 16 years of age," and even when the word "white" was stricken from the qualifications for membership, a provision was inserted that "persons of African decent [sic] shall be organized in separate local unions." Even on this segregated basis, few blacks were actually organized. Thus, while Hickey and other Texas socialists were talking loudly about economic equality for blacks and were bitterly opposing any concession to "social equality," they did little to help black sharecroppers achieve some measure of economic equality. "Their ideology and tactics," writes Donald Graham, "were determined far more by prudent concession to white racism rather than a sincere Socialist defense of the working class." [2]

In part, this situation was the result of the absence of a socialist press in the South that stood unequivocally against racism and for Negro equality, and that could educate the party on the need to be socialists first and Southerners second. (Of course, it is open to question whether such a press could have long maintained an existence in the South.) Now and then, a socialist paper in the South, such as the *Laborer*, published in Dallas, Texas, would speak out on the issue. But in its ten years of existence as a socialist weekly, from 1904 to 1914, the *Laborer* carried only two editorials on the Negro question: "For Justice to the Negro and to Ourselves" in its April 24, 1909, issue, and "The Lynching Orgy in Dallas" in the March 12, 1910, issue. Both were strong condemnations of lynching, but, as usual, offered as the socialists solution: "A complete change from the present system wherever the supreme force is property, to a system based on *humanity*, the common good, will end all of these evils. And education for this purpose is our solution." If this theme had been repeated regularly, it might have accomplished some good. But once having raised it, the *Laborer* promptly dropped it.

Another case in point is the *National Rip-Saw*, the popular socialist monthly directed at farmers and tenants in the South and Southwest. Beginning in 1912, [3] the monthly was edited by Frank O'Hare, with his wife, Kate Richards O'Hare, a dynamic socialist speaker and writer, as co-editor and regular contributor. [4] Kate O'Hare, in particular, did not hesitate to deal with the Negro question, but her approach was hardly

conducive to furthering respect either for blacks among Southern socialists or for socialism among Southern blacks. Mrs. O'Hare kept repeating
how much better off the Negro had been under chattel slavery, and what
a terrible nightmare white Southerners had been forced to endure during
the era of "Negro domination" following the Civil War. 5 This approach,
of course, played right into the hands of the Southern socialists who were
opposed to waging any campaign to eliminate the laws disfranchising
the Negro. Much of Mrs. O'Hare's discussion, moreover, was geared to
the concept that the Negro was not the equal of the white, but that since
his inferiority had been shaped by capitalist exploitation, it was the duty
of all workers, and especially of the socialists, to treat him as an equal. In
the February 1913, issue of the *Rip-Saw*, she wrote:

> "Only a Nigger." Yes, only a negro with black skin, vicious,
> depraved, ignorant and diseased, the product of our system, but
> his blood is red, he is a human being, he is bound with ties that
> can not be severed to every other human being on earth, black
> and white. 6

In her most widely distributed writing on the Negro question (published originally in the *Rip-Saw* and reprinted as a pamphlet), *Nigger
Equality*, Kate O'Hare insisted that socialism did not stand for any
equality for the Negro except

> equality of opportunity. Socialists want to put the Negro where
> he can't compete with the *white man*. The whole aim of Socialism
> is that every human being, white, black, red or yellow, shall have
> equal opportunity to have access to the natural resources which
> nature has supplied and to the machinery which man has created
> and then to have the full social product of his labor.

No other equality was involved in the socialist program for the Negro. In
fact, even under socialism there would be no "social equality" between
the superior white and inferior black races. That the Negro might not
even be capable of taking advantage of the opportunities offered by
socialism was not beyond the realm of possibility, but that was his own
affair:

> But you ask what is the solution of the race question?

> There can be but one. Segregation. If you ask me what I am
> going to work and speak and write and vote for on the race ques-
> tion when it is to be settled under a Socialist form of government,

I can tell you very quickly. Let us give the blacks one section in the country where every condition is best fitted for them. Free them from capitalist exploitation; give them access to the soil, the ownership of their machines and let them work out their own salvation. If the negro rises to such an opportunity, and develops his own civilization, well and good; if not, and he prefers to hunt and fish and live idly, no one will be injured by him and that will be his business. [7]

Thus, the 150,000 subscribers to the *National Rip-Saw* and additional thousands who obtained Mrs. O'Hare's pamphlet were treated to a discussion of the Negro question which helped strengthen existing racist concepts.

In sharp contrast to the *Rip-Saw*, *The Rebel*, and other Southern Socialist papers on the Negro question was the *Oklahoma Pioneer*. Although it was not without a strong racist element, the Socialist party of Oklahoma was the only consistent champion of Negro equality among Southern locals.

## EARLY RELATIONS BETWEEN OKLAHOMA SOCIALISTS AND THE NEGRO

The Oklahoma socialists tried to alleviate the economic problems of the small landholding farmers and tenants: the power of marketing agencies, railroads, moneylending firms, and absentee landlords. To remedy these conditions, the socialists demanded that the state take control of credit, marketing, and land distribution. The two major parties bitterly opposed these demands as state socialism. In their struggle against the Republican and Democratic parties, Oklahoma's socialists sought to enlist the aid of the Negro voters. Unlike the blacks in most Southern states, who were all but eliminated from politics by various forms of disfranchisement, the Negroes of Oklahoma retained their full legal rights to the franchise—at least until 1910. While black voters accounted for only 10 percent of the state's electorate, they were able to swing an election in a close contest. [8]

Since many blacks in Oklahoma were tenants, the socialists felt that the party's demands on behalf of the tenants would help overcome the traditional ties that bound the Negro to the Republicans. Moreover, since Oklahoma had a number of all-black towns—in fact, some blacks even nourished the dream of making it an all-black state—the socialists hoped to build an effective political base in these communities. [9] Hence, Oklahoma's socialists advanced the Negro's cause from the beginning of the party's existence in the area late in 1899, when it was still a territory. Reporting the formation of the Socialist party of Oklahoma, the *Daily Oklahoman* noted that among the thirty-two delegates present was Professor William Gibbs, "a colored teacher from Guthrie," who "delivered a very able address on the relations of the Negro to Socialism." (Gibbs was elected to the party's Executive Committee.) The Socialist party demanded that the following be included among the provisions of the Oklahoma constitution: "That the suffrage shall rest in all native or naturalized persons of legal age, irrespective of sex, color or creed." [10]

With statehood imminent, Oklahoma Republicans and Democrats joined forces to write a state constitution that would eliminate the Negro as a political factor in the new state. Oklahoma blacks, joined by the Socialist party, protested these attempts. Their protests forced President Theodore Roosevelt to prevent discriminatory laws from being written into the state constitution. [11] After Oklahoma achieved statehood in 1907, the Socialist party felt that the time was ripe for attracting Negro members. Many local party leaders, true to the Southern tradition, opposed black recruitment. But during this period, a new group of party leaders had moved into Oklahoma, including several from the Wisconsin state organization. [12]

## OSCAR AMERINGER AND THE *OKLAHOMA PIONEER*

Among them were party secretary Otto E. Branstetter and labor organizer Oscar Ameringer. While both were from the Wisconsin party, neither shared Victor Berger's white supremacist views. On the contrary, both wanted to recruit farmers and workers into the party regardless of color. Ameringer, in fact, was probably one of the outstanding white champions of racial equality in the Socialist party. Prior to coming to Oklahoma, he had been a union and socialist organizer in New Orleans, where he became involved in the activities of the biracial brewery and dock workers' unions. He emerged from this experience with many of his prejudices eliminated.

> What a book, what a whole library of enlightenment that experience was to me! It gave me my first insight into the true nature of the thing called the race problem. Among the many, many things I learned was that these black men were men even as you and I. Beneath black skins beat the same hearts, gnawed the same hunger, circulated the same blood. Below their kinky hair lodged the same dreams, longings and aspirations. Like you and me, they sought pleasure and evaded pain. What they asked from life was

living. Happiness within four walls, a loving mate, children, and the chance to rear them better than they had been reared. Health, laughter, beauty, peace, plenty, a modest degree of security in sickness and age. [13]

In Oklahoma, Ameringer took over the editorship of the leading party organ, the *Oklahoma Pioneer*, and he consistently and vehemently fought racial inequality. He argued that the Negro's degradation was the fault of the capitalist system, and not of any inherent racial inferiority. He pointed out that he had seen the Negroes at "their lowest, in the land of sharecropping and in the Negro slums of Northern cities," yet he had also seen Negroes who were "hard-working, intelligent, law-abiding farm owners on free soil." If the black man was "inferior," it was "not because he was black skin but because he works for a living." Once rid of the burdens of economic oppression, the Negro could function as capably as the white. It was the duty of the Oklahoma Socialist party to give him that opportunity by including him in its ranks and involving him in its program. Ameringer stated, moreover, that he did not believe in separate branches for blacks since this would only encourage the forces in Oklahoma favoring the continuation of legal segregation. He was referring to the fact that soon after statehood was granted, an alliance of Democrats and Republicans in the state legislature had passed a segregation statute over the protests of both the blacks and spokesmen for the Socialist party. Jim Crow locals in the Socialist party, Ameringer felt, would only make the task of ending Jim Crow legislation more difficult. [14]

Ameringer's all-out advocacy of racial equality met with opposition in the Oklahoma party. The *Industrial Democrat*, another socialist organ in Oklahoma City, warned that Ameringer was antagonizing many potential white members by his opposition to segregation. "Socialism," it insisted, "does not teach nor assume that all men or all races are equal." All socialism did was to offer all races the opportunity "to work and for each to get the full value of what he would produce." Furthermore, since "socially the negro can never expect to reach a position of equality with the whites," for the Socialist party to attempt "social equality" was to attempt the impossible. In reply to an attack on the socialist in Tom Watson's *Jeffersonian Magazine*, accusing the Reds of "dividing up," warring on "the marriage system," and (worst of all) "racial and social equality," the *Industrial Democrat* made it very clear that "social equality is not a demand of socialism." The editor argued that one could compare racial differences to those between men born with "a small sluggish brain" and those possessing "a large brain of fine quality. One Oklahoma socialist even insisted that there would be a segregated afterlife. He envisioned a "Negro heaven" that was "one vast watermelon patch," dotted with shade trees, dancing platforms, and numerous other recreational facilities, "where they can play and dance and shout themselves throughout eternity." This vision appeared in a pamphlet entitled *Why I Am a Socialist.* [15]

In 1910, W. T. Lane, a Negro lecturer from Omaha, began to spread the socialist gospel among Oklahoma blacks and to sell subscriptions to the *Pioneer.* He did recruit blacks, but they were usually organized into separate locals. However, in the coal districts, where the United Mine Workers drew no color line bars for their membership and voted heavily socialist, Negro miners attended mixed rallies with red buttons adorning their coats. Ameringer praised the United Mine Workers for allowing Negro participation "in all union matters." "The result," he pointed out, "is solidarity." [16]

On one point Ameringer and most of his critics in the party agreed: the need to resist attempts to disfranchise the black voters of Oklahoma. While Ameringer and his supporters took this stand as part of their egalitarian principles, the segregationist socialist knew from experiences in other parts of the South that attempts to deprive the black man of his political rights were usually extended to the poor whites as well. Consequently, quite a few segregationist socialists joined Ameringer and his followers in opposing the Democratic party's attempt to disfranchise the state's black voters. [17]

## OKLAHOMA SOCIALISTS AND THE "GRANDFATHER CLAUSE"

In the spring of 1910, the Oklahoma legislature passed and submitted to a referendum vote, to be held in August, a franchise amendment (modeled after the "Grandfather Clause" in Louisiana and North Carolina) which read:

> No persons shall be registered as an elector of this State, or be allowed to vote in any election held herein, unless he be able to read and write any section of the Constitution of the State of Oklahoma; but no person who was, on January 1, 1866, or at any time prior thereto, entitled to vote under any form of government, or who at that time resided in some foreign nation, and no lineal descendant of such person, shall be denied the right to register and vote because of his inability to so read and write sections of such Constitution. [18]

Since very few blacks had voted before January 1, 1866, *the law ex-*

*empted every male voter, except the black man, from the literacy test.*
And since the literacy test would be administered by white racist registrars, even those blacks who could read and write could be disfranchised
by trickery.

Party secretary Otto Branstetter immediately denounced this
"nefarious law" because it would "disfranchise thousands of working
men because they are negroes." In June 1910, he formed a committee to
fight against the clause, headed by Oscar Ameringer and Jack Hazel,
both editors of the party paper, *Oklahoma Pioneer*. Party lawyer Pat S.
Nagle filed suit to prevent the "Grandfather Clause" from appearing in a
referendum. He explained that the socialists opposed the clause not because they could thereby win black votes, but because they were a proletarian party committed to defending the rights of all "sections of the
working class, regardless of color." Party members who might not be
ready to accept such an argument were urged to oppose the franchise
amendment on the basis that "the literacy test for blacks was just a first
step toward a poll tax that would disfranchise whites as well." [19]

While there is no copy in existence of the Socialist party's petition
against the proposed Grandfather Clause, an excerpt from it appears in
the record of the court hearings on the petition. In addition, there exists
the argument submitted by Otto Branstetter, Jack Hazel, Oscar Ameringer, W. L. Reynolds, and Pat Nagle, Committee of the Oklahoma Socialist party. (Both documents are in the Oklahoma Archives.) The first
maintained that the proposed Grandfather Clause conflicted with a
section of the Enabling Act establishing the state of Oklahoma which
stated: "That said State shall never enact any law restricting or abridg-
ing the right of suffrage on account of race, color, or previous condition of
servitude." But the clear purpose of the Grandfather Clause was "to deprive electors of the African or colored race of the right of suffrage, and
not deprive any person of the white race of such privilege." The argument by the Committee of the Socialist party insisted that the purpose of
the new legislation was "to disfranchise a large section of the working
class," and that under such legislation, "the working class of many
states both white and black have been almost wholly disfranchised."
Since the chairman of the Democratic Executive Committee had denied
that "the intent was to disfranchise the negroes *solely*," it was logical to
conclude that "the purpose must be to disfranchise in connection with
the negro, the Russian, the Bohemian, the Irishman, the Jew, the
Catholic or some other group." The document denied that there was even
such a thing as "social equality" and stated that the socialists did not
make this an issue. It then closed with an appeal to the working class of
Oklahoma that assured the white workers that the socialists did not
assert that the Negro and white man "are equal—they are not equal—

and the inequality is not so much in color as in years—something between twenty-five thousand and two hundred and fifty thousand years."
(Just where the Oklahoma socialists obtained these statistics was not
disclosed, but they suggest that even this forward-looking socialist
leadership could not free itself of racist concepts.) The document continued in a bolder vein:

> But they do say that the negro is entitled to equal opportunity
> for access to the means of life and the full social value of his own
> labor. And he should not be deprived of the ballot, because the
> ballot is an instrument with which he can fight his way to indus-
> trial freedom. And it can not be said that he has always voted
> wrong—he has voted right more often than the white section of
> the working class—he has unswervingly voted against those
> who murdered his father, outraged his mother and raped his
> sister.
>
> They tell you that the negro belongs to the working class, and
> the working class must stand by the negro. If the white section of
> the working class abandons the negro he will become a scab and
> strike breaker on the industrial fields and in times of unrest the
> armed and uniformed mercenary of the ruling class. [20]

These two paragraphs represent the most advanced statement by any
group of Southern socialists!

In an intraparty referendum, the Oklahoma socialists voted to include
a demand for "unrestricted suffrage" in the party's 1910 platform. During the summer, the state leadership worked actively against the Grandfather Clause. Oscar Ameringer wrote the 2,500-word party statement
against the clause, and it was circulated as part of the referendum process. It charged that "the state's Democrats had initiated a measure in-
famously and undemocratically known as the 'Grandfather Clause'
intended to rob the Negroes of Oklahoma of the franchise." It called on
every right-thinking citizen to defeat the measure. [21]

As the August 2 deadline for the vote on the Grandfather Clause drew
near, Stanley J. Clark, socialist editor, rushed into print a special "Liberty Edition" of the *Industrial Democrat*, which quickly sold out its full
press run of 25,000 copies. Another special edition appeared a week later.
Both issues carefully spelled out the class analysis of disfranchisement,
printed detailed instructions on how and where to hunt down the elusive
registrars, and explained the complicated procedure for voting down the
amendment. These "Liberty Editions," which sold for only ten cents per

hundred, in themselves involved a huge outlay for a party that drew its revenue from small contributions of hard-pressed tenants. They were only part of the well-coordinated campaign the Socialist party of Oklahoma mounted against the Grandfather Clause. What made it even more remarkable was the fact that no assistance whatsoever was forthcoming from the National Executive Committee. [22]

Quite a few Oklahoma socialists, especially in the Southern portion of the state, began to express concern over the boldness and extent of the party's defense of black voting rights. They feared that it would lead many to believe that the socialists stood for complete "social equality." Therefore, when the Democrats began to charge that all Oklahoma socialists, like the "nigger loving Dutchman" Ameringer, favored "social equality," some Oklahoma socialists abandoned all their efforts to defeat the Grandfather Clause. Nevertheless, a large number of socialist voters, when they could manage to vote in the face of the most vicious interference by the registrars, cast their ballots against the clause. The socialists (and a few Republican leaders) were the only whites who actively opposed the measure, and the Republicans made only "half-hearted efforts." The results showed stronger opposition to the amendment in socialist precincts than even in Republican ones. Students of the results have concluded that the socialists proved more dedicated to defending Negroes' political rights than their traditional white allies, the white Republicans. [23]

In view of the massive fraud involved, it was not surprising that the referendum was approved. "The 'Grandfather Clause' has carried," Ameringer reported in the *Pioneer*. It carried by a 30,000-vote margin (135,443 votes to 106,222) amidst loud and justifiable charges of fraud by both the black and socialist leadership. Although saddened by the outcome, Ameringer was proud that the white cottonpickers of the state, "most of whom are Socialists, voted for the franchise for the colored man like a stone wall." And this was because "the Socialists of Oklahoma stand for economic and political equality, irrespective of sex, race, color or previous condition of servitude." [24]


## OKLAHOMA NEGROES ENDORSE SOCIALIST PARTY

"Negroes Favor the Socialist Party" was a headline in a number of socialist papers in late October 1910 as they reported that, on October 14, black leaders from all over Oklahoma had gathered in Chickasaw to express their anger at the Republicans and their gratitude to the Socialist party. The meeting represented the State Constitutional League, the

Oklahoma Protective League, and the Protective League of the 4th and 5th congressional districts. The blacks who represented these organizations met in convention to form a new association that would voice the aspirations of the Negroes of Oklahoma based on their recent experience. As soon as the convention opened, the chairman, Reverend J. A. Johnson, president of the Oklahoma Protective League, introduced a resolution denouncing the Republicans for their failure to seriously oppose the "nefarious legislation" that deprived Oklahoma blacks of their voting rights. The statement contained the signatures of representatives from all the congressional districts in which blacks resided, including those of the chairman and secretary of the Resolutions Committee. It was quickly ratified by the angry black delegates at the Chickasaw convention. The resolution endorsed the socialists as strongly as it denounced the Republicans. Its concluding articles declared:

> Whereas, the Socialist Party has invited us to affiliate with them for the reason that the Socialist Party believes in the Social Equality of all the races; and,

> Whereas, the Colored Race of Oklahoma believes with the Socialists that all men are born free and equal in every sense of the word;

> Therefore, Be It Resolved, That we hereby endorse the platform put out by our Socialist brothers and recommend that all the colored people of Oklahoma vote the Socialist ticket and align themselves with our Socialistic brethren. [25]

"We stand for a nationwide revolution in politics," W. R. Fulbright, one of the black leaders, declared at an open-air meeting. "The sentiment has been going on for some time in many states, but no colored organization has heretofore had the courage to break away." The black man sold his "political birthright" to the party of Lincoln after the Civil War for a "mess of pottage," but now he was "tired of being the tool of Republican bosses." Fulbright continued: "The republicans are to blame for the negro being disfranchised. The only party that has been our friend all along is the Socialist party. Who are our friends, my countrymen? The Socialists are our friends, and I am for them right or wrong." [26]

Later, Republican blacks rallied their forces and passed a counter-resolution favoring the Republicans. The news that was featured in the press, however, was that Negroes had endorsed the Socialist party. The *Oklahoma Pioneer* editorialized: "We welcome this action on the part of the negroes, not because it will increase our voting strength in the fall election, but because the negro is part of the working class and we stand for the whole of it." [27]

## OKLAHOMA ADOPTS THE "GRANDFATHER CLAUSE"

On the eve of the election, the Socialist party lawyer Pat Nagle issued a broadside "What the Black Section of the Working Class Must Do to Be Saved." In it, he warned Negro voters that they would be harassed and even attacked when they sought to cast their ballots against the Grandfather Clause. He cautioned them against going to the polls armed. Instead, he advised, "If a red card Socialist lives in your precinct, ask him to go the polls with you. If he is a southern man it will make no difference with him. Cumbie, the Socialist nominee for governor, fought for years in the Confederate army." Nagle assured black Oklahomans that they could count on the socialists to vote against the Grandfather Clause. "We stand for you because you belong to the working class," he insisted. "Here we take our stand and from this rock we will never be shaken." [28]

On election eve, John C. Wills, socialist nominee for lieutenant governor, reaffirmed his party's allegiance to the black working class. A former Pullman striker who had been blacklisted, Wills' experience had taught him that "when treated right," the Negroes' "fidelity to the cause of labor was of the highest order." In an open letter to Charles West, attorney general of Oklahoma, Wills publicly defended Negroes as a "race with a future"—a deserving people who "have made wonderful progress and are struggling to uplift themselves." He declared that "history is replete with examples of noble traits of character displayed by the negro in his association with whites," and he insisted that white capitalists were to blame for fomenting race hatred. Wills also replied to the charge that Negroes were still too backward to warrant their active participation in the political affairs of the state:

> The comparison between them [Negroes] and races with centuries of civilization back of them redounds to their credit, and despite the fact that the march of modern civilization suddenly thrust them upon their resources, and forced thousands of them into vicious environments, they have made wonderful progress and are manfully struggling to uplift themselves.
>
> There is hope in the future for a race that has produced a Dumas, a Douglas [sic], a Washington and others who have shed lustre on the black skin. And now a gang of political tricksters, henchmen of the capitalist system, seek, as in the past to inflame

the minds of the ignorant, gullible whites with race hatred, the fruit of which has ever been strife, outrage and bloodshed. [29]

The Grandfather Clause was passed, and at least two-thirds of Oklahoma's blacks were disfranchised. Despite the Chickasaw declaration, a fair number of those who could still vote continued to vote Republican. The *Oklahoma Pioneer* explained this with the observation that, while the black man in Oklahoma was "race conscious," "the transition to class consciousness will not be easy for him." [30]

Predictably, the Socialist party's prominent role in opposing the Grandfather Clause sparked a debate in the socialist press. In the *Oklahoma Pioneer* of February 10, 1912, H. H. Stallard led off with the charge that socialist opposition to disfranchisement had cost the party 10,000 sorely needed white votes in the 1910 campaign: "If enlisting one negro or pushing him to the front will prevent ten white men from studying Socialism we have done the negro as well as the white man an injury. Socialism is what we want, then let us adopt a resolution declaring for segragation [*sic*] of the negro and let him work out his own destiny." Such a resolution, he maintained, would "line up every white worker in the south" and simultaneously "deprive the southern demogogue of the weapon he has been using to perpetuate himself in office."

The letter provoked an immediate stinging rebuke from John B. Porter, a black socialist from Cogar. Porter regretted that a modern-day "Brutus" like Stallard should stab the Negroes in the back at a time when many blacks were joining the Socialist party, believing that it alone "stood for collectivism, democracy and equality." He asked why Comrade Stallard wanted the Negro disfranchised in the Socialist party. Answering his own question, he said:

> It is to line up the white workers of the South. In this he resorts to the tactics of the curbstone politician, putting the office above principles. Such a victory is in reality a defeat for International Socialism.
>
> The voters thus secured bring with them their prejudice and disregard for human rights so characteristic of this part of our beloved country.

Porter argued that he and his people would "utterly despair were it not for those Socialists whose convictions probed deeper than bread and butter" issues to the essential unity and equality of all mankind. The party may have lost white votes in 1910, but it had proved itself worthy to be called socialist. [31]

John C. Wills, who, it will be recalled, had already demonstrated his belief in "the essential unity and equality of all mankind," joined the debate with a scathing attack on Red racists entitled "The Socialist Jim Crow Car." In it, he denounced Democratic politicians like Stallard who blundered into the Socialist party "before shedding their hidebound convictions," and who felt uneasy mixing with Negroes at state conventions. The triumph of socialism, he declared, would never come as a result of its followers' succumbing to "a mania for exclusion seggregation [sic] or decentralization." Wills maintained that instead victory required a steadfast commitment to the black worker, who, in past outbreaks of industrial warfare, had "sensed his class interests and was a hero in comparison with the backward races." He curtly dismissed Stallard's claim that support for the political rights of Negroes had cost the party votes. "If we did lose 10,000 votes they were well lost," he insisted, "such reactionary element having no place in the socialist movement." [32]

The assault on Stallard's racism was intensified when the socialists in the coal and mining town of Wilburton published a resolution of censure in the *Pioneer*, citing as justification the February 10 issue of that paper which contained his offensive proposal. [33]

In his reply, Stallard upheld literacy as a prerequisite for voting and defended private property. When letters denouncing him continued to appear in the socialist press, however, Stallard complained to the *Pioneer* that, as a result of his stand on the race question, he had endured "the most complete lambasting . . . that any Socialist has had to take over a long time." Maintaining that the Socialist party had no right to "fix a social standard for its members," he pledged to "step down and out" if it "goes where I can't follow." "Good riddance, then," the *Pioneer* commented in closing the debate. [34]

## OKLAHOMA SOCIALISTS BATTLE TO RESTORE BLACK VOTING RIGHTS

The Oklahoma socialists continued to battle for the restoration of black voting rights. Article 28 of the 1912 Oklahoma socialist platform set a very high standard for its members. The state platform, approved by referendum, included a special article on the status of blacks in American society that reemphasized the identity of the Negroes' interest with that of the white workers in the class struggle. "At this time," Donald Graham points out, "the majority of Oklahoma Negroes were legally and extralegally disfranchised; the article could not, then, be interpreted as a mere tactical ploy to attract their votes." [35]

The platform explained that the evolution of Negroes from slavery through virtual serfdom to capitalism had been telescoped into a brief historical period compared to the centuries-long evolution of the working class. Nevertheless, they shared in the historical experience of white American workers and suffered the same forms of oppression. Black men and women had thus earned with their sweat and blood "a future . . . in the realm of civilization." Workers, who were the bearers of that future, and the Socialist party, their political vehicle, were the only haven for Negroes in a hellish white racist capitalist society. Accordingly, Oklahoma socialists resolved to "protest against the lawlessness, oppression and violence to which the negro is subjected in this state" and to "sympathize with the negro race in its present helpless struggle." The Oklahoma socialists proclaimed that:

> The safety and advancement of the working class depends on its solidarity and class consciousness. Those who would engender or foster race hatred or animosity between the sections of the white and black working class are the enemies of both; and we assure the black section of the working class that under the coming civilization, which is Socialism, they will be accorded every political and economic right which we now demand and eventually shall secure for ourselves, and that then they will no longer be driven in terror from the homes of their childhood and the graves of their murdered dead.

The platform then denounced the racism of the old parties: the cowardice of the Republicans who had struck a "corrupt bargain" with the Southern Democrats in 1877 which "delivered the negro naked and defenseless to his enemies"; the "pharasaical attitude" of the Progressives who only "pretended to offer the negro recognition"; and the viciousness of the Democrats, who still defended the enslavement of blacks and sought to play them off against whites to benefit the Southern ruling class.

The article closed with the warning that Negro disfranchisement was but the first step in the gradual disfranchisement of all workers. It forecast that even if white workers ignored blacks, the capitalists would not, and black and white would encounter each other, as they had so often in the past, across picket-lines, with the Negro serving as a strikebreaker and an "armed and uniformed mercenary of the ruling class." Hence the need for "class conscious solidarity" among workers of both races. White farmers and workers must therefore defend black voting rights in order to protect their own.

The platform promised the same political and economic rights to all workers regardless of race, but it did not promise "social equality."

Indeed, it blamed the Democratic party for a policy of forced racial mixing. [36] With this clause included, a majority of the membership accepted Article 28 in a party referendum, and the article became one of the most advanced, if not *the* most advanced, statement on the Negro question by any division of the Socialist party since the adoption of the 1901 resolution. The article was reaffirmed in 1914 and 1916.

In a leaflet "Why We Want the Negro to Vote" (reprinted in a number of socialist papers), Ameringer explained the reasoning behind Article 28:

> We want the negro to vote because he is a working man.

> If the black man has enough sense to feed, clothe and shelter mankind then he has enough sense to vote . . . .

> The Socialists will vote to a man against disfranchisement of any section of the working class, be he white, black, yellow or red. If this stand will earn us the usual title "nigger lover," then be it so.

"We Socialists," Ameringer insisted, "are blind as bats concerning race, color, or nationality. All we see is classes and class interests." [37]

Three years after putting through the Grandfather Clause, Oklahoma Democrats took steps to curtail the franchise further. Early in the state legislature's 1913 session, they proposed a Texas-style poll tax. (The 1902 poll tax had taken a heavy toll of black voters in Texas.) One outraged socialist wrote Senator John Thomas of Lawton, inquiring about the proposal, and received the assurance that it was merely intended to supplement the Grandfather Clause, "to assist in keeping the negroes from voting in the eastern counties." Not satisfied with this reply, the comrade wrote to *The Rebel* in Halletsville, Texas, about the effect of the poll tax in that state. Editor Tom Hickey replied with an editorial, "Striking the White Through the Negro," in which he demonstrated that his racism did not entirely blind him. He warned Oklahoma Reds that "while it disfranchises large numbers of negroes the poll tax also disfranchises the white brother in a proportion of about five to one." [38] The socialists then joined forces with the Republicans in Oklahoma and organized sufficient support to compel the Democrats to retreat. The poll tax bill was allowed to die. [39]

In the 1914 general election, the socialists continued their campaign to restore an unrestricted suffrage, demanding the return of political rights to Negroes. [40] Although they were unable to alter the situation, the United States Supreme Court, in the summer of 1915, declared the 1910

Grandfather Clause to be in clear conflict with the Fifteenth Amendment's guarantee of the right to vote. Enraged by this turn of events, the Democrats responded by passing a rigid literacy test for voters and submitted it to a referendum. After combining with the Republicans in the legislature in a vigorous but fruitless effort to prevent the bill's passage, the socialists began a campaign to rally citizen support for a "fair election law." "Fair election law" petitions were mailed out from party headquarters in Oklahoma City on March 11, 1916. In two weeks, 20,000 signatures were obtained, with endorsements continuing to pour in at the rate of 2,000 a day. As we shall see below, Eugene V. Debs toured the state for a week in March, speaking at rallies on behalf of universal suffrage. [41]

Despite widespread intimidation of blacks and white socialists alike, the Democrats suffered a crushing defeat in the August referendum. After a socialist-Republican campaign, Oklahoma voters decisively rejected the literacy test by a vote of 133,140 to 90,605. In the November election, the socialists' "fair election law" was on the ballot. The mail campaign in behalf of the law actually paid off at the polls, as the voters supported the constitutional amendment by 147,067 to 119,062. But the Democrat-dominated State Election Board introduced a new method of calculating a *majority* of the total votes cast and ruled that the "fair election law" amendment had fallen short of the votes required for passage. Socialists and Republicans joined in a court appeal against the decision which dragged on until September 1918, when the board was upheld. Actually, the appeal to the courts made little difference. The Democratic control over the election machinery enabled them to achieve the aims of the Grandfather Clause and the literacy test — the total disfranchisement of black voters. [42]

## PRAISE FOR OKLAHOMA SOCIALISTS

Since 1910, Oklahoma socialists had fought a consistent and unequivocal battle for the Negro's right to vote. This campaign did not bring the party any substantial support at the polls. However, many northern socialists pointed to the role of the Oklahoma socialists in the defense of black voting rights, and the endorsement of the party by leading Oklahoma blacks, as proof that there were socialists in the South who stood up for the Negro in deeds as well as words and that Negroes could be convinced that only the socialists were their *true* friends. [43] W.E.B. Du Bois published an account of the Chicasaw convention in *The Crisis*, reprinting the *Call*'s report, and he hailed the endorsement of the socialists by the black Oklahomans as "epoch-making." He continued:

It is a principle universally acknowledged by Socialists that although Socialism is primarily the movement of the working class
for the overthrow of capitalist rule, it nevertheless must rush to
the assistance of every oppressed class or race or nationality. The
working class cannot achieve its ultimate grand aim of freeing
itself from exploitation unless it frees all other elements of the
community from exploitation. It cannot put an end to its own
oppression unless it puts an end to all forces of oppression.

Clearly, the Oklahoma socialists understood this genuine socialist position and had acted in accordance with its principles. Therefore, it was
only fitting that black leaders of that state had "advised all the colored
people of Oklahoma to vote the Socialist ticket." [44]

# Southernism or Socialism—Which?

## THE SOUTHERN PICTURE

For many socialists, the events in Oklahoma were no cause for rejoicing, especially since the outcome was that Oklahoma Negroes could not vote the socialist ticket even if they wanted to, any more than they could in any other Southern state. More than ever before, the racist, segregationist socialists in the South used these developments to justify their doing nothing to recruit blacks. Why bother to spend time and money appealing to blacks, they asked, when they were now more or less totally disfranchised, and when such efforts would only antagonize those who could vote for the socialist ticket?

While the Socialist party in the South did not indeed present a uniform picture, it could be said that, with few exceptions, the Negro was ignored and rarely recruited. In Alabama and Kentucky, socialists in mining camps did make an effort to include Negroes in their ranks. Few such attempts were made in South Carolina, Georgia, Mississippi, and Florida, and even in most of the states of the upper South, Negroes were enrolled only if they asked to join; campaigns to recruit them were few and far between.[1]

The 1912 platform of the Tennessee Socialist party declared that "the question of race superiority" had been "injected into the mind of the white wage-worker" only as a "tactical method" of the "capitalist class to keep the workers divided on the economic field." The platform called upon Negro workers to join the party "in the political field as the only avenue of abolishing wage slavery, and the solution of the race question." A year later, the state secretary of the Tennessee party conceded that all the party had done was to wait for the Negroes to respond, and since most blacks were "stand-pat" Republicans, nothing much happened. [2]

At its 1909 convention, the Socialist party of Virginia voted "to make a special appeal to the Negro voters," and resolutions were adopted urging the party "as a whole to pay more attention to the solidarity of the white and colored workers." The Virginia socialists voted to make a special effort "to break down the race prejudice existing in their own state by particularly inviting colored workers into the organization." The *Richmond Planet*, the leading black weekly in Virginia, headlined the story, "Socialists Will Make Bid for Va. Negro Vote." It observed:

> The Republicans are denying that they want the Negro, the Democrats hint that they would like to have him on condition that he only vote and demand nothing, and the Socialists say, come on in on terms of absolute political equality — vote and participate in our party councils. This is indeed a choice morsel held out to Negro voters. [3]

But the *Planet* was unable to report any socialist action to make good on their promise to the Negro. Indeed, whatever confidence the black weekly had in the Virginia socialists vanished a year later, when it discovered that white party members joined racists in mourning Jack Johnson's defeat of Jim Jeffries, "the great white hope," in the heavyweight championship bout. Socialist party member B. Charney Vladeck, recently arrived from Russia, was in Norfolk the day Johnson beat Jeffries and watched with horror as "a band of sailors invaded the streets of the city insulting & beating up any colored man or woman they came across. It had the appearance of an anti-Jewish pogrom in Czarist Russia." He was infuriated to see that many of the beatings of Negroes took place in front of houses on the porches of which sat Russian Jews — members of the Socialist party of Virginia. He reminded them that they had escaped from Russia because of such persecution. He asked: "How can you stand watching such outrages without trying to protect the innocent people? Why this is exactly what you fled from only a few years since." He noted sadly in his autobiography: "The people would just nod their heads with a little guilty smile and say: 'Well, you are still a greenhorn — in time you will learn better — they are nothing but animals.'" [4]

This was one version of a theme common among any Southern socialists: Northern comrades did not really know the bestial and backward qualities of the Negro and should let the Southern party comrades handle the question without interference.

## DEBATE ON THE NEGRO QUESTION

On June 29, 1910, the *Chicago Daily Socialist* reported that the National Executive Committee of the Socialist party had agreed to send organizers at once into the Southern states for the purpose of increasing the number of locals. A special objective was to recruit Negroes, who were to be organzied into locals regardless of color, so that "the Negro will be educated to know that the Socialist party stands for equality of opportunity to all." It turned out that the report was greatly exaggerated; indeed, the only matter remotely related to it was the discussion of the appointment of a "colored organizer" to reach Negroes in the South, and even that proposal was shelved.

Nevertheless, the mere publication of the report initiated a most intensive debate on the Negro question in the socialist press, which was to continue for almost four years. The ink was barely dry on the *Chicago Daily Socialist*'s edition carrying the original report when the first protest came to the socialist paper. It was from Sumner W. Rose of Biloxi, Mississippi, state secretary of the Mississippi Socialist party. It condemned the National Executive Committee for having passed the resolution without first consulting "Southern state committeemen." "Let me tell you, comrades," Rose continued, "that organizing the locals 'with no respect to color' will not work." He advised the committee to remember the evils caused by "Negro domination" during Reconstruction, when Northern carpetbaggers took advantage of Negro ignorance. The Negro, he insisted, was still ignorant and could easily be led in any direction by designing persons if he were again enfranchised. The best friends of the Negro were those who did not try to lift him above his potential. Then Rose got to the heart of the issue:

> The executive committee has got the cart before the horse. Through an over-amount of sentiment they propose to reach those who have no vote and render it difficult to reach those who have a vote. Now, I do not wish to be considered in the light of a mere vote catcher, but without votes how are we to do anything? To my mind in the south this is a white man's fight, and must be made so, for the white man has the vote.

This did not mean that the Negro should be denied socialist literature—at least as much as he was capable of absorbing—but it was for the white socialists of the South to help him in this regard—without interference from their Northern comrades. 5

Rose predicted that he would be charged with "Southern prejudice," and the charge was not long in coming. George H. Goebel of Newark, New Jersey, a member of the National Executive Committee, assured Rose that there was no truth to the report that had so alarmed him. But he condemned Rose for his prejudice and declared that it was high time the party met the issue "face to face, call it by its right name, and not dodge it."

> Either the Socialist party stands for equal rights to the entire working class, and is an organization of that working class, re-gardless of creed, color, or nationality, against the capitalist class, or it does not. When it does not it should have the good sense to die and make way for a working class party that will. 6

Five comrades supported Rose, while an equal number criticized his stand. His supporters took the position that the Northern comrades, knowing nothing of the " 'nigger' question" in the South, should leave it to be dealt with by the Southern socialists. There was enough for the party to do in the South to organize whites, they said, without taking on the burden of recruiting illiterate blacks who could not vote and who, even if they could, did not have "intelligence sufficient to vote for their true interests in voting for Socialism." 7

Four of Rose's critics were Southerners. Reverend George D. Coleman of Tennessee said he did not favor "social equality." He insisted, how-ever, that the party should recruit blacks throughout the South and prove that it stood for "equal political and economic rights to all citizens irrespective of sex, race or color," and that it was founded upon the prin-ciple of the "brotherhood of man." If socialism did not mean this, he, for one, was willing to wait "until a party is formed that does mean that." Similarly, Emma Riddle Singer, born and raised in the South, said flatly that if socialism meant what Rose represented it to be, it would never have brought her into the party:

> The idea of requiring a black working brother to sit around and read Socialism, not daring to put it into action but depending on us to do that for him, is the most preposterous thing for a Social-ist to suggest. If that is Socialism, I am not a Socialist.

Thomas N. Freeman, secretary of the Alabama Socialist party, agreed with Rose that the Negro question should be left to the Southern social-ists. He differed with him on the readiness of the Negro for socialist re-

cruitment, arguing that blacks were more than eager to join and that it
was up to the party to fight for rights so that they could vote once again.
He reminded Rose that during the era of the Populist movement in
Alabama—which he knew about from personal experience—blacks
stood with the white farmers in a combined movement to wrest control
from the "capitalist rulers of Alabama." Moreover, he said, it was precisely because blacks and whites had joined together that the frightened
capitalists had moved to disfranchise the Negro in order to split that
threatening alliance. The Populist experience proved that blacks could
be relied upon to "vote with the working class when there is an issue between them and the capitalists." Therefore, it was necessary for Southern socialists to campaign persistently to restore the suffrage to the
blacks, knowing that they could be convinced to vote the socialist ticket.

   A. H. Dennett of Virginia condemned socialists like Rose for betraying
the principles of socialism. Dennett declared that if the Socialist party
stood for segregation of its members along a color line, then "let it die, for
it will be false to the International Socialist movement." Going even further, he wrote:

> Let the local that refuses comradeship to the black man because
> he is a black man, have the charter revoked. If any individual
> member of the Socialist party refuses comradeship to the black
> man because of his color, let him be expelled from the party, for
> they [sic] are guilty of cowardice and treason.[8]

   The letters published in the *Chicago Daily Socialist* proved that the
party members in the South were not all racists. Unfortunately, the
egalitarianism expressed in the letters of Rose's Southern critics was
rarely reflected in the policies and practices of Southern locals.

   While the letters in the *Chicago Daily Socialist* provoked by the reported action of the National Executive Committee ceased after August
17, 1910, another series on the same theme began in the *New York Call*
early in 1911. It was launched by an editorial in the *Call* announcing that
it was abandoning its former opposition to "social equality" and urging
the Socialist party to come out unequivocally for complete equality for
the Negro—including "social equality." The *Call*, undoubtedly influenced by Isaac Max Rubinow's definition in his *Internationalist Socialist Review* study, defined "social equality" as completely equal access to
public facilities. The editorial quickly produced a vicious letter from a
"Southern Socialist," denouncing the paper, accusing it of opening the
door to "marriages between whites and blacks," and charging that its
stand would make it easier for the Negro to achieve his real goal in life:
"Any man who knows the Negro knows that it is the all-absorbing, over-

powering desire of every Negro to possess a white woman. That's the real reason they are so anxious to secure 'social equality.'" He closed with the warning: "Whenever the capitalist exploiters succeed in branding Socialism as the Negro party it is absolutely dead so far as America is concerned."9

Here in all their nakedness were the fundamental arguments of Southern socialist racists—the danger of miscegenation if Negroes achieved equality, and the necessity of establishing without equivocation that the Socialist party was the "white man's party." Of course, as we have seen, such racism was not confined to Southern comrades; William E. Walling, for one, often pointed to the fact that it was characteristic of the party in various sections of the country. Too many comrades, Walling noted, like a socialist professor of political science who told him that he would kill his daughter if she asked permission to marry a Negro, justified their racism with the view: "Socialism has nothing to do with the brotherhood of man."10

Apart from Walling's criticism, however, such statements usually went unchallenged or unrebuked. What was different about the discussions in the *Call* was that the socialist paper refused either to remain silent or to retreat in the face of the Southern racists' criticism of its stand on "social equality." It charged that the Southern socialist's concern for the purity of the white race was sheer hypocrisy, since he ignored the fact that Negro women in the South were objects of white Southern men's desires. If there was any mixture of the races, it stated, it was more because Southern whites forced black women to sleep with them than because black men hungered for white women. "Social equality," it insisted, did not mean that one was obliged to be on terms of "personal intimacy" with a Negro, although if he wished to be, he had a perfect right to do so. It meant that the Negro was

> to have the same economic opportunities as the white man, that his vote is to be of equal effect with the white man's, that the educational opportunities offered by school, college and university are to be open to him on the same conditions as to the white man, and that in all other respects he is to be treated as the peer, and not as the inferior, of the white man.

It meant, too, that the Negro should have an equal right with white workers to join a union of his trade. Granted that equality for the Negro under capitalism could at best mean only "equality with his fellow workers in wage slavery," and that only under socialism would the "Negro . . . be given, for the first time in recorded history, the opportunity to develop all that is best in him, physically and mentally," it would not do for the

Socialist party to take the position that it was, therefore, necessary to wait for the coming of socialism before the Negro question could be solved. While the struggle for socialism was being waged every single day, "it is the duty of the Socialist movement everywhere to champion the rights of the Negro, which are the same as those of the white man, in every possible way, and to demonstrate to the millions of Negro workers that their only friend in this country is the Socialist Party." This would unquestionably retard the party's growth in the South. There was no alternative, however, for "steadfast adherence to principle has been demonstrated again and again to be the only course that leads to Socialist success"—even in the South! [11]

Mary White Ovington praised the *Call* for its "able and convincing editorial," [12] and one Jewish comrade expressed gratitude that he had lived to see so strong an affirmation of correct socialist principles in the leading socialist organ. He condemned the "hollow arguments" and "fallacious conclusions" that ran through the letter of the "Southern Socialist," noting that the same was "dished up by the reactionaries and blind Slavophiles of Russia in defense of the social ostracism and political suppression of the Jew." [13]

The *Call* devoted two more editorials to the subject, both in answer to critics. The first was in response to a letter from Nat L. Hardy, one of the key leaders of the Texas Socialist party. Hardy argued that, aside from the "Southern Socialist," none of those who discussed the Negro question in the *Call*, including its editor, knew anything about the nature of the race question in the South. He insisted that all the talk about Southern socialists neglecting the Negro was "bosh," and that if the Northern comrades would just leave it to the party members in the South, they would liberate the South and in the process emancipate the Negro. The kind of liberation he meant was that from economic oppression, and not the opportunity to "enter the parlors of the whites, ride in the cars with the whites, send their children to the same school as the whites—in short, guarantee a general mix-up with the whites." If that was what the Northern comrades and the party leadership expected Southern socialists to do, they had better count them out! [14]

Since Hardy's letter was written months before he and Tom Hickey organized the all-white Renters' Union in Texas, ignoring the black tenants in the process, the *Call* could not charge its critic with hypocrisy when he insisted that all Southern socialists stood for the economic liberation of the Negro. However, it did meet Hardy's challenge head on, accused him of being "imbued with anti-Negro prejudices," and declared that there was no room in the Socialist party for a man who professed allegiance to socialism and yet insisted that Negroes should occupy an inferior status in society: "Socialism without the idea of democratic equality is unthinkable, except as a reactionary nightmare. The equality of all the workers in the struggle for emancipation from wage-slavery, as well as in the emancipated society itself, lies at the root of the entire Socialist movement." [15]

If the *Call*'s editorials indicated that its definition of "social equality" for the Negro meant only a commitment to equal access to public facilities, Hardy's letter also revealed that leading Southern socialists, in opposing "social equality," opposed an end to a Jim Crow society in the South.

A few days later, the *Call* replied to another critic—one who insisted that, even "under a Socialist government in Washington," municipal matters would remain in the hands of the municipality, and since the race war between white and colored laborers would continue in the South even under socialism, these municipalities could continue segregation of the Negro in the cooperative commonwealth. The *Call* denied that this argument had any validity since it assumed that a race war would continue between black and white workers under socialism. But this was impossible since the first thing a socialist government would do would be to take possession of the great industries of the nation, abolish the distinction between capitalist and laborer, and "put an end to the competition between laborers. What, then, would become of the 'race war between white and colored laborers?'" [16]

In answering its critics, the *Call* wrote in some surprise: "The Negro question seems to be giving Socialists more trouble than we could have thought possible." This situation was by no means confined to New York. By the summer and fall of 1911, there was hardly a local in which differing points of view on the Negro question was not causing some conflict. Even in far-off Garden City, Kansas, the local socialist organ, *Prolucutor*, announced on April 13, 1911: "The Negro question has been an issue among Garden City Socialists for almost a year." Acknowledging that "nigger haters" in the local were determined to expel him because he demanded the "solidarity of all races," the hard-pressed editor declared: "It is now time to be plain. Any man who claims to be a Socialist and denies equal rights to the Negro is a weak exponent of the cause which would free him from bondage." [17]

In his letter to the *Call*, Nat L. Hardy had referred to a "very unwise" stand by the National Executive Committee and had warned that it would "bring great injury to the cause should they try to push their ideas in the South." He was referring to the report that, in August 1910, the committee had voted to challenge the Grandfather Clause adopted in New Mexico to disfranchise the Negro, and at the same time had elected Lena Morrow Lewis and George H. Goebel to "a sub-committee to study and prepare plans for propaganda among negroes in the South, it being contended that they are a big factor in the South and that special work must be done among them."[18] Probably as a result of criticism by Southern socialists, of which Hardy's was typical, the National Executive Committee did not do anything beyond passing the resolution and appointing the committee. But in December 1911, the socialist press reported that national organizer Theresa Malkiel was touring the South and Southwest and would do what she could to implement the committee's pledge to conduct "propaganda among negroes of the South."

Nothing much was heard from Comrade Malkiel until August 21, 1911, when the New York *Call* published her sensational report under the headlines:

## "SOCIALISTS" DESPISE NEGROES IN SOUTH

"Comrades" Refuse to Allow Colored Men in Meeting Halls or Party.

Writing from Memphis, Tennessee, Malkiel told of a shattering experience at Bald Knob, Arkansas, which "sent my blood boiling." She had spoken at a picnic ground to a thousand farmers and their wives and children. A delegation approached her, representing over a thousand Negroes who were also holding a picnic, and invited her to address the blacks on socialism. She had readily agreed, but the white comrades had refused to permit her to leave for the Negro picnic, arguing that if she went, "it would break up their organization." "Lord preserve us from this kind of Socialists," she wrote, reporting that she had been kept from speaking "to the darkies." She left Bald Knob angry and sick at heart, and arrived in Earl, Arkansas, in a pouring rain. She was met by a dozen white comrades and "at least a couple of hundred Negroes who came from far and near to hear a Socialist speaker."

Again she was shocked and saddened. Even though it was pouring, the blacks pleaded with her to speak to them outside since they would not be allowed to enter the hall where she was to address the white people that evening. So, even though the white comrades were not happy, she decided to address the blacks then and there in the rain. While she spoke from under a shelter, about 600 Negroes, most of them tenant farmers, stood in the pouring rain for over an hour, "listening to the message of Socialism so different from what the people around them were practicing." That evening, she was further angered to learn that the white comrades who had organized the first socialist local in Earl refused to allow any of the blacks to join, even though they pleaded for an opportunity to become members. The white comrades even rebuffed blacks who just asked for the chance to sit and listen to the proceedings of the meeting of the new local. "To my pleadings," Malkiel reported, "to let them sit in the adjoining room so that they could listen to our work of organization, they would not listen." When one of the Negroes tiptoed into the meeting "and sat in the further corner of the room," he was ordered out by the whites. When she remonstrated, Malkiel was told that if the "darky" was allowed to remain in the room, it "would precipitate a riot and kill the movement."

"The poor, poor darkies," Malkiel wrote bitterly, "they are turning to the Socialist party as their only hope. And to the ever-lasting shame of our Southern comrades, they treat them like dogs."

Despite her use of the derogatory term "darkies," Comrade Malkiel's report was a bombshell. Never before had a party member unleashed so bitter an attack on the Southern racists who called themselves socialists. Never before had Southern comrades been accused so badly of deliberately and consciously alienating a potential Negro membership. So burning an indictment of the Socialist party in the South was her report that it was reprinted gleefully, word for word, in *The People*, the organ of the Socialist Labor party, as proof of Daniel DeLeon's charge that the Socialist party was a racist organization. [19] Anarchist Emma Goldman, writing in *Mother Earth*, observed that Malkiel's report proved "that the black men receive far worse treatment at the hands of Socialists than from conservatives," and that "the party consists chiefly of national and racial philistines, moral eunuchs, and religious soul savers." All this was a logical result of "a Socialist propaganda limited to vote baiting." [20]

Although the Malkiel report aroused some indignation among party members, it was not as widespread as one might expect. The Southern reaction was typified by an article in *The Rebel* by E. R. Meitzen of Texas, a former Populist turned socialist who had become a leading advocate of segregation in the party. After rebuking Theresa Malkiel for intruding into Southern affairs, he accused the New York comrades of having done nothing themselves for the last thirty years "to alleviate the sufferings of the negroes." "Methinks even Tammany has been kinder to the sons of Ham," he declared, since the political machine had "organized more negro locals in one year than all the Socialist party in the north as in 18 years." Moreover, Northern socialists had done nothing to prevent "the wholesale northern lynchings" of Negroes, and until they could point to something that they had accomplished on this score, their pious criticism of Southern comrades would arouse little response. On the issue of lynching, Meitzen claimed, Southerners did not have to apologize: "In the North, they lynch 'em en masse," whereas in the South, "they lynch individually for the nameless crime." He conveniently failed to mention

that while the number of lynchings in the entire nation declined somewhat between the decades 1890-1899 and 1900-1909, the percentage that
took place in Southern states rose from 82 percent to 92 percent. [21]

Only a few letters came to the *Call* denouncing the socialists in Knob
and Earl, as well as all others who shunned "Negroes because of their
color." One that did referred to them not as "comrades," but as
"brutes": "They are out of place in the Socialist party and such narrow-
minded individuals should be expelled as soon as possible." At the very
least, this correspondent went on, the Knob and Earl charters should
"immediately be repealed." Comrade Malkiel was even criticized for continuing to speak to such comrades after their vicious behavior toward the
Negroes. [22] When a Virginia comrade defended the Arkansas socialists
in the *Call*, insisting that segregated locals were the only possible way to
operate in the South and reminding the readers of the socialist press that
"Socialism does not mean SOCIAL EQUALITY," he was called to
account. It was time that Southern socialists made up their minds that
they must confront the race question like socialists, a number of comrades wrote, even if this meant delaying the party's growth in the South.
In the long run, the cause would be benefited: "To win we must convert
the colored people to Socialism. You cannot do it by ignoring or shunning
them." [23]

Comrade William Morris of Washington, D.C., was unhappy because
so few letters had condemned the Southern socialists after the publication of Comrade Malkiel's account and because the *Call* had published no
editorial on the subject. "Last spring," he observed, "there was a series
of letters on the same subject, which stopped after a short while. And so
we stand. Nothing definite has resulted, and the question is still as open
as it ever was." [24] However, Nils Uhl, a black member of Branch 5, while
reminding the party that "Socialism is the one gospel that can afford to
indorse Southernism," maintained that, judging from its understanding
of the Negro question, perhaps it was best that the *Call* had carried no
editorial. He reminded his readers that, despite the fact that he had
called attention a year before to the *Call*'s use of a small "n" for Negro,
nothing had changed. The *Call*, for its part, simply repeated its previous
stand, insisting that it was not "the style of this paper, nor of 99 per cent
of the papers of this country, to capitalize a common noun, as a rule." [25]

Venting their anger in letters to the *Call* did not satisfy the members of
Branch 1 of Local New York. They unanimously adopted a resolution
which read:

> Resolved, that Branch 1 deplores the stated disqualification of
> the negroes by Socialists in the South as contained in the letter of
> National Organizer Malkiel . . . , and requests the General Com-

mittee to consider the matter with a view to calling on the National Executive Committee to confirm the facts and to proceed
against locals so offending against the constitution and spirit of
the party.

After it was received by Local New York's Executive Committee, a
substitute resolution was adopted recommending that, after ascertain-
ing the truth of the report, the National Executive Committee "consider
what action can be taken to do away with this condition which Local New
York regards as contrary to the spirit of Socialism." [26] Even though it
was toned down, this resolution was the most far-reaching stand in opposition to racism yet taken by a leading Socialist party group.


## 1912 SOCIALIST PARTY NATIONAL CONVENTION

On May 12, 1912, the Socialist party's national convention met in
Indianapolis. For months prior to the convention, a small group of socialists had been insisting that this time the Negro question, including the
racist policies of a number of Southern locals, should be tackled head on
instead of being totally ignored as in the past several conventions. Black
socialists, in particular, demanded such action. Referring specifically to
the "dirty diatribes" against the Negro in *The Rebel*, the organ of the
Texas socialists, and "the experience of Mrs. Theresa Malkiel" and "certain other exhibitions of the thing called southernism," Hubert H. Harrison put the issue squarely:

> Southernism or Socialism—which? Is it to be the white half of
> the working class against the black half, or all the working class?
> Can we hope to triumph over capitalism with one-half of the
> working class against us? Let us settle these questions now—for
> settled they must be. [27]

At Isaac Max Rubinow's request, the *Call* reprinted the concluding
article of his series that had appeared in the *International Socialist Review* between 1908 and 1910. In this article, he had called upon the party
to take concrete steps to convince the Negro that it was truly an organization that stood for blacks as well as whites. Rubinow introduced the
reprint with the note:

> It is the humble opinion of the writer that a proper attitude to-
> ward the Negro problem is one of the most important problems
> before the Socialist movement in America. It is the sacred duty

of the National Convention to form a policy and frame a plank in regard to the Negro. 28

"Race Problem Is Coming Up" read the headline in the *Chicago Daily Socialist* of May 9, 1912. It went on to explain: "The negro problem is coming up at the national Socialist convention, which starts a week from Sunday at Indianapolis." It also informed its readers that a group of socialists, led by Charles E. Russell and William E. Walling, were prepared to do everything in their power to bring the issue before the convention and try to get the party to take a definite stand against racism in every form.

But the only mention of the Negro at the convention was by William D. Haywood in his speech praising the support of industrial unionism. When the resolution was endorsed by the convention, Haywood said that he could now tell the four million black workers in the country that the Socialist party stood with them. For the industrial union strategy—the strategy of the IWW—was the way to organize the Southern blacks, despite almost total disfranchisement. Only Haywood made this point, however; no other delegate mentioned the Negro. 29

Eleven years before, in the same city of Indianapolis, at its founding convention, the Socialist party had devoted several days to the Negro question and had finally adopted a forward-looking resolution on the subject. But in 1912, apart from Haywood, there was only silence.


## VICTORY OF SOUTHERNISM

In November 1906, Mary White Ovington wrote to Ray Stannard Baker, the famous reform journalist who was about to depart for the South to study the Negro problem (a study that resulted in *Following the Color Line*):

> I hope myself to go South in two or three weeks and to make some study of labor conditions. I mean to meet the socialists in the different cities. That is the only party that has any Democracy about it, and it is hated by the white man who uses the Negro to exploit labor. You may remember that Tilman [sic] said, "What shall we do with the socialists? Shoot 'em like we do the 'niggers.'" 30

Seven years later, Ovington had a different view of the Southern socialists. In the *New Review* of September 1913, she wrote:

> There are two organizations in this country that have shown that they care about full rights for the Negro. The first is the National Association for the Advancement of Colored People. . . . The second organization that attacks Negro segregation is the Industrial Workers of the World. . . . The I.W.W. has stood with the Negro. 31

Ovington pointed specifically to the Brotherhood of Timber Workers in Louisiana, affiliated with the IWW. The Brotherhood had organized black and white timber workers in a common front against the powerful lumber barons and had defied the segregated pattern of life in the Deep South by holding meetings of black and white in the same halls. "Only one familiar with the South can appreciate the courage of their position, and the bravery demanded of both races," Ovington noted. 32

Ovington regretted that she could not list her party, the Socialist party, as a force in American life that stood "aggressively for the Negro's full rights." Its record made that impossible. In the South, there were some white socialists, like those in Oklahoma, who supported the blacks, but too many had "shown a race prejudice unexcelled by the most virulent Democrats." And what had the 1912 convention of the party to say to the Negro? The truth was that "no word, save that of Haywood, was uttered in appreciation of the existence of this most exploited race. . . . To this convention, the United States Negro, comprising one-fifth of all the workingmen in the Union, did not exist." Ovington was forced to conclude, to her sorrow, that Southernism had triumphed over socialism. 33

Ida M. Raymond, state secretary of the Mississippi Socialist party, fiercely disputed this criticism of the Southern comrades. In a thoroughly racist statement, she justified the disfranchisement of the Negro because of the use blacks had made of the ballot during Reconstruction. Giving the Negro the right to vote, she said, risked

> a repetition of the time when the Ku Klux Klan had to take matters in their own hands and save their women, their homes, and their country from the terrible outrages that were perpetrated by the Negroes as long as they were allowed the constitutional rights without limitation.

Like most Southern socialists, Raymond insisted that the party should confine itself to offering the Negro economic liberation. Agitation for anything more, she said, would simply doom the socialist movement south of the Mason-Dixon line. 34

In a previous chapter, we noted that earlier that year in the same magazine, the *New Review*, W.E.B. Du Bois had voiced the fear that the

Socialist party would move along the same path followed earlier by Southern racists like James K. Vardaman and Ben Tillman, and even use the hatred of the Negro to win Southern whites to its banner. Raymond's letter provided further evidence of what Du Bois had in mind.

A woman comrade in Washington, D.C., suggested to the state secretary of the Mississippi party, and to all socialists who shared her views, that there was plenty of room for them in the major parties. She observed: "But so long as Socialism is understood to signify a fundamental conviction for Equality, Democracy and Human Brotherhood, how can anyone holding these contrary convictions conscientiously remain in the ranks of the Socialist Party?"[35]

In April 1913, the national office of the Socialist party developed sufficient interest in its Negro membership to query the state secretaries as to the status of Negroes in their organizations. All the secretaries from Northern states who replied reported Negroes in their organizations in mixed locals, but they could supply little information since membership records did not specify race. Secretaries of nine Southern states and the District of Columbia replied. Florida, Georgia, and Mississippi reported some Negro members either in segregated locals or as members-at-large. South Carolina reported no Negro members: the state secretary commented that strong racial feeling in the state made it unwise to permit Negores to join white locals. Arkansas, Kentucky, Louisiana, Maryland, Tennessee, and the District of Columbia all reported that they allowed mixed locals. Of these, however, Arkansas had no known Negro members, and only Kentucky had more than a handful of active Negroes. In that state, the locals in the mining camps were mixed.

The data supplied by the party secretaries in the nine states and the District of Columbia reveal that there could not have been a Negro membership of more than two or three hundred at the most; that there were, in fact, only three organized separate Negro locals; and that, although six of the state organizations did not specifically prohibit Negroes from joining white locals, there were effective "social barriers" in those areas which, in practice, would tend to discourage Negro membership in the party. Finally, the correspondence showed that none of the party secretaries expected the situation to improve in the immediate future as far as Negro membership was concerned. W. F. Dietz, the state secretary of the Louisiana party, spoke for most of the party secretaries in the South when he stated that "it is almost unanimously agreed that the time has not come to try to organize the negroes. . . . the cause will make greater progress by not trying to organize them at the present time."[36]

At the May 1913 meeting of the Socialist party's National Executive Committee, a proposal was received from black socialist Reverend George W. Slater, Jr., "concerning the election of a secretary for the colored race." Although the National Executive Committee had stated in 1910 that the organization of the Negro was an issue of prime importance and although Kate O'Hare (even though she opposed a separate "colored department" in the national office) favored further cooperation with the Negroes and the working out of some plan to achieve this goal, Slater's proposal was filed away. In opposing the whole idea, Morris Hillquit declared: "There is no reason why we should not do the same thing with a Jewish secretary to be in touch at all times with the Jewish population and so all along the line with all races. We do not recognize such distinctions, and we make our appeal broadly to the working class generally." [37] This was the majority viewpoint. In other words, more than a decade after its founding, the Socialist party still had nothing special to offer the Negro.

# 12

# Some Changes in the Socialist Party Approach to the Negro Question, 1913-1916

## SIGNS OF CHANGE

The indifference to the Negro at the 1912 Socialist party convention and the lack of interest displayed by the National Executive Committee shortly thereafter to the need for a special organizing drive among blacks appeared to doom any chance for a change in the party's traditional indifference to the Negro question. In the next few years, however, there were signs of change. For example, white party members became more sensitive to derogatory jokes and cartoons about blacks in the socialist press, and were more ready to speak out rather than ignore this tendency as in the past. Thus, a party member sharply criticized "the way in which the negro race" was portrayed in cartoons in *The Masses*, the famous literary and political publication edited by Max Eastman. She complained:

> If I understand The Masses rightly, its general policy is to inspire the weak and unfortunate with courage and self-respect and to bring home to the oppressors the injustice of their ways. Your pictures of colored people would have, I should think, exactly the opposite effect. They would depress the negroes themselves and confirm the whites in their contemptuous and scornful attitude. [1]

The entire editorial boad of *The Masses* met to consider this criticism. While some believed that the artists criticized were "not guilty," the majority agreed that "because the colored people are an oppressed minority, a special care ought to be taken not to publish *anything* which their race-sensitiveness, or the race-arrogance of the whites, would mis-interpret." It was indeed new to find a socialist publication sensitive to criticism about the way blacks were portrayed in its pages. The view that one had to apply a "special" approach when dealing with the Negro was also rare in a socialist journal.

In the fall of 1914, a comrade in West Virginia wrote jubilantly that "the colored workingmen of Fayette County have at last awakened to the fact that their interests lie with their fellow workers of the mines and mills and not with the powerful capitalists who own and control the Republican party." He was referring to the fact that, for the first time since it was organized, the Socialist party of West Virginia was begin-ning to attract blacks. This observation appeared in the *Huntington* (W. Va.) *Socialist and Labor Star* of September 11, 1914. In the previous week's issue, the paper had announced the formation of a colored social-ist local in Huntington and had stated that the "new organization starts off with quite a large membership and unbound enthusiasm." [2] The local imported Ross D. Brown, "the famous colored socialist orator of Muncie, Ind[iana]" to launch an organizing drive among blacks in the area. The Huntington socialist journal reported that Brown had achieved fine re-sults and that an "earnest attempt" would be made "to thoroughly orga-nize the colored workers into the Socialist Party." The paper urged all blacks to respond:

> As Socialists, and as a party organization, you are welcome to be-come one of us and we exclude none on account of color, race or previous conditions. We are workers and the Socialist party, composed as it is of the working class, is opposed to the disfran-chisement of the workers, either white or black, because it will re-quire all workers to get Socialism. [3]

Here was another indication that something new was happening in the Socialist party.

Still another sign of the times was the formation of the first Intercolle-giate Socialist Society (ISS) chapter at a black college. The ISS was established in 1905 "to promote an intelligent interest in socialism among college men and women." By the spring of 1912, it boasted active chapters in forty-seven undergraduate colleges and universities, includ-ing Yale, Harvard, Princeton, Columbia, Chicago, and Brown, and re-ported that it was "increasing its numbers rapidly." [4] No attempt had

been made, however, to recruit black college students. Indeed, the first
black to attend an ISS convention was sent by the Delta Sigma Theta
sorority of Howard University to the organization's fifth annual convention in December 1913. She reported to her fellow students at Howard
that she had been cordially received and had participated in a discussion
on the topic "Of the Negro Problem in the South." After a heated debate,
the discussion ended with agreement all around that "economic causes
were at the bottom of racial friction and that whatever prejudice existed
was the result of ignorance and a thing not to be tolerated by Socialists."
She recommended that all college students devote some time to "an im-
partial study" of socialism, and she noted that the "young colored student [should] be interested in it because of its fair attitude toward racial
issues."[5]

This report led to the formation of an ISS chapter at Howard. In an
article entitled "Socialism at a Colored University" in the *New York
Call* of December 26, 1915, William H. Foster, president of the chapter,
reported that in less than two years, the chapter had held public meetings, distributed literature, sent delegates to the ISS annual conventions, and interested "the student body and professors of the university
in general concerning the study of Socialism."

Another aspect of a change was the socialist press's greater attention
to the problem of lynching. Not only was it now being denounced regularly, but in contrast to earlier periods, lynching was rarely defended on
the basis that it was meant to preserve the honor of white womanhood in
the South. On the contrary, more attention than ever before was now
paid to the violation of the honor of *black* womanhood. On the front cover
of its August 1915 issue, *The Masses* featured Robert Minor's magnifi-
cent cartoon showing blacks being lynched in Georgia with the heading
"The Southern Gentleman Demonstrates His Superiority." A few issues
later, it published Mary White Ovington's moving story, "The White
Brute," which told of how a black bride was taken from her black husband and outraged by a white man. The story was reprinted and distributed widely by the NAACP and contributed significantly to punctur-
ing the defense of the lynching of blacks.

Two other notes were struck in the socialist press with relation to
lynching: (1) upholding of the rights of Negroes to defend themselves
against lynch mobs, even if it involved violence; and (2) insistence that
the federal government act against lynch mobs and protect their innocent victims.[6] At the same time, socialists were in full agreement that
only socialism would solve the problem. Writing in the *Ballot Box*, a
socialist paper published in Fallon, Nevada, one comrade put it this way:

> Slavery, race-prejudice, a race-war are the legitimate fruits of an
> industrial system of capitalism based on competition or the prac-

tice of exploiting from others the value of their labor without returning an equivalent therefore.

Socialism proposes to establish and maintain a co-operative commonwealth. Under such a system race antagonism will in due time fade away because Socialism has for its four corner-stones justice, reciprocity, universal brotherhood and universal peace.

When the people of the South put more Socialism into practice and less competition, strife and hate, they will have fewer lynchings and will advance several notches in the estimation of right-thinking and peacefully disposed persons. 7

The socialist press emphasized this same theme at the time of Booker T. Washington's death late in 1915. Said the *Appeal to Reason*:

The career of Booker T. Washington is undoubtedly an inspiring indication of the possibilities of Negro development under favorable conditions. But it also reminds us that the salvation of the Negro race is not possible through the work of individual benefactors like Washington, or even through united racial action which is only a means of intensifying racial prejudice, but through united economic and political action to secure industrial and social freedom and opportunity for all men, regardless of race or color. 8

Another sign of change in the socialist position on the Negro question is found in the criticism that was now leveled at the party and its spokesmen in the Southern press. When the *New York Call* published a description of two young girls in one of the biggest public schools of New York City — one with "the fairest skin, blue eyes and blond curls," the other "black . . . with her kinky hair brushed into an orderly pig-tail," embracing each other as close friends — and then called the scene "the America of our dreams," the *Louisville* (Kentucky) *Times* denounced the socialists as "hysterical sentimentalists . . . who prate of the 'ecstatic intimacy' of the white girl and the negro." The *Times* declared that in the process they were defiling what America really stood for. 9 When deaf, mute, and blind socialist Helen Keller published a plea for equality for black Americans, the *Selma* (Alabama) *Times* attacked her. It pointed out that, although she was born in Alabama, she had forfeited her right to be honored by her native state because of her pro-Negro "fawning and bootlicking" statement. Further, the paper urged that any appearance she might make in the state be boycotted. Helen Keller refused to retreat. As she wrote to the editor of the *Selma Times*, she stood "for the equality of all men before the law, which the Constitution of the United States is supposed to guarantee to every American citizen." And she went on:

> I believe we should never do unto a son or daughter of God what one would not have done unto his own son or daughter. That is my idea of the teachings of Christ. In my spoken and written words I try always to be faithful to the truth as I understand it. If my words written in this spirit, result in the loss of engagements in any part of the country, I shall regard that loss as an offering to the cause of honest thought, and the sacrifice will afford me true happiness. 10

As we shall see, some party members did not stand up for equality as resolutely as this individual who could not see, hear, or speak.


## DEBS' NEW APPROACH TO THE NEGRO QUESTION

Still another important development during this period was the change in Eugene V. Debs' approach to the Negro question. Until about 1915, he had confined himself to calling on the Negro to reject the false doctrines of meekness and humility. He had left it up to the blacks themselves to combat discrimination and terrorism while he did nothing to call upon the Socialist party to participate in such activities. While touring the South, Debs had even begun to retreat from his earlier position against all discrimination. He never mentioned the Negro in his frequent speeches at the great encampments in Texas, Arkansas, and Oklahoma, and he did not protest the segregation practiced at these meetings. Considerable publicity was given in the socialist press to the fact that a black comrade, Sam Pruett, traveled fifty miles in a wagon to hear Debs speak at the encampment in Fort Smith, Arkansas, in May 1910. When the local police forced Pruett to leave the auditorium, since it was against the law for blacks to be present with whites in the same hall, the *Appeal to Reason* reported the fact, but said nothing about any protest by Debs. It was certain, however, that Comrade Pruett's "understanding that the Socialists were not responsible" had made him "a better Socialist than when he came." 11

Debs was outraged by the racist nature of the majority report of the Committee on Immigration to the 1910 Socialist party congress. In a letter to the *International Socialist Review* shortly after the congress — which, typically, he did not attend — he called it "utterly unsocialist, reactionary, and in truth outrageous." He warned:

If Socialism, international revolutionary Socialism, does not stand staunchly, unflinchingly, and uncompromisingly for the working class and for the oppressed masses of all lands, then it stands for no one and its claim is a false pretense and the profession a delusion and a snare. [12]

Yet, he did not add "of all races and colors" to "of all lands." Nor did he say anything about the failure of the 1910 congress to endorse industrial unionism as a means of reaching the disfranchised blacks with the socialist message. Although he was probably the foremost champion of industrial unionism in the land and the most bitter critic of the AFL's craft unionism, his alienation from the IWW, to which he had belonged for a brief period, was probably the reason for his silence. It is true that he announced that he was still an "industrial unionist, but . . . not an industrial anarchist," in criticizing the anarchosyndicalist influences in the IWW. [13] But he does not appear to have realized that his uncompromising criticism of the IWW weakened the battle against racism. Since Debs' position on the Negro question was that it all boiled down to the "labor question" and that only through organized struggle in the labor and socialist movements would the Negro win equality, his lack of interest in what the IWW was accomplishing in building interracial solidarity was certainly strange.

Actually, after his discussion of the Negro question during the presidential campaign of 1908, in which he reiterated his familiar stand that the Socialist party had no special message for blacks, Debs did not say a word on the subject for the next seven years. He broke his silence in the summer of 1915 to condemn *The Birth of a Nation*, the racist film released that year which became an immediate financial success. The film, based on Thomas Dixon's novel, *The Clansman*, characterized the Negro, according to *The Crisis*, as an "ignorant fool, a vicious rapist, a venal and unscrupulous politician, or a faithful but doddering idiot." [14] It glorified the Ku Klux Klan for having saved "civilization" by restoring white supremacy during the Reconstruction era.

Debs conceded that David W. Griffith, the film's director, had made an advance in motion picture art and technique. Debs charged, however, that if his purpose "was to insult the black race and to revive and intensify the bitter prejudices which grew out of the Civil war, he could not have better succeeded, and it was to be passing strange if the colored people did not protest against certain shocking features of the drama as doing their race grossest injustice." Debs called upon all socialists to join in protest. When the blacks of Terre Haute, Indiana, under the leadership of the NAACP, picketed the theater showing the film, Debs joined their picket line. [15]

In taking this position, Debs was far in advance of the Socialist party leadership, which maintained complete silence on *The Birth of a Nation*. In a letter to the *New York Call*, a comrade praised Debs' position and asked why the *Call*'s readers had "not raised their voices in protest against the picture." Having seen the film, she could say unequivocally: "A more outrageous yet cunningly devised piece of slander and breeder of race prejudice I have rarely come across." She urged all socialists to join the NAACP in protesting the film. [16] Evidently, her appeal brought some results, for the *Call* reported the Socialist party members were engaged in picketing the film in several cities. [17]

Once he had broken his silence on the Negro question, Debs began to write editorials on various aspects of the subject in the *National Rip-Saw*, of which he was co-editor. [18] In 1916, the front page carried Debs' byline on editorials like "The Crime of Lynching and 'White Supremacy,'" "The Color Line," and "Unmitigated Barbarity," in which he denounced lynching and upheld the right of the Negro to full equality. He continued also to denounce *The Birth of a Nation* in *Rip-Saw* and to call upon its readers to protest the showing of the film in their communities.

In 1915 and 1916, Debs worked closely with the Oklahoma socialists to defeat new devices introduced by the Democrats to achieve Negro disfranchisement. In 1915, the Supreme Court had declared the Grandfather Clause unconstitutional (Guinn *vs.* 238 U.S. 347). The Democrats, who dominated the Oklahoma legislature, then introduced the poll tax device to replace the Grandfather Clause. The socialists rallied so much opposition to the poll tax that it was defeated, whereupon the Democrats tried to use a literacy test requirement specifically directed at the "illiterate negro." By dint of hard campaigning, the socialists were also able to defeat the literacy test in 1915, [19] but the following year the legislature again pushed through the literacy test (and other changes in the election procedure) and submitted the issue to a referendum vote in August 1916. In the *National Rip-Saw*, Debs urged the socialists to mobilize again to defeat the proposal and called upon black and white workers to "rally behind the Socialists in defeating the capitalist conspiracy." Oklahoma socialists plastered the state with circulars (printed in red) reading: "Danger! You are to be disfranchised! . . . Unless you go to the Polls . . . and vote down the Literacy test proposed by the Williams machine." The *Black Dispatch*, a Negro paper published in Oklahoma City, called attention to the posters and to the fact that the Socialist party invited all Negroes to be present and to be registered, and that the party would see to it that they were protected in exercising this right. W.E.B. Du Bois reprinted the *Dispatch*'s article along with other evidence of the Oklahoma socialists' activity in defense of Negro rights. Du Bois concluded that Debs was "right" when he wrote in the *National Rip-Saw* that the Socialist party was the only political organization in the United States that did not draw "the color line." He attributed the defeat of the literacy test largely to the Oklahoma socialists' tireless campaign against the measure. [20]

## SPECIAL CHARACTER OF THE NEGRO QUESTION

In a series of angry editorials published in 1915, the New York *Call* declared that it was time to discard the view that blacks were just part of the working class like all other workers. The truth was, it insisted, that the Negro suffered special forms of persecution in American society to which no other group was subjected. "The whole Negro race," it cried, "is suppressed, robbed, outraged, insulted, debauched, ground down in a manner that makes the blood of those not blinded by race passion to boil. And this is a regular thing, not in isolated cases of passion." It was not enough for socialists to feel that they had done their duty by the Negro people by promising them equality of opportunity in the new society of the future. "It IS necessary to fight that the rights of citizenship, of the franchise, of education, of the right to live their own lives be given to the Negroes."

This acknowledgment — that Negroes suffered a special form of discrimination and that it was no answer to hold out the hope that socialism would solve the problems of all workers, including blacks — was being expressed quite frequently in important socialist circles and marked a new phase of socialist ideology on the Negro question. At its 1916 convention, the New York Socialist party declared that blacks were the "most oppressed portion of the population of the United States" and that they were "especially discriminated against in economic opportunity."

> However much white workingmen are the victims of the present system it must be remembered that Negro workmen, because of their former enslavement are more liable to exploitation, low wages and wretched working conditions. To this must be added the fact that a number of labor organizations have excluded colored people from the trade union movement and have then condemned them for scabbing.

The convention denounced lynchings. It called on the federal government to protect blacks against the lawless mobs and to bring to trial and punish local authorities who refused to enforce the laws. After observing that the persecution and oppression of Negroes was attributable "to the denial of fundamental political and social equality," the convention demanded the "enactment of federal legislation to put an end to the wrongs." 21

The Socialist party of New York had traveled quite a distance in just a few years. References to the special oppression of the Negro, to brutal lynchings, and to the necessity of federal government protection of the rights of blacks, including "social rights," as well as denunciations of racism in the trade unions, would have sent a shudder through a Socialist party convention a few years before.

By 1916, criticism of AFL racism was being heard frequently in the socialist press. There were even instances of a split on this issue between the AFL and the socialists in communities where previously the two had been closely linked. A case in point is St. Louis.

Although some black workers were permitted to join existing unions in St. Louis, and some even sat in the Central Trades and Labor Union, in general the St. Louis unions were Jim Crow and the Socialist party had never challenged this racist practice. In fact, the party in St. Louis was reluctant to criticize the AFL unions on any issue. 22 Therefore, it came as a surprise in 1916 when the Socialist party broke with the AFL unions over the proposal to segregate the city into defined black ghettoes. While the Central Trades and Labor Union supported the segregation measure, the Central Committee of the Socialist party of St. Louis voted to oppose it. *St. Louis Labor*, the official socialist organ, edited by Gustave Hoehn and usually uncritical of the AFL, emphasized that it was "the duty of every Socialist voter to stand by his Socialist principles and by his party, and vote against the segregationist proposition." It also carried a lengthy appeal to white workers, urging them to vote against the measure. Warning that "if we can segregate the negro, why not the Jew, Greek, Pole, Slav, other foreign races or those of religious sects?," the appeal declared:

> The education of the negro, and providing him with proper means for a living to raise his standard of living, is more worthy of the thought of good people than to crowd him into conditions where life is unbearable. Crowding him back into the alleys and slums will not make for a better condition for the white man than for the black man. The negro is here, not by choice. We brought him here when he served our purposes. If he was good enough for us to live with in the same city or on the same plantation when he was a slave, and a means of profit to the owner, we will have to tolerate his existence now. How choice the segregators were in the selecting of their parents is another question. Would it not be Hell—if, when we enter heaven, we should find that God was black! 23

When St. Louis real estate agents, in order to rally support for the segregation proposal, distributed literature favoring it to audiences as they left the theater showing *The Birth of a Nation*, Socialist party members countered by distributing copies of the above appeal which appeared in the *St. Louis Labor.*[24] The socialists were voices crying in the wilderness, for the vote was overwhelmingly in favor of the segregation proposal.

## BEGINNING OF THE "GREAT MIGRATION"

These voices were being increasingly listened to in the black community. For this was the period of the "Great Migration," when hundreds of thousands of blacks moved from the South to the North to escape the lack of political rights, social subordination, economic peonage, poor educational facilities, intimidation, and segregation, and to obtain employment in Northern industry. In the past, the immigrant masses had provided the industrial North with a cheap, readily available labor supply. World War I, however, drastically curtailed the flow of immigrants: the volume declined from 1,218,480 in 1914 to only 326,700 in 1915, 298,826 in 1916, 295,403 in 1917, and 110,618 in 1918. Moreover, half a million immigrants already in the United States left for Europe between 1915 and 1918 to serve in the armed forces of their native lands. With more than four million men drafted into the armed services of the United States when war was declared on Germany in April 1917, the need for workers to fill the jobs of the draftees became acute.

In the absence of new immigrant workers, Northern firms flooded the South with recruiters seeking to hire blacks. According to one authority, the Pennsylvania Railroad alone brought 12,000 Negro men north to maintain track and equipment. Another estimate claims that 50,000 blacks arrived in Chicago in an eighteen-month period in 1917-1918. Actually, between 1910 and 1920, the black population of Chicago increased from 44,000 to 109,000; of New York from 92,000 to 152,000; of Detroit from 6,000 to 41,000; and of Philadelphia from 84,000 to 134,000. The same decade saw a net increase of 322,000 in the number of Southern-born blacks living in the North, exceeding the aggregate increase of the preceding forty years. Richard A. Easterlin expresses it well when he writes: "With foreign labor supply largely cut off, a period of high labor demand in the North began increasingly to generate large movements of blacks out of the South."[25]

While the major political parties were indifferent as this migration got under way, and while the AFL and its affiliates were mainly concerned with barring migration on the ground that the blacks would be used to fill the "places of union men demanding better conditions," socialists viewed the migration as inevitable and irreversible. [26] They realized, too, that a new political phenomenon was under way. No longer was the Negro, in the main, politically impotent as he had been in the South since the beginning of disfranchisement. Now there was emerging a substantial Negro population in the North armed with the ballot. If convinced that the Socialist party was the only organization that stood squarely for Negro rights, they might very well contribute to a substantial increase in socialist votes.

Writing in the *International Socialist Review* of July 1916, Palmer Hoke Wright predicted that "by the end of 1917 the number of Negroes in the north will be double." This increase would mean little for the Socialist party, he maintained, for it would only result in an increase in "racial opposition and prejudice and disturbance" as the "natural outcome" of the Great Migration, since unorganized blacks, "used to working for small wages," would "accept less than the white man for the same work, and that spells trouble." [27] However, Ida Crouch-Hazlett, a black socialist, urged the party to take full advantage of this migration of the Negro population. To do this, it was necessary to recognize the need for the blacks to form their own independent bodies within the Socialist party:

> Were this any considerable number of blacks, they should have their own organizations in whatever they undertake, in the same method as foreign-speaking bodies. They work better that way. They have a different psychology, different way of doing things, and cannot develop a freedom when forced to adopt methods that are not natural to him. [28]

Several years earlier, Hubert H. Harrison had made the same point and had been instrumental in organizing the Colored Socialist Club in New York under the auspices of Local New York. Although that effort failed, Harrison's experience influenced a group of New York blacks during the period of the Great Migration to launch a black socialist movement. While this movement was linked to the Socialist party, it was also an independent expression of black radicalism. Moreover, these black socialists gave their movement the important backing of a black socialist press. [29]

# 13

## The New Harlem Radicals and *The Messenger*

In October 1919, the *New York Times* reported that there was a new mood in black America. Out of World War I had come "a new negro problem," with the emergence of a new crop of black leaders who, unlike the old-style, pre-World War I Negro leaders, "still under the influence of Booker Washington," were anything but docile and accommodating. On the contrary, the new black spokesmen were radicals and revolutionaries— men and women who favored the overthrow of the existing social system and its replacement by a socialist society.

These new black radicals, the *New York Times* continued, were making their influence felt in every Northern community in which the black population had experienced enormous growth during the great flow northward in the years of World War I. Nowhere were they as influential as in New York City's Harlem. Here, the *Times* insisted, was the center of radical black agitation. [1]

### THE HARLEM RADICALS

The *Times* was correct on both scores. There was indeed a new, radical mood in black America, and its center was indeed Harlem. It was in Harlem that a group known as the Harlem (or New Negro) radicals came into existence during World War I. With rare exceptions, they were all socialists, and they met frequently to discuss the relationship of socialist doctrine to the solution of the Negro question. Just as regularly, they discussed this relationship in the halls or on the street corners of Harlem. One thing the discussions and the speeches revealed most clearly: these black men and women had no doubt whatsoever that socialism was the only solution to the Negro question.

In Harlem, too, during this period there appeared every month a crop of ultramilitant, radical magazines—the *Challenge*, the *Crusader*, *The Emancipator*, and especially *The Messenger*, which at first carried the subtitle "The Only Radical Negro Magazine in America." This subtitle was soon replaced by "A Journal of Scientific Radicalism." By "Scientific Radicalism" was meant, of course, socialism.

As we have already seen, Hubert H. Harrison was the pioneer radical in Harlem on the eve of World War I. He was the community's leading street-corner orator and the outstanding black in the Socialist party of New York. But this man, called both the "father of Harlem radicalism" and the "father of socialism in Harlem," had broken with the Socialist party. In 1917, no longer convinced that socialism held the answer to the race problem, he began to propound the doctrine of "race first." Proclaiming his own variety of radicalism—an amalgam of black nationalism and socialism, in which the former predominated—Harrison now argued that it was the duty of all black radicals to sever their ties with the socialist movement, join his Afro-American Liberty League, and spread the doctrine of race first. 2

An impressive group of New Negro Harlem radicals disagreed with Harrison, even though they respected his contributions to the common struggle and admired his abilities as a soap-box orator and writer. They were enthusiastic in their support of socialism and considered the Socialist party the best avenue for putting this belief into practice. (Some, however, were later to break with the Socialist party and join the newly formed Communist party.) Among these black socialists were men like Richard B. Moore, Otto Huiswood, Cyril V. Briggs, William Bridges, W. A. Domingo, and Lovett-Fort-Whitman, and women like Helen Holman, Williana Burroughs, Hermie Huiswood, and Layle Lane. Many of the New Negro Harlem radicals had come from the British West Indies, the Dutch West Indies, and the Virgin Islands. But it was two black men born in this country who became the leaders among the New Negro Harlem radicals and the most important black socialists in the United States: A. Philip Randolph and Chandler Owen.

Both Randolph and Owen had grown up in the South, had known its discrimination, ridden its Jim Crow cars, attended its segregated schools, and had been disfranchised. Owen, a native of Warrenton, North Carolina, made his way to Virginia Union University in Richmond, a remarkably liberal school for that time and place. (Among the noted graduates of the Baptist-supported institution during that period, in addition to Owen, were Charles S. Johnson, Eugene Kinckle Jones, Abram L. Harris, James W. Ivy, and T. Arnold Hill.) From Union University, Owen went North to study sociology, political science, and law at Columbia University.

Asa Philip Randolph was born in Jacksonville, Florida, where his father was minister to three small African Methodist Episcopal congregations. He received a high school education at Cookman Institute (now Bethune-Cookman College) and, following his graduation in 1907, worked for four years as a post office delivery worker, grocery store clerk, delivery wagon driver, and in other menial jobs. In the spring of 1911, Randolph left Jacksonville for black Harlem, which was then bounded by 128th and 145th Streets and Fifth and Seventh Avenues. Soon he was attending City College at night and doing various odd jobs during the day. One position was with an employment agency known as the Brotherhood of Labor. Another, as a waiter on a Fall River Line steamer, lasted no longer than the first trip: he was fired when he was discovered organizing a protest against the miserable living conditions of the waiters and hallmen.

Meanwhile, on City College's campus, Randolph heard the evening session students talk of radicalism, of the Industrial Workers of the World and their militant strikes in Lowell, Massachusetts, in 1912 and in Paterson, New Jersey, the following year, and of the Socialist party, whose presidential candidate, Eugene V. Debs, had polled nearly a million votes in the 1912 election. It was in a history course at City College that Randolph was introduced to the history of socialism. He became so intrigued by it that in his spare time, as he later recalled, he "began reading Marx as children read 'Alice in Wonderland.'"

It was in New York's lively black intellectual circles that the two migrants from the South—Owen and Randolph—met. (They were introduced by Randolph's wife, Lucille, who had met Owen at a party and was impressed by his seriousness and political interests which so resembled those of her new husband.) Owen, however, knew nothing yet of socialism and was under the influence of the writings of the sociologist Lester F. Ward, to which he introduced Randolph. Randolph, for his part, contributed the writings of Marx to the partnership. By now fast friends, the two spent their time together studying "the theory and history of Socialism and working-class politics" and "their application to the racial problem." Together, too, they attended socialist and labor forums in the evening at the Rand School and at branches of the party, and, at the corner of Lenox Avenue and 135th Street, listened with rapt attention to Hubert H. Harrison as he spoke on the importance of socialism to black

Americans. In due time, with Marx, Ward, and Harrison as their guides, these two black radicals, as Randolph phrased it later, talked themselves into joining the Socialist party. [3]

## THE INDEPENDENT POLITICAL COUNCIL

Randolph and Owen became party members sometime during the late spring of 1916 and immediately became involved in New York City socialist politics. Not long after arriving in New York, Randolph and a few of his free-thinking friends had formed a current affairs group, the Independent Political Council. By sponsoring lectures and conducting debates in the black churches on the need for blacks to break away from their dependence on the Republican party, the council gained a reputation for political independence and militancy. However, it did not espouse socialism. After they joined the party, Randolph and Owen decided to devote full time to the cause. They dropped their studies at City College and Columbia and reorganzied the Independent Political Council with the aim of turning it into a vehicle for advancing the interests of the Socialist party in the black community. With Randolph as president and Owen as executive secretary, the council stepped up its activities. The two, however, still kept their basic aim secret in order not to alienate sections of the black community. They advanced the concept that the council's objective was to campaign for clean, honest, and progressive government, coupled with justice for blacks. [4] The aims of the moderately radical program were:

First, to create and crystallize sentiment against the present unrighteous conditions, through an organized educational campaign.

Second, to compile and distribute literature and to conduct public lectures on the vital issues affecting the colored people's economic and political destiny.

Third, to appraise men and measures in public life.

Fourth, to examine, expose and condemn cunning and malicious political marplots in the legislative, judicial and executive departments of the city, state and nation.

Fifth, fearlessly to criticise and to denounce selfish and self-styled leaders.

Finally, to devote its influence uncompromisingly to the advocacy of all principles, to the endorsement of all men, and to the
support of all movements working for justice and progress.[5]

Actually, the council was an adjunct of the Socialist party's presidential campaign of 1916. With Debs refusing to run for president for the
first time since 1900, the Socialist party nominated another standard
bearer—Allan J. Benson—through party referendum. Although comparatively unknown compared to Debs, Benson was gaining a reputation
because of his vigorous opposition to military preparedness as a scheme
for bringing the United States into the war then raging in Europe, and
because of his proposal for a constitutional requirement of a popular
referendum to declare war.[6] To Randolph and Owen, Bensom may have
lacked Debs' emotional and humanitarian appeal, but since they were
becoming more and more opposed to war preparations themselves, they
found his antimilitarist position attractive.[7]

The names of Randolph and Owen made their first appearance in the
socialist press in the October 23, 1916, issue of the New York *Call*. Under
the headlines "Harlem Colored Residents Are for Benson. Independent
Political Council Indorses Socialist Candidate for U.S. Presidency," the
*Call* announced that 600 members of the Independent Political Council—
"the most important organization of the colored residents of Harlem"—
had endorsed the candidacy of Benson and was "conducting an extensive
campaign in Harlem to get colored men to split their ticket in favor of
Benson if they will not vote the entire ticket." Describing the council as
made up of 400 blacks and 200 whites (men and women), with Randolph as president and Owen as executive secretary, the paper reported
that it was leading a campaign against the enlistment of blacks in the
national guard regiment and distributing leaflets outlining reasons why
they should not enlist. One of these reasons was that they would be called
upon "to 'fight for their country,' not a foot of whose land is theirs." Randolph was quoted as praising Benson for being the only presidential
candidate who knew no "color line" and as urging all blacks to vote for
him. At the same time, he emphasized that this support did not mean a
blanket endorsement of the Socialist party by the council he headed: "It
would not give a wholesale endorsement to the Socialist Party, while a
half dozen or more Socialist candidates in Iowa, Kansas and other States
favor race segregation in cars and like." Randolph was referring to a poll
conducted by *The Crisis* on the attitude of the candidates of the different
parties toward segregation of blacks in housing, transportation, and
other facilities. Among those who responded as favoring such segregation were socialist candidates in a number of Northern and Western, as
well as Southern states.[8]

The name of the Independent Political Council appeared once more in the columns of the *Call* prior to election day. This time the article announced that the council was leading a "political revolution" in Harlem by swinging "colored voters to socialism." Interviewed at the council's headquarters at 436 Lenox Avenue, Randolph and Owen came out for the single tax and socialism as the solution for high rents and high food prices, which they viewed as "the chief clouds on our domestic horizons." They also denounced "military preparedness" as a "Trojan horse" aimed at piling taxes upon the poor while blinding them to the process by which the United States would be dragged into the war. Finally, they called for legislation to make lynching a federal crime. Asked why the council did not support "the whole Socialist ticket," Randolph replied that they were not socialists and that even if they were party members, they would not endorse socialists who had indicated they "favored segregation among races." But they were impressed by the socialist program for solving the Negro question, and they were certainly interested in advancing Benson's candidacy. [9]

Editorially, the *Call* hailed the report of the interview as marking the "Awakening of the Negro." It noted that what was truly significant was not that the "more intelligent" of the Independent Political Council would vote for Benson, but that the council's existence indicated "the growing perception among Negroes that in Socialism lies the only real and final emancipation, not only for them, but for the entire human race." [10] Clearly, the *Call* did not expect a large vote for Benson in Harlem. Indeed the socialist candidate did run as poorly in that community (against Woodrow Wilson, seeking reelection as the man who had "kept us out of war") as he did elsewhere in the nation. What the *Call* was really referring to was the fact that, despite the denial that they were socialists, the work of Randolph and Owen indicated that a new radical force was emerging in the black community. This fact received nationwide attention when *The Public*, in its November 10, 1916, issue, under the heading "Radical Movement Among New York Negroes," noted the existence of the Independent Political Council—"a New York organization consisting mainly of Negroes who have broken away from the Republican Party" and were beginning to gravitate toward socialism.

No sooner was the presidential election over than the *Call* reported that a big drive was getting under way in Harlem in preparation for the municipal campaign the following year. The Independent Political Council, it stated, was expected to play a leading role in these activities. [11] Indeed, in the months that followed, Randolph and Owen regularly mounted the soap box on the corners of Lenox Avenue and 135th Street and of Seventh Avenue and 132nd Street to advocate socialism; they called upon their audiences first to join the Independent Political Council and then the Socialist party. By the time the mayoral election campaign of 1917 was in full swing, Randolph and Owen were functioning actively as an integral part of the drive to elect Morris Hillquit, the socialist candidate. Hillquit's campaign was being promoted by literature distributed widely throughout Harlem in the name of the Independent Political Council, and in the columns of a new magazine edited by Randolph and Owen, the first issue of which hit the streets on the eve of election day.

## THE FOUNDING OF *THE MESSENGER*

The new magazine emerged out of a search for larger headquarters for the Independent Political Council. When Randolph and Owen were offered sufficient space in the office of the Headwaiters and Sidewaiters Society if they would edit a monthly magazine for the new black union, the two socialists, unemployed at the time, agreed. For the next eight months in the society's headquarters on Lenox Avenue, they brought out the *Hotel Messenger*, the name they chose for the magazine, and held daily meetings with members of the Political Council and with other black radicals. But in August 1917, the last issue of the *Hotel Messenger* appeared. Once the editors began to interview black hotel workers, they discovered that from the common waiters' and pantrymen's point of view, the headwaiters were as much an enemy as the employers. The headwaiters lorded it over their "inferiors" and coerced them into purchasing their uniforms through them at exorbitant prices while pocketing kickbacks from the uniform dealers. This was in addition to the grievances of inadequate wages and poor working conditions. When Randolph and Owen wrote stinging editorials against those who employed them, the two young black editors quickly found themselves out of a job. But Randolph and Owen decided to keep their periodical going. So, in addition to organizing a union of elevator and switchboard operators, agreeing to coordinate Hillquit's mayoral campaign in Harlem, and forming a socialist political club in Harlem's Twenty-First Assembly District, they issued, in November 1917, the first number of *The Messenger*. 12 They announced under the "Editors' Statement":

We are no longer the "Hotel" Messenger. . . .

The steady and numerous requests by the intelligent, radical forward-looking and clear-eyed thinking patrons of the editors to rid themselves of the hindering name, have borne this fruit—The Messenger. . . .

The Messenger shall be forward, aggressive, militant, revolutionary.

The Messenger shall ever fight for the economic and intellectual emancipation of the workingman.

It shall ever fight for peace—a durable, permanent and democratic peace.

It shall ever fight the hydra-headed monster—race prejudice.

It shall ever champion the cause of free speech, free press and free assemblage. 13

The Messenger started out as a socialist publication, and at the time it was launched, it was the only black socialist magazine in the country. But it was not, as one student of The Messenger asserts, "the first socialist magazine edited by and for blacks in America." 14 That honor belongs to the American Negro Socialist, of whose existence we know because of two items in the Cleveland Citizen, a socialist weekly. The first, in the issue of September 11, 1915, read:

> J.B. Reed is the editor of the American Negro Socialist, the first issue of which has just appeared at Butte, Mont[ana]. Its purpose is to carry the message of socialism to the negroes of the United States. The excellence of the first number indicates that it will do a big and useful work in the Socialist movement.

The following week, the Citizen published a letter Reed had sent out to the general membership of the party:

> Our aim and object is to create an impression on the Negro's mind, that he must identify himself with the class struggle, the sooner the better. The United States Supreme Court has now decided that the Negroes of the South have the right to the franchise, and if such is the case, the [American] Negro Socialist predicts that the time is not far off when the Negro shall make application to the Socialist Party for his absolute favor since the U.S. Court has ruled in his favor.

Unfortunately, no copies of this short-lived black journal appear to have survived. An effort to locate copies in the Butte Public Library brought a reply from the librarian that "the few copies we had of the

American Negro Socialist" were destroyed in a fire in March 1960, and that she did not know "of any place in Butte that you might find one." 15

## WORLD WAR I AND THE BOLSHEVIK REVOLUTION

The first issue of *The Messenger* appeared seven months after the United States entered World War I and in the same month as the October (Bolshevik) Revolution in Russia. Jervis Anderson accurately observes in his biography of A. Philip Randolph: "These two events — one in the demand it made upon the patriotism of black citizens and the other in the impulse it gave to American radicalism — would have a powerful impact upon the racial and political militancy of the magazine's tone." 16 Before examining how the magazine and its editors reacted to these developments, it would be well to consider the general impact they had on black radicalism.

When the United States entered the war, the majority of black Americans were eager to prove their patriotism and loyalty. Nearly 400,000 Afro-Americans served in the armed forces during the struggle, while on the home front, black civilians enthusiastically purchased Liberty Bonds and stamps. The great majority of the Negro press gave strong support to the war. Black editors were not completely willing to forget the injustices of American life, but they concentrated on winning the war, in the hope that a record of loyal service in the world struggle for democracy would be rewarded by the extension of some of that democracy at home. Even W.E.B. Du Bois advised blacks to "close ranks" and put aside their grievances in the effort to win the war, insisting that the loyal participation of blacks would win an end to discrimination. 17

Not all blacks shared this optimistic outlook, and none less so than the black socialists. At an emergency Socialist party convention held in St. Louis in April 7, 1917, when the entrance of the United States into the war appeared to be only days away, the majority report adopted overwhelmingly by the delegates attacked the "capitalists' war" and condemned American involvement. Black socialists were among the first to applaud the St. Louis antiwar manifesto, and when prowar socialists Charles Edward Russell and William English Walling tried to use their influence among blacks to persuade their black comrades to join them in opposing the Socialist party's antiwar stand, they were rejected.

Unlike most black leaders, black socialists viewed the war as useless bloodshed of gain only to the war profiteers. They had little hope that participation in the war effort would benefit black people at all. The war, they insisted, was against the interests of the working class, and since 99 percent of blacks were workingmen, they would be among the first whose interests would be adversely affected. 18

It did not take long after the United States joined the Allied forces in the war "to make the world safe for democracy" before black Americans found that the situation of their race at home was worsening instead of improving. The number of lynchings took an upward turn, with thirty-eight black victims in 1917. Anti-Negro riots met blacks migrating from the South to aid the war effort through their contributions to industrial production. In July 1917, in East St. Louis, Illinois, enraged white mobs, determined to drive Negroes out of industrial jobs, engaged in an orgy of shooting, lynching, and burning blacks wherever they found them, killing men, women, and children. For almost two days, the rioting raged until order was finally restored. At least thirty-nine blacks lost their lives in the riot, with a hundred or more injured. Black property damages ran into the hundreds of thousands of dollars. In terms of lives lost, this was one of the worst anti-Negro riots of the twentieth century. 19

From the outset of the war, Negro soldiers training in the South were subjected to constant goading and insults by white Southerners. Police brutality against blacks in uniform was a common complaint of the black soldiers. In several communities, these practices caused indignant outbursts on the part of black soldiers, and in Houston, Texas, they led to a riot. In September 1917, the men of the Twenty-fourth Infantry, fed up with police harassment and insults by white civilians, beat up a few whites. The Negro soldiers were disarmed when it was feared that they would use their weapons in defending themselves. But the soldiers seized arms and in a battle with whites, killed seventeen of them. With the merest pretense of a trial, thirteen black soldiers were hanged for murder and mutiny, and forty-one others were imprisoned for life. The Northern press joined the Southern newspapers in justifying the execution of the thirteen blacks and the imprisonment of the others, but black Americans were furious at the "legal lynching" of the black soldiers. 20

On November 15, 1917, the Bolsheviks triumphed in Russia. The formation of the first socialist government thrilled and inspired American radicals. Subjected to unprecedented harassment because of their antiwar stand, many of them were becoming discouraged about their ability to continue their activity. Now, in backward Russia, the symbol of oppression, had occurred the most successful socialist revolution the world had yet seen. And now, at long last, the champions of socialism could point to an example of success.

With but few exceptions, almost all Socialist party members, officials, and journals alike praised the Russians for what they had achieved and expressed their enthusiasm for the Bolsheviks. Black socialists had special reasons for joining their comrades in supporting the Bolshevik Revolution. They soon learned from reports by such socialists as John Reed, then in Soviet Russia, that V. I. Lenin, the leader of the October Revolution, had long considered the solution of the national question in Russia as a key Bolshevik demand; that he viewed the Czarist Empire as the "prison of nations"; that of the seventy measures presented by the Bolshevik deputies under his leadership to the Duma, or Russian parliament, from 1912 through July 1914, twenty supported the struggles of oppressed nations. They also read in Reed's dispatches to the *New York Call* and *The Masses* that to Lenin, national oppression was an assertion of privileged status of one nationality over another by restricting national and individual rights of members of the oppressed nationality; that he insisted that the Marxist program was to enforce both "equality of nations and languages" and "prohibitions of all privileges whatever in this respect"; and that in the socialist state all citizens of all nationalities would be subject to the same regulations. Each nationality would have a chance to develop and cultivate its national life within a working-class internationalism, and none would have any privileges not available to the others.

As the Bolsheviks moved to consolidate their control, the dispatches from Soviet Russia described how they put Lenin's interpretation of the national question into practice by adopting his doctrine of "national self-determination." According to this doctrine, every nationality within Russia could be autonomous, or, if it wished, enjoy independent political and cultural existence. At the same time, the Bolsheviks put an end to Czarist pogroms against the Jewish people and guaranteed them equality along with all other peoples who had been oppressed by Czarism. 21

Various American blacks were quick to contrast the rights accorded oppressed minorities and nationalities in the new Soviet Republic with the lynchings and mob violence directed against Negroes in the United States. If anti-Jewish pograms could be wiped out in Russia, they asked, why was it not possible to put an end to lynchings in the United States? If equality could be granted to all oppressed nationalities by the new system in Russia, why could not the Negro people in the United States achieve such equality? Black socialists did not hesitate to answer that all this was possible, but only if socialism was established in the United States. The events in Russia since November 1917, they insisted, gave further evidence that blacks had to support the movement for a new social and economic system in this country. 22

## MESSAGE AND IMPACT OF *THE MESSENGER*

This, then, was the political and social climate at the time of the birth and infancy of *The Messenger*. The magazine reflected the ideological currents of the period but added its own interpretation of events to the usual socialist viewpoint. It was militantly antiwar, agreeing with the party resolution that it was basically an imperialist war. It went even further by emphasizing that colonial rivalries and the exploitation of colored peoples were the real issues of the war. It vigorously opposed the restoration of the status quo after the conclusion of hostilities, both at home and abroad. It favored the Bolshevik Revolution, calling it "the greatest achievement of the twentieth century" and announcing that it felt that such a revolutionary upheaval might be good for the United States. It favored the peace proposals the Bolsheviks had advanced as early as April 1917 which called for no annexations, no indemnities, and the self-determination of all peoples. It bitterly opposed the Versailles Peace Treaty and the League of Nations, calling both "imperialist," and proposed the establishment of an "International Council on the Conditions of Darker Races" to administer, educate, and insure the self-determination of oppressed peoples in the postwar world. Speaking for the black radicals it represented, it declared in its March 1919 issue: "The New Crowd would have no armistice with lynch-law; no peace with jim-crowism and disfranchisement, no peace until the Negro receives complete social, economic and political justice." [23]

*The Messenger* opposed both major parties and vented its hatred of all so-called black leaders who occupied positions in them. It had nothing but scorn for "old-line" black spokesmen, viewing them as traitors to their people. It stood for absolute social equality, including intermarriage, and for the right of all blacks to defend themselves. It called for positive actions by the government to protect the civil and political rights and the civil liberties of blacks. It urged all blacks to leave the despised South as quickly as possible, even though it recognized that the North was not much better. Denouncing the bourgeois methods of the NAACP and the National Urban League as having failed completely to come to grips with the need for fundamental change, it insisted that new forms of social protest must be evolved. It called for the unionization of all workers, black and white, favored industrial over craft unionism, and the IWW over the AFL. And, of course, in issue after issue it supported socialism as the only feasible solution for the many ills facing black Americans:

> The Negro, like any other class, should support that party which represents his chief interests. Who could imagine a brewer or saloonkeeper supporting the Prohibition party?
>
> It is like an undertaker seeking the adoption of a law, if possible, to abolish death.

Such is not less ludicrous, however, than that of a Negro living in virtual poverty, children without education, wife driven to the kitchen or wash-tub; continually dispossessed on account of high rents, eating poor food on account of high cost of food, working 10, 12, 14 hours a day, and sometimes compelled to become sycophant and clownish for a favor, a "tip," supporting the party of Rockefeller, the party of his employer, whose chief interests are to overwork and underpay him. Let us abolish these contradictions and support our logical party—the Socialist Party. [24]

There certainly had never been anything in the black experience in the United States quite like this magazine which Randolph and Owen launched in November 1917 and which they edited with the assistance of two key "New Crowd" Negroes, George Schuyler and W. A. Domingo, and the long-time black socialist, Reverend George Frazier Miller. Despite the pressure of his wealthy parishioners, Miller opposed the war and wrote regularly on socialism for the revolutionary magazine. In its militancy, *The Messenger* was far in advance of anything up to that point in the history of black radicalism. In fact, it was even in advance of the very Socialist party to which it advised its readers to turn.

It is difficult to determine with any degree of accuracy how many readers *The Messenger* influenced, partly because the magazine's records were destroyed years ago in a fire. The Socialist party claimed that the magazine's circulation in 1918 was 43,000 copies per month. The editors themselves never gave such a high figure; they claimed that in the period from June to November 1919, sales rose to a peak of 26,000. (In its August 1919 issue, however, the magazine claimed a total of 33,000 black and white readers.) Whichever figure is correct, the fact is that in the summer of 1919, *The Messenger* enjoyed nearly nationwide distribution, with copies being sold by the thousands in New York, Los Angeles, San Francisco, Chicago, Philadelphia, Pittsburgh, Washington, D.C., Seattle, Detroit, Richmond, Atlanta, and Boston. To this should be added a fairly large unpaid circulation among the prisoners at Fort Leavenworth, including the "Houston Martyrs"—the forty-one black soldiers of the Twenty-fourth Infantry who had been imprisoned for life. [25]

While it may be difficult to determine just who in the black community read *The Messenger*, it is clear that it left an impact on its readers. William L. Patterson, later an important black leader in the Communist party, recalled coming across *The Messenger* in a bookstore in San Francisco where he was studying law:

I was stirred by its analyses of the source of Black oppression and the attempt to identify it with the international revolution against working-class oppression and colonialism. This was an enriching and exhilarating experience. For the first time I was being made aware that the study of society and the movement to change it constituted a science that had to be grasped if Black America was ever to attain equal rights. 26

As Theodore Kornweibel, Jr., points out, *The Messenger* was "more than a magazine." 27 There developed around it a circle of black radical intellectuals who discussed and debated how to develop the best approach to the important issues of the day—the neglect of black rights; the struggle for civil rights; the war and government oppression of antiwar dissenters; the attempts of the Allied powers, together with the United States, to destroy the infant Soviet Union; and the subjects of black labor, black politics, and black leadership. The fruits of these discussions found their way into the pages of *The Messenger* and, later, of such black radical periodicals as the *Crusader*, *Emancipator*, and *Challenge*. (Unfortunately, aside from *The Messenger*, only scattered copies of these journals produced by black socialists survive.) But these bright, earnest, militant blacks were not content merely to discuss and write. They were all involved in radical political activities, doing what they could to reach black Americans with the message that, while it was necessary to fight for the achievement of "full citizenship" in a capitalist society, this goal was rendered meaningless as long as Negroes remained an economically oppressed group. In the end, they said, only socialism could solve this problem. They brought this message to black Americans at street-corner rallies, in churches, and wherever else they gathered, to mobilize them in opposition to the establishment. In fact, Randolph and Owen were so deeply involved in antiwar activities and in honoring speaking engagements at antiwar rallies that it was difficult for them to issue *The Messenger* on a regular schedule until the war was over.

As Harlem coordinators for the Socialist party of Morris Hillquit's campaign for mayor of New York in the fall of 1917, Randolph and Owen launched a brilliant "educational campaign." Thousands of pamphlets headed "Some Reasons Why Negroes Should Vote the Socialist Ticket" were distributed in the name of the Independent Political Council. The pamphlet, reprinted in *The Messenger*, listed twenty-five reasons why blacks should support Hillquit and the Socialist party. A victory for the socialist candidates, it claimed, would result in "the abolition of high rents," "the city ownership and operation of the subway, elevated and surface car lines, the electric, gas and telephone companies," "a more efficient police system which will use more brains than billies," and what the *New York Age* called the "absurd promise . . . to furnish free food and free clothing for school children." The twenty-fourth reason given was that the Socialist party was "for peace." 28 In their street-corner meetings, Randolph and Owen raised and emphasized these same issues. They made special note of the fact that Hillquit was *the antiwar candidate* who called for an immediate convocation of an international conference to end the war on the socialist principles of "no annexations and no indemnities." They also read to their black audiences the resolutions adopted by the city convention of the Socialist party which had nominated Hillquit, denouncing the "outrages" of the East St. Louis mobs against the Negro population and calling for the prosecution and punishment of "the perpetrators of these fiendish deeds, as well as the local authorities who failed to give the Negroes sufficient protection." 29 What political party in New York other than the socialists, they asked, had taken so forthright a stand against the racist lynch mob? To ask the question, they said, was to answer it.

With the aid of Negro radical members of the Twenty-first Assembly District Socialist Club in Harlem, organized especially for the campaign, Randolph and Owen canvassed the black community for Hillquit. The black socialists made front-page news in the *New York Age* of November 1, 1917, with the headline "Law-Abiding Citizens Condemn Rowdyism at Political Meeting." The reference was to the fact that at a meeting at Palace Casino in Harlem in support of John Purroy Mitchell, the fusion mayoral candidate, a group of Hillquit's supporters, organized by Randolph and Owen, hissed and heckled the speakers. When Theodore Roosevelt, who saw in every opponent of the war "the Hun within our gates," rose to speak, the black radicals started to walk out in protest. The *Age* condemned the "rowdies who espouse the cause of the Socialist candidate," and it predicted that "the disgraceful actions of the Socialists will act as a boomerang at the polls next Tuesday."

The *Age* proved to be a poor prophet. Although John P. Hylan, the Tammany candidate, was elected by a plurality of 147,975, Hillquit received 145,332 votes, the largest tally a socialist candidate had ever polled in New York City. 30 *The Messenger* exulted over his strong showing and especially over the fact that, as it estimated (an estimate accepted in political circles), 25 percent of the votes in Harlem had been cast for Hillquit. This black socialist vote, it declared, was "a thing which gives the Negro . . . political respect." The journal expressed the hope that in the next election in 1918, 50 percent of the Negro voters would cast their ballots for socialists. 31

The first issue of *The Messenger* went to press before the country received the news of the Bolshevik Revolution. Therefore, there was no mention of this epic event until a later issue. But in an antiwar pamphlet they published late in 1917, *Terms of Peace and the Darker Races*, Randolph and Owen had already identified themselves with the anti-imperialist program of the Bolsheviks. "Russia has repeatedly proclaimed her peace terms," they wrote. "She has called on her Allies to do likewise. Russia speaks in clear, unequivocal language. . . . Again Russia has renounced all secret diplomacy. All of her Allies have dark lantern diplomacy." They called for a peace treaty that would be based on the principle that "government by the consent of the governed must be accorded to all peoples whether white or black or brown," a right that had to be given to "Africa, China, and the Islands held by Great Britain, by the United States, and by other nations." Such a treaty, in addition to embodying freedom and independence for Africa and other colonies, should also guarantee an end to lynching, Jim Crowism, segregation, discrimination, and disfranchisement in the Southern states. The pamphlet concluded:

> in the words of the Petrograd Council of Workers and Soldiers' Deputies: Workers of all countries—black and white! In extending to you our fraternal hand over mountains of corpses of our brothers, across rivers of innocent blood and tears, over smoldering ruins of cities and villages, over destroyed treasures of civilization, we beseech you to re-establish and strengthen international unity without regard to race or color. [32]

## RANDOLPH, OWEN, AND WORLD WAR I

Hubert H. Harrison was enthusiastic in his praise of the two black socialists, even though he hardly shared their fervor for the party from which he had resigned. He wrote in his paper, *Voice*:

> We often find Negro leaders who are radicals on the subject of their race. But frequently they know so little of anything else that they have no real attitude, no opinions worth while on anything else. . . . The authors are bold—perhaps too bold for safety's sake—but in these days of cowardly compromising and shifting surrender we cannot find it in our heart to condemn opposing qualities. [33]

The pamphlet made Randolph and Owen so renowned in radical antiwar circles that they were invited to present the viewpoint of black labor at the convention of the antiwar peace center, People's Council of America for Democracy and Terms of Peace. Because of uncertainty over whether any city would allow the antiwar group to meet in it, owing to the hysteria whipped up against the organization, the two did not attend the convention when it finally met in Chicago. They wrote thanking the group for its invitation and stating that, while they regretted being unable to attend in person, they reaffirmed their position that the war was being fought over the lands and labor of darker peoples throughout the world. ("The real bone of contention in this war is darker peoples for cheap labor and darker peoples' rich lands.") In a stirring plea against imperialism, they wrote:

> So long as African territory is the object of unstinted avarice, greed and robbery, while its people with dark skin are considered as just objects of exploitation—now here and now there in slavery, enforced labor, peonage and wage slavery—just so long will the conditions smolder and brew which needs must be prolific in the production of war. [34]

At the same time that they were mobilizing the black community in opposition to the war, Randolph and Owen were advancing peace terms that would benefit American blacks. These were later incorporated into a pamphlet which they issued after the Armistice, *The Negro and the New Social Order: Reconstruction Program of the American Negro*. In it, the two black socialists proposed the following postwar program: planned demobilization, beginning with an immediate cessation of war works; public work projects; a thirty-four-hour work week; and social insurance to prevent the hardships of unemployment. They insisted that conditions would not be permanently improved until peonage, the company store, tenant farming, and the private ownership of elevators, stockyards, and packinghouses was eradicated. Other reforms they proposed included the single tax, agricultural unions, agricultural labor laws, the admission of blacks and whites into labor unions on an equitable basis, an end to child labor, limits on women's labor, equal pay for equal work (referring to both sex and race), equal employment opportunity in government, a minimum wage, social security, woman suffrage, federal antilynching legislation, abolition of Jim Crow, full social equality and repeal of all laws prohibiting it, and an end to the private domination of industry for private gain:

> The private domination of industry for private gain has brought such disastrous consequences both among and within the nations of the world as to make public ownership for public service the first necessity in any forward-looking plan of reconstruction both for the nation and the Negro. [35]

Having decided to bring their antiwar and postwar program to a wider public audience, Randolph and Owen left New York late in the spring of 1918 to tour the Midwest. In addition to rallying the antiwar movement, their intention was to help build the Socialist party by trying "to get colored people interested in Socialism." Bundles of *The Messenger* were shipped ahead to be sold at different points on the tour.

As they left, 113 IWW officials, including Ben Fletcher, the black Wobbly leader, were brought to trial in Chicago, accused of violating the Espionage Act. Leaders of the Socialist party were being imprisoned under the same act for advocating opposition to the war and resistance to the draft. Kate Richards O'Hare was convicted because of an antiwar speech in North Dakota and sent to the penitentiary, and Rose Pastor Stokes was sentenced to ten years for saying that she was "for the people while the government is for the profiteers." Eugene V. Debs was arrested and sentenced to the federal penitentiary for an antiwar speech in Canton, Ohio. 36

According to the record compiled by civil libertarian Roger Baldwin, during the first year of the war most of the socialist papers were either held up by the Post Office Department or had their second-class mailing rights revoked. Early in the spring of 1918, federal agents raided the offices of *The Messenger*, ransacked the files, and took all its back issues with them.

As conscientious objectors themselves, Randolph and Owen were under no illusions as to what might happen to them as they set out on their antiwar lecture tour. Nevertheless, the two young black radicals did not mince any words in their speeches. They insisted that blacks should not be expected to support the war when they were still being lynched, Jim-Crowed, disfranchised, and segregated. While one inveighed against the war, the other brought the same message to the audience by hawking copies of *The Messenger*. Justice Department agents were usually in the crowd, taking notes of the speeches and purchasing copies of *The Messenger*.

In Cleveland, the Justice Department did more than take notes. During the first meeting, a Justice Department agent approached the podium while Randolph was speaking and placed him under arrest. Owen was similarly apprehended while selling *The Messenger* to the audience. The charge was violating the Espionage Act. The two spent three days in jail; bail offered by a wealthy black woman was refused. Finally, Seymour Stedman, a leading Socialist party lawyer, arrived to handle the defense and the two were released on bail. They were also freed because the judge refused to believe that two young blacks could write the inflammatory articles in the July issue of *The Messenger*, and was convinced that they were being used by white socialists. He threw out the charges and told Randolph and Owen to leave town immediately.

After their release, they proceeded to Chicago to fulfill a prearranged engagement. They found that news of their arrest had preceded them and that the minister of the church at which they were to have spoken had shut the doors to them and left town. "He wanted no part of us," Randolph later recalled. "So we just got ourselves a soap-box, set it up on the steps of the church, and went right on blasting the war. We couldn't sell any *Messengers* because they had been confiscated in Cleveland."

They visited other cities and held street meetings there. Invariably, federal agents were in the crowds and delivered orders to them to tone down their rhetoric and stop their attacks on President Wilson. They were also forbidden to set foot in Washington, D.C., but they took this warning as an invitation, hastened to the capital, and proceeded to lambaste the president in his own backyard. Their tour was cut short when Owen received notice from his draft board; he reluctantly went into the army, from which he was released early in 1919. Randolph, who was classified 4-A, was able to keep *The Messenger* going, although rather irregularly, until Owen returned. [37]

In his biography of Randolph, Jervis Anderson tries to explain how (except for the brief incident in Cleveland) the two black socialists were able to stay out of jail, despite the vigorous antiwar tone of their speeches and the even sharper one in the July issue of *The Messenger*. Anderson's theory is that the Justice Department may have felt that it had only a weak case against them, and that Wilson did not want to act against Negro antiwar dissenters. Since the president showed no such sensitivity to black opinion when it came to the indictment and sentencing of Ben Fletcher, who was given ten years at Leavenworth, it is hardly likely that the second part of this theory was the explanation. More likely is the reaction of the Cleveland judge—namely, the feeling that the two blacks could not have written such moving and effective articles as appeared in *The Messenger*, and that they were only the tools of white socialists. In fact, the high literary quality of *The Messenger*, in general, caused considerable comment among a wide circle of critics. [38]

The antiwar socialists did not get off without some punishment, however. They had barely returned to New York when they learned that Postmaster General Burleson had denied second-class mailing privileges to *The Messenger*.

While they were in Chicago for the church meeting that was never held, Randolph and Owen appeared before a session of the Socialist party's National Executive Committee to urge "the carrying on of Socialist propaganda among the Negroes." Based on their experiences in

New York and other cities, they felt they could assert with confidence that since 99 percent of Negroes had lost faith in the Republicans—they never had any in the Democrats—the opportunities for the spread of Socialist propaganda among the Negroes were never better, and that work should be stepped up in the expanding black communities of the North. In New York City, where 25 percent of the Negro vote had gone to Hillquit, the party's influence among blacks was growing rapidly. It not only now had in Harlem "a strong publication advocating the cause of Socialism among the colored people," but also a black had been nominated there for Congress on the socialist ticket. [39]

The congressional program adopted by the National Executive Committee after the meeting with the two young black socialists had a section dealing with the Negro that was a milestone in Socialist party history. For the first time, the national leadership of the party broke with the view that the Negro question was no more than a class question. The Negro section of the 1918 platform termed the Negroes "the most oppressed portion of the American population," the victims of "lawlessness," widespread political disfranchisement and loss of civil rights, and "especially discriminated against in economic opportunity." The Socialist party demanded that blacks be "accorded full benefits of citizenship, political, educational and industrial," and that Congress enforce the provisions of the Fourteenth Amendment by reducing the representation in Congress of those states that "violate the letter or spirit of the amendment." [40]

Randolph and Owen took special pleasure in the nomination of a black socialist candidate for Congress in Harlem. In the 1917 election, the Republican party had nominated and elected a black, Edward A. Johnson, to represent one of the Harlem districts in the New York State Assembly. After the election, *The Messenger*'s editors promised Harlem that in 1918 there would be not just one, but several, "able colored men" on the socialist ticket, and that "it will be difficult to prevent the ticket from receiving 75% of the Negro vote." [41] And indeed there were several "able colored men" on the socialist ticket in Harlem. Randolph and Owen were chosen for the New York Assembly, and Reverend George Frazier Miller was nominated for Congress. The *Cleveland Citizen* reported these nominations under a headline that proclaimed: "No Ostracism in Socialist Party. Socialist Party Draws No Color Line." It reminded its readers that Randolph and Owen were "the two cultured colored speakers who were denied the privilege of addressing the people of Cleveland a few months ago. They were thrown into jail and kept there for three days without any charge being preferred against them other than that they are Negroes." [42]

In a leaflet issued jointly by Miller, Randolph, and Owen, the Negro citizens of Harlem were reminded that "the Socialist party was the only party in the United States which condemned the East St. Louis lynching of Negroes," that in Oklahoma the socialists had defeated the Grandfather Clause disfranchising Negroes, and that in Germany and France the socialists had stood up for the rights of African people. That the socialists should be "abused and maligned" by reactionaries was logical, they declared; after all, the same had been true of the abolitionists: "All who live off cheap Negro labor will be opposed to Socialism, just as all slaveholders were opposed to Abolitionism." 43

When the *New York Age* warned hysterically that a vote for the three black socialist candidates would be a vote for "the reign of terror, the arson, the rape and pillage of Bolshevism," the *Crusader* magazine replied: "Every Negro who is pro-Negro before anything else will vote for these colored men." Their nomination, it said, was an historic event: "For the first time in the history of politics in this state a political party has of its own free will chosen three Negroes to represent it before the people." Black Harlemites would no doubt be told that they would be throwing away their vote by voting for them, but the magazine's response was: "Well, then, throw it away! Is it not better to throw it away on a party who recognizes you and on candidates of your own than to throw it away on an ungrateful party, and on white candidates who never represent you?" 44

*The Messenger*'s prediction a year earlier of a 75 percent socialist vote in Harlem proved to be wishful thinking. Every one of the black socialist candidates was defeated, although the socialist vote remained at about the same 25 percent level it had reached in 1917. The *New York Call* was not discouraged. In an editorial on "Negro Socialists," it argued that the events in Harlem since 1917 augured well for the future influence of the Socialist party among blacks: "The new Negro is here — and there will be many more of them to enrich the Socialist movement in the United States." 45

## *THE MESSENGER* ON THE SOCIALIST PARTY

In view of the involvement of Randolph and Owen in socialist affairs from the launching of *The Messenger*, it seems strange that criticism of the party rarely appeared in its pages. *The Messenger* did condemn socialists like Walling, Stokes, Russell, and Spargo who refused to support the St. Louis antiwar resolution, left the party, and became shrill propagandists for the war. The magazine called them "Radical Renegades" and accused them of throwing mud at the socialist movement. 46 But it never criticized those in the party who gradually abandoned the spirit of the St. Louis resolution, became champions of the Liberty Loan, and either gave qualified support to the war or, as in the case of the socialist needle trades unions, came out openly in favor of it. And only rarely did the magazine have anything critical to say about the socialist position on the Negro question. In the first two years of its existence, only one adverse comment appeared. This was a reference to the socialist opposition to lynching which, it charged, began only when white men were lynched. Even "that fearless champion of the rights of the workingmen and the cause of democracy"—the New York *Call*—was "practically silent" on the subject until a white man was lynched. [47]

Before they launched *The Messenger*, Randolph and Owen had emphasized that they would not support any socialist candidates who endorsed Jim Crow. But they paid no attention in their magazine to the socialist version of this evil. What is truly startling is that *The Messenger* did not even publish the text of Eugene V. Debs' criticism of racism in the party. Now that Debs, who had in the past refrained from criticizing party members for their indifference to the Negro question, was breaking his silence, the story should certainly have merited space in "the only magazine of Scientific Radicalism in the World Published by Negroes."

Debs' criticism was inspired by the publication of "The Problem of Problems" by W.E.B. DuBois in *The Intercollegiate Socialist*. Debs' article, "The Negro: His Present Status and Outlook," published in the same journal in its April-May issue and reprinted in the *Call*, praised DuBois for his courage in addressing a socialist audience and pointing out that many socialists failed to deal firmly with racism. "Even among Socialists," Debs wrote, "the Negro question is treated with timidity bordering on cowardice which contrasts painfully with the principles of freedom and equality proclaimed as cardinal in their movement." He continued:

> The Socialist who will not speak out fearlessly for the negro's right to work and live, to develop his manhood, educate his children, and fulfill his destiny on terms of equality with the white man misconceives the movement he pretends to serve or lacks the courage to live up to its principles.

Debs' message to his comrades was clear. He himself spurned any right denied the Negro, "and this must be the attitude of the Socialist movement if it is to win the negro to its standard and prove itself worthy of his confidence and support." By "any right," Debs unequivocally meant "social equality" as well as economic and political equality. Until the Negro's access to these rights was the same as that of the white man, he said, and "until these are fully recognized and freely accorded, all our talk about democracy and freedom is a vulgar sham and false pretense." 48

None of this message found its way into the pages of the foremost black socialist journal in the United States. As Randolph later explained, the editors reasoned that airing the movement's weaknesses on the Negro question was not likely to encourage blacks to join, and, in fact, might have brought about the opposite. 49 Whatever the reason, the result was a sharp curtailment of any influence *The Messenger* might have exerted in eradicating these backward tendencies in the Socialist party.

# 1919: The Red Summer, the Red Scare, and the Split in the Socialist Party

The peace ending World War I came to the United States in November 1918. The year following the Armistice, 1919, has been called the "Red Year"—the year of the witch-hunting Lusk Committee in New York, of the nationwide "Red Scare" under Attorney General A. Mitchell Palmer, of the "Red Summer" of racial conflict, and of the split in the Socialist party and the founding of the Communist party of the United States. While each of these events has been the subject of many individual studies, few scholars have examined their relationship to black radicalism. [1]

Although the anti-Red hysteria emanating from government and patriotic organizations focused mainly on white "Bolshevik" and "Anarchist" activities, the black population also came under suspicion. Despite the fact that most blacks had patriotically supported the war and that 400,000 blacks had served in the armed forces, there was a widespread belief during the war that German propaganda was achieving alarming success among the black population. There were reports of enemy agents, operating through the Lutheran church, who "not only followed the negroes into the cotton fields and mills, but also into the army," with the aim of inciting blacks to rise up in revolt against a defenseless home front. [2]

During the war, labor shortages brought hundreds of thousands of blacks to Northern cities, and, upon arrival, many found more freedom than they had ever known before. In the same period, a third of a million Negroes entered the armed forces, and many served in France in units of the American Expeditionary Force. There they developed both a new faith in their ability to defend themselves and an awareness that segregation was not a universal way of life. Those who served in France often found that white Frenchmen (and women) did not accept the social proscriptions underlying Jim Crow. Friendly relations with the French, combined with a pride in the battlefield achievements of black units, gave the returning soldier a confidence he had not had before. In an editorial entitled "What the Negro Expects Out of the War," the *Washington Bee* declared bluntly: "Out of this war the Negro expects — he demands — justice, and can not and will not be content with less."3

It was the tragic gap between expectation and reality that accounts for the postwar black militancy. Coming North to live as men, blacks too often found white communities seething with the same hatred they thought they had left behind. They found labor unions that begrudged them the opportunity to earn a living, and white homeowners who sought to confine them to crowded ghettoes. They were forced to remain in these ghettoes with substandard housing and to pay exorbitant rents and high prices for food, while being subjected to continuing discrimination on the job and in their everyday life. The 1919 report of the Research Bureau of Associated Charities of Detroit told a typical story:

> There was not a single vacant house or tenement in the several Negro sections of this city. The majority of Negroes are living under such crowded conditions that three or four families in an apartment is the rule rather than the exception. Seventy-five percent of the Negro homes have so many lodgers that they are really hotels. Stables, garages and cellars have been converted into homes for Negroes. The pool rooms and gambling clubs are beginning to charge for the privilege of sleeping on pool tables overnight.4

Black disillusionment was increased still further by the heavy unemployment among black industrial workers brought about by the slackening demand for labor during the postwar demobilization. Exacerbating the bitterness still more was the fact that when black soldiers and sailors returned home from fighting "to make the world safe for democracy," they had to face unemployment, Jim Crow veterans' organizations, and the lynching of black men who dared to wear their uniforms publicly in certain parts of the country. In short, they found a nation proceeding toward "normalcy," which translated itself into a repetition of the assaults and indignities that had been their lot in the past. Black veterans who were fortunate enough to find work were given only the most menial and lowest paying jobs. Even Negro veterans with college degrees ended up as common laborers.[5]

During the war years, the membership of the NAACP increased considerably. In 1919, on its tenth birthday, the organization had 220 branches and 56,345 members, the majority of whom, for the first time, were in the South. The circulation of *The Crisis* stood at 100,000.

In June 1919, when the NAACP listed 56,345 members, another organization of blacks claimed over two million members. This was the Universal Negro Improvement Association, founded and led by Marcus Garvey. The bulk of Garvey's followers were the former black peasants of the South, recently proletarianized in the Great Migration to the Northern communities, and also recently disillusioned and embittered by the evaporation of the promise of a better life in postwar America.

When blacks protested against the nation's failure to provide democracy for its Negro citizens, they were answered by a series of attacks, lynchings, and race riots in both North and South. From May through September 1919, major race riots broke out in Charleston, Longview (Texas), Knoxville, Omaha, Washington, D.C., Chicago, and Phillips County, Arkansas. In addition, these same months produced no fewer than thirteen lesser conflicts between blacks and whites, excluding lynchings that were not met with physical resistance.[6]


RACE RIOTS

The immediate causes of the seven major race riots varied somewhat from place to place. In Charleston, an altercation between a Negro and two sailors sparked the outbreak, but in Washington, Knoxville, and Omaha, the triggering incident was an allegation that a Negro had assaulted a white woman. White servicemen played the leading roles in the Washington disturbance, which began when they tried to enter the black section in search of the alleged assailants. The Knoxville and Omaha disturbances broke out when mobs attempted to lynch black prisoners charged with the crime of rape. The Chicago riot started when a young Negro swimmer drowned after whites stoned him for crossing the imaginary boundary line separating white and Negro beaches on Lake Michigan.[7] The white attack on the section of Longview had a dual origin: (1) the publication of an "offensive" article in the *Chicago Defender* protesting the disappearance of a local Negro charged with having an affair with a white woman, which was angrily attributed by the white community to another local black; (2) the desire of the whites to put a halt to the local Negro Business Men's League, which was marketing cotton. The riot in Phillips County, Arkansas, also arose from attempts of whites to quash any economic independence among blacks. In the fall of 1919, Negro sharecroppers, attempting to improve their economic situation by forming the Progressive Farmers and Household Union of America, demanded an accounting from landlords. The reaction of the whites triggered a riot resulting in the death of five whites. Estimates of the number of Negroes who lost their lives ran into the hundreds, as white mobs ranged through Phillips County for three days, slaughtering any Negroes they could find. The sharecroppers' union was destroyed.[8]

Despite the varied nature of the immediate causes, one fact stands out clearly: in each of the major 1919 race riots, the initial violence came from whites. Equally clear is the fact that white society was determined to prevent Negroes from changing the status quo. The Chicago riot had many root causes, but foremost among them were the activities of "neighborhood improvement associations" bent on keeping Negroes out of white residential areas. The outbreak in Elaine, Arkansas, the only rural community to experience a major riot in this period, was caused by the whites' determination to prevent blacks from improving their status by organizing a sharecroppers' union. Through one riot after another, whites made it known that as far as they were concerned, the war had made no difference: Negroes were and would remain segregated, deprived of the right to vote and to organize in the South, and of the right to move into white neighborhoods in the North. In both North and South, they were to remain an outcast race with no rights a white man was bound to respect.

None of this, of course, was really new. What was relatively new about the "Red Summer" of 1919, as compared with previous anti-Negro riots, was the fact that, to a greater degree than ever before, the Negro responded by fighting back. Indeed, there had been instances of armed self-defense by Negroes in riot situations before; reports of such actions are to be found in the accounts of most of the major race riots in the twentieth century. Two whites were killed in the defense of the Negro district of Brownsville in Atlanta in 1906. Negro soldiers took the offensive in Houston in 1915 in an attempt to retaliate against whites who had beaten their comrades, and only quick police action succeeded in halting their march into the city and averting a riot. The East St. Louis riot of 1917 followed a Negro attack on plainclothes policemen whom the assailants mistook for white marauders who had earlier fired into their homes. While the ensuing violence was predominantly one-sided, isolated groups of Negroes armed to defend themselves, and the white mobs forebore from attacking the main Negro residential districts.[9]

Nevertheless, in practically all of these riots, as the casualty figures show, black violence was minor compared with the extent of white violence toward blacks. In the Washington and Chicago riots of 1919, however, Negro defensive actions and retaliation were extensive. Blacks frequently responded with arms to white attacks, and any whites found in black neighborhoods were often beaten or shot. Even whites in Longview, Texas, were killed, and the blacks in Phillips County, Arkansas, although they were far outnumbered, killed a few white attackers before they were crushed bloodily. The Chicago casualty figures tell their own story. In thirteen days of riots, thirty-eight persons were killed and 537 wounded; of these, fifteen of the dead and 178 of the injured were white. [10] The exact figures for Washington are not available, but it is known that on the afternoon of July 21, when some of the most severe fighting took place, four persons were killed, and eleven seriously or fatally wounded. [11] Ten of the dead and injured were white, while five were Negro. In the remaining disturbances, Negroes also fought back against their white tormentors, inflicting a proportionate share of injury and death. [12]

All this made it apparent that Negroes could no longer be attacked with impunity. To paraphrase the poet Claude McKay, they were determined that if they must die, it would not be like hogs but like men—fighting back.

So novel was the idea of black resistance that the New York State legislature, the Justice Department, Representative James F. Byrnes of South Carolina, and much of the nation's press all insisted that it could only be explained by Bolshevik influence.

## PALMER'S REPORT

In November 1919, Attorney General A. Mitchell Palmer submitted a report to the Senate Judiciary Committee on the investigative activities of the Department of Justice. Included in it was a section, apparently written by J. Edgar Hoover, [13] entitled "Radicalism and Sedition Among the Negroes as Reflected in Their Publications." [14] The purpose of this document was "to give a substantial appreciation of the dangerous spirit of defiance and vengeance at work among Negro leaders and, to an ever increasing extent, among their followers." [15]

The report itself consisted of extracts from such Negro publications as the *Negro World, Veteran, Challenge, Crusader, Messenger, New Negro, Crisis, Broad Axe, Favorite Magazine, Half-Century Magazine, Baltimore Afro-American,* and *Cleveland Gazette.* (In the case of some of these publications, these extracts are the only material extant.) The most substantial extracts were from *The Messenger,* which occupied twelve of the report's twenty-five pages. Palmer was convinced that it was the most dangerous of the black publications. He charged that, while its early issues might have been harmless, by its publication of the May-June 1919 issue, it was definitely an "exponent of open defiance of sedition," for here was to be found "the first counsel of the Negro to align himself with Bolshevism . . . in the editorial 'Negro Mass Movement.' " [16] (That the editorial in question did not once use the word "Bolshevism," but rather "socialism." apparently made no difference.) The same issue had five other articles that were deemed offensive: an editorial entitled "The March of Soviet Government"; another commending the Civil Liberties Bureau and its jailed former director, Roger Baldwin; a piece entitled "Political Prisoners," which condemned the conviction and sentencing of such radicals as Eugene V. Debs, Kate Richards O'Hare, and Ben Fletcher; an editorial criticizing nearly every nationally known black public figure for having failed to provide militant leadership; and finally, an article proclaiming that "We Want More Bolshevik Patriotism"—a patriotism that "springs from the beast of the people," one which would "attract rather than coerce," and where "the people are more articulate and the profiteers less articulate." The article concluded: "What we really need is a patriotism of liberty, justice and joy. That is Bolshevik patriotism, and we want more of that brand in the United States."

Palmer considered the July 1919 issue "particularly radical." [17] He cited a poem describing in graphic detail the lynching of a black man on a Sunday in a "Christian" country, the verse illustrated by a drawing of a victim hanging from a telegraph pole, being burned in a fire fueled by an American flag; an editorial entitled "The Hun in America"; an article urging blacks to inform themselves about American exploitation of the natural resources of Mexico as well as about American efforts to spread race prejudice there; a long analysis comparing the AFL and the IWW and emphasizing that since white workers are also wage slaves to the capitalist system, the only way to combat it was to affiliate with the union that drew no color line; an article by W. A. Domingo explaining the proposition "Socialism the Negroes' Hope" and concluding that the fact that the worst oppressors of blacks, men like Hoke Smith and Lee Overman, were the most vigorous opponents of socialism was sufficient reason for blacks to support it; and an article by black former army officer William N. Colson discussing "Propaganda and the American Negro Soldier," which concluded that "the consensus of opinion among thinking colored people is that the war ended too soon. They believe that the American Negro would have gotten a status [sic] had America been chastised more severely." The July 1919 issue of *The Messenger*, incidentally, was held up for several days by Postmaster General Bureleson pending a determination of whether it was seditious and thereby subject to the denial of mailing privileges.

The September 1919 *Messinger* was considered "more insolently offensive" than any other issue. [18] Cited as proof were the lead editorial, authored by W. A. Domingo, entitled "If We Must Die." Besides including the text of Claude McKay's poem of that name, it expressed both excitement and exultation over the news of blacks fighting back against their white persecutors in the recent Washington and Chicago riots. Also cited were two cartoons: one, caricaturing W.E.B. Du Bois, James Weldon Johnson, and Robert Russa Moton, depicted them as advocating submissiveness and passiveness in the face of rioting and lynching. The other cartoon showed the "New Crowd Negro" armed and firing on a white mob, "giving the 'Hun' a dose of his own medicine." Palmer then cited Domingo's article which pointed out that the Bolshevik regime had ended race riots and pogroms in Russia, and an article on the Washington riots by W. E. Hawkins which voiced "pride and jubilation" that the Negroes had fought back and had "shot a lynching bee into perdition."

The October issue was cited as being significant "for one thing above all." This, Palmer charged, was the first time a black publication had openly approved of interracial sex, and was "marked throughout by a spirit of insolent bravado." [19] He was referring to the long article, "A Reply to Congressman James F. Byrnes of South Carolina."

Byrnes, later secretary of state and justice of the U.S. Supreme Court, had delivered his speech in Congress on August 25, 1919, [20] only a month after the July riots in Washington, Chicago, Longview, and other communities. To Byrnes, the recent violence indicated a general antagonism between the races, but it was clear to him, as he said it would be to anyone who read the daily newspapers, that of late there had been no propaganda coming from the white press that would serve to antagonize white men toward the black population. In other words, racist feelings were not being spread by whites. On the other hand, they were being disseminated by so-called black leaders through the black press. These persons were radicals who rejected the conservative advice of men who followed in the tradition of Booker T. Washington, like Moton, and instead stirred up passions and incited to violence. Most unfortunately, some of the theretofore conservative leaders, too, had become radical. The example Byrnes gave of this type was W.E.B. Du Bois. At one time, he argued, *The Crisis'* editor had rendered good and intelligent leadership, but lately he had become more radical. As proof, Byrnes cited the stirring editorial, "Returning Soldiers," in the May 1919 *Crisis* (which had also aroused both Palmer and the Lusk Committee.) Byrnes was convinced that the language in it violated the Espionage Act which prohibited encouraging resistance to or abuse of the government. (The country was still at war, so the act could be applied to suppress dissent.) He also objected to articles in *The Crisis* that alluded to social contact between black soldiers and white women in France.[21]

To Byrnes, however, *The Crisis* was not nearly as dangerous as *The Messenger* (These were the only two black publications Byrnes discussed.) *The Messenger* was condemned for supporting the IWW, praising Debs, and praying for a Bolshevik government in the United States. The fact that it was printed on fine-quality paper and had few advertisements was proof to Byrnes (as it was to Palmer) that it must be financed by the IWW, although neither of them bothered to explain where the hard-press IWW could get the money to subsidize the publication. Referring to a *Messenger* prediction that there would be more riots, Byrnes commented that such statements "show that the negro leaders had deliberately planned a campaign of violence." An example of such an incendiary statement was the August 1919 article on "How to Stop Lynching," which advocated that blacks form armed self-defense groups. If there was no legislation to keep such pernicious doctrines from the mails, Byrnes maintained, then some should be enacted: "We can all believe in a free press, but we can recognize the distinction between a free press and a revolutionary and anarchistic press." The time was at hand for stopping the Bolsheviks of Russia and the IWW from using the black press for their "nefarious purposes." Still more such incendiary statements were found in the articles by Lieutenant Colson, particularly the story of black troops at bayonet drill. Byrnes insisted that Colson should be prosecuted for his articles since peace had not yet been proclaimed; furthermore, they should lead one to consider carefully whether any more black troops and officers should be enlisted.

Byrnes explained why he had given so much free publicity to such heinous doctrines. The whites, he said, should know what the blacks were doing, and responsible black leaders should be warned not to do rash things for the purpose of furthering their own ambitions. Rather, he wanted to counsel them to encourage their race that to expect political and social equality was a false hope. Byrnes emphasized that the war had not changed the attitudes of whites on the question of equality. Then followed a long dissertation on the exemplary treatment of blacks in the South, including an assertion that lynching was almost universally condemned. The congressman then spoke to the North: he granted that that section could treat blacks as it saw fit, but he predicted that as soon as the proportion of blacks reached the level where they might play a significant role in politics, the North, too, would restrict the suffrage, for "this is a white man's country, and will always remain a white man's country. So much for political equality. . . . As to social equality, God Almighty never intended [it]."

In their reply to the Southern racist, Owen and Randolph readily admitted that they "would be glad to see a Bolshevik government substituted in the South in place of our Bourbon, reactionary, vote stolen, misrepresentative Democratic regime." On the issue of social equality, *The Messenger* did not equivocate: "As for social equality, there are about five million mulattoes in the United States. This is the product of semi-social equality. It shows that social equality galore exists after dark, and we warn you that we expect to have social equality in the day as well as after dark." Political and social equality were inevitable, they continued, and they promised that the day would yet come when Byrnes would sit with blacks in a railroad car in South Carolina. 22

It is easy to understand why Palmer was so upset by the reply to Representative Byrnes.

After extracting from each of the issues from May-June to October 1919 the material that he considered clearly "subversive," Palmer complained that "no amount of mere quotation could serve as a full estimate of the evil scope attained by the *Messenger*. Only a reading of the magazine itself would suffice to do this." 23 He did not add that a reading would also disclose that in the extracts he published, he omitted essential material that often cast a different light on the argument he was making; that he frequently failed to capitalize "Negro," whereas this was done in every case in the original publication; and that he reproduced sentences so sloppily at times that their point was missed completely.

In his conclusion, Palmer accused the Negro of " 'seeing red' " and charged that the object of the militant black journals was to encourage this vision in others. Nor could the power of this black press be ignored. Palmer was sure that some of the periodicals had wealthy backers and that many had also taken deliberate advantage of the race riots during the summer of 1919 to publish inflammatory sentiments that sometimes had "reached the limits of open defiance and a counsel of retaliation": "Defiance and insolently race-centered condemnation of the white race is met with in every issue of the more radical publications." There could be little doubt that there existed a "well-concerted movement among a certain class of Negro leaders of thought and action to constitute themselves a determined and persistent source of a radical opposition to the Government, and to the established rule of law and order." Underlying all their attitudes, Palmer saw an increased emphasis on feelings of race consciousness, "always antagonistic to the white race and openly, defiantly assertive of its own equality and even superiority." Such assertions were to be read most frequently in those journals edited by educated men, and therefore "the boast is not to be dismissed lightly as the ignorant vaporing of untrained minds."24

What, then, was the solution? The one Palmer recommended was a strong domestic sedition law. Such a law, he claimed, was needed because deportation could only be used against aliens, and blacks were citizens. Moreover, Palmer doubted that the courts would uphold either the use of the Espionage Act in peacetime or various old sedition laws that dated from the Civil War period. The only current federal legislation of use was that prohibiting treason, rebellion, and conspiracy to commit sedition, but what was needed was legislation making individual acts of preaching or publishing seditious ideas punishable. 25

## THE LUSK COMMITTEE REPORT

At the same time that the federal government was investigating "subversive" influences in the Negro community, the state of New York, through the Lusk Committee, was conducting a similar investigation. The Joint Legislative Committee Against Seditious Activities, headed by Clayron R. Lusk, a freshman senator from an upstate urban community, and made up almost entirely of lawyers and businessmen, grew out of an investigation conducted by a committee of the Union League Club of New York City to study radicalism in the state. Headed by New York lawyer Archibald Stevenson, the committee made a two-month investigation and, on March 13, 1919, reported to the Union League Club's membership. In its report, the committee emphasized, among other things, that an attempt was being made to arouse discontent among Negroes in the United States by circulating Bolshevik doctrines among them. As proof the committee cited a number of editorials and articles in *The Messenger*. After hearing the committee's report, the league's membership voted unanimously to petition the legislature to appoint a special committee "to determine the extent of the revolutionary movement in New York with a view to the enactment of laws necessary to protect the Government." On March 20, 1919, the Lusk Committee was officially formed when the legislature passed a resolution providing for a legislative investigation to trace "secret information received from official sources" that Bolshevism, with heavy financial backing, "was making rapid headway in New York and was soon to become a menace to organized government in the state and nation." 26

The report of the Lusk Committee (*Revolutionary Radicalism*), published in four volumes in April 1920, took up 4,500 pages. Chapter 5 of Volume 2 bore the title "Propaganda Among Negroes." The Lusk Committee defined as one of its tasks that of investigating groups "at work to stimulate race hatred in our colored population, and to engender so-called class consciousness in their ranks." [27] By this, Lusk did not mean a major irritant to race relations after World War I—the Ku Klux Klan. The Klan had reorganized in 1915 and was spreading rapidly to the West and into many Northern cities as well, disseminating vicious anti-Negro (as well as anti-Jewish and anti-Catholic) propaganda. [28] In the entire 4,500-page report, the Klan is not mentioned once. What the committee obviously had in mind were the radical organizations, particularly their publications.

Like the Palmer report, most of "Propaganda Among Negroes" was devoted to verbatim extracts from various black militant periodicals. It also included reports of meetings submitted by the committee's spies in Harlem, [29] and documents obtained in the course of the committee's raids on the socialist Rand School. [30]

"The most interesting as well as one of the most important features of radical and revolutionary propaganda is the appeal made to those elements of our population that have a just cause of complaint with the treatment they have received in this country." So began the forty-four pages devoted to "Propaganda Among Negroes." This problem was said to be especially serious in New York, for in recent years a great number of blacks had migrated from both the West Indies and the American South. Generally speaking, claimed Lusk, they were treated well in New York. However, the fact that they were often ill-treated where they had previously resided meant that they brought their resentments with them, and these resentments had "been capitalized by agents and agitators of the Socialist Party of America, the IWW and other radical groups." The radical groups were encouraged by "well-to-do liberals" in "social uplift organizations," such as the NAACP. Since many of the complaints of blacks were genuine, spreading radical propaganda among them was all the more serious. Lusk warned that this "should encourage all loyal and thoughtful negroes in this State to organize to oppose the activities of such radicals, which cannot but lead to serious trouble if they are permitted to continue the propaganda which they now disseminate in such large volume." [31]

Unable to perceive the different currents within the black community, the Lusk Committee treated all black leaders who were to the left of Booker T. Washington as potential Bolsheviks. Marcus Garvey was called "one of the most violent agitators among the negroes . . . who in addition to stirring up violent race hatred among the negroes, is an excellent business man"(?). In fact, the quotations from Garvey's speeches and from the *Negro World* showed nothing that even remotely resembled socialism or Bolshevism. [32] The committee found four articles in *The*

*Crisis* to which it objected—one from the March 1920 issue describing the good treatment of black soldiers in France and their relationships there with French women; and three articles from the following month, one of which condemned American intervention in Haiti, one which ridiculed the misuse of the term *Bolshevism*, and the third which proposed a voting alliance between socialists, blacks, and aliens. In none of these articles, however, was there a call for a socialist or communist form of society. Actually, to Lusk, what was most damning about *The Crisis* was its association with the NAACP, "an organization which has done considerable good for the negro race and which at the same time has been led to take a decidedly radical stand through the influence of certain members of its board." These unnamed individuals were said to have "extended their sympathy and support to the Socialistic group headed by Randolph and Owen." [33] At the end of the second volume there appeared a table listing the "Revolutionary and Subversive Periodicals Published in New York City." Here, *The Crisis* appeared alongside of *The Messenger*, the *Anarchistic Soviet Bulletin*, *Voice of the Worker*, and *Weekly Industrial Worker*. [34] Clearly, since the Lusk Committee could not establish the "revolutionary and subversive" content of *The Crisis* from the extracts, it tried to do so through guilt by association.

The Lusk Committee believed that propaganda among blacks was dangerous, partly because some of their grievances were valid. The primary reason, however, was because the radicals were not really interested in remedying the conditions causing the grievances but were only using them for their own purposes of appealing to class consciousness and eventually establishing a socialist commonwealth. [35] The committee argued that the radical spirit in America was not an indigenous social reform movement, but something imported from abroad, and that radicalism was being spread purely as an ideology, not as a means of solving problems rooted in the concrete conditions in the country:

> A study of the tactics and methods employed by revolutionary groups and organizations makes it clear that the present social unrest, with its revolutionary implications, is not the spontaneous development of economic causes. The growth of the radical and revolutionary movement is due largely to the effect of propaganda. False ideas respecting government and the present social order are being sold to the people of this country, as well as other countries, in much the same manner as a manufacturer or merchant sells his wares through the medium of advertising. [36]

Unlike Palmer, Lusk did not feel that any new repressive legislation was needed, although he did think that the existing federal deportation program and New York's criminal anarchy statute should be strengthened and more vigorously enforced. Lusk also stressed that not all of the current problems having to do with "subversion" could be solved by legislation alone. For example, since the Soviet Union was the ultimate source (to Lusk) of most current radicalism, a policy of nonrecognition and no trade would help bring down the communist government, after which there would be little threat of radicalism in the United States. Part of the blame for domestic unrest, according to Lusk, was attributable to economic dislocation, which ultimately was the fault of influential persons in industry and government who had failed to deal intelligently with economic problems. Finally, combatting subversion would be much easier if the country returned to religion and moral training. 37 Lusk hardly set an example of "moral" conduct by the illegal raids and seizures, the wholesale deprivations of rights guaranteed in the first ten amendments to the Constitution, and the "carnival atmosphere" that characterized his committee's conduct throughout its existence. 38

## NATIONAL CIVIC FEDERATION REPORT

The investigations of black radicalism discussed above were all governmental, but there was also one private investigation during this period. 39 The National Civic Federation, a powerful alliance of big business, conservative labor leaders, and various public figures, troubled by reports of radicalism among blacks, decided to find out the real situation for itself. Charles Mowbray White was assigned to investigate the subject and report his findings to the federation. Over a period of a few days, White visited and interviewed Marcus Garvey, W.E.B. DuBois, Frederick Moore of the black weekly, *New York Age*, and Chandler Owen and A. Philip Randolph.

On one point all the blacks interviewed by White agreed: that the Negro had to secure equal rights regardless of the means required to achieve them, and if the only route to equality was through violence, then so be it. As DuBois put it: "To be frank the war has increased my radicalism, and from now on my one ambition will be toward a world improvement for the Negro by whatever means available."

White accompanied the report of his interviews with an analysis of the extent and influence of Negro radicalism. In this document, he observed that the vast majority of blacks were patriotic, loyal Americans and that "despite widespread agitation by whites and blacks among the colored Americans not more than a small fraction of their twelve millions has been turned from their proverbial loyalty." Still, he insisted, it was impossible to ignore the opinion of black leaders that about a quarter of a million Negroes belonged to the radical movement, and

> that of this 250,000, a great many probably a substantial major-
> ity constitute a dangerous menace in that they are energetic
> propagandists, very well informed on their various theories, and
> are deeply embittered against the white race. Through the use of
> fifty or one hundred thousand of them as agitators of the blacks
> throughout the nation, it is easy to see what a formidable force is
> thus created for the purpose of exciting a race and class con-
> sciousness.

White informed the National Civic Federation that all of the men he had interviewed—Owen, Randolph, Garvey, DuBois, and Moore—belonged to "the category of extreme Socialists or Bolshevists." Of these, he said, the socialists were the most dangerous, for they were part of a Negro socialist membership in the Bronx and Harlem of 50,000, had an effective propaganda organ among the blacks, *The Messenger*, and were assisted by many white Americans. White was convinced that "a preponderant majority of the white people cooperating with negroes in their various and numerous institutions for their improvement, are of a Socialist turn."

When it came to informing the National Civic Federation as to what the socialist and Bolshevik doctrines consisted of, White fell into the same camp as the government investigators. The real danger, he as-serted, was the demand for equality for blacks in American society. This demand was turning loyal blacks disloyal:

> Undoubtedly there are still many loyal Americans among
> negroes but the hope at least seems very general among them . . .
> the hope, I saw, seems deeply imbedded in their consciousness
> that sometime in the near future they will by some measure come
> into the fullest and most complete equality with the whites. [40]

And this was socialism and Bolshevism!

*        *        *

None of the reports defined such terms as radicalism, sedition, subver-sion, socialism, or Bolshevism. The Lusk Committee came closest to a definition of radicalism when it called it a movement "seeking to under-mine and destroy not only the government under which we live, but also

the very structure of American society." [41] As far as black radicalism
was concerned, the reports did not even suggest what it meant, and by
lumping together Randolph, Owen, Du Bois, and Garvey, they did more
to confuse than to enlighten. Little wonder, then, that the *New York Age*
concluded, after reading the Palmer and Lusk Committee reports on
black radicalism, that "the Negro is a 'dangerous radical' because he is
demanding the common fundamental rights that are accorded to all
other citizens of the country." [42] The *Pittsburgh Courier*'s observation
was even more bitter: "As long as the Negro submits to lynchings, burnings, and oppressions — and says nothing he is a loyal American citizen.
But when he decides that lynchings and burnings shall cease even at the
cost of some bloodshed in America, then he is a Bolshevist." [43] The Chicago Commission on Race Relations said it all when it declared that radicalism in the racial context meant "any advocacy of changes which to the
general white public appears undesirable." [44]

## THE SPLIT IN THE SOCIALIST PARTY

In August 1919, during the height of the "Red Summer," the *Baltimore Afro-American* carried an editorial entitled "Listening to
Socialism," in which it declared:

> No one can shut his eyes to the fact that the Socialist party, the
> party of discontent in the United States, is making a successful
> drive for colored supporters . . . . The Negro will take little pains
> to learn what the Socialist party hopes to accomplish in toto. It
> will be sufficient for him to know that the party platform con-
> tains a plank pledging its candidates to equal and exact justice
> and opportunity for all men, white and black. So long as no other
> party even remotely promises anything of the kind except the
> Socialists, the time can hardly be long before the radical group
> will count more and more on its colored supporters." [45]

Soon after this editorial appeared, the black weekly sent the following
question to leading black men and women throughout the country: "In
view of the rapid rise of the Socialist party and in view of the plank pledging Socialist candidates to work for exact justice and equality of opportunity for all regardless of race, what stand, in your opinion, ought we to
take toward the Socialist party?"

The response must have disappointed the *Afro-American*. Only one
black — Ida Wells-Barnett — came out for support of the Socialist party.
The militant black woman leader wrote that "so long as that party has

pledged itself to work for exact justice and equality of opportunity for all regardless of race, it should at least be given a trial by a large number of thinking and aggressive Negroes." Most of those who replied took the position of W.E.B. DuBois, that a vote for the Socialist party "is thrown away." Others argued that to vote socialist would help maintain the Wilson administration in power. [46] So bitter and widespread was the disillusionment of blacks with the Wilson administration, and so determined were they to defeat his party, that this argument alone was almost enough to persuade most of them against casting their vote for the Socialist party. [47] One black spokesman who responded insisted that to vote socialist would be "taking a chance—a gambler's chance," since a question existed as to whether the Socialist party would even be able to continue. Apart from the government harassment during the Red Scare, the party itself was being torn apart by a split between the right and left wings. The division had become so intense by the summer of 1919 that it was an open question as to whether there would be socialist candidates for blacks to vote for in the fall elections of 1919. [48]

The split in the Socialist party in the summer of 1919 was no sudden development. There had been a bitter inner conflict in the party even before the war was over industrial versus craft unionism, syndicalism versus reliance on political action, working within the AFL versus supporting the IWW, and the restriction of immigration. But it was the Bolshevik Revolution of November 1917 that snapped the last bonds holding the left and right socialists within one party. While all socialists at first welcomed the Russian Revolution and defended it, a difference of approach soon developed between the right and left wings. Many on the left believed that the Bolsheviks' success could be duplicated in the United States, but Berger and Hillquit (the leaders of the right and center, respectively) argued that the war had "strengthened capitalism, reaction and *treason* within the *working class*, making the prospect of immediate revolution even bleaker than before." "While we can learn from the Bolsheviks," Berger wrote, "we cannot transfer Russia to America." The left wing, now led by Louis C. Fraina, Charles E. Ruthenberg, John Reed, James Larkin, Rose Pastor Stokes, and Ludwig Lore, disagreed. They were supported by a group that had emerged during the war with increasing influence—the foreign-language federations. This group, which had made up only 35 percent of the Socialist party members in 1917, had grown by 1919 to 53 percent.

In February 1919, representatives of twenty left wing locals in New York met in conference. After listening to reports by John Reed, James Larkin, Rose Pastor Stokes, and representatives of the foreign-language federations, they organized themselves as the left wing section of the Socialist party and voted to publish a manifesto and issue a paper. All the major centers of the party now took their cue from New York and followed its example. It soon became clear that an overwhelming majority of the membership was with the left wing. In referendum votes for national officers in the spring of 1919, the left wing elected twelve out of the fifteen members of the National Executive Committee.

Meeting during May 24-30, the lame-duck National Executive Committee refused to relinquish its position, voted to suspend several foreign-language federations, threatened to expel locals that supported the left wing, and decided to hold an emergency convention in Chicago on August 30. In the weeks that followed, the state organizations of Massachusetts and others, Local Chicago, and many locals in New York were expelled, and their charters were granted to the "loyal members." In all, a minimum of 55,000 members were "drummed" out of the party as part of the right wing's preparation for the emergency convention, while others left in disgust.

On June 24, 1919, after three days of debate, a national conference of the left wing voted down the proposition of abandoning the Socialist party and resolved that "this Conference shall organize as the Left Wing Section of the Socialist Party for revolutionary socialism." The conference also decided that if, with the aid of the courts and the police, the right wing held on to the emergency convention, then a Communist party should be launched at once. The conference made provision for the publication of its manifesto and program, established headquarters in New York, and designated the *Revolutionary Age* as its official organ. But the Michigan language federation group told the conference that it was not going along with its decision and that for its part it was going to forget the Socialist party and launch a Communist party in Chicago on September 1.

On September 1, 1919, not one, but two, Communist parties opened their conventions in Chicago. The Communist party was set up by the language federations and the Michigan organization, with approximately 27,000 members. The Communist Labor party was organized by delegates to the emergency convention led by John Reed, Benjamin Gitlow, and Edward Wagenknecht, and represented about 10,000 members. They had tried to attend the Socialist party convention which opened in Chicago on August 30, but were barred by right wing socialists, assisted by the Chicago Police Department. The alliance with the Chicago police against the left symbolized the profound change that had taken place in the party.

As a critic of the left has admitted, "the Right Wing had saved its hold on the party name and machinery, but had lost two-thirds of its membership." Expulsions and secessions depleted the Socialist party ranks. [49]

All this occurred during the "Red Summer" of 1919, and the left wing journals carried several editorials on the race riots. In general, they placed the blame for the riots on the whites, condemned the white race for having "denied the Negro not only his rights as guaranteed by the federal constitution, but even the simplest human rights," and called for the unity of white and black workers. "The Negro constitutes a large portion of our proletariat," declared *Revolutionary Age*. "The white workers must realize that there can be no emancipation for them without the cooperation of the Negro just as there can be no emancipation for the white workers if the Negro is allowed to become the reactionary tool of the capitalist interests." While the left wing socialist press did point out that the Negro was "a vital problem of our revolutionary movement," it saw it as "simply a phase of the social problem, which the communist revolution alone can solve." 50 This statement was nothing more than a rewording of a traditional socialist position.

With this type of philosophy, it is not surprising that not once did the left wing mention the Negro question as a factor in the sharpening conflict between the right and left. In *The Class Struggle* of February 1919, Louis Fraina wrote on "Problems of American Socialism." In his conclusion, he indicated that he had dealt with "some of the problems of American Socialism — there are others, but these are fundamental." 51 He made no mention of the Negro question. On the eve of the emergency convention, an article entitled "The Left Wing and the Socialist Party" was published in *Revolutionary Age* by authority of the National Council of Left Wing Sections. It criticized the right for attacking the influence of the foreign-language sections in the left, and declared:

> The Industrial proletariat in the United States is predominantly of foreign birth. Of the native elements, the largest group are the negroes, more alien than any of the aliens. But even this is beside the point, for the struggle against capitalism is not a national but a world struggle. 52

This was the only reference to the Negro. The "Left-Wing Manifesto" contained a ten-point criticism of the policies and practices of the right wing, but not one dealt with the Negro. The same was true of the "Program of the Left Wing," adopted at the National Left Wing Conference. 53

There is no evidence that blacks participated in founding either the Communist or Communist Labor party, and not a single Negro delegate attended either convention. The platform of the Communist Labor party was silent on the Negro, but the program of the Communist party did include a paragraph on the Negro question. It read:

> In close connection with the unskilled worker are the problems of the negro worker. The negro problem is a political and economic problem. The racial question of the negro is simply the expression of his economic bondage and oppression, each intensifying the other. This complicates the negro problem but does not alter its proletarian character. The Communist Party will carry an agitation among the negro workers to unite them with all class conscious workers. [54]

While this statement did acknowledge that the racial factor made some difference, it still viewed the Negro question as simply one aspect of the broader labor question. Moreover, the paragraph provoked no discussion. Indeed, in a detailed report published in *The Liberator* on the three conventions in Chicago—Socialist, Communist, and Communist Labor—Max Eastman never once mentioned a discussion of the Negro question at any of the gatherings. [55]

## BLACK SOCIALISTS ON THE SPLIT

*The Messenger*, the leading black socialist journal in the United States, exerted practically no pressure on either the right or the left wing. Instead, it remained almost totally silent as the split in the Socialist party reached the breaking point in 1919. Only one article appeared in the magazine dealing with the debates between the two wings of the party—"The Right and Left Wing Interpreted," published in the May-June 1919 issue. Discussing these differences, the editors acknowledged that they were worldwide and were present in the socialist parties of every country. In the United States, too, the Socialist party was "in the midst of a keen and sharp discussion as to tactics and policies." The editors then proceeded to analyze and dismiss as unrealistic each of the ten points of the "Left-Wing Manifesto." They then suggested that there be a halt to rhetorical attacks between the two wings, a continuation of rational dialogue, and finally a vote, and if the left wing won, the party should move to the left. [56]

The article was written before the National Executive Committee, led by Morris Hillquit, began a series of expulsions of entire state, city, and national group socialist federations, climaxed by the police action against the left wing at the Chicago emergency convention. *The Messenger* remained silent all during these events. Having implied in the May-June article that they had no intention of supporting the left wing, Randolph and Owen were not eager to publicize the ruthless and dictatorial policies and practices of the right wing. In addition, they were in full agreement with the platform adopted by the Socialist party after the expulsion of the left wing, which declared that there was no immediate revolutionary potential in the United States and that there was therefore no need to break sharply with the methods of the war period. Even though *The Messenger* continued to express admiration for Soviet Russia, and the editors created a sensation in the summer of 1919 by upholding the "ideals of the Bolsheviki" at a YMCA forum, they made it clear that they were not pushing for a Russian-Communist style upheaval in the United States and that the Socialist party continued to hold out the best hopes for black Americans. The Negro, they said, "must support it with his dollars and his votes." [57]

Nor did *The Messenger* have anything to say about the conventions of the Socialist, Communist, and Communist Labor parties in Chicago. To have criticized the left wing for failing to deal adequately with the Negro question would have required it to comment on the right wing's neglect of the same issue. So the editors decided to say nothing. With their faith in the Socialist party undiminished, Randolph and Owen taught a course on "Economics and Sociology of the Negro Problem" at the Rand School, lectured for the party throughout the city, especially in Harlem, and published articles on "Why Negroes Should Be Socialists" in *The Messenger* and the *New York Call*. [58]

A contributing editor to *The Messenger* decided to call attention to the failure of both the right and left wings of the Socialist party to deal adequately with the Negro question. He was W. A. Domingo, a native of Jamaica and a leader of the West Indian community in New York, who was both a socialist and a prominent supporter of Garvey's Universal Negro Improvement Association. In a long document entitled "Socialism Imperilled, or the Negro — A Potential Menace to American Radicalism," Domingo set out to warn both the right and left wings that failure to deal with the Negro question and to concentrate on raising the class consciousness of black workers might lead to the Negroes being "formed by the capitalists into a mercenary army" for the suppression of the social revolution in the United States. Conceding that he was drawing an "imaginative picture," Domingo warned both the right and left wings against complacency: "The Negro has race consciousness. We must transmute that race consciousness into class consicousness." To fail to do so was to imperil the revolution, whether it would be carried out by the right or the left.

Domingo criticized the Socialist party for following the example of the AFL and "leaving the negro severely alone." He had warm praise for the IWW for having made special efforts to organize "the despised negro," and he urged the party, whether it came under the control of the right or the left, to profit from its own and the AFL's mistakes. The AFL, he said, had succeeded in making the Negro an enemy of that organization and "the scab of America," and he criticized both the right and left wing's approaches to the Negro. The right, he maintained, ignored the Negro "except in northern urban centers where their vote is needed to elect a municipal official," while the left clung to the view that the Negro, as a part of "the lowest stratum of the American proletariat," was still basically only a worker whose problems would be solved like those of all other workers and required no special attention. He urged the left to learn from the experience of the Bolsheviks, under the influence of the "great Lenin," who had stressed "the needs of the poorest peasants and the industrial workers" and cemented "their loyalty by placing them in the first class" in plans for the revolution. In like manner, he insisted, the left should begin to place the Negro in the United States in the category of those whose education in the class struggle and whose needs required priority: "Since it is the avowed object of the Left Wing to establish Socialism through the medium of a dictatorship of the proletariat, how can they expect to accomplish it with a large portion of the American proletariat untouched by revolutionary propaganda?"

Unless the Negro was incorporated into all plans for the revolution, Domingo warned, it would not matter which faction gained control of the Socialist party. The capitalists would simply use the Negro to prevent the establishment of a socialist society in the United States. The spectacle would then exist of one section of the working class—the black workers—being armed by the capitalists to be used against the other workers in order to defeat the revolution. It was essential, first, for all socialists, whether right or left wingers, to recognize this danger and then to take steps to remove it. To this end, Domingo proposed the following program to be adopted by American radicals:

1. Condemn all facts of injustice to the Negro. 2. Give Negroes more prominence in the discussions and in publications. 3. Report and denounce all cases of racial discrimination, especially by the labor unions. 4. Do everything to attract Negroes to meetings. 5. Launch a special propaganda drive among Negroes to show them the benefits they would derive from a radical change in the existing economic system. 6. Subsidize radical Negro newspapers. 7. Send radical white speakers to spread radical propaganda among the Negroes, especially in the South, where the black masses were most likely to be organized into a "mercenary army" by the capitalists. 8. Induce intelligent Negroes to attend radical meetings of whites and impress upon them that the socialists are their friends. 9. Avoid stressing problems of race and emphasize the advantage to all, black and white, of the cooperative commonwealth. [59]

Domingo's proposals came to light only because the document was seized by agents of the Lusk Committee in a raid on the Rand School where Domingo was teaching. It was partially summarized in the *New York Times* of June 20, 1919, at which time Senator Lusk was quoted as saying that it was the "most important piece of evidence" unearthed by the committee, and that it indicated that a "detailed plan" existed "for the spreading of Bolshevist propaganda among negroes in the South." When it was finally published, the document hardly supported this conclusion, since it called for methods of making Negroes more socially conscious and more receptive to the message of socialism. Nowhere in it was there any suggestion of violence; rather, the stress was on the danger of violence from the reactionary forces, intent upon crushing the social revolution.

## AFRICAN BLOOD BROTHERHOOD

Domingo himself became the editor of Garvey's *Negro World* and later joined the semisecret African Blood Brotherhood as its director of publicity. The African Blood Brotherhood, a name derived from the African rite of fraternization by mingling drops of blood, was founded by Cyril V. Briggs. It evolved out of the political climate created by World War I and the conflict within the international socialist movement over member-party support for the war policies of their respective national governments. A number of the Harlem black socialists who viewed the war largely as a struggle for colonial conquest believed that the Socialist party in the United States was not sufficiently active in exposing and opposing the redivision of colonial empires by the leading imperialist powers. They were searching for a new organization through which they might conduct this struggle more effectively.

Briggs had been an editor of the *New York Amsterdam News* but had resigned when the U.S. Intelligence Department demanded censorship of his editorials condemning segregation in the armed forces and the use of a Negro regiment in the capacity of stevedores. In the fall of 1917, he founded the African Blood Brotherhood as "a revolutionary secret order" and became its "paramount chief." As its title indicates, the organization was strongly linked to the struggle for "a free Africa." But it considered the fight for fulfilling the democratic rights of American blacks a vital prerequisite for developing a strong political force to campaign for the liberation of Africa.

The platform of the African Blood Brotherhood, under the general heading of "immediate protection and ultimate liberation," called for armed resistance to lynching, unqualified franchise rights for blacks in the South, a struggle for equal rights and against all forms of discrimination, and the organization of Negroes into established trade unions. It also protested against trade-union discrimination and advocated the organization of Negro unions where blacks were banned by white unions. Most significant, the Brotherhood called for self-determination for Negroes in states where they constituted a majority.

Actually, this was not the first time the liberation of Negroes in America had been linked to the anticolonialist concept of "self-determination." On November 13, 1918, the New York *Call* reported that the Socialist party had concluded that, if the principle of self-determination for subject people, races, nationalities, and small nations included in Wilson's Fourteen Points for the peace program was to mean anything, it should also be applied in the Southern states of the country over which Wilson was president and where in certain areas blacks constituted a majority of the population. Self-determination was called a major way to redress "the wrongs of which Negroes complain." Evidently the African Blood Brotherhood, tired of waiting for the Socialist party to do more than merely affirm its belief in the principle, decided to make "self-determination" a major issue.

At its inception, the Brotherhood linked anticolonialism and militant protest against the treatment of blacks in the United States. It bitterly attacked Du Bois' call for Negroes to "close ranks" in support of the war, arguing that the Negro had no interest in a "white man's war . . . for things he [the black man] is not enjoying in America." The first duty of blacks, it insisted, was to fight against lynch violence at home. Moving from opposition to the colonialist character of the war and a call for a worldwide struggle for a "free Africa," the Brotherhood championed independence for blacks within the United States. In its view, the same corporate power that stood behind the imperialist conquests of Africa was the enemy of the black masses of this country. The demand for self-determination for the American Negro in areas where the race constituted a majority of the population was seen as part of the worldwide struggle against corporate domination. Since the oppression of Negroes in America, particularly in the Southern Black Belt, was analogous to the total and systematic political, economic, and cultural oppression of blacks in the colonies of Africa and the West Indies, the battle against that oppression had to be both anticapitalist and anti-imperialist.

The Brotherhood demanded the complete achievement of equal rights and the destruction of all forms of segregation in American society. It believed strongly in the organization of black workers but opposed any servile relationship to the white labor movement. It maintained that blacks should unite with whites where possible, but should form separate unions where necessary. Publishing a thirty-page monthly, the *Crusader*, and organizing campaigns against discrimination in industry and unions, as well as for black socialist candidates, the African Blood

Brotherhood exercised some influence among the black masses. At its peak, it claimed 2,500 members in fifty-six posts throughout the nation, including areas of strength among the black coal miners in West Virginia. [60]

But that was in 1921. Before that, the organization had been forced to operate underground throughout the South, isolating it from the mainstream of the Negro population.

The African Blood Brotherhood had originally emerged as a left wing breakaway from the Harlem Section of the Socialist party. The founders, most of them West Indians like Briggs, Richard B. Moore, Otto Hall, and Otto Huiswood, had left the Socialist party because they regarded its program in the struggle against colonialism and for Negro liberation as too moderate. Nevertheless, they did not immediately join the communist movement when it was formed in 1919. They were repelled by the failure of both Communist parties to deal with the Negro question in their platforms and by the fact that when the Communist party did begin to deal with the question in its early stages, it continued the traditional thinking of the socialist movement that the Negro problem was basically an aspect of the class question. Eventually, however, this small but significant group of black socialists-nationalists became affiliated with the communist movement.

# 15

# After the Split, 1920-1928

The hysterical climate of the postwar Red Scare reached its climax late in 1919. In a hunt for "alien radicals" to be deported, the federal government began a series of mass raids in which thousands of people were arrested. The raids were ordered by Attorney General Palmer and executed under the direction of his special assistant, J. Edgar Hoover. A trial run on November 7, 1919, the second anniversary of the Soviet Revolution, netted 452 arrests in eleven cities. The major sweep took place on New Year's Day 1920, when 2,758 were arrested in thirty-three cities. The Palmer raids continued over protests until about 10,000 people had been arrested—most of them unjustly, since only some 300 were deported.

On January 11, 1920, Socialist Congressman Victor Berger of Milwaukee was denied his seat in Congress. Four days earlier, five New York State assemblymen, all socialists, had their seats challenged by the legislature; they were finally excluded in April 1920.

The American Communist and Communist Labor parties had been founded just before the Red Scare reached its height. Soon, most of the leaders of the two parties were either in jail, having been sentenced to long terms in the penitentiary, or were being summarily deported with scores of others and sent to Russia on the infamous "leaking boat," the U.S.S. transport *Buford*. Under these circumstances, the communist movement was driven underground and forced to operate secretly.

When the two Communist parties decided to merge into the United Communist party in 1920, the delegates to the unity convention traveled in great secrecy. It was not until December 1921 that the young, unified communist movement, having weathered the Palmer raids and the police persecution, was ready to emerge as the Workers (later to be called the Communist) party.

The heated factionalism that wracked the Socialist party after the questions of support for the war, the Bolshevik Revolution, and the concept of a revolutionary party, culminating in the split in the party, did not weaken Randolph's and Owen's faith in it as the vehicle for achieving black liberation. In addition to teaching at the Rand School, the party's educational institution in New York City, lecturing for the party, and publishing articles on why Negroes should become socialists, they sought to bring the message of socialism to blacks throughout the country through a number of organizations they either created or helped to create.

From its inception, *The Messenger* radicals favored the promotion of independent black unionism. They had helped in the formation of the National Association for the Promotion of Labor Unionism Among Negroes and the National Brotherhood Workers of America (NBWA). At the founding convention of the latter organization, Randolph and Owen were appointed to its board of directors, and their monthly journal served as the organization's official mouthpiece. But NBWA officials were soon charging them with being more interested in securing support for their magazine than in building the new organization; hence, *The Messenger* editors and the NBWA parted ways. The NBWA continued on its own until its demise in 1921. [1] Meanwhile, *The Messenger* editors founded the Friends of Negro Freedom. The new group sought to distinguish itself from the leading organizations fighting in the interest of the Negro, such as the NAACP and the National Urban League. Even though the NAACP finally had a black secretary, Randolph and Owen still regarded it as being top-heavy with whites at the national leadership level. They accused it of having no program for economic improvement or for the fundamental reorganization of American society, and of placing its branches under the guidance of upper class blacks, in an attempt to become respectable. The Urban League was considered even worse: several of its branches were supported by industrialists for the purpose of using them as antiunion allies, and they reciprocated by providing scabs when needed. In short, as *The Messenger* editors repeatedly emphasized, both the NAACP and the Urban League were run by individuals who were neither of the black race nor of the working class. In their opinion, the white, conservative type of leaders that dominated these organizations made it impossible for them to function effectively in the Negro's behalf. Randolph and Owen insisted that if any organization was to be successful in bringing about a fundamental improvement in the condition of the Negro masses, it would have to be controlled by those who knew the problems of the Negro workers best—namely, the black workers themselves.[2]

The March 1920 issue of *The Messenger* announced the formation of a new organization. At the same time, the editors noted that many concerned Negroes in all parts of the country had asked them to form some group that would carry out the "New Crowd Negro" principles and function more effectively in the Negro's interest. A convention was called for May in Washington, D.C. Among the signers of the call were Archibald Grimké, the NAACP leader in the capital; black historian Carter G. Woodson; Robert W. Bagnall, former pastor of a Detroit church and president of that city's NAACP branch; and *Baltimore Afro-American* editor Carl Murphy. The convention adopted the name Friends of Negro Freedom (FNF). Bagnall was chosen to head the Executive Committee, which included Grace Campbell, George F. Miller, T. J. Free, and several others. Resolutions were passed calling for rent strikes and boycotts of high-priced and unfair merchants and of motion pictures that presented unflattering stereotypes of the Negro. They also urged a national Chatauqua (lecture society) for increasing black education, and the freeing of black colleges from white control, since this molded the students' minds in a way more suited to the interests of the white community than those of the black. A national black holiday was to be celebrated, strangely enough, on John Brown's birthday. The resolutions also condemned unquestioning obedience to the major parties, and the Socialist party was recommended without being mentioned by name. Finally, the resolutions declared that "destruction precedes construction, and that the country needs some destruction: of lynching, peonage, and other practices."[3]

While welcoming international affiliates, the FNF was intended to be primarily a national body made up of local branches in cities and towns across the country. Membership was open to all races, but control of the group was to rest with the Negroes since it was in their interest that the organization was founded. It would seek to unionize Negro workers, insure better housing for black workers' families through the formation of Tenant Leagues, reduce the cost of food, fuel, clothing, and other necessities by organizing consumer cooperatives, and acquaint the colored population with the fundamental problems concerning their race through the establishment of educational forums. Special committees would be established to organize boycotts against those stores and businesses that practiced racial discrimination. It was hoped that, by employing such tactics as boycotts, rent strikes, labor agitation, and other "direct action" techniques, the FNF would organize the black masses into a force powerful enough to protect their interests both on the job and in their communities. The educational programs were designed to bring to them a clear understanding that socialism was the real solution to their problems, as it was to those of all workers. [4]

The FNF undertook several enterprises, but first the black radicals who founded it had to deal with the elections in the fall of 1920.


ELECTION OF 1920

On the eve of the Socialist party's national convention in May 1920, the *New York Call* noted that the Republican party in the South was engaged in the process of "eliminating the Negro." Black delegates were no longer a common sight at Republican conventions in the Southern states. [5] Evidently, some leading socialists decided to take their cue from the Republicans. For example, in a detailed analysis of the actions to be taken at the party's forthcoming national convention, Victor Berger did not once mention the Negro question. "Why omit the Negro?" a comrade asked in the *New York Call*, reminding the party for the hundredth time: "For the Socialist movement in America to succeed it must have at least the good will of the Negro in America, if not his cooperation." [6] Despite this advice, the *Souvenir Journal* of the national convention made no mention of the Negro, not even in an article by Joe Hodes, state secretary of the Georgia Socialist party, entitled "The Movement in a Southern State." [7]

Two black delegates, both from Indiana, were present at the convention; they urged the adoption of a strong plank dealing with the Negro. The plank finally adopted read: "Congress should enforce the provisions of the 14th Amendment with reference to the Negroes, and effective Federal legislation should be enacted to secure to the Negroes full civil, political, industrial and educational rights." [8] Even this rather innocuous stand angered a party member in Pittsburgh who wrote to the *Call*: "No self-respecting white man would vote the socialist ticket with this clause in the platform. When I say this, I not only express my own opinion, but, I believe, the opinion of every white man who respects his race." The *Call* denied this, insisting that, to the contrary, "hundreds of thousands" of white workers would "vote the Socialist ticket knowing this demand is made and they would refuse to vote a Socialist ticket if the party did not take this stand." As in the past, it read its correspondent a lecture to the effect that "in the class struggle there is no color line," that white workers, even in the South, were "slowly beginning to appreciate the necessity of black and white solidarity," and that the correspondent, having been won over by the economic argument of socialism, had yet to learn another aspect of its ideology—"the solidarity of all workers regardless of their color, the language they speak or the country in which they are born."9

The report of the Committee on Organization and Propaganda called upon the convention to support special efforts for spreading socialist propaganda among Negroes. The National Executive Committee was requested to put into immediate effect a resolution calling for the employment of two Negro organizers and one Negro woman to work among black women. 10 The first proposal was the only one adopted by the convention, and shortly after it adjourned, a pamphlet was issued entitled "Why Negroes Should Be Socialists." They were advised to join the party in their capacity as workers since the party was the only one that represented the workingman. The pamphlet stressed that race was not the issue. It gave examples of white employers exploiting white workers:

> The IWW's are mostly white men, yet, are they not clubbed, deported, jailed, lynched, and outraged just as Negroes are? . . . . Is not Eugene V. Debs, the presidential candidate on the socialist ticket, denied his freedom by white Democrats and Republicans? Were not the steel and coal strikers beaten down by white soldiers and policemen when they committed the crime of striking for a living wage? Both the strikers were white men and the employers were white men, yet their interests were opposed and they fought. How do you explain that MR. NEGRO WORKER?

All this, the pamphlet contended, was proof that the oppression of the Negro was attributable to class rather than to race and that the remedy lay in working-class solidarity and the triumph of the Socialist party— "the only hope of the worker, and the salvation of the Negro." 11

While it was true that white workers were being subjected to an unprecedented degree of violence and repression in post-World War I America, the violence meted out to blacks during this same period—including physical attacks on returning black veterans, the race riots in over a score of cities, and the increased rate of lynchings—was both quantitatively and qualitatively different from that experienced by the whites. The failure of the Socialist party to understand this fact is an indication of the continued weakness of its approach to the Negro question. Like the resolution adopted at the national convention dealing with Negro rights, the Socialist party's pamphlet simply refused to understand the dimensions of the injustices experienced by black Americans.

*The Messenger* ignored everything that took place at the 1920 national convention except the nomination of Eugene V. Debs as the Socialist party standard bearer in the presidential campaign. "Debs is our candidate," it exulted. "Let us elect Debs. Let us release Debs. Long live Debs!" 12 Emphasizing the fact that Debs was the first man in American history to run for president while in prison, it proudly displayed a letter from the Atlanta Federal Penitentiary addressed to *The Messenger*, in which the socialist presidential candidate called for political and economic equality for all workers: "The Socialist Party proposes in accordance with its fundamental principles, that the Negro shall have the same political, economic and civil rights that the white man has to life, liberty and the pursuit of happiness." Debs, *The Messenger* assured the black voter, was not only "the modern Abe Lincoln of the workingmen"; he was "greater than Lincoln". Lincoln "merely nominally freed the bodies of Negroes . . . but Debs would free the bodies and minds of the Negroes." 13

The Socialist party's national vote in 1920 was 920,000. In light of the split of the previous year and the 410,000 votes cast for the Farmer-Labor ticket 14 —a party with a nearly identical platform—it would seem that popular support for the party was still strong. Moreover, the Socialist party ran well in several urban centers, including New York City. Randolph, the party's candidate for state comptroller, ran less than a thousand votes behind Debs. *The Messenger* editor polled more votes than any other socialist candidate for statewide office, and he was the only black on the state ticket. His strongest support came from New York City; in the Bronx, he received 18.5 percent of the vote. 15

Even though it was acknowledged that an unknown number of socialist ballots had been deliverately uncounted, the increased socialist vote in the Twenty-first Assembly District, which included Harlem (center of the party's strength among blacks in the country), was encouraging. To be sure, Republican Warren Harding had run first in the district, with its overwhelming Negro population, but in four areas, Debs had defeated Democratic James C. Cox for second place. 16 Pointing to an increase of 300 percent in the socialist vote, the socialists of the Twenty-first Assembly District declared:

> The members of this branch point with pride to the deep inroad they have made into the territory that has heretofore been known as a "Republican stronghold." Organized a little over two years ago and composed mainly of colored workers, they have succeeded in establishing themselves in spite of the many obstacles they had and still have to contend with. 17

In the New York elections of 1922, blacks again found a place on the ballot, this time on the American Labor, or combined Socialist and Farmer-Labor line. (This was a coalition of socialists and the more progressive unions.) A. Philip Randolph ran for secretary of state, Frank R. Crosswaith, who was increasingly becoming known as a leading black socialist, for Congress, and Clarence A. Carpenter for Assembly. Both Crosswaith and Carpenter ran in Harlem's Twenty-first Assembly District, which still had the reputation in 1922 of having "more Negro Socialists than can be found anywhere else in the country." [18]

## THE NEXT EMANCIPATION

It was the members of the Twenty-first Assembly District, Local New York—"the greater number of them being members of the Negro race"—who initiated the move that provided the Socialist party with its chief campaign appeal to blacks. This was the pamphlet by James Oneal entitled *The Next Emancipation* which, according to the New York *Call's* announcement at the height of the campaign, had gone into several printings and was "recognized as one of the most scientific and sound expositions of Socialism as an interpretation of the struggles of the Negro workers." [19] In a circular letter issued to the Socialist party's National Executive Committee in May 1922 on behalf of the members of the party branch in the Twenty-first Assembly District, Frank R. Crosswaith and G. Ollendorf informed the body that it had invited Oneal to write a propaganda booklet which could bring the party's message to the Negro and at the same time help in overcoming the five obstacles to recruiting blacks into the party. These were listed as follows:

> First—The well founded distrust of the Negro of any so-called white man's proposition, he having learned by bitter experience that the white man's proposition is seldom to his advantage.

> Second—The Lincoln tradition and the supposed debt of gratitude to the Republican party.

> Third—The Marcus Garvey "Back to Africa" doctrine.

> Fourth—The Booker T. Washington "good Negro" theory, as upheld by the National Association for the Advancement of Colored People, finding its culmination in the "Keep-the-Negro-in-his-place speech" of President Harding at Birmingham, on October 18, 1921.

> Fifth—The want of a proper recognition of the psychology of the Negro in our propaganda publications. [20]

*The Next Emancipation* was widely distributed to blacks during the campaign, and excerpts were reprinted in the leading black weeklies. (*The Messenger*, which hailed it as containing "more valuable subject matter on the Negro problem than any publication of its size yet written," reprinted it in its entirety.) [21] In it, Oneal contended that the Negro problem was fundamentally a labor problem, that the Negro was a worker exploited in the same manner as the white worker, and that the anti-Negro prejudice engendered and fostered by the exploiting class was aimed at preventing the solidarity of all labor, black and white, which was essential for its emancipation. He pointed out that at one period of American history, white workers were enslaved by white masters, just as were the Negroes; that at another period, the anti-Irish prejudice was just as deep-seated as the anti-Negro prejudice, and that the same might also be said, at one time or another, of anti-German and anti-East European prejudice — all springing from the same source. It was for this reason, Oneal declared, that the socialists rejected the programs of both Booker T. Washington and Marcus Garvey as futile efforts to achieve emancipation. Washington's plan to have the Negro educate himself in a trade or profession and then invade the business world was not workable, since, even if it was effective, it could only create a relatively small number of Negro capitalists who would exploit the large mass of Negro workers in the same manner as they were being exploited by white capitalists. Garvey's program, calling for the establishment of a Negro republic in Africa, would not even, if successful, abolish the exploitation of Negro labor, but would limit the exploitation to a small Negro capitalist class. A black capitalist class would make the same use of government, police power, military control, the injunction, and the courts against the Negro workers as the white capitalist class had against white workers.

Oneal then indicated by concrete example the sham role that the Republican party had played as the friend of the Negro, and how the "First Emancipation" of blacks from slavery had been reluctantly adopted by the Republicans, including "even Lincoln." After the Civil War, it had been betrayed by Republican administrations, and blacks were left to the mercy of the white supremacy South. "In the face of this record of pretense and hypocrisy," Oneal complained, "many Negro workers have sincerely believed that the Republican Party represented them!" He concluded by insisting that the only way for the Negro worker to secure real emancipation was by organizing with white workers and bringing about this emancipation together with that of these workers through the achievement of the socialist program:

> *The Socialist party admits workingmen and women of all races, colors and creeds into the organization.* All have equal rights and

privileges in the organization. It fraternizes with the workers of all countries. It calls upon the workers of the nation to desert the parties of capitalism, to unite under the banner of the Socialist party.

> *The Socialist party summons the useful workers, Negro and white, skilled and unskilled, to the struggle for the Next Emancipation. It is a glorious struggle, and for the greatest prize humans ever fought for, the liberation of all humanity from servitude, social degradation, and political impotence!*

However, Oneal stressed that one thing the "Next Emancipation" would not institute would be "social equality" of the races. The Socialist party, he said, recognized that white workers, especially in the South, were reluctant to vote socialist because they feared that, under socialism, "the emancipation of Negro and white workers would bring about some intimate personal and social relations of the two races by force of law or legal compulsion":

> Nothing of the kind. The matter of intimate associates and companions is a matter of personal choice and will always remain such. No law can compel one Irishman to associate with another Irishman if he does not want to. No law can compel one Negro to associate with another Negro if he does not want to. On the other hand, if an Irishman chooses a Negro for a personal friend and both find each other's company congenial, that is their affair and nobody else's. 22

This, then, was *The Next Emancipation*, the only Socialist party pamphlet issued from the time of the split until 1935 that was directed exclusively to Negroes. (*The Next Emancipation* was reprinted repeatedly after 1922, but it remained substantially the same as when it was first published.) In several respects, Oneal actually retreated from the position the Socialist party developed on the Negro question during World War I. For example, he stressed that the vast majority of Negroes in the United States were workers and that "the real division of humanity is between mastery and slavery. Color, religion and humanity are mere incidents." But, as discussed earlier, this position, quite common in socialist literature before World War I, had undergone considerable modification with the recognition that "color and race" did make a difference and that, while blacks were workers, they were both especially exploited and subjected to much greater persecution because of racism. All this went out of the window in Oneal's analysis. Then again, while its literature usually avoided the issue of social equality, by the eve of World War I, the party, at least in New York and other Northern cities, was proclaiming that it stood for complete social equality and would not be intimidated by the charge that it was encouraging miscegenation. During these same years, socialist literature linked the battle against segregation in every aspect of American life with the struggle for social equality. Oneal's only comment on the fight against segregation was the weak statement that it would require another booklet "to consider the Jim Crow car, the theater, the hotel, amusements, and a hundred other institutions around which cluster racial prejudices." 23 Apart from the fact that he was dodging the issue, the "other booklet" was never written, and the same meaningless remark continued to appear in every subsequent edition of *The Next Emancipation*. Plainly, the section on "social equality" in Oneal's widely heralded and frequently reprinted pamphlet could have been published in 1902 without the alteration of a single sentence.

Oneal was correct in emphasizing that the plight of the white indentured servant (whom he incorrectly called a slave) was hardly an enviable one in Colonial America. However, to equate his status, as he did, with that of the black slave was to display a total lack of understanding of the nature of slavery. White indentured servants did not, as Oneal contended, suffer the same punishments as black slaves; their families were not broken up, despite Oneal's claim to the contrary, and, bad as their lot was, it was far better than that of the Negro slave. Oneal's failure to acknowledge these differences might be understandable since he sought to prove that there was no special Negro problem, but for black socialists to accept this interpretation and to uncritically hail *The Next Emancipation* is truly incredible.

The disappointing 1922 returns revealed that the Socialist party was on the wane. Randolph collected 129,461 votes, or 5 percent of the vote cast for the secretary of state. Two years earlier, when he ran for comptroller, he received 7 percent of the vote. In the Bronx, where he received the highest percentage of votes, the figure was 12.3 percent compared to 18.5 percent in the previous election. 24

## THE RETURN OF EUGENE V. DEBS

Commenting on the 1922 election returns, black weeklies observed that the party was fast disappearing as the place around which black radicals rallied and that the "Workers (Communist) Party" had fallen heir to this tradition. Oneal denied this claim, but he did concede that the party was growing weaker in black circles. However, there was new hope in the offing. Early that year, the Socialist party's great spokesman,

Eugene V. Debs, had been released from prison and was about to begin a lecture tour to recruit new members. With his reputation for racial equality already established before he went to prison and further enhanced by his conduct while in the Atlanta Federal Penitentiary, Debs, the party felt, should sign up a goodly number of black comrades. [25]

On Christmas Day 1921, Debs, along with twenty-three other political prisoners, was pardoned by President Harding. The headline in a leading black weekly during the first week of January 1922 read: "Radical Man Kissed Black Man at Parting and Both Broke Down." Pointing out that Debs had been known as the "guardian of the Negro inmates" at Atlanta, the newspaper conceded that he had "won the silent, as well as active admiration of thousands of Negroes throughout the United States," and that his "influence" in recruiting blacks into the Socialist party was "feared." [26]

Debs' reputation as an able counselor to the Negro prisoners at Atlanta grew largely out of his association with Sam Moore, a Negro serving a twenty-year sentence for assault. [27] Debs also helped many other black prisoners, a fact duly reported in the black press. So was the news that *The Messenger* had nominated Debs as the black American's "standard bearer in the next Presidential election." Debs declined the honor in a letter to the black monthly, adding, however, that "coming from my Negro comrades this is a recognition of special value to me." [28]

For several months after his release from prison, Debs rested and enjoyed long visits with old friends. Ill health forced him to enter a sanitarium in Illinois in the summer of 1922, but by the end of the year, he was sufficiently recovered to contemplate a national speaking tour for the Socialist party. He began the tour during the winter and spring of 1922-1923 and continued it until November, when he became ill and canceled the rest of his speaking engagements. Broken in health, he returned to Terre Haute, Indiana. The last speech of the tour before his breakdown was delivered in Harlem at the Commonwealth Casino at 135th Street and Madison Avenue. Entitled *Appeal to Negro Workers* and reprinted in pamphlet form by the national office of the Socialist party, it represents both Eugene V. Debs' last pronouncement on the Negro question and an almost desperate effort by the party to use his warm personality and prestige to regain influence in the black community.

"The old speeches will not do," Bertha Hale White, national secretary of the Socialist party, told Debs. [29] But Debs' last speech on the Negro question had nothing new to say. Much of it was made up of personal reminiscences of the labor movement, with examples of how racism had retarded organized labor; his stand against segregation during pre-World War I Southern tours for the party; and his relationship with Sam Moore during his stay in prison. In addition, there was a summary of highlights on American Negro history from Crispus Attucks to the Civil

War, with special attention paid to Debs' heroes, Wendell Phillips and John Brown. (There was no mention of Frederick Douglass.) None of this, however, was new, and the only references to the contemporary scene were to the Ku Klux Klan, in which Debs made the rather startling statement that if the "colored people" would continue to exercise "self restraint," the Klan would "spend its force"; to the election coming up in New York City within a few days and the plea for blacks to vote for the socialist ticket; and to a call for support for *The Messenger* and the *New York Leader*, the party's daily paper, formerly the *Call*. 30 Debs called *The Messenger* "a true champion of the colored workers" and worthy of their "encouragement and support." 31 Ironically, the copy he held in his hand was the November 1923 issue which was devoted entirely to a panegyric to black business. It featured an editorial, "Business and Labor," condemning "superficial radicals" who argued that "there is nothing in common between the employer and employee." 32

Debs had no word of criticism for the bourgeois ideology displayed in the black magazine he praised so lavishly. Unfortunately, this was the tone of the entire speech insofar as it related to the Socialist party and the Negro. Missing was the criticism he had voiced in 1918 concerning the Socialist party's failure to address itself to the special needs of the Negro, or his bold assertion that any socialist who failed to speak out "for the Negro's right to work, live and develop his manhood, educate his children, and fulfill his destiny" equally with whites "misconceives the movement he pretends to serve or lacks the courage to live up to its principles." There was no place for racists in the Socialist party, he had said in 1918—an obvious thrust at Southern locals that practiced segregation. But in 1923, all was well with the Socialist party's approach to the Negro question.

In his 1923 speech, Debs did not repeat, word for word, his 1903 statement that the Socialist party had "nothing special to offer to the Negro, and we cannot make separate appeals to all the races." However, much of his Commonwealth Casino speech was in keeping with this approach. He emphasized that blacks were basically workers, just like white workers, and would solve their problems, like white workers, by joining unions and voting socialist. The laws of capitalism applied "to white and black alike." There was no race question: "At bottom it is a class question." 33 Debs had said the same thing in 1903; clearly he had learned little in two decades about the significance of racism in American society. Ernest Rice McKinney, a black socialist and a contributing editor of *The Messenger*, observed: "As understanding as Debs was of these problems, he apparently didn't understand this one: that Negroes had two disabilities, one being Negroes, and one being workers; that Negroes had to struggle on both fronts and probably more vigorously on the front against discrimination." 34

James Oneal, editor of the *New York Leader* and party ideologist on the Negro question, was quite content with Debs' speech. In his review of it in the socialist press, Oneal declared that it presented "the Socialist position of no color line in the struggle of the working class to be free." He predicted that "the reprint of this speech should be of considerable service in Socialist educational work among Negro workers. The argument is clear and eloquent and the Socialist message stands in bold outline." [35]

*The Messenger* was much more cautious. It called Debs' speech one of his "most brilliant and moving orations," heralded the fact that the Negro press gave it wide circulation "to Negroes throughout the country," and left it at that. [36] Unlike Oneal, *The Messenger* editors refused to delude themselves. Despite their sentimental attachment to Debs, they knew there was nothing in his speech that would bolster the influence of the Socialist party in the black community. The party was sinking fast, and all prospects for a renewal of its strength were rapidly receding. Owing to lack of funds, the *New York Leader* became a weekly in the summer of 1924, and *The Messenger*, having anticipated this outcome, could only comment "Too bad!" At about the same time, it reported that the Twenty-first Assembly District Socialist Club in Harlem was defunct; this, too, came as no surprise. [37] Nor for that matter was the report of the demise of the Friends of Negro Freedom, the organization Randolph and Owen had founded. As the socialist press explained, the FNF had engaged in a variety of activities, including helping migrants adjust to the North; trying through negotiations with employers to open up new jobs for blacks in theaters, on the railroads, and in organized baseball; and even issuing a FNF union label to signify to the black community that a particular union welcomed black membership and offered employment opportunities to Negroes. Its main work, however, had been educational and was conducted mainly through weekly forums sponsored by the fourteen branches established across the country. The most frequent topic at these educational forums was what the socialists, black and white alike, called "the Garvey menace." Soon the FNF acquired the reputation of being "an organization which had been formed to speed the retirement of Marcus Garvey from public life." Once that goal had been achieved, it appeared to have nothing to live for and so passed out of existence. [38]

## "GARVEY MUST GO!"

The "Marcus Garvey Must Go" campaign of the Socialist party, spearheaded by Randolph and Owen of *The Messenger*, must have come as a surprise to some contemporaries inasmuch as the black socialist editors were among Garvey's earliest associates in Harlem. When Garvey settled in Harlem, after a whirlwind tour of thirty-eight states, he soon joined one-time socialist and leading Harlem intellectual, Hubert H. Harrison, and socialists A. Philip Randolph and Chandler Owen as a "soap-box and step ladder" orator on the corner of 135th Street and Lenox Avenue. It was Randolph who introduced him to his first Harlem audience in the spring of 1917, and on June 12, 1917, at the invitation of Harrison, Garvey addressed a Harlem mass meeting in the Bethel African Methodist Episcopal Church. On July 8, 1917, Garvey shared the platform with Chandler Owen at a meeting in Harlem's Lafayette Hall at 131st Street and Lenox Avenue. [39]

By 1918, when he decided to remain in the United States rather than return to his native land, Jamaica, Garvey was already known as one of Harlem's leading black orators. His eloquent speaking style and magnetic personality made a deep impression on his audiences. On July 2, the Universal Negro Improvement Association (UNIA), originally founded in Jamaica in July 1914, was incorporated under the laws of New York, and in August, the *Negro World*, edited by Garvey, made its appearance. The earliest issues were slipped under people's doors in the early hours, but soon it was being sold with a growing circulation as more and more blacks were won over by the power of Garvey's call for African self-rule and an African homeland for American Negroes. [40]

On November 10, 1918, Garvey presided at a meeting of 5,000 UNIA members at the Palace Casino. The purpose of the meeting was to generate interest in securing a black representative at the upcoming Paris Peace Conference and to stimulate awareness among blacks of international issues in general. Among those who spoke were A. Philip Randolph and Ida Wells-Barnett. The UNIA named Randolph as one of its delegates to the peace conference, but he never attended, partly because black Americans, with few exceptions, were being denied passports to France by the U.S. government. [41]

In June 1919, Garvey incorporated his Black Star Line. Its purpose was to place ships on the seas which would provide a worldwide link of black communities through trade. It would also facilitate the movement of blacks, fleeing the racism of white nations, to a new and independent life of freedom in Black Africa. This was on the eve of the "Red Summer" of 1919, and, as we have seen, during the next few months, more than a score of American cities were to be scarred by racial conflicts. The bloody events of these months caused many blacks to believe that Marcus Garvey had the only logical answer to their problems. By regaining Africa for the black man, by organizing Negroes so as to make them self-reliant and proud of their blackness and their great historical past, and by establishing black business enterprises, the UNIA, according to Garvey, would liberate blacks from their inferior status in American society. So great was the appeal of this program that the UNIA enjoyed a phenomenal growth. It purchased Liberty Hall in New York City for its central meeting place, put both the Black Star Line and the Negro Factories Corporation into operation, established branches of the organization both in the United States and abroad, and distributed the *Negro World* internationally, despite efforts of the imperalist powers to suppress the black weekly in their colonies. 42

In its claim of a membership of two million in 1919, the UNIA undoubtedly included sympathizers as well as members in the strict sense, and even the figure itself is questionable. Nevertheless, it was already the largest black mass organization ever formed in America. During his interview with Charles Mowbray White of the National Civic Federation in August 1920, Garvey regaled him with stories of the UNIA's sympathy with the Bolsheviks in Russia and the Irish liberationists, repeating his public statement that, if necessary, blacks should seek the aid of Lenin and Trotzky in liberating Africa from imperialism. He also explained that he did not advocate the return of all black people to Africa. He relegated W.E.B. DuBois to the status of an "antebellum Negro." Garvey showed White the UNIA colors and explained the red-green-black. Red, he said, showed "sympathy with the Reds of the world, and the Green their sympathy for the Irish in their fight for freedom, and the Black [is for] the Negro."

It was during White's interview with Randolph and Owen at the office of *The Messenger* that the rift between Garvey and the black socialist leaders surfaced. Owen did most of the talking, but White reported that Randolph concurred in his associate's sentiments. Garvey, Owen insisted, could not possibly be Bolshevik in outlook because "he has made no effort to study the socialist movement headed by us." In fact, he maintained that the Jamaican was an uneducated ignoramus who knew nothing of the Afro-American, being the leader of a "purely West Indian" movement. Owen and Randolph even advanced the hypothesis that Garvey might be working with the Justice Department to destroy black solidarity by siphoning money from rival organizations. They also expressed the conviction that Garvey's slogan of "Africa for the Africans" was unscientific, whereas they were scientific internationalists. They predicted that Garvey's schemes would collapse within three months; if he should somehow prove successful, they warned, "it would set back ten years at least the Socialist movements we are leading among the blacks." 43

These comments remained buried in the archives of the National Civic Federation, and it was not until the September 1920 issue of *The Messen-*

*ger* that their first public criticism of the UNIA appeared. [44] While it did not mention Garvey by name, the article "Africa for the Africans" clearly applied to him. It stated that Garvey's African panacea was based on simplistic reasoning, since the oppression throughout the world knew no color line. As proof, the authors cited the persecution of the Israelites by the Egyptians in ancient times. Nations oppressed others out of lust for profit, they insisted, and black nations were as prone to do this as any others. Capitalistic gain was what motivated imperialism in Africa. Since England was the chief exploiter of that continent and only very few in that country benefited from the exploitation, a more sensible program of African redemption would be to fight against British and other imperialists by boycotting their goods. Only practical methods should be used. In order to really help Africa, one would have to consult, in secret, with its native leaders. Emotion, personal ambition, and ignorance of the true conditions in Africa were poor weapons against British capital and munitions. The magic word "unity" would be of little value by itself. [45]

At precisely the same time, the *New York Call* also published its first criticism of Garvey, and it likewise refrained from mentioning him by name. Its editorial, "Colonizing Africa," warned that substituting black for white control of Africa would mean little as long as "the capitalistic system of production is not changed in its essentials. . . . Capitalism dominated by Negroes in the same as capitalism dominated by whites." Those who sought to "maintain Africa for the Africans" had better learn that the emancipation of the black worker, whether in Africa or in the United States, was "bound up with the emancipation of the worker of all races." [46]

Garvey was first mentioned critically by name in the October and December 1920 issues of *The Messenger*, where the answer to the question, "The Garvey Movement: A Promise or a Menace," was given emphatically in favor of the latter. In a detailed, five-page analysis, "Garveyism," written by Randolph in the September 1921 issue, and in "Black Zionism," also by Randolph, in the January 1922 issue, the theoretical basis for black socialist criticism of Garvey was set down. First, there was an attack on his proposal for an all-black party. Since such a party could never become the majority party in the United States, it would never be effective either in winning national elections or in outlawing Jim Crow and lynching. Such a party would surely produce its own counterforce, an all-white party, which would play into the hands of racists like Tom Watson and Hoke Smith. The answer did not lie in racial parties, for parties were based on economic interests, not race lines. Instead, blacks should organize economically, along socialistic lines. [47]

Randolph recognized and acknowledged that Garvey had made a

useful contribution by his "necessary and effective criticism of Negro leadership; by his stimulation of pride and interest in black history and traditions, thereby helping to bury the old slave-psychology of Negro inferiority; by instilling an attitude of resistance toward whites; and by motivating black people to follow black leadership." Moreover, the UNIA had demonstrated the ability of blacks to organize a large mass movement under their own leadership, had done much to popularize the international character of the race problem, and, as a propaganda organization, had been effective in awakening blacks to the issues of modern times. Finally, despite the fact that his business operations were unsound, Garvey had done much to stimulate black business initiative.

But, the critique continued, these positive points were far overshadowed by the fundamental fact that the Garvey movement was based on fallacies and guided by poor judgment. The crux of its program—the redemption of Africa and the building of an African empire—was unrealistic. All of Africa, except Abyssinia and Liberia, was held by white imperalists. To divest them of their empires would require arms and revolution, but only the imperialists possessed the means of modern warfare. And since they had fought to seize Africa and continued to profit from their possession of it, they certainly were not about to surrender meekly to an emotional appeal. To win Africa, Randolph argued in "Black Zionism," would require defeating the armies and navies of England, France, Belgium, Portugal, Italy, and Spain:

> It ought to be apparent to even the most ardent and superficial Garveyite that the interest of the [imperialist] Power in preventing the establishment of an African State is the interest of all the Powers; and if all the Powers are interested in maintaining the status quo in Africa, that the redemption of Africa by Negroes who are unarmed, unorganized, uneducated, a minority in numbers to their oppressors, divided, both in and out of Africa by languages, custom, history, and habits, is a will-o'-wisp, an iridescent dream which could only be born in the head of an irresponsible enthusiast.

Furthermore, Randolph asked, if the colonial administrations could somehow be overthrown, would they then be replaced by a Negro emperor and an equally despotic rule?

Randolph questioned the economic wisdom of an all-black shipping line. For one thing, the postwar shipping industry was depressed, owing to wartime overbuilding and the consequent excess of tonnage over goods to be shipped. For another, the entire industry was controlled by a shipping trust. The Black Star Line would soon be at its mercy, with severe losses resulting for those blacks naive enough to have invested in the enterprise.

Thus, Randolph concluded, while it was possible to say a few good things about Garvey, basically, he was definitely a menace. Not only was his ideology false, but it also seriously hindered the march of black radicalism. Blacks were finally beginning to be radicalized, to demand all justice, and to be accepted by organized labor, and along came Marcus Garvey to divert them from all this and from their fundamental problems in American society with his "pipedreams" of Africa. What other conclusion could there be but that Garvey was a tool of racist whites, capitalists, and Bourbons, who gave him the widest publicity and help in order to get blacks to follow him instead of moving toward genuine radicalism? The falsity of Garvey's charge that all whites were engaged in a conspiracy to exploit blacks was demonstrated by the fact that white socialists, at least, were color blind. In any case, Garveyism only widened the gap between black and white workers, the only result of which would be more race hatred and ultimately more race violence. [48]

These attacks were only the prelude to the real campaign. The lead editorial of *The Messenger* for July 1922 was headed: "Marcus Garvey! The Black Imperial Wizard Becomes Messenger Boy of the White Ku-Klux Kleagle." It was disclosed that Garvey had met with the head of the Ku Klux Klan, Kleagle Clark, in Atlanta early in 1922, and although he promised to make public the substance of their conversation, it had remained secret. Then again, Garvey had made a speech in New Orleans on his 1922 Southern trip in which he asserted that since blacks had not built the railroads, they should not insist on riding in the same cars with whites. This was too much for *The Messenger*. Expressing regret that Garvey had been treated leniently for so long, the magazine promised an unremitting editorial campaign, to begin the following month, to expose in detail all of Garvey's spurious schemes, "from his row-boatless steamship line to his voteless election to the Presidency of a non-existent nation." All "ministers, editors and lecturers who have the interests of the race at heart" were urged "to gird up their courage, put on new force, and proceed with might and main to drive the menace of Garveyism out of this country." And just in case its message had still not been made clear, the following declaration appeared in italics: "Here's notice that the MESSENGER is firing the opening gun in a campaign to drive Garvey and Garveyism in all its sinister viciousness from the American soil." [49]

Clearly, the ultimate goal would be to deport Garvey. As an alien, Garvey could not only be jailed but deported, and his imprisonment and deportation became the main objectives of *The Messenger* campaign. Garvey had been arrested in January 1922 and indicted the following

month for using the mails to defraud in connection with his promotion of
the Black Star Line. [50] *The Messenger*'s editors were eager to bring him
before a jury. In fact, in a speech on August 27, 1922, Owen announced
that the Friends of Negro Freedom would soon petition the Department
of Justice to bring Garvey to an early trial. [51]

On January 16, 1923, Reverend Robert W. Bagnall, FNF member and
NAACP official, wrote to Arthur B. Spingarn, national vice-president
and chairman of the legal committee of the NAACP:

> The enclosed is an open letter to Attorney General Daugherty
> which we plan to have signed by influential colored people in
> various parts of the country. It was drawn up by a group of us,
> among whom Owen, Randolph, Pickens, and I were the princi-
> pals. We wish to guard against any illegal statement, and we
> shall appreciate your advice on that point and as to the whole
> matter. [52]

After several sections were deleted, [53] the letter to U.S. Attorney General Harry M. Daugherty was made public. [54] It urged the government
to proceed with its prosecution of the year-old mail fraud case against
Garvey. The letter accused Garvey and the UNIA of stirring up prejudice against whites: "There are in our midst Negro criminals and potential murderers, both foreign and American born, who are moved and
actuated by intense hatred against the white man. These undesirables
continually proclaim that all white people are enemies of the Negro."
They were guilty also, it was charged, of creating dissension within the
black race. The UNIA was described as "just as objectionable and even
more dangerous" than the Ku Klux Klan, "inasmuch as it naturally
attracts an even lower type of cranks, crooks and racial bigots, among
whom suggestibility to violent crime is much greater." The organization
was accused of approving of violence to achieve its ends, and of perpetra-
ting thirteen specific acts of violence or intimidation against its opponents. "The UNIA," the letter continued, "is composed chiefly of the
most primitive element of West Indian and American Negroes." It
closed:

> For the above reasons we advocate that the Attorney-General
> use his full influence completely to disband and extirpate this
> vicious movement, and that he vigorously and speedily push the
> government's case against Marcus Garvey for using the mails to
> defraud. This should be done in the interest of justice; even as a
> matter of practical expediency.

The letter came from a committee of eight individuals, of whom Chandler Owen was secretary. The other seven signatories were Harry H. Pace, president of the Black Swan Phonograph Corporation and active in the National Urban League; John E. Nail, also of the Urban League and president of a New York real estate company; Dr. Julia P. Coleman, president of a black cosmetic manufacturing company; Robert S. Abbott, publisher of the *Chicago Defender* and a long-time opponent of Garvey; William Pickens and Reverend Bagnall of the NAACP; and George W. Harris, editor of the *New York News* and a member of the New York City Board of Aldermen. [55] The group was closely associated with the Friends of Negro Freedom.

When no reply was received to their letter, Carl Murphy, editor of the *Baltimore Afro-American* and a founder and active member of the FNF, inquired of the attorney general as to what steps had been taken to disband the UNIA in accordance with the expressed request of the eight signers. [56]

The attorney general was requested to address his reply to Owen. On February 20, 1923, the attorney general's office drafted a detailed reply to him, endorsing the group's analysis of the Garvey movement and promising possible further legal action against him. Although the draft was not sent, its concluding paragraph is worth quoting. It read: "The details of your letter are being given very careful attention and if sufficient evidence can be obtained on the several instances recited, you may rest assured that still additional action will be taken." [57]

The draft was replaced by a brief, more formal note of two sentences which ended: "Please keep us advised in the event additional facts come to your attention." [58] Owen thanked Assistant Attorney General Joseph Crim for his reply and reminded him that the eight represented "the most distinguished and responsible businessmen, educators and publicists among the colored people of the United States." [59] This note came from the man who only a few years before had proudly proclaimed himself a revolutionary and a Bolshevik, and had condemned the same "distinguished and responsible businessmen" as traitors to the black masses. Now he was cooperating with the attorney general of the United States and inviting the Justice Department to persecute and deport a black spokesman whose ideas he found repugnant. Yet, Owen still called himself a socialist.

Garvey's long-delayed trial finally began in May 1923. A guilty verdict was returned in late June, and on June 21, Garvey was given the maximum sentence of five years, together with a $1,000 fine, and was ordered to pay the entire cost of the trial. (Garvey had been the main target; his three codefendents were acquitted.) *The Messenger* exulted:

"Our work is bearing fruit. The Black Star Line is completely gone. Every one of his stores is closed. His *Negro World* is suspended, and well-nigh all of his former employees are suing him for pay." All that remained was to send "The Well Known Jackass" to a long sojourn in federal prison and then deport him. 60

*The Messenger* editors got their wish, but it took some time. After his short imprisonment in New York's Tombs until bail could be raised, Garvey enjoyed relative freedom, much to *The Messenger*'s annoyance, until February 1925, when, his appeals exhausted, he was committed to the federal penitentiary in Atlanta. In January 1928, his sentence was commuted and he was deported.

Thousands, possibly millions of black Americans found a prophet in Marcus Garvey. He preached black pride and a return to Africa, but the latter part of his message was much less important than the sense of identity and meaning he infused into the lives of so many blacks. At one time, *The Messenger* editors understood this aspect of Garvey's appeal. The April 1922 issue mentioned Garvey's contribution in "putting into many Negroes a backbone where for years they have had only a wishbone." But never again did *The Messenger* editors display such understanding of what lay behind Garvey's mass appeal or why his program struck such a responsive chord among the black masses. Undoubtedly, Garvey's enormous popularity as a leader of the black masses at precisely a time when their own influence was declining irked *The Messenger* editors. Randolph and Owen had linked the fate of black Americans to that of the Socialist party. When that party declined steadily after 1919, they refused to seek out the reasons for its loss of influence in the black community. Instead, they made Garvey the scapegoat.

Nevertheless, given Garvey's insistence that the United States was and would and should be a white man's country, his endorsement of Ku Klux Klan members as "better friends to my race" than those who favored integration, his increasingly reactionary positions vis-à-vis labor unions, socialism, and domestic politics in the United States, his basically capitalistic orientation, his opposition not only to socialism and communism (or, as he put it, "Miscegenationist Socialists and Miscegenationist Communists") but even trade unionism—at least as it was practiced in the United States—and his advice to black workers to organize by themselves, accept lower wages from white employers, and eventually become their own employers, and given what they believed to be glaring weaknesses in his program for Africa, the break between Garvey and *The Messenger* editors was, as Jarvis Anderson puts it, "inevitable." 61 What was not inevitable, however, was the unprincipled nature of their attacks and the depths to which Randolph and Owen sank in their campaign against Garvey. As it mounted in intensity, it became characterized by personal attacks, biting sarcasm, and tactics that could only be called "hitting below the belt." Garvey was described as a "half-wit, low grade moron, whose intellectual presumption is only exceeded by his abysmal ignorance"; his newspaper writings were called " the wild vaporings, imbecile puerilities and arrant nonsense of a consummate ignoramus"; his speeches were depicted as displaying an "erratic rampage of mendacity and bigoted, groundless braggadacio," and the UNIA was "the Most Dishonorable Order of Skinners, Fakirs, Hot-Air and Buncombe Dispensers." [62] More than once, Randolph called Garvey a crook who had laid away a fortune, although there was not the slightest evidence that this charge was true. It was reprehensible for *The Messenger* editors—radicals and socialists as they proclaimed themselves—to join with the ruling class in having Garvey sent to jail and deported. Their denigration of West Indian Negroes was bad enough, [63] but this was a betrayal of all that radicals believed in. When one reads the correspondence between "radical socialist" Chandler Owen and Attorney General Harry M. Daugherty in the Department of Justice files, it is hard to believe that Owen was the same man who had condemned Attorney General Palmer in 1919 and 1920. [64] The sad truth is that it was this same Chandler Owen who implored the attorney general to prosecute an outspoken black leader. It is indeed ironical that when Daugherty was forced out of office in June 1924, *The Messenger* hailed the departure of this personage from "the political underworld . . . [who] is notorious for his crooked, shady political dealings." [65] Naturally, no mention was made of the appeal of one of its own editors to this same "notorious" official to deport Marcus Garvey.

## THE LAFOLLETTE CAMPAIGN AND THE SOCIALIST PARTY

In the 1924 presidential election, the socialists joined forces with the Progressives to support Robert LaFollette, a Progressive Republican, for the presidency on an independent ticket—the Progressive Farmer-Labor party. This action was a radical departure from the party's oft-expressed principle of nonsupport of "capitalist parties" of whatever political complexion. The Farmer-Labor party and the American Federation of Labor also officially endorsed the LaFollette candidacy. The platform of the Progressives was mildly socialistic and strongly liberal. It advocated government ownership of railroads, abolition of private monopoly, popular election of federal judges, generous relief for farmers, the prohibition of injunctions, outlawing of war, a child labor amend-

ment to the Constitution, the power to override a Supreme Court decision declaring a law unconstitutional, and various government reform
measures (recall, initiative, referendum, and direct primaries.)

Along with the NAACP, *The Messenger* editors had sought to extract
from the Progressive party some recognition of the particular needs and
terrible grievances of black Americans, but their efforts were in vain.
Nevertheless, the LaFollette movement did get the support of both the
NAACP and *The Messenger*. For both it was a first. This was the only
time the NAACP endorsed a presidential candidate. *The Messenger*, for
its part, had always in the past urged voting the straight socialist ticket.
As late as February 1923, in its lead editorial entitled "Politics and the
Negro," Randolph had rejected the view that there was anything to be
gained from disregarding party labels. Only a socialist victory could
have meaning for blacks, he insisted, because only socialists in office
"would abolish lynching, the Jim Crow car, disfranchisement and peonage." [66] Eighteen months later, Randolph was not only not so sure but
completely confused. As the 1924 campaign progressed, he first advised
blacks to split their votes among the three parties—Republican, Democratic, and Progressive: ("Coolidge, Davis and LaFollette are all splendid men.") He then reversed himself and advised a vote for LaFollette,
not necessarily because he was the best candidate, but to show that
blacks were intelligent and independent. [67]

In contrast, the *Baltimore Afro-American* did not hesitate to announce
its support for LaFollette. It assured blacks that if they "would be free
there is nowhere then to turn but to the so-called radical party—LaFollette." Ignoring the fact that LaFollette had refused to speak out on any
issue facing blacks, the *Afro-American* declared that "America wants as
her next president no silent dummy." It assured its readers that the
Progressive candidate promised "a square deal to every man without
regard to race, color or religion," "to use the influence of his office to
stamp out the Ku Klux Klan," "to wipe out discrimination in Federal departments," and to eliminate most of all the other grievances of the
Negro. [68] Had this view of LaFollette been true, *The Messenger* editors
would have been much less confused and uncertain. Nevertheless, by
election day they had made up their minds. Even though he was supported by the lily-white Machinists' Union and had remained silent on
the race and Klan issues throughout the campaign, and even though the
coalition he headed would probably sponsor few if any fundamental political or economic changes, they halfheartedly preferred LaFollette.
How far the magazine had traveled in less than two years was indicated
by the fact that it could not even wholeheartedly endorse socialist guber-
natorial candidate Norman Thomas. That Frank R. Crosswaith was the
socialist candidate for New York secretary of state was not even men-

tioned. Apparently, the editors had lost all faith in the viability of the Socialist party.

LaFollette polled 4,882,856 popular votes and the thirteen electoral votes of his own state of Wisconsin. He got about 17 percent of the total national vote—a bitter disappointment to Progressives and socialists who expected a much higher vote. Analyzing the election results, Randolph blamed LaFollette's "surprisingly poor" showing on his failure to speak out on the Negro question. ("It is quite probable that LaFollette would have polled a much larger Negro vote had he made a single speech to them.") He attributed most of the candidate's weakness at the polls, however, to lack of money and the endorsement by the socialists. The latter, Randolph argued, "invited some unfavorable comment, alienated a number of farmers and workers, as well as quasi-liberal supporters," and was "a source of much confusion to the public." [69]

## RETREAT OF RANDOLPH AND OWEN

Clearly, when *The Messenger*'s editor could view a socialist endorsement as a liability, it was a sign that the "World's Leading Radical Black Magazine" no longer regarded the Socialist party as the hope of the Negro. But then the editors of *The Messenger* were in the process of moving away from the Socialist party. By 1925, Owen had gone to Chicago, although he kept his name on *The Messenger*'s masthead, and had moved into Republican politics. In 1926, he challenged white Republican incumbent Congressman Martin Madden for representation of Chicago's "Black Belt." *The Messenger* urged blacks to send Owen to Congress and, in briefly tracing his career, omitted the fact that he had formerly been a radical. Owen made a dismal showing: he finished last among five candidates in the primary, garnering less than 1 percent of the vote. Nonetheless, he continued his association with the Republicans and in later life filled several party positions. [70]

Owen's drastic about-face was hastened by the bitter experience his brother Touissaint suffered at the hands of the socialist-dominated needle trades' unions. A master tailor from Columbia, South Carolina, Touissaint had been encouraged to come to New York by his brother, who was confident that the same unions that praised *The Messenger* and lauded its socialist editors for calling for black-white unity would open their membership to the black tailor. But Touissaint failed to find work of any sort, and he died poverty-stricken in March 1923. Chandler Owen was embarrassed and disillusioned by his futile effort to secure work for his brother. [71]

*The Messenger*'s obituary notice to "Our Fallen Comrade, Touissaint

L. Owen," said he had been "one of the Race's most gifted, skilled and able artisans," and had possessed "one of the largest tailoring establishments in the South." But it said nothing of his sad experience with the Socialist needle-trade unions. In its July 1923 issue, however, it did carry a veiled criticism of these unions in an editorial entitled "The Needle Trades Unions and the Negro Worker," suggesting that these unions might yet "serve as a constructive model for the labor movement in adjusting and co-ordinating the sensitive and explosive materials of race." That was the last reference to the subject.

Randolph, as is well known, accepted the call to be chief organizer of the fledgling union of Pullman porters, and he began to unionize the black workers in this occupation into the Brotherhood of Sleeping Car Porters. [72] He continued writing editorials for *The Messenger*, which became the official organ of the Brotherhood. Having severed his connection with the Socialist party in 1925, his editorials reflected little of his former revolutionary outlook. Randolph noted the death of Eugene V. Debs in the fall of 1926 and even informed his readers of his acquaintanceship with the "Grand Old Man." While he paid tribute to Debs as the "Negro race's most faithful friend" and as a militant labor leader, he did not, as the *Pittsburgh Courier* did in an editorial six times the size of the one in *The Messenger*, refer to him as a socialist. [73] In the spring of 1927, about a year before it succumbed, *The Messenger* ran an essay contest on solutions to the race problem. The winning essay mentioned socialism as one of the proposed solutions and dismissed it as only part — and a small part — of the answer. [74]

Writing in *Current History* of June 1923, Abram L. Harris observed that it was "claimed in some circles that *The Messenger* editors have receded from their ultra-radical and Socialist position." [75] He was referring to Randolph's and Owen's increasingly bitter attacks on the Communist party in general and to black communists in particular. Harris was somewhat concerned that, like many members of the Socialist party, *The Messenger* editors were becoming so dominated by a categorical anti-communist position that they had little time to devote to offering black Americans a viable radical alternative. [76]

And, indeed, in a 1926 letter to Morris Hillquit, Norman Thomas did point out that a paranoid opposition to communism seemed to be all that concerned the Socialist party:

> It is thoroughly unhealthy that the one issue in which a great many of our Comrades tend to arouse themselves, the one thing that brings into their eyes the old light of battle, is their hatred of Communism. . . . A purely negative anti-Communist position will ultimately kill the Socialist Party body and soul. [77]

# 16

# The Socialist Party and Black Americans, 1928-1939

## ON THE EVE OF THE GREAT DEPRESSION

Since the early 1920s, the Socialist party had been declining as a national organization and had had a great deal of difficulty keeping its members, black and white, much less attracting new ones. Its poorest years followed the attempt to support LaFollette in the 1924 presidential campaign. "The four years between 1924 and 1928," Norman Thomas commented in 1931, ". . . were hard for the socialists to live through." In 1928, the party had fewer than 8,000 members. With Norman Thomas as its standard bearer in the election of 1928, the party polled 267,420 votes, less than 1 percent of the total vote cast. A socialist paper commented gloomily that the Thomas vote

> shows a tremendous drop from the vote of 1920, the last election in which the Socialists had a ticket of their own. In New York, for instance, where Eugene V. Debs, the Socialist candidate in 1920, polled 203,201 votes in 1920, Norman Thomas received 170,332 last November. Illinois, which in 1920 gave Debs 74,747, gave only 19,138 to Thomas in November. Wisconsin, which accorded Debs 85,041, gave Thomas 18,213. The same states in 1924 gave LaFollette, who ran on an independent progressive and Socialist ticket, 467,293 in New York, 432,027 in

Illinois, and 453,678 in Wisconsin. . . . In Arkansas Debs polled
5,111 in 1920 whereas Norman Thomas polled only 317. In Ken-
tuckey where Debs drew 6,400, Thomas got only 837. [1]

So low were the prospects for the Socialist party that a movement
arose for it to change its name so that it might have a chance to revive.
But Thomas argued cogently that big business, in control of "big
media," would soon make any new name as obnoxious as the old, and the
proposal was dropped. [2]

One socialist was not discouraged by the 1928 returns. He was Frank
R. Crosswaith who had stepped into A. Philip Randolph's shoes when
the latter stopped working actively for the Socialist party. Crosswaith
soon became the leading black socialist in the United States.

Crosswaith's long and active life began in the Virgin Islands in 1892.
He came to the United States when he was in his teens and spent about
eight years in the Navy as a mess boy. On his return to civilian life, he got
a job as an elevator operator. As he pointed out years later, even before
he obtained this job, he became "affiliated with a union." While working,
he attended the Rand School of Social Science; later in his life, he was to
teach at the socialist school.

By the early 1920s, Crosswaith had established himself as a leading
black socialist, and in 1924, the New York State Socialist party nominated him for secretary of state of New York. (He had been nominated for
Congress on the socialist ticket for the Twenty-first District, in Harlem,
but declined when LaFollette nominees replaced socialist candidates.)
Although he polled few votes in the 1924 race, the nomination indicated
that he was a rising star in the party and was already being viewed as
"one of the most effective Socialist speakers in the party." [3]

To Crosswaith, the fact that over 1,000 votes had been cast for Norman Thomas in Harlem in 1928 "without any effort whatsoever" was
proof that the Socialist party had a great future among black Americans.
Shortly after the election, he announced the formation of the United
Colored Socialists of America and the launching of a drive to recruit
blacks into the Socialist party. The *Pittsburgh Courier* featured the
statement and acknowledged that this, "coupled with the fact that the
Socialist Party has opened a special office for Negro work in Harlem,
aroused renewed interest in what the Socialist program can mean for the
Negro." It went on:

> For many years the Socialists have made determined efforts to
> build up a Negro following but without any appreciable results.
> Here and there it attracted some Negroes better known for their
> enthusiasm and oratory than for their knowledge and good

sense, but the bulk of Negroes, young and old, have passed the party by.

The *Courier* was skeptical that even these new efforts would bring about any change. 4

Since the only propaganda literature distributed by the United Colored Socialists of America was a reprint of James Oneal's 1922 pamphlet, *The Next Emancipation*, with a new introduction by Frank Crosswaith that added only an emotional appeal to Negroes to join the United Colored Socialists or the Socialist party, 5 it did not take long before the *Courier*'s prediction became a reality.

## BLACK SOCIALISTS

From 1926 to 1936, Crosswaith won the nomination of the Socialist party for a number of local, state, and national offices, including those of lieutenant governor of New York and member of the House of Representatives. Beginning in 1930, he was used on national speaking tours of the North and West with a frequency second only to Norman Thomas. 6 All this activity outside of Harlem weakened his influence in the leading black community. In 1937, Claude McKay reported that "Frank Crosswaith, chairman of the Negro Labor Committee, stated frankly to me that it was in 1935 only that he started active labor organization work in Harlem. Until then he was busy with labor organization elsewhere and as a Socialist lecturer throughout the United States."7 Crosswaith founded the Trade Union Committee for Organizing Negro Workers in 1925 and edited the Negro Labor News Service from 1932 to 1934. But in a letter to Norman Thomas on December 18, 1934, Crosswaith conceded that the news service was so "handicapped by a lack of resources, financial and otherwise" as to be incapable of much activity. 8

Apart from Crosswaith, the Socialist party had only a handful of Negro spokesmen during 1926-1936. In late 1927, Ethelred Brown, a Unitarian minister in Harlem and organizer for the Brotherhood of Sleeping Car Porters, and V. C. Gaspar, also a Brotherhood organizer, began speaking for the party as members of the Harlem socialist branch. In 1929, Frank Poree, who had been a candidate on the socialist ticket in the early 1920s, returned to the party and joined Crosswaith, Brown, and Gaspar as socialist street speakers in Harlem. By 1930, when Crosswaith was a candidate for Congress in the Twenty-first Congressional District, Brown ran as a socialist candidate for the New York Assembly from the Harlem area, and Poree ran for Congress on the socialist ticket in the Twentieth Congressional District. In the early 1930s, they were joined by two other Negroes—Noah C. A. Walter and Arthur C. Parker. These six blacks—Brown, Gaspar, Poree, Walter, Parker, and, of course, Crosswaith—were the leaders of a group in Harlem with some influence until 1934, when the New York City local was split by intraparty bickering. 9

In a few instances, the Harlem black socialists deviated from the official Socialist party program regarding Negroes. For one thing, in their own campaigns, they added their own demands to the limited program of the national platforms, calling for a thorough investigation of racial discrimination in the federal government; for new funds for education, with special facilities regardless of race, creed, or color; for admission of Negroes to juries; and for equal voting rights in all states, with proportional reductions of representation if the Fourteenth Amendment was not adhered to. 10 The black Harlem socialists were also much sharper in their attacks on racism in organized labor than were the white socialists; they not only attacked unions that excluded blacks but also those that allowed some to join but then treated them as second-class members. They stayed clear of criticizing the socialist-led needle trades' unions, however. 11 Indeed, an article in *Opportunity* in April 1934 noted that "until last year Negro workers, in an organizational sense, had been distinctly on the outer side of the periphery in the great women's garment industry. . . . En mass [*sic*] . . . the Negroes in the garment trades were considered as poor organizable material." 12 The situation changed during the garment workers' general strike in the summer of 1933, in which Negroes, for the first time, participated in large numbers. But during all the years before 1933, neither Crosswaith nor any other black socialist ever criticized these socialist-oriented unions for their failure to work actively to get Negro members. Nor did they, after 1933, ever once raise the issue that the Negro members of the needle trades' unions under socialist leadership were "not accorded all of the rights and privileges exercised by other union men." Like the Socialist party, even though these unions espoused Negro equality, they were often indifferent when it came to backing up their pronouncements. It was difficult for black workers to summon much enthusiasm for black leaders who gave unstinting praise to such unions and never voiced a word of criticism over the disparity between their words and deeds.

## THE GREAT DEPRESSION

A section entitled "The Negroes" in the party's 1930 congressional election program advanced three proposals: passage of the Berger antilynching bill, denial of government aid to schools that discriminated against Negroes, and enforcement of the Thirteenth, Fourteenth, and Fifteenth Amendments to the United States Constitution. [13]

The Great Depression was already under way when this program was adopted. The Socialist party had passed resolutions on the unemployment issue, and its election platform of 1928 had a major plank dealing with unemployment insurance. However, as one student of the unemployed movement points out: "the party did nothing to mobilize working people on this and other related issues." [14] All workers suffered from this lack of socialist activity, but blacks suffered the most. The U.S. Bureau of Census Special Unemployment Census showed the following unemployment percentage figures by race and nativity among male workers in thirteen U.S. cities for January 1931: manufacturing and mechanical industries—white (native-born), 31.7; white (foreign-born), 29.9; Negro, 52.0. The figures for domestic and personal service (including female workers) were: white (native-born), 17.7; white (foreign-born), 12.4; Negro, 30.7. A National Urban League summary in 1931, based on reports from investigators in 106 cities, showed that the proportion of Negroes unemployed was from 30 to 60 percent greater than that of whites, and that the percentage of Negroes among the unemployed sometimes four, five, or six times as high as their population percentage. [15]

In June 1931, the Socialist party distributed a five-page leaflet, "The Negro and Socialism," by Frank Crosswaith. The only reference to the deplorable situation pointed up by the above reports was the statement:

> Unemployment insurance will enable a worker who is laid off to get a part of his pay just as a worker who is hurt on the job today gets a part of his pay through workmen's compensation. This measure will especially benefit Negroes for, owing to prejudice existing in many places, Negroes are the first to be fired and the last to be hired. And the same thing applies to the various other measures that Socialists favor for the immediate benefit of labor. The Negro will be benefitted to a greater degree than other workers. [16]

Later that same month, in an issue of his *Negro Labor News Service*, Crosswaith discussed the nine Scottsboro Negroes who had been sentenced to death in Alabama on the trumped-up charge of raping two white girls while riding a train in search of work. Crosswaith wrote: "If these boys in Scottsboro could have had decent unemployment relief where they lived, through a system of unemployment insurance, as we Socialists want, they would not have had to bum the trains hunting for jobs." [17] But the paper did not say what the unemployed, starving black workers should do until unemployment insurance was achieved. Two months later, the *Negro Labor News Service* reported that "a representative group of colored people" had met under the leadership of Arthur C. Parker, formed the Massachusetts Unemployed Council, and had been addressed at their meeting in Roxbury by Crosswaith. It reported:

> The Council will try to find, create, and secure opportunities for employment for worthy unemployed persons. It will appeal to proprietors of stores and other business institutions in locations predominantly colored, who employ one or more clerks or attendants, to keep regularly employed at least one Negro. When necessary, it will attempt to force disinterested, prejudiced, or obstinate proprietors to cooperate with the Council by picketing and critical publicity when necessary.

This was the only reference to an organization of unemployed blacks founded and led by black socialists, and it seems to have disappeared immediately after it was organized. "Socialists Organize Unemployed" read a headline in a socialist paper in December 1932. The article told of "unemployed councils" formed by socialists "all over the country," but even apart from the absence of any specific localities in which such councils existed, there was no mention in the entire article of any work done among blacks. [18]

The position of the Socialist party on the issue was even worse. The 1932 national platform, under the heading "The Negro," simply said:

> The enforcement of constitutional guarantees of economic, political, and legal equality for the Negro.

> The enactment and enforcement of drastic anti-lynching laws. [19]

There was nothing in the 1934 Socialist party election platform on the Negro. A special convention was held in Detroit that year at which a bitter debate broke out between the right wing and left wing factions of the party that ended when the right wing quit the party. The debate centered largely on "The Declaration of Principles" adopted at the special convention, which contained no mention of the Negro. [20]

Between 1926 and 1936, the New York State and New York City party organizations did not write a specific plank for Negroes in any of their platforms [21] —even though the Empire City had the largest potential membership in Harlem. Most of the states which did include a Negro plank (and they were few and far between) simply echoed the national platforms, sometimes adding a clause deploring racial discrimination in the trade unions.

As the Depression deepened, the gap between white and Negro unemployed widened. In Cincinnati, 28 percent of the white and 54.3 percent of the Negro workers were unemployed in 1933. A survey in Pittsburgh revealed that in February 1934, "48 per cent of the Negroes were entirely without employment . . . while only 31.1 per cent of the potential white workers were unemployed." The following year the situation was even worse. Precisely at that time, Frank Crosswaith and Alfred Baker Lewis published the pamphlet, *Negro and White Labor Unite for True Freedom*, which concluded: "The injustice from which the Negro suffers is basically the same evil, only somewhat worse in degree, that is meted out to all those who are the bottom of our industrial life whenever they seek to improve their economic conditions." [22]

". . . Only somewhat worse in degree . . ."! One wonders what country these men are living in in the year 1935.

Even more amazing was Morris Hillquit's response when his communist opponent for mayor of New York City, William L. Patterson, asked him in October 1932 why nothing was said about the terrible plight of the vast number of unemployed blacks in the metropolis in the ten planks adopted by the Socialist party for its municipal platform. Hillquit answered: "To us Negroes are just workers and human beings. Any seeming discrimination in their favor would be as offensive to self-respecting Negroes as discrimination against them." [23] Of a piece was Norman Thomas' statement a month later that "the thoughtful Negro should not and will not ask" anything more than the demands for an antilynching bill and enforcement of constitutional guarantees. "They want to be treated on a level with whites," he went on. The solution to the Negroes' problem, which was basically economic and the same as that faced by the white workers—exploitation by the owning class—was the same solution that was proposed for the white workers: production for use, not for profit. "What the Socialist Party offers the Negro . . . [is] neither more nor less than it offers the workers of every race." [24] It was put succinctly by Ernest Doerfler in the *New Leader* of November 5, 1932:

> The stand of the Socialist Party on the Negro question remains that enunciated by Eugene V. Debs: "We have nothing special to offer the Negro, and we cannot make appeals to all races. The Socialist Party is the party of the whole working class—the working class of the whole world."

It was this approach which came to be known as the "Debsian view" of the Negro question. Only once did the Socialist party officially adopt the position that Negroes were especially exploited. This was in 1918 when the National Executive Committee and the New York State party advanced the view that Negroes were "the most oppressed portion of the United States." [25] But this stance was soon abandoned, and while the Old Guard and the militants in the Socialist party fought each other on a wide variety of issues, both accepted the "Debsian view" of the Negro question. Negro recruits were informed that the socialists appeals to them were being made "fundamentally for the same reason and in the same way as we appeal to white workers. We do not seek to bribe him [the Negro] with jobs or to cultivate his favor by condescending patronage," as, the socialists argued, the major parties did. Common sense demanded that the exploited Negro workers join with and vote for the Socialist party, since it was the only party of the exploited workingman. Only a party that recognized them as workers, treated them as equal to whites, and sought a solution to their problems was deserving of their support. [26]

Even if the Negro might not benefit immediately in every sense from joining the Socialist party, he would do so ultimately when the party succeeded in establishing industrial democracy and with it an end to race prejudice. Since prejudice was the tool of the exploiters, designed to keep the working class in slavery, the solution for prejudice was to eliminate class lines. For the white worker, elimination of class lines meant the end to oppression by the owner, but to the Negro it held an even greater promise—that of racial equality. However, there seemed to be a difference of opinion within the party as to how quickly that promise would be fulfilled. Some hinted that the very struggle for the socialist society would bring about racial equality. In the process of the class struggle, workers of both races would find that they could not desert each other: "A sense of equality will inevitably ripen. . . . The white man and the Negro will be forced to adopt a class, not a race consciousness." Thus, race discrimination and Jim Crow would end immediately with the establishment of a truly socialist government, since the workers, black and white, would have built a close unity in the course of achieving the new society: "A socialist society would destroy it ['the shameful racial discrimination'] root and branch and the Negro masses would share in the ample incomes, healthful homes, and the cultural advantages to which all workers are entitled." [27]

Not all socialist appeals to the Negro were that optimistic. In fact, most of them indicated that the end to racial discrimination would not be so immediate, nor was it so certain; they would not promise anything more specific than an end to racial discrimination, lynching, and Jim Crow. (Until the 1936 platform, there was no indication that the new society would include social equality.) In his 1922 pamphlet, which became the bible for socialist speakers and writers on the Negro question, Oneal stated several times that the unity of the Negro and the white worker and the abolition of class ownership would "not immediately, but eventually" bring the end to race prejudice. [28]

In any case, since the class struggle would bring into existence a new society that would end the Negro's problems sooner or later, special demands for blacks were not only unnecessary but self-defeating: "If we were to make special demands for all oppressed national and racial minorities in the United States we should soon lose the class struggle in the struggle." [29]

Inasmuch as the Negro problem was at bottom essentially only one variation of the total labor problem, since the solution of the Negro's problems could only come about through a new society created by the whole working class, black and white, and since organized labor was, along with the Socialist party, the vehicle of emancipation, the Negro had to be part of the trade-union movement. The problem was how to achieve this when the American Federation of Labor discriminated against blacks in all but six of its forty-five international unions, and when the Railroad Brotherhoods totally excluded them. [30] What was the point of urging Negroes to be class- and not race-conscious, to cease being scabs and join the unions of their trades, when they could not enter? The solution seemed to be to educate the discriminating unions. The Negro resolutions of 1926 and 1928, without naming either the AFL or the Railroad Brotherhoods, called attention to trade-union discrimination, its injustice to Negroes, and the harm it did to the objectives of the labor unions. The 1936 resolution went further and instructed "Socialist members in the unions to work actively to end such discrimination." [31] Some party organs were less equivocal; they called the AFL by name and coupled it with a call upon party members to fight discrimination in their own unions. [32]

However, Socialist party members in the AFL did nothing to implement the resolutions. When, after a long struggle, the Brotherhood of Sleeping Car Porters was admitted to the AFL, A. Philip Randolph led a persistent, if futile, battle against racism in the AFL. But Randolph had left the party in 1925, and he did not return to it until 1936. Until that time, the most vigorous socialist opponent of AFL racist policies was Frank Crosswaith. Moreover, while other socialists, when they criticized at all, only attacked the exclusionary policies of the trade unions, Crosswaith went further and particularized the racist practices of unions toward Negro members: white leadership in unions made up predominantly of Negroes; the monopoly of the best jobs by white members; and the practice of white unemployed members returning to work before their Negro counterparts. [34] However, he stopped short of criticizing socialist-dominated unions for these practices. As a result, black members of the

New York needle trades' unions viewed his stand against trade-union racism with some cynicism, especially since he himself was on the payroll of several of these unions, including the largest one, the International Ladies' Garment Workers' Union. [35]

## THE SOUTH

In 1918, it will be recalled, the Socialist party stated that, if self-determination for subject people, races, nationalities, and small nations included in Wilson's Fourteen Points for the peace program was to mean anything, it should also be applied in the Southern states of the country over which Wilson was president and where in certain specific areas blacks constituted a majority of the population. Self-determination was called a major way of redress "the wrongs of which Negroes complain." [36] Never again, however, was the issue of self-determination for the Negro people raised, Indeed, the Socialist party immediately dismissed the Communist party's assertion in the early 1930s that the black people in the United States constituted a separate nation in the Black Belt of the South and that that nation was entitled to self-determination. At no time did the socialists even debate the question of whether blacks constituted a nation. As for self-determination in the Black Belt, Norman Thomas dismissed the issue for the party in the *New Leader* of October 29, 1932, with the observation that "at best it suggests segregation for the Negro tenth of our population, at the worst it invites race war." So much for an issue which, despite the difference of views that might exist on the subject, was one of the most important questions to emerge in the relationship of American radicals and black Americans in our entire history.

During the early 1920s, the Socialist party and its press unquestionably played an important part in exposing the terrible plight of Southern Negroes and the horrors of peonage and lynchings, especially in Georgia and Arkansas, as well as in exposing the Ku Klux Klan. [37] The *New York Call* could say with justifiable pride on September 7, 1921:

> For more than a year The Call has been calling attention to the rise of the Ku Klux Klan, a sinister organization of malign purposes and foul deeds. . . . The Call was one of the first publications to recognize the character of the Klan. . . . In a period of hate, fear, terrorism and black reaction it was natural that the Klan should crawl out into the open and offer its services for any dirty work in the North. The Catholic, the Jew, the alien, the So-

cialist, the Negro were its targets. We wrote of it as "bands of
Black Hundreds." We continuously stressed its slimy history.
We urged the Federal government to outlaw it.

All this was true, but when it came to mobilizing black and white in the
South to join the Socialist party and challenge the Klan, the peonage system, and the lynchers, the record was quite different. In March 1921,
James Oneal, the *Call*'s editor, argued that the idea of carrying on "intensive agitation among the Negroes" in the South was utopian. (This was
partly a criticism of the proposal by the late John Reed, a delegate to the
second congress of the Communist International [Comintern] held in
Moscow in 1920 urging such agitation.) As Oneal saw it, the entire South
was now so completely reactionary and such a stronghold of the Ku Klux
Klan, and so thoroughly were the illiterate poor whites under the influence of racism, that to attempt to carry the socialist message to blacks
was both to invite "a bloody race war in the South" and "to further
retard the possibility of reaching the South with the message of economic
and political organization." [38]

Oneal was criticized by a Jewish comrade who reminded him that in
prerevolutionary Russia, the ruling class had employed all sorts of prejudices to divide and weaken the masses, yet Russia had had its revolution.
Why not the United States, even including the South? Oneal brushed the
criticism aside with the observation that the color issue was peculiar to
the United States, and that this made "all the difference in the world between the workers of Russia and the South." [39]

There was only one socialist paper in the South and Southwest during
the early 1920s—the *Oklahoma Leader*, published in Oklahoma City.
This weekly paid considerable attention to the problems of women and
women workers but almost entirely ignored the Negro, including Negro
women. In the years between 1921 and 1926, there was only one reference
to the Negro in the *Leader*—an article entitled "Harlem, New Negro
Mecca" in its issue of March 13, 1925. It was a Federated Press dispatch
that described briefly the contents of the March 1925 issue of the *Survey
Graphic* devoted to the "New Negro." During these six years, there was
not a single reference in the paper to the problems of blacks in Oklahoma
or to any effort to interest them in the Socialist party—a far cry indeed
from the role which the Socialist party of Oklahoma played on the eve of
World War I.

In 1921, Oneal had written off the South. [40] In 1927, he argued that it
would still take a long time before "a possibility of a Socialist movement" would exist in that section, although he did hold out the prospect
that an economic depression might offer such a "possibility": "It will

tend to make the workers forget the race prejudice which has been used by their white exploiters to keep them allied to reaction in politics." Until then, it would be best to forget about the South. [41]

This was precisely what the Socialist party proceeded to do. In the states from Maryland to Texas, there were about 900 members in 1933, or 5 percent of the national total, and about 700 in 1935, or about 4 percent of the national total. In the six states of the Deep South—North and South Carolina, Georgia, Alabama, Mississippi, and Louisiana—where the largest number of Negroes lived, there were 270 party members in 1933 and about 80 in 1935. None was a Negro. [42]

Between mid-1926 and mid-1928, the *New Leader* printed five reports from a socialist working in Mississippi, none of which mentioned Negroes or the problems and possibilities of getting them into the party. [43] In September 1928, Thomas made a speaking tour through Virginia, Tennessee, Kentucky, Arkansas, and Oklahoma, and in early 1929, August Claessens, socialist organizer and columnist, leaving from New York, covered the Southern states on the Atlantic Coast. In neither of their reports were Negroes mentioned. [44] In a 1930 article on rebuilding the party in Virginia, it was pointed out that since almost all Southerners believed in segregation, "the southern socialists must adjust their tactics to this state of affairs. It is certain that there will never be a thriving Socialist movement in the South unless it is conducted Southern style." This required particularly their own literature, since Northern literature was "frequently useless, if not harmful" in the South. Other socialists were assured, however, that "the Socialists of Virginia are good Socialists as well as Southerners and can be trusted to solve the intricate problem involved." [45] How it would be solved was explained by J. D. Sayers, Southern Socialist party organizer:

> Lay off that TNT mine in the South for the present. I mean the race question. That is a problem that must be left to evolution. . . . A white man, or even a Northern Negro Socialist, speaking to and organizing Southern Negroes, for Socialism is not only risking his life . . . and sometimes their lives, but creates an antagonism born of suspicion among the whites which shuts the door hard and fast against winning the latter. WIN THE WHITE SOUTHERNER TO SOCIALISM AND THE RACE PROBLEM WILL SOLVE ITSELF NATURALLY. [46]

As could be expected, Crosswaith never went into the South during his speaking tours for the party. In fact, no socialist organizer visited all the states of the lower South until early 1931, and in 1932 none of the thirteen paid organizers working out of the national office was in the South. [47]

In 1932, however, there was also evidence of change. In their convention that year, the Virginia socialists decided to make an appeal to the Negro voters and adopted resolutions urging the party as a whole to pay more attention to the solidarity of white and Negro workers. Deciding to make a "special effort" to break down race prejudice in their own state, they invited black workers into the organization. The socialist press service reported that the Virginia convention received a great deal of attention from black papers in the state and that "colored visitors were received royally by the Socialist delegates . . . and made very favorable impressions." [48] In May of the same year, David George, a party organizer in Virginia and North Carolina, reported that the black newspapers continued to devote considerable attention to Socialist party activity, that Negro leaders were "coming with us," and that "within the party we have been able to effectively squelch whatever race prejudice has shown its ugly face, so that Negroes find a hearty welcome awaiting them." [49] A progress report from Richmond later in the year told of a series of meetings in the Negro sections of the city and a growing Negro membership. [50]

The Virginia situation began to influence other states as well. Integrated meetings held by socialists in several Southern cities were reported as being the first of their kind in their states; and sometimes meetings were called off because of inability to get places that could be integrated. [51] Returning from a Southern speaking tour in March 1933, Thomas was pleased at "the way in which Socialist locals are welcoming Negroes and trying to work with Negroes." [52] Two months later, the *New Leader* reported that

> southern socialists representing North Carolina, Louisiana, Kentucky, Georgia and Tennessee held a meeting . . . at Washington in which it was decided that Socialism in the South would recognize only two classes, the exploited and the exploiters. No racial lines are to be considered. Negro comrades are to be welcomed into the party and treated as fellow workers. [53]

## SOUTHERN TENANT FARMERS' UNION

In May 1933, over the objections of its conservative elements, the Socialist party sponsored a "New Continental Congress" in Washington, D.C. Local Committees of Correspondence were established, and on March 19, 1933, a call was issued for a "Continental Congress for Economic Reconstruction" to draw up a program for submission to President Roosevelt and Congress. About 4,000 delegates responded to the call and poured into Washington on May 6 by train, bus, truck, auto, and by hitchhiking. With Emil Rieve, president of the American Federation of Full-Fashioned Hosiery Workers, in the chair, the Continental Congress proceeded to adopt a new Declaration of Independence that "would assure the return of the government and democratic control of the nation's industries and resources to the proletariat." It called for taking from bankers, landowners, merchants, and industrialists their "tyrannical powers, and returning to the people the control of government and industry"; a steady income and shorter hours for everyone; and the right to build a world of comfort and independence. The Congress then declared independence from "the profit system" which had "enthroned economic and financial kings . . . more powerful, more irresponsible and more dangerous to human rights than the political kings whom the fathers overthrew." [54]

Although the Congress did not pass any resolution on any aspect of the Negro question and the new Declaration of Independence did not specifically mention blacks, the Continental Congress did strike a blow against Jim Crow. Most of the New York delegates were originally housed in the Cairo Hotel. When it was reported that the hotel had barred Florian Pinkney, a Negro delegate, hundreds of the delegates marched in a body to the hotel, canceled their reservations, and demanded the return of the money they had paid in advance. When the hotel refused to return the money, Norman Thomas arranged with several lawyer delegates to bring suit, whereupon the hotel gave in and returned the money. When the delegates sought other accommodations, however, they discovered that the Tourist Camp owned by the federal government and operated by the War Department's Quartermaster Bureau also discriminated against Negroes. Unable to reach any government officials because of the weekend holiday, Thomas publicized the Jim Crow policy in letters to the press. He pledged to continue the fight against the Cairo Hotel and to "insist that the administration abolish discrimination against Negroes by departments of the federal government." He felt that "one of the important results of the Continental Congress . . . was to shed light on the extent to which discrimination against Negroes is being carried on in Washington." [55]

One other important result was that the Congress helped stimulate a movement which led soon after the Socialist party's most effective effort to reach Negroes in the South, and indeed anywhere in the country — the Southern Tenant Farmers' Union in Arkansas, organized and run largely by socialists. One of the delegates to the Congress was Harry L. Mitchell, a socialist from Arkansas, and he joined in picketing the Cairo Hotel against its Jim Crow policy. "This was the first demonstration I was ever in," he recalled years later. When he returned to Arkansas from the Continental Congress, he became secretary of the state's Socialist party and began the movement that led to the formation of the Southern Tenant Farmers' Union. The Washington experience had opened Mitchell's eyes to the possibility of uniting black and white in a joint struggle for common objectives, and he sought to apply this experience to the organizing drive among the tenant farmers and sharecroppers of Arkansas. [56]

The need was crutial. Rural poverty in Arkansas during the Great Depression is vividly illustrated by one incident that was typical of thousands like it:

> One women, her name was Ollie Strong, . . . died begging for a cup of coffee. She was the mother of eleven children. . . . I have seen her hack crossties and haul them fifteen and twenty miles to sell them so she could get herself and the children something to eat. . . . She chopped cotton on various plantations when she was with child. . . . She went to picking when she was swelled so large she couldn't stoop over. She would have to crawl on her knees so as to be able to pick. . . . When she died there wasn't anything to eat at all in the one-room pole cabin. The last thing she called for was a cup of coffee, but there wasn't any.

If a tenant was "shiftless" or "troublesome," or was simply no longer wanted by the landlord for any reason, he was unceremoniously evicted. One landlord, in order "to enforce eviction, tried in mid-winter to pull the doors and shutters off a cabin in which the cropper's wife and children huddled in thin cotton clothes. The cropper tried to resist; the landlord shot him."

In the summer of 1933, the situation grew even worse. Cotton prices had plunged during the Depression, and to raise prices the Agricultural Adjustment Act (AAA), passed in 1933, required that some cotton land be plowed under to create scarcity. In eastern Arkansas, the poverty became more acute than in other cotton-producing areas, since the growing mechanization of agriculture, combined with the effects of the new AAA program, left proportionately more sharecroppers without either homes or work. Under the AAA, the government compensated for the financial loss of "plowing under" by sending benefit payments to the planters who signed yearly cotton acreage reduction contracts. Benefits were to be shared by the landlord and tenant according to their interest in the crop (50-50 in the case of sharecroppers, and varying proportions for other tenants, depending on their rental arrangements). But since the landlord signed the contract and the money was sent to him to distribute, few tenants ever received their share. It was useless to complain to the Department of Agriculture; the planters and their friends comprised the local committees in control of the situation.

It was against this background that the Southern Tenant Farmers' Union (STFU) was organized. In 1931, the communists had organized an all-Negro Sharecroppers' Union in Alabama which became involved in a battle with the authorities that led to an anti-Negro massacre at Camp Hill. In 1933, a Socialist party organizer, writing from northeast Arkansas, informed Norman Thomas that he would "find the true proletariat... moving irresistibly toward revolution and no less." Communists, he warned, might "sweep these bottom-lands like wildfire. We *must* have a Socialist program for sharecroppers." Meanwhile, two socialists, Harry L. Mitchell and Henry Clay East, were organizing socialist locals in Arkansas. Black and white sharecroppers, disenchanted with the AAA, responded to their appeals. With Thomas' encouragement, and assisted by Mitchell and East, a small group of them organized the first local of the STFU in July 1934. Several of them had been members of the Negro union wiped out in the Elaine massacre of 1919, and some of the whites were former Ku Klux Klan members. But they united, black and white, and elected a white sharecropper as chairman and a Negro minister as vice-chairman. 57

On August 2, 1934, Mitchell informed Thomas that "the sharecroppers black and white are going down the line with us. . . . The Union is growing." 58 And it did grow rapidly. It held mass meetings throughout Arkansas' rich delta land during the summer and fall of 1934, and all efforts of the planters to divide the blacks and whites failed. The Socialist party provided both moral and financial support; indeed, without its support, the organization might well have collapsed. 59 Norman Thomas visited Arkansas and addressed integrated meetings of the union. When he spoke in Memphis during his presidential campaign of 1936, the *Memphis Press-Scimitar's* account noted that "socialist ideals" were "still vivid for those who attended with more than 100 negro members of the Southern Tenant Farmers' Union yesterday at the Labor Temple." It concluded:

> "Brother Brookings," a negro with something of the preacher about him, was called on by J. R. Butler president of the Southern Tenant Farmers Union, and Socialist candidate for governor in Arkansas. Mr. Butler called for the union song.
>
> Mr. Thomas stood up with the crowd. Everybody stood. "Brother Brookings" gave the opening line: "We shall not be moved." The crowd took up the words. There were not 12 white

people in the hall. The music took on a camp meeting rhythm.
   "Come and join the Union," sang "Brother Brookings," and
the crowd sang the line and added, "We shall not be moved."
Each time the leader gave the opening line, such as We're tired of
bein' 'victed," the chorus answered enthusiastically. The singing
climax was reached with "Norman Thomas is our leader." [60]

Thomas wrote and spoke frequently on behalf of the union and its interracial policies. He thereby helped focus nationwide attention both on
the miserable conditions on the plantations and the terror launched by
the planters to crush the union.

After a year of organization, the STFU claimed 10,000 members. As it
grew in size and effectiveness, the repressive measures against it increased. The union could no longer hold public mass meetings in the field,
and its officers were warned that they would be lynched if they remained
in eastern Arkansas. The STFU's headquarters were moved to
Memphis, where its officers, black and white, could live in relative safety
and the membership could hold rallies and conventions.

Despite the repression, the union conducted a series of mass struggles.
In September 1935 it staged a strike in northeastern Arkansas to demand payment of sixty-five cents a hundredweight for picking cotton—
about twice the going rate. The strike was successful in raising wage
levels, but it did not bring about union recognition. In May 1936, the
STFU organized cotton pickers' strikes in the delta, and through the
cameras of the popular *March of Time* newsreel, the nation saw the
drama of the "marching picket lines"—groups of a hundred or more
workers, black and white, tramping through the fields and pleading with
nonstrikers to join them. The strike spread the union into five other
states—Texas, Mississippi, Tennessee, Oklahoma, and Missouri—and
resulted in an increase in union membership to over 25,000. [61]

While the STFU was interracial, its locals were composed mainly of
workers of one race. "Of the 103 locals 63 were all-Negro or all-white,"
Jerold S. Auerbach observes; "of the remaining 30, 7 had only one Negro
or white member." [62] By 1937, an overwhelming percentage of the mem-
berhsip (over 80 percent) was black. Most of them were wage workers
and day laborers rather than tenants. [63]

Many of the local leaders were ministers in the black churches, E. B.
McKinney, the union's first vice-president, was a black Baptist minister.
During the period from 1934 to 1937, relations between Mitchell, Butler,
Howard Kester, and other white leaders of the union and the blacks had
been fairly harmonious. The union had been able to raise wage levels in
the field, secure some relief for its members, and, even though it accom-
modated itself to the Southern way of life by rarely challenging racial

segregation and never advocating social equality, it did attack poll taxes, inferior educational facilities, and discrimination in the distribution of relief—each part of the social control structure of the plantations. In appealing for "better school houses with decently paid teachers," textbooks, and transportation to and from school provided by the state, and demanding that "no child goes hungry," the organization declared: "The Southern Tenant Farmers' Union pleads alike for white child and Negro child, for the Negro man as well as the white man. It asks that all men and their children be allowed to have a full and complete chance to become intelligent and useful citizens." [64]

Nevertheless, blacks in the union became discontented over the domination of policy-making by a small group of whites, and the preaching of socialism failed to obscure the fact that the union's president and leadership cadre were white. Again, the conditions of the leadership, insofar as salaries and expenses were concerned, contrasted sharply with those of the black membership in the field. This problem was compounded by the union's failure to stand up firmly against racial segregation (even within its own offices) and to fight for social equality. "There are no ones thinking of the Negroes condition," E. B. McKinney complained early in 1937, "everybody is out for themselves and if the Negro just keeps on sleeping at this time, it will be too late for him to wake up after awhile." [65]

After 1937, more and more black members ceased their activity in the organization, and several important black leaders, led by McKinney, defected. A general disenchantment set in among the blacks over a situation in which whites dominated an organization that was over 80 percent black. The Socialist party leaders in Memphis, Arkansas, and New York attributed their defection more to a "Communist conspiracy" to wreck the union than to legitimate grievances on the part of the black membership. [66]

The STFU was further weakened by a dispute with the Congress of Industrial Organizations (CIO) international union with which it affiliated—the United Cannery, Agricultural, Packing and Allied Workers of America (UCAPAWA). Conflicts between UCAPAWA president Donald Henderson and Mitchell and Butler diverted the organization's attention from the need to continue the struggle against the planters. Local organization deteriorated, and no mass struggles were initiated either in 1937 or 1938. By 1939, the STFU was little more than a paper organization. [67]

Contemporary journalists and some historians have tended to exaggerate the interracial character of the Southern Tenant Farmers' Union under white socialist leadership. Nevertheless, it did represent the most important contribution of the Socialist party to the achievement of black-white unity. The fact that it occurred in the South made it especially significant. Indeed, a number of socialists expressed the hope that the STFU would set an example for other Southern party sections. 68 But apart from the action taken by the Virginia socialists, it proved to be unique. In the reports of the eleven Southern states to the National Socialist party convention in 1934, only five of them mentioned work with Negroes or with the problems of organizing them. In the report of the secretary of the Jacksonville (Florida) local, the following interesting comment on the work of a party speaker from New Jersey appears: "Certain questions full of dynamite, especially at outdoor meetings in Dixie, such as questions about Communism and Negro, were met by Comrade Seidman without compromising Socialist principles and yet without offense to the most conservative Southerner." 69 It would seem that only a socialist could accomplish such a wondrous feat!

Northern party leaders were particularly adept at "hedging" when they were in the South. August Claessens, a leading New York socialist, related his experiences as a speaker in a Florida town. In doing so, he illustrated how socialists, both North and South, avoided raising any hackles on the issue of social equality:

> In one Florida town our comrades were a bit timid about arranging a meeting. Upon arrival I discovered that they were worried about my attitude on the race problem. I assured them my lecture was not on that topic. "But if you will be asked?" "Then," I replied, "I give the unequivocal Socialist answer, and that is Socialists stand for complete economic, social and political equality of all races." I had speedily to qualify that social equality does not mean forced moral relations—either between races or within our own tribe. Even with complete abolition of all segregation, discrimination and artificial distinctions, I would still be at liberty to choose my own personal friends and associates. 70

Claessens' report reveals that, as late as 1934, the Socialist party still lacked the political courage to face up to the race problem in terms of complete racial equality. Moreover, when party spokesmen like Claessens and Oneal said that social equality was not enforceable by legislation, to the Southern socialist this meant not merely interracial marriage, but integrated housing, washrooms, education, transportation, and the like. By begging the question of exactly what social equality meant, the Socialist party allowed the white Southern socialists to furnish their own definitions and to remain "good Socialists as well as Southerners." Little wonder that, despite the publicity it received for the interracial Southern Tenant Farmers' Union, and despite the work of a few individual socialists, and, in the case of Virginia, of a state organization, the Socialist party never succeeded in attracting Negro members in any large numbers.


CRITICISM OF THE SOCIALIST PARTY POSITION ON THE
NEGRO QUESTION

This failure both disappointed and puzzled party leaders. Crosswaith frequently professed his inability to understand the lack of Negro interest in the Socialist party. In an article in *The Crisis* of February 1931, Norman Thomas wrote that, although his party had "espoused the cause of Negro rights without errors in tactics of Communists," it had reaped few benefits: "In general, Socialists have earned a degree of Negro support they have not yet received." [71]

This was by no means the first time this issue had been raised. In 1922, for example, Frank Crosswaith had complained to W.E.B. Du Bois about his critical attitude towards the Socialist party, specifically his contention that the party had for too long played "the 'ostrich' so far as the Negro is concerned." Crosswaith insisted that from "the formation of the First International under the direct guidance of Karl Marx until today," its record was "persistently spotless . . . on the Negro question":

> Every unprejudiced man and woman who reads and thinks, knows that the Socialist Party has always taken the right stand in regards to the Negro. In the dark and barbarous Southland, the Socialist movement has made but little progress, due, in large part, to the fact that it must first break down barriers of prejudice, ignorance and hate, erected chiefly against the Negro. Most Southerners are bitterly opposed to Socialism and the Socialist Party for no other reason than it has taken the right attitude on the Negro question.

After detailing the number of Negroes nominated for office on the socialist ticket from 1918 to 1922, Crosswaith called upon Du Bois to abandon his carping attitude and answer the following question: "Is it, or is it not, to the best interest of the race to espouse the cause of Socialism and the social revolution, or will the best interest of the race be served by further aligning ourselves with the Republican and Democratic parties?"

The New York *Call* published the full text of Crosswaith's letter to Du Bois. It did not publish Du Bois' reply, in which the former member of the Socialist party read Crosswaith a short lecture:

> I know the record of the Socialist Party toward the Negro very well. On the whole it has been exceptionally good as I have said

from time to time. But for the most part its theoretical attitude has never been put to a practical test. Even the nominations which you speak of were of very little importance since there was not the slightest chance for any of these gentlemen and the Socialist [party] knew this well.

On the other hand, the question of segregated Locals in the South is of tremendous practical importance and it is here that the Party is wavering and, I am afraid, failing to stand up to its ideals. [72]

Despite the brushoff this reply received, Du Bois continued to try to explain to Socialist party spokesmen, including Norman Thomas (whom he admired and respected, and had endorsed for president in 1932), why the socialists had not won more black adherents. Again and again, he mentioned that in their platforms and literature the socialists referred to the Negro only "vaguely and as an afterthought." He added rather bitterly, since this was hardly the first time he had made the point: "If American socialism cannot stand for the American Negro, the American Negro will not stand for American socialism." [73]

Hence, Du Bois threw out his challenge, but none of the white socialist leaders took it seriously. Indeed, the only time they even bothered to answer him was in 1929, when Du Bois noted that not once from 1872 to 1924 had the Socialist party passed a resolution at a party convention dealing with "the Negro plight in the United States." Although he also pointed out the party's failure in the 1920s to deal adequately with the Negro issue, especially in the South, it was the reference to the resolution that brought forth a response. This was in the form of a sharp rejoinder from James Oneal, in the *New Leader* (the socialist weekly which replaced the daily *New York Leader*), in which Du Bois' speech appeared. Oneal, the leading Socialist party theoretician on the Negro question, noted that Du Bois was evidently not aware that at the party's founding convention in 1901 there had been three black delegates, and that after much discussion, "the special problem of Negro workers . . . was embodied in a resolution which was printed and distributed as a leaflet throughout the country." Oneal actually distorted the events at the 1901 convention, either through his own ignorance or because it suited his approach to the Negro question. For one thing, he did not give William Costley the credit for the special resolution that was adopted. Also, he did not mention that Costley's original resolution had been changed to eliminate the clause attacking lynching. Finally, he had Costley leading the opposition to the whole idea of a special resolution on the Negro question. Oneal put into Costley's mouth his own erroneous theoretical approach to the Negro question. In that same year, 1929, Oneal wrote in

*The Next Emancipation*: "There is no color line in exploiting the workers." In answering Dr. Du Bois, he wrote:

> The reason why Costley and his two colored colleagues took this position [of opposing the singling out of Negro workers for special mention] was this. They contended that Negro workers were a part of the whole working class and that when the Socialist Party adopted a program for the liberation of the working masses it carried with it the liberation of the workers of all nationalities, colors and creeds. Costley especially resented special mention of Negro workers as suggestive of the white man's patronizing attitude toward them. [74]

The editor of the *New Leader* was completely in error: it was Costley who fought for a special resolution on the Negro question, and the resolution that was finally adopted included his words noting the "peculiar position" of black workers in the working class.

Neither Frank Crosswaith nor most of the other Negro socialists ever gave any support to Du Bois' criticism of socialist racial policies or voiced their own. In fact, the only criticism of the party from a Harlem Negro socialist came from Arthur C. Parker, when he wrote in the *New Leader* of October 31, 1931, that he had *one criticism* to make of the party:

> Heretofore, we have not given the colored group and their potential political economic importance the amount of consideration and concentration necessary to assure the party an understanding welcome by thinking colored people.
>
> Frank Crosswaith ran for the Assembly in 1927 and again in 1929-30 and despite fused opposition from Democrats and Republicans, the daily press and other agencies he polled a tremendous vote. Thousands of dollars were sent by the party for the campaigns conducted by Thomas, Panken and Broun, and although Crosswaith nearly fought his battle unaided, he was well up among the leaders in the number of votes received.

Only one other criticism of the party was voiced by a Negro socialist during 1926-1936. This was at the 1934 national convention. When consideration of the resolution on trade-union policy was just about completed, Crosswaith moved an addition to it, directing the socialists in the labor movement to work against race discrimination in the unions. After the resolution had been passed without discussion, George Streator, a Negro delegate from North Carolina, stood up, evidently quite agitated, and commented:

Although that resolution was agreeably adopted unanimously without any question, I would like to emphasize, here, the import of that which I am certain and convinced our party has allowed to glide by rather than face squarely. I would have preferred some opposition, which would have brought out some debate.

There has always been a policy on the party of the American Federation of Labor to discriminate against negro workers. . . . That is a very real problem when we think of organizing the colored people of the United States in the Socialist Party.

Always we who have attempted to sway sentiment in that direction must face the question of, how can a party which works hand in hand with the AFL, have the genuine interests of the negro workers at heart? . . . How in the name of God can we adopt a policy toward the organization of workers unless some time and some day the Socialist Party is going to face squarely the question of the exclusion of the negro worker either by direct legislation or subterfuge in the AFL? [75]

Streator's complaint failed to provoke any discussion, and the convention moved on to other matters.

In the whole decade under discussion, only one white party member published a critical analysis of the weaknesses of the party's stand on the Negro question. This was Margaret L. Lamont in "The Negro's Stake in Socialism," published in the *American Socialist Quarterly* of March 1935. In language that was fairly common in the writings of white socialists before World War I but was rarely heard since the early 1920s, she declared: "It is not pleasant to have to say that socialists have often failed to press vigorously their demands for civil, legal, political and social rights for the Negro." The fundamental reason for this failure, as she saw it, was the party's reluctance to alter "the line laid down by Debs on the race issue . . . that the Socialist party would act in the interests of all workers, white and black alike, and that a particularized appeal to Negroes would not, therefore, be in keeping with party principles": "As a result of the development of this noble, but perhaps inadequate, party line, the main emphasis of Socialists in practical activity among Negroes has been a somewhat passive insistence that trade union discrimination against them be removed."

Lamont criticized the party's frequent statements that race prejudice could only be eliminated when socialism was achieved, because it carried the implication that there was not much use in fighting for the Negro's social and political rights before this battle was won. While she conceded that "fundamental human rights" could not be achieved without a complete socialist victory, she emphasized that it was important to conduct a persistent struggle for immediate improvements for the Negro within a capitalist society. These improvements would "slowly add to the strength and confidence of the exploited group; while the denial of basic rights . . . [would] increase the sense of solidarity within the particular group and other exploited groups." Focusing on the deplorable situation of Negroes in this country, she urged concentration on a campaign for immediate improvement for blacks: "The struggle for rights withheld on grounds of race must go on as part and parcel of the struggle for the basic rights of all workers." This called for more than an affirmation of belief in racial equality. It demanded an active and militant stand against, and participation in the day-to-day struggle to end lynching, all forms of Jim Crowism, and discrimination in education; and, a program to provide relief benefits for unemployed blacks and to wipe out the crime of disfranchisement. It also required increased social activity for industrial unionism. She pointed out that "when the jealously guarded sanctity of special crafts disappears, most of the false notions about lack of capacity of the Negro for skilled and semi-skilled work will also vanish."

Turning to the work of socialists in the fight against racism in the trade unions, Lamont was noncommittal about the needle trades' unions "where Socialists have had influence." She admitted, however, that "in new unions in which Socialists have played a part . . . Negroes have been admitted without any question and given responsibility." There were not many such unions, and she cited only the Building Service Employees' Union and the Southern Tenant Farmers' Union, "which, like the communist-controlled Share-croppers' Union of Alabama, is organizing white and Negro workers together in the face of grave terror." On the whole, the socialist record in the trade unions they influenced with respect to racial discrimination could be listed only as "modestly creditable." The same, however, could not be said for the role of socialists in unions where they were a minority. "It must be recognized," Lamont wrote bluntly, "that many individual socialists in the American Federation of Labor have remained passive or criminally indifferent in the face of open or veiled discrimination against Negroes." While she was critical of other aspects of their approach to the Negro, she conceded that in this respect, at least, the communists were in advance of the members of her own party, and she urged cooperation with their forces in the AFL to end racism.

Lamont proposed a twofold policy which she urged the Socialist party to endorse in place of its existing one of neutrality and/or collaboration with racists in the AFL: (1) to urge unions in newly organized fields to remain independent and unaffiliated until the AFL recognized the admission of black workers on "absolutely equal terms with white workers"; and (2) for socialists in the AFL to insist that the AFL withhold and revoke the charters of unions and locals which did discriminate. Both suggestions had been mentioned by Randolph, but Lamont's article was the only one in the 1926-1936 period in which socialist collaboration with the AFL to maintain racism was conceded, and in which a party member made anything but rhetorical exhortations for ending discriminatory practices in the AFL. She was also unique in stating that the socialists had something to learn from the activity of communists in behalf of the Negro people.

Finally, Lamont called for the abandonment of the "Debsian formula" and for a complete overhaul of the party's approach to the Negro question. Observing that the Socialist party would never win support from Negroes for its efforts to create "a workers' government" if it clung to its traditional approach to black Americans, she wrote: "Socialists must be constantly awake to the fact that the allegiance of Negroes in the future will be granted to that political group which shows itself most able to keep faith with the Negro workers in the rigorous conflicts of their day-to-day living. [76]

## FAILURE OF THE SOCIALIST PARTY TO RESPOND

Lamont's long and keen analysis had no effect whatsoever on the Socialist party. When W.E.B. Du Bois made many of the same points early in 1929, his words, too, had produced no results, but at least then the *New Leader* had headlined the fact: "Noted Editor Wants Party to Take More Vigorous Stand for Rights of Colored People." [77] In 1935, to Lamont's criticism there were only silence and a smug reaffirmation of the traditional party stand on the Negro question. "Our general Socialist position on the race question is admirable," Norman Thomas wrote in July 1935. "Its needs in some communities to be more vigorously and consistently illustrated by action by Socialists." [78]

The same attitude is reflected in the pamphlet published by the Socialist party late in 1935, *True Freedom for Negro and White Labor* by Frank Crosswaith and Alfred Baker Lewis, for which Thomas wrote the introduction. The pamphlet was fundamentally a restatement of the "Debsian formula," as developed by James Oneal in *The Next Emancipation*, with some additions noting developments since that 1922 publication had first appeared. Thus, there was praise for the Southern Tenant Farmers' Union, but no criticism of the socialist role in the AFL in collaborating with the racist leadership. The needle trades' unions, especially the International Ladies Garment Workers Union, "in which the Socialists have a great deal of influence," were rated excellent on the Negro question. In short, nothing in the sixty-page pamphlet reflected anything that Lamont had stressed in urging a reevaluation of the party's program on the Negro question.

It is hardly surprising, then, that George Streator, the Negro socialist from North Carolina who had already criticized the party's position at the 1934 national convention, continued his criticism in an article entitled "The Negro: Step-Child of Socialism." Praising Lamont's attack on the party for its stand on the Negro question, Streator wrote caustically: "The Socialist Party in recent years has printed nothing on the Negro question beyond certain speech outlines accredited to Frank Crosswaith, the Party alibi on the race question." The party had also done nothing in the trade unions to break down barriers against black workers: "In spite of the longtime influence of Socialists in the Machinists International, that body has the most overt clause barring Negroes." As a result, the Communist party had gained almost a "monopoly" among radicals over the Negro masses and would continue to exercise its influence as long as the Socialist party refused to get "informed and *aroused* about the Negro question." [79]

Early in 1936, Streator followed up his criticism with the charge that since the split in 1919, and especially since the beginning of the Great Depression, "the Socialists, hampered by a moth-eaten Old Guard leadership had lost influence among the Negro masses." [80] His words went unheeded. In that same year, 1936, the militants were in control of the Socialist party's convention. In their *Draft for a Program for the United States*, which they adopted in September 1935, they had included a plank on "Negro Equality" which read:

> The fifteen million Negroes in the United States suffer not only from brutal economic exploitation, but also from racial, social and legal inequality and deadly race prejudice. The Socialist Party advocates and will consistently fight for complete equality for the Negroes. It will expose and fight against all forms of discrimination against the Negroes, Jim-Crowism, segregation. It will campaign incessantly against lynching and for extreme punishment of all those participating in it. It will work for the unity between white and Negro workers and farmers for a common fight against capitalism and for Socialism. [81]

At the 1936 Socialist party convention, the militants abandoned their "Negro Equality" plank and substituted for it a statement that was adopted by the convention as plank 8 of the Socialist party platform, the one dealing with "Civil Liberties." This statement urged the abolition of all laws that interfered with the right of free speech, free press, free assembly, and the peaceful activities of labor "in its struggle for organization and power." It called for "the enforcement of constitutional guarantees of economic, political, legal and social equality for the Negro and all other oppressed minorities, and the enactment and enforcement of a Federal anti-lynching law." [82]

Except for one provision, the same single stilted clause had appeared in every platform dealing with the Negro since 1926. The only new idea was the addition of the words "and social equality for the Negro and all other oppressed minorities."

This was the way things stood in the Socialist party on the problems of black Americans thirty-five years after the party was founded. The picture was indeed a dismal one.

## ON THE EVE OF WORLD WAR II

As criticism of the failure of the 1936 convention to present any new position on the Negro question mounted, the Socialist party hastened to set up a national subcommittee on Negro work. With great fanfare, it announced that it would be headed by A. Philip Randolph, thus marking the black labor leader's return to the party. [83] Actually, at the time Randolph was much too involved in his activities as president of the Pullman porters' union and of the National Negro Congress, [84] which was founded in 1936, to be able to do much for the new subcommittee. The work fell on the shoulders of Frank R. Crosswaith. The presence of Margaret Lamont on the subcommittee suggested that it would not defend the party's position on the Negro uncritically. [85]

The Negro Work Subcommittee announced a fourfold program:

> (1) That locals and branches be urged to appoint Negro Work Committees; (2) That Socialist trade unionists should work for the passage of the Randolph resolution at the American Federation of Labor convention against race discrimination in unions; (3) That the National Association for the Advancement of Colored People be supported in any effort they make for justice to Negro workers; (4) That a Harlem Labor Center be established through which the Negro Labor Assembly might carry the trade union message to hundreds of thousands of Negro workers in every type of employment. [86]

The "Randolph Resolution," introduced annually at AFL conventions by A. Philip Randolph since the early 1930s (and just as regularly rejected by the conventions), called upon the delegates to order "the elimination of the color clause and pledge from the constitution and rituals of the trade and industrial unions" and the explusion of all unions that maintained "said color bar." [87] The inclusion of the call for "Socialist trade unionists" to work for passage of the "Randolph Resolution" in the Negro Work Subcommittee's program was an advance over the Socialist party's traditional policy of "no interference" in AFL operations. Even so, it reflected a total indifference to a development under way when the program was adopted in 1937 that was of the greatest significance to the black worker. This, of course, was the emergence of the CIO (formed after the 1935 AFL convention when the resolution for industrial unionism was rejected), and the organizing drives launched by the new industrial union movement that brought hundreds of thousands of hitherto unorganized black workers into the labor movement for the first time. [88] Yet, no one reading the Negro Work Subcommittee's program would even guess that such an unprecedented development affecting the black community was taking place. At the very time the Negro Work Subcommittee was drawing up its program, T. Arnold Hill, director of the Department of Industrial Relations of the National Urban League, published *The Negro and Economic Reconstruction*, in which he wrote: "The CIO is unique among existing American labor movements, not only in its philosophy, but in its policy of equality for all workers, Negro as well as white." [89] But at no time before World War II did the Negro Work Subcommittee of the Socialist party show any awareness of this historic development affecting black workers, nor did it seek to aid in its advance. Indeed, at the very time that the National Negro Congress was forging an alliance with the CIO that was crucial for the success of the industrial union movement in a number of key mass production industries where Negroes formed an important element, Frank R. Crosswaith, on behalf of the Socialist party's Negro Work Subcommittee, was warning Norman Thomas that any help given to the National Negro Congress in this activity would only redound to the credit of the "irresponsible extremists on the left," meaning, of course, the communists. Crosswaith rejected an invitation to join the New York Sponsoring Committee, and although he finally agreed, after repeated visits from the Committee members, to send observers to the Congress' founding convention, he also advised several trade unions that he worked with not to participate in the movement and to reject the Congress' plea for financial support. Crosswaith's actions helped influence the Socialist-dominated Amalgamated Clothing Workers Union and the International Ladies' Garment Workers' Union, both by now "with sizable black membership," to decline invitations to sponsor the Congress. [90]

The National Negro Work Subcommittee did chalk up two achievements. It assisted in the launching of the Harlem Labor Center in March 1937 under the direction of Crosswaith, [91] and it proposed a resolution on Negro work to the Socialist party's national convention in April 1937. Upon adoption, this resolution became the first on the Negro question since 1901 to deal with it in anything more than brief generalities. While it still reflected the party's unwillingness to break with the traditional view that there was nothing different between the exploitation of the Negro and that of the white worker—both being equally exploited under capitalism—it did at least observe that the task of breaking down the barriers between black and white workers was "one which will require special handling." It came out for "complete equality" for the Negro in every aspect of American life:

> The so-called Negro problem is not one of physical inheritance, but of social environment. It is not a problem which can be solved on anything other than a non-segregated basis of complete equality. . . .

> Absolute freedom of opportunity for all workers to join and function in trade unions regardless of race or color must be a cornerstone of Socialist Party trade union policy. This program must be actively pushed as an educational tactic for white and Negro workers alike.

> The fight for Negro civil liberties must be aggressively launched. The Socialist Party must realize that the basis of race prejudice is economic. As such, it is as potential in the north, as in the south and must be dealt with accordingly.

> In matters of equality before the law, at the polls, before relief boards, not to mention the field of educational and cultural opportunities, employment and professional discrimination, this work can offer activity to any number of Socialist locals anywhere in the country.

The resolution called for support of such organizations as the National Negro Congress and the National Association for the Advancement of Colored People, in both of which "disciplined Socialist work" could be of value. But such work was no substitute for "an active program of Socialist education, rooted in the heart of the Negro struggle for a genuine emancipation," for only in this way could "the problem of the American Negro and his similarly exploited white brother" be solved. [92]

"Your best interests are reflected in the program of the Socialist

Party," Crosswaith pleaded in the fall of 1938, in his last appeal to Negro voters before the outbreak of World War II. *"If you would be true to yourself and your class—even as your economic masters are true to theirs—you will cast your ballot in the Socialist column on election day. You have nothing to lose by so doing. You have everything to gain."* [93]

The *Boston Guardian*, the black weekly founded by William Monroe Trotter, published a letter from its editor (Maude Trotter Steward) to Frank Crosswaith, assuring Crosswaith that such appeals would bring a meager response so long as he clung to his red-baiting. Crosswaith was advised to "close the page on red-baiting," and to turn his pen to "Socialism and broad, allied subjects of race discrimination." [94] A study of the Socialist press reveals that, between the April 1937 convention and the outbreak of World War II in September 1939, not a single report was published indicating any concrete implementation of the resolution adopted on Negro work. The failure to report any activity on behalf of the National Negro Congress' campaigns to organize black workers into the CIO is not surprising in view of Crosswaith's obsession with the idea that this would only help the communists—and this even though A. Philip Randolph, the socialist, was president of the Congress.

The Negro Work Subcommittee was represented at the Southern Socialist Conference in Rochdale, Mississippi, in April 1939. The only position the conference adopted with regard to black Americans was the endorsement of the subcommittee and the urging of all Southern socialists "to work as closely as possible with the branches of the National Association for the Advancement of Colored People in their communities." [94] Coming two years after the adoption of the Negro work resolution by the 1937 Socialist party national convention (the 1938 convention did not adopt a position on the Negro), this stand, the socialists' last public position on the Negro question before World War II, is indeed a classic example of the mountain laboring and producing a mouse.

# Notes

PREFACE

1. August Meier, *Negro Thought in America, 1880-1915* (Ann Arbor, Mich., 1963).
2. August Meier, Elliott Rudwick, and Francis L. Broderick, *Black Protest Thought in the Twentieth Century* (Indianapolis and New York, 1965).
3. Herbert Aptheker, *A Documentary History of the Negro People in the United States from Colonial Times to 1910* (New York, 1951).
4. June Sachen, *The Unbridgeable Gap: Blacks and Their Quest for the American Dream* (New York, 1972).
5. Jervis Anderson, *A. Philip Randolph: A Biographical Portrait* (New York, 1972).
6. Charles V. Hamilton, *The Black Experience in American Politics* (New York, 1973).
7. Tony Thomas, ed., *Black Liberation and Socialism* (New York, 1974).
8. Morris Hillquit, *History of Socialism in the United States* (New York, 1903).
9. John Hope Franklin, *From Slavery to Freedom: A History of Negro Americans* (New York, 1955).
10. Daniel Bell, *Marxian Socialism in the United States* (Princeton, N.J., 1952).
11. Howard H. Quint, *The Forging of American Socialism* (Columbia, S.C., 1953).
12. David A. Shannon, *The Socialist Party of America* (New York, 1955), p. 52.
13. Ira Kipnis, *The American Socialist Movement, 1897-1912* (New York, 1952).
14. James Weinstein, *The Decline of Socialism in America, 1912-1925* (New York, 1969).
15. I have omitted reference to my own articles on Reverend George Washington Woodbey, early twentieth-century black socialist, and Caroline H. Pemberton, Philadelphia socialist champion of black equality, published in the *Journal of History* and *Pennsylvania History* in 1976, since they are parts of the present work. I have also omitted the late Oakley C. Johnson's article, "Marxism and the Negro Freedom Struggle, 1876-1917," *Journal of Human Relations* 13 (First Quarter, 1965): 21-39, since it is quite superficial in its treatment of the subject and adds little to what was already known.
16. Earl Ofari, "Marxism, Nationalism, and Black Liberation," *Monthly Review* 18 (March 1971): 18-33.
17. Earl Ofari, "Black Activists and 19th Century Radicalism," *Black Scholar* 5 (February 1974): 19-25.
18. R. Lawrence Moore, "Flawed Fraternity—American Socialist Response to the Negro, 1901-1912," *Historian* (November 1969): 1-14.

19. Sally M. Miller, "The Socialist Party and the Negro, 1901-1920," *Journal of Negro History* 56 (July 1971): 220-39.


CHAPTER 1

1. See, in this connection, E. P. Hobsbawm, *Primitive Rebels* (Manchester, 1959); E. P. Thompson, *The Making of the English Working Class* (London, 1963); Charles Tilly, *The Vendee*, (New York, 1967); George Rudé, *Crowd in History: A Study in Popular Disturbance in France and England, 1730-1848* (New York, 1964).

2. For a good summary of these movements, see Mark Holloway, *Heavens on Earth: Utopian Communities in America, 1680-1880* (New York, 1951).

3. The term *utopian socialism* was given to the views of Owen and Fourier among others by Frederick Engels in his masterly study, *Socialism: Utopian and Scientific*, to distinguish them from Marxism which he called scientific socialism.

4. For a discussion of Robert Owen and Charles Fourier, their socialist principles and their influence in the United States, see Philip S. Foner, *History of the Labor Movement in the United States*, Vol. #1, (New York, 1947), pp. 167-78.

5. Hermann Schlüter, *Die Anfange der deutschen Arbeiterbewegung in Amerika* (Stuttgart, 1907), pp. 13-17, 83-96, 226-33. Carl Wittke's biography of Weitling is entitled *The Utopian Communist* (Baton Rouge, 1950).

6. Karl Obermann, *Joseph Weydemeyer: Pioneer of American Socialism* (New York, 1947), pp. 11-30.

7. Hermann Schlüter, *Die Internationale in Amerika: Ein Betrag zur Geschichte der Arbeiterbewegung in den Vereinigten Staaten* (Chicago, 1918), pp. 410-13.

8. Obermann, op. cit., pp. 92-93; Schlüter, *Die Anfange*, pp. 161-62.

9. *New Harmony Gazette*, October 1, 1825.

10. *The Liberator*, October 13, 1854.

11. Ibid., August 1, 1845; *New York Tribune*, June 20, 1845; *Working Man's Advocate*, June 22, 1845.

12. *Statueten des Kommunisten-Klubs in New York*, manuscript copy in Wisconsin State Historical Society, US MSS. 15 A, Box 4.

13. *Sociale Republik*, vol. 1, no. 14, New York, July 24, 1858, copy in New York Public Library.

14. Schlüter, *Die Anfange*, pp. 160-62.

15. There are two useful biographies of Frances Wright: William Randall Waterman, *Frances Wright* (New York, 1924), and A.J.G. Perkins and Theresa Wolfson, *Frances Wright, Free Enquirer* (New York, 1939). For Wright's connection with the labor movement of the Jacksonian era, see Foner, op. cit., vol. 1, pp. 129-32, 136-38.

16. *New Harmony Gazette*, February 21, 1827.

17. Edd Winfield Parks, "Dreamer's Vision, Frances Wright at Nashoba, 1825-1830," *Tennessee Historical Magazine*, series 2, no. 2 (1973): 77; O. B. Emerson, "Frances Wright and Her Nashoba Experiment," *Tennessee Historical Quarterly* 6 (1947): 292-93; William H. Pease and Jane H. Pease, *Black Utopia: Negro Communal Experiments in America* (Madison, Wis., 1963), p. 36.

18. Waterman, op. cit., pp. 128-31.

19. *New Harmony Gazette*, October 1, 1825.

20. *The Liberator*, June 6, 1845.

21. *The Harbinger*, June 21, 1845.

22. *The Condition of Labor. An Address to the Members of the Labor Reform League of New England, by One of the Members* (Boston, 1847), p. 16; *New York Tribune*, June 20, 1845; *The Liberator*, September 5, 1845.

23. *Phalanx* (Paris), reprinted in *National Anti-Slavery Standard*, November 4, 1843; also reprinted in John R. Commons, *A Documentary History of American Industrial Society*, vol. 7 (Cleveland, 1910), pp. 207-8.

24. *Working Man's Advocate*, June 22, July 4, 6, August 17, 24, 1844.

25. Ibid., September 27, 1845.

26. Herman Schlüter, *Lincoln, Labor and Slavery* (New York, 1913), p. 61.

27. *Working Man's Advocate*, March 16, 1844; *Young America*, January 3, 1846; *New York Tribune*, February 16, 1850.

28. *Natinal Anti-Slavery Standard*, May 8, 1851.

29. Philip S. Foner, *The Life and Writings of Frederick Douglass*, vol. 1 (New York, 1950), pp. 41, 48, 51, 53, 55-57, 110-12; *Life and Times of Frederick Douglass*, Collier ed. (New York, 1962), p. 228.

30. *The North Star*, March 16, 1849; *Frederick Douglass' Paper*, January 29, 1852.

31. *National Anti-Slavery Standard*, December 28, 1848.

32. Schlüter, *Lincoln*, pp. 72-73; Wittke, *The Utopian Communist*, pp. 159-60. W.E.B. Du Bois is incorrect when he states that there "was no condemnation of slavery" in Weitling's paper (*Black Reconstruction in America, 1860-1880* [New York, 1935], p. 23).

33. Obermann, op. cit., pp. 50-51, 85-88, 109-11; Frederich Kapp, *Geschichte der Sklaverei in den Vereinigten Staaten von Amerika* (New York, 1860), pp. 177-84, 184-85n. Knapp noted that he considered the series of six articles Wedemeyer published in the *Illinois Staats-Zeitung* so "valuable" that he had based his analysis of the economic issues involved in the slavery controversy upon them.

34. Schlüter, *Lincoln*, pp. 75-77. For a discussion of the opposition to the bill among other workers, see Foner, *History of the Labor Movement*, vol. 1 pp. 279-82.

35. C. F. Huch, "Der Sozialistiche Turnerbund," *Mitteilungen des Deutschen Pionier-Vereins von Philadelphia*, Seschundzvantzigstes Heft, 1912, pp. 1-15.

36. L. P. Hennighausen, "Reminiscences of the Political Life of the German-Americans in Baltimore During 1850-1860," *Seventh Annual Report of the Secretary of the Society for the History of the Germans in Maryland, 1892-1893*, pp. 54-57.

37. A. E. Zucker, ed., *The Forty-Eighters: Political Refugees of the German Revolution of 1848* (New York, 1950), 102-4.

38. Herbert Aptheker, *The Labor Movement in the South During Slavery* (New York, n.d.), p. 16; William D. Overdyke, *The Know-Nothing Party in the South* (Baton Rouge, 1950), pp. 17-18.

39. Frederick Law Olmsted, *A Journey Through Texas* (New York, 1860), pp. 433-34. The other two classic works on the antebellum South are *The Cotton Kingdom* and *A Journey in the Seaboard Slave States*. Frederick Law Olmsted, of course, is the famous landscape architect who designed many public parks, including Central Park in New York.

40. Douai's biography appeared after his death in English in the *Workmen's Advocate* and in German in the *New Yorker Volkszeitung* of January 28, 1888. Both were official organs of the Socialist Labor party. Douai was coeditor of both papers.

Douai's first name was variously spelled Adolf and Adolph. Before the Civil War, it was commonly Adolf and afterward, Adolph.

41. Joseph Dorfman, *The Economic Mind in American Civilization*, vol. 3 (New York, 1959), pp. 44-45.

42. Sorge paid tribute to Douai for his antislavery activities in Texas where he notes "Douai achieved great honor through fearless behavior and personal courage which even forced his slaveholding opponents to respect him." He also gave Douai credit for popularizing the principles of Karl Marx after the Civil War, but he criticized him for his acceptance of monetary reforms as a major solution for workers' problems. (Friedrich A. Sorge, *The Labor Movement in the United States*, translated from the German by Brewster and Angela Chamberlin, edited by Philip S. Foner and Brewster Chamberlin, and with a bio-

graphical essay by Philip S. Foner [Westport, Conn., 1977], pp. 6, 7, 12, 34, 134, 154, 165, 201, 202, 312, 327, 339, 346, 350, 355, 359.)

43. Dr. Adolf Douai, *Das ABC des Sozialismus* (Altenburg, 1851), pp. 91-94. The pamphlet shows that Herbert Aptheker is in error in describing Dr. Douai as a Marxist when he was editor of the *San Antonio-Zeitung* (Aptheker, op. cit., p. 15).

44. Billy D. Lebetter, "White Over Black in Texas: Racial Attitudes in the Anti-Bellum Period," *Phylon* 34 (1973): 406-18. This is an excellent presentation of the strong hold slavery had over Texans and the small room that existed for antislavery activity. But it fails to mention the antislavery German socialists, especially Dr. Adolph Douai.

45. *San Antonio-Zeitung*, August 27, 1853.

46. Dr. Adolf Douai to Dr. John Hull Olmsted, September 4, 1854, and to "Dear Friends," December 16, 1854, Frederick Law Olmsted Papers, Library of Congress, Manuscripts Division; Rudolph L. Biesele, *The History of the German Settlements in Texas, 1831-1861* (Austin, 1922), pp. 196-99.

47. Rudolph L. Biesele, "The Texas State Convention of Germans in 1854," *Southwestern Historical Quarterly* 33 (April 1930): 247-55; *Western Texan*, June 1, 1851; *San Antonio-Zeitung*, June 1, 1851.

48. *Texas State Gazette*, June 17, 1854; Biesele, "The Texas State Convention," pp. 257-59; Overdyke, op cit., p. 18; Gilbert Giddings Benjamin, *The Germans in Texas: A Study in Immigration* (Austin, 1974), p. 100

49. Dr. Adolf Douai to Dr. John Hull Olmsted, September 4, 1854; Dr. Adolf Douai to "Dear Friends," November 17, December 6, 1854; Dr. Adolf Douai to "Dear Friends," December 16, 1854, Olmsted Papers, Library of Congress; Laura Wood Roper, "Frederick Law Olmsted and the Western Texas Free-Soil Movement," *American Historical Review* 56 (October 1950): 58-60; Laura Wood Roper, *FLO: A Biography of Frederick Law Olmsted* (Baltimore and London, 1973), pp. 96-105. Although Roper's accounts are the only other detailed treatment of Douai's role in Texas, she never once mentions the fact that he was a socialist. The Olmsteds themselves were unable to aid Douai financially, but they solicited financial support for his paper from Henry Ward Beecher and others, persuaded Theodore Parker and other friends to subscribe, and secured new type for the publisher in New York on liberal terms. On October 31, 1853, most of the money had been raised, and on November 17, Douai acknowledged he had received it.

50. Dr. Adolf Douai to "Dear Friends," December 7, 1855, Olmsted Papers, Library of Congress.

51. Biesele, "The Texas State Convention," p. 260.

52. *San Antonio-Zeitung*, February 24, March 10, May 12, 19, 26, 1855.

53. Ibid., May 12, 1855.

54. *Texas State Gazette*, June 12, 1855.

55. Ibid., July 25, 1855; Biesele, "The Texas State Convention," p. 261.

56. Dr. Adolf Douai to "My Dear Friends," August 4, 1855, Olmsted Papers, Library of Congress.

57. Ibid.

58. Frederick Law Olmsted to E. E. Hale, August 23, 1855, January 17, 1856, New England Emigrant Aid Company Papers, Kansas State Historical Society, Topeka. Olmsted, then raising money for arms for Kansas, approached some of the contributors for funds to sustain Douai (Roper, op. cit., p. 61).

59. *San Antonio-Zeitung*, February 16, 1856. See also issues of December 20, 1855, February 9, 16, 23, March 1, 1856.

60. Benjamin, op cit., p. 101; Douai in *Der Pionier*, July 13, 1856. Although he never returned to Texas, Douai was not indifferent to events taking place in the state which had expelled him for his principles. When he learned that Jacob Waelder, a proslavery German member of the Texas House of Representatives, had been appointed consul to Frankfurt

on the Main, he was furious, and he gave vent to his feeling in a letter to the *New York Tribune*. Douai charged that Waelder was a disgrace to the German people, that he had once even defended a slaveowner who had assaulted an antislavery German on the ground that "to kill a man who assailed the institution of slavery was no crime." To allow such a man to represent the United States abroad was to shame the American Republic before all of Europe. "If the American Government insists upon sending so hateful an individual, a man who is so totally unrepresentative of all that is best in the German people," Douai concluded, "then it is up to the people of Germany to send him packing back to the slaveowners whose cause he has so cherished and so contemptibly defended." The *Tribune* praised Douai's letter as exactly what one would expect from a man who had almost lost his life in defending the cause of antislavery. The paper also expressed agreement with Douai's suggestion to the German people: "This miserable renegade has been sent to disgrace us abroad. We trust, however, the mark we thus stamp upon him will secure him repudiation in Germany, such as his conduct in America has amply deserved" (*New York Weekly Tribune*, May 9, 1857).

61. *New Yorker Volkszeitung*, January 18, 1888; *Workmen's Advocate*, January 28, 1888; Morris Hillquit, *History of Socialism in the United States*, New York, 1903, p. 191.

62. Adolf Douai, "Der Gute Alte Zeit," *Der Pionier*, July 13, 1856; Adolf Douai, "Der Kindergarten," *Der Pionier*, September 17, 1859; Louise Hall Thorp, *The Peabody Sisters of Salem* (New York, 1968), pp. 320-28.

63. *New Yorker Staatszeitung*, July 25, August 30, 1856.

64. Heinzen bitterly opposed Marxism. His relations with Douai cooled considerably when Douai established close relations with the German-American Marxists. In a lengthy debate with Heinzen in *Der Pionier*, stretching from October 1857 through March 1858, Douai accused Heinzen of being hostile to Marxism because he was essentially an idealist and did not understand the materialist conception of history. See issues of October 18, November 1, December 6, 13, 1857, January 3, 10, 17, 24, February 14, 21, 28, and March 7, 14, 21, 1858. See also Adolf Douai, *Heinzen, Wie Er Ist* (New York, 1869).

65. *Der Pionier*, August 10, 1856.


CHAPTER 2

1. *Der Pionier*, June 1, 18, 1859. In a letter to Olmsted, Douai described himself proudly as an "infidel," writing at length of his belief that "all religious opinions" have been demonstrated "to be phantasies and entire[ly] unfounded." He referred to a pamphlet he had published in Germany expounding on his antireligious sentiments (Douai to "Dear Friends," December 16, 1854, Olmsted Papers, Library of Congress). This pamphlet was *Volkskatechismus der Altenburger Republikaner* (Altenburg, 1848).

2. Adolf Douai, "Humboldt and Agassiz," *Der Pionier*, July 2, 9, 16, 23, 1859. Agassiz' essay appeared in *The Christian Examiner and Religious Miscellany* 49 (July 1850): 110-45. For the influence of Agassiz' racist thought, see William Stanton, *The Leopard's Spots: Scientific Attitudes Toward Race in America, 1815-1859* (Chicago, 1960).

3. *Der Pionier*, May 31, June 7, 14, July 5, 12, 19, August 2, 9, 16, 23, 30, 1857.

4. Ibid., December 6, 1860.

5. *Sociale Republik*, September 10, 17, 24, 31, 1858.

6. Frank I. Herriot, *The Conference of German-Republicans in the Deutsches-Haus, Chicago, May 14-15, 1860*, reprinted from *Transactions of the Illinois Historical Society for 1928* (Chicago, n.d.), pp. 48-49, 63-64, 85-86, 93; W. L. Baringer, *Lincoln's Rise to Power* (Boston, 1937), pp. 273-74.

7. Philip S. Foner, *Business and Slavery: The New York Merchants and the Irrepress-*

*ible Conflict* (Chapel Hill, N.C.: 1940), pp. 190-95; *New Yorker Demokrat*, October 31, 1860.

8. "What Democrats Understand as People's Sovereignty" and "The Prohibition of Slavery by Nature," *New Yorker Demokrat*, October 5, 15, 1860.

9. Ibid., October 29, 1860.

10. Ibid., October 29, 31, November 2, 1860.

11. *New York Herald*, November 5, 1860.

12. *New York Times*, November 9, 1860; Foner, *Business and Slavery*, p. 206.

13. Max Birnbaum, "Northern Labor in the National Crisis, 1860-1861," B.S. thesis, University of Wisconsin, 1938, pp. 54-57; Joseph Shafer, "Who Elected Lincoln?" *American Historical Review* 57 (October 1941): 51-63; Eric Foner, *Free Soil, Free Labor, Free Men* (New York, 1970), p. 259.

14. Adolf Douai, "Der Abolitionist, Eine Novelle," *Der Pionier*, January 6, 13, 20, 27, February 5, 12, 19, 26, 1859.

15. *New Yorker Demokrat*, November 19, 27, 28, December 10, 1860.

16. W.E.B. DuBois, *Black Reconstruction*, p. 50.

17. Foner, *History of the Labor Movement*, vol. 1, pp. 297-301.

18. *The Liberator*, December 13, 1860.

19. Carl Sandburg, *Abraham Lincoln: The War Years*, vol. 1 (New York, 1936), p. 428. Lincoln assured the delegates that he agreed with these sentiments. He observed that "the workingmen are the basis of all governments for the plain reason that they are the most numerous."

20. *Der Wecker* (Baltimore), December 15, 1860; Virgil C. Blum, "The Political and Military Activities of the German Element in St. Louis, 1859-1861," *Missouri Historical Review* 42 (1948): 111-29; Robert J. Rombauer, *The Union Cause in St. Louis, 1861* (St. Louis, 1909), pp. 129-40. For a more critical view of the stand taken by Germans in Missouri on the slavery issue, see Walter D. Kamphoefner, "St. Louis Germans and the Republican Party, 1848-1860," *Mid-America* 57 (April 1975): 69-88.

21. Frank Moore, *Rebellion Record*, vol 1 (New York, 1862), pp. 107, 109, 235; Foner, *History of the Labor Movement*, vol. 1, pp. 308-9; Carl Wittke, *Refugees of Revolution: The German Forty-Eighters in America* (Philadelphia, 1952), pp. 221-25.

22. *The Liberator*, September 4, 1863.

23. *The Iron Platform* (New York), June 1864.

24. Obermann, op. cit., pp. 124-27; Sceva Bright Laughlin, *Missouri Politics During the Civil War* (Salem, Ore., 1930), pp. 42-46; *Neue Zeit*, St. Louis, December 2, 9, 1863.

25. Edward Conrad Smith, *The Borderland in the Civil War* (New York, 1927), p. 383.

26. Karl Marx and Frederick Engels, *The Civil War in the United States* (New York, 1937), pp. 25-30.

27. Foner, *History of the Labor Movement*, vol. 1, pp. 25-30.

28. Royden Harrison, "British Labor and American Slavery," *Science & Society* 25 (December 1961): 291-318.

29. *Bee-Hive*, October 4, 1862.

30. *Manchester Guardian*, January 3, 1863; *Bee-Hive*, January 3, March 28, 1863; Richard Greenleaf, "British Labor Against American Slavery," *Science & Society* 17 (Winter 1953): 42-58; Charles J. Glicksburg, "Henry Adams Reports on a Trades Union Meeting," *New England Quarterly* 15 (1948): 724-28; Ephraim Douglass Adams, *Great Britain and the American Civil War*, vol. 2 (New York, 1926), p. 292n.

31. "Proclamation of the London German Workers Educational Society, December, 1863," *Archiv für die Geschichte des Sozialismus und der Arbeiterbewegung* 6 (1916): 191, 210; Royden Harrison, *Before the Socialists: Studies in Labour and Politics, 1861-1881* (London, 1965), p. 69.

32. *Documents of hte First International: The General Council of the First International 1864-1866: Minutes* (Moscow, n.d.), pp. 22-23. Royden Harrison takes issue with Marx's evaluation of the importance of the British workers in preventing Palmerston from declaring war upon the United States. He argues that what "apparently restrained Palmerston in October 1862, was not that intervention would be unpopular, but that its advantages could not be clearly demonstrated" (*Before the Socialists*, p. 67). But suppose the "advantages" had outweighed the risks, would not the opposition of the British workers have been a significant factor for the ruling class to have weighed before making a decision? Ephraim Douglass Adams has shown that British workers organized five pro-Union meetings in 1862, forty-six such meetings in 1863, and eleven in 1864 (op. cit., vol. 2, p. 223). Recently, in her book *Support for Secession* (Chicago, 1972), Mary Ellison has demonstrated that meetings were also held in working-class districts in Lancashire in support of the Confederacy, but these meetings were never as reflective of working-class sentiment as those held in support of the Union. Ellison's conclusion, that they were even more so, is not, in my opinion, merited by the evidence she presents.

33. *Bee-Hive*, January 7, 1865; *Documents of the First International: The General Council of the First International 1864-1866: Minutes*, pp. 48-54.

34. Karl Marx, *Capital*, edited by Frederick Engels, vol. 1 (New York, 1939), p. 329.

35. *Documents of the First International: The General Council of the First International 1864-1866: Minutes*, pp. 294-95, 307-12.

36. Marx to Engels, May 1, 1865; Marx and Engels, *The Civil War in the United States*, p. 274.

37. Under these codes, adopted in all of the Southern states, a Negro who was not at work was arrested and imprisoned. In order to pay off the prison charges and fine, he was hired out. If a Negro quit work before his contract expired, he was arrested and imprisoned for breach of contract, and the reward to the person performing the arrest was deducted from his wages. Some of the codes also provided that if a Negro laborer left his employer, he was to "forfeit all wages to the time of abandonment." For these and other provisions of the "black codes," see Walter L. Fleming, *Documentary History of Reconstruction, Political, Military, Social, Religious, Education and Industrial, 1865 to the Present Time*, vol. 1 (Cleveland, 1906-1907), pp. 273-314.

38. James S. Allen, *Reconstruction: The Battle for Democracy* (New York, 1937), pp. 390-91.

39. Translated from the German and published in English in *National Anti-Slavery Standard*, August 19, 1865. In another address, the *Unionbund* called for reconstruction of the Union "on the basis of equal rights for *all* citizens," and condemned the German Union Leagues for failing to take a stand in opposition to Johnsonian Reconstruction (ibid., October 21, 1865).

40. *Boston Daily Evening Voice*, February 17, 1866.

41. Johann Philip Becker to Friedrich A. Sorge, Geneva, May 30, 1867, Sorge Papers, New York Public Library, Manuscripts Division.

42. Allen, op. cit., p. 39.

43. Sanuel Berstein, *The First International in America* (New York, 1965), p. 39.

44. The call for the convention was published in the leading papers.

45. *New York World*, September 14, 1871; *Workingman's Advocate*, September 23, 1871.

46. *New York World*, December 18, 1871.

47. See, for example, *Nashville* (Tenn.) *Republican Banner*, October 29, 1871.

48. *Galveston Daily News*, June 7, 1871.

49. Ibid., February 20, 28, March 3, 11, 21, April 14, 1872; James Verde Reese, "The Worker in Texas, 1821-1876," Ph.D. dissertation, University of Texas, 1964, pp. 256-59;

James V. Reese, "The Early History of Labor Organization in Texas, 1838-1876," *Southwestern Historical Quarterly*, 62 (July 1968): 13.

50. Letterbook, IWA Papers, State Historical Society of Wisconsin; Bernstein, op. cit., p. 66. In a survey of the black workers in New York City in 1869, the *New York Times* (March 2, 1869) reported that the Germans were the only ones in the city "who appear to be really uninfluenced by this intolerant spirit of prejudice against the color of the negro," that in shops dominated by the Germans, a black worker received "fair wages—quite as much as . . . a whiteman of equal skill and powers of work," and that the German workers treated the black "properly, and not simply as *the nigger*."

51. *New National Era*, January 13, April 4, 1870; October 19, 1871.

52. *The General Council of the International Working Men's Association, Minutes: 1866-1868* (Moscow, n.d.), pp. 304-10.

53. *The General Council of the International Working Men's Association, Minutes: 1870-1871* (Moscow, n.d.), pp. 52-54.

54. Ibid., pp. 81-82.

55. Karl Marx to Siegfried Meyer and August Vogt, April 9, 1870; Karl Marx and Frederick Engels, *Letters to Americans, 1848-1895* (New York, 1952), pp. 77-80.

56. Daniel Mason, "On Negro-White Unity," *Political Affairs* (August 1954): 61-62.

57. Marx and Engels, *Letters to Americans*, p. 78.

58. Ibid. Emphasis added.

59. Karl Marx, *Capital*, vol. 1 (New York, 1886), p. 528.

60. When Section 12 of New York City joined actively in the nomination of the flamboyant Victoria C. Woodhull for president and Frederick Douglass, the black liberator, for vice-president on the Equal Rights party ticket in 1872 and hailed "The Woman's, Negro's and Workingmen's Ticket," Sorge reported that the action had made "a laughing stock" of the International. At the May 28, 1872, meeting of the General Council, Frederick Engels called the whole business an example of "middle-class humbug in America." Karl Marx spoke of "a so-called convention . . . held at the Apollo Music Hall, ostensibly to nominate Mrs. Woodhull to the presidency and Douglass, a colored man, for Vice-President. The proceedings had become the laughing stock of America."

While there is not much about the Equal Rights party that a Marxist could endorse, the fact is that no party which nominated a woman for president, Frederick Douglass for vice-president of the United States in 1872 was mere "humbug." (For the convention proceedings which nominated Woodhull and Douglass, see *Woodhull & Claflin's Weekly*, April 20, May 11, 18, June 1, 8, 15, 1872; Philip S. Foner, *Frederick Douglass* (New York, 1964). For Engels' and Marx's reaction, see *The General Council of the International Workingmen's Association: Minutes, 1871-1872* (Moscow, n.d.), pp. 250-51, 323-32.

61. *National Anti-Slavery Standard*, January 1, 1870.

62. Harvey Klehr, "Marxist Theory in Search of America," *Journal of Modern History* 33 (June 1970): 122-24.

63. *Vorbote*, July 29, 1876.

64. The disciples of Ferdinand Lassalle, the German socialist and advocate of producers' cooperatives with state aid, viewed the ballot as the chief instrument for lifting "the yoke of capital" from labor. They put little value on trade unions and strikes. The Marxists believed in political action but believed that the most immediate task confronting the working class was to organize into trade unions and struggle for improvements under capitalism. Believing with Lassalle that the worker could never gain more than was "necessary for subsistence" by the iron law of wages, the Lassalleans viewed such activities on the economic front as a waste of time.

65. The only indication that Sorge was aware of Reconstruction is his reference to "carpetbaggers" in describing the middle-class reformers who joined the American sections of

the First International, especially Section 12. They were "carpetbaggers" in the North dispatched by the bourgeoisie to confuse the workers (*The Labor Movement in the United States*, p. 144). Sorge also accepted the view that "carpetbaggers" who went South during Reconstruction were all despicable characters. (Ibid., p. 133).

66. Philip S. Foner, ed., *The Formation of the Workingman's Party of the United States: Proceedings of the Union Congress Held at Philadelphia, July 19-22, 1876* (New York, 1976), p. 34.

67. Morris Hillquit, *History of Socialism in the United States* (New York, 1903), p. 225.

68. For a discussion of the Compromise of 1877, see C. Vann Woodward, *Reunion and Reaction*, 2d rev. ed. (New York, 1956).

69. Neither G. M. Stekloff in *History of the First International* (London, 1921) nor Hermann Schlüter in *Die Internationale in Amerika* mentions the Negro. Samuel Bernstein in *The First International in America* has two references.

## CHAPTER 3

1. Dovie King Clark, "Peter Humphries Clark," *Negro History Bulletin* (May 1942): 176; *Dictionary of American Biography*, vol. 4 (New York, 1946), p. 143.

2. Carter G. Woodson, "The Negroes of Cincinnati Prior to the Civil War," *Journal of Negro History* 1 (January 1916): 120-42; Charles B. Galbreath, *History of Ohio*, vol. 1 (New York, 1925), pp. 167-202; Philip S. Foner, *History of Black Americans: From Africa to the Emergence of the Cotton Kingdom* (Westport, Conn., 1975), p.. 516.

3. Merrill Goozner, "Peter H. Clark of Cincinnati," unpublished seminar paper, Afro-American History, University of Cincinnati, March 1974, pp. 1-2; William J. Simmons, *Men of Mark: Eminent, Progressive and Rising* (Cleveland, 1890), p. 374.

The Cincinnati High School was founded by Hiram S. Gilmore, who became its principal. Gilmore was a utopian socialist, and his ideas may have "had an influence" on his students. (Goozner, op. cit., p. 2.) The school's graduates included P.B.S. Pinchback, lieutenant governor (and for a brief period governor) of Louisiana, John M. Langston, dean of Howard University and a leading champion of civil rights, Thomas C. Ball, artist, and J. Monroe Trotter, active in the struggle for black rights in the twentieth century.

4. L. D. Easton, "The Colored Schools of Cincinnati," in Isaac M. Martin, ed., *History of the Schools of Cincinnati and Other Educational Institutions, Public and Private* (Cincinnati, Ohio, 1900), pp. 185-87.

5. Wm. Wells Brown, *The Rising Son; or the Antecedents and Advancement of the Colored Race* (Boston, 1882), p. 521.

6. *Proceedings of a Convention of the Colored Men of Ohio, Held in the City of Cincinnati on the 23d, 24th, 25th and 26th Days of November, 1858* (Cincinnati, 1858), pp. 28-32; Benjamin Quarles, *Black Abolitionists* (New York, 1969), pp. 3-4.

7. *Workingman's Advocate* (Chicago), August 27, 1870.

8. James M. Morris, "William Haller, 'The Disturbing Element,'" *Cincinnati Historical Society Bulletin* 28 (Winter 1970): 120-32.

9. James M. Morris, "The Road to Trade Unionism: Organized Labor in Cincinnati, 1800-1893," Ph.D. dissertation, University of Cincinnati, pp. 87-90.

10. Wendell Phillips Dabney, *Cincinnati's Colored Citizens* (Cincinnati, 1926), pp. 187-89; *New Natinal Era and Citizen*, December 18, 1873; Goozner, op. cit., p. 13.

11. *Proceedings, Convention of Colored Newspaper Men, Cincinnati, August 4, 1875* (Cincinnati, 1875), pp. 3-4.

12. The Sovereigns of Industry was founded in January 1874 by Edward Martin Chamberlin (1835-1892), a member of an English-speaking section of the First International in

Boston, as a means of abolishing the wage system. Chamberlin outlined his system in his book, *The Sovereigns of Industry* (Boston, 1875). The Sovereigns mainly operated cooperative stores. The total membership in 1875-1876 was said to be 40,000, of whom 75 percent were in New England. The organization was dead by 1878.

13. *Cincinnati Commercial*, November 27, 1875.

14. Ibid., June 17, 26, 1876.

15. Ibid., December 11, 1876.

16. Ibid., March 27, 1877.

17. *The Emancipator*, March 31, 1877.

18. *Cincinnati Commercial*, June 12, 15, 1877.

19. For discussions of the great strike, see Robert W. Bruce, *1877: Year of Violence* (Indianapolis, 1958), and Foner, *History of the Labor Movement*, vol. 1, pp. 464-74.

20. *Cincinnati Enquirer*, July 23, 1877.

21. Ibid.; *Cincinnati Commercial*, July 23, 1877.

22. *Cincinnati Commercial*, July 23, 1877; *The Emancipator*, July 28, 1877. The speech is reprinted in Philip S. Foner, ed., *The Voice of Black America: Speeches by Blacks in the United States, 1797-1973*, vol. 1 (New York, 1975), pp. 481-87.

23. *Cincinnati Commercial*, July 24, 1877.

24. Ibid., July 26, 1877.

25. *The Emancipator*, August 4, 1877.

26. Karl Marx to Frederick Engels, July 25, 1877; Karl Marx and Friedrich Engels, *Werke* 34 (Berlin, 1967), p. 59.

27. Foner, *History of the Labor Movement*, vol 1. pp. 470-73; Bruce, op. cit., pp. 212-59.

28. *Labor Standard*, August 4, 1877.

29. *St. Louis Globe-Democrat*, July 25, 1877; David T. Burbank, *Reign of the Rabble: The St. Louis General Strike of 1877* (New York, 1966), pp. 50-53; Bruce, op. cit., pp. 258-60.

30. *Scranton Republican*, July 26, 1877; *St. Louis Globe-Democrat*, July 26, 1877.

31. *St. Louis Missouri Republican*, July 26, 27, 28, 29, 1877; *St. Louis Globe-Democrat*, July 25-27, 1877; Russell M. Nolen, "The Labor Movement in St. Louis from 1860 to 1890." *Missouri Historical Review* 24 (January 1940): 170-72.

32. *St. Louis Times*, August 2, 12, 1877; Burbank, op. cit., pp. 72-73.

33. *Labor Standard*, August 12, 19, October 7, 1877; *The Emancipator*, August 18, 1877.

34. *The Emancipator*, July 21, August 4, 1877.

35. There is no adequate study of the early years of the Socialist Labor party. Hillquit's account in his *History of Socialism in the United States* is too general, while specialized studies of American socialism in later decades merely summarize the party's early history. The party records and correspondence in the archives of the State Historical Society of Wisconsin—recently made available on microfilm—have not yet been submitted to careful study.

36. *Socialistische Arbeiter-Partie, Platform, Constitution and Beschluss, welche von der 26, 27, 28, 30, and 31, December 1877 zu Newark, N.J.* (Cincinnati, 1878); *Socialistic Labor Party, Platform, Constitution and Discussion from 25, 26, 27, 28, December, 1879* (New York, 1880), pp. 3, 22.

37. *The Socialist* (Chicago), January 11, 1879.

38. The same could be said of the socialist position regarding the Chinese. *The Socialist* carried articles attacking Kearneyism, the anti-Chinese movement in San Francisco led by Denis Kearney, an Irish drayman, which attracted wide support in working-class circles (December 21, 1879 and January 11, 1879). But it did not criticize members of the party in California who joined forces with Kearney.

39. For the plight of the migrants stranded in St. Louis, see Glen Schwendemann, "St. Louis and the 'Exodusters' of 1879," *Journal of Negro History* 41 (January 1961): 32-46. The full story may be found in Nell Irvin Painter, *Exodusters: Black Migration to Kansas After Reconstruction* (New York, 1977).

40. The May 10, 1879, issue of *The Socialist* carried a brief article entitled "The Fleeing Negroes." It was a reprint of a New Orleans letter to the *New York Sun*. It dealt mainly with the fact that Negroes were being tempted to leave for Kansas by bright-colored pamphlets "containing tempting illustrations of highly-colored life in Kansas, which readily take captive the colored man's fancy," and "the country colored man being devoid of the quality of suspicion, finds his imagination filled with the El Dorado described by the pamphlets, and being a creature of impulse and given to follow, he is easily induced to action." This racist account did not mention that the exodus was well organized by blacks themselves, nor did it cite the reasons for the migration. Moreover, *The Socialist* did not add any further information in publishing the dispatch from New Orleans.

*The Socialist*, another Socialist Labor party English-language organ published in Detroit, totally ignored the Negro exodus. Indeed in its entire career, this party organ only once mentioned the Negro. In its issue of February 9, 1878, under the heading "The Color Made the Difference," it reprinted a story of a black woman in Pittsburgh who, despite scoring the highest mark in penmanship was turned down for a position in the office of the city recorder when it was discovered she was a Negro.

41. *The Socialist* (Chicago), May 10, 24, 1879.

42. Ibid., November 23, 1878, May 3, 1879; C. G. Clemens in *The Whim-Wham*, October 1, 1881; and Michael J. Brodhead and O. Gene Clanton, "C. G. Clemens: The 'Sociable Socialist,'" *Kansas Historical Quarterly* (Winter 1974): 483.

43. *Cincinnati Commercial*, July 22, 1879.

44. Morris, "William Haller," op. cit., pp. 128-29.

45. *Cincinnati Enquirer*, July 4, 11, 12, 18, August 11, 15, 1879.

46. *Cincinnati Commercial*, July 22, 1879.

47. *Cincinnati Enquirer*, March 3, 4, 1881; *Cincinnati Commercial*, March 3, 1881.

48. As William Wells Brown wrote in 1882: "No man has been truer to his oppressed people than Peter H. Clark and none are more deserving of their unlimited confidence than he" (Brown op. cit., p. 524).

After 1881, Clark moved in and out of the Republican party; in 1885, he supported the Democratic party (*Washington Bee*, March 14, 1885; August Meier, *Negro Thought in America, 1880-1915* [Ann Arbor, 1963], p. 28). Clark's support of the Democratic party infuriated blacks in Cincinnati. He was forced to move to St. Louis where he lived and taught school until 1926 when, at the ripe age of ninety-seven, he died. There was an unsuccessful attempt by members of the Cincinnati black community to have his remains brought back to their city. As Wendell P. Dabney observes: "Dead he was no longer dangerous; therefore more desirable" (op. cit., p. 116). While August Meier discusses Clark's move from the Republican to the Democratic party, he does not devote any attention to his role in the socialist movement.

49. Cf. *Platform and Constitution of the Socialist Labor Party, October, 1885* (New York, 1886), p. 3; *September, 1887* (New York, 1887), p. 3; and *October, 1889* (New York, 1890), p. 3.

The conclusion regarding the Social Labor party press is based on a study of the files of the *New Yorker Volkszeitung*, issues of the *Arbeiter-Zeitung*, and *Die New Yorker Yiddishe Volkszeitung* still in existence, and of the *Workmen's Advocate*, the party's English-language organ.

50. Hillquit, op. cit., pp. 199-205; David Herreshoff, *American Disciples of Marx: From the Age of Jackson to the Progressive Era* (Detroit, 1967), p. 104.

51. Heinrich Gemkow and Associates, *Frederick Engels, A Biography* (Dresden, Germany, 1972), pp. 437-38.

52. Marx and Engels, *Letters to Americans*, pp. 160-65.

53. For a discussion of Swinton and his paper, see Philip S. Foner, *History of the Labor Movement in the United States*, vol. 2 (New York, 1955), pp. 29-31; Marc Ross, "John Swinton, Journalist and Reformer: The Active Years, 1857-1887," Ph.D. dissertation, New York University, 1968; Sender Garlin, "The Challenge of John Swinton," *Masses & Mainstream* (December 1951): 40-47. For Swinton's acquaintance with and opinion of Marx, see Philip S. Foner, ed., *When Karl Marx Died: Comments in 1883* (New York, 1973), pp. 46-52, 220-28.

54. Marx and Engels, *Letters to Americans*, pp. 7, 42, 131-200; Gemkow and Associates, op. cit., p. 438.

55. Edward and Eleanor Marx Aveling, *The Working-Class Movement in America*, 2d ed. enlarged (London, 1891), Chapter 9 and p. 33.

56. Marx and Engels, *Letters to Americans*, p. 163.

57. For a general discussion of the Negro and the Knights of Labor, see Foner, *History of the Labor Movement*, vol. 2, pp. 66-74, and Philip S. Foner, *Organized Labor and the Black Worker 1619-1973* (New York, 1974), pp. 47-63. For a more detailed treatment, see Sidney H. Kessler, "The Negro in the Knights of Labor," M.A. thesis, Columbia University, 1939, which is summarized in his article, "The Negro in the Knights of Labor," *Journal of Negro History* 37 (July 1952): 250-82. For a more recent treatment of the subject, see Melton A. McLaurin, "The Racial Policies of the Knights of Labor and the Organization of Southern Black Workers," *Labor History* 17 (Fall 1976): 568-85, and Kenneth Kann, "The Knights of Labor and the Southern Black Worker," ibid., 18 (Winter 1977): 49-70.

58. Terence V. Powderly, *Thirty Years of Labor, 1859-1889* (Columbus, Ohio, 1889), p. 464; Irwin M. Marcus, "The Southern Negro and the Knights of Labor," *Negro History Bulletin* 30 (March 1967): 5-7; McLaurin, op. cit., pp. 577-79; *John Swinton's Paper*, December 13, 1885; *Journal of United Labor*, August 25, 1886, July 2, 1887, and June 9, 1888; *Knights of Labor*, October 2, 1886.

59. *John Swinton's Paper*, May 16, 1886.

60. The District Assembly was organized in July 1882 and took in most of the locals of New York and Brooklyn. It had a membership of 60,000 in the mid-1880s. Most of the socialists in the district's leadership were Lassalleans; they functioned through an inner circle called the Home Club. The Lassallean composition of the socialists in District Assembly 49 may account for the lack of attention paid to the district's activities by Engels and other leading Marxists, including Friedrich A. Sorge.

61. Cf. *The Freeman* (Indianapolis), February 8, 1890, page one of which carried a portrait of Frank Ferrell.

62. *Union Printer*, May 31, 1887. The strike involved a "large force" of hop-pickers in Kern County, California. The employers planned to replace the Chinese strikers with Negroes, but the scheme fell through largely because the blacks refused to act as strikebreakers. See Stuart Jamiesen, "Labor Unionism in American Agriculture," U.S. Department of Labor, Bureau of Labor Statistics, Bulletin No. 836, Washington, D.C., 1945, p. 46n.

63. *John Swinton's Paper*, July 10, 1887.

64. *Journal of United Labor*, September 25, 1886; *New York Freeman*, October 2, 1886.

65. *Richmond Whig*, October 2, 1886; *New York Times* quoted in George Talmadge Starnes and Edwin Hamm, *Some Phases of Labor Relations in the South* (New York, 1934), p. 74.

66. *New York Tribune*, October 11, 1886; *Philadelphia Press*, October 6, 1886; Pow-

derly, *Thirty Years of Labor*, pp. 652-53; *Proceedings*, General Assembly, Knights of Labor, 1886, p. 254.

67. *Proceedings*, General Assembly, Knights of Labor, 1886, p. 254.

68. Cf. "Knights of Labor and the Color Line," *Public Opinion* 2 (October 1886): 1-3.

69. *Cleveland Gazette*, October 23, 1886.

70. *New York Freeman*, October 2, 1886.

71. *Richmond Dispatch*, October 17, 1886; *Pittsburgh Dispatch*, October 15, 1886.

72. *Workmen's Advocate*, January 31, April 4, 1886.

73. *Report of Proceedings, Sixth Congress of the Socialist Labor Party, Turn Hall, Buffalo, N.Y., September 17-20, 1887* (New York, 1887), p. 12.

74. Hillquit, op. cit., pp. 264-69.

75. For a general discussion of these trends, see Rayford W. Logan, *The Negro in American Life and Thought: The Nadir, 1877-1901* (New York, 1954).

CHAPTER 4

1. The literature on Daniel De Leon is immense and is growing by leaps and bounds. Revisionist articles continue to be published. They vary from uncritical, adulatory studies by his disciples to bitter, denunciatory ones by those who argue that his dogmatism and sectarian policies made more enemies than converts to American socialism, to recent studies which insist that De Leon has been misunderstood or deliberately falsified. One common denominator in all studies of De Leon is their entire omission or superficial treatment of his position on the Negro question.

For a critical view of De Leon's methods and philosophy, see Foner, *History of the Labor Movement*, vol. 2, pp. 279-81, 296-97, 388-99. For a defense of De Leon, see *Daniel De Leon: The Man and His Work: A Symposium* (New York, 1935); Carl Reeve, *The Life and Times of Daniel De Leon* (New York, 1972); Bernard Bortnick, "De Leon's Role in the Labor Movement," *Weekly People*, December 15, 22, 1973; and issues of *Labor History*, 1972-1976.

2. Lucien Sanial had also been editor of the *Workmen's Advocate*.

3. See, for example, *The People*, April 5, 12, 19, May 3, 1891.

4. Eric Hass, *Socialism, A World Without Prejudice* (New York, n.d.), p. 19.

5. Foner, *History of the Labor Movement*, vol. 2, pp. 157-66.

6. *The People*, November 26, 1893.

7. For a terrifying picture of the desperate conditions of black sharecroppers and wage hands in the late 1880s, see the speech of Frederick Douglass in Foner, *The Voice of Black America*, vol. 1, pp. 550-64.

8. C. G. Baylor to Daniel De Leon, Providence, R.I., December 8, 1895, Daniel De Leon Correspondence, State Historical Society of Wisconsin. Even though he himself was an anti-imperialist and viewed the war waged by the United States against Spain in 1898 as an imperialist war, and though he devoted considerable space in *The People* to denunciation of the war, De Leon did not bother to reprint Baylor's anti-imperialist articles published in the *Richmond Planet* of July 30 and August 13, 1898. The *Planet* was a militant black weekly.

9. *The People*, November 3, 1895, April 5, 1896.

10. Ibid., April 24, 1898. In 1896, the Socialist Labor party adopted the constitutional provision that "no section or subdivision shall be designated by race or nationality" (Socialist Labor Party, *Proceedings of Convention of 1896*, p. 43). Despite the highly centralized structure of the party, the provision does not appear to have been enforced. Apart from the colored section in Virginia, there was an Italian section in Houston between 1896

and 1898 (*Unione Socialiste de La Laboratore Italiani "Guffrida Defelice"*). The section had "20 active members" (Malcolm Sylvere, "Sicilian Socialists in Houston, Texas, 1896-98," *Labor History* 11 [Winter 1970]: 77-81).

11. *The People*, May 12, July 8, December 15, 1901.

12. Foner, *History of the Labor Movement*, vol. 2, pp. 378-80.

13. *Proceedings of the Tenth Convention of the Socialist Labor Party, Held in New York City, June 2 to June 8, 1900* (New York, 1901), pp. 115-18.

14. For details of the strike and the return to work, see Melton A. McLaurin, *Paternalism and Protest: Southern Cotton Mill Workers and Organized Labor, 1875-1905* (Westport, Conn., 1972), pp. 88-97.

15. *Proceedings of the Tenth Convention. . . . .* p. 34.

16. *Daily People*, October 25, 1903.

17. *Weekly People*, January 30, September 3, 1904.

18. Ibid., May 23, 1908.

19. Daniel De Leon, *Flashlights of the Amsterdam Congress* (New York, 1906), pp. 117-18.

20. *Weekly People*, May 25, July 13, 1907.

21. Foner, *Organized Labor and the Black Worker*, p. 112.

22. Quoted in Hass, op. cit., pp. 19, 28.

23. Arnold Peterson, *Daniel De Leon: Social Architect*, vol. 1 (New York, 1941), p. 232.

24. There is a brief discussion by Frank Bohn, Socialist Labor party organizer, of the "race consciousness among our Southern comrades," which appeared in the *Weekly People* of December 10, 1904, but it actually said very little.

25. *Weekly People*, September 4, 23, 30, November 11, 1911. The participants in the debate were K. E. Choate of Houston, Texas, Arnold Peterson and Olive Johnson, leading figures in the party, and a Comrade Palmer of Paterson, New Jersey.

26. Henry David, *The History of the Haymarket Affair* (New York, 1936), pp. 12-45; Foner, *History of the Labor Movement*, vol. 2, pp. 37-38; Alan Calmar, *Labor Agitator, The Story of Albert R. Parsons* (New York, 1937), pp. 57-62.

27. David, op. cit., pp. 64-69; Foner, *History of the Labor Movement*, vol. 2, p. 39.

28. This conclusion is based on a study of existing copies of *The Anarchist* and *Liberty*, published in Boston, *Arbeiter-Zeitung, Vorbote*, and the *Alarm*, published in Chicago.

29. Parsons was one of the four anarchists executed in the Haymarket frameup of 1886. His wife, Lucy Parsons, was a beautiful dark-skinned woman who was a Mexican-Indian with Negro blood. Even while it condemned her anarchist views, the black press viewed Lucy Parsons as a member of the race. When Professor Jesse Lawson, New Jersey black leader, boasted in 1898 that "there are no anarchists among the colored people, and we thank God for it," the Indianapolis *Freeman* reminded him that he had overlooked Lucy Parsons. It introduced her to its readers as "A Quadroon Anarchist" (*The Colored American*, November 5, 1898; *Indianapolis Freeman*, December 12, 1898).

In her fine biography of Lucy Parsons, Carolyn Ashbaugh does not mention these articles in the black press. See Carolyn Ashbaugh, *Lucy Parsons, American Revolutionary* (Chicago, 1976).

30. *Alarm*, April 4, 1885.

31. Ibid., April 3, 1886.

32. *The Rebel* (Boston), January, 1896.

33. Foner, *Organized Labor and the Black Worker*, p. 90.

34. "Black Dynamiters in Boston," reprinted in *Richmond Planet*, May 28, 1892. See also "Anarchist Doctrines" and "No Dynamite," ibid., June 11, July 2, 1892.

35. *The Appeal* (St. Paul), June 11, 1892.

36. John F. Bruce, "The Anarchists," *The Colored American*, January 18, 1902; Earl

Finch, "A Remedy for Anarchy," ibid., February 15, 1902; Joshua T. Small to Editor, ibid., March 8, 1902.

37. "Anarchist Views of Lynching," *Literary Digest*, September 12, 1903.

38. *Mother Earth*, October 1911.

39. Ibid., August 1907.

40. In her autobiography *Living My Life*, Emma Goldman does not once mention either blacks or the Negro question. In *Red Emma Speaks: Selected Writings and Speeches by Emma Goldman*, compiled and edited by Alix Kates Shulman, there is only the following reference to the Negro by Emma Goldman: "The history of progress is written in the blood of men and women who have dared to espouse an unpopular cause, as, for instance, the black man's right to his body, or the woman's right to her soul" (New York, 1972, p. 35).

41. *The Nationalist*, May and December 1889; *The New Nation*, January 31, 1891.

42. Bellamy did not discuss the Negro in either of the two books he published after *Looking Backward: Looking Forward* which appeared in 1889 and *Equality* which was published in 1897.

43. "The National Party" in *Public Opinion*, October 22, 1896, p. 523. The December 13, 1890, and March 12, 1892, issues of *True Nationalist* carried without comment accounts of lynchings of Negroes in the South.

44. "The Negro's Part in Nationalism," *The Nationalist* 2 (1890): 91-97.

45. Hillquit, op. cit., pp. 291-92.

46. *American Fabian* 2 (March 1896): 11.

47. Cf. R. Seymour, "Was Christ a Socialist?" *The Christian Recorder*, November 8, 1894; W. H. Coston, "The Negro and Socialism," ibid., February 18, 1897.

48. *AME Church Review* 3 (October 1886): 165-67.

49. Rev. James Theodore Holly, "Socialism from the Biblical Point of View," *AME Church Review* 9 (1892-1893): 244-58.

50. Rev. R. C. Ransom, "The Negro and Socialism," ibid., 3 (1896-1897): 192-200. In his study *Black Religion and Black Radicalism* (New York, 1972, pp. 187, 188, 220), Gayraud S. Wilmore mentions Reverend Ransom and lists him as a militant, but makes no mention of his advocacy of socialism. There is, in fact, no discussion of the influence of Christian Socialism among blacks.

51. *AME Church Review* 13 (1896-1897): 442.

52. Ibid., 1 (January 1895): 287.

53. *Railway Times*, January 1, 1897. For an analysis of socialist recruitment from the Populists in the Southwest, see James R. Green, "Socialism and the Southwestern Class Struggle 1898-1918: A Study of Radical Movements in Oklahoma, Texas, Louisiana, and Arkansas," Ph.D. dissertation, Yale University, 1972, pp. 3-5, 15-17. For the full study of Populism, see Lawrence Goodwyn, *Democratic Promise: The Populist Movement in America* (New York, 1976).

54. *Railway Times*, June 15, 1897; *The Social Democrat*, July 1, November 4, 1897; Foner, *History of the Labor Movement*, vol. 2, pp. 388-90. *The Coming Nation* and the *Appeal to Reason* were both founded by Julius A. Wayland, an Indiana Republican who had grown wealthy as a printer and real estate man and had become an advocate of the socialism of Edward Bellamy before joining the Social Democracy.

55. Bernard J. Brommell, "Debs's Cooperative Commonwealth Plan for Workers," *Labor History* 12 (Fall 1971): 560-69; H. Wayne Morgan, "The Utopia of Eugene V. Debs," *American Quarterly* 11 (Summer 1959): 120-35.

56. *The Social Democrat*, June 16, July 16, 1898.

57. Foner, *Organized Labor and the Black Worker*, pp. 112-13.

58. "The Race Problem: A Suggestion," *The Coming Nation*, January 7, 1899.

59. *Milwaukee Sentinel*, July 25, 1897; *Milwaukee News*, July 31, 1897.

60. *Social Democratic Herald*, May 27, June 17, 1899, February 24, 1900.

61. Ibid., February 24, 1900.

62. Marvin Wachman, *History of the Social-Democratic Party of Milwaukee, 1898-1910* (Urbana, Ill., 1945), pp. 63-64; Thomas W. Gavett, *Development of the Labor Movement in Milwaukee* (Madison and Milwaukee, 1965), pp. 112-12.

63. Cf. "The Labor Problem," *Appeal to Reason*, September 15, 1900; "The Negro Problem," *International Socialist Review* 1 (October 1900): 204-11; (February 1901): 464-70; "The Negro and His 'Rights,'" *The Workers' Call*, March 9, 1901.

64. Rayford W. Logan, op. cit., pp. 132-64; C. Vann Woodward, *Origins of the New South, 1877-1913* (Baton Rouge, 1951), pp. 147-74, 321, 365; Floyd J. Miller, "Black Protest and White Leadership: A Note on the Colored Farmers' Alliance," *Phylon* 32 (First Quarter 1972): 174.

65. See Herbert G. Gutman, "Black Coal Miners and the Greenback-Labor Party in Redeemer, Alabama, 1878-1879," *Labor History* 10 (Summer 1969): 506-35.

66. There is a growing body of literature dealing with the Colored Farmers' National Alliance and the relations between white and blacks in the Populist Revolt. See especially Martin Dann, "Black Populism: A Study of the Colored Farmers' Alliance Through 1891," *Journal of Ethnic Studies* 2 (Fall 1974): 58-71, and William F. Holmes, "The Leflore County Massacre and the Demise of the Colored Farmers' Alliance," *Phylon* 34 no. 3 (1974): 267-74.

67. William W. Rogers, *The One-Gallused Rebellion: Agrarianism in Alabama* (Baton Rouge, 1971), pp. 131-46; Lawrence D. Rice, *The Negro in Texas, 1874-1900* (Baton Rouge, 1971), pp. 70-110. For a strained effort to establish full and lasting relations between whites and blacks in the Alliance and Populist movements, see Judith Stein, "'Of Mr. Booker T. Washington and Others': The Political Economy of Racism in the United States," *Science & Society* 38 (Winter 1974-1975): 422-63.

68. *New York Freeman*, February 14, 1885.

69. T. Thomas Fortune, *Black and White: Land, Labor and Politics in the South* (New York, 1884), p. 93.

70. Ibid., pp. 222-23.

71. Ibid., pp. 241-42.

72. Ibid., pp. 157, 176.

73. *New York Age*, August 2, 1890.

74. Emma Lou Thornbrough, *T. Thomas Fortune, Militant Journalist* (Chicago, 1972), pp. 240-52.

75. Quoted in Jack Abramowitz, "John B. Rayner—A Grass Roots Leader," *Journal of Negro History* 35 (April 1951): 162.

76. Booker T. Washington, "The Awakening of the Negro," *Atlantic Monthly* 88 (September 1936): 326.

77. Booker T. Washington, "Negro Disfranchisement and the Negro in Business," *The Outlook* 18 (October 9, 1909): 310-11, 315.

78. Booker T. Washington, "The Negro and the Labor Problem in the South," reprinted in Howard Brotz, ed., *Negro Social and Political Thought, 1850-1920* (New York, 1966), p. 404; Booker T. Washington, "Address before the Southern Industrial Convention, Huntsville Alabama, October 12, 1899," in E. L. Thornbrough, ed., *Booker T. Washington—Great Lives Observed* (Englewood Cliffs, N.J., 1969), pp. 46-47; Louis R. Harlan, *Booker T. Washington: The Making of a Black Leader* (New York, 1972), pp. 90-91.

79. Charles Alexander, Tuskegee, Alabama, "The Socialism of the Negro," *The Christian Recorder*, July 5, 1900.

80. Charles H. Vail, "The Negro Problem," *International Socialist Review* 1 (February 1901): 470.

CHAPTER 5

1. *Social Democratic Herald*, December 10, 1898, February 18, 1899, March 17, 1900.

2. *The Workers' Call*, Chicago, August 3, 1901; *The Worker*, August 4, 1901. In her study "The Socialist Party in Indiana Since 1896," Ora Ellen Cox mentions John Adams of Brazil but not Edward D. McKay (*Indiana Magazine of History* 12 [June 1916]: 99n).

3. *Cleveland Citizen* quoted in Howard H. Quint, *The Forging of American Socialism* (Columbia, S.C., 1953), p. 42.

4. *The Worker*, August 11, 1901. M. Winchevsky, the correspondent, was three years off on the date on which a Boston mob seized Garrison, dragged him with a rope around his neck through the streets, and might have lynched him had he not been whisked off to jail. The incident occurred on October 21, 1835.

5. *The Worker*, August 4, 1901.

6. "Proceedings of the Founding Convention of the Socialist Party, 1901," typewritten copy in Tamiment Institute, Bobst Library, New York University.

7. *The Worker*, August 4, 1901.

8. *Appeal to Reason*, August 10, 17, 1901. Emphasis in original. Neither *The Worker* nor *Appeal to Reason* mentioned that, in the discussion of the resolution on the organization of the party, Delegate Goebell had used the expression "nigger in the woodpile" without any rebuke from any other delegate.

9. William E. Walling, *The Socialism of Today* (New York, 1916): 504-05.

10. C. Vann Woodward, "Flight from History: The Heritage of the Negro," *The Nation*, 100th Anniversary Issue (September 20, 1965): 144.

11. "Proceedings of the Founding Convention of the Socialist Party, 1901," Tamiment Institute.

12. For a detailed discussion of the steel strike of 1901, see Philip S. Foner, *History of the Labor Movement in the United States*, vol. 3 (New York, 1964), pp. 78-86. The use of strikebreakers, including blacks, was a feature of the methods used by the U.S. Steel Corporation to smash the strike. However, the degree of strikebreaking is difficult to estimate. According to *The Worker*, the socialist weekly in New York City, few of the men imported as strikebreakers actually agreed to take the places of strikers. It noted that the most "encouraging feature of this development was that blacks joined whites in refusing to scab" (September 22, 1901).

13. *The Colored American*, August 18, 1901.

14. Ibid., August 31, 1901. *The Freeman*, a black weekly published in Indianapolis, the very city in which the Socialist party's Unity Convention was held, did not publish the "Negro Resolution" or even carry a single report on the convention.

15. *The Worker*, September 22, 1901.

16. *The Christian Recorder* on August 22, 1901, fully endorsed the position of *The Colored American*.

17. *The Colored American*, August 31, 1901. Booker T. Washington insisted that the barriers imposed against black labor by trade unions could be overcome by appealing to employers to use black labor. Negro labor's great advantage was that it was "not inclined to trade unionism"; the black worker "is almost a stranger to strife, lock-outs and labor wars; [he] is labor that is law-abiding, peaceable, teachable . . . labor that has never been tempted to follow the red flag of anarchy." Washington advocated black strikebreaking as a means by which black workers could obtain entrance into industry. (Foner, *Organized Labor and the Black Worker*, p. 79).

18. *The Colored American*, September 14, 1901.

19. The assassination of President William McKinley by an anarchist who shot him on September 6, 1901, led to furious attacks on anarchism; little effort was made to distinguish between it and socialism.

20. *The Colored American*, September 28, 1901.

21. Ibid., October 26, 1901.

22. See Foner, *Organized Labor and the Black Worker*, pp. 144-46.

23. Foner, *History of the Labor Movement*, vol. 3, pp. 369-70, 381-83.

24. *The Carpenter*, September, 1903, pp. 6, 10.

25. *The Worker*, September 22, 1901.

26. In August 1902, *The Colored American* magazine reprinted, without comment, an editorial from the socialist *Appeal to Reason* denouncing the "continuation of lynching outlawry."

27. "Negro Socialist Talks," *Chicago Socialist*, March 29, 1902.

28. Charles H. Vail, *Socialism and the Negro Problem* (New York, 1902), pp. 10-12.

29. "The Misfortunes of the Negroes," *Social Democratic Herald*, May 31, 1902.

30. Edward John Muzak, "Victor L. Berger, A Biography," Ph.D. dissertation, Northwestern University, 1960, pp. 163-65.

31. William Noyes, "Some Proposed Solutions of the Negro Problem," *International Socialist Review* 2 (December 1, 1901): 402-3.

32. Ibid., 4 (June 1903): 271-73.

33. *Wilshire's Editorials*, Los Angeles, Calif., 1906.

34. *The Voice of the People* (Atlanta), November 1, 1902; *The Colored American*, November 4, 1902.

35. *Literary Digest*, July 4, 18, 1903; *The Colored American*, July 20, 1903. See also New York *Age*, July 16, 1903, and Philip S. Foner, "Black-Jewish Relations in the Opening Years of the Twentieth Century," *Phylon* (February 1976): 6-15.

36. *The Freeman*, July 25, 1903.

37. E. U. (Ernest Untermann), "The American Kishineff," *Appeal to Reason*, July 25, 1903.

38. Ibid., August 24, December 31, 1901, July 15, August 2, 1902.

39. Ibid., July 2, September 2, 1903.

40. Reynolds *v.* Board of Education of City of Topeka, *Kansas Reports*, vol. 66, p. 672; *In the Supreme Court of Kansas. William Reynolds, Plaintiff v. The Board of Education of the City of Topeka, of the State of Kansas, Defendant, Brief for Plantiff, G. C. Clemens, and F. J. Lynch, Attorneys for Plaintiff* (Topeka, n.d.), pp. 8, 10-11, 12-13, 15, 17-19; Cartwright *v.* Board of Education of the City of Coffeyville, *Kansas Reports*, vol. 72, p. 32; Michael J. Brodhead and O. Gene Clanton, "G. C. Clemens: The 'Sociable Socialist,'" *Kansas Historical Quarterly* (Winter 1974): 498-99. For Clemens' earlier anti-Negro views, see above, p. 59.

41. Harvey P. Moyer, ed., *Songs of Socialism* (Chicago, 1902), pp. 35-36.

42. A. T. Cruzner, "The Negro or the Race Problem," *International Socialist Review* 4 (November 1903): 264.

43. *The Worker*, July 19, 1903.

44. Ira Kipnis, *The American Socialist Movement, 1897-1912* (New York, 1952), p. 133; *The Worker*, July 26, 1903.

45. Eugene V. Debs, "The Negro in the Class Struggle," *International Socialist Review* 4 (November 1903): 258-59; "The Negro and His Nemesis," ibid. (January 1904): 396.

46. Clarence Meily, "Socialism and the Negro," ibid., 4 (November 1903): 267.

47. *Fort Worth* (Texas) *Register*, October 10, 1903.

48. Newspaper clipping from the *Indianapolis World*, Eugene V. Debs Scrapbooks, Tamiment Institute, Bobst Library, New York University.

49. Cable's *The Silent South*, published in 1885, aroused white supremacist opposition to him, an opposition that increased after publication of *The Negro Question* in 1888.

50. Newspaper clipping from the *Indianapolis World*, Eugene V. Debs Scrapbooks,

Tamiment Institute, Bobst Library, New York University.

51. *The Worker*, July 26, 1903.

52. *The Workers' Call* (Chicago), October 26, 1901; *The Worker*, May 18, 1902, July 26, 1903, October 2, 1904; *Social Democratic Herald*, July 25, 1903.

53. Eugene V. Debs, "The Negro in the Class Struggle," op. cit., pp. 259-60; "The Negro and His Nemesis," op. cit., pp. 395-96; Ray Ginger, *The Bending Cross: A Biography of Eugene Victor Debs* (New Brunswick, N.J., 1949), p. 260.

54. *Social Democratic Herald*, January 1904.

55. *International Socialist Review* (November 1903): 259.

56. *Chicago Socialist*, July 9, 1902.

57. Henry R. Pemberton to author, Wayne, Penn., April 10, 1970.

58. Caroline H. Pemberton, *Stephen the Black* (Philadelphia, 1899), pp. 13-14, 174-75. *Stephen the Black* was reprinted by Books for Libraries Press in 1972 as part of the Black Heritage Library collection. The reprint contains no discussion of either the author or the book.

Caroline H. Pemberton also published a novel, *The Charity Girl*, serialized in the *International Socialist Review* in 1901. One chapter was devoted to the Negro and revealed again Pemberton's scorn for the upper-class ladies of Philadelphia, who were devoting themselves to furthering "Special Schools to Train Negroes in Habits of Industry." She described a scene in which these ladies were upset when Negroes suggested that these ladies employ them. The ladies were asked: "How is the negro to become industrious and self-supporting if he is persistently refused employment?" To which one lady replied: "They seemed to be actually *hinting* at us to employ them! Imagine!" (Chapter X, *International Socialist Review*, vol. II, August 1901, p. 27.)

59. Ibid., pp. 176-77. For a more detailed discussion of the novel, see my article "Caroline Hollingsworth Pemberton: Philadelphia Socialist Champion of Black Equality," *Pennsylvania History* 43 (July 1976): 229-34.

60. *Stephen the Black*, pp. 204-5.

61. Ibid., pp. 211-13.

62. Ibid., pp. 214-15.

63. Ibid., pp. 216-17.

64. Ibid., pp. 240-43.

65. Ibid., pp. 246-47.

66. For an analysis of *Doctor Huguet*, see John Patterson, "Alliance and Antipathy: Ignatius Donnelly's Ambivalent Vision in Doctor Huguet," *American Quarterly* 22 (Winter 1970): 824-45.

67. The letters are discussed in some detail in Foner, "Caroline Hollingsworth Pemberton," op. cit., pp. 235-38.

68. *Springfield Republican*, April 17, June 6, 1899, September 11, 1890; *The Christian Recorder*, May 11, 1899; *The Public*, May 16, 1899; *City and State*, May 11, 1899.

69. *Springfield Republican*, May 14, 1900.

70. *Literary Digest* 11 (May 26, 1900): 630, and *Boston Transcript* reprinted in ibid.

71. Pemberton's conversion to socialism, as she explained in her article, "How I Became a Socialist," was almost by accident. One of her letters in the *Springfield Republican* brought a response from a socialist who "pointed out the overwhelming power of wealth—the plutocratic nature of our government—and suggested that a study of Socialism would throw light on the political situation." At his advice, she read *The Fabian Essays on Socialism* with George Bernard Shaw's opening chapter, "The Economic Basis of Socialism," a work that had already revolutionized the opinion of the British public toward socialism. Although she went on to read William Morris and Edward Bellamy, she had already been converted to socialism by her reading of the work of the British evolu-

tionary socialists. After a good deal of searching—she did not yet know a single socialist—she hunted out the Socialist party of Philadelphia, paid her membership dues, and began attending party meetings (*Springfield Republican*, June 16, 1899, September 11, 1900; Caroline H. Pemberton, "How I Became a Socialist," *The Comrade* 1 [May 1902]: 202).

72. The reference is probably to Pemberton's visit to the "heart of the Black Belt" in 1897.

73. This view of slavery was given circulation not only in contemporary historical works such as John Fiske's *Old Virginia and Her Neighbors* (Boston, 1897) and Ulrich B. Phillips' *Georgia and State Rights* (Washington, D.C., 1902), but also in the novels of Thomas Nelson Page. It has been revived with great fanfare in Robert William Fogel and Stanley L. Engerman, *Time on the Cross: The Economics of American Negro Slavery* (Boston, 1974).

74. *The Worker*, November 7, 1901.

75. A. M. Simons, "Economic Aspects of Chattel Slavery," *International Socialist Review* (July 1, 1903): 25-33; (August 1903): 95-105; (September 1903): 163-73.

76. Ibid. (September 1903): 173.

77. Such studies include Herbert Aptheker, *American Negro Slave Revolts* (New York, 1943); Bell I. Wiley, *Southern Negroes, 1861-1865* (New Haven, Conn., 1938); Kenneth M. Stampp, *The Peculiar Institution: Slavery in the Ante-Bellum South* (New York, 1956).

78. With an insight rare among socialist papers, *The Worker* pointed out that a vital flaw of Reconstruction following the Civil War was that "when the government—actuated partly by humane sentiment, but more by economic necessity—set the slaves free forty years ago, it carefully refrained from providing them with land or other means of production" (May 18 1902). For a more typical view, see *Appeal to Reason*, July 13, 1903. Paul M. Buhle points out that the typical socialist historiography dealing with Reconstruction could be summed up as follows in relation to blacks: "At best, they were viewed as passive in the critical events during and after the Civil War; at worst, a writer like Simons was capable of sentimentalism toward the beleaguered white South during Reconstruction. In general, Blacks were the props of history" (Paul M. Buhle, "Marxism in the United States, 1900-1940," Ph.D. dissertation, University of Wisconsin, 1975, p. 33).

79. *The Worker*, November 24, 1901.

80. Ibid., December 1, 1901.

81. For a summary of these views, see Lawrence J. Friedman, *The White Savage: Racial Fantasies in the Postbellum South* (Englewood Cliffs, N.J., 1970).

82. *Social Democratic Herald*, September 14, 1901, May 11, 1902.

83. *International Socialist Review* 4 (November 1903): 258-59.

84. See Frederick Douglass, "*Why Is the Negro Lynched?*" *The Lesson of the Hour*, in Philip S. Foner, ed., *The Life and Writings of Frederick Douglass*, vol. 4 (New York, 1955), pp. 491-523, and Ida B. Wells, *Southern Horrors* (New York, 1892); *A Red Record* (New York, 1895); and *Mob Rule in New Orleans* (New York, 1900), all three reprinted in Ida Wells-barnett, *On Lynchings* (New York, 1969).

85. *The Worker*, December 8, 1901.

86. Ibid., December 1, 1901.

87. International Socialist Bureau, "To the Laborers of all Countries," *International Socialist Review* 4 (July 1903): 46; "Resolution on Lynching," *Chicago Socialist*, November 28, 1903; George Haupt, ed., *Bureau Socialiste Internationale: Comptes rendus des reunions manifestes et circulaires, 1900-1907* (Paris, 1969), pp. 90-93. The signers were from England, Germany, Argentina, Australia, Belgium, Bohemia, Bulgaria, Denmark, Spain, the United States, Finland, France, Holland, Hungary, Italy, Japan, and Luxembourg.

88. *International Socialist Review* 4 (1904): 743-44.

CHAPTER 6

1. Jo. A. Parker to James W. Baird, Dallas, December 5, 24, 1902, James W. Baird Papers, Barker Library, University of Texas at Austin.

2. William Mailly to Eugene V. Debs, March 27, 1903, William Mailly Letterpress Book, Socialist Party Papers, Duke University Library.

3. William Mailly to John Chase, March 13, 1903, ibid.; *The Worker*, May 1, 1903.

4. James R. Green, "Socialism and the Southwestern Class Struggle, 1898-1918," op cit., pp. 38-39; William Mailly to A. W. Ricker, March 23, 1903, William Mailly Letterpress Book, Socialist Party Papers, Duke University Library.

5. Green, op. cit., pp. 30-34; Harold A. Shapiro, "The Labor Movement in San Antonio, Texas, 1865-1915," *Southwestern Social Science Quarterly* 36 (1955): 65-68; William Mailly to E. B. Latham, March 19, 1903, William Mailly Letterpress Book, Socialist Party Papers, Duke University Library; *The Southern Socialist*(Bessemer, Ala.) 1, no. 1 (July 1903), photostat copy in Tamiment Institute, Bobst Library, New York University.

6. *The Worker*, May 1, 1903.

7. Ibid., December 20, 1903.

8. Ibid.

9. A. W. Ricker, "Socialism and the Negro," *Appeal to Reason*, September 12, 1903.

10. See ibid., January 24, March 7, April 25, May 2, 9, 16, June 6, 27, September 10, 26, October 24, November 7, 14, 1903.

11. *The Southern Socialist* 1, no. 2 (September 1903): 3, 6, 10; *Birmingham Labor Advocate*, May 9, 1903.

12. *The Worker*, March 29, 1903.

13. Ibid., January 25, 1903.

14. William Mailly to C. J. Johnson, February 27, June 8, 1903, Mailly Letterpress Book, Socialist Party Papers, Duke University Library.

15. *New Orleans Daily Picayune*, September 18, 1903.

16. Ibid., September 20, 1903. The *Daily Picayune* stated that its observations on the "Negro Clause" did not mean it would approve of socialism if a different approach was adopted by the Louisiana party. Socialism might be useful in Europe, but it was "not for the American people" (September 27, 1902).

17. *Dallas Morning News*, September 26, 1903.

18. *Edinburgh Review*, reprinted in Gunnan Johnson, *Racial Ideologies*, vol. 2 (New York, 1905), p. 344.

19. *The Worker*, November 6, 1903.

20. Foner, *Organized Labor and the Black Worker*, pp. 70-73.

21. *Social Democratic Herald*, November 21, 1903; *The Worker*, December 6, 1903.

22. *The Worker*, December 6, 1903.

23. Ibid., November 15, 1903.

24. Ibid., December 6, 1903.

25. Edwin Arnold Brenholz in *Seattle Socialist*, January 17, 1904.

26. *The Worker*, December 20, 1903.

27. A. H. Floaten in *Socialist Party Weekly Bulletin*, December 17, 1903.

28. Eraste Virden, "Negro Locals," *International Socialist Review* 5 (January 1, 1905): 389-92.

29. Ibid., 4 (April 1, 1904): 649.

30. Ibid., p. 626.

31. Ibid., p. 635.

32. Ibid., p. 640.

33. Ibid., p. 645.

34. Ibid., pp. 613-14.

35. Ibid., p. 638.

36. Ibid., pp. 632-33.

37. Ibid., pp. 645-46.

38. National Committee of the Socialist Party, *Proceedings of the National Convention of the Socialist Party Held at Chicago, Illinois, May 1 to 6, 1904* (Chicago, 1904). See also *Wayland's Monthly* (November 1905): 41-45, and Kirk H. Porter and Donald Bruce Johnson, Comps., *National Party Platforms, 1840-1956* (Urbana, Ill., 1956), pp. 140-63.

39. *The Comrade* 3 (August 1904): 132-33.

40. *The Voice of the Negro* (Atlanta), June 1904.

41. For Taylor's address accepting the nomination for president by the National Liberty party, see Philip S. Foner, ed., *The Voice of Black America*, vol. 2 (New York, 1975), pp. 31-35.

42. "The Negro and Socialism," *The Worker*, July 3, 1904.

43. Foner, *History of the Labor Movement*, vol. 3, pp. 395-400.

44. Herbert Shapiro, "The Muckrakers and Negroes," *Phylon* 21 (1970): 80.

45. Upton Sinclair, *The Jungle* (New York, 1961), pp. 270-71.

46. In his appeal for support for Sinclair's publishing venture in the *Appeal to Reason* of November 18, 1905, Jack London made no mention of the racism in *The Jungle*. But then Jack London was himself a leading white supremacist in the Socialist party. See Philip S. Foner, *Jack London: American Rebel* (New York, 1947).

47. The *Chicago Daily Socialist* of December 29, 1906 carried a front-page story on the report of the committee of Atlanta businessmen on the Atlanta Riot which condemned the white mob. However, the paper made no editorial comment.

48. The best study of the Brownsville Affair is John D. Weaver, *The Brownsville Affair* (New York, 1970).

49. The first real comment in the socialist press on the Brownsville Affair came years after the incident had occurred. On June 18, 1910, the *New York Call*, in an estimate of Theodore Roosevelt, noted: "A booster of the square deal, he dismissed a regiment of negro troops, because they refused to tell what in all likelihood they did not know." On October 16, 1912, the *Chicago Evening World*, successor to the *Chicago Daily Socialist*, had a brief piece on the Brownsville Affair. It consisted of an answer to the question from a reader inquiring if any of the "colored soldiers" had ever been reinstated after they were discharged. The *Evening World* simply informed the reader that, after an investigation by the military, fourteen soldiers of the three companies were declared eligible for reenlistment and entitled to back pay for the entire time of their dismissal. Nothing was said about the 153 blacks who might still be alive and interested in resuming their careers as soldiers. Nor was anything said about what socialists might do to help rectify the injustice.

50. Socialist Party, *Weekly Bulletin*, January 2, 24, 1907. There were a large number of abstentions on the vote.

51. Socialist Party, *Weekly Bulletin*, March 23, 1907.

52. Ibid., April 6, 13, 1907.

53. *Monthly Bulletin of the Socialist Party*, November 1904; *Weekly People*, December 3, 1904; De Leon, op. cit., pp. 117-18.

54. Sally M. Miller, "Americans and the Second International," *Proceedings of the American Philosophical Society* 120 (October 1976): 383-84.

55. Morris Hillquit, "Emigration in the United States," *International Socialist Review* 8 (July 1907): 74-75; Victor Berger, "We Will Stand by the Real American Proletariat," *Social Democratic Herald*, October 12, 1907; Ernest Untermann, "As to Special Exclusion," ibid., November 9, 1907; *Chicago Daily Socialist*, November 1, 14, 18, 1907; *The Worker*, January 25, February 22, 1908.

56. *Monthly Bulletin of the Socialist Party*, December 1907; Kipnis, op. cit., pp. 277-79.

57. *Proceedings, National Congress of the Socialist Party, Held at Chicago, Illinois, May 10 to 17, 1908* (Chicago, 1908), p. 105.

58. Ibid., pp. 110-11.

59. Ibid., pp. 107, 111.

60. Ibid., pp. 116, 121.

61. *New York Evening Call*, July 2, 1908.

62. Socialist Pamphlet No. 25, Wilshire Book Co., New York, 1908, copy in Tamiment Institute, Bobst Library, New York University. It is a measure of the contradictions in the Socialist party on the Negro question that Gaylord Wilshire who published this pamphlet wrote in 1907: "We may talk as much as we please of the brotherhood of man, but under the competitive system the brotherhood of man has no place. Every man for himself and the devil take the hindmost is the rule today" (*Wilshire's Magazine*, January 1907, p. 6).

63. Debs' biographer, Ray Ginger, devotes twenty-three pages of *The Bending Cross* to the 1908 campaign but fails to mention the Passage pamphlet.

64. Passage combined extracts from both the *International Socialist Review* articles under the general heading "The Negro in the Class Struggle."

65. Roosevelt's order dismissing the Negro soldiers during the Brownsville Affair and disqualifying them for service in either the military or the civil service of the United States had been executed by Secretary of War William Howard Taft who became the Republican presidential candidate in 1908. Because of the Brownsville Affair, blacks were more ready than ever before to bolt the Republican party.

66. For a discussion of the proslavery argument that the chattel slave was better off than the wage slave, see Wilfred Carsel, "The Slaveholders' Indictment of Northern Wage Slavery," *Journal of Southern History* 6 (November 1940): 514-20.

67. Clyde J. Wright, "The Colored Man's Chance," *Chicago Daily Socialist*, September 15, 1908.

68. See, for example, John Ellis, "The Lesson of Garrison's Life," *The Worker*, December 30, 1905, and *Chicago Daily Socialist*, May 12, 1911.

69. "Sojourner Truth a Great Woman," *New York Call*, February 12, 1911.

70. Weaver, op. cit., p. 275.


CHAPTER 7

1. *Ohio Socialist Bulletin*, February 1909. This is the only reference to Reverend Euell in the socialist press.

2. *Chicago Daily Socialist*, May 11, 1908; John Mather, *Who's Who of the Colored Race* (Chicago, 1921); A. W. Ricker in *Appeal to Reason*, October 31, 1903.

3. Rev. George W. Woodbey, *What to Do and How to Do It or Socialism vs. Capitalism*, *Wayland's Monthly* no. 40 (August 1903): 4; A. W. Ricker in *Appeal to Reason*, October 31, 1903. Correspondence with the Omaha Public Library, the University of Nebraska Library, the Nebraska State Historical Society, and the United Methodist Historical Society at Nebraska Wesleyan University has failed to turn up any information on Reverend Woodbey and his role as a Populist and socialist in Nebraska.

4. *Los Angeles Socialist*, July 12, 1902.

5. Ibid., December 17, 1904; *Common Sense* (Los Angeles), October 27, 1906.

6. *Los Angeles Socialist*, May 2, 1903.

7. *Common Sense* (Los Angeles), August 5, 1905. The *San Diegan-Sun* carried one item on the case. Under the headline "Battery Charge," it reported on July 11, 1905, that officer George H. Cooley was served with a warrant charging him with battery. "The complaining witness was Rev. G. W. Woodby, the colored Socialist orator, who has frequently

been heard at the gathering of the adherents of the party in this city."

8. *Common Sense* (Los Angeles), October 8, 1904, March 7, April 11, 1908.

9. A. W. Ricker in *Appeal to Reason*, October 31, 1903.

10. Ibid. Robert Blatchford's *Merrie England*, published in London in 1894, was a book of twenty-six chapters and 210 pages in which the superiority of socialism over capitalism is brilliantly set forth in clear, plain language.

11. Woodbey, op. cit., p. 3.

12. *Chicago Daily Socialist*, May 11, 1908.

13. Woodbey, op. cit., pp. 5-7.

14. Ibid., pp. 15-19.

15. Ibid., p. 20.

16. Ibid., pp. 20-21.

17. Ibid., p. 24.

18. Ibid., pp. 37-38.

19. Ibid., p. 44.

20. Compare, for example, Woodbey's discussion of an international credit system under socialism (pp. 36-37) with Bellamy's discussion of the same system in Chapter 8 of *Looking Backward*.

21. In a letter to William Dean Howells a few months after the publication of *Looking Backward*, Bellamy wrote that "the word socialist is one I could never well stomach. In the first place it is a foreign word in itself, and equally foreign in all its suggestions. . . . Whatever German and French reformers may choose to call themselves, socialist is not a good name for a party to succeed with in America. No such party can or ought to succeed which is not wholly and enthusiastically American and patriotic in spirit and suggestions." Quoted in Arthur E. Morgan, *Edward Bellamy* (New York, 1941), p. 374.

22. For a discussion of *The Iron Heel*, see Philip S. Foner, *Jack London: American Rebel* (reprint, New York, 1964), pp. 87-97.

23. Woodbey, op. cit., p. 7.

24. G. W. Woodbey, *The Bible and Socialism: A Conversation Between Two Preachers* (San Diego, 1904), Preface.

25. Ibid., p. 7.

26. Ibid., pp. 69, 83, 90.

27. Ibid., p. 69.

28. Ibid., p. 96.

29. G. W. Woodbey, *The Distribution of Wealth* (San Diego, Calif., 1910), p. 7.

30. Ibid., pp. 41, 44-45.

31. Ibid., pp. 54-55.

32. Ibid., p. 68. Woodbey's fellow-Californian socialist closed his letters, "Yours for the Revolution, Jack London."

33. *Proceedings of the National Convention . . . 1904*, pp. 47-48.

34. Ibid., p. 182.

35. *Proceedings, National Convention . . . 1908*, pp. 208-9.

36. Ibid., pp. 290-91.

37. Ibid., p. 106.

38. Ibid., pp. 106-7.

39. Ibid., pp. 107-8.

40. The most detailed discussion of the 1908 convention in relation to the immigration issue is Charles Leinenweber, "The American Socialist Party and 'New' Immigrants," *Science & Society* 32 (Winter 1968): 6-12. It does not even mention Woodbey's speech in opposition to the resolution calling for a study of the necessity for immigration restriction.

41. *Proceedings, National Convention . . . 1908*, p. 163.

42. Ibid., p. 164.

43. Neither Ira Kipnis nor Ray Ginger mentions Woodbey's nomination in their discussion of the 1908 convention.

44. *New York Evening Call*, November 2, 1908.

45. Rev. G. W. Woodbey, "Why the Negro Should Vote the Socialist Ticket," four-page leaflet, undated, copy in Socialist Party Papers, Duke University Library.

46. G. W. Woodbey, "The New Emancipation," *Chicago Daily Socialist*, January 18, 1909.

47. G. W. Woodbey, "Socialist Agitation," ibid., January 4, 1909.

48. Philip S. Foner, *History of the Labor Movement in the United States*, vol. 4 (New York, 1965), p. 173.

49. *San Francisco Call, San Francisco Chronicle*, February 1-8, 1908.

50. *Chicago Daily Socialist*, May 11, 1908.

51. *San Francisco Call*, June 12, 1908.

52. In a letter to the author, Harland B. Adams of San Diego summarized a conversation he had with Dennis V. Allen, a black San Diegan who in the years 1912 to 1916, as a postal clerk, delivered mail to the home of Reverend Woodbey. According to Mr. Allen, Reverend Woodbey lived at 12 Twenty-Ninth Street, San Diego. He described Woodbey as "a rather dark Negro slender and abut 5 feet 11 inches. Mrs. Woodbey was extremely stout, almost to the point that with her age and weight, it was difficult for her to get about. She was known by nearly everyone in the small Negro population of San Diego at that time, as Mother Mary or Mother Woodbey. She was a devout Baptist Christian and regularly attended the Baptist Church at 29th and Clay, which still exists." The Woodbeys, Allen continued, owned the property where he lived, as well as the house next door which he rented to a Negro who was a veteran of the Civil War.

According to Allen, he was in a group that drafted Reverend Woodbey as pastor of the Mt. Zion Baptist Church, and was also part of the group that had him removed. Although he was extremely popular and drew large crowds to his sermons, his dismissal "was a direct result of mixing too much Socialist with his Bible, and this the members of his church resented."

Allen organized the San Diego Race Relations Society in 1924 and held the post of president for thirty-six years.

53. Foner, *History of the Labor Movement*, vol. 4, pp. 194-95.

54. Ibid., pp. 199-200.

55. *San Diego Union*, February 22, 1912. The authorities ignored the charges.

56. *The Citizen*, reprinted in *St. Louis Labor*, April 27, 1912. In her study "The I.W.W. Free Speech Movement San Diego, 1912," *Journal of San Diego History* (Winter 1973): 25-33, Rosalie Shanks does not once mention Reverend Woodbey.

57. *Industrial Worker*, October 17, 1912; *The Wooden Shoe* (Los Angeles), January 22, 1914.

58. *California Social Democrat*, December 12, 1914.

59. *New York Call*, December 16, 1911.

60. Rev. George W. Slater, Jr., "How and Why I Became a Socialist," *Chicago Daily Socialist*, September 8, 1908.

61. Cf. Rev. George W. Slater, Jr., "The Cat's Out," and "An Eye-Opener," *Chicago Daily Socialist*, September 29, October 20, 1908.

62. Rev. George W. Slater, Jr., "Booker T. Washington's Error," ibid., September 22, 1908.

63. At a conference held at Hampton (Virginia) Industrial School in 1908, black educators pointed out that graduates of Hampton who had been trained as skilled workers "complained that they had not been able to work at their trades because (they are) ex-

cluded from the union." Quoted in Foner, *Organized Labor and the Black Worker*, p. 79.

64. Ida Wells-Barnett, "The Negro's Quest for Work," *Chicago Daily News*, reprinted in *New York Call*, July 23, 1911.

65. Quoted in Foner, *Organized Labor and the Black Worker*, p. 124.

66. W.E.B. Du Bois, *The Negro Artisan* (Atlanta, 1902), pp. 180-85.

67. Foner, *The Voice of Black America*, vol. 1, pp. 640-43.

68. Rev. Geo. W. Slater, Jr., "Pullman Porter Pity," *Chicago Daily Socialist*, December 22, 1908.

69. Rev. George W. Slater, Jr., "Abraham Lincoln a Socialist," ibid., October 6, 1908. For Lincoln's statements on labor and capital, see Roy F. Basler, et al., eds., *The Collected Works of Abraham Lincoln* (New Brunswick, N.J., 1942), vol. 2, p. 384, vol. 3, p. 478, vol. 8, pp. 259-60. For a discussion of Lincoln's position on labor and capital, see Foner, *History of the Labor Movement in the United States*, vol. 1, pp. 291-92, and Eric Foner, *Free Soil, Free Labor, Free Men: The Ideology of the Republican Party Before the Civil War* (New York, 1970), pp. 12, 16, 20, 23, 29-30, 32.

70. Rev. George W. Slater, Jr., "The Cat's Out," *Chicago Daily Socialist*, September 29, 1908.

71. Rev. George W. Slater, Jr., "Reaching the 1,000,000," ibid., November 4, 1908.

72. Rev. George W. Slater, Jr., "Mine Eyes Have Seen It," ibid., November 9, 1908.

73. Rev. George W. Slater, Jr., "The New Abolitionists," ibid., January 4, 1909.

74. Rev. George W. Slater, Jr., "The Colored Strikebreaker," ibid., January 14, 1909.

75. "The Colored Man Welcome," ibid., January 4, 1909.

76. Rev. George W. Slater, Jr., "Race Problems' Socialist Cure," ibid., March 27, 1909.

77. *New York Call*, December 16, 1909. For the efforts of Local New York to recruit Negro members and win Negro votes for the Socialist party, see below, pp. 211-14.

78. Boris Newell, Assistant Director, Clinton Public Library to author, March 9, 1966. There is no information about Reverend Slater in the State Historical Society of Iowa.

79. *Cleveland Citizen*, September 14, 1912.

80. Rev. Geo. W. Slater, Jr., "The Negro and Socialism," *The Christian Socialist*, July 1, 1913.

81. Rev. Geo. W. Slater, Jr., "Lincoln and the Laborer," ibid., February 1915.

82. Rev. Geo. W. Slater, Jr., "Socialism and Social Service," ibid., February 1915.

83. George W. Slater, Jr., to John Fitzpatrick, Clinton, Iowa, 3/37/1921, John Fitzpatrick Papers, Chicago Historical Society.

84. Rev. S. C. Garrison, "The Lover of Humanity," *The Christian Socialist*, February 1915.

85. "Was He a Failure," ibid.

86. Of all the black socialists mentioned in this chapter, only one, Reverend George W. Slater, Jr., appears in any history of American socialism, and then only his 1913 article in *The Christian Socialist* ("The Negro and Socialism") is mentioned. See James Weinstein, *The Decline of Socialism in America 1912-1915* (New York, 1969), p. 71.

87. *Amsterdam News* (New York), June 19, 1943. In *The Crisis* of September 1918, W.E.B. Du Bois wrote: "Miller is a clean, frank fighter, a radical Socialist and a clear speaker and writer" (pp. 235-36).


CHAPTER 8

1. W.E.B. Du Bois, "Of Mr. Booker T. Washington and Others," in *The Souls of Black Folk* (New York, 1903), pp. 47-60. For an effective answer to the frequent defense of Wash-

ington on the ground that he strove secretly to achieve equality for blacks while publicly seemingly to surrender the struggle for equality, see Louis R. Harlan, "The Secret Life of Booker T. Washington," *Journal of Southern History* 37 (August 1971): 393-416.

2. Herbert Aptheker, ed., *A Documentary History of the Negro People in the United States* (New York, 1951), pp. 900-1.

3. Ibid., pp. 902-10. See also Elliott M. Rudwick, "The Niagara Movement," *Journal of Negro History* 43 (July 1957): 177-82.

4. For an excellent survey of the reviews of *The Souls of Black Folk* at the time of publication, see the introduction by Herbert Aptheker to the 1973 reprint of the book, pp. 14-35.

5. *Conservator* (May 1903): 43-44. The review is signed "T," but there is no doubt it was by Traubel. It is listed as his work in Henry Saunders, comp., *Complete Index to "The Conservator"* (Toronto, 1920).

6. André Tridon, "Socialism and the Race Question," *The Worker*, October 20, 1906.

7. As treasurer of the Cosmopolitan Club, Tridon was authorized to accept inquiries. Ovington later listed Tridon as the club president, but contemporary accounts called him treasurer.

Reverend George Frazier Miller, who was recruited into the Socialist party by Tridon, later mentioned that Tridon had told him that he decided to devote himself to the battle against racism after a visit to the South where he observed that the black man who would not work was the only man he saw working. (Rev. George Miller, *A Reply to the Political Plea of Bishop Cleland K. Nielson and Bishop F. Gaelon, at Cathedral of St. John the Divine in the City of New York, Saturday Evening, October, 1913*, p. 8. Copy in Howard University Library.) Ovington listed Reverend Miller as "one of the best members" of the Cosmopolitan Club (Mary White Ovington, "Reminiscences," *Baltimore Afro-American*, October 1, 1932).

8. Mary White Ovington to Oswald Garrison Villard, October 8, 1906, Oswald Garrison Villard Papers, Houghton Library, Harvard University.

9. The early history of the Cosmopolitan Club movement is described in a paper by Louis Lochner, one of its founders, presented at 1911 First Universal Races Congress. See Gustav Spiller, ed., *Papers on Inter-Racial Problems Communicated to the First Universal Races Congress Held at the University of London July 26-29, 1911* (London, 1911), pp. 439-42, reprint edition with an introduction by Herbert Aptheker (New York, 1970).

10. Charles Flint Kellogg, *NAACP: A History of the National Association for the Advancement of Colored People*, vol. 1, 1909-1920 (Baltimore, 1967), pp. 3-7. John E. Milholland, a wealthy New Yorker, was active in promoting primary election reform, prison reform, pacifism, labor reform, woman suffrage, and federal aid to education as well as political rights for Negroes. There is still no biography of Milholland, but there is an obituary biography in the *New York Times* of July 1, 1925, and a sketch in Charles Edward Russell, *Bare Hands and Stone Walls* (New York, 1933), pp. 231-35.

11. For discussions of the relationship between imperialism and intensification of racism in the United States, see Philip Wayne Kennedy, "The Concept of Racial Superiority and United States Imperialism, 1890-1910," Ph.D. dissertation, St. Louis University, 1962; Herbert Aptheker, "American Imperialism and White Chauvinism," in *Afro-American History: The Modern Era* (New York, 1971), pp. 99-108, and Robert C. Beisner, *Twelve Against Empire: The Anti-Imperialists, 1898-1900* (New York, 1968), pp. 232-33.

Some anti-imperialists started out as racists and as a result of their anti-imperialist experience became involved in the battle against racism in the United States. See Daniel B. Schirmer, *Republic or Empire: American Resistance to the Philippine War* (Cambridge, Mass., 1972), pp. 255-60.

12. Mary White Ovington, "Reminiscences," *Baltimore Afro-American*, September 17, 24, 1932. Ovington's "Reminiscences" appeared in twenty-four installments between

September 1932 and February 1933 in the *Afro-American*. A partial summary appears in the sketch by Gilbert Osofsky, "Progressivism and the Negro: New York, 1900-1915," *American Quarterly* 16 (Spring 1964): 159-63.

13. James M. McPherson, *The Abolitionist Legacy: From Reconstruction to the NAACP* (Princeton, N.J., 1975). McPherson is very weak on the role of the socialists in the founding of the NAACP. He calls Mary White Ovington a "romantic racialist" and a social worker, but does not indicate that she was an active member of the Socialist party (p. 343). He discusses the Cosmopolitan Club without once mentioning its socialist origins (pp. 374-76). On the racial question, he generally accepts the simplistic approach to the role of the socialists by linking the "Left in American politics" to the view, common in America, that Negroes were "altogether inferior to the whites," observing that "the Left in American politics thought no differently." He continues: "'Almost all socialists,' writes an historian of the Socialist Party of America, regarded the Negro 'as occupying a lower position on the evolutionary scale than the white'" (p. 339). His sole source for this sweeping assertion is R. Laurence Moore's very meagerly researched study "Flawed Fraternity—American Socialist Response to the Negro, 1901-1912," *Historian* 32 (1969): 12. But the present chapter also reveals how totally one-dimensional is this approach.

14. Ibid.

15. Mary White Ovington to W.E.B. Du Bois, June 10, 1904, in Herbert Aptheker, ed., *The Correspondence of W.E.B. Du Bois, 1877-1934*, vol. 1 (Amherst, Mass., 1973), pp. 76-77. Du Bois' articles on New York City appeared in the *New York Times Magazine* of November 17, 24, 1901.

16. *Baltimore Afro-American*, September 24, 1932.

17. Mary W. Ovington, "The Negro Family in New York," *Charities*, October 7, 1905, pp. 132-34.

18. Mary White Ovington, *The Walls Came Tumbling Down* (New York, 1947).

19. *Baltimore Afro-American*, October 1, 1932.

20. *New York Herald*, April 30-May 1, 1908; *New York World*, April 28, 1908.

21. Oswald Garrison Villard to F. J. Garrison, April 29, 1908, Oswald Garrison Villard Papers, Houghton Library, Harvard University.

22. *New York World*, April 28, 1908.

23. *New York Herald, New York American, New York Times*, April 28, 1908.

24. *New York American*, April 28, 1908.

25. *New York Times*, April 29, 1908; Oswald Garrison Villard to Mary White Ovington, April 20, 1908, Oswald Garrison Villard Papers, Houghton Library, Harvard University.

26. *New York Herald*, April 30, 1908; *Washington Evening Post*, April 29, 1908; *Richmond Times-Dispatch*, May 1, 1908; *Savannah News*, April 30, 1908; *Charleston News & Courier*, May 1, 1908; *Birmingham Age-Herald*, May 1, 1908.

27. Ovington, *The Walls Came Tumbling Down*, p. 46.

28. Ibid.

29. *Birmingham Age-Herald*, May 1, 1908.

30. Mary White Ovington in *New York Evening Post*, April 29, 1908; Hamilton Holt in *New York Times*, April 29, 1908; André Tridon in *New York Herald*, April 30, 1908.

31. Mary White Ovington in *New York Evening Post*, April 29, 1908.

32. Kellogg, op. cit., pp. 71-72. "The Cosmopolitan Club Dinner taught me how to read the morning paper," Ovington commented later (*The Walls Came Tumbling Down*, p. 46).

33. James F. Morton, Jr., "On the Promotion of Race Antipathy," *The Public*, May 5, 1908.

34. "Colored Woman Protests," *New York Times*, April 30, 1908, and John B. Syphox in *New York World*, April 30, 1908.

35. "Yellow Journalism and Race Prejudice," *New York Age*, May 14, 1908.

36. *Horizon*, March 1908. The article also reprinted the text by James F. Morton, Jr., in *The Public*, calling it one of the few that had "given a true account of the dinner."

37. *Chicago Daily Socialist*, May 5, 1908.

38. *New York Call*, June 1, 1908.

39. Undated document, Socialist Party Papers, Duke University Library.

40. *New York Herald*, April 29, 1908.

41. Oswald Garrison Villard to Mary White Ovington, April 29, 1908, Oswald Garrison Villard Papers, Houghton Library, Harvard University.

42. Kellogg, op. cit., pp. 71-72.

43. Harlan, op. cit., p. 414.

44. Mary White Ovington in *New York Evening Post*, April 29, 1908.

45. *Baltimore Afro-American*, October 22, 1932.

46. *New York Herald*, April 29, 1908.

47. *Baltimore Afro-American*, October 15, 1932.

48. Herbert Aptheker, ed., *The Autobiography of W.E.B. DuBois. A Soliloquy on Viewing My Life from the Last Decade of Its First Century* (New York, 1968), p. 168; Arnold Rampersad, *The Art and Imagination of W.E.B. DuBois* (Cambridge, Mass., 1976), pp. 45-46.

49. Aptheker, ed., *The Correspondence of W.E.B. DuBois*, vol. 1, pp. 81-82.

50. W.E.B. DuBois, "Socialist of the Path," and "Negro and Socialism," *Horizon*, February 1907, and *Horizon*, June 1907, February 1908.

51. Kellogg, op. cit., p. 23*n*.

52. Henry L. Slobodin, "The Niagara Movement," *New York Call*, August 27, 1909.

53. For a study of the forces that led to the Springfield riot and the events during the riot, see James L. Crouthamel, "The Springfield Race Riot of 1908." *Journal of Negro History* 45 (July 1960): 164-81.

54. *Dictionary of American Biography*, vol. 23 (New York, 1958), pp. 689-90; William English Walling to Eugene V. Debs, December 14, 1909, William English Walling Papers, Wisconsin State Historical Society; William English Walling, *Socialism As It Is: A Survey of the World-wide Revolutionary Movement* (New York, 1912), pp. 79-80. For Anna Strunsky's relations with Jack London, see Foner, *Jack London: American Rebel*, pp. 39-40.

55. William English Walling, "The Founding of the N.A.A.C.P.," *The Crisis* (July 1929): 226.

56. *Chicago Daily Socialist*, August 19, 20, 25, 1908.

57. Ibid., August 19, 22, 1908.

58. *New York Evening Call*, August 18, 1908. On August 22, the *Call* reprinted an editorial on the riot published in the *Chicago Daily Socialist*.

59. William English Walling, "The Race War in the North," *The Independent*, September 3, 1908, pp. 539-34. Benjamin R. Tillman of South Carolina and J. K. Vardaman of Mississippi were both outspoken white racists and open advocates of Negro disfranchisement and second-class status for blacks. They regularly vilified the Negro people in speeches in the U.S. Senate.

60. *New York Evening Call*, September 8, 1908.

61. Mary White Ovington, "Reminiscences," *Baltimore Afro-American*, November 26, 1932; Ovington, *The Walls Came Tumbling Down*, pp. 102-03; Mary White Ovington, *How the National Association of Colored People Began*, pamphlet (New York, 1914), p. 1. Walling had already outlined his plan for a national biracial organization to Charles Edward Russell; see Russell, *Bare Hands and Stone Walls*, p. 224.

62. E. C. Stickel to Chas. E. Russell, May 14, 1904, Charles Edward Russell Papers, Library of Congress; Charles Edward Russell, "The Faith Upon Which I Stand," speeches delivered in Quinn Chapel, Chicago, November 29, 1912, copy in ibid.

For Russell's tribute to his abolitionist father, see Charles Edward Russell, *A Pioneer Editor in Early Iowa: A Sketch of the Life of Edward Russell* (Washington, D.C., 1941).

63. Kellogg, op. cit., pp. 11-12; Walling, "The Founding of the N.A.A.C.P.," op. cit., p. 226; Mary White Ovington, "William English Walling," *The Crisis* (November 1936): 335.

64. Kellogg, op. cit., pp. 12-13; Josephine Goldmark, *Impatient Crusader: Florence Kelley's Life Work* (Urbana, Ill., 1953), p. 143.

65. For the text of Villard's "Call" and the full list of signers, see Kellogg, op. cit., pp. 297-99.

66. Ibid., pp. 297-98; *Chicago Daily Socialist*, February 13, 1909.

67. Villard's "Call" also received little attention. The *New York Age* of February 18, 1912, simply mentioned that a call had been issued for a conference "for the discussion of the present state of the Negro."

68. Kellogg, for example, does not even mention the Russell-Walling "Call" (op. cit., pp. 12-15).

69. *Survey* 22 (June 12, 1909): 407-9; Philip S. Foner, ed., *W.E.B. Du Bois Speaks: Speeches and Addresses, 1890-1919* (New York, 1970), p. 187. Writing in *Horizon* in November 1909, Du Bois called the National Negro Conference the most significant event of the year.

70. Cf. *Proceedings of the National Negro Conference, New York, May 31 and June 1, 1909*, n.d., n.p.

71. Ibid., pp. 79-92; Aptheker, ed., *A Documentary History of the Negro People*, pp. 916-24.

72. *New York Call*, June 1, 2, 1909.

73. Robert Hunter, "The Emancipation of the Negro," *New York Call*, May 31, 1909; *Chicago Daily Socialist*, May 31, 1909.

74. *New York Evening Call*, June 3, 1909.

75. Oswald Garrison Villard to Francis Jackson Garrison, May 17, 1910, Oswald Garrison Villard Papers, Houghton Library, Harvard University.

76. *The Crisis* (March 1920): 241; B. Joyce Ross, *J. E. Spingarn and the Rise of the NAACP, 1911-1939* (New York, 1972), pp. 19-22.

77. As we shall see below, for a brief period in 1912 Du Bois was a member of the Socialist party. Charles Edward Russell delivered two speeches at the conference: "How the National Association for the Advancement of Colored People Was Born," and "The Faith Upon Which I Stand."

78. *Chicago Daily Socialist*, April 27, 1912. According to Nancy J. Weiss, several of the "most influential board members of the . . . (National) Urban League were self-declared Socialists." But she mentions only Ruth Standish Baldwin, wife of the railway magnate, as a member of the Socialist party. She does not note that, quite unlike nearly all socialists, Mrs. Baldwin was a fervent admirer of Booker T. Washington (Nancy J. Weiss, *The National Urban League* [New York, 1974], pp. 39-40, 51, 56, 61, 62).

In his article "Progressivism and the Negro: White Liberals and the Early NAACP," *The Historian* 38 (November 1975): 58-78, William Stueck makes only one reference to the role of socialists in founding the NAACP, and that is in a footnote on page 70.

CHAPTER 9

1. Aptheker, ed., *The Correspondence of W.E.B. Du Bois*, vol. 1, pp. 81-82.

2. Charles E. Kerr, editor of the *Review*, probably had not bargained for such an extensive study. In his conclusion, Rubinow admitted that he might have played "a successful confidence game" with the editor, noting half humorously: "For surely Comrade Kerr

would never have agreed to accept a series of fifteen articles about the forsaken negro, for whom we have until now shown so very little concern." See *International Socialist Review* (May 1910): 1010.

3. Du Bois first used the passage in the Address *To the Nations of the World* which he wrote in 1900 for the Pan-African Association Conference in London. It became famous when it appeared in the first paragraph of *The Souls of Black Folk* in 1903: "Gentle Reader; for the problem of the Twentieth Century is the problem of the color-line."

4. I. M. Robbins, "The Economic Aspects of the Negro Problem," *International Socialist Review* (February 1908): 480-81.

5. Ibid., June 1910, pp. 1113, 1115-16.

6. Ibid., p. 1117.

7. *New York Call*, November 2, 1908, July 12, November 29, 1909, April 11, 1910, January 25, 1911.

8. Gilbert Osofsky, *Harlem: The Making of a Ghetto* (New York, 1963), pp. 80-88, 105.

9. *The Worker*, June 9, August 18, 1906.

10. *New York Call*, January 6, 1911.

11. Ibid., January 11, 1911; Nils Uhl in *New York Call* and *Call*'s editorial comment in issue of October 2, 1911.

12. Ibid., October 23, 1911. In its issue of September 1908, *Horizon*, the official organ of the Niagara Movement, reprinted an excerpt from an editorial in the single-tax weekly, *The Public* (September 18, 1908), entitled "Negro with a Capital 'N.'" Explaining why it spelled Negro with a capital "N," when so few other publications did, *The Public* declared: "The spelling of Negro with a little 'n' may well be offensive to sensitive persons of that race, and we see no other reason for refusing to capitalize the word than a positive intention to offend or indifference to giving offence, unless it be the ignorance of English usage."

13. A week after publishing Du Bois' letter, the *Call* carried an article in which the word Negro was spelled throughout with a small "n." For an excellent discussion of the historical development of the use of the capital "N" in Negro, see Donald Grant and Mildred Bricker Grant, "Some Notes on the Capital 'N,'" *Phylon* 36 (December 1975): 435-43.

14. *New York Call*, January 17, 20, 1911.

15. Samuel M. Romansky to Julius Gerber, New York, October 12, 1911, Local New York, Socialist Party Papers, Tamiment Institute, Bobst Library, New York University.

16. Julius Gerber to Samuel M. Romansky, October 17, 1911, Minutes of the Executive Committee, Local New York, October 18, 1911, ibid.

17. There is a need of a biography of Hubert H. Harrison.

18. By the *Tuskegee Machine* is meant the power exerted by Booker T. Washington and his allies in dominating segments of the Afro-American press and institutions (through supplying money) and in using political influence with the Republican party leadership to reward pro-Washington blacks with jobs and punish those who opposed his views. While the term *Tuskegee Machine* was not used publicly, it was universally understood.

19. Charles W. Anderson to Booker T. Washington, September 10, October 30, 1912, Booker T. Washington Papers, Box 15, Library of Congress.

20. *New York Call*, December 16, 1911.

21. John Burfeind to Julius Gerber, November 25, 1911, Local New York, Socialist Party Papers, Tamiment Institute, Bobst Library, New York University.

22. Minutes of the Executive Committee, Local New York, November 8, 1911, ibid.

23. *New York Call*, November 28, December 4, 16, 26, 1911.

24. The original of "An Appeal" in the form of a circular is in New York, Socialist Party Papers, Tamiment Institute, Bobst Library, New York University.

25. Minutes of the Executive Committee meeting, Local New York, February 28, 1912, ibid.

26. *New York Call*, December 16, 1911. See also issue of December 29, 1911.

27. Ibid., December 6, 1911.

28. Ibid., December 27, 1911.

29. Ibid., January 9, 1912.

30. Ibid., December 6, 1911.

31. Ibid., January 20, 24, 27, February 12, 1912.

32. Ibid., January 20, 1912.

33. Minutes of the Executive Committee meeting, Local New York, February 28, 1912, Local New York, Socialist Party Papers, Tamiment Institute, Bobst Library, New York University.

34. Incomplete letter by Hubert H. Harrison, undated but probably February 20 or 21, 1912, ibid.

35. Report of Secretary of Local New York for the Year 1912 to the Central Committee, Local New York, ibid.

36. Harrison also published articles in *The Masses* under the pseudonym "Piet Vlag," but these were usually of a literary nature.

37. *New York Call*, February 28, 1912; copies of leaflets announcing lectures by Hubert H. Harrison under the auspices of Branches 4 and 5, in ibid.

38. Foner, *The Voice of Black America*, vol. 2, pp. 82-85.

39. Hubert H. Harrison, "Socialism and the Negro," *International Socialist Review* 12 (March 1912): 65-72; "The Black Man's Burden," ibid. (April 1912): 660-63; (May 1912): 762-64.

40. Joel August Rogers, *World's Great Men of Color*, vol. 2 (New York, 1943), pp. 611-19. Rogers' biographical sketch of Harrison is the only useful study of the man published. A briefer sketch is Irwin Marcus, "Hubert Harrison: Negro Advocate," *Negro History Bulletin* 34 (January 1971): 18-19.

41. *New York Call*, November 19, 27, 1912.

42. *International Socialist Review* (July 1912): 832.

43. *New York Call*, December 26, 1911.

44. Philip S. Foner, *History of the Labor Movement in the United States*, vol. 4 (New York, 1965), pp. 124-27, 396-97; William D. Haywood, *Big Bill Haywood's Book* (New York, 1927), p. 246.

45. "Resolutions of Protest," in Local New York, Socialist Party Papers, Tamiment Institute, Bobst Library, New York University. Among the other party members who signed were William English Walling, Walter Lippmann, Margaret M. Sanger, Max Eastman, and J. Phelps Stokes.

46. Marcus, op. cit., p. 18.

47. Minutes, Central Committee, Local New York, December 13, 1913, Tamiment Institute, Bobst Library, New York University; Hubert H. Harrison, "Socialism and the Negro," *International Socialist Review* 12 (March 1912): 69-70; "What Haywood Says on Political Action," ibid. (February 1913): 623.

48. Minutes, Meeting of the Executive Committee of Local New York, August 25, 1913, Tamiment Institute, Bobst Library, New York University.

49. Minutes of the Executive Committee of Local New York, October 6, 1913, ibid.

50. Minutes, Central Committee of Local New York, April 11, 16, 21, May 6, 1914, ibid.

51. Minutes, Central Committee of Local New York, May 18, 1914, ibid.

52. Hubert H. Harrison, *The Negro and the Nation* (New York, 1917), Preface, pp. 21-29.

53. Elliott M. Rudwick, *W.E.B. Du Bois: A Study in Minority Group Leadership* (Philadelphia, 1960), p. 263.

54. Introduction by Herbert Aptheker to 1973 edition of W.E.B. Du Bois, *The Souls of Black Folk* (Milwood, N.Y., 1973), p. 30.

55. Alice Hyneman Sotheran, "The Negro and Socialism," *New York Call*, January 19, 20, 1911.

56. W.E.B. Du Bois to "My Dream Madame," New York, November 6, 1912, original letter in Local New York, Socialist Party Papers, Tamiment Institute, Bobst Library, New York University; reprinted in Aptheker, ed., *The Correspondence of W.E.B. Du Bois*, vol. 1, p. 180. See also Kenneth M. Glazier, "W.E.B. Du Bois' Impressions of Woodrow Wilson," *Journal of Negro History* 58 (January 1973): 454.

57. *New York Call*, January 21, 1911. For the charge, denied by the editor, that the *Call* distorted what Du Bois had said, see "Justice" in ibid., January 25, 1911.

58. See Foner, ed., *W.E.B. Du Bois Speaks*, pp. 258-67; *Speeches and addresses, 1920-1963* (New York, 1971), pp. 43-46.

59. W.E.B. Du Bois, "A Field for Socialists," *New Review* (January 11, 1913): 54-57; "Socialism and the Negro Problem," ibid. (February 1, 1913): 138-41. Arnold Ramparsad suggests that Du Bois' resignation from the party was hastened by his objection "to two aspects of radical socialism, its basis in dogma and its acceptance of revolution as necessary for change" (op. cit., p. 158). Since "radical socialism" was in no respect dominant in the leadership of the Socialist party in 1912, this hardly could have been an influence. Actually, Ramparsad says nothing of Du Bois' criticism of racism in the Socialist party; he does not even mention his articles in *New Review* where this is made clear.

CHAPTER 10

1. Texas socialists seemed obsessed by the desire to prove that Democrats were responsible for miscegenation. Arch Lingan, a party member in Beaumont, wrote to the Socialist party national office, asking "if you have anything out along the line of the number of cases of miscegenation (intermarriage of whites and negroes) especially in 'Democratic' strongholds, I am anxious for quite a number" (Arch Lingan to Carl D. Thompson, September 29, 1913, Socialist Party Papers, Duke University Library). See also Donald Graham, "Red, White and Black: An Interpretation of Ethnic and Racial Attitudes of Agrarian Radicals in Texas and Oklahoma, 1880-1920," M.A. thesis, University of Saskatechewan, Regina Campus, February 1973, pp. 145-47.

2. *The Rebel* (Halletsville, Tex.), October 7, November 11, 18, 1911; November 16, 1912; T. A. Hickey, "The Land Renters Union in Texas," *International Socialist Review* 13 (1913): 239-44; Nat L. Hardy in *New York Call*, November 13, 1911; James P. Green, "Socialism and the Southwestern Class Struggle, 1898-1918," op. cit., p. 101; Graham, op. cit., p. 158.

3. For an attack on the *Rip-Saw* in 1910 as being a "negro hater and negro baiter," and the defense of the paper, see *New York Call*, November 3, 8, 1910.

4. Kate Richards O'Hare was the most prominent woman socialist lecturer and organizer. During World War I, she was imprisoned because of her antiwar speeches and writings. Indicted under the Espionage Act, she was sentenced to five years' imprisonment in the Missouri State Penitentiary at Jefferson City. See Bernard J. Brommel, "Kate Richards O'Hare: A Midwestern Pacifist's Fight for Free Speech," *North Dakota Quarterly* 44 (Winter 1976): 5-19.

5. *National Rip-Saw*, August 1914, p. 5.

6. Ibid., September 1914, p. 7.

7. Kate Richards O'Hare, "'Nigger Equality,'" pamphlet, copy in Michigan State University Library.

8. Green, op. cit., p. 13; H. L. Meredith, "Agrarian Socialism and the Negro in Okla-

homa, 1900-1918," *Labor History* 11 (Summer 1970): 277-79.

9. See Mozell C. Hall, "The All-Negro Communities of Oklahoma: The Natural History of a Social Movement," *Journal of Negro History* 31 (1946): 254-68; William L. Battle and Gilbert Geis, "Racial Self-Fulfillment and the Rise of an All-Negro Community in Oklahoma," *Phylon* 18 (1957): 247-60.

10. *Daily Oklahoman*, December 28, 1899; H. E. Farnsworth, "Oklahoma Socialists on Deck," January 27, 1900, copy in Morris Hillquit-Socialist Labor Party Papers, Tamiment Institute, Bobst Library, New York University.

11. Nathaniel J. Washington, *The Historical Development of the Negro in Oklahoma* (Tulsa, 1948), pp. 48-50.

12. Meredith, op. cit., p. 280.

13. Oscar Ameringer, "To Rise Together," in Samuel Colton, ed., *Sagas of Struggle: A Labor Anthology* (New York, 1951), p. 44.

14. Oscar Ameringer, *If You Don't Weaken: An Autobiography* (New York, 1940), pp. 112-30, 279; *Oklahoma Pioneer*, March 30, August 27, 1910; H. L. Meredith, "Oscar Ameringer and the Concept of Agrarian Socialism," *Chronicles of Oklahoma* 45 (Spring 1967): 82-84.

15. *Industrial Democrat* (Oklahoma City), March 12, June 25, 1910.

16. Graham, op. cit., p. 219, quoting from Marion Hughes, *Why I Am a Socialist*.

17. Green, op. cit., p. 18.

18. "The Grandfather Clause in Oklahoma," *The Outlook*, August 20, 1910, pp. 853-54.

19. Green, op. cit., p. 93; *Appeal to Reason*, April 16, 1910; *Daily Oklahoman*, June 2, 20, August 7, 1910.

20. "In the Matter of Initiative Petition, No. 10, Field by Fred P. Branson," 10th day of June 1910, signed by Patrick S. Nagle, and including "Argument Submitted by O. F. Granstreeter, John Hegel, Oscar Ameringer, W. L. Reynolds, and P. S. Nagle.—Committee," Oklahoma Department of Libraries, Archives and Records Division, Oklahoma City.

21. Ameringer, *If You Don't Weaken*, p. 279; Meredith, *Labor History*, op. cit., p. 282; Green, op. cit., p. 94.

22. *Industrial News* (Oklahoma City), July 23, 30, 1910; Graham, op. cit., p. 285 and *n*.

23. James R. Scales, "Political History of Oklahoma, 1907-1949," Ph.D. dissertation, University of Oklahoma, 1949, pp. 128-29; *Oklahoma Pioneer*, August 27, 1910; *Appeal to Reason*, August 13, 1910; Green, op. cit., p. 95; Graham, op. cit., pp. 286-87.

24. *New York Call*, June 11, 1911; *Chicago Daily Socialist*, January 9, 1912.

25. "Negroes Favor Socialist Party," undated broadside, Socialist Party Papers, Duke University Library.

26. *Chicago Daily Socialist*, October 18, 1920; *New York Call*, October 21, 1910.

27. *Oklahoma Pioneer*, October 22, 1910.

28. Ibid., November 5, 1910.

29. Ibid.

30. Ibid., June 1, 1910.

31. Ibid., March 2, 1912.

32. Ibid., March 6, 1912.

33. Ibid., March 30, 1912.

34. Ibid., April 20, 1912.

35. Graham, op. cit., p. 228.

36. "State Platform of the Socialist Party of Oklahoma, 1912," Socialist Party Papers, Duke University Library.

37. *Ballot Box* (Fallon, Nev.), November 2, 1912.

38. *The Rebel* (Halletsville, Tex.), March 22, 1913.

39. Graham, op. cit., p. 296.

40. Ibid., p. 297.

41. Ibid., pp. 327-29.

42. Ibid., pp. 335-36.

43. *New Yorker Volkszeitung*, August 1, 1910; *New York Call*, August 5, October 25, 1910; *Chicago Daily Socialist*, July 19, August 5, 1910.

The *Volkszeitung* and the *Call* were both critical of the Socialist party's National Executive Committee for having done nothing to help the Oklahoma socialists in their battle to defeat the Grandfather Clause.

44. *The Crisis* (December 1910): 6-8.

In *When Farmers Voted Red: The Gospel of Socialism in the Oklahoma Countryside 1910-1924* (Westport, Conn., 1976), Garin Burbank has a chapter entitled "Local Socialists and 'Nigger Equality.'" It is devoted mainly to the segregationist forces among Oklahoma Socialists, and argues that "all of the Socialist spokesmen who defended the Negro as a worker and a human being were either outsiders who had moved to Oklahoma or were proponents of the northern Civil War traditions." (p. 87.) Apart from the difficulty of knowing just who "outsiders" were in Oklahoma at this time, this statement does not mention that the stand taken by these "Socialist spokesmen" was consistently endorsed in party referendums in which most voters were "insiders."

CHAPTER 11

1. See H. Grady McWhiney, "The Socialist Vote in Louisiana, 1912: An Historical Interpretation of Radical Sources," M.A. thesis, Louisiana State University, 1951, pp. 12-18; Covington Hall, "Labor Struggles in the Deep South," unpublished manuscript in Howard-Tilton Library, Tulane University, pp. 54-56, 98-120.

2. *Chicago Daily Socialist*, May 20, June 20, 1908, April 22, 1912; *New York Call*, May 24, 1913; *Appeal to Reason*, April 20, 1912; "State Platform of the Socialist Party of Tennessee Adopted July, 1912," copy in Tamiment Institute, Bobst Library, New York University; Jos. R. Boss, State Secretary, Socialist Party of Tennessee, to Bureau of Information, Socialist Party, 5-14, 1913, Socialist Party Papers, Duke University Library.

3. "Virginia Socialists Protest Prove Prejudice Absent," typed copy in Socialist Party Papers, Duke University Library.

4. *Richmond Planet*, June 8, 1910; "Autobiography," B. Charney Vladeck Papers, Section 2, Box 7, Tamiment Institute, Bobst Library, New York University. For reactions to the Johnson-Jeffries fight in the *New York Call*, see issues of June 9, August 4, 1910. In the August 4 issue, Reverend Ronald D. Sawyer saw Johnson's victory as a great boost for the Negro. "It will help him get over his licked spirit, help him get on his feet." However, the Jeffries-Johnson fight gave Gaylord Wilshire the opportunity to write a viciously racist editorial in his magazine in which he argued that if blacks were given "perfect freedom to vote as they pleased," they would elect "men so incompetent or so dishonest or both that there would be no value to any kind of property in the South, public or private." Having just returned from a visit to Haiti, Wilshire insisted that blacks were simply not capable of functioning intelligently in public life. To show that he was both a socialist and a racist, Wilshire concluded that under socialism, the Negro would be able to play a role in the government, "for I consider that under Socialism, with its organization giving justice and equal political and economic rights to all, the Negro problem will be no problem at all. The Negro Problem is one of the many Problems of Capitalism that will automatically disappear with Socialism" (Gaylord Wilshire, "Reno and the Negro Problem," *Wilshire's*, August 1910, pp. 6-7). The Jeffries-Johnson fight took place in Reno. Nev.

5. *Chicago Daily Socialist*, July 14, 1910.

6. Ibid., July 27, 1910.

7. Alving Porter, New Orleans, D. Burgess, Seattle, J. C. Fitts, Astoria, Ore.,

Charles F. Schneider, Ocala, Fla., and Tersiliner, Tenn., in ibid., July 27, 28, August 2, 13, 1910.

8. Ibid., July 26, August 2, 15, 17, 1910.

9. *New York Call*, January 24, 1911.

10. Walling in *The Independent*, reprinted in *Weekly People*, July 10, 1909.

11. "The Negro and Socialism," *New York Call*, January 24, 1911.

12. Mary White Ovington in ibid., January 30, 1911.

13. Lee Weinstein in ibid., Febrary 1, 1911.

14. Ibid., February 11, 1911.

15. Ibid., February 14, 1911.

16. Ibid., February 21, 1911.

17. On April 13, 1911, under the headlines "A Warning to 'Nigger' Haters. There is no place in the Socialist movement for men with race lines, boundary lines, or color lines," the *Prolucutor* reprinted the Negro resolution adopted at the 1901 (founding) convention of the Socialist party.

18. *New York Call*, August 8, 1910.

19. *The People*, September 5, 1911.

20. *Mother Earth* 6 (October 1911): 198.

21. *The Rebel* (Halletsville, Tex.), September 2, 1911; C. Vann Woodward, *Origins of the New South* (Baton Rouge, 1951), p. 351; Graham, op. cit., pp. 120, 162.

22. B. Jack and L. Schaskin in *New York Call*, August 28, 1911.

23. Jack Rocova and Harry D. Smith in ibid., September 12, 1911.

24. Ibid., September 12, 1911.

25. Ibid., October 2, 1911.

26. Minutes of Meeting, City Executive Committee, Local New York, August 30, 1911, Local New York Socialist Party Papers, Tamiment Institute, Bobst Library, New York University.

27. Hubert H. Harrison, "Socialism and the Negro," *International Socialist Review* 12 (March 1912): 834.

28. *New York Call*, May 19, 1911.

29. *National Convention of the Socialist Party, Held at Indianapolis, Ind., May 12 to 18, 1912, Stenographic Report*, Chicago, 1912, p. 100. For the policies and practices of the IWW with respect to black workers, see Foner, *Organized Labor and the Black Worker*, pp. 106-19.

30. Mary White Ovington to Ray Stannard Baker, November 12, 1906, Ray Stannard Baker Papers, Box 89, Library of Congress.

31. Mary White Ovington, "The Status of the Negro in the United States," *New Review* 1 (September 1913): 748-49. Joseph Ettor, a popular IWW leader, declared that "Miss Ovington sums up correctly the I.W.W. position on the Negro question" (*Solidarity*, September 20, 1913).

32. *New Review* 1 (September 1913): 749. For the full story of the Brotherhood of Timber Workers and the courageous struggle led by it and the IWW in uniting black and white timber workers, see Foner, *History of the Labor Movement in the United States*, vol. 4, pp. 233-57; Melvyn Dubofsky, *We Shall Be All: A History of the IWW* (Chicago, 1969), pp. 209-10; Vernon L. Jensen, *Lumber and Labor* (New York, 1944), pp. 71-89; Ruth A. Allen, *East Texas Lumber Workers: An Economic and Social Picture* (Austin, Tex., 1964), pp. 165-90; James R. Green, "The Brotherhood of Timber Workers, 1910-1913: A Radical Response to Industrial Capitalism in the Southern U.S.A.," *Past and Present* no. 60 (1973): 161-200; Charles H. McCord, "A Brief History of the Brotherhood of Timber Workers," M.A. thesis, University of Texas, May 1959.

33. *New Review* 1 (September 1913): 749.

34. Ibid. (December 1913): 90-91.

35. Ibid. (January 1914): 64.

36. Carl D. Thompson to State Secretaries and Replies, May 1913, Socialist Party Papers, Duke University Library.

37. *The Party Builder*, May 1913, pp. 3-8. Hillquit declared he had never heard of Slater and wondered if the proposal was made simply to give himself a job. The fact that a leading national figure of the Socialist party had never heard of Reverend Slater speaks much of the attention to the Negro displayed by such socialist leaders as Hillquit.

CHAPTER 12

1. *The Masses* (May 1915): 6.

2. *Huntington (W.Va.) Socialist and Labor Star*, September 4, 1914.

3. Ibid., September 11, 18, 1914.

4. *The Bulletin of the Intercollegiate Socialist Society, April-May, 1912*, p. 3.

5. "Delta Sigman Theta Sends Delegate to Convention of Intercollegiate Socialist Society," *Howard University Journal* (January 16, 1914).

6. Max Eastman, "Niggers and Night Raiders," *The Masses* (February 1913): 6; *The Crisis* (January 1916): 144.

7. R. A. Dague, "Shall Negroes Be Burned at the Stake?" *Ballot Box* (Fallon, Nev.), February 22, 1913.

8. *Appeal to Reason*, reprinted in *The Crisis* (January 1916): 177.

9. *The Crisis* (July 1915): 123-24.

10. Ibid. (July 1916): 133. For a study of Helen Keller as a socialist, see Philip S. Foner, *Helen Keller: Her Socialist Years* (New York, 1967).

11. *Appeal to Reason*, May 21, 1910.

12. "A Letter from Debs on Immigration," *International Socialist Review* 11 (July 1910): 16-17.

13. Foner, *History of the Labor Movement*, vol. 4, pp. 13-16, 61-62, 74-75, 105, 107; Eugene V. Debs to John Brown, Eugene V. Debs Mss., Indiana State University Library, Terre Haute.

14. *The Crisis* (May 1915): 33. The Afro-American Civic League of Terre Haute adopted a resolution praising Debs for his "attitude . . . concerning the movie, 'The Birth of a Nation'" (*Terre Haute Post*, June 18, 1916 in Eugene V. Debs Scrapbooks, Book 18, Tamiment Institute, Bobst Library, New York University).

15. *New York Call*, June 16, 1915.

16. Verne E. Sheridan in *New York Call*, April 8, 1915.

17. Ibid., April 22, 1915.

18. Ray Ginger, *The Bending Cross*, p. 325.

19. *Appeal to Reason*, April 17, 1915, March 15, 1916.

20. *National Rip-Saw*, April 1916; *New York Call*, August 4, 12, 1916; *The Crisis* (June 1916): 75-76.

21. *New York Call*, August 19, 1915, July 8, 1916; *The Crisis* (January 1916): 177.

22. Gary M Fink, *Labor's Search for Political Order: The Political Behavior of the Missouri Labor Movement, 1890-1940* (Columbia, Mo., 1970), pp. 56-57.

23. *St. Louis Labor*, February 12, 19, 1916. For a discussion of the segregation law which, however, makes no mention of the socialist opposition to the ordinance, see Daniel T. Kelleher, "St. Louis' 1916 Residential Segregation Ordinance," *Bulletin, Missouri Historical Society* 26 (April 1970): 239-48.

24. *The Crisis* (June 1916): 187.

25. U.S. Department of Labor, *Negro Migration in 1916-1917* (Washington, D.C., 1919), pp. 120-26; Ray Stannard Baker, "The Negro Goes North," *World's Work* 34 (July

1917), pp. 311-15; Foner, *Organized Labor and the Black Worker*, pp. 129-35; Richard A. Easterlin, "The American Population," in *American Economic Growth: An Economist's History of the United States,*(New York, 1972), p. 137; Reynolds Farley, *Growth of the Black Population* (Chicago, 1970), pp. 46-47.

26. Foner, *Organized Labor and the Black Worker*, p. 136.

27. Palmer Hoke Wright, "The American Negro and the War," *International Socialist Review* 17 (July 1916): 166-67.

28. Ida Crouch-Hazlett, "The Negro and the Socialists," *New York Call*, July 22, 1917.

29. Rogers, op. cit., vol. 2, p. 615.


CHAPTER 13

1. *New York Times*, October 5, 1919.

2. Rogers, op. cit., vol. 2, pp. 613-15; *New York Evening Call*, December 22, 1917.

3. There is nothing of a biographical nature on Chandler Owen other than occasional scraps of information in *The Messenger*. (See, for example, the October 1919 issue, p. 11.) There is a biography of Randolph (Jervis Anderson, *A. Philip Randolph, A Biographical Portrait*, New York, 1972) which is especially useful for his early life. There is also a useful five-part series of articles in the *New York Post*, December 28-31, 1959, and January 3, 1960. This may be supplemented by Alan Morrison, "A Philip Randolph: Dean of Negro Leaders," *Ebony*, November 1958, pp. 103-4, 108, 110-12, 114, and Richard Bardolph, *The Negro Vanguard* (New York, 1959), pp. 189-90.

The present account of Randolph's career up to his joining the Socialist party is based on the above sources as well as a personal interview with Randolph, October 13, 1972.

4. Interview with A. Philip Randolph, October 13, 1972.

5. *The Messenger*, November 1917.

6. James Weinstein, *The Decline of Socialism in America, 1912-1925* (New York, 1969), pp. 106, 125.

7. Interview with A. Philip Randolph, October 13, 1972.

8. *The Crisis* (September 1916): 180-83.

9. *New York Call*, November 2, 1916.

10. Ibid.

11. Ibid., December 22, 1916.

12. *New York Post*, December 29, 1959.

13. *The Messenger*, November 1917, p. 1.

14. Theodore Kornweibel, Jr., "The *Messenger* Magazine: 1917-1928," Ph.D. dissertation, Yale University, 1971, p. 285.

15. Letter of Joyce Bouchard to author, February 23, 1965. Bouchard suggested my trying the Montana Historical Society Library in Helena, but this produced an answer that no copies of the journal were in the institution. Advertisements placed in the Butte newspapers also produced no positive results, nor did notices of inquiry for copies in a wide variety of journals.

Although there was scarcely a large black population in Butte in 1915, there was a strong socialist movement; the militant Western Federation of Miners was also an important force in the city. Thus, it is not entirely surprising that the first black socialist magazine should have appeared in Butte.

16. Anderson, op. cit., p. 85.

17. H. C. Peterson and Gilbert C. Fite, *Opponents of War, 1917-1918* (Madison, Wis., 1957), pp. 74-80.

18. *The Crisis* (May 1918): 7.

19. Foner, *Organized Labor and the Black Worker*, pp. 137-39.

20. *The Crisis* (July 1918): 111.

21. Philip S. Foner, *The Bolshevik Revolution: Its Impact on American Radicals, Liberals, and Labor* (New York, 1967), pp. 20-21, 53-55.

22. Ibid., pp. 20-21. V. I. Lenin, leader of the Bolshevik Revolution, wrote extensively on the situation of black Americans. He advanced the concept that they were an "oppressed nation" in the United States. "Shame on America for the plight of the Negroes!" he ended an article in February 1913 on the high illiteracy rate among Negroes in the United States. For these and other writings of Lenin on the Negro before the Bolshevik Revolution, see *Lenin on the United States: Selected Writings by V. I. Lenin* (New York, 1970), pp. xiii, 58-59, 115-206.

It is possible that Levin's writings on the Negro were brought to the attention of black socialists. The *New York Call* of October 26, 1918, reported that at a meeting of "Negro Socialists," Alexander Trachtenberg spoke on "The Relation of the Russian Revolution to the Negro." Since Trachtenberg read Lenin's writing in Russian, he may have referred to them during his lecture.

23. *The Messenger*, March 1919, pp. 9-12. See also issues of November 1917, pp. 10, 19, January 1918, p. 12, July 1918, pp, 8-9, 23, May-June 1919, p. 14.

24. *The Messenger*, May-June 1919, pp. 9-10. See also March 1919, pp. 9-12.

25. Weinstein, op. cit., p. 71; Frederick T. Detweiler, *The Negro Press in the United States* (Chicago, 1922), p. 171; Kornweibel, op. cit., pp. 16-17. Black troops of the 24th Infantry stationed in Houston, Texas, goaded by white civilians, took up their weapons and killed seventeen of the local citizens. After a farcical trial, thirteen of the troops were hanged for murder and mutiny, and forty-one were imprisoned for life. See Edgar A. Shuler, "The Houston Race Riot, 1917," *Journal of Negro History* 29 (July 1944): 300-38.

26. Interview quoted in Kornweibel, op. cit., pp. 19-20.

27. Ibid., p. 26.

28. "Some Reasons Why Negroes Should Vote the Socialist Ticket," By the Independent Political Council, copy in Tamiment Institute, Bobst Library, New York University; *The Messenger*, November 1917, p. 11; *New York Age*, November 1, 1917.

29. *New York Call*, July 9, October 30, 1917. For comments in the *Call* on the East St. Louis riots, see issues of July 5, 7, 11, 12, 22, 1917.

30. Hillquit's vote represented a nearly fivefold increase over the normal socialist vote. For the first time the party elected members of the Board of Aldermen, putting seven on the body; and elected a municipal court judge and ten assemblymen, an increase of eight over the previous high (Weinstein, op. cit., p. 154).

31. *The Messenger*, January 1918, p. 11; *New York Call*, August 14, 1918.

32. A Philip Randolph and Chandler Owen, *Terms of Peace and the Darker Races* (New York, 1917), pp. 30-32.

33. Quoted in Anderson, op. cit., p. 80. For Harrison's attack on Owen, charging him with "duplicity" for having accused Harrison of standing for the doctrine of "Negroes First," see *New York Evening Call*, December 22, 1917, and *New York Call*, January 7, 1918.

34. *The Messenger*, November 1917, pp. 10-11. The convention finally was held in Chicago after Mayor Thompson granted permission.

35. *The Messenger*, March 1919, Supplement.

36. William Preston, Jr., *Aliens and Dissenters: Federal Suppression of Radicals, 1903-1933* (Cambridge, Mass., 1963), pp. 88-117.

37. *New York Post*, December 30, 1959; *The Messenger*, April 1922, p. 310; Kornweibel, op. cit., pp. 3-5; Anderson, op. cit., pp. 106-8.

38. Anderson, op. cit., pp. 108-9; Philip S. Foner, "The I.W.W. and the Black Worker," *Journal of Negro History* 55 (Spring 1970): 24.

39. *New York Call*, August 14, 1918.

40. Four-page leaflet, Tamiment Institute, Bobst Library, New York University. The reference was to Section 2 of the Fourteenth Amendment.

41. *The Messenger*, January 1918, p. 11.

42. *Cleveland Citizen*, October 19, 1918. Jervis Anderson seems to be unaware that Randolph was nominated on the socialist ticket in 1918. He writes that the socialists nominated blacks, including Randolph, to office in Harlem for the first time in 1920 (op. cit., p. 96).

43. *New York Call*, November 4, 1918.

44. *New York Age*, September 19, 1918; *Crusader*, reprinted in *New York Call*, September 23, 1918.

45. *New York Call*, November 4, 1918.

46. *The Messenger*, May-June 1919, p. 12.

47. Ibid., November 1917, p. 8.

48. *Intercollegiate Socialist*, April-May 1918, pp. 11-14; *New York Evening Call*, June 3, 1918. For Du Bois' discussion, see *The Intercollegiate Socialist*, December-January 1917-1918, pp. 5-9, and reprinted in Foner, *W.E.B. Du Bois Speaks . . . , 1890-1919*, pp. 258-67.

49. Interview with A. Philip Randolph, October 13, 1972.

CHAPTER 14

1. See for example, Preston, op. cit., which devotes scores of pages to the "Red Year" of 1919 without once mentioning the Negro. A more recent example is the heavily documented article, "Federal Suppression of Leftwing Dissidence in World War I" by Leslie Fishbein (*Potomac Review*, Summer 1974, pp. 47-67), which also contains not a single mention of the Negro.

2. W. M. Lewis to Ralph M. Easly, May 2, 1918, National Civic Federation Papers, Gen. Corr. 1918 "N," New York Public Library, Manuscripts Division.

3. *Washington Bee*, April 26, 1919.

4. Quoted in Kenneth G. Weinberg, *A Man's Home, A Man's Castle* (New York, 1971), p. 5.

5. Foner, *Organized Labor and the Black Worker*, pp. 146-47.

6. Arthur I. Waskow, *From Race Riot to Sit-In, 1919 and the 1960's: A Study in the Connections Between Conflict and Violence* (New York, 1966), pp. 12, 305-7.

Waskow describes seven of some twenty-five racial incidents of 1919, with particular emphasis on the Washington, Chicago, and Elaine, Arkansas, outbreaks. He lists eleven incidents for these months of the "Red Summer"; two more are described in the *New York Times*, July 20, September 16, 1919.

7. Ibid., pp. 13, 22-23, 38, 106, 110-11.

8. Ibid., pp. 16-17, 121-24, 128; B. Boren McCool, *Union, Reaction and Riot: A Biography of a Rural Race Riot* (Memphis, 1970), pp. 12-13, 17-40. For an amazingly arrogant defense of the white mobs on the ground that the Negroes in Phillips County had "begun a planned insurrection . . . against the whites in that area," see J. W. Butts and Dorothy James, "The Underlying Causes of the Elaine Riot of 1919," *Arkansas Historical Quarterly* 12 (May 1973): 95-104.

9. Elliott Rudwick, *Race Riot at East St. Louis: July 5, 1917* (Carbondale, Ill., 1964), pp. 46-54. Waskow errs in failing to point out these earlier self-defense efforts and in emphasizing that the 1919 riots were a "new departure" in the sense that they marked the first time the Negro fought back since Emancipation.

10. Chicago Commission on Race Relations, *The Negro in Chicago: A Study of Race Relations and a Race Riot in 1919* (Chicago, 1922), p. 10.

11. Lloyd M. Abernathy, "The Washington Race War of July, 1919," *Maryland Historical Magazine* 58 (December 1963): 318-20. Noting the failure of the police to defend the Negro community from the white mob, Abernathy points out that "the significance of the Washington riot is not that the Negro was left to his own defenses but that he did not run away and hide as he had on previous occasions; for the first time he fought back at his persecutors."

12. Waskow, op. cit., pp. 27, 41-42.

13. Hoover's authorship of this section of the report is suggested in a letter he wrote to Assistant Attorney General Robert P. Stewart, November 7, 1919, in which he stated: "I have received communications from several Senators requesting to be supplied with a complete report upon negro agitation in the Untied States and I am preparing the same at the present time." Case no. 152860, sub 1 (Box 1230 XH), Justice Department Central Files, Straight Numerical File, National Archives, RG 60.

14. "Radicalism and Sedition Among Negroes as Reflected in Their Publications," Exhibit 10 of A. Mitchell Palmer, *Investigative Activities of the Department of Justice*, 66th Cong., 1st Sess., 1919, Senate Document 153, vol. 12, pp. 162-87.

15. Ibid., p. 162.

16. Ibid., pp. 172-73.

17. Ibid., p. 173.

18. Ibid., p. 179.

19. Ibid., p. 181.

20. *Congressional Record*, 66th Cong., 1st Sess., vol. 58, pp. 4303-5.

21. After the editorial appeared, the Post Office threatened to bar *The Crisis* from the mails. FBI agents visited DuBois' office, asking him "what he was up to" (Herbert Aptheker, ed., *A Documentary History of the Negro People in the United States, 1910-1932* [Secaucus, N.J., 1973], p. 271n).

22. *The Messenger*, October 1919.

23. *Investigative Activities*, p. 184.

24. Ibid., p. 162.

25. Ibid., pp. 6-9, 14.

26. Lawrence H. Chamberlin, *Loyalty and Legislation Action, A Survey of Activity by the New York State Legislature 1919-1949* (Ithaca, N.Y., 1951), pp. 4-6; Thomas A Vadney, "The Politics of Repression: A Case Study of the Red Scare in New York," *New York History* 49 (January 1968): 56-58; Julian E. Jaffe, *Crusade Against Radicalism: New York During the Red Scare, 1914-1924* (Port Washington, N.Y., 1972), pp. 119-20.

27. New York (State) Legislature, Joint Legislative Committee Investigating Seditious Activities, *Revolutionary Radicalism: Its History, Purpose and Tactics, with an Exposition and Discussion of the Steps Being Taken and Required to Curb It*, vol. 2 (Albany, N.Y., 1920), p. 1476.

28. For the resurgence of the Ku Klux Klan, see David M. Chalmers, *Hooded Americanism: The History of the Ku Klux Klan* (Garden City, N.Y., 1965), and Kenneth J. Jackson, *The Ku Klux Klan in the City, 1915-1930* (New York, 1967).

29. The reports of the committee's spies in Harlem are in Lusk Committee Papers, New York State Library, Manuscripts Division, Albany, N.Y., Box 4, Folder 1. A summary of these reports is in J. M. Pawa, "Black Radicals and White Spies: Harlem, 1919," *Negro History Bulletin* 35 (October 1972): 129-32, and J. M. Pawa, "The Search for Black Radicals: American and British Documents Relative to the 1919 Red Scare," *Labor History* 16 (Spring 1975): 272-84.

30. The Lusk Committee raided the Rand School twice and removed vast quantities of books and records. On the second occasion, the committee brought in an expert to open the school's safe.

31. *Revolutionary Radicalism*, vol. 2, p. 1476. Several of the articles from *The Messen-*

*ger* chosen for inclusion in the Justice Department reports also appeared in the Lusk Committee report. Yet, it is interesting that the Lusk Committee ignored the reply to Congressman Byrnes and other articles dealing with social equality, as well as those that encouraged fighting back against rioters and lynching, both themes of special interest to the Justice Department. "The emphasis of the Lusk Committee, on the other hand, seems to be directed toward the possibility of blacks becoming socialistic and part of a world-wide movement towards Bolshevism" writes Theodore Kornweibel, Jr., in his study of *The Messenger* (op. cit., p. 65).

32. See *Revolutionary Radicalism*, vol. 2, pp. 1492-95.

33. Ibid., p. 1518.

34. Ibid., pp. 2004-5.

35. Ibid., pp. 1519-20.

36. Ibid., p. 1143.

37. Ibid., vol. 3, pp. 2011-14, 2075.

38. Jaffe, op. cit., pp. 125-42.

39. There is also a British government report on radicalism among Negroes in the United States, but it deals primarily with the influence of Marcus Garvey and his *Negro World* in the British colonies. See W. F. Elkins, "Unrest Among the Negroes: A British Document of 1919," *Science & Society* 32 (Winter 1968): 66-79.

40. Report on Negro Radicalism by Charles Mowbray White to National Civic Federation, The Negro Folder, Box 152, National Civic Federation Papers, New York Public Library, Manuscripts Division.

41. *Revolutionary Radicalism*, vol. 1, p. 7.

42. Robert T. Kerlin, ed., *The Voice of the Negro, 1919* (New York, 1920), p. 185.

43. *Pittsburgh Courier*, October 12, 1919.

44. Chicago Commission on Race Relations, *The Negro in Chicago: A Study of Race Relations and a Race Riot in 1919* (Chicago, 1922), p. 476.

45. *Baltimore Afro-American*, August 8, 1919.

46. Ibid., August 22, 1919.

47. As presidential candidate in 1912, Wilson had solicited black votes and had assured "my coloured fellow citizens of my earnest wish to see justice done them in every matter, and not mere grudging justice, but justice executed with liberality and cordial good feeling." But once elected, he completely forgot his promise. Even worse, he instituted segregation dining and toilet facilities in the Bureau of Printing and Engraving, the Post Office Department, and offices of the Treasury Department. Later, Wilson's inaction during the East St. Louis race riot of 1917 was another reason for black dislike of his administration. See Henry Blumenthal, "Woodrow Wilson and the Race Question," *Journal of Negro History* 48 (January 1963): 1-21; Foner, *The Voice of Black America*, vol. 2, pp. 86-90 (speech of William Monroe Trotter).

48. Ralph W. Tyler in *Baltimore Afro-American*, August 22, 1919.

49. William Z. Foster, *History of the Communist Party of the United States* (New York, 1952), pp. 143-85; Theodore Draper, *The Roots of American Communism* (New York, 1957), pp. 131-225; James Weinstein, op. cit., pp. 177-234. The critic of the left is Daniel Bell; he is quoted in Irving Howe and Lewis Closer, *The American Communist Party: A Critical History* (New York, 1962), pp. 370-78.

50. *Revolutionary Age*, July 5, 12, 1919.

51. Louis G. Fraina, "Problems of American Socialism," *The Class Struggle* (February 1919): 46.

52. *Revolutionary Age*, July 5, 1919.

53. Ibid.

54. Alexander Trachtenberg, ed., *American Labor Year Book, 1919-1920* (New York, 1921), p. 419.

55. Max Eastman, "The Chicago Conventions," *The Liberator* (October 1919): 5-19.

56. *The Messenger*, May-June 1919, pp. 21-22.

57. Ibid., August 1919, pp. 12-13; *Baltimore Afro-American*, June 13, 1919.

58. *New York Call*, November 27, 1919; The Rand School of Social Science, *Bulletin for 1919-1920*: "Why Negroes Should Be Socialists," *The Messenger*, October, December 1919; A Philip Randolph, "The Socialist Message and the Negro," *New York Call*, November 9, 1919 (Magazine Section).

59. *Revolutionary Radicalism*, pp. 1489-1510. For a superficial critique of Domingo's piece which distorts what he said, see Harold Cruse, *The Crisis of the Negro Intellectual* (New York, 1967), pp. 128-29.

60. Offord, op. cit.; Mark Solomon, "Red and Black: Negroes and Communism," Ph.D. dissertation, Harvard University, 1972, pp. 79-84.


CHAPTER 15

1. For reasons for the collapse of the NBWA, see Foner, *Organized Labor and the Black Worker*, pp. 151, 160-61.

2. *The Messenger*, March 1920, p. 3; April-May 1920, p. 4; September 1920, pp. 90-91.

3. Ibid., September 1920, pp. 88-90.

4. Ibid., March 1920, pp. 12-13, April-May 1920, pp. 3-5, September 1920, pp. 88-89.

5. *New York Call*, April 22, 1920.

6. Victor Berger, "Let Us Drop the 'Revolutionary' Jargon," ibid., May 9, 1920 (Magazine Section); Ernest Murray in ibid., May 16, 1920.

7. *Souvenir Journal of the National Convention, Socialist Party, New York City*, (1920), unpaged.

8. *New York Call*, May 14, 1920.

9. Ibid., June 29, 1920.

10. *New York Times*, May 15, 1920.

11. *Why Negroes Should Be Socialists* (Chicago), copy in Tamiment Bobst Library, New York University. As demonstrated by internal evidence, the pamphlet appeared in the summer or fall of 1920.

12. "Eugene Debs—Candidate for President," *The Messenger*, April-May 1920; "Special Letter Sent to the *Messenger* by Eugene V. Debs," ibid., November 1920.

13. "Debs and the Negro," ibid., November 1920.

14. The Farmer-Labor party grew out of the labor parties in Chicago and New York and the Farmers' Non-Partisan League. It refused to soft-pedal the Negro issue.

15. *The Messenger*, November 1920, pp. 138-39.

16. Weinstein, op. cit., pp. 73n., 236-38; James B. Rhodes, "The Campaign of the Socialist Party in the Election of 1920," M.A. thesis, American University, 1965, pp. 64-68; James Malcolm, ed., *The New York Red Book: An Illustrated State Manual* (Albany, N.Y., 1921), pp. 530, 534-40, 569, 570-71.

17. *New York Call*, March 2, 1921.

18. Ibid., October 7, 9, November 4, 1922.

19. Ibid., October 7, 1922. Oneal was the Socialist party-Farmer Labor party candidate for Assembly in the 14th district, Brooklyn.

20. *New York Call*, May 24, 1922. On October 26, 1921, in a widely publicized speech in Birmingham, Alabama, President Harding, after asserting that American democracy was

a "sham unless the Negro is granted political and economic equality," proceeded to quote with approval Lothrop Stoddard, the leading ideologist of white supremacy, and then to proclaim: "Men of both races may well stand uncompromisingly against every question of social equality" (*New York Times,* October 27, 1921).

21. *Baltimore Afro-American,* June 9, July 7, 1922. The excerpts were headed "Socialist Party Appeals to the Colored Workers." For *The Messenger's* comment, see issue of September 1922.

22. James Oneal, *The Next Emancipation* (New York, 1922).

23. Ibid., p. 19.

24. *The Messenger,* December 1922, p. 539; Malcolm, ed., op. cit., p. 522.

25. *The New York Call,* May 20, 1923.

26. *Baltimore Afro-American,* January 6, 1922.

27. There is a moving tribute to Debs by Sam Moore in the Theodore Debs Papers, Cunningham Memorial Library, Indiana State University. It is entitled "Sam Moore, 'Eugene Victor Debs. The Superman—A Close Up View of Him.'"

28. *The Messenger,* April 1923, p. 18, May 1923, p. 15.

29. Weinstein, op. cit., pp. 242-43.

30. The last issue of the *New York Call* was September 30, 1923. It became the *New York Leader* on October 1, 1923.

31. *The Negro Workers by Eugene Victor Debs. Address Delivered Tuesday, October 30, 1923, Commonwealth Casino, 135th Street and Madison Avenue, N.Y.C.* (New York, 1924), pp. 26-27. Copy in Tamiment Institute, Bobst Library, New York University.

32. *The Messenger,* November 1923, p. 12.

33. *The Negro Workers by Eugene Victor Debs,* p. 12.

34. Anderson, *A. Philip Randolph,* p. 149.

35. *The New York Call,* October 9, 1922; *New Leader,* August 16, 1924.

36. "Debs Speaks in Harlem," *The Messenger,* December 1923, p. 16.

37. Ibid., July 1924, p. 64; August 1924, p. 78.

38. *New York Call,* June 26, 29, 1923.

39. Amy Jacques-Garvey, *Philosophy and Opinions of Marcus Garvey,* vol. 2 (New York, 1925), p. 129. Garvey's early life before he came to the United States is discussed in Edmund David Cronin, *Black Moses: The Story of Marcus Garvey and the Universal Negro Improvement Association* (Madison, Wis., 1960), pp. 3-20; Amy Jacques-Garvey, *Black Power in America* (Kingston, Jamaica, 1968), pp. 2-13; Joel August Rogers, *World's Great Men of Color* (New York, 1943), vol. II, pp. 599-615; Tony Martin, *Race First: The Ideological and Organizational Struggles of Marcus Garvey and the Universal Negro Improvement Association* (Westport, Conn., 1976), pp. 3-12.

40. Peter Gilbert, ed., *The Selected Writings of John Edward Bruce: Militant Black Journalist* (New York, 1971), pp. 8-9.

41. *New York Times,* November 11, 1918; *The Messenger,* December 1920, p. 170.

42. *Negro World,* October 26, 1918, January 29, April 15, 1919.

43. Report of interview with Chandler Owen and A. Philip Randolph, editors of *The Messenger,* August 20, 1920, by Charles Mowbray White, National Civic Federation Papers, New York Public Library, Manuscripts Division, "Negro Folder," Box 152.

44. White reported that Owen had told him that an editorial in the September 1920 issue of *The Messenger* "will deal in a lengthy and scientific manner with the Garvey movement and will clearly state what we think of him and it" (ibid.).

45. *The Messenger,* September 1920, pp. 83-84.

46. *The New York Call,* September 1, 1920.

47. *The Messenger,* October 1920, pp. 114-15, December 1920, pp. 170-72.

48. Ibid., September 1921, pp. 448-52, January 1922, pp. 330-35.

49. Ibid., July 1922, p. 437.

50. The trial began one year after Garvey had been arrested on the charge of using the mails to defraud. Garvey was initially indicted alone, after which the authorities seized books and records of the Black Star Line and the UNIA. Upon realizing that the Black Star Line was a corporation rather than a private firm, the original indictment against Garvey alone was withdrawn; two new ones were substituted which named three codefendants with Garvey.

51. *New York Times*, August 28, 1922.

52. Robert W. Bagnall to Arthur B. Spingarn, January 16, 1923, Arthur B. Spingarn Papers, Library of Congress.

53. The changes noted in the latter are included in the NAACP files, Box-304, and in Walter White to James Weldon Johnson, May 17, 1923, Papers of National Association for the Advancement of Colored People, Library of Congress, Manuscripts Division.

54. Chandler Owen wrote to Attorney General Daugherty on January 26, 1923, on the letterhead of the Friends of Negro Freedom, suggesting that the letter not be given to the press since the plans were to release it all over the country on February 1 (Owen to Daugherty, Department of Justice Files, Record Group 60, 198940, National Archives).

55. Chandler Owen, et al., to Hon. Harry M. Daugherty, January 15, 1923, ibid. The full text of the letter is also published in Amy Jacques-Garvey, *Philosophy and Opinions of Marcus Garvey*, vol. 2, pp. 293-300.

56. Carl Murphy to Daugherty, January 30, 1923, Record Group 60, 198940, Department of Justice Files, National Archives.

57. Assistant Attorney General John W.H. Crum to Chandler Owen, February 20, 1923, ibid.

58. Assistant Attorney General John W.H. Crum to Chandler Owen, February 23, 1923, ibid.

59. Chandler Owen to Assistant Attorney General W.H. Crum, February 20, 1923, ibid.

60. *The Messenger*, March 1923, p. 747, April 1923, p. 748; August 1923, p. 782.

61. Harold Cruse points out that "Garvey's nationalism was more bourgeois than it was revolutionary" (op. cit., p. 330). For Garvey's generally conservative political and economic values, see Cronin, *Black Moses*, pp. 132-33, 142; Jacques-Garvey, op. cit., *Philosophy and Opinions of Marcus Garvey*, vol. 2, pp. 11, 172-73.

Randolph's hostility to Garvey was intensified after he received a package in the mail postmarked New Orleans which was found to contain a human hand of a white man. An accompanying letter scolded Randolph for not being able to unite with his own and gave him a week to join the "nigger improvement association." It was signed "K.K.K." Randolph concluded that "the Klan had come to the rescue of its Negro leader, Marcus Garvey" (*New York Times*, September 6, 11, 1922).

62. Anderson, op. cit., p. 126.

63. For the conflict between W. A. Domingo and *The Messenger* editors on this issue, see *The Messenger*, March 1923, pp. 639-45.

64. Although DuBois denounced the Garvey movement as spiritually bankrupt and futile, and its leader as "the most dangerous enemy of the Negro race in America and in the world," he refused to become an agent for the most reactionary forces in the United States because of his dislike for Garvey. For DuBois' view of Garvey, see DuBois, "A Lunatic or a Traitor," *The Crisis* 28 (May 1924): 8-9; for his refusal to join in the conspiracy with the federal government against Garvey, see his letter to W. A. Domingo, January 8, 1923, in Herbert Aptheker, ed., *The Correspondence of W.E.B. DuBois*, vol. 1, pp. 263-64.

65. *The Messenger*, June 1924, p. 178. Daugherty was a small-time lobbyist for tobacco, meat, and utility interests who first launched the Harding presidential boom and was rewarded with the attorney generalship. While in office he made a business of selling liquor permits, pardons, and paroles to criminals at fancy prices; he was dismissed by

President Coolidge when these activities were revealed.

66. *The Messenger*, February 1923, and reprinted in *New York Call*, March 18, 1923.

67. *The Messenger*, August 1924, p. 247; September 1924, pp. 290-91, 293-94, 296, 298-99; October 1924, pp. 325-28.

68. "The *Afro* for La Follette," *Baltimore Afro-American*, October 24, 1924.

69. *The Messenger*, November 1924, pp. 339, 340, 345-47.

70. Anderson, op. cit., pp. 142-43; George S. Schuyler, *Black and Conservative* (New Rochelle, N.Y., 1966), p. 138; *The Messenger*, February 1926, p. 37, September 1926, p. 273.

71. Anderson, op. cit., p. 142.

72. Foner, *Organized Labor and the Black Worker*, pp. 177-80.

73. *Pittsburgh Courier*, October 30, 1926; *The Messenger*, November 1926, p. 15.

74. *The Messenger*, May 1927, p. 138.

75. *Current History* (June 1923): 415.

76. For the type of approach Harris was referring to, see *The Messenger*, September 1923.

77. Norman Thomas to Morris Hillquit, December 21, 1926, Morris Hillquit Papers, Milwaukee Historical Society.

CHAPTER 16

1. Norman Thomas, *America's Way Out* (New York, 1931), p. 289; David A. Shannon, *The Socialist Party of America* (New York, 1955), p. 185; *Oklahoma Leader*, December 28, 1928.

2. Norman Thomas, "Why Not a New Party?" *North American Review* 207 (February 1929): 143-50.

3. Irwin M. Marcus, "Frank Crosswaith: Black Socialist, Labor Leader & Reformer," *Negro History Bulletin* 37 (August-September 1974): 287; speech of Frank R. Crosswaith at Negro Labor Committee Conference, Freedom House, June 28, 1952, copy in Harlem Labor Committee Archives, New York City.

4. *Pittsburgh Courier*, March 26, 1929.

5. Oneal, *The Next Emancipation*, with an introduction by Frank Crosswaith (New York, 1929). See also Harry W. Laidler, "The Socialist Message for the Negro," *New Leader*, June 1, 1929.

6. Franklin S. Roberts, "Frank R. Crosswaith: Harlem's Eugene V. Debs," *Political World* (July 1942): 8; *A Socialist Plan for New York: Official 1933 Campaign Handbook of the Socialist Party*, p. 8; *New Leader*, August 22, 28, February 21, 1931, March 4, 1933; *Labor and Socialist Press News*, February 16, 1934.

7. Claude McKay, "Negro Extinction or Survival: A Reply to George S. Schuyler," *Amsterdam News*, November 20, 1937.

8. Foner, *Organized Labor and the Black Worker*, p. 174.

9. *New Leader*, November 12, 1927, November 16, 1929, August 23, 1930. There is mention of Jesse Taylor, a black candidate for city council in Buffalo, New York, and John Gardner, for councilman in Norwalk, Connecticut (*New Leader*, November 2, 1930, August 5, 1931).

10. *New Leader*, October 29, 1929, October 13, 1930, June 20, 1931; *The Crisis* (September 1932): 279.

11. *New Leader*, April 11, 1925.

12. Edith Kline, "The Garment Union Comes to the Negro Worker," *Opportunity*, April 1934, pp. 107-8.

13. The Socialist Party of America, "Declaration of Principles (Chicago, Ill., 1930).

14. Albert Prago, "The Organization of the Unemployed and the Role of the Radicals, 1929-1935," Ph.D. dissertation, Union Graduate School, 1976, pp. 59-60. Prago points out that, in Chicago, the socialists "engaged in militant struggles on behalf of the unemployed" (p. 116). But there is no evidence that they did anything special for the unemployed blacks. Moreover, the movement in Chicago got under way late in 1932. See *New Frontier* 1, no. 1 (December 12, 1932).

15. Foner, *Organized Labor and the Black Worker*, pp. 189-90.

16. Frank R. Crosswaith, "The Negro and Socialism," Socialist Party of America, Chicago, Ill., copy in Tamiment Institute, Library of New York University.

17. "The Scottsboro Frameup," *Negro Labor News Service*, June 20, 1931.

18. "Unemployed Council Formed," ibid., August 1, 1931; "Socialists Organize Unemployed," *American Guardian*, December 16, 1932.

19. The Socialist Party of America, "1932 Election Platform" (Chicago, Ill., 1932).

20. Kirk Porter and David B. Johnson, *National Party Platforms, 1890-1956* (Urbana, Ill., 1956), p. 372.

21. *American Labor Yearbook*, 1926, pp. 235-40; 1930, pp. 118-22; *New Leader*, July 26, 1930, January 23, 1932, July 22, 1934, May 25, 1935; *Socialist Call*, February 21, 1936.

22. Foner, *Organized Labor and the Black Worker*, p. 190; Frank R. Crosswaith and Alfred Baker Lewis, *Negro and White Labor Unite for True Freedom* (New York, 1935), pp. 7-8, 17-21.

23. *New Leader*, October 8, 1932.

24. Ibid., October 29, 1932; *Opportunity*, November 1932, p. 340.

25. *New York Call*, November 13, 1918.

26. Norman Thomas, speech in St. Louis, *Labor and Socialist Press News Service*, September 18, 1936.

27. Frank Crosswaith, "For Whom Should the Negro Vote?" *Opportunity*, September 1932, p. 279; Frank Crosswaith in *New Leader*, December 20, 1930, and Alfred C. Parker in ibid., March 19, 1932; V. F. Calverton, "Critical Cruisings," ibid., October 23, 1926, and editorial in ibid., April 30, 1927; James Oneal in ibid., February 27, 1926; editorial in ibid., December 5, 1931.

28. James Oneal, *The Next Emancipation*, pp. 27, 30; Norman Thomas, "The Candidates Speak," *Opportunity*, November 1932, p. 340.

29. Ernest R. Doerfler, "Socialism and the American Negro Problem," *American Socialist Quarterly* (Summer 1933): 33-34.

30. For a discussion of the exclusionary racist practices in the AFL and the Railroad Brotherhoods during the 1920s and 1930s, see Foner, *Organized Labor and the Black Worker*, pp. 158-76, 188-215.

31. See *Proceedings of the National Convention of the Socialist Party*, 1926, p. 13; 1928, p. 151; 1936, pp. 621-22.

32. *Socialist Call*, October 5, 1935, p. 10; Doerfler, "Socialism and the American Negro Problem," op. cit., p. 35.

33. See Foner, *Organized Labor and the Black Worker*, pp. 149-50, 172-73, 179.

34. See Crosswaith and Baker, op. cit., p. 55; Crosswaith in *New Leader*, January 25, 1930, in *Negro Labor News Service*, January 18, 1930, and in *Socialist Call*, May 1, 1935, p. 4.

35. Foner, *Organized Labor and the Black Worker*, pp. 332, 341-45.

36. *New York Call*, November 23, 1918.

37. See "The Ku Klux Klan," *New York Call*, January 10, 1921; "Butchering Georgia Negroes," ibid., March 30, 1921; "Georgia in the Spotlight," ibid., April 28, 1921; "Race Relations in the South," ibid., May 21, 1921, and Chandler Owen, "Peonage, Riots, and Lynchers," *The Messenger*, August 1921.

38. James Oneal, "The Socialist Movement in the United States," *New York Call*, March 27, 1921.

39. Ibid., May 8, 1921.

40. Ibid., March 27, 1921.

41. *New Leader*, December 17, 1921.

42. *Proceedings, National Convention of the Socialist Party*, 1934, pp. 134-36; 1936, pp. 310-13.

43. Ibid., May 22, September 25, 1926, September 17, 1927, March 17, 1928, June 30, 1928.

44. Ibid., August 4, 1928, June 8, 1929.

45. Ibid., June 21, 1930.

46. Ibid., December 3, 1932.

47. *Labor and Socialist Press News*, December 27, 1930; David A. Shannon, *The Socialist Party of America* (New York, 1967), p. 209.

48. *Labor and Socialist Press News*, March 25, 1932; *New Leader*, March 19, 1932.

49. *New Leader*, May 17, 1932.

50. Ibid., August 13, 1932.

51. *Labor and Socialist Press News*, February 23, 1934.

52. *New Leader*, March 18, May 26, November 1, 1933.

53. Ibid., May 20, 1933.

54. *New York Times*, March 20, May 7, 1933.

55. Norman Thomas, "Jim-Crowism in the Capital," *New Republic* (May 31, 1933): 75.

56. "Reminiscences of H. L. Mitchell, Co-Founder, Southern Tenant Farmers' Union," Oral History Project, Columbia University during 1956 and 1957; interview with H. L. Mitchell, April 26, 1975, University of the Pacific, Stockton, Calif. Mitchell cites the Mayflower Hotel as the one picketed. It was the Cairo Hotel.

57. The account of the Southern Tenant Farmers' Union is based on an extensive study of the Southern Tenant Farmers' Union Papers, originals in the Southern Historical Collection, University of North Carolina, Chapel Hill, microfilm copies, Tamiment Institute, Bobst Library, New York University.

58. H. L. Mitchell to Norman Thomas, August 2, 1934, Southern Tenant Farmers' Union Papers, Microfilm, Reel 1.

59. Jerold S. Auerbach, "Southern Tenant Farmers: Socialist Critics of the New Deal," *Labor History* 7 (Winter 1966): 5-13.

60. Newspaper clipping (undated) in Southern Tenant Farmers' Union Papers, Microfilm, Reel 4.

61. H. L. Mitchell to Chester Hunt, March 24, 1936; Mitchell to A. S. Bayne, April 7, 1936, ibid., Microfilm, Reel 5.

62. Auerbach, op. cit., p. 17n.

63. Mark D. Naison, "Black Agrarian Radicalism in the Great Depression: The Threads of a Lost Tradition," *Journal of Ethnic Studies* 1 (Fall 1973): 57.

64. Circular, May 1936, Southern Tenant Farmers' Union Papers, Microfilm, Reel 3.

65. E. E. McKinney to Bob Miller, February 10, 1937, ibid., Microfilm, Reel 4.

66. Naison, op. cit., pp. 60-62.

67. The complex relationship between STFU and UCAPAWA can be traced in the Southern Tenant Farmers' Union Papers. For a summary of these relations, see Mark Naison, "The Southern Tenant Farmers' Union and the CIO," in Staughton Lynd, ed., *American Radicalism: Testimonies and Interpretations* (New York, 1973), pp. 75-99, and Lowell K. Dyson, "The Southern Tenant Farmers Union and Depression Politics," *Political Science Quarterly* 88 (February 1973): 230-52.

68. See, for example, Frank N. Trager, Labor and Organization Secretary, Socialist

Party, to J. R. Butler, February 5, 1937, Southern Tenant Farmers' Union Papers, Microfilm, Reel 4.

69. *Journal of the National Convention of the Socialist Party*, 1934; *New Leader*, December 24, 1932.

70. *New Leader*, December 22, 1934.

71. Ibid., September 20, 1930; *The Crisis* (February 1931): 45.

72. *New York Call*, July 4, 1923. The letter also appears in *The Correspondence of W.E.B. DuBois* with some slight change, vol. 1, pp. 266-70.

73. *New Leader*, February 9, 1929; *The Crisis* (August 1928), p. 257, November 1928, p. 368, September 1931, p. 315. See also Foner, *W.E.B. DuBois Speaks, 1920-1963*, pp. 43-46.

74. *New Leader*, February 9, 1929; Oneal, *The Next Emancipation*, p. 12. For Costley's role at the 1901 Socialist party convention, see above, pp. 94, 96, 100.

75. *Proceedings of the National Convention of the Socialist Party*, 1934, pp. 269-70.

76. Margaret L. Lamont, "The Negro's Stake in Socialism," *American Socialist Quarterly* (March 1935): 41-51. None of this discussion enters into Frank A. Warren's *An Alternative Vision: The Socialist Party in the 1930's* (Bloomington and London, 1974). Indeed, there is not a single mention of Negroes or blacks in the entire book.

77. *New Leader*, February 9, 1929.

78. *Socialist Call*, July 13, 1935.

79. George Streator, "The Negro: Step-Child of Socialism," *Revolutionary Socialist* 1 (Summer 1935): 15-20. See also George Streator, "The Negro, the South and the Socialist Party," ibid. (Autumn 1935): pp. 6-7.

80. *Socialist Call*, February 15, 1936.

81. *Draft for a Program for the United States, as formulated by the Left Wing at the Socialist Call Institute, Bound Brook, N.J., Sept. 7-8*. Published by the *Socialist Call*, November 1935.

82. *Socialist Call*, June 6, 1936.

83. Ibid., December 5, 1936.

84. The National Negro Congress was organized in 1936 with A. Philip Randolph as president and John P. Davis as executive secretary. It was organized at a founding convention in Chicago, February 14-16, 1936, attended by 817 delegates representing 585 organizations from twenty-eight states. The original Executive Board included men and women like Ralph Bunche, Maude White, and James W. Ford, the black communist leader.

85. Other members of the committee were Elizabeth Gilman of Baltimore, Eloise O. Fickland of Philadelphia, Alfred Baker Lewis and Ralph M. Harlow of Massachusetts, and Norma Taylor and C. A. Walters of New York.

86. *Socialist Call*, February 6, 1937.

87. In 1934 and 1935, the AFL convention had rejected what came to be known as the "Randolph Resolution," despite the endorsement of the National Negro Congress, Cleveland Metal Trades Council, the District Council of Painters, the Cleveland Federation of Labor, the Ohio Council, the Buffalo Central Labor Union, and the Maritime Federation of the Pacific Coast. Thereafter until 1939, the annual AFL convention regularly turned down the "Randolph Resolution." In 1939, the delegates adopted a weak resolution calling upon affiliated unions whose constitutions had discriminatory clauses to report on the question of the color bar and various forms of racial discrimination at the next convention. Nothing was done thereafter. (See Foner, *Organized Labor and the Black Worker*, pp. 236-37.

88. Foner, *Organized Labor and the Black Worker*, pp. 215-37.

89. Quoted in Herbert Aptheker, ed., *A Documentary History of the Negro People in the United States, 1933-1945* (New York, 1974), p. 274.

90.  Frank (Crosswaith) to Dr. Norman Thomas, January 28, 1937, Norman Thomas Papers, New York Public Library, Manuscripts Division; Mark D. Naison, "The Communist Party in Harlem, 1928-1936," Ph.D. dissertation, Columbia University, 1975, p. 410.

91.  *Socialist Call*, March 20, 1937.

92.  Ibid., April 17, 1937.

93.  Ibid., October 1, 1938.

94.  Ibid., April 29, 1939.

# Bibliography

MANUSCRIPTS

Chicago Historical Society:
  John Fitzpatrick Papers.
Columbia University Oral History Project:
  Reminiscences of H. L. Mitchell, Southern Tenant Farmers' Union.
Cunningham Memorial Library, Indiana State University:
  Theodore Debs Papers.
  Sam Moore, "Eugene Victor Debs, The Superman—A Close Up View of Him."
Duke University Library:
  Socialist Party of America Papers.
  William Mailly Letterpress Books, Bureau of Information, Socialist Party.
Harlem Labor Committee Archives, New York City:
  Speech of Frank R. Crosswaith at Negro Labor Committee Conference, Freedom House,
      June 28, 1952.
Houghton Library, Harvard University:
  Oswald Garrison Villard Papers.
Library of Congress:
  Ray Stannard Baker Papers.
  Papers of the National Association for the Advancement of Colored People.
  Frederick Law Olmsted Papers.
  Charles Edward Russell Papers.
  Arthur B. Spingarn Papers.
  Booker T. Washington Papers.
National Archives:
  Department of Justice Files, Record Group 60, 1940.
New York Public Library:
  Friedrich A. Sorge Papers.
  National Civic Federation Papers.
  Norman Thomas Papers.
New York Public Library, Schomburg Collection:
  "Cyril Briggs and the African Brotherhood," WPA Writers' Project No. 1, Reporter:
      Carl Offord.

New York State Library, Albany:
  Lusk Committee Papers.
Oklahoma Department of Libraries, Archives and Records, Oklahoma City:
  In the Matter of Initiative Petition, No. 10, Filed by Fred P. Bronson, 10th day of June,
    1910, signed by Patrick S. Nagle, and including Argument submitted by O. F.
    Granstreeter, John Hegel, Oscar Ameringer, W. L. Reynolds, and P. S. Nagle,
    Committee.
State Historical Society of Wisconsin, Madison:
  Daniel DeLeon Correspondence, Socialist Labor Party Papers.
  Letter Book, IWA Papers.
  Statuten des Kommunisten Klubs in New York, US Mss, 15A, Box 4.
  William English Walling Papers.
Tamiment Institute, Elmer Holmes Bobst Library, New York University:
  Eugene V. Debs Scrapbooks.
  Morris Hillquit Papers (microfilm).
  Local New York, Socialist Party Papers.
  Socialist Labor Party Papers (microfilm).
  Southern Tenant Farmers' Union Papers (microfilm).
  B. Charnney Vladeck Papers.
  Proceedings of the Founding Convention of the Socialist Party, 1901.
Tulane University, Howard-Tilton Library:
  Covington Hall, "Labor Struggles in the Deep South."
University of Texas, Austin:
  James W. Baird Papers.


UNPUBLISHED DISSERTATIONS

Birbaum, Max. "Northern Labor in the National Crisis, 1860-1861." B.S. thesis, University of Wisconsin, 1938.
Buhle, Paul M. "Marxism in the United States, 1900-1940." Ph.D. dissertation, University of Wisconsin, 1975.
Dancis, Bruce. "The Socialist Woman's Movement in the United States, 1901-1917." Senior Thesis, American Radicalism in the Twentieth Century, University of California, Santa Cruz, 1973.
Goozner, Merill, "Peter H. Clark of Cincinnati." Unpublished Seminar Paper, Afro-American History, University of Cincinnati, 1974.
Graham, Donald. "Red, White and Black: An Interpretation of Ethnic and Racial Attitudes of Agrarian Radicals in Texas and Oklahoma, 1880-1920." M.A. thesis, University of Saskatchewan, Regina Campus, 1975.
Green, James R. "Socialism and the Southwestern Class Struggle, 1898-1918, A Study of Radical Movements in Oklahoma, Texas, Louisiana, and Arkansas." Ph.D. dissertation, Yale University, 1972.
Kennedy, Philip Wayne. "The Concept of Racial Superiority and United States Imperialism, 1890-1910." Ph.D. dissertation, St. Louis University, 1962.
Kornweibel, Theodore, Jr. "The Messenger Magazine: 1917-1918." Ph.D. dissertation, Yale University, 1971.
McCord, Charles H. "A Brief History of the Brotherhood of Timber Workers." M.A. thesis, University of Texas, 1959.
McWhiney, H. Grady. "The Socialist Vote in Louisiana, 1912: An Historical Interpretation of Radical Sources." M.A. thesis, Louisiana State University, 1951.

Muzak, Edward John. "Victor L. Berger, A Biography." Ph.D. dissertation, Northwestern University, 1960.

Naison, Mark, "The Communist Party in Harlem, 1928-1936," Ph.D. dissertation, Columbia University, 1975.

Prago, Albert. "The Organization of the Unemployed and the Role of the Radicals, 1929-1935." Ph.D. dissertation, Union Graduate School and Institute for Policy Studies, 1976.

Reese, James Verde. "The Worker in Texas, 1821-1876." Ph.D. dissertation, University of Texas, 1964.

Rhodes, James B. "The Campaign of the Socialist Party in the Election of 1920." M.A. thesis, American University, 1965.

Ross, Marc. "John Swinton, Journalist and Reformer: The Active Years, 1857-1887." Ph.D. dissertation, New York University, 1968.

Scales, James R. "The Political History of Oklahoma, 1907-1949." Ph.D. dissertation, University of Oklahoma, 1949.

Solomon, Mark. "Red and Black: Negroes and Communism." Ph.D. dissertation, Harvard University, 1972.

## GOVERNMENT DOCUMENTS

*Cartwright v. Board of Education of the City of Coffeyville, Kansas Reports.* Vol. 72.

New York (State) Legislature. *Joint Legislative Committee Investigating Seditious Activities, Revolutionary Radicalism, Its History, Purpose and Tactics, with an Exposition and Discussion Being Taken and Required to Curb It.* Vol. 2. Albany, 1920.

Palmer, A. Mitchell. *Investigative Activities of the Department of Justice.* 66th Cong., 1st Sess., 1919, *Senate Document 153.* Vol. 12.

*Reynolds v. Board of Education of City of Topeka, Kansas, Reports v. 66, in the Supreme Court of Kansas, William Reynolds, Plaintiff, The Board of Education of the City of Topeka, of the State of Kansas, Defendant, Brief of Plaintiff, G. C. Clemens, and F. J. Lynch, Attorneys for Plaintiff.* Topeka, n.d.

## NEWSPAPERS AND MAGAZINES

*Alarm, The* (Chicago).
*AME Church Review* (Washington, D.C.).
*American Fabian* (Boston).
*American Guardian* (Oklahoma City).
*American Socialist Quarterly.*
*Amsterdam News* (New York).
*Anarchist, The* (Boston).
*Appeal, The* (St. Paul).
*Appeal to Reason* (Girard, Kans.).
*Arbeiter-Zeitung* (Chicago).
*Arbeiter-Zeitung* (New York).
*Ballot Box* (Fallon, Nev.).
*Baltimore Afro-American.*
*Bee-Hive* (London).
*Birmingham Age-Herald.*
*Birmingham Labor Advocate.*
*Boston Daily Evening Voice.*
*Bulletin of the Intercollegiate Society.*

*California Social Democrat* (Los Angeles).
*Carpenter, The.*
*Charleston News & Courier.*
*Chicago Daily News.*
*Chicago Daily Socialist.*
*Chicago Evening World.*
*Cincinnati Commercial.*
*Cincinnati Enquirer.*
*City and State* (Philadelphia).
*Class Struggle, The* (New York).
*Cleveland Citizen.*
*Colored American* (Washington, D.C.).
*Colored American Magazine, The* (Washington, D.C.).
*Common Sense* (Los Angeles).
*Comrade, The* (New York).
*Conservator, The* (Philadelphia).
*Crisis, The* (New York).
*Daily Oklahoman* (Oklahoma City).
*Daily Worker* (New York).
*Dallas Morning News.*
*Der Pionier* (Boston).
*Die New Yorker Yiddish Volkszeitung.*
*Die Wecker* (Baltimore).
*Emancipator, The* (Cincinnati).
*Fort Worth Register.*
*Frederick Douglass' Paper* (Rochester).
*Freeman, The* (Indianapolis).
*Galveston Daily News.*
*Harbinger, The* (Boston).
*Herald of Freedom* (Concord, N.H.).
*Horizon, The* (Nashville).
*Howard University Journal* (Washington, D.C.).
*Huntington Socialist and Labor Star.*
*Industrial Democrat* (Oklahoma City).
*Industrial Worker* (Spokane).
*Intercollegiate Socialist, The* (New York).
*International Socialist Review* (Chicago).
*Iron Platform, The* (New York).
*John Swinton's Paper* (New York).
*Journal of United Labor.*
*Knights of Labor* (Chicago).
*Labor Standard* (New York).
*Liberator, The* (Boston).
*Liberty* (Boston).
*Literary Digest, The* (New York).
*Los Angeles Socialist.*
*Manchester Guardian.*
*Masses, The* (New York).
*Messenger, The* (New York).
*Milwaukee News.*
*Milwaukee Sentinel.*
*Monthly Bulletin of the Socialist Party* (New York).
*Mother Earth* (New York).

*Nashville Republican Banner.*
*National Anti-Slavery Standard* (New York).
*National Rip-Saw* (Kansas City).
*Negro World* (New York).
*Neue Zeit* (St. Louis).
*New Harmony Gazette* (Indiana).
*New Leader* (New York).
*New Nation, The* (Boston).
*New Orleans Daily Picayune.*
*New Review* (New York).
*New York Age.*
*New York American.*
*New York Call.*
*New York Evening Call.*
*New York Freeman.*
*New York Herald.*
*New York Post.*
*New York Times.*
*New York Tribune.*
*New York World.*
*New Yorker Demokrat.*
*New Yorker Staatszeitung.*
*New Yorker Volkszeitung.*
*North Star, The* (Rochester).
*Ohio Socialist Bulletin.*
*Oklahoma Leader* (Oklahoma City).
*Party Builder, The.*
*People, The* (New York).
*Philadelphia Press.*
*Pittsburgh Courier.*
*Pittsburgh Dispatch.*
*Prolocutor* (Nevada).
*Public, The* (Chicago).
*Railway Times* (Chicago).
*Rebel* (Halletsville, Tex.).
*Rebel, The* (Boston).
*Revolutionary Age* (New York).
*Revolutionary Socialist* (New York).
*Richmond Dispatch.*
*Richmond Planet.*
*Richmond Times-Dispatch.*
*Richmond Whig.*
*St. Louis Globe-Democrat.*
*St. Louis Labor.*
*St. Louis Missouri Republican.*
*St. Louis Times.*
*San Antonio Zeitung.*
*San Diegan-Sun.*
*San Francisco Call.*
*San Francisco Chronicle.*
*Savannah News.*
*Scranton Republican.*
*Seattle Socialist.*

*Social Democrat, The.*
*Sociale Republik* (New York).
*Socialist, The* (Chicago).
*Socialist, The* (Detroit).
*Southern Socialist, The* (Jackson, Miss.).
*True Nationalist* (Boston).
*Union Printer* (Washington, D.C.).
*Voice of the Negro, The* (Atlanta).
*Voice of the People, The* (New Orleans).
*Vorbote* (Chicago).
*Washington Bee.*
*Washington Evening Post.*
*Wayland's Monthly* (Girard, Kans.).
*Western Texan.*
*Whim-Wham, The* (Kansas City).
*Wilshire's Magazine* (Los Angeles).
*Wooden Shoe, The* (Los Angelex).
*Worker, The* (New York).
*Workers' Call, The* (Chicago).
*Working Man's Advocate* (New York).
*Workingman's Advocate* (Chicago).
*Workmen's Advocate* (New Haven).
*Young America* (New York).

## PAMPHLETS AND LEAFLETS

Aptheker, Herbert. *The Labor Movement in the South During Slavery.* New York, n.d.
Crosswaith, Frank. "The Negro and Socialism." Socialist Party of America, Chicago, Ill.,
     n.d.
——, and Lewis, Alfred Baker. *Negro and White Labor Unite for True Freedom.* New
     York, 1935.
*Delcaration of Principles, Issued by the Socialist Party of America.* Chicago, 1930.
De Leon, Daniel. *Flashlights of the Amsterdam Congress.* New York, 1906.
Douai, Dr. Adolf. *Das ABC des Sozialismus.* Altenburg, Germany, 1851.
——. *Heinzen, Wie Er Ist.* New York, 1869.
——. *Volkskatechismus der Altenburger Republinaner.* Altenburg, Germany, 1848.
*Draft for a Program for the United States as Formulated by the Left Wing at the Socialist
     Call Institute, Bound Brook, N.J., Sept. 7-8.* New York, 1935.
Herriott, Frank T. *The Conference of German-Republicans in the Deutsches-Haus, Chi-
     cago, May 14-15, 1860.* Chicago, n.d.
*Journal of the Convention of the Socialist Party, 1934.*
Miller, Rev. George. *A Reply to the Political Plea of Bishop Cleland K. Nielson and Bishop
     F. Gaelon, at Cathedral of St. John the Divine in the City of New York, Saturday
     Evening, October, 1913.* New York, 1914.
National Committee of the Socialist Party. *Proceedings of the National Convention of the
     Socialist Party Held at Chicago, May 1 to 6, 1904.* Chicago, 1904.
——. *Proceedings, National Congress of the Socialist Party, Held at Chicago, Illinois,
     May 10 to 17, 1908.* Chicago, 1908.
——. *Proceedings, National Convention of the Socialist Party, Held at Indianapolis,
     Ind., May 12 to 18, 1912, Stenographic Report.* Chicago, 1912.

———. *Proceedings of the National Convention of the Socialist Party.* 1926, 1928, 1934.

*The Negro Workers by Eugene Victor Debs, Address Delivered Tuesday, October 30, 1923, Commonwealth Casino, 135th Street and Madison Avenue, N.Y.C.* New York, 1924.

*1932 Election Platform. Issued by the Socialist Party of America.* Chicago, Ill., 1932.

O'Hare, Kate Richards. *"Nigger Equality."* Chicago, 1912.

Oneal, James. *The Next Emancipation.* New York, 1922.

———. *The Next Emancipation.* With an introduction by Frank Crosswaith. New York, 1929.

Ovington, Mary White. *How the National Association for the Advancement of Colored People Began.* New York, 1914.

*Platform and Constitution of the Socialist Party, October, 1881.* New York, 1881.

*Proceedings of the Convention of Colored Men of Ohio, Held in the City of Cincinnati on the 23d, 24th, 25th & 26th Days of November, 1858.* Cincinnati, 1858.

*Proceedings, Convention of Colored Newspaper Men. Cincinnati, August 4, 1975.* Cincinnati, 1875.

*Proceedings, General Assembly, Knights of Labor.* 1886. Washington, D.C., 1886.

*Proceedings of the Tenth Convention of the Socialist Labor Party, Held in New York City, June 2 to June 8, 1900.* New York, 1901.

*Proceedings of the National Negro Conference, New York, May 31 and June 1, 1909.* n.p., n.d.

*The Rand School of Social Science, Bulletin 1919-1920.*

Randolph A. Philip, and Owen, Chandler. *Terms of Peace and the Darker Races.* New York, 1917.

*Report of Proceedings, Sixth Congress of the Socialistic Labor Party, Turn Hall, Buffalo, N.Y., Sept. 17-20, 1887.* New York, 1887.

*Socialist Pamphlet No. 25.* New York, 1908.

*Socialistic Labor Party, Platform, Constitution, and Discussion from 25, 26, 27, 28 December, 1879.* New York, 1880.

*Socialistische Arbeiter-Partei, Platform, Constitution, und Beschluss, welche von der 26, 27, 28, 30, und zu Newark, N.J.* Cincinnati, 1878.

"Some Reasons Why Negroes Should Vote the Socialist Ticket, by the Independent Political Council."

*Souvenir Journal of the National Convention, Socialist Party.* New York, 1920.

"State Platform of the Socialist Party of Oklahoma, 1912." Oklahoma City, 1912.

"State Platform of the Socialist Party of Tennessee, Adopted July, 1912." Nashville, 1912.

Vail, Charles H. *Socialism and the Negro Problem.* New York, 1902.

"Virginia Socialist Protest Proves Prejudice Absent." Richmond, 1900.

"Why Negroes Should Be Socialists." Chicago, 1920.

Woodbey, Rev. George W. *The Bible and Socialism: A Conversation Between Two Preachers.* San Diego, Calif., 1904.

———. *The Distribution of Wealth.* San Diego, Calif., 1910.

———. *What to Do and How to Do It. or Socialism vs. Capitalism, Waylands Monthly, No. 40, August, 1903.*

## MISCELLANEOUS

Labor and Socialist Press News Service.

Negro Labor News Service.

[424] BIBLIOGRAPHY

BOOKS

Adams, Ephraim Douglas. *Great Britain and the American Civil War.* Vol. 2. New York, 1926.
Allen, James S. *Reconstruction: The Battle for Democracy.* New York, 1937.
Allen, Ruth V. *East Texas Lumber Workers: An Economic and Social Picture.* Austin, Tex., 1964.
*American Labor Year Book.* New York, 1926.
Ameringer, Oscar. *If You Don't Weaken, An Autobiography.* New York, 1940.
Anderson, Jervis. *A. Philip Randolph: A Biographical Portrait.* New York, 1972.
Aptheker, Herbert. *American Negro Slave Revolts.* New York, 1943.
— — —, ed. *The Autobiography of W.E.B. DuBois, A Soliloquy on Viewing My Life from the Last Decade of Its First Century.* New York, 1968.
— — —, ed. *The Correspondence of W.E.B. DuBois, Vol. 1, 1877-1934.* Amherst, Mass., 1973.
— — —, ed. *A Documentary History of the Negro People in the United States.* New York, 1951.
— — —, ed. *A Documentary History of the Negro People in the United States, 1910-1932.* Secaucus, N.J., 1973.
— — —, ed. *A Documentary History of the Negro People in the United States, 1933-1945.* Secaucus, N.J., 1974.
Ashbaugh, Carolyn, *Lucy Parsons, American Revolutionary.* Chicago, 1976.
Aveling, Edward, and Marx, Eleanor. *The Working Class Movement in America.* London, 1891.
Bardolph, Ralph. *The Negro Vanguard.* New York, 1959.
Baringer, W. L. *Lincoln's Rise to Power.* Boston, 1937.
Bellamy, Edward. *Equality.* Boston, 1897.
— — —. *Looking Backward.* Boston, 1884.
— — —. *Looking Forward.* Boston, 1887.
Benjamin, Gilbert Giddings. *The Germans in Texas: A Study in Immigration.* Austin, Tex., 1974.
Bernstein, Samuel. *The First International in America.* New York, 1965.
Blatchford, Robert. *Merrie England.* London, 1894.
Brown, Wm. Wells. *The Rising Son; Or the Antecedents and Advancement of the Colored Race.* Boston, 1882.
Bruce, Robert W. *1877: Year of Violence.* Indianapolis, Ind., 1958.
Burbank, David. *Reign of the Rabble: The St. Louis General Strike of 1877.* New York, 1966.
Calmar, Alan. *Labor Agitator, The Story of Albert R. Parsons.* New York, 1937.
Chalmers, David M. *Hooded Americanism: The History of the Ku Klux Klan.* Garden City, N.Y., 1965.
Chamberlin, Edward Martin. *The Sovereigns of Industry.* Boston, 1875.
Chamberlin, Lawrence H. *Loyalty and Legislative Action, A Survey of Activity by the New York State Legislature, 1919-1949.* Ithaca, N.Y., 1951.
Chicago Commission on Race Relations. *The Negro in Chicago: A Study of Race Relations and a Race Riot in 1919.* Chicago, 1922.
Commons, John R., ed. *A Documentary History of American Industrial Society.* Vol. 7. Cleveland, 1910.
Cronin, Edmund David. *Black Moses: The Story of Marcus Garvey and the Universal Negro Improvement Association.* Madison, Wis., 1960.
Cruse, Harold. *The Crisis of the Negro Intellectual.* New York, 1967.
Dabney, Wendell Phillips. *Cincinnati's Colored Citizens.* Cincinnati, 1926.

David, Henry. *The History of the Haymarket Affair*. New York, 1936.

Detweiler, Frederick T. *The Negro Press in the United States*. Chicago, 1912.

*Dictionary of American Biography*. Vol. 4. New York, 1946. Vol. 23. New York, 1958.

*Documents of the First International: The General Council of the First International 1864-1866: Minutes*. Moscow, n.d.

Dorfman, Joseph. *The Economic Mind in American Civilization*. Vol. 3. New York, 1959.

Draper, Theodore. *The Roots of American Communism*. New York, 1957.

Dubofsky, Melvin. *We Shall Be All: A History of the IWW*. Chicago, 1969.

Du Bois, W.E.B. *Black Reconstruction in America, 1860-1880*. New York, 1935.

— — —. *The Souls of Black Folk*. New York, 1903. Reprinted with a preface by Herbert Aptheker. New York, 1973.

Ellison, Mary. *Support for Secession*. Chicago, 1972.

Engels, Frederick. *Socialism: Utopian and Scientific*. New York, 1935.

Esterlin, Richard A. *American Economic Growth: An Economist's History of the United States*. New York, 1972.

Farley, Reynolds. *Growth of the Black Population*. Chicago, 1970.

Fink, Gary M. *Labor's Search for Political Order: The Political Behavior of the Missouri Labor Movement, 1890-1940*. Columbia, Mo., 1970.

Fiske, John. *Old Virginia and Her Neighbors*. Boston, 1897.

Fleming, Walter L. *Documentary History of Reconstruction, Political, Military, Social, Religious, Educational and Industrial, 1865 to the Present Time*. Vol. 1. Cleveland, 1906-1907.

Fogel, Robert William, and Engleman, Stanley L. *Time on the Cross: The Economics of American Negro Slavery*. Boston, 1974.

Foner, Eric. *Free Soil, Free Labor, Free Men: The Ideology of the Republican Party Before the Civil War*. New York. 1970.

Foner Philip S. *The Bolshevik Revolution: Its Impact on American Radicals, Liberals, and Labor*. New York, 1967.

— — —. *Business and Slavery: The New York Merchants and the Irrepressible Conflict*. New York, 1940.

— — —. *Helen Keller, Her Socialist Years*. New York, 1967.

— — —. *History of Black Americans: From Africa to the Emergence of the Cotton Kingdom*. Westport, Conn., 1975.

— — —. *History of the Labor Movement in the United States*. Vol. 1. New York, 1947.

— — —. *History of the Labor Movement in the United States*. Vol. 2. New York, 1955.

— — —. *History of the Labor Movement in the United States*. Vol. 3. New York, 1964.

— — —. *History of the Labor Movement in the United States*. Vol. 4. New York, 1965.

— — —. *Jack London: American Rebel*. New York, 1947.

— — —. *The Life and Writings of Frederick Douglass*. Vol. 1. New York, 1950.

— — —. *Organized Labor and the Black Worker, 1691-1973*. New York, 1974.

— — —, ed. *The Formation of the Workingmen's Party of the United States: Proceedings of the Union Congress Held at Philadelphia, July 19-22, 1876*. New York, 1976.

— — —, ed. *The Voice of Black Americans: Speeches by Blacks in the United States, 1797-1974*. 2 vols. New York, 1975.

— — —, ed. *W.E.B. Du Bois Speaks: Speeches and Addresses, 1890-1919*. New York, 1970.

— — —, ed. *W.E.B. Du Bois Speaks: Speeches and Addresses, 1920-1963*. New York, 1970.

— — —, ed. *When Karl Marx Died: Comments in 1883*. New York, 1973.

Fortune, T. Thomas. *Black and White: Land, Labor and Politics in the South*. New York, 1884.

Foster, William Z. *History of the Communist Party of the United States*. New York, 1952.

Friedman, Laurence J. *The White Savage: Radical Fantasies in the Postbellum South*. Englewood Cliffs, N.J., 1970.

Galbreath, Charles B. *History of Ohio*. Vol. 1. New York, 1925.

Gavett, Thomas W. *Development of the Labor Movement in Milwaukee*. Milwaukee, Wis., 1965.

Gemkow, Heinrich, and Associates. *Frederick Engels, A Biography*. Dresden, Germany, 1972.

Genovese, Eugene D. *Roll, Jordan, Roll: The World the Slaves Made*. New York, 1974.

Gilbert, Peter, ed. *The Selected Writings of John Edward Bruce, Militant Black Journalist*. New York, 1971.

Ginger, Ray. *The Bending Cross: A Biography of Eugene Victor Debs*. New Brunswick, N.J., 1949.

Goldmark, Josephine. *Impatient Crusader: Florence Kelley's Life Work*. Urbana, Ill., 1953.

Goodwyn, Lawrence. *Democratic Promise: The Populist Movement in America*. New York, 1976.

Harlan, Louis R. *Booker T. Washington: The Making of a Black Leader*. New York, 1972.

Hass, Eric. *Socialism, A World Without Prejudice*. New York, n.d.

Haupt, George, ed. *Bureau Socialiste Internationale: Comptes rendus des reunions manifestes et Circulares, 1900-1907*. Paris, 1969.

Haywood, William D. *Big Bill Haywood's Book*. New York, 1927.

Herreshoff, David. *American Disciples of Marx: From the Age of Jackson to the Progressive Era*. Detroit, 1967.

Hillquit, Morris. *History of Socialism in the United States*. New York, 1903.

Hobsbawm, E. P. *Primitive Rebels*. Manchester, England, 1959.

Holloway, Mark. *Heaven on Earth: Utopian Communities in America, 1680-1880*. New York, 1951.

Howe, Irving, and Closer, Lewis. *The American Communist Party: A Critical History*. New York, 1962.

Jackson, Kenneth J. *The Ku Klux Klan in the City, 1915-1930*. New York, 1967.

Jacques-Garvey, Amy. *Black Power in America*. Kingston, Jamaica, 1968.

— — —. *Philosophy and Opinions of Marcus Garvey*. Vol. 2. New York, 1925.

Jaffe, Julian E. *Crusade Against Radicalism: New York During the Red Scare, 1914-1924*. Port Washington, N.Y., 1972.

Jamieson, Stuart. "Labor Unionism in American Agriculture." U.S. Department of Labor, Bureau of Labor Statistics, Bulletin No. 836. Washington, D.C., 1945.

Jensen, Vernon L. *Lumber and Labor*. New York, 1944.

Johnson, Gunnan. *Racial Ideologies*. Vol. 2. New York, 1905.

Kapp, Friedrich. *Geschichte der Sklaverei in den Vereinigten Staaten von Amerika*. New York, 1860.

Kellogg, Charles Flint. *NAACP: A History of the National Association for the Advancement of Colored People, vol. 1, 1907-1920*. Baltimore, 1967.

Kerlin, Robert T., ed. *The Voice of the Negro, 1919*. New York, 1920.

Kipnis, Ira. *The American Socialist Movement, 1897-1912*. New York, 1952.

Laughlin, Seiva Bright. *Missouri Politics During the Civil War*. Salem, Ore., 1930.

*Lenin on the United States: Selected Writings, by V. I. Lenin*. New York, 1970.

*Life and Times of Frederick Douglass*. Collier edition. New York, 1962.

McCool, B. Boren. *Union Reaction and Riot: A Biography of a Rural Race Riot*. Memphis, Tenn., 1970.

McLaurin, Melton A. *Paternalism and Protest: Southern Cotton Mill Workers and Organized Labor, 1875-1905*. Westport, Conn., 1972.

McPherson, James H. *The Abolitionist Legacy: From Reconstruction to the NAACP*. Princeton, N.J., 1975.

Malcolm, James, ed. *The New York Red Book: An Illustrated State Manual.* Albany, N.Y., 1921.

Martin, Tony. *Race First: The Ideological and Organizational Struggles of Marcus Garvey and the Universal Negro Improvement Association.* Westport, Conn., 1976.

Marx, Karl. *Capital.* Vol. 1. New York, 1939.

Marx, Karl, and Engels, Frederick. *Werke.* Band 34. Berlin, 1967.

Mather, John. *Who's Who of the Colored Race.* Chicago, 1921.

Meier, August. *Negro Thought in America, 1880-1915.* Ann Arbor, Mich., 1963.

Moore, Frank, ed. *Rebellion Record.* Vol. 1. New York, 1962.

Moyer, Harvey P., ed. *Songs of Socialism.* Chicago, 1902.

Obermann, Karl. *Joseph Weydemeyer: Pioneer of American Socialism.* New York, 1947.

Olmsted, Frederick Law. *A Journey Through Texas.* New York, 1860.

Osofsky, Gilbert. *Harlem: The Making of a Ghetto.* New York, 1963.

Ovington, Mary White. *The Walls Came Tumbling Down.* New York, 1947.

Painter, Nell Irwin. *Exodusters: Black Migration to Kansas After Reconstruction.* New York, 1977.

Pease, William H., and Pease, Jane H. *Black Utopia: Negro Communal Experiments in America.* Madison, Wis., 1963.

Pemberton, Caroline H. *Stephen the Black.* Philadelphia, 1899.

Peterson, Arnold. *Daniel De Leon: Social Architecht.* Vol 2. New York, 1941.

Peterson, H. C., and Fite, Gilbert C. *Opponents of War, 1917-1918.* Madison, Wis., 1957.

Phillips, Ulrich B. *Georgia and State Rights.* Washington, D.C., 1902.

Porter, Kirk H., and Johnson, Donald Bruce. *National Party Platforms, 1840-1956.* Urbana, Ill., 1956.

Powderly, Terence V. *Thirty Years of Labor, 1859-1889.* Columbia, Ohio, 1889.

Preston, William, Jr. *Aliens and Dissenters: Federal Suppression of Radicals, 1903-1933.* Cambridge, Mass., 1933.

Quarles, Benjamin. *Black Abolitionists.* New York, 1969.

Quint, Howard H. *The Forging of American Socialism.* Columbia, S. C., 1953.

Rampersad, Arnold. *The Art and Imagination of W.E.B. Du Bois.* Cambridge, Mass., 1976.

Reeve, Carl. *The Life and Times of Daniel DeLeon.* New York, 1972.

Rice, Lawrence D. *The Negro in Texas, 1874-1900.* Baton Rouge, La., 1971.

Rogers, Joel August. *World's Great Men of Color.* Vol. 2. New York, 1943.

Rogers, William W. *The One-Gallused Rebellion: Agrarianism in Alabama.* Baton Rouge, La., 1971.

Rombauer, Robert J. *The Union Cause in St. Louis, 1861.* St. Louis, 1909.

Roper, Laura Wood. *FLO: A Biography of Frederick Law Olmsted.* Baltimore and London, 1973.

Ross, B. Joyce. *J. E. Spingarn and the Rise of the NAACP, 1911-1939.* New York, 1972.

Rude, George. *Crowd in History: A Study in Popular Disturbance in France and England, 1730-1848.* New York, 1964.

Rudwick, Elliot M. *Race Riot at East St. Louis, July 5, 1917.* Carbondale, Ill., 1964.

— — —. *W.E.B. Du Bois: A Study in Minority Group Leadership.* Philadelphia, 1960.

Russell, Charles Edward. *Bare Hands and Stone Walls.* New York, 1933.

Sandburg, Carl. *Abraham Lincoln, The War Years.* Vol. 1. New York, 1936.

Saunders, Henry, comp. *Complete Index to "The Conservator."* Toronto, 1920.

Schirmer, Daniel B. *Republic or Empire: American Resistance to the Philippine War.* Cambridge, Mass., 1972.

Schlüter, Hermann. *Die Anfange der Deutschen Arbeiterbewegung in Amerika.* Stuttgart, 1907.

— — —. *Die International in Amerika: Ein Betrag zur Geschichte der Arbeiter Bewegung in den Vereinigten Staaten.* Chicago, 1918.

— — —. *Lincoln, Labor and Slavery.* New York, 1913.

Schuyler, George S. *Black and Conservative.* New Rochelle, N.Y., 1966.

Shannon, David A. *The Socialist Party of America.* New York, 1955.

Shulman, Alex Kates, ed. *Red Emma Speaks: Selected Writings and Speeches by Emma Goldman.* New York, 1972.

Simmons, William J. *Men of Mark: Eminent, Progressive and Rising.* Cleveland, 1890.

Sinclair, Upton. *The Jungle.* New York, 1906.

Smith, Edward Conrad. *The Borderland in the Civil War.* New York, 1927.

Sorge, Friedrich A. *The Labor Movement in the United States.* Trans. by Brewster and Angela Chamberlin, ed. by Philip S. Foner and Brewster Chamberlin. Westport, Conn., 1977.

Spiller, Gustav, ed. *Papers on Inter-Racial Problems Communicated to the First Universal Races Congress, Held at the University of London, July 26-29, 1911.* London, 1911. Reprinted with an introduction by Herbert Aptheker, New York, 1970.

Stampp, Kenneth M. *The Peculiar Institution: Slavery in the Ante-Bellum South.* New York, 1955.

Stanton, William. *The Leopard's Spots: Scientific Attitudes Toward Race in America, 1815-1859.* Chicago, 1960.

Starnes, George Talmadge, and Hamm, Edwin. *Some Phases of Labor Relations in the South.* New York, 1934.

Stekloff, G. M. *History of the First International.* New York, 1923.

Thomas, Norman. *America's Way Out.* New York, 1931.

Thompson, E. P. *The Making of the English Working Class.* London, 1963.

Thornbrough, Emma Lou. *T. Thomas Fortune—Militant Journalist.* Chicago, 1972.

Thorp, Louise Hall. *The Peabody Sisters of Salem.* New York, 1968.

Tilly, Charles. *The Vendee.* New York, 1967.

Trachtenberg, Alexander, ed. *American Labor Year Book, 1919-1920.* New York, 1920.

U.S. Department of Labor. *Negro Migration in 1916-1917.* Washington, D.C., 1919.

Wachman, Marvin. *History of the Social-Democratic Party in Milwaukee, 1898-1910.* Urbana, Ill., 1945.

Walling, William English. *Socialism As It Is: A Survey of the World-Wide Revolutionary.* New York, 1912.

— — —. *The Socialism of Today.* New York, 1916.

Warren, Frank A. *An Alternative Vision: The Socialist Party in the 1930's.* Bloomington, Ind., and London, 1974.

Washington, Nathaniel J. *The Historical Development of the Negro in Oklahoma.* Tulsa, Okla., 1948.

Waskow, Arthur I. *From Race Riot to Sit-In, 1919 and the 1960's: A Study in the Connections Between Conflict and Violence.* New York, 1966.

Waterman, William Randall. *Frances Wright.* New York, 1924.

Weaver, John D. *The Brownsville Affair.* New York, 1970.

Weinstein, James. *The Decline of Socialism in America, 1912-1915.* New York, 1969.

Weiss, Nancy J. *The National Urban League.* New York, 1974.

Wells-Barnett, Ida. *On Lynchings.* New York, 1969.

Wiley, Bell I. *Southern Negroes, 1861-1865.* New Haven, Conn., 1938.

Wilmore, Gayraud S. *Black Religion and Black Radicalism.* New York, 1972.

*Wilshire's Editorials.* Los Angeles, Calif., 1906.

Wittke, Carl. *Refugees of Revolution: The German Forty-Eighters in America.* Philadelphia, 1952.

— — —. *The Utopian Communist: A Life of Wilhelm Weitling.* Baton Rouge, La., 1950.

Woodward, C. Vann. *Origins of the New South, 1877-1913.* Baton Rouge, La., 1951.
———. *Reunion and Reaction.* New York, 1956.
Zucker, A. E. *The Forty-Eighters: Political Refugees of the German Revolution of 1848.* New York, 1950.


ARTICLES

Abernathy, Lloyd M. "The Washington Race War of July, 1919." *Maryland Historical Magazine* 58 (1963): 318-24.
Abramowitz, Jack. "John B. Raynor—A Grass Roots Leader." *Journal of Negro History* 3 (1951): 160-93.
Alexander, Charles. "The Socialism of the Negro." *The Cristian Recorder,* July 5, 1900.
Ameringer, Oscar. "To Rise and Fall Together." In Colton, Samuel, ed., *Sagas of Struggle: A Labor Anthology.* New York, 1951. pp. 66-85.
"Anarchist Views of Lynching." *Literary Digest,* September 12, 1903.
Aptheker, Herbert. "American Imperialism and White Chauvinism." In *Afro-American History: The Modern Era.* New York, 1971. Pp. 99-108.
Auerbach, Kerold S. "Southern Tenant Farmers: Socialist Critics of the New Deal." *Labor History* 7 (1966): 5-13.
Baker, Ray Stannard. "The Negro Goes North." *World's Work* 34 (1917): 311-15.
Battle, William L., and Geis, Gilbert. "Racial Self-Fulfillment and the Rise of an All-Negro Community in Oklahoma." *Phylon* 8 (1957): 247-60.
Berger, Victor. "Let us Drop the 'Revolutionary' Jargon." *New York Call,* May 9, 1912 (Magazine Section).
———. "We Will Stand by the Real American Proletariat." *Social Democratic Herald,* October 12, 1907.
Biesle, Rudolph L. "The Texas State Convention of Germans in 1854." *Southwestern Historical Quarterly* 33 (1930): 247-61.
Blum, Virgil C. "The Political and Military Activities of the German Element in St. Louis, 1859-1861." *Missouri Historical Review* 42 (1948): 111-29.
Blumenthal, Henry. "Woodrow Wilson and the Race Question." *Journal of Negro History* 47 (1963): 1-21.
Bortnick, Bernard. "De Leon's Role in the Labor Movement." *Weekly People,* December 15, 22, 1973.
Brodhead, Michael J., and Clanton, O. Gene. "C. G. Clemens: The 'Sociable Socialist.'" *Kansas Historical Quarterly* 40 (1974): 475-502.
Brommell, Bernard J. "Debs's Cooperative Commonwealth Plan for Workers." *Labor History* 12 (1971): 560-69.
———. "Kate Richards O'Hare: A Midwestern Pacifist's Fight for Free Speech." *North Dakota Quarterly* 44 (1976): 5-19.
Bruce, John F. "The Anarchists." *Colored American,* January 18, 1902.
"Butchering Georgia Negroes." *New York Call,* March 30, 1921.
Butts, J. W., and James, Dorothy. "The Underlying Causes of the Elaine Riot of 1919." *Arkansas Historical Quarterly* 12 (1973): 95-114.
Carsel, Wilfred. "The Slaveholders' Indictment of Northern Wage Slavery." *Journal of Southern History* 6 (1940): 514-20.
Clark, Dovie King. "Peter Humphries Clark." *Negro History Bulletin* 6 (1942): 176-77.
"Colored Woman Protests." *New York Times,* April 30, 1908.
Coston, W. H. "The Negro and Socialism." *The Christian Recorder,* February 18, 1897.
Cox, Era Ellen. "The Socialist Party in Indiana Since 1896." *Indiana Magazine of History* 12 (1916): 12-32.

Crosswaith, Frank. "For Whom Should the Negro Vote?" *Opportunity* 12 (1932): 279.

Crouch-Hazlett, Ida. "The Negro and the Socialists." *New York Call*, July 22, 1907.

Crouthamel, James L. "The Springfield Race Riot of 1908." *Journal of Negro History* 45 (1960): 164-81.

Cuzner, A. T. "The Negro or the Race Problem." *International Socialist Review* 4 (1903): 261-64.

Dague, R. A. "Shall Negroes Be Burned at the Stake?" *Ballot Box* (Fallon, Nev.), February 12, 1913.

Dann, Martin. "Black Populism: A Study of the Colored Farmers' Alliance Through 1891." *Journal of Ethnic Studies* 2 (1974): 58-71.

Debs, Eugene V. "The Birth of a Nation." *Terre Haute Post*, June 18, 1916.

———. "The Negro and His Nemesis." *International Socialist Review* 4 (1904): 391-97.

———. "The Negro in the Class Struggle." *International Socialist Review* 4 (1903): 258-59.

"Debs and the Negro." *The Messenger*, November 1920.

"Debs Speaks in Harlem." *The Messenger*, December 1923.

"Delta Sigma Theta Sends Delegate to Convention of Intercollegiate Society." *Howard University Journal*, January 16, 1914.

Doerfler, Ernest R. "Socialism and the American Negro Problem." *American Socialist Quarterly* 4 (1933): 23-36.

Douai, Adolf. "Der Abolitionist." *Der Pionier*, January 6, 13, 20, 27, February 5, 12, 19, 26, 1859.

———. "Humboldt und Agassiz." *Der Pionier*, July 2, 9, 16, 23, 1859.

Douglass, Frederick. "Why Is the Negro Lynched? The Lesson of the Hour." In Foner, Philip S., *The Life and Writings of Frederick Douglass*. Vol. 4. New York, 1955. Pp. 491-523.

DuBois, W.E.B. "A Field for Socialists," *New Review* 1 (1913): 54-57.

———. "A Lunatic or Traitor." *The Crisis* 28 (1924): 8-9.

———. "Negro and Socialism." *The Horizon* 3 (1908).

———. "Of Mr. Booker T. Washington and Others." In *The Souls of Black Folk*. New York, 1903. Pp. 41-54.

———. "Socialism and the Negro Problem." *New Review* (1913): 138-41.

———. "Socialist of the Path." *The Horizon* 2 (1907).

Dyson, Lowell K. "The Southern Tenant Farmers' Union and Depression Politics." *Political Science Quarterly* 85 (1973): 230-52.

Eastman, Max. "The Chicago Convention." *The Liberator*, October 1919, pp. 5-19.

———. "Niggers and Night Riders." *The Masses*, February 1913, p. 6.

Easton, L. D. "The Colored Schools of Cincinnati." In Martin, Isaac M., ed., *History of the Schools of Cincinnati and Other Educational Institutions. Public and Private*. Cincinnati, Ohio, 1900. Pp. 160-85.

Elkins, W. F. "Unrest Among the Negroes: A British Document of 1919." *Science & Society* 32 (1968): 66-79.

Ellis, John. "The Lessons of Garrison's Life." *The Worker*, December 30, 1905.

Emerson, O. B. "Frances Wright and Her Nashoba Experiment." *Tennessee Historical Quarterly* 6 (1947): 290-310.

"Eugene Debs—Candidate for President." *The Messenger*, April-May 1920.

Finch, Earl. "A Remedy for Anarchy." *Colored American*, February 15, 1902.

Fishbein, Leslie. "Federal Suppression of Leftwing Dissidence in World War I." *Potomac Review* 3 (1974): 47-67.

Foner, Philip S. "Black-Jewish Relations in the Opening Years of the Twentieth Century." *Phylon* 37 (1976): 6-15.

— — —. "Caroline Hollingsworth Pemberton, Philadelphia Socialist Champion of Black Equality." *Pennsylvania History* 43 (1976): 229-52.

— — —. "The I.W.W. and the Black Worker." *Journal of Negro History* 55 (1970): 45-64.

— — —. "Rev. George Washington Woodbey: Early Twentieth Century California Black Socialist." *Journal of Negro History* 61 (1976): 136-57.

Fraina, Louis G. "Problems of American Socialism." *The Class Struggle*, February 1919, p. 46.

Garlin, Sender. "The Challenge of John Swinton." *Masses & Mainstream*, December 1951, pp. 40-47.

Garrison, Rev. S. C. "The Lower Humanity." *The Christian Socialist*, February 1915.

"Georgia in the Spotlight." *New York Call*, April 28, 1921.

Glazier, Kenneth M. "W.E.B. Du Bois' Impressions of Woodrow Wilson." *Journal of Negro History* 58 (1973): 32-54.

Glicksburg, Charle J. "Henry Adams Reports on a Trades Union Meeting." *New England Quarterly* 15 (1948): 724-28.

Grant, Donald, and Grant, Mildred. "Some Notes on the Capital 'N.'" *Phylon* 36 (1975): 435-43.

Green, James R. "The Brotherhood of Timber Workers, 1910-1913: A Radical Response to Industrial Capitalism in the Southern U.S.A." *Past and Present* 60 (1973): 161-200.

Greenleaf, Richard. British Labor Against American Slavery." *Science & Society* 27 (1953): 42-58.

Gutman, Herbert G. "Black Coal Miners and the Greenback-Labor Party in Redeemer, Alabama, 1878-1879." *Labor History* 10 (1969): 506-35.

Hall, Mozell C. "The All-Negro Communities of Oklahoma: The Natural History of a Social Movement." *Journal of Negro History* 31 (1946): 254-68.

Harlan, Louis R. "The Secret Life of Booker T. Washington." *Journal of Southern History* 37 (1971): 393-416.

Harrison, Hubert H. "The Black Man's Burden." *International Review* 12 (1912): 660-63, 762-69.

— — —. "Socialism and the Negro." *International Socialist Review* 12 (1912): 65-72.

Harrison, Royden. "British Labor and American Slavery." *Science & Society* 25 (1961): 291-318.

Hennighausen, L. P. "Reminiscences of the Political Life of the German-Americans in Baltimore During 1850-1860." *Seventh Annual Report of the Secretary of the Society for the Study of Germans in Maryland* (1892-1893): 194-235.

Hickey, T. A. "The Land Renters Union in Texas." *International Socialist Review* 13 (1912): 239-44.

Hillquit, Morris. "Emigration in the United States." *International Socialist Review* 8 (1907): 64-75.

Holly, Rev. James Theodore. "Socialism from the Biblical Point of View." *AME Church Review* 9 (1892-1893): 244-58.

Holmes, William F. "The Leflore County Massacre and the Demise of the Colored Farmers' Alliance." *Phylon* 33 (1972): 267-74.

Huch, C. F. "Der Sozialistische Turnerbund." *Mitteilungen des Deutschen Pionier-Vereins von Philadelphia* 62 (1912): 1-15.

Hunter, Robert. "The Emancipation of the Negro." *New York Call*, May 31, 1909.

International Socialist Bureau. "To the Laborers of All Countries." *International Socialist Review* 4 (1903): 46.

Johnson, Oakley C. "Marxism and the Negro Freedom Struggle, 1876-1917." *Journal of Human Relations* 13 (1965): 21-39.

Kamphoefner, Walter D. "St. Louis Germans and the Republican Party, 1848-1860." *Mid-

*America* 57 (1975): 69-88.

Kann, Kenneth. "The Knights of Labor and the Southern Black Worker." *Labor History* 18 (1977): 49-70.

Kelleber, Daniel T. "St. Louis 1916 Residential Segregation Ordinance." *Bulletin, Missouri Historical Society* 26 (1970): 239-48.

Kessler, Sidney H. "The Negro in the Knights of Labor." *Journal of Negro History* 37 (1952): 250-82.

Kline, Edith. "The Garment Worker Comes to the Negro Worker." *Opportunity* 12 (1934): 107-8.

"Knights and the Color Line." *Public Opinion* 2 (October 1886): 1-3.

Laidler, Harry W. "The Socialist Message for the Negro." *New Leader*, June 1, 1929.

Lamont, Margaret L. "The Negro's Stake in Socialism." *American Socialist Quarterly* 4 (1935): 41-51.

Lebetter, Billy D. "White Over Black in Texas: Radical Attitudes in the Ante-Bellum Period." *Phylon* 34 (1973): 406-18.

Leinenweber, Charles. "The American Socialist Party and 'New' Immigrants." *Science & Society* 32 (1968): 6-12.

McKay, Claude. "Negro Extinction or Survival: A Reply to George S. Schuyler." *Amsterdam News*, November 20, 1937.

McLaurin, Melton A. "The Racial Policies of the Knights of Labor and the Organization of Southern Black Workers." *Labor History* 17 (1976): 568-85.

Marcus, Irwin M. "Frank Crosswaith: Black Socialist, Labor Leader & Reformer." *Negro History Bulletin* 37 (1974): 287-89.

— — —. "Hubert Harrison." *Negro History Bulletin* 34 (1971): 18-19.

— — —. "The Southern Negro and the Knights of Labor." *Negro History Bulletin* 30 (1967): 5-7.

Mason, Daniel. "On Negro-White Unity." *Political Affairs*, August 1954, pp. 61-62.

Meilly, William. "Socialism and the Negro." *International Socialist Review* 4 (1907): 265-67.

Meredith, H. L. "Agrarian Socialism and the Negro in Oklahoma, 1900-1918." *Labor History* 11 (1970): 12-35.

— — —. "Oscar Ameringer and the Concept of Agrarian Socialism." *Chronicles of Oklahoma* 45 (1967): 46-68.

Miller, Floyd J. "Black Protest and White Leadership: A Note on the Colored Farmers' Alliance." *Phylon* 3 (Summer 1972): 169-74.

Miller, Sally M. "Americans and the Second International." *Proceedings of the American Philosophical Society* 120 (1976): 372-87.

— — —. "The Socialist Party and the Negro, 1901-1920." *Journal of Negro History* 46 (1971): 220-29.

Moore, R. Laurence. "Flawed Faternity: American Socialist Response to the Negro, 1901-1912." *Historian* (1969): 1-14.

Morgan, H. Wayne. "The Utopia of Eugene V. Debs." *American Quarterly* 11 (1959): 120-35.

Morris, James M. "William Haller, 'The Disturbing Element.'" *Cincinnati Historical Society Bulletin* 28 (1970): 120-32.

Morrison, Alan. "A. Philip Randolph: Dean of Negro Leaders." *Ebony*, November 1958, pp. 103-4, 108, 110-12, 114.

Morton, James F., Jr. "On the Promotion of Race Antipathy." *The Public*, May 5, 1908.

Naison, Mark D. "Black Agrarian Radicalism in the Great Depression: The Threads of a Lost Tradition." *Journal of Ethnic Studies* 1 (1973): 47-65.

"Negro Socialist Talks." *Chicago Socialist*, March 29, 1902.

Noyes, William. "Some Proposed Solutions of the Negro Problem." *International Socialist Review* 2 (1901): 106-09.

Ofari, Earl. "Black Activists and 19th Century Radicalism." *Black Scholar* 5 (February 1974): 19-25.

———. "Marxism, Nationalism, and Black Liberation." *Monthly Review* 18 (1971): 18-33.

Osofsky, Gilbert. "Progressivism and the Negro: New York, 1900-1915." *American Quarterly* 16 (1964): 153-68.

Ovington, Mary White. "The Negro Family in New York." *Charities*, October 7, 1905, pp. 132-34.

———. "Reminiscences." *Baltimore Afro-American*, September 1932-February 1933.

———. "The Status of the Negro in the United States." *New Review* 1 (1913): 248-49.

Owen, Chandler. "Peonage, Riots, and Lynchers." *The Messenger*, August 1921.

Parks, Edd Winfield. "Dreamer's Vision, Frances Wright at Nashoba (1825-1830)." *Tennessee Historical Magazine*, Series 22 (1970): 42-54.

Patterson, John. "Alliance and Antipathy: Ignatius Donnelly's Ambivalent Union in *Doctor Huguet*." *American Quarterly* 22 (1970): 824-45.

Pawn, J. M. "Black Radicals and White Spies: Harlem 1919." *Negro History Bulletin* 35 (1972): 129-32.

———. "The Search for Black Radicals: American and British Documents Relative to the 1919 Red Scare." *Labor History* 16 (1975): 272-84.

Pemberton, Caroline H. "How I Became a Socialist." *The Comrade* 1 (1902): 202.

"Race Relations in the South." *New York Call*, May 21, 1921.

Randolph, A. Philip. "The Socialist Message and the Negro." *New York Call*, November 9, 1919 (Magazine Section).

Ransom, Rev. R. C. "The Negro and Socialism" *AME Church Review* 3 (1896-1897): 192-200.

Reese, James V. "The Early History of Labor Organization in Texas, 1838-1876." *Southwestern Historical Quarterly* 72 (1968): 1-20.

"Resolution on Lynching," *Chicago Daily Socialist*, November 28, 1903.

Ricker, A. W. "Socialism and the Negro." *Appeal to Reason*, September 12, 1903.

Robbins, I. M. "The Economic Aspects of the Negro Problem." *International Socialist Review* 8-10 (1908-1910).

Roberts, Franklin S. "Frank Crosswaith: Harlem's Eugene V. Debs." *Political World*, July 1942, p. 8.

Roper, Laura Wood. "Frederick Law Olmsted and the Western Texas Free-Soil Movement." *American Historical Review* 56 (1950): 58-64.

Rudwick, Elliott M. "The Niagara Movement." *Journal of Negro History* 43 (1957): 177-82.

Schafer, Joseph. "Who Elected Lincoln?" *American Historical Review* 57 (1941): 51-63.

Schwendermann, Glen. "St. Louis and the 'Exodusters' of 1879." *Journal of Negro History* 41 (1961): 32-46.

Seymour, R. "Was Christ a Socialist?" *The Christian Recorder*, November 8, 1894.

Shanks, Rosalie. "The I.W.W. Free Speech Movement, San Diego, 1912." *Journal of San Diego History* 8 (1973): 25-33.

Shapiro, Harold A. "The Labor Movement in San Antonio, Texas, 1865-1915." *Southwestern Social Science Quarterly* 36 (1955): 220-42.

Shapiro, Herbert. "The Muckrakers and Negroes." *Phylon* 31 (1970): 76-88.

Shuler, Edgar A. "The Houston Race Riot of 1917." *Journal of Negro History* 29 (1900): 300-38.

Simons, A. M. "Economic Aspects of Chattel Slavery." *International Socialist Review* 4

(1903): 25-33, 95-105, 163-73.

Slater, Rev. George W., Jr. "Booker T. Washington's Error." *Chicago Daily Socialist*, September 22, 1908.

—— —. "The Cat's Out." *Chicago Daily Socialist*, September 29, 1908.

—— —. "The Colored Strikebreaker." *Chicago Daily Socialist*, January 14, 1909.

—— —. "An Eye-Opener." *Chicago Daily Socialist*, October 20, 1908.

—— —. "How and Why I Became a Socialist." *Chicago Daily Socialist*, September 8, 1908.

—— —. "Lincoln and the Laborer." *The Christian Socialist*, February 1915.

—— —. "The Negro and Socialism." *The Christian Socialist*, July 1, 1913.

—— —. "The New Abolitionists." *Chicago Daily Socialist*, January 4, 1909.

—— —. "Pullman Porter Pity." *Chicago Daily Socialist*, December 22, 1908.

—— —. "Race Problem's Socialist Cure." *Chicago Daily Socialist*, March 27, 1909.

—— —. "Reaching the 1,000,000." *Chicago Daily Socialist*, November 4, 1908.

—— —. "Socialism and Social Service." *The Christian Socialist*, February 1915.

Slobodin, Henry L. "The Niagara Movement." *New York Call*, August 27, 1909.

"Socialist Party Appeals to the Colored Workers." *Baltimore Afro-American*, June 9, July 7, 1920.

"Socialists Organize Unemployed." *American Guardian*, December 16, 1932.

"Sojourner Truth a Great Woman." *New York Call*, February 12, 1911.

Sotheran, Alice Hyneman. "The Negro and Socialism." *New York Call*, January 19, 20, 1911.

"Special Letter Sent to the *Messenger* by Eugene V. Debs." *The Messenger*, November 1920.

Stein, Judith. "'Of Mr. Booker T. Washington and Others: The Political Economy of Racism in the United States." *Science & Society* 38 (1974-1975): 422-63.

Streator, George. "The Negro, the South and the Socialist Party." *Revolutionary Socialist* 1 (Autum 1935): 6-7.

—— —. "The Negro: Step-Child of Socialism." *Revolutionary Socialist* 1 (Summer 1935): 15-20.

Stueck, William. "Progressivism and the Negro: White Liberals and the Early NAACP." *Historian* 38 (1975): 58-78.

Sylvere, Malcolm. "Sicilian Socialists in Houston, Texas 1896-98." *Labor History* 11 (1950): 77-81.

"The *Afro* for La Follette." *Baltimore Afro-American*, October 24, 1924.

"The Colored Man Welcome." *Chicago Daily Socialist*, January 4, 1909.

"The Grand Father Clause in Oklahoma." *The Outlook* 95 (August 20, 1910): 853-54.

"The Ku Klux Klan." *New York Call*, January 10, 1921.

"The Labor Problem." *Appeal to Reason*, September 15, 1900.

"The Misfortunes of the Negroes," *Social Democratic Herald*, May 31, 1902.

"The National Party." *Public Opinion* (October 22, 1896): 523.

"The Negro and His 'Rights.'" *The Workers' Call*, March 9, 1901.

"The Negro and Socialism." *The Worker*, July 3, 1904.

"The Negro and Socialism." *New York Call*, January 24, 1911.

"The Negro Problem." *International Socialist Review* 1 (October 1900), (February 1901): 464-70.

"The Negro's Party in Nationalism." *The Nationalist* 2 (1890): 91-97.

"The Race Problem: A Suggestion." *The Coming Nation*, January 7, 1899.

"The Scottsboro Frameup." *Negro Labor News Service*, June 20, 1931.

Thomas, Norman. "The Candidates Speak." *Opportunity* 10 (November 1932): 340.

—— —. "Jim-Crowism in the Capital." *New Republic* 75 (May 31, 1933): 75.

—— —. "Why Not a New Party?" *North American Review* 207 (1929): 143-50.

Tridon, André. "Socialism and the Race Question." *The Worker*, October 20, 1906.

"Unemployed Council Formed." *Negro Labor News Service*, August 1, 1931.

Untermann, Ernest. "The American Kishineff." *Appeal to Reason*, July 25, 1933.

Vadney, Thomas A. "The Politics of Repression: A Case Study of the Red Scare in New York." *New York History* 49 (1968).

Vail, Charles H. "The Negro Problem." *International Socialist Review* 1 (February 1901).

Vidrine, Eraste. "Negro Locals." *International Socialist Review* 5 (January 1, 1905): 89-92.

Walling, William English. "The Founding of the N.A.A.C.P." *The Crisis* (July 1929).

— — —. "The Race War in the North." *The Independent*, September 3, 1908, pp. 529-34.

Washington, Booker T. "Address Before the Southern Industrial Convention, Huntsville, Alabama, October 12, 1899." In Thornbrough, E. L., ed., *Booker T. Washington-Great Lives Observed*. Englewood Cliffs, N.J., 1969.

— — —. "The Awakening of the Negro." *Atlantic Monthly* 48 (September 1906): 302-24.

— — —. "The Negro and the Labor Problem in the South." Reprinted in Brotz, Howard, ed., *Negro Social and Political Thought, 1850-1920*. New York, 1966. Pp. 401-5.

— — —. "Negro Disfranchisement and the Negro in Business." *The Outlook* 17 (October 9, 1909): 310-11, 315.

Wells-Barnett, Ida. "The Negro's Quest for Work." *New York Call*, July 23, 1911.

"What Haywood Says on Political Action." *International Socialist Review* 13 (February 1913): 622-24.

"Why Negroes Should Be Socialists." *The Messenger*, October, December 1919.

Woodbey, Rev. G. W. "The Next Emancipation." *Chicago Daily Socialist*, January 18, 1909.

— — —. "Socialist Agitation." *Chicago Daily Socialist*, January 4, 1909.

Woodson, Carter G. "The Negroes of Cincinnati Prior to the Civil War." *Journal of Negro History* 1 (1916): 120-42.

Woodward, C. Vann. "Flight from History: The Heritage of the Negro." *The Nation* (100th Anniversary Issue, September 20, 1965): 142-46.

Wright, Clyde J. "The Colored Man's Chance." *Chicago Daily Socialist*, September 15, 1908.

Wright, Palmer Hoke. "The American Negro and the War." *International Socialist Review* 17 (July 1916): 166-67.

"Yellow Journalism and Race Prejudice." *New York Age*, May 14, 1908.

# Index

of Sleeping Car Porters, 335; opposes
League of Nations, 276; opposes Versailles peace treaty, 276; opposes
World War I, 276; Palmer calls most
dangerous of black publications, 292;
promotes independent black unionism, 313-14; raided, 282; refrains from
criticizing Socialist party, 285-87; on
split in Socialist party, 306-09; supports Bolshevik Revolution, 276; supports Debs for president, 316-17; supports LaFollette for president, 334;
supports Socialist party in split, 306-
07; target of Palmer report, 292-97;
theoretical basis for opposing Garvey,
327-29; urges blacks to form self-defense groups, 295
Mexican-Americans, 20
Mexican war, 13-14
Meyer, Siegfried, 40
Miller, Floyd J., 89
Miller, Reverend George Frazier: advocates Socialism at National Negro
Conference, 201; at Cosmopolitan
Club criticizes Colored Socialist Club,
212; and Friends of Negro Freedom,
314; joins Socialist party, 181; mem-
ber Cosmopolitan Club, 184; nomi-
nated for Congress, 284; opposes
World War I, 277; praised, 392; writes
for *Messenger*, 277
Milholland, John E., 185-86, 188, 192, 198,
393
Miller, Guy E., 147
Miller, Sally M., x, xi
Minor, Robert, 256
Miscegenation, 243, 399
Mississippi, 240, 366
Mitchell, Harry L., 312, 350, 351
Mitchell, John Purroy, 279
Molyneaux, P. Aloysius, 132-33, 134
Moore, J. M., 88
Moore, Richard B., 266, 310
Moore, R. Lawrence, x, xi, 394
Moore, Sam, 322
Morris, William, 248, 385
Morton, James F., Jr., 191
Moskowitz, Henry, 198
*Mother Earth*, 82
Mother Jones, 128
Moton, Robert Russa, 294
Mt. Zion Baptist church, 391

"Movement in a Southern State, The," 315
Moyer, Harvey P., 110
Mullatoes, 220
Murphy, Carl, 314

Nael, John E., 331
Nagle, Pat S., 227, 231
Nashoba, 7-8
National Association for the Advancement
of Colored People (NAACP): accused
of helping radicals, 298-99; and cam-
paign against Garvey, 331; criticized,
276, 313; early leaders mostly Social-
ists, 201; in election of 1924, 334;
growth, 290; origins, 195-200; Social-
ists urged to work with branches, 366;
Socialists work to establish, 195-200
National Association for the Promotion of
Labor Unionism, 313
National Association of Cosmopolitan
Clubs, 185
National Association of Manufacturers,
112
National Civic Federation, 300-01, 326
National Civic Federation report, 300-01
National Conscription Act, 31
National Council of Left Wing Sections,
305
National Executive Committee, Socialist
party, 143-44, 192, 240, 245-46, 283-84,
285, 304, 316
National Labor Union, 47
National Left Wing Conference, 305
National Liberty party, 140-41
National Negro American Political League,
148, 195
National Negro Committee, 199-200
National Negro Conference, 197-200
National Negro Congress, 363, 364, 415
National Negro Work Subcommittee, 365
*National Reformer*, 13
National Reformers, and slavery, 4, 10, 109
*National Rip-Saw*, 221-23, 260
"National Self-Determination," 275
National Urban League, 276, 313, 331, 341,
396
National Women's Trade Union League,
195
*Nationalist, The*, 83
Nationalist clubs, 82
Nationalist party: DeLeon joins, 70; dis-
cussion in of Negro question, 83;

200-01; recruits Populists in South, 129; revival of work in South, 349; role in formation of NAACP, 193-201; said to be carrying on Abolitionist tradition, 149-50; said to be winning black converts, 302-03; St. Louis members oppose residential segregation, 262; segregation in Southern locals, 144-45; segregation advocated in, 109-110; segregation under Socialism, 203-04; separate branches in South, 130-31; significance of 1901 Negro Resolution, 99-100; simplistic view of role on Negro, 394; some in take advanced position on Negro question, xi, 183-201; Southern drive of, 128-29; and Southern Tenant Farmers' Union, 349-53; split in, 288, 303-04; stand by National Executive Committee on Negro issues, 143-44; stand at Southern Socialist Conference, 366; and unemployment of blacks during depression, 413; view of Negro question in 1920s and 1930s, 344-45; welcomes Russian Revolution, 303
Socialists: accused of favoring intermarriage, 190; compared with Abolitionists, 150
"Socialists Organize Unemployed," 342
*Socialist Thought*, 3
Socialist Trades and Labor Alliance, 76, 94
Social Party of New York and Vicinity, 37
Social Revolutionary clubs, 78
Society of Christian Socialists, 83
Society of Universal Inquiry and Reform, 12
Socrates, 67
Solid South, 128
"Some Reasons Why Negroes Should Vote the Socialist Ticket," 278-79
*Songs of Socialism*, 109-10
Sorge, Friedrich Adolph: advised how to advance cause of IWA in U.S., 36-37; arrival in U.S., 5; becomes General Secretary IWA, 42; criticizes Douai, 16; criticizes Equal Rights party, 374; describes black participation in IWA demonstration, 39; does not become Marxist until 1860s, 5; early life, 5; ignores blacks, 42; and Knights of Labor, 378; meets Marx, 5; on Reconstruction, 374-75; role at convention of

Radical Germans, 32; sends Marx reports, 40
Sotheran, Alice Hyneman, 218
*Souls of Black Folk, The*, 182, 218
South: blacks lose out as skilled craftsmen in, 175; call for Socialists to recruit blacks in, 58; counterrevolution in, 42; how to win, 348; revival of Socialist party in, 349; separate branches in, 130-31; Socialist fear of antagonizing, 96-97; Socialist influence in Southern Tenant Farmers' Union, 349-55; Socialist Labor Party, in, 73-74, 81; Socialist party abandons, 348; Socialists in rarely recruit blacks, 238
Southern drive, 128-29
*Southern Socialist, The*, 129, 130
"Southern Socialist," 242-43, 244
Southern Socialist Conference, 366
Southern Socialist press, and Negro, 220-23
Southern Tenant Farmers' Union, 350-53, 360-62
Sovereigns of Industry, 48, 375-76
Soviet Union, 54, 300, 414
*Sozialistiche Turnerbunds*, 15
Spargo, John, 146, 189, 194
Spencer, Clarence K., 129
Spies, August, 78
Spingarn, Arthur B., 330
Split, in Socialist party, 288, 303-11
*Springfield Republican*, 119
Springfield riot, 195-97
*Staatszeitung*, 22
Stallard, H. H., 232, 233
Standard Oil Company, 74-75
State Constitutional League, 229-30
Stedman, Seymour, 282, 355
Steel strike of 1901, 100, 102, 383
Steffens, Lincoln, 198
Stephens, Alexander H., 30
*Stephen the Black*, 115-17
Stevenson, Archibald, 297
Stephenson, George, 172
Steward, Maude Trotter, 366
Stoddard, Lothrop, 106, 410
Stokes, Rose Pastor, 282, 303
Stolvey, James Benjamin, 72
Streator, George, 358-59, 362
Strikebreaking: black press on, 100-03; blacks used in, 106, 383
Strikes, of black workers, 43-44

About the Author

Philip S. Foner, Independence Foundation Professor of History at Lincoln University, is the author of many works, including *When Karl Marx Died: Comments in 1883, Labor and the American Revolution* (Greenwood Press, 1976), and *History of Black Americans: From Africa to the Emergence of the Cotton Kingdom* (Greenwood Press, 1975).